THE CULTURE OF NATURE IN BRITAIN
1680–1860

THE CULTURE OF NATURE IN BRITAIN

1680–1860

P. M. HARMAN

YALE UNIVERSITY PRESS

NEW HAVEN AND LONDON

Published with assistance from the Annie Burr Lewis Fund

For information about this and other Yale University Press publications, please contact:
U.S. Office: sales.press@yale.edu   www.yalebooks.com
Europe Office: sales@yaleup.co.uk   www.yaleup.co.uk

Set in Minion by J&L Composition, Scarborough, North Yorkshire
Printed in Great Britain by TJ International, Padstow, Cornwall

ISBN 978–0–300–15197–8

Library of Congress Control Number: 2009935588

A catalogue record for this book is available from the British Library.

10 9 8 7 6 5 4 3 2 1

Contents

Figures

✳

Preface

TAKING AS ITS THEME the culture of 'nature' in Britain in the period 1680–1860, spanned by Newtonian science and natural theology, Charles Darwin's *Origin of Species* (1859) and John Ruskin's *Modern Painters* (1843–60), this book explores the accommodation, interaction and cultural context of conceptions of 'nature'. Historical study of concepts of nature in this period has conventionally fragmented into a focus on disparate topics in the sciences, art, landscape, philosophy, natural theology and literature. Romanticism is generally seen as marking a cultural divide at the turn of the nineteenth century, and this has led to the imposition of chronological limits defining the scope of historical inquiry. Studies have bifurcated into a focus either on cultural patterns in the eighteenth-century Enlightenment or on nineteenth-century Romantic art, literature, science and natural theology. Some studies have crossed (modern) disciplinary boundaries, and there has been recent interest in the interactions of art and literature with the sciences; my references attest to the interest and value of this work. But there has nevertheless been a fragmentation of outlook, which it is the aim of the present work to confront: to discuss 'nature' – in terms shaped by the linked themes of design, exploration, landscape, flora and fauna, colour and vital forces (but not here addressing the large topics of human nature and the self) across conventional disciplinary and chronological boundaries, and within common terms of debate.

Taking a broader thematic range and longer time span than is customary, this book considers the impact of Romanticism in terms of the web of interactions joining art, science, literature and natural theology. The links between the aesthetics of nature and natural theology, forged in the era of Newtonian science, established norms of cultural orthodoxy common to the arts and sciences, utilising the language of 'design' to counteract claims that the culture and science of modernity posed a challenge to traditional values. It is here argued that Romanticism disrupted these links between natural theology and the aesthetic appreciation of nature.

Changes in agrarian and industrial practices shaped the material and social environments in which the natural world was experienced, depicted in art and literature, and interpreted by science. The language of 'design' was questioned, challenging the conventional representation of the natural world based on the aesthetics of nature and natural theology. Expanding geographical exploration fostered travel and encounters between disparate cultures, enlarging knowledge of landscape and natural history, made exotic in the reports of scientific travellers such as Alexander von Humboldt and Darwin. Travelling as tourists to the English Lake District and Italy (the latter forming part of the Grand Tour) became an important cultural entertainment, where the form and structure of mountain landscapes were interpreted aesthetically.

In the eighteenth century the aesthetics of nature was based on a painter's eye for a balanced landscape; through the study of paintings, the appreciation of landscape views was shaped by the appeal to familiar visual forms harmonising with the environment. In the Romantic age this aesthetic yielded to the valorisation of naturalism and realism. John Constable appealed to the authority of science to establish fidelity to nature as the aim of the landscape painter; William Wordsworth described the aesthetics of the Lake District landscape in terms of the natural history and geology of the mountains. With the turn to realism, the Romantics emphasised that rocks and flowers were not encountered as passive objects in the laboratory. The forms of the natural world, landscape and natural history were given immediacy in being experienced through impressions of colour and the effects of active forces. Ruskin applauded J.M.W. Turner's capacity as an artist to depict the natural world as suffused with the vividness of colour and energised by inherent active powers. Ruskin regarded colour as the mark of 'nature and life', and envisioned mountain landscapes as shaped by the throbbing energy and pulse of swirling patterns of flowing rock. In the face of natural selection, and Darwin's reduction of the human aesthetic sense to the physical sensations of animals, Ruskin asserted the primacy and uniqueness of human judgement in the aesthetic appreciation of nature.

The argument in each chapter is presented in historical sequence, concluding with summary statements drawing attention to the main themes discussed; these statements indicate how the individual chapters fit into the structure of the book as a whole. Given its wide coverage the discussion here is far from exhaustive; the selection of topics has been shaped by the thematic structure adopted, and the argument is illustrative rather than systematic.

The chronological span of the book, from the time of Isaac Newton through the Romantic age, is determined by the impact of the terms of a cultural debate – exemplified by Jonathan Swift's *Gulliver's Travels* (1726) – concerned with the order of nature, the status of natural philosophy, and the capacity of the contrivances of the human arts to manipulate and control the natural world. With Romanticism, nature came to be seen as transcending artificial aesthetic categories derived from the construction of human arte-facts. The immediacy of the natural world was located in the experience of nature as dynamically evolving; its powers were conceived as the source of spiritual and artistic illumination, and were contrasted with the artificial products of human civilisation. The link between the aesthetics of nature and natural theology was disrupted: the language of design faltered as an embracing theme. In concluding the book with Darwin's *Origin of Species* and Ruskin's *Modern Painters,* the terminal date of 1860 indicates the change in intellectual culture at around that time – the rise of professional and secularised forms of knowledge. I do not intend to imply that 'after Darwin' the connections between the sciences and the arts splintered into 'two cultures', though Darwinian scientific naturalism undoubtedly posed a severe challenge to the conventions of natural theology and the aesthetics of nature. Rather I suggest that there then emerged a new framework of argument, shaped by different social forces and intellectual assumptions within which interactions flourished, with new patterns changing the terms of cultural criticism and debate.

This book has been of long gestation, having its origin in work I commenced many years ago, and though I pursued other studies more urgently, these early interests were continued parenthetically, set aside rather than aborted. I am grateful to Janet Browne and Robert Fox for generous encouragement, and to Michael Wheeler for fostering discussion of Ruskin and *Modern Painters* at a time when I was beginning to contemplate pursuing this topic more directly. I gratefully acknowledge a research grant from The Royal Society, and a Research Leave Award from the Arts and Humanities Research Council in 2005–6.

CHAPTER 1

✳

Themes and Contexts

In the watercolour drawings that J.M.W. Turner made in the 1820s and 1830s for the series of engravings of *Picturesque Views in England and Wales*, he recorded the impact of technology and industry on the landscape. He departs from traditional rural nostalgia, which had been dominant in shaping the aesthetics of nature in the eighteenth century. This was the image of the national landscape shaped by a golden age of the earth's bounty and the vision of the fertility of the soil and the virtues of rural life. Turner shows smoky industry and jostling urban life intruding into the countryside and seashore, and gives human figures unusual prominence. These themes are apparent in *Lancaster, from the Aqueduct Bridge* (c. 1825), which shows the bridge over the River Lune at Lancaster with labourers fishing, resting and sleeping in the foreground (Fig. 1). The Stainton–Preston canal, one of the numerous canals recently constructed to foster the growth of trade and mechanised industry, represents contemporary industrial and technological improvement, and contrasts with the surrounding pre-industrial agricultural landscape. The focus on varied human activities marks a distinct contrast with the timelessness and harmony of the aesthetics of eighteenth-century landscape paintings, which symbolised the politics of rural ownership, stability and benevolence.[1]

In contrast to the landscape painters of the eighteenth century, Turner responds directly to the agrarian and industrial transformation of Britain. More conventional landscape paintings had deployed an imagery displaying the continuity of the traditions of rural life, evoking the harmony between man and nature, and the permanence and order of the social landscape. Agricultural innovations and the depiction of farming practice were subordinated to the representation of English agrarian life by adapting and enlarging traditional rural themes, portraying the order of society in the order of the landscape, and evoking the harmony with nature in the classical golden age. Landscape painters portrayed agrarian continuity and change through symbolic depictions of social relations and landscape, but did not directly focus on the social and agricultural transformations in the countryside. In

1   J.M.W. Turner, *Lancaster, from the Aqueduct Bridge.*

Mr and Mrs Andrews (*c.* 1750) Thomas Gainsborough emphasises possession, the ownership of the well-managed Suffolk estate. Although the farm
shows signs of modern agricultural improvements, the painting focuses on
landownership in a parkland setting and the pleasures of rural life rather
than the cultivation of the surrounding farmland. In *Landscape: Ploughing
Scene in Suffolk* (1814) John Constable provides no hint of the ownership of
the land; the figures of ploughmen are set in a wide prospect, a landscape
dominated by a vast sky. The scene suggests the continuity of rural life in the
preservation of traditional husbandry, and evokes the harmony between man
and nature.[2] By transgressing this traditional aesthetics of nature in the
representation of landscape, Turner's watercolours suggest the social and
cultural transformations engendered by the agricultural and industrial revolutions that shaped the perception of 'nature'. In his famous painting *Rain,
Storm and Speed – The Great Western Railway* (1844), which became an icon
for the French Impressionists, Turner made a symbolic contrast between the
train and the countryside, capturing the immeasurable power of steam – the
very embodiment of the industrial revolution, with its capacity to generate
undreamt-of speed.[3]

Nature and the Culture of Modernity: Science, Agriculture and Industry

Similarly to current contemporary usage, 'nature', as the product of cultural and social categories, had a range of associations and meanings: it was 'the work of the mind' built from 'strata of memory'.[4] In the universal sense 'nature' denoted the cosmos as designed by God, the structure of material reality and more particular features of the material environment – landforms and organisms, all subject to scientific explanation in terms of laws of nature. 'Science' (commonly termed 'natural philosophy' in this period) established an ordered and structured knowledge of natural phenomena, delimiting the meaning and boundaries of 'nature' and the 'natural'. With the establishment of the conceptual and cultural framework of modern science in the seventeenth century, this scientific meaning came to shape understanding of the natural world. But 'nature' also had a non-scientific reference, being contrasted with human culture, the artefacts of civilisation, distinguishing the features and products of the earth from the contrivances of mankind. While a distinction was made between untamed wilderness and the humanised landscape subjected to cultivation (the pastoral and agricultural work of farming), the notion of 'nature' had a breadth of reference, which incorporated, as it still does, both untamed wilderness and the humanised landscape of human habitation – the 'countryside' cultivated, farmed and managed for human needs.

With the scientific revolution of the seventeenth century, science, especially Newtonian science as set out in *Principia* (1687) and *Opticks* (1704), became an important element of intellectual life. The physical cosmos came to be seen as intelligible in terms of Newtonian laws and as amenable to control through technological innovation. Science expressed the values and achievements of modernity, and its methods offered the models for technological innovation and rational agriculture. The emergent faith in science as a road to understanding rested on confidence in progress and the possibility of discovery, improvement and innovation. The 'moderns' adhered to the belief that the world of natural phenomena was transparent to investigation and that new methods of discovery could be forged; they urged that these discoveries be applied to exercise power over the natural world.

Understanding the natural world became entwined with natural theology: God was the lawgiver, with design and divine wisdom evidenced in the natural order. Older views that made appeal to miraculous (supernatural) interventions or (preternatural) wonders and marvels became supplanted by constructions of 'nature' as subject to laws of nature and open to controlled rational investigation. A fundamental shift in sensibility occurred with the visualisation of the universe as a clockwork mechanism comprising cogs, wheels and pulleys rather than a living organism. For Descartes and Robert

Boyle, particles of matter and motion defined reality; the world of sensory appearances, of colours and tastes, was reduced to a secondary status, explained as the result of the interaction of the particles on the human senses. By the early eighteenth century the scientific world view in Britain was enlarged from the analogy with clockwork (in the discourse of Newtonians, this was disparaged as a representation of nature), to embrace the conceptual structure of the ordered Newtonian system permeated by divine power. The concept of gravitational force, unique to the Newtonian system, was incorporated into the discourse of natural theology by appeal to God's design and continued active presence in the world. The notion of 'machine' came to function as a metaphor for intertwined concepts of order, system and laws of nature.

'Natural philosophy' was understood to be the inquiry into the phenomena of nature and their causes. Its values and philosophical structure, conditioned by natural theology, utilised the language of the aesthetics of nature, appealing to principles of harmony, order, design and beauty. System, harmony, analogy and unity were taken to be the fundamental principles of natural philosophy, and shaped the unifying systems developed in the late eighteenth century by Joseph Priestley, Erasmus Darwin and James Hutton. These natural philosophers rejected the potency of divine agency; but their influence, in helping to form an enlightened intellectual milieu, waned with the reaffirmation of philosophical, theological and scientific orthodoxies in the train of the British government's repressive political policy in the 1790s during the protracted war with France. Scientific knowledge became fragmented and codified into specialised divisions. The *Bridgewater Treatises* of the 1830s embodied this shift in sensibility, in seeking to reaffirm the hegemony of traditional forms of knowledge as shaped by the natural theology of design and in appealing to divine wisdom as evidenced in the natural order. The subject division of the *Treatises* marked the reordering of the sciences into new and specialised discourses pursued by expert practitioners. But the *Treatises* illustrate the weakened capacity of natural theology to provide a convincing and unifying intellectual structure, and functioned rather as a vehicle for the communication of science without threat to religious orthodoxy.[5]

The intellectual revolution of the seventeenth century established the cognitive structures of modern natural science; in the early nineteenth century the image of the 'natural philosopher' as one who probes nature's mysteries was succeeded by that of the 'scientist', the professional investigator working within a specialised scientific discipline.[6] It was at the 1833 meeting of the recently formed British Association for the Advancement of Science that William Whewell, the most philosophically acute of the *Bridgewater* authors, noted the poet Samuel Taylor Coleridge's complaint that the term 'philosopher' was 'too wide and lofty' to describe the activities of contemporary men of science. In response Whewell coined the term 'scientist'; this neologism served to demarcate 'science' (natural philosophy) from 'philosophy' (moral and metaphysical) and to emphasise the communality of the scientific enterprise.[7] By the 1830s social structures were being established which provided a basis for the integration of science into the fabric of social life. The new outlook was shaped by the industrial revolution, symbolised by the railway, and made the object of polite scrutiny in the Great Exhibition of 1851. There was a shift in the practice of natural philosophy from speculation and system building to more cautious and circumscribed forms of knowledge. New levels of precision were being achieved in the construction and use of scientific instruments – electrometers, dip circles, barometers and thermometers – and quantitative experimentation and mathematical theory became features of research in natural philosophy.

Technological control was an important element in the new commercial society of the eighteenth century. Science expressed the philosophical counterpart to the ordered nature of the countryside and landscape gardens, where landscapes were shaped for human ends. Cultivated landscapes evidenced order, as manifested in God's design of the natural world. The concern with the new aristocratic taste for landscape parks prompted discussion of the relation between the ordering of landscape gardens and the craft of the painter. In the late seventeenth century the traditional social order based on landowner-ship and aristocratic patronage began to give way to institutions of a commercial and centralised society. There was a shift from power based on landed property to an urbanised world based on the financial power of the commercial classes. Cultural patronage moved to the commercial class. The new commercial society was in part shaped by technological innovations; contemporary rhetoric associated technology (seen to be based on the new science of the seventeenth century) with financial speculation. The cultural values of this new consumer society fostered cultivation of the aesthetic pleasures of the natural world: the countryside, through the enclosure of land, was brought ever more systematically under the control of farmers and gardeners, as landscape was moulded to human convenience and the scenes of nature were transformed and polished in landscape gardens. The representation of 'nature' in terms of aesthetic categories and the glorification of cultivated rural life was a response to the rise of refined urban society; the commercial class incorporated and transformed the values and social mores of the traditional aristocratic elite.[8]

In an essay printed as an introduction to John Dryden's translation of Virgil's *Georgics* in 1697, Joseph Addison responded to the achievements of contemporary science in establishing the aims and procedures of inquiry into nature. A didactic poem on the contemporary scientific world view would be complex in its argument, he suggested, but the agricultural poetry of the *Georgics*, concerned with husbandry, was more amenable to poetic expression. For Addison, the promotion of agricultural improvement through the application of natural philosophy had Virgilian sanction; and in modern context this implied the association of the world view of the scientific revolution with agricultural and technological improvement in the countryside.

The progress of agriculture transformed the physical appearance of the countryside in the eighteenth century: nature was regularised, 'barren wilderness erased, or disappearing' as Wordsworth expressed it in *The Excursion* (1814), bemoaning the general preference for crops and pasture over mountain landscape.[9] Writing in the *Edinburgh Review* in 1811, the critic Francis Jeffrey noted the common contemporary aesthetic preference for cultivated rural landscape over rugged wilderness: 'There is scarcely any one who does not feel and understand the beauty of smiling fields and comfortable cottages; but the beauty of lakes and mountains is not so universally distinguishable.'[10] The aesthetic and moral veneration of untamed landscape wilderness, integral to the modern sensibility, has its origins in the writings of the Romantic poets. Concluding the first volume of *Modern Painters* (1843), in a passage offering advice to the prospective landscape painter, John Ruskin valorised untouched pristine wilderness, the source of spiritual illumination and artistic and moral truth, as embodying the 'real works of nature' unconstrained by human intervention; this was 'nature in her liberty . . . the pure wild volition and energy of the creation . . . not subdued to the furrow . . . of the agriculturist'.[11]

The shift in taste in Britain, from formal gardens to 'natural' ('picturesque') parkland, and for mountainous terrain and romantic wilderness, was consequent on the process of the rigorous cultivation of the countryside, the erasure of heaths and the enclosure of arable land and pasture.[12] At the end of the seventeenth century Gregory King estimated that about half of England and Wales was under cultivation, as arable, pasture or meadow; allowing for three million acres of woods and coppices and a further three million of 'forests, parks and commons', he calculated that there were ten million acres of 'heaths, moors, mountains and barren land'. In the eighteenth century commentators emphasised human interactions with the rural landscape: the cultivated landscape of ordered farmland was applauded, the wilderness deplored as barren. Touring England in the 1720s Daniel Defoe found Yorkshire moorland to be bristling with frightful hazards, and he described Surrey heathland as a barren desert.[13] This conception of landscape was shaped by cultural meanings drawn from traditional representations: the biblical paradise and the injunction, at the expulsion from the Garden of Eden, to cultivate the land, and the life of agricultural toil and moral virtue portrayed in the *Georgics*. In *Gulliver's Travels* (1726) Jonathan Swift applauded agricultural improvement but was scornful of fanciful modern schemes of agricultural innovation; only when an estate was cultivated in traditional fashion would agriculture flourish. Swift envisaged the management of the land to be free of innovations, preferring an environmental superintendence based on the traditional ethic of benevolence.

In the period 1750–1850 English agriculture underwent major changes: these have been described as an agricultural revolution involving the transformation in output and productivity brought about by changes in farming practice and technology; and, more broadly, as an agrarian revolution, a transformation of the rural economy and society, of the institutional framework of farming. Agricultural improvement led to a transformation in values, from rural benevolence to a commercial economy. The practice to be adopted, urged the proponent of agricultural improvement Arthur Young in 1767, was 'to cultivate that crop, whatever it be, which produces the greatest profit Valued in Money'. Technological change in agricultural practice had an important impact on the rural economy, leading to an increase in cereal yields per acre following the introduction in the later eighteenth century of the Norfolk four-course crop rotation, described by William Marshall in *The Rural Economy of Norfolk* (1787) as: 'No dung – no turnips – no bullocks – no barley – no clover – nor . . . wheat.'[14] This enabled the agricultural sector to sustain the increasing population. In its cultural and political transformation of the rural environment, the agricultural revolution was shaped by technological innovation and a tradition of agricultural literature deriving from classical antiquity.

A key development was the introduction of forage crops (clover and lucerne) as the essential element (causing nitrogenation) in the four-crop rotation. The use of such forage crops is discussed in works of Latin writers on agriculture: Columella, Palladius, Virgil and the elder Pliny. In England the replenishment of soil had hitherto been maintained through manure rather than through forage crops: this encouraged the growth of weeds, which were controlled through summer fallow with tillage. But the cultivation of clover as fodder for cattle led to the reclamation of wasteland and the employment of labour throughout the year. In the early eighteenth century interest in classical agriculture was fostered by Dryden's translation of Virgil's *Georgics* as noted earlier and by the landowning class's experience of the Italian landscape during the Grand Tour. Virgil was read as an agronomist as well as a poet, and while Dryden's translation was admired for poetic expression, it was, however, criticised as inaccurate in its use of agricultural terms. To remedy this defect William Benson published *Virgil's Husbandry* in 1725, a new translation of the first book of the *Georgics*, concerned with field crops. The cultivation of lucerne and clover required seed-sowing by hand: early in the eighteenth century the agricultural reformer Jethro Tull introduced planting with the seed-drill and horse hoe, substantially diminishing the quantity of seed that needed to be planted. In his *Horse-Hoeing Husbandry* (1731) he developed a theory of cultivation directed to the problems of the new agronomy; he argued that soil should be broken up by ploughing to facilitate the development of the root system and that the beneficial effect of spreading manure really lay in tilling the soil. These ideas lay at the core of the Norfolk four-course rotation of turnips, barley, clover and wheat. Agricultural innovations, based on appeal to classical agronomy, proceeded alongside the transformation of the estates of landed gentry; the availability of forage crop seeds (clover) imported from the Continent utilised a seed resource long preserved by the peasantry, and adapted to the cultivated environment.[15]

As with the industrial revolution, however, a focus on technological change is insufficient to characterise the agrarian revolution. Between 1550 and 1850 most of the common land of England came to be held as private property. The transformation of a subsistence economy into a capitalist agricultural system was facilitated by changes in the institutional structure of landownership, by the enclosure of common lands and the reclamation of wasteland, and by changes in employment patterns and property rights, especially as the result of parliamentary enclosure.[16] Arthur Young observed in 1809 that with enclosure 'a vast amelioration has been wrought . . . men have been taught to think'. He found a 'glorious spirit' of improvement among the farmers of Norfolk in 1768: 'instead of boundless wilds and uncultivated wastes . . . the country is all cut into enclosures, cultivated in a most husbandlike manner . . . yielding a hundred times the produce that it did in its former state'.[17] The enclosure of common pasture into small, hedged fields was established by the sixteenth century; the fastest rate of enclosure occurred in the seventeenth century; but from the mid-eighteenth century the process was sanctioned by acts of parliament. This process involved the ending of customary land tenure and the establishment of leaseholds; the removal of common rights over the use of land, often through a specific act of parliament for the enclosure of a particular locality, and the removal of open fields with the establishment of a farming landscape of hawthorn hedges or drystone walls in the uplands. And some two million acres of heathland were enclosed and brought under cultivation – lamented in the poetry of John Clare.

This process of enclosure often resulted in a switch in the use of land, from arable to livestock farming when enclosure involved the loss of common rights and the enlargement of farms, and from pastoral to arable farming when poor-quality pasture was brought under cultivation. Enclosure transformed the agrarian economy and facilitated farming innovations through the reduction of costs and the improved use of land through reclamation and drainage, but also led to the depopulation of the countryside and to the creation of a class of labouring poor. The transformation in the ownership and control of the land and new technological developments led to changes in social relations, cultural patterns and the economy of the countryside. In the widespread 'Captain Swing' riots in 1830 the rural poor destroyed threshing machines and burned ricks and barns.[18] These agrarian innovations – enclosed fields, the loss of common land, new farms, reclaimed heaths and newly introduced crops – were not depicted in the work of the great English landscape painters of the eighteenth century. Nor did these artists directly confront the social conflicts and environmental changes that transformed the agrarian landscape and shaped the experience of the natural world.[19]

In the eighteenth century a series of technological changes transformed the production of goods. Mechanisation became part of everyday life, transforming an agrarian economy based on traditional craft manufacture to an economy shaped by the growth of the factory system, machine production and urbanisation. The common experience of the natural world of the countryside was changed with the substitution of mechanical devices for human skills; the introduction of inanimate power, especially steam power, took the place of human and animal strength. These developments, termed the 'industrial revolution', occurred approximately between 1750 and 1850 in Britain.[20] The process and chronology of industrialisation in Britain shows diversity. Innovative techniques of manufacture coexisted with traditional workshop industry, and technological innovation was directed to the improvement of hand skills as well as the mechanisation of production. Important elements in industrialisation include: the provision of investment capital by stock companies and local banks; new transport systems, canals and turnpikes, which facilitated the movement of raw produce and manufactured artefacts; growing imperial expansion, which in this period was generally in the hands of mercantile companies, creating sources of the raw produce (especially cotton) and colonial and overseas markets for the products of the manufacturing industry; urbanisation, fostered by rural depopulation and the transformation of the agrarian economy; and the growth of the urban population and industrial manpower.

Although industrial change was fostered by the development of the economy rather than through technological innovations, science did provide inspiration and elements of the knowledge base for technological invention. Science shaped values, assumptions and motivations, rather than providing applicable knowledge in a form readily transferred to technology and industry.[21] Steam technology was developed and applied in the eighteenth century, by Thomas Newcomen, Thomas Savery and James Watt; but its development was not directly founded on the application of secure scientific principles. The innovations and improvements in the technology of the steam engine helped rather to generate the science of 'thermodynamics' that served to explain the principles of the steam engine. This scientific theory was only fully explicit by 1850, by which time Britain was in the age of steam-powered locomotives and the railway. By now the railway system had reached high standards of performance, using a novel and science-based technology, the electric telegraph, as a means of communication. The creation of a formally coherent scientific theory and its systematic application were not necessary for industrial use, because more limited applications of fragmentary scientific knowledge could be of value.[22]

A significant minority of manufacturers were alert to the utility of science and its prospective implications for technological improvement. But only after 1850 was science significantly integrated into technology so as to shape industrial development: the age of steam yielded to the age of electricity and chemistry. New science-based industries were developed: the chemical dyestuffs industry followed the discovery of aniline dyes by W.H. Perkin in 1856, and the electrical industry came with the development of the electric telegraph and the invention of the dynamo which could generate electric currents. The relationship between science and industrial technology may best be seen as cultural: attitudes to nature were shaped by the perception that scientific knowledge did have practical import, and that nature could be transformed by technological ingenuity.[23] This belief shaped the foundation of the Royal Institution in 1799: many of the founders were landowners with a strong interest in philanthropy and agrarian reform. Humphry Davy's work there on agricultural chemistry and the scientific basis of tanning was performed in response to an interest in agricultural improvement and hope for the practical application of scientific research. The establishment of the informal Lunar Society of Birmingham in the 1770s (its members included Joseph Priestley, James Watt, Josiah Wedgwood and Erasmus Darwin), and of literary and philosophical societies, especially the productive and influential Manchester Literary and Philosophical Society founded in 1781, provided the meeting place and the arena for cultural expression for a network of industrialists, natural philosophers and engineers. The association of scientists and industrialists may have had little effect in directly furthering invention and innovation; the significance of the patronage of science by industrialists is that science expressed the cultural values of the new manufacturing elite. Science joined the hope of technological progress to intellectual enlightenment and moral and spiritual edification. Although the impact of scientific research on technological innovation was limited prior to 1850, the cultural values associated with science and industry, promoted to a huge public in the display of artefacts at the Great Exhibition of 1851,[24] were a significant characteristic of the society that produced the industrial revolution.

While landscape artists of the eighteenth century did not directly focus on transformations in the countryside, poets and writers considered that the new industrial technology, especially the railway, would radically shift the relation-ship between man and nature.[25] As Walter Benjamin put it, 'technology is the mastery of not nature but of the relation between nature and man'.[26] In a celebrated essay on the 'Signs of the Times' the prophet of the Victorian age, Thomas Carlyle, wrote in 1829 that a new 'Age of Machinery, in every outward and inward sense of that word' had dawned. This was a spiritual transforma-tion: 'men have lost their belief in the Invisible, and believe and hope and work only in the visible . . . only the material, and the immediately practical, not the divine and spiritual, is important to us'. Therefore 'old modes of exertion are all discredited and thrown aside', machines would ensure that 'nothing follows its spontaneous course'.[27] From the 1830s there seemed to be no more potent example of the age of machinery than the railway. In 1844, on learning of the proposed railway line between Kendal and Windermere, Wordsworth asked, 'Is then no nook of English ground secure/From rash assault?'[28] In the second volume of *Modern Painters* (1846) John Ruskin lamented that the 'men who thus feel will always be few', for their views would always be ignored in favour of the mercenary demands of Wordsworth's opponents. Drawn into correspondence following this negative comment on the railways, he wrote in June 1846 that 'I am quite at a loss to conjecture what can be said in their defence', but found a small crumb of comfort: 'all that you can know, at best, of the country you pass is its geological structure and general clothing'.[29] An unforeseen consequence of railway cuttings was the exposure of strata of rock sections and fossils, encouraging a scientific window on the past – made popular in the writings of geologists such as William Buckland and Charles Lyell;[30] but for Ruskin, geological enthusiast that he was, this was by no means an approbation of the railways. In July 1845 the botanist Joseph Dalton Hooker had commented to Charles Darwin that 'Cutting open railways causes a change in vegetation in two ways, by turning up buried live seeds, & by affording space & protection for the growth of transported seeds'.[31] Hooker and Darwin were to reflect on the effects of the environment and geographical distribution on the fecundity of species ten years later, in the context of discussing Darwin's evolutionary theory.

From the 1770s the new factories and mills began to change the face of the landscape. Matthew Boulton opened his 'Soho Manufactory' near Birmingham in 1765, and with James Watt he began the manufacture of steam engines; and Josiah Wedgwood opened a large factory at 'Etruria' near Stoke-on-Trent in 1769; Richard Arkwright erected spinning mills, initially at Preston in Lancashire; and the Darbys established ironworks at Coalbrookdale in Shropshire. The new factories were first built in open country, close to a regular supply of water, and new villages grew up around them. But by the early nineteenth century the growth of the industrial towns and the expansion of mechanisation powered by steam generated industrial and urban blight.

Areas of native ground were certainly left in ruins during the age of steam, but industrial blight was confined. Woodlands retained ecological diversity; hedgerows kept their utility. The new forms of transport promoted intensive and sustainable arable farming, brought about by crop rotation and the use of animal fertilisers and skilled labour. Much of the 'traditional' English landscape remained. But there were complex relations between industrial and agricultural changes and the shape of the landscape. The use of coal and coke in iron and steel manufacture led collieries to follow seams deeper; to do so steam-pumping engines were needed, which required precisely tooled cylinders manufactured by the new metalworking industry. Steam engines became more efficient, fuelling the grouping of manufacturing machines in factories. Production and labour were coordinated. After 1850 there was a chemical revolution in which coal was used, directly and indirectly, to produce artificial acids, alkalis, dyes and fertilisers. Chemicals, metal products, machines and textiles were exported, and carried to the overseas empire by steam power, directed by the telegraph and expedited by financial services and marketing – each technology intersecting with the others, a cluster of technologies impacting on the environment.

In contrast to the landscape painters of the eighteenth century, artists of the nineteenth century began to respond to the industrial transformation of Britain. In *The Last Judgement* (1853) John Martin depicts a railway train falling into Chaos, setting the new technology within the framework of traditional religious imagery; and in *Rain, Storm and Speed – The Great Western Railway* (1844) Turner captured the power of steam with its capacity to generate undreamt-of speed.[32] Artists now set images of industry and urban life alongside representations of the countryside, responding to the social transformations brought about by the agricultural and industrial revolutions, and a changing aesthetics of nature.

'Ancients' and 'Moderns': Jonathan Swift and Gulliver's Travels

The conceptual and cultural framework of modern science developed in the seventeenth century made appeal for its intelligibility to the establishment of laws of nature, investing the culture of nature with a scientific reference. As a cultural movement science was associated with the values and achievements of modernity, and its methods offered a model for the progress of knowledge and the possibility of future discovery, improvement and innovation. But the value claims and implications of the new science were often found to be controversial in offering a challenge to traditional culture. The terms of Jonathan Swift's conservative and nostalgic critique of the 'moderns' and ridicule of the fads of modernity, made at the turn of the eighteenth century, bear on this contemporary debate and offer a foretaste of future discussions.

Swift's argument was rooted in contemporary developments; in joining science's claims to knowledge, the rise of a commercial society and changes in the ownership and use of land, he illuminated the debate over the culture of nature. Swift judged, as did others, that the claims of the new science to intellectual authority, and the associated emphasis on natural theology, compromised the hegemony of revelation as the basis of religion; and that the aspiration to the control and manipulation of the rural and urban environment through agricultural improvement and commercial innovation would fail to reshape the relation between man and the natural world. For Swift these innovations rested on the values of the 'moderns'; in their place he urged a traditional and nostalgic outlook, where 'science' is opposed to 'nature' and 'nature' is interpreted as an unchangeable reality.

Swift's satiric genius first came to public notice with the anonymous publication of *A Tale of a Tub* and its appendage *The Battle of the Books* in 1704. At Moor Park in Surrey, Swift had been the secretary of the retired diplomat Sir William Temple, whose 'Essay upon Ancient and Modern Learning', published in a collection of his writings in 1690, sparked a controversy which shaped Swift's literary career. On his retirement from public life in 1680 Temple had cultivated the life of a country gentleman and man of letters, writing elegant essays on moral and political philosophy in Ciceronian style. He was indifferent to the sciences and did not write as a classical scholar; his knowledge of Greek had faded and he was dismissive of modern textual scholarship as disruptive, as it thwarted his ideal of reading ancient authors as the basis for gentlemanly education and public life. Temple offered his essay as the reflections of a man of taste rather than a man of learning. He was provoked by the publication of two recent works: Thomas Burnet's *Sacred Theory of the Earth* (1681–9) and Pierre Fontenelle's essay on the ancients and the moderns (1688). In responding to these works Temple did not altogether disallow the merits of the moderns but asserted the cultural primacy of ancient models; denying the possibility of progress or improvement in literature and the sciences, he insisted on the superior achievements of the ancients. Burnet had sought to integrate the providential history of the Bible with an interpretation of the history of the earth derived from René Descartes, aiming to illuminate and interpret received biblical truths through advances in modern, rational understanding – and declaring that greater enlightenment could be anticipated as knowledge advanced. In his brief essay Fontenelle had emphatically applauded the achievements of the moderns, not only in philosophy and science, but also in literature. Temple demurred, contesting the ambitious claims of contemporary philosophy and science; in his view the work of Descartes, Thomas Hobbes and Nicolaus Copernicus was inconsequential and essentially unoriginal, resting on themes advanced in antiquity. Temple's argument regarding literature hinged on the assumption of the constancy of human nature (so no improvement in human wit could be expected) and his claim that the circumstances of modern life – disruptions caused by religious and civil strife, and the prevalence of scholarly pedantry – were inimical to the moderns in seeking to match the writings of their predecessors; for these reasons the moderns could only hope to imitate, not to surpass, the superior achievements of the ancients.

Temple's argument soon received a rebuttal. In his *Reflections upon Ancient and Modern Learning* (1694) William Wotton, a scholar of wide accomplishment and learning, contested Temple's pessimistic assumptions about the prospects of future knowledge and literary achievement; as befitted a fellow of the Royal Society, he paid special attention to the range of achievement of contemporary natural philosophy. Wotton conceded the literary accomplishments of Cicero, Horace and Virgil, and agreed with Temple that their achievements were dependent upon the circumstances of the ancient world; but unlike Temple, he drew the conclusion that under favourable circumstances those achievements might well be matched in the future. He believed that the great natural philosophers of the seventeenth century had surpassed the achievements of antiquity; here he was able to bolster his case by drawing upon an impressive range of contemporary work, offering an authoritative and systematic response to Temple's uninformed assertions. As the pamphlet war developed Wotton enlisted the support of his friend Richard Bentley, a classical scholar of awesome accomplishment. Temple had dismissed classical scholarship as intrusive 'modern' pedantry that threatened his conventional assumptions about the timeless nature of the classics. But Bentley considered that Temple had made a major error in showering praise on letters by custom attributed to an ancient Greek tyrant Phalaris (who was said to have roasted his enemies alive in a brazen bull). Bentley could show Temple's supposition that the *Epistles of Phalaris* was among the earliest prose works to be false; the letters were fictitious and had been written centuries after the time of Phalaris. For Bentley, Temple's evaluation of the *Epistles* on purely literary grounds (and only on the basis of a translation from the Greek original), while ignoring and dismissing any possible insights from philological criticism, exposed the superficiality of his regard for classical authors and the incoherence of his contempt for classical scholarship. Bentley gave a summary account of his argument for the spurious composition of the letters in a new edition of Wotton's *Reflections* in 1697. His unambiguous statement of the importance of critical scholarship for the understanding and appreciation of classical literature generated accusations of pedantry and ill manners, to which he responded with a systematic analysis demolishing the authenticity of the *Epistles of Phalaris*, a stunning exhibition of his scholarly methods.[33]

The weight of Bentley's scholarship did not end the quarrel between the 'ancients' and 'moderns'. The 'ancients' would not be dislodged from their core intuition, as put succinctly by Swift's associate Alexander Pope: 'Now Nature being still the same, it is impossible for any Modern Writer to paint her otherwise than the Ancients have done.'[34] In *A Tale of a Tub* Swift amplified the ridicule of scholarly pedantry; this became the central theme in the collective work of his circle, the satirical *Memoirs of Martin Scriblerus* (1741), and was exemplified most famously in Pope's *Dunciad* (1728–9; revised 1742–3). In *A Tale of a Tub* the allegory of three brothers representing Roman Catholicism, Anglicanism and Calvinism is interrupted by 'digressions', pseudo-scholarly satires on the absurdities of modern scholarly practice larded with references to Bentley and Wotton. Swift proceeds by imaginative flights of fancy and parody, contending that the critical arguments of the moderns had been so convincing that there was 'grave Dispute, whether there have been ever any *Antients* or no', declaring that the matter should be resolved by 'the most useful Labours and Lucubrations of that Worthy *Modern*, Dr B[en]*tly*'. The pretensions of the 'moderns' are exposed: he remarks that all branches of knowledge have improved since antiquity, a seeming concession ridiculed in his blithe assertion that such improvements have been achieved 'especially within these last three Years, or thereabouts'. He mocks the moderns by inverting scholarly reasoning: he criticises 'a certain Author called Homer' for his 'gross Ignorance in the *Common Laws of this* Realm, and in the Doctrine as well as the Discipline of the Church of England', while praising him as the 'Inventor' of the compass, gunpowder and the circulation of the blood; he caps the parody by regretting Homer's deficiency in matters of the latest research, his 'long Dissertation upon *Tea*' and his 'Method of *Salivation without Mercury*'. In a manner he later developed and perfected in *Gulliver's Travels* Swift pokes fun at the natural philosophers for their pointless inversion of natural processes, alluding to an experiment by Paracelsus who '*try'd an Experiment upon human Excrement, to make a Perfume of it*'.[35] In his satire Swift celebrated the virtues of classical imitation, extolling (with Temple) classical rhetoric over 'modern' pedantic classical philology and pretentious natural philosophy.

Gulliver's Travels (1726) provides a complex satire on contemporary English society and politics; the comedy and parody of *Martin Scriblerus* and *A Tale of a Tub* are given a more biting political edge. The sharpened tone is a response to the political culture that emerged after the Hanoverian succession in 1714 and the 1715 Jacobite rebellion. This new mood was shaped by the political and religious developments following the Glorious Revolution of 1688–9. The revolution settlement led to the Toleration Act of 1689, which modified penal laws against religious dissenters, and to the Protestant succession excluding the Catholic Stuart 'pretenders' from the throne. The opposition between the two broad political groups, known popularly as Whigs and Tories, hardened into party conflict, shaping the adversarial divide that came to characterise British parliaments. However, formal party organisation and division did not develop until the nineteenth century; in the eighteenth century the disposition of government and political power was strongly determined by the exercise of royal favour and by the personal associations and antipathies of the politicians.

The Glorious Revolution had been supported by a broad spectrum of political views, but in the course of time it came to have partisan associations. The Whigs were brought into power by the revolution, and while they included many leading aristocratic landowners, they presented themselves as merchants and were well represented among the directors of the Bank of England founded in 1694. The Whigs favoured the Low Church tendency within Anglicanism, emphasising the heritage of the Reformation. They were more open to accommodations between revelation and the claims of reason, and were more likely to be sympathetic to dissenters excluded from political life by the Toleration Act. As firm supporters of the Hanoverian succession the Whigs achieved a long period of political power, notably with the rise to primacy of Sir Robert Walpole, monopolising public life. Representing mercantile and financial interests, they allied themselves to the 'projectors' of financial and technological schemes, the banking and commercial enterprises which greatly expanded in size; the Bank of England, the national debt, the widespread use of paper currency and credit, and the financing of joint stock companies effected a new economic order. The Whigs defined the public interest in terms of the rhetoric of improvement, urging that financial and commercial expansion would be achieved through technological innovation generating wealth and control over nature.

The Tories had major support among the smaller rural gentry, a class subject to particular financial straits at the time, but also included among their ranks large landowners and merchants. Their loyalty to Church and King led to division over the Glorious Revolution; many Tories remained supporters of the deposed James II and some supported the Jacobite cause in 1715, discrediting the party's claims to government. In religion they favoured the High Church faction within Anglicanism which was opposed to the toleration of dissenters and suspicious of the claims for reason which they believed compromised the authority of revealed religion. The Tories looked to traditional cultural and religious values, emphasising ownership of land as the basis for political interest, and contesting the new economic order and consequent shift in political power. Tories defined the wider public interest in terms of the values and interests of landed society, a politics of nostalgia reaching back to cultural and religious values that had been shaken during the course of recent English history.

In Part III of *Gulliver's Travels*, 'A Voyage to Laputa', Swift develops his theme of satirising the pretensions of the new science. In England the values of the scientific revolution of the seventeenth century were first expressed in the writings of Francis Bacon, notably in the unfinished *Instauratio Magna* (*The Great Instauration*) published in 1620 and *The New Atlantis* (1626) which present a critique of traditional learning and education, offering the hope of a new method for gaining knowledge and power over nature.[36] Bacon asserts that the true end of knowledge is the benefit of humanity, and his work is pervaded by a sense of renewal and restoration (*instauratio*) and of modernity. *Atlantis* took its name from the fabled island mentioned by Plato, and Bacon's text belongs to a tradition of utopian narratives, most famously Thomas More's *Utopia* (1516). Salomon's House in the fictional island of Bensalem (a Hebrew word signifying 'son of peace') is an institution dedicated to scientific investigation. Bacon's tale of a society devoted to the cultivation of natural knowledge had a seminal influence in shaping the outlook of the founders of the Royal Society of London. After the Restoration of the monarchy and the foundation of the Royal Society in 1660 the promoters of the new science were careful to associate the cultural value of knowledge of the natural world with religious imperatives. In a manner that became characteristic of the new natural theology of mechanism, of order and design in nature, Robert Boyle argued that the laws of nature, exemplified by Descartes' laws of matter in motion, were to be construed as divine decrees. There was a harmony between God's works and God's word, the study of nature and the revealed truths of the Bible; so reason and revelation were complementary in providing comprehension of God's intentions. Despite Boyle's insistence on the primacy of revelation over reason, the rise in importance of natural theology in this Christian apologetic led to a shift in religious sensibility, to a stress on natural religion, the demonstration of God's existence from the order of nature. The natural philosophy of Isaac Newton in *Principia* (1687) and *Opticks* (1704) became emblematic in glorifying the achievements of science; science became part of the framework of public culture, the 'moderns' triumphing over the 'ancients'.

As noted, in the early years of the eighteenth century the traditional social order and power structure based on landownership and aristocratic patronage was yielding to institutions of a commercial and centralised society, in which aristocratic magnates remained important but power began to be shared with the rising financial and commercial classes. There was a shift from power based on landed property to an urbanised world where power was based on money. This new commercial and consumer society was in part shaped by technological innovations based on the new science of the seventeenth century, encouraging the rise of new professional classes seeking to join technology and financial speculation. Writing to Robert Boyle in 1667, the Secretary of the Royal Society Henry Oldenburg noted the advantages of Baconian experimental science 'both *for light and use*, above that of former times'. Public presentation of the values of the new science in the rhetoric of members of the Royal Society incorporated the Baconian stress on achieving technological power over nature, where experiments of 'light' (generating knowledge) would be followed by experiments of 'fruit' (yielding power). The pursuit of natural philosophy came to embody these economic and political tensions, as in the association of the entrepreneur James Brydges, Duke of Chandos and the Newtonian lecturer, author and cleric J.T. Desaguliers in a project by the York Buildings Company in the 1720s to bring a water supply to London. The Company drew upon Desaguliers' expertise in hydraulics to assist in the construction of pipes and reservoirs, and his familiarity with the Newcomen steam engine (developed at this time) used to raise water. The project ran into difficulties and was attacked in a mysterious, anonymous pamphlet (the author may even have been Desaguliers), *The York-Building Dragons* (1726), satirising the technology of steam power and water management. The steam engine monster would produce 'two such vast dense and opaque Columns of Smoak, that those who live in the Burrough will hardly see the Sun at Noon-day'; more improbably, 'the dragon . . . dipping his two heads into the Thames, will suck out thence such a prodigious quantity of water, that barges will never after be able to go through bridges . . . and the tide will not rise high enough . . .'.[37]

Swift associated the activities of inventors and 'projectors' with the new commercial order as manifested in the birth of the Bank of England and the growth of the national debt. The period witnessed a striking growth of joint-stock companies, notably the South Sea Company and the East India Company. He considered that these financial innovations, accompanied by new values and powers, contributed to the destruction of traditional society: 'so that power which according to the old maxim was used to follow land, is now gone over to money'. In political pamphlets Swift charted the relations between the Whigs, the Bank of England and the new class of moneyed men operating business and credit. The creation of this system of debt was basic to the political support of the government; and the new class that acquired wealth through public debt and stockjobbing took over estates of impoverished gentry, buying their way into parliament. Swift saw this brew of political and financial corruption as endemic to the new political order of the Hanoverian succession. For the Scriblerians the South Sea bubble of 1720, when the Company's stock rose to dizzy heights before the bubble of speculation collapsed with the burst of public confidence, epitomised the corrupted political and social order. The fortunes gained and lost in the deluge of speculation diseased the traditional social hierarchy which had maintained the fabric of the English Constitution; in Pope's words, 'peer and butler share alike' in a speculation that saw 'corruption, like a general flood' submerge 'Britain sunk in lucre's sordid charms'.[38] In the 1720s Robert Walpole became established as the dominant political leader of the Whigs; and to his Tory critics, money and the corruption it engendered became the very rule and sinew of government, prevailing over traditional social bonds and elevating private over public interest. Walpole's supporters affirmed the new power of money but challenged this judgement of the implications of corruption, maintaining that the smooth working of government and the public interest was dependent on corruption, for only through patronage could the offices of the state be properly distributed to the advantage of the functioning of the Constitution.

These themes are explored in *Gulliver's Travels*. In Part I, 'A Voyage to Lilliput', the voyager Gulliver is shipwrecked: the affairs of contemporary England are ridiculed by being mirrored in the activities of tiny Lilliputians. The kingdom had once had a balanced, traditional Constitution, which had degenerated through 'the most scandalous Corruptions into which these people are fallen by the degenerate Nature of Man'. Swift and his circle thought that under Walpole the differences between the parties had vanished and that Walpole used these meaningless distinctions simply to perpetuate Whig control. The meaningless party struggle is satirised in Lilliput, the parties taking their titles 'from the high and low Heels on their Shoes, by which they distinguish themselves'. In Lilliput only the 'low Heels' (corresponding to the Low Church Whigs) form the government, but 'it is alledged indeed, that the high Heels are most agreeable to our ancient Constitution'. The schism in religion between Catholic and Protestant versions of Christianity is satirised in the Lilliputian dispute over their religious injunction about the breaking of eggs at the '*convenient End*', the two parties holding divergent views as to whether the text meant the larger or smaller end. In Part II, 'A Voyage to Brobdingnag', the land of giants, Gulliver encounters a country free of political dispute, its monarch a statesman above parties, solicitous for his people. The king could not understand the basis of English government or the national debt, 'at a Loss how a Kingdom could run out of its Estate like a private Person'.[39] Although the king, a representative of the 'ancients', a statesman like Sir William Temple, reacted with horror to Gulliver's offer to explain the principles of gunpowder and cannon to ensure his power over his people, Gulliver on his next voyage encounters the scientific 'moderns' and finds that the Laputans can use their flying island (literally) to crush insurrections in the territory of Balnibarbi over which it floats.

In Part III, 'A Voyage to Laputa', the name of the island suggests *la puta* (the whore), with the hinted association of spiritual degeneracy.[40] Swift finds a parallel between the moral corruption of science and finance, and vents his wrath on the 'projectors'; in the absurdities of the flying island of Laputa and the Grand Academy of Lagado in Balnibarbi he parodies the absurdities of the 'moderns', exposing the pretensions of the new science. Swift pours merciless scorn on the association between science and financial projects that had created a market for information about air pumps, barometers and steam engines, as devices to be exploited. Lecturers and instrument makers such as Desaguliers provided the expertise that was drawn upon by 'projectors' such as the Duke of Chandos, who sought financial gain and political influence. Swift associated the Royal Society, the standard-bearer of the 'moderns', with the ephemeral schemes of 'projectors' dedicated to the production of rapid profits, and therefore saw it as embedded in modern commercial society.

Swift portrays the Laputans as living in a scientific utopia, parodying Bacon's *New Atlantis*. The Laputans excel in mathematical theorems that are quite useless when put to practical application: they prove unable to fit Gulliver with a suit of clothes; they ludicrously cut food into geometrical shapes; they are absorbed in pointless higher abstractions. For Bacon science was envisaged as the central activity of a good community, but in Laputa it is ridiculed, or indeed seen as the agent of oppression, which the Laputans use to tyrannise the inhabitants of the territory of Balnibarbi. Although the Laputans profess rationality (as in mathematics) they are superstitious, having fear of the sun and comets: here Swift alludes to well-known contemporary speculations on the history of the earth by Thomas Burnet, John Woodward and William Whiston. The allusion to comets is especially telling, for here Swift associates science with religious heterodoxy. In his *New Theory of the Earth* (1696) Whiston, subsequently notorious for his expulsion from his Cambridge chair for denying the doctrine of the Trinity, had tried to provide a mechanism for the deluge and the conflagration in terms of the past and future motions of Halley's comet (tracked in 1680).

Gulliver then visits Balnibarbi, the territory below the flying island. The Grand Academy of Lagado is a satirical portrayal of the Royal Society of London, where the academicians devote themselves to unproductive and pointless experiments in seeking to reverse productive natural processes. Many of the experiments described are comic versions of work published in the *Philosophical Transactions of the Royal Society*.[41] The most famous of these, the extraction of sunbeams out of cucumbers, was derived from a sequence of rather more sober experiments reported by Stephen Hales on the effect of the sun's rays on the sap of plants; his work on plant transpiration was an important contribution to the study of the relation between vegetation and the atmosphere, bearing on understanding the effects of deforestation on rainfall. Hales had argued that due to the agency of the sun's heat, water is transpired through the sap vessels of plants, passing into the leaves to be 'perspired'. In Swift's satirical inversion the experimenter, sorely in need of funding in the form of a ready supply of cucumbers, 'had been Eight Years upon a Project for extracting Sun-Beams out of Cucumbers, which were to be put into Vials hermetically sealed, and let out to warm the Air in raw inclement Summers'; Swift transposes Hales' experiments into the realm of the ridiculous. The extraction of sunbeams from cucumbers, experiments on the extraction of food from excrement (an idea that Swift had already exploited in A Tale of a Tub) and the production of naked sheep, represent fruitless reversals of productive natural processes, ludicrous 'experiments' that invert and degrade nature. Swift illustrates the political dimension of his critique of 'projectors', seeking to show that upstart money men and their scientific confederates could not be fit persons to undertake the government of the country.

Gulliver meets a nobleman called Munodi who shows him the effect that the mania for projects has had in ruining the country. Munodi himself, who represents traditional cultural values based on the ownership and customs of the land, has, like Sir William Temple, aimed to avoid modern innovations: 'he was content to go on in the old Forms; to live in the Houses his Ancestors had built, and act as they did in every Part of Life without Innovation'. Unlike other inhabitants of Balnibarbi, 'every Thing about him was magnificent, regular and polite'. However, even Munodi has succumbed to the current fashion: he recounts the episode of his construction of a new water mill at the instigation of 'a Club of those Projectors' who induced him to replace his excellent old mill with a new scheme based on a complex management of water flow, but 'the Work miscarryed'.[42] Here Swift may be alluding to the project for the management of a water supply in London. The effrontery of the Royal Society and the false utopia promised by science, the collusion of speculators and natural philosophers to destroy tradition and religion, is confronted in Swift's conservative critique and nostalgic vision of the past golden age of the traditional Constitution. In the battle between 'ancients' and 'moderns' Swift followed his mentor Sir William Temple in his continued commitment to the 'ancients', and in Gulliver's Travels he identifies projectors with the 'moderns'. His is a nostalgic ideology, where 'science' is opposed to 'nature', and 'nature' is interpreted as an unchanging reality, an analogue of a traditional social order and of permanent cultural and religious values.

In Gulliver's Travels Swift shows a broad interest in and acquaintance with the contemporary literature of travel and exploration, such as writings by Richard Hakluyt, and with Herodotus and Strabo, the sources of classical ethnography. Most famously this interest is manifest in his account of the Yahoos, a savage and uncouth form of humanity; but the entire work is shaped around the narrative of an extended voyage.[43] This concern with exploration and travel is a feature of contemporary engagement with the culture of nature, joining geography, ethnography, and the mapping and scientific investigation of the landscape and environment. This interest took sophisticated form in the writings of Alexander von Humboldt and Charles Darwin in the nineteenth century; climate and vegetation provide the aesthetic and scientific framework for the appreciation of nature.

CHAPTER 2

✳

Design

In October 1857 William Dyce recorded the scene of a family holiday by the seaside near Ramsgate in Kent in a watercolour drawing, which he worked up into an oil painting, *Pegwell Bay, Kent – A Recollection of October 5th 1858*, exhibited at the Royal Academy in 1860 (Fig. 2).[1] The title is seemingly misleading, for the recollection of the scene alluded to cannot have been Dyce's own remembrance of what he saw at Pegwell Bay a year before the date specified in the painting's title; yet Dyce seemingly depicts his own presence, as observer and artist, carrying artist's equipment at the foot of the cliffs. The clue to the meaning of the 'recollection' is given in the date ascribed to the scene depicted. Dyce has introduced a comet, not present in October 1857, which is unseen by his family (his wife, her two sisters and the artist's son), and which is only seen by the painter himself, who is given privileged access to the significance of the 'recollection'. The comet can be identified as Donati's Comet, first observed on 2 June 1858 and seen at its brightest on 5 October 1858,[2] which excited the interest of the public and aroused the curiosity of astronomers. The 'recollection' therefore is not the remembrance of a scene observed by the artist, even though he is portrayed as an observer, but the product of his reflective contemplation of the scene as it would have been, where he has pondered the meaning for humanity of a celestial phenomenon. The painting's title draws implicit attention to the sublime nature of astronomy in revealing divine creativity and to the observation of celestial events in enlarging the imagination of human observers; as an aesthetic category the 'sublime' was conventionally associated with altitude and vastness, and with the awe and terror inspired by the immensity of the celestial worlds revealed by astronomy.

Dyce's family are oblivious to the cosmic and sublime scene enacted over their heads; they are concerned with the innocent task of gathering seashells, or perhaps with the currently fashionable investigation of rock pools, marine molluscs and sea anemones. Dyce's depiction of his wife and her sisters innocently pursuing conchology is restrained, emphasising their innocent and demure engagement (consistent with the serious intellectual emphasis of

2   William Dyce, *Pegwell Bay, Kent – A Recollection of October 5th 1858.*

the painting); but his viewers at the Royal Academy would no doubt have recollected cartoonists' lampoons of the incongruous sight of women picking over rock pools while wearing balloon skirts – their costumes presenting a sight oddly analogous to the grotesque forms of sea anemones.[3] This interest had its serious scientific side: Charles Darwin's study of barnacles, lauded by the Royal Society, played into his evolving theory of the origin of species. Dyce's viewers may have been familiar with the popular literature of marine zoology, notably the works of Philip Gosse who had emphasised that the study of shells and marine zoology revealed the work of the Creator, placing the observation of sea life into the prevailing tradition of natural theology, the doctrine that divine creativity and benevolence were manifest in the objects of nature. Dyce's seemingly innocent portrayal of the gathering of seashells has significant bearing on contemporary natural history and natural theology.[4]

The central part of the painting is occupied by a detailed depiction of the cliffs, showing a minute attention to the details of the geological formations. As Dyce will have known, sea cliffs provided prime sites for the study of geological strata and fossils, and his painting records details of the erosion of the chalk, emphasising the passage of geological time, and places quotidian human activities in a framework of the immense timescale of geological history. Astronomy, with its imagery of clockwork and the mechanism of the heavens, had long provided the basis for discussion of God's design as manifested in nature; but in the nineteenth century geology, evoking the historical and progressive development of the earth – raising questions of the reality of the flood, the age of the world and the origin of mankind – came to be regarded as a fruitful resource for reflection on natural theology. The two most scientifically authoritative of the *Bridgewater Treatises* of the 1830s, presenting up-to-date scientific information with reference to natural theology, were by William Whewell on astronomy and William Buckland on geology. Dyce's depiction of the sublime heavens above and the eroding terrestrial strata below, which shaped human existence while human beings unknowingly went about their carefree lives, placed human activity within the time frame of astronomy and geology and within an intellectual outlook that joins science to natural theology and the aesthetics of nature. These were themes that shaped the culture of nature in the eighteenth and nineteenth centuries.

Nature and Culture: Natural Theology

The mechanisation of the natural world was a key feature of seventeenth-century philosophy and science: the traditional organic analogies, of nature as purposive, of planets as endowed with principles of life, of the cosmos connected by a web of interacting powers linked by correspondences, affinities and influences, were displaced by images of clockwork. This mechanical universe raised questions about the role of God in nature – of design, divine intervention, and God's providence and government of the world – questions about God's existence and attributes. These issues were fully discussed in the correspondence between Newton's spokesman the theologian Samuel Clarke and Gottfried Wilhelm Leibniz in 1715–16. Among other matters Leibniz voiced objections to Newton's theory of gravity: that the attractive force of gravity could be conceived as a mathematical construct, unexplained by a mechanism of particles; that the force of gravity was construed as the direct expression of God's continued active presence in the world; and that the solar system would require occasional reformation by divine providence to restore irregularities developing over time. This theory, argued Leibniz, was philosophically incoherent as it implied that God is obliged to 'clean' and 'even to mend' the 'machine of God's making', a doctrine that 'would not sufficiently show his *wisdom*' in foreseeing and making provision for the future course of events in the solar system. Moreover, if the attraction of the sun and planets 'cannot be explained by the nature of bodies' – that is by a mechanism of particles in motion – then the Newtonian concept of attraction is 'a miraculous thing'. For Leibniz the universe is 'a watch, that goes without wanting to be mended', for God's 'machine lasts longer, and moves more regularly, than those of any other artist whatsoever'. In reply Clarke maintained that the

Newtonian concept of the force of gravity is 'natural' because it is shown to act 'regularly and constantly' according to the law of gravitational attraction. Newton did not deny that gravitational attraction had a cause, but this cause was 'invisible and intangible'; thus 'gravitation may be effected by regular and natural powers, though they be not mechanical'. Indeed, Newton's rejection of the simplicities of the analogy between the world and a clock (for all Leibniz's talk of the omniscient clockmaker) reinforced the role of providence in the cosmos: the concept of the world as a clock operating 'without the interposition of God, as a clock continues to go without the assistance of a clockmaker' is, according to Clarke, 'the notion of materialism.'[5]

The correspondence exposes a central theme of debate in natural theology: what role could, and should, be left for God in a clockwork universe? By the early eighteenth century the scientific world view in Britain had become emphatically Newtonian, a 'mechanical philosophy' transformed by concepts such as gravitational force, unique to the Newtonian system, and which was explained in terms of divine involvement in the workings of the universe. The notion of 'mechanism' was enlarged to embrace the conceptual structure of the Newtonian system; and 'machine' could function as a metaphor for intertwined concepts of order, system and laws of nature. By emphasising gravity as the manifestation of divine agency, and as demonstrating divine omnipotence, the Newtonians sought to defeat charges of 'materialism', of excluding God from the world of matter and motion.

By contrast, a group of thinkers known as 'deists' who were contemptuous of Christian doctrines of revelation and providence – Anthony Collins, Matthew Tindal and John Toland – used the concept of the clockwork universe to argue for the restriction of the divine role to the initial creation of a law-bound system. Despite the insinuations of the Newtonians to the contrary, this was not Leibniz's position: he affirmed God's providence but found it in the perfection of the created order, in divine foresight not in the imperfections of the natural order which – as he saw it – Newton sought to remedy by divine interventions. For Leibniz, God works miracles for the salvation of sinners and to manifest divine favour, not to mend deficient clockwork. But the emphasis on natural theology by the scientific 'moderns' could raise problems for Christian apologists. Appeal to design, to God as the architect of the natural world, does not in itself distinguish Christian theism from deism – lending support to the suspicion that science could readily slide into 'materialism'. And if, as David Hume was to argue, the design argument fails, then the claims of theism (and indeed deism) based on the divine craftsman would crumble.[6]

In his *Notion of Nature* (1686) and *Christian Virtuoso* (1690) Robert Boyle set out a classic formulation of the meaning of laws of nature as a 'system of rules' of God's devising. In espousing the mechanical philosophy he supposed that the 'aggregate of bodies that make up the world' are defined by 'mechanical affections' of size and figure. He was careful to explain that the expression 'the law of God prescribed to [nature]' must be understood as 'improper and figurative', for a 'law' is 'a notional rule of acting according to the declared will of a superior' and only intelligent agents could respond to laws. Laws of nature are therefore to be understood as the language of the divine will. The laws of nature do not themselves generate the motions of matter constituting the universe, for these motions are produced 'by real power, not by laws', this power being divine agency. Boyle rejects the doctrine that the active powers of matter are immanent in its fabric; his mechanical philosophy supposes that the particles of bodies were created and given due motions 'according to the laws of motion prescribed by the Author of things', and natural phenomena would follow in an orderly manner through the assistance of God's providence, by 'his ordinary and general concourse'. Nor would this exclude 'God's special providence', miraculous interventions wrought by supernatural means.[7] In this 'voluntarist' theology, as subsequently further elaborated by Newton, the activity of matter is maintained by the continual exertions of God's will, thus emphasising divine omnipotence. This voluntarist theology shaped Samuel Clarke's objections to Leibniz's appeal to divine omniscience and foresight, and Newton's refusal to explain gravity in physical terms as a property of matter. To allow Leibniz's notion of the universe as a perfect clock and his theory of gravity as explained by a mechanism of particles would diminish God's presence in nature and open the way to materialism and atheism. In supporting this Newtonian doctrine William Whiston maintained that gravity was an 'immechanical power', for it was not 'any power belonging to body or matter at all'; gravity was the expression of God's continual activity in the universe.[8]

An early platform for the dissemination of Newtonian natural theology emerged in the lectures founded under the will of Robert Boyle. These *Boyle Lectures*, envisaged as sermons to prove the Christian religion against its opponents with an injunction to avoid controversies among Christians, were delivered between 1692 and 1714. Several of the lecturers took the opportunity to utilise, and thereby popularise, key features of the Newtonian system of the world – notably the first lecturer Richard Bentley in the *Confutation of Atheism from the Origin and Frame of the World*, the last two of his series of eight lectures delivered in 1692; Samuel Clarke in his *Demonstration of the Being and Attributes of God* and *Discourse Concerning the Unchangeable Obligations of Natural Religion* delivered in 1704–5; and William Derham in his *Physico-Theology* delivered in 1711–12. These works became widely familiar in the eighteenth century as sources of scientific knowledge: the Newtonian construction of the natural order was communicated within a framework of natural theology, which established norms of cultural orthodoxy. While natural theology, culminating in the *Bridgewater Treatises* of the 1830s, provided an enduring framework for scientific communication, the balance between the exposition of science and the apologetics of natural theology changed.

Both Bentley and Clarke were leading 'moderns'. Bentley became the standard-bearer of modern critical classical scholarship (see p. 14); and Clarke translated Newton's *Opticks* (1704) into Latin, the *Optice* (1706), including Newton's lengthy 'query' on gravity and providence that prompted Leibniz's objections, to which Clarke responded in corresponding with him. Clarke was (correctly) suspected of disbelieving the doctrine of the Trinity, a view privately held by Newton, publicly espoused by Whiston; the orthodoxy of these men and the natural theology they avowed was often perceived as suspect by High Church clerics. Clarke's emphasis in his *Demonstration of the Being and Attributes of God* on natural religion, on order and design as demonstrating the existence of God, leading to the inference of the divine attributes of intelligence, wisdom, power and free will from the evidence of the divinely designed universe, gave rise to suspicion among the orthodox (despite protestations to the contrary) that revelation was given insufficient weight by the Low Church theologians in their emphasis on natural theology. In the case of the first series of *Boyle Lectures*, by Richard Bentley in 1692, there is unequivocal evidence of Newton's direct participation. As he prepared the manuscript of his final two lectures for publication, Bentley applied to Newton to help clarify points in his exposition of natural philosophy. The four letters that Newton wrote to Bentley, first published in 1756, contain some of his most famous statements on understanding gravity: his denial that gravity could be 'innate, inherent and essential to matter' (rejecting mechanistic and materialistic explanations), and his affirmation that 'Gravity must be caused by an Agent acting constantly according to certain Laws; but whether this Agent be material or immaterial, I have left to the Consideration of my Readers'.[9] These statements shaped Bentley's argument in his published lectures; his demonstration of God's existence from the origin and frame of the world served to give an accessible account of Newtonian natural philosophy, shown to be theologically safe.

A century later Immanuel Kant found the spirit of rational inquiry to be the characteristic of 'Enlightenment': *sapere aude* (dare to know). For the philosophers of the Enlightenment – Voltaire, Denis Diderot, David Hume and Kant – the scientific revolution provided the model in their quest to assert the autonomy of humanity and reject the shackles of religion, to provide rational understanding through unrestricted inquiry, to examine all preconceptions and shibboleths, to embrace discovery, criticism and innovation. For the philosophers of the Enlightenment nature was seen as a self-regulating system of laws, man could study himself only as part of the natural world and the present age was more enlightened than past ages; they espoused the doctrine of historical progress. Their historiography valorised the achievements of Newton and the moderns as having roots in classical antiquity; they repudiated the Christian millennium and credited the Greeks with inventing the spirit of inquiry. The appeal to the values of modernity and to Greek antiquity as the fount of civilisation subverted traditional Christian historiography – the human past was treated as a secular not as a sacred record. In the famous chapters 15 and 16 of the first volume of his *History of the Decline and Fall of the Roman Empire* published in 1776, Edward Gibbon explained the rise of Christianity by exclusive reference to secular, human causes. He considered the self-reliant civic virtues and tolerant paganism of the Roman state, where sceptical philosophers regarded religious beliefs with irony and magistrates found the superstitions of the populace socially useful, to have been subverted and corrupted by the infusion of Christianity.

These attitudes undermined the value systems that natural theology aimed to defend. In the essay on miracles published in his volume of *Philosophical Essays Concerning Human Understanding* in 1748, David Hume slyly remarks that 'the *Christian Religion* not only was at first attended with miracles, but even at this day cannot be believed by any reasonable person without one'; that is never, for 'no human testimony can have such force as to prove a miracle, and make it a just foundation for any system of religion'. The claims of revelation did not withstand sceptical scrutiny. In his essay on providence, the 'religious hypothesis', he treats with contempt the appeal to the evidence of nature to establish the attributes of the deity. The conventional analogical argument, beloved of the natural theologians, is devoid of content: 'with our reasonings from the works of nature . . . we can, by analogy, infer any attribute or quality in [the Deity]', with the consequence that 'every supposed addition to the works of nature makes an addition to the attributes of the Author of nature'.[10] He subjected the argument from design to an exhaustive critique in his *Dialogues Concerning Natural Religion* published posthumously in 1779. Hume did not deny that the universe had a first cause, but questioned that this cause was either the transcendent God of Christian theology or the creator God of the deists. The design argument rested on analogies, but analogies could at best be suggestive and could not be proved. Consider the common analogy between nature and a machine, which purported to establish that the cosmos was a created artefact; but 'the world plainly resembles more an animal or a vegetable than it does a watch or a knitting-loom', and its 'origin ought rather to be ascribed to generation or vegetation than to reason or design'. The design argument fails: the god of natural theology would (on this argument) be analogous to a seed rather than a clockmaker. Examples of design might be illusory, for the 'adjustment of means to ends', the adaptation to use or need, showed that there was an 'order, an economy of things' in nature, but did not prove design. Nor did nature show a beneficent creator at work; on the contrary, natural history gave examples of 'curious artifices of nature in order to embitter the life of every living being'. All was not for the best in the best of all possible worlds. Even if it were conceded that the cause of the universe bore a '*remote analogy to human intelligence*', having disposed of the power of analogy Hume maintained that such a proposition did not bear on human life or action and that 'the dispute between the sceptics and dogmatists is entirely verbal': it 'affords no inference that affects human life', a conclusion satisfactory to the sceptic but not to the theist. Hume's cool scepticism left the claims of both revealed and natural religion resting on shaky foundations.[11]

Hume's critique did not dispose of natural theology. His sceptical philosophy was not understood, and he was dismissed and disregarded by the influential Scottish 'common sense' philosophy, inaugurated by Thomas Reid in his *Inquiry into the Human Mind on the Principles of Common Sense* (1764) and developed by Dugald Stewart in volumes of essays published from the 1790s. These philosophers held that the common-sense principles taken for granted in human life rest on the constitution of human nature, and that Hume's scepticism about causality and natural theology was sophistry and could be refuted by the common sense of personal experience and social circumstances. But as Kant pointed out in his *Prolegomena to any Future Metaphysics* (1783), where he acknowledged that Hume had awoken him from his 'dogmatic slumber' and dismissed the confused opinions of his common-sense critics, Hume did not deny that the concept of causality was indispensable and useful; his point was that knowledge consists in connections between ideas, and that our perception of cause and effect is no more than the product of repeated experience. The outlook of the common-sense philosophers scarcely grappled with Hume's sceptical critique of causal reasoning and natural theology, but was compatible with an untroubled assumption of theism and the logic of the design argument that professed to offer independent and rational proof of the existence and attributes of God also, and primarily, revealed in biblical testimony. The authors of the *Bridgewater Treatises* made only occasional reference to Hume, 'that ablest champion of the infidel cause', as Thomas Chalmers described him in 1833.[12]

Natural theology remained resilient because it served the wider ends of Christian apologists, providing parallels between the operations of providence in the natural world, in maintaining the stability of the natural order through laws of nature, and in the political Constitution through the operation of laws in sustaining social and political stability. Arguments of this kind were made in the *Boyle Lectures*, delivered in the aftermath of the 1688 Glorious Revolution, where the intervention of providence was seen in the displacement of a Catholic monarch, James II, and in the establishment of the

Constitution and the Protestant succession. The post-1688 settlement was seen in terms of an analogy between the laws of England, preserving political and civil liberty, and the mechanical laws determining the stability of nature. In his *Commentaries on the Laws of England* (1765–9) William Blackstone set out the system of checks and balances provided by the two Houses of the legislature, the executive of government and the monarchy, within a Constitution that served to guarantee liberty; and he drew the analogy with the operation of a machine and the interaction of mechanical powers: 'Like three distinct powers in mechanics, they jointly impel the machine of government in a direction different from what either, acting by itself would have done ... a direction which constitutes the true line of the liberty and happiness of the country.'[13] These arguments, not entirely accurate as a description of the realities of the political process, defended a Constitution that protected the interests of the inherited social hierarchy determined by family, rank and property, and were important in shaping the response to the French Revolution and its Napoleonic aftermath, where the maintenance of the Constitution and of social stability was seen as vital to the political authority of the government. The course of events in France, which had initially evinced some sympathy among the political elite (Edmund Burke excepted), had by 1792–3 turned from revolution against autocracy to terror and dictatorship; and French foreign policy became aggressive in encouraging revolution across Europe and the declaration of war against Britain. The government began a policy of repression of seditious ideas; and the arguments of natural theology became a weapon in rescuing science from the grasp of radicals sympathetic to the new order in France, such as the Unitarian Joseph Priestley and the sceptic Erasmus Darwin. Their conceptions of matter and nature, condemned by the orthodox as materialism and atheism, blurred the conventional (and Newtonian) disjunctions between the active and the passive, between matter and spirit, constructions of nature that had shaped the arguments of the natural theologians in asserting the role of providence, law and stability in nature and the Constitution.

One of the most popular works in the natural theology tradition, Archdeacon William Paley's *Natural Theology* (1802), was written at this crucial historical moment. Paley tirelessly uncovered instances of mechanism in the natural world as evidence of design, providing a summation of many eighteenth-century themes: 'Our business is with mechanism' throughout animate and inanimate nature, he declares. He opens his book with the famous contrast between a watch and a stone encountered on walking over a heath: while the watch contains moving parts indubitably 'framed and put together for a purpose', the stone seemingly might have 'lain there for ever'. But Paley maintains that the stone is, like the watch, also framed by mechanism. This indicates the major thrust of his argument, the depiction of nature as a mechanism, asserting the analogy between the works of nature, created and designed, and a contrivance of the mechanical arts such as a watch: 'contrivances of nature surpass the contrivances of art, in the complexity, subtlety, and curiosity of the mechanism ... yet ... are not less evidently mechanical, not less evidently contrivances, not less evidently accommodated to their end'. In advancing this argument, Paley's procedure is, as he declares, 'cumulative', based on a series of interlocking inferences, where he appeals especially to anatomy, seeking to establish that every part of every organism had been designed for its function, being especially taken with the eye which he discusses in great anatomical detail, remarking that God must have known 'the most secret laws of optics' to create such a perfect structure for its intended purpose. His overall conclusion is emphatic: 'The marks of *design* are too strong to be got over. Design must have had a designer. That designer must have been a person. That person is God.' But Paley and the natural theologians were concerned to demonstrate the attributes as well as the existence of the deity from design in nature: he infers the unity of God from 'the *uniformity* of plan observable in the universe'. He is particularly concerned to establish divine beneficence, noting that divine goodness can be inferred because 'the Deity has superadded *pleasure* to animal sensations'.[14]

These comfortable arguments do not attend to Hume's sceptical refutation of their cogency. Paley was well known as a moral and political philosopher, the author of *The Principles of Moral and Political Philosophy* (1785), in which he maintained that moral rules had their only justification in utility, employing this principle as the basis of a defence of existing political institutions. He incorporates his moral utilitarianism into the argument of *Natural Theology*, along with his claim (in a pamphlet) that labourers enjoyed a happier lot than the wealthy – on which Coleridge had caustically commented, 'Themes to debauch Boys' minds on the miseries of rich men & comforts of Poverty'.[15] Paley maintains that the inequalities of wealth in society did not compromise divine beneficence, that disproportionate social distinctions 'may be endured', and that 'artificial distinctions sometimes promote real equality', so that the stratification in the social order could be seen as beneficial to the community as a whole. Natural theology had a range of apologetic uses.[16]

For the first generation of Romantics who became publicly prominent around 1800, Paley's natural theology represented a complacent and stultifying religious and political ethic; but Coleridge demurred at the extremity of William Wordsworth's vehement dismissal of natural theology, recording surprise and dismay in October 1803 over 'a most unpleasant Dispute' with Wordsworth and William Hazlitt on the design argument as developed by John Ray, William Derham and William Paley: 'they spoke so irreverently so malignantly of the Divine Wisdom ... But *thou*, dearest Wordsworth – and what if Ray, Durham, Paley, have carried the observation of the aptitudes of

Things too far, too habitually – into Pedantry? – O how many worse Pedantries! ... O dearest William! Would Ray, or Durham have spoken of God as you spoke of Nature?'[17] Coleridge was to remain suspicious of Wordsworthian pantheism, Wordsworth's 'vague misty, rather than mystic, Confusion of God with the World & the accompanying Nature-worship', as he put it in 1820.[18] His notebook entry suggests that for Wordsworth the spontaneous contemplation of 'nature' would be compromised by natural theology: the aesthetics and language of the natural theology of design yielded to the aesthetics of nature, the assertion of the power of nature's immediacy and of the primacy of nature as immeasurable and unfettered by the forms and constraints of scientific theory.

For the natural theologians the language of natural theology, the assertion of order in nature through mechanism and design, had joined the discourses of aesthetics and natural philosophy; the metaphor of mechanism on which Paley grounded his natural theology now came under attack. Coleridge wrote of the 'philosophy of mechanism, which, in everything that is most worthy of the human intellect, strikes *Death*'.[19] In the 1870s John Ruskin was later to encapsulate the Romantic distaste for mechanism and its associated aesthetic in commenting on a passage in Charles Darwin's *Descent of Man* (1871, second edition 1874), where Darwin had used a mechanical analogy to describe the coloured pattern of the wing feathers of the Argus pheasant: 'All these materialisms, in their unclean stupidity, are essentially the work of human bats; men of semi-faculty or semi-education, who are more or less incapable of so much as seeing, much less thinking about, colour; among whom, for one-sided intensity, even Mr. Darwin must be often ranked, as in his vespertilian treatise on the ocelli of the Argus pheasant which he imagines to be artistically gradated, and perfectly imitative of a ball and socket.'[20] For Ruskin, in Darwin's hands the primacy of nature's beauty had been displaced by the imagery of mechanism.

The Romantics offered a new philosophy and theology of nature as a radical alternative to the mechanism and Newtonian science of the Enlightenment. Friedrich Schelling, Henrik Steffens and Novalis in Germany, and Coleridge in Britain, sought to establish the harmony of self and nature; they urged a unified view of the cosmos that would permit the integration of material and spiritual elements in the world, restoring that which had been lost at the Fall. Aesthetics provided the basis for the reunion of self through nature; understanding and knowledge of nature would be achieved by the immediate engagement with sensory experience unmediated by the abstract categories of science that were seen as deadening to the imagination. There was general hostility to the mechanical natural philosophy associated with Newton and the formalistic, descriptive, taxonomic natural history of Carolus Linnaeus. Newton in particular, as the primary representative of the natural philosopher, became an ambiguous figure, his experiments on colours drawing diverse comment. Johann Wolfgang von Goethe attacked Newton's prism experiments and theory of spectral colours as abstract and artificial, divorced from the true range of experience of colours in nature; while Coleridge, who rejected Newton's natural philosophy as materialistic, on reading the *Opticks* found that he admired 'the beauty and neatness of his experiments' and 'the accuracy of his *immediate* deductions from them'.[21] In *The Prelude* (1805; revised 1850) Wordsworth voiced respect for Newton's power of abstract thought, recollecting his statue in the chapel of Trinity College, Cambridge 'with his prism and silent face'; while for the younger poet John Keats in *Lamia* (1820), Newton's theory of spectral colours would 'clip an Angel's wings . . . unweave a rainbow'. In the history of science Johannes Kepler rather than Newton was admired: the creative act of discovery was venerated as an act of 'genius' (a crucial Romantic concept) over Newton's formulation of the deductive structure of the laws of mechanics. William Blake portrayed Newton as the spirit of geometry and measurement, as a desiccated calculating machine. For the German 'nature philosophers' the cosmos was treated like a living being and described in terms of organic metaphors of growth, development and decay, rather than the imagery of clockwork and Newtonian mechanistic laws. Science itself was not rejected, but new forms of knowledge were sought based on the interaction and conflict of forces (termed dynamism) rather than the interactions of matter (reviled as mechanism); dynamical process and development became the new motifs, ideas that the 'nature philosophers' found in embryo in the writings of Leibniz and Kant.

Nevertheless, natural theology continued to serve apologetic ends in complementing revealed religion and in using the order of nature as the analogy for a political Constitution, and for hierarchy and stability in society. The language of mechanism, design, order and stability had moreover become commonplace for both Christians and deists; its ambiguity could provide a comfortable cloak under which scientific ideas could be communicated and rendered safe. For the Romantics, however, the 'Newtonian' cosmology of designed mechanism, Paley's moral utilitarianism, the political economy promoted by Thomas Malthus and the complacent benevolence of natural theology formed interweaving discourses, a world view at odds with their emphasis on imagination, nature's immediacy and the union of the self and nature, subject and object. Reflecting on the account of the ravages of mosquitoes and horseflies (bulldogs) in John Franklin's *Narrative of a Journey to the Shores of the Polar Sea* (1823), Coleridge noted that he would 'recommend these pages to the ingenuity of the physico-theological *minute* Final-cause men –. Their Teleology, I suspect, would have a hard job of it with the American Musquitos, and winged Bull-dogs "that range in the hottest glare of the Sun, and carry off a portion of flesh at each attack"'.[22] In the face of the 'one great Slaughter-house the warring world' of struggling organisms, as Erasmus Darwin put it in *The Temple of Nature* (1803),[23] and the social and political instabilities of the early nineteenth century, the stable and benevolent model of the natural world and society promoted by the natural theologians ultimately withered.

Yet the natural theology tradition, while faltering, showed spasms of further development because it continued to serve apologetic purposes, to shape and unify scientific theorising and to incorporate new scientific developments. Natural theology provided a vocabulary that continued to be used to support the scientific enterprise and to counteract claims that science posed a challenge to orthodoxy, its language being sufficiently diverse to embrace different religious cultures and philosophical positions.[24] In the early nineteenth century, with the rapid development of the science of geology, forms of argument in natural theology shifted from utilising the imagery of clockwork and mechanism (a static model of nature with which deists had become comfortable) to evoking the historical and progressive development of the earth as evidenced in the rocks and fossils. A rising generation of Christian geologists argued that fossils and the uncovering of geological strata displayed the progressive nature of the earth's development since its creation. The static vision of the natural order espoused by Paley (with his emphasis on mechanism in the contrivances of nature) yielded to a dynamic model of the earth's development over time, shown by the introduction of new species and the succession of strata. Geology testified to successive acts of creation rather than the eternity of stony and living forms, but also raised questions about the authority of the account of creation in Genesis. In *Vindiciae Geologicae* (1820), his inaugural lecture at Oxford, William Buckland claimed that a universal flood (as in Genesis) was necessary to explain the deposition of fossils and strata. He was concerned to show that science was a safe form of knowledge for the believer, arguing that geology had now 'added largely to the evidences of natural religion in that kingdom of nature, where proofs of design and order are most obscurely developed'.[25]

In the 1830s eight books were commissioned under the will of the eighth Earl of Bridgewater, to present a wide range of scientific information to be 'considered with reference to natural theology', and to be accessible to the educated (rather than the expert) reader. The authors of the *Bridgewater Treatises*, each paid £1,000, did not share a common religious position, though four were ordained; they formed a diverse group, but were appointed as leading representatives of the scientific and religious establishment, and they expressed the natural theology as held, in its various forms, by the gentlemanly elite. Several of the authors display discomfort with Paley's confident moral utilitarianism and optimism deduced from design. While Paley had sought to demonstrate divine attributes by a cumulative argument, appealing to endless examples of design and mechanism, the argument of the *Treatises* is more muted about demonstrative natural theology, which is disclaimed or subordinated to the exposition of authoritative surveys of the natural world. The purpose of the *Treatises* was to communicate science and to establish its religious tendency, thereby rendering it intellectually safe;[26] but the apparent discomfort of the authors in confidently asserting the apologetic arguments of traditional natural theology, consequent on philosophical caution or their religious outlook, is nevertheless marked and striking. The *Athenaeum* reviewer of William Whewell's account of *Astronomy and General Physics* (1833) declared that he would have 'recommended it to youth . . . as a safe guide to science, and as worthily inculcating . . . sublime truths' had the book been published in a cheaper format.[27] Natural theology provided norms of cultural orthodoxy within which science could be safely communicated to the public, rather than a body of philosophical argument to be confidently asserted.

The diversity of the authors' outlook and their caution over apologetic argument can be seen in the (rather different) strategies adopted by the Scottish evangelical cleric Thomas Chalmers, the entomologist and High Church cleric William Kirby, and the chemist and physician William Prout. In his *Moral and Intellectual Constitution of Man* (1833) Chalmers developed a form of natural theology compatible with his evangelical outlook, departing from the traditional form of reasoning based on mechanism and design as followed by Paley. Chalmers denied that natural theology was the 'foundation of the edifice' of religion for it could not provide demonstrative proof of the existence and attributes of God. He presented natural theology rather as 'a prompter to enquiry' for it created 'an appetite which it cannot quell' which could only be satisfied by revelation: it is 'a preliminary to the gospel' rather than a rational foundation for the acceptance of revelation.[28] In his account of *Animals* (1835) Kirby made little reference to natural theology in the body of his massive text, religious matters being largely confined to his ninety-page introduction. Born in 1759, he wrote from a distinctive High Church theological position; in his introduction he urged a literal reading of Genesis and voiced suspicion of modern geology; and he considered natural theology to be significant in its relation to revelation rather than as a form of apologetic argument. His book reads like a text on natural history given a distinctive religious packaging; but he concluded his work with the conventional claim that in describing the 'nice adaptation [of animals] to their several functions' he had 'traced . . . the footsteps of an infinite Wisdom, Power, and Goodness'.[29] In his account of *Chemistry, Meteorology* (1834) William Prout rested his case for design and a designer on the limping appeal that the molecular arrangements of matter described in his text would be illustrative of design: the 'numerous instances of prospective arrangement' of matter recorded in his text provide 'evidences of design'. God is envisioned as 'the Great Chemist of nature' adjusting and arranging the molecules of matter; and he stated that he had avoided a full exposition of the design argument as irrelevant to his purpose.[30] The work reads like a chemistry text with gestures towards natural theology.

In the *Treatises* written by Buckland and Whewell, prominent men of science who provided intellectual leadership at the time, their strategy of philosophical caution and adroit withdrawal from the task of proffering an apology for natural religion makes explicit the fragmentation of natural theology in the *Treatises*. In *Geology and Mineralogy* (1836) written at the prompting of the Archbishop of Canterbury, William Howley, William Buckland the Canon of Christ Church and Reader in Geology at Oxford, strove to accommodate his science with his religious creed. He repeated arguments from his Oxford inaugural lecture of 1820 in striving to reconcile geology and Scripture, to establish a theologically safe time for geological history. He argued that the word *beginning* in the first verse of the Book of Genesis should be understood as separated by 'an undefined period of time', perhaps 'millions of millions of years', from the creation of the 'surface of the earth and . . . of its present animal and vegetable inhabitants' subsequently recounted in the biblical text. The geological history of the earth, recorded in its strata and fossils, was antecedent to the biblical account of the earth and the human race. Thus he maintains that all 'the phenomena of Geology . . . are passed over in silence' in the biblical narrative of the earth and its inhabitants. This was a liberal Anglican response to the literalist strictures of William Kirby, but was hardly an uncontroversial opinion – and Buckland's opponents were quick to equate his notion of unlimited time with eternity – but this argument was expounded in his introductory chapter and occupied only a small portion of his text. Nearly six hundred pages of detailed instruction in geology follow, presented within a framework of natural theology broadly drawn from Paley; and in finally summarising the implications of his exhaustive survey of geological facts, Buckland declared that 'in all of these phenomena, considered singly, we have found evidence of Method and Design'; moreover, he finds 'a never failing Identity . . . of . . . construction' which points to the 'existence of One supreme Creator of all things'.[31] In Buckland's hands biblical scholarship served to create an intellectual space in which the geologist can safely work; while natural theology provided a context for the interpretation of geological discoveries. In his *Bridgewater Treatise* natural theology is denuded of its demonstrative claims: it provides a safe framework for the presentation of geological science.

In writing on *Astronomy and General Physics* (1833) the Cambridge scientist, cleric and scholar William Whewell, whose religious position embraced Buckland's liberal Anglicanism and elements of evangelicalism, did address the traditional philosophical issues raised by natural theology, his philosophical sophistication apparent in showing tacit awareness of the critiques of natural theology mounted by Hume and Kant. His basic point is that Paley's 'train of deductive reasoning', that 'design must have had a designer', would 'be of no avail to one whom the contemplation or the description of the world does not impress with the perception of design'. Adaptations to use or need might suggest that there was an order in nature, but could not prove design. The conviction that the universe manifests 'design and purpose' can only be impressed on the mind by 'such combinations as we perceive, immediately and directly', but cannot be deduced from scientific observations of nature. The 'truth' that the order of nature is such as to 'imply a Being endowed with consciousness, design, and will' stands 'among original principles' of reasoning, a (Kantian) regulative principle that orders our experience of phenomena, and that does not belong 'at the end, but at the beginning of our syllogisms'. He explains that his purpose was 'not to show that Natural Theology is a perfect and satisfactory scheme', but states that his objective was more limited: 'to bring up our Natural Theology to the point of view in which it may be contemplated by the aid of our Natural Philosophy'. Natural theology serves an illustrative rather than a demonstrative purpose, for divine power and wisdom were displayed in the laws and design of the natural world, and could not be deduced from them.

This approach is sustained in the threads of argument that pervade and unify Whewell's exposition, especially his emphasis on the 'mutual adaptation in the laws of nature', in the 'power by which they were established'. He declares that '*Nature acts by general laws*' and that 'wise and benevolent design' can be seen in the 'interweaving . . . of . . . adaptations'. In contrast to Paley's reiterated appeal to examples of mechanism and mechanical structure, which do nothing to establish design and a designer, Whewell places emphasis on the complexity of the laws that shape and unify the order of nature, which suggests design and purpose to the mind. He also draws the analogy between natural and moral laws: the 'power by which . . . the laws which prevail in nature' was established offers evidence of 'selection, design, and goodness'; and God is also 'the Governor of the moral world', the author of the intellectual, aesthetic, moral and religious powers of man. Whewell distances himself from Paley's emphasis on mechanism and moral utilitarianism. He makes it clear that natural religion was not in 'itself sufficient for our support and guidance', and in appealing to 'lights derived from revelation' his argument was wholly orthodox in subordinating natural to revealed religion; this was also a stance consistent with his diminution of the authority and demonstrative power of natural theology.[32]

The subject matter of Whewell's *Treatise* lies within the compass of Newtonian astronomy and mechanics, the sciences that provided the basis for Paley's appeal to mechanism and design in the natural world, but Whewell departs from what he judges to be the demonstrative deductive claims of Paley's natural theology, from his emphasis on mechanism, and from his moral utilitarianism. He turns the core argument of natural theology around: design and purpose could not be deduced or proved from whatever order the universe may seem to possess, but are convictions impressed on the mind 'immediately and directly' by interweaving powers, by the variety and complexity of nature, and its likeness to a system of embedded laws. Natural philosophy is prior to natural theology: the 'truth' that there is a designer shapes and is revealed by the comprehension of nature's fecundity, the interweaving of adaptations through natural laws. The fragmentation of demonstrative natural theology apparent in the *Bridgewater Treatises*, the dissipation of its authority and unifying grip, is especially clear in Whewell's adroit philosophical argument which had its counterpart in the aesthetics of nature of Romanticism: the assertion of the primacy of the order of nature over the metaphors of design and mechanism that had shaped the aesthetics and language of traditional natural theology.

The Aesthetics of Nature

Philosophical reflection on the aesthetic appreciation of nature in the eighteenth century was shaped by natural theology. The works of nature, like works of art, were considered to be artefacts, the products of acts of creation and design: the human craftsmanship manifest in the production of a work of art had its counterpart in the order of nature created by God. In his essay 'On the Beautiful', included in *Philosophical Essays* (1810), Dugald Stewart, who retired from lecturing at Edinburgh that year, illustrated, but also qualified, the analogy between works of art and the works of nature, contrasting the finite capacities of humanity with God's infinite power. While the creative imagination of the artist was determined and limited by human faculties and works of art were contrived on a human scale, the works of nature are products of a being endowed with infinite power and creativity. While the 'works . . . of Nature [are] impressed . . . with the signature of Almighty Power, and of Unfathomable Design', works of art were produced by artists following 'that obvious uniformity of plan which we expect to find in the production of beings endowed with the same faculties, and actuated by the same motives as ourselves'. Nature necessarily transcends art, for narrowly human criteria of design and beauty were not to be expected in the works of nature, where a 'deviation from uniformity . . . appears perfectly suited to that *infinity* which is associated, in our conceptions, with all her operations'.[33] The language and assumptions of natural theology shaped the terms of discussion of the aesthetics of nature. Reflections on the nature of beauty and standards of taste (the term 'aesthetics' only became current in the nineteenth century) were a product of the culture of civilised manners. There was a widespread assumption that just as the ownership of land and the possession of independent means was the qualification for unbiased judgement of the public interest and participation in government, education and the leisured pursuit of the arts would provide the conditions for exercising the generalising judgements necessary for the appreciation of beauty and the exercise of taste. In his *Essays on the Nature and Principles of Taste* (1790) Stewart's friend Archibald Alison voiced the opinion that it was 'only in the higher stations ... or in the liberal professions of life, that we expect to find men either of a delicate or comprehensive taste' necessary for the appreciation of art, for the 'inferior situations of life, by contracting the knowledge and affections of men, within very narrow limits, produce insensibly a similar contraction in their notions of the beautiful or the sublime'. And in similar fashion, the 'sensibility to the beauties of the country' would be unattainable to those professing the 'mechanical arts', for men passing their earliest years in urban commercial pursuits would 'lose all those sentiments of tenderness and innocence' which gave the 'foundation of much the greater part of the associations we connect with the scenery of Nature'.[34] The aesthetic appreciation of nature was accessible only to the leisured and educated elite.

The writings on aesthetics by Joseph Addison, Francis Hutcheson, George Turnbull, Edmund Burke, Richard Payne Knight, Archibald Alison and Dugald Stewart take the relation between works of art and works of nature to be a central element of their discourse. Hutcheson's *Inquiry into the Original of our Ideas of Beauty and Virtue* (1725, second edition 1726) set out an aesthetic theory that shaped subsequent philosophical debate, discussing the appreciation of beauty in nature in relation to design and natural theology. A central work in the tradition is Burke's *A Philosophical Enquiry into the Origin of Our Ideas of the Sublime and Beautiful* (1757, with a second edition in 1759). Burke's distinction between beauty and the sublime, and especially his emphasis on the sublime as a crucial aesthetic category, shaped subsequent writing on aesthetics in philosophy (by Kant) and literary criticism (by Coleridge). Discussion of the sublime was fostered by Nicolas Boileau's French translation in 1674 of the classical literary treatise *On the Sublime* (*Περί ὕφους*) that was attributed to the third-century rhetorician and philosopher Cassius Longinus (though now thought to have been written two centuries earlier). In the treatise *Peri Hupsous* by 'Longinus' the sublime is equated with altitude or loftiness and is associated with rules and procedures in literature and rhetoric; but in the eighteenth century the sublime came to denote the vastness, awe and terror inspired by altitude and greatness in nature, and for the Romantics the sublime came to be associated with emotion and the imagination, with the spontaneity of genius.

In his famous series of essays on the 'Pleasures of the Imagination' published in *The Spectator* in June and July 1712, Joseph Addison explained that these pleasures 'arise originally from sight' and 'from the actual view and survey of outward objects', echoing Locke's doctrine that ideas are not innate but are occasioned by sensations; and he gives aesthetic priority to the 'bold and masterly [and] . . . rough careless strokes' of nature over the 'nice touches and embellishments of Art'. The pleasures of the imagination are prompted by visual experience and 'proceed from the sight of what is *Great, Uncommon* or *Beautiful*'. He associates beauty with the 'delight in colours', for there is no 'more glorious or pleasing show in nature, than . . . the rising and setting of the Sun, which is wholly made up of those different strains of light that shew themselves in clouds of a different situation'; the allusion to Newton's theory of spectral colours is clear. By 'greatness' Addison means the 'largeness of a whole view', the feeling of awe induced by 'stupendous works of nature' such as 'a vast uncultivated desert, of huge heaps of mountains, high rocks and precipices, or a wide expanse of waters', the 'rude kind of magnificence which appears in these stupendous works of nature'. He also associates 'greatness' with the enlargement of the imagination induced by the ideas of immensity and infinity due to 'the Authors of the new philosophy': 'we are lost in such a labyrinth of suns and worlds, and confounded with the immensity and magnificence of Nature'.[35] Aesthetic pleasure is derived from the visual experience of nature and expressed in terms of the language of natural philosophy. The earth's vast deserts, mountains and oceans are associated with the plurality of worlds in the immensity of the universe, all regarded as symbols of greatness and awe – in subsequent usage, the 'sublime'. In 1728 Alexander Pope published a satire on 'true modern poetry' – its title 'Peri Bathous: or, Martin Scriblerus, His Treatise of the Art of Sinking in Poetry' making satirical allusion to 'Longinus', *Peri Hupsous*, the sublime as '*Altitude*' – and explained that 'the Sublime of Nature is the Sky, the Sun, Moon, Stars, etc'.[36]

In his *An Inquiry into the Original of our Ideas of Beauty and Virtue* (1725, second edition 1726) Francis Hutcheson, who held the chair of moral philosophy at Glasgow in the 1730s, linked the aesthetic category of beauty to natural philosophy and natural theology. Hutcheson was concerned to establish why it is that nature, designed by God, is perceived as beautiful. He maintains that there is an internal sense suggesting ideas of beauty, order, harmony and design to the mind when artefacts and scenes exhibiting uniformity amid variety are perceived. Education and custom may influence and shape 'our *internal Senses*', but 'this presupposes our *Sense of Beauty* to be *natural*'. His aesthetics of nature rests on the assumption that nature is an artefact; that nature is therefore analogous to a work of art; that as an artefact nature has been created and designed by an artificer; and that nature manifests the power and wisdom of its creator, God. He distinguishes between absolute or 'original' beauty, and relative or 'comparative' beauty; while absolute beauty is perceived without relation to any other object, relative beauty is the beauty that results from comparison. He states his criterion of 'original' beauty in the following terms: 'The Figures which excite in us the Ideas of Beauty, seem to be those in which there is *Uniformity amidst Variety*.' But 'comparative' or 'relative beauty' takes the form of an imitation of an original by a copy; it is perceived in 'objects commonly considered as *imitations* or *resemblances* of something else', and is judged in relation to correspondence to the '*Intention* in the Artificer' – he gives as an example the imitation of landscape in gardens. The '*Beauty* arising from correspondence to *Intention*' opens a 'new scene of *Beauty* in the Works of Nature', because it raises the question of the relation between the perfection of parts to the perfection of the whole: 'considering how the *Mechanism* of the various Parts known to us, seems adapted to the Perfection of that Part, and yet in Subordination to the Good of some *System* or *Whole*'.

Hutcheson's answer is given in terms of design and natural theology: the uniformity of nature and the perfection and contrivance of both its parts and its system as a whole manifests '*Reason* and *Design*' which arise from the '*Intention* of the Author of *Nature*'. There is an analogy between the artifice and intention of the landscape gardener and the creative power and design of God: judging the works of nature aesthetically in terms of the intention of the deity grounds the aesthetics of nature in natural theology. Our pleasure in the beauty of nature depends upon our 'constitution [which has been] adapted to preserve the regularity of the universe'. Our senses have been so contrived that we find beauty in the 'uniformity, proportion and similitude thro all the parts of nature which we can observe'. The sense of beauty in nature arises from an awareness of design and intention: the 'evidences of wisdom in the adminis-tration of nature' generates 'a sense of beauty'. The beauty perceived in nature is grounded in design: the 'divine goodness ... has constituted our sense of beauty as it is at present', and 'the Great Architect' has similarly adorned 'this vast theatre in a manner agreeable to the spectators', contriving to harmonise our innate sense of beauty with the regularity and mechanism engendered in the order of nature.[37] The aesthetics of nature is entwined with natural theology.

Some of Hutcheson's terms of argument are deployed in the *Treatise on Ancient Painting* published in 1740 by George Turnbull, who taught at Marischal College, Aberdeen, in the 1720s. The bulky volume is resplendently illustrated with engraved plates of classical art, which however bear little rela-tion to the verbose and stodgy text (dismissed as waste paper by both William Hogarth and Johann Winckelmann); but there is a significant centrepiece, 'a philosophical Consideration of the Fine Arts', where Turnbull argued that painting is a language conveying scientific information about nature. He aimed to establish the value of painting in education and in the promotion of moral and civic virtue, maintaining that the purpose of education is to bring to perfection the 'Sense of Beauty' by which nature can be enjoyed, for 'the Beauty and Perfection of Arts, of Life, and of Nature, is the same'; the aesthetics of nature and art alike rest on 'the Wisdom and Goodness of our Maker, the Creator and Upholder of all things'. The imitative arts therefore seek to emulate the 'Beauty, the Harmony, the Grandeur, and Order of Nature'. Turnbull's aesthetics of art rests on the aesthetic appreciation of nature, construed in terms of natural theology. As a uniform system 'observing general Laws', nature 'becomes orderly and the Object of Science'; natural philosophy is knowledge of 'the general Analogies and Harmonies which take place in Nature'; the laws of nature manifest 'Wisdom, Goodness, and Benevolence'; and these laws, harmonies and analogies are discovered through 'our natural Sense of Beauty arising from Regularity and Order, or, in other words, from Uniformity amidst Variety'. These words echo Hutcheson, and Turnbull follows Hutcheson's argument that the aesthetics of nature is intertwined with natural theology and natural philosophy.

Turnbull recognises a close link between nature and landscape art: nature is 'the sole Object of Knowledge, and of Imitation whether in Arts or Life'. He describes landscape paintings as 'Samples or Experiments in natural Philosophy' because they 'fix before our Eyes beautiful Effects of Nature's laws'. Even paintings of imaginary landscapes, not copied from 'any particular appearance in Nature', if they are 'conformable to Nature's Appearances and Laws' would be 'still the Study of Nature itself', for 'if the Composition be agreeable to Nature's settled Laws and Properties, it may exist'. Conformity to the laws of nature, not the faithful replication of nature's appearances, is the criterion of truth and reality. If landscape paintings succeed in representing 'the Effects of Nature in the visible World', they may be considered as 'proper Samples and Experiments' and may therefore assist in the scientific under-standing of nature, for 'Pictures may bring Parts of Nature to our View, which could never have been seen or observed by us in real life'. And the argument cuts both ways: the study of landscape paintings will sharpen the appreciation of nature itself, awakening 'superior Pleasures' in the aesthetic appreciation of nature for an observer 'who hath an Eye formed by comparing Landscapes with Nature'. An observer accustomed to 'observing and chusing picturesque Skies, Scenes, and other Appearances, that would be really beautiful in Pictures' will be 'more attentive to Nature'. The language of landscape painting is the language of natural philosophy; both convey scientific information about the world of nature. The key theme linking nature and its imitation in painting is the connection between aesthetics and natural philosophy: there is an 'inseparable necessary Connexion . . . between the reality of Beauty, Unity, Order, Grace and Greatness in Nature . . . and in all ingenious Imitations of

Nature by Arts'; this connection 'is the chief Scope of true Philosophy'. The aesthetics of nature is consequent on the enlarged view of natural philosophy established by natural theology: 'those who content themselves with reducing Effects to their physical Causes, without any Reflections upon the Wisdom, Goodness, and Benevolence, that appear in the Laws of Nature, deprive them-selves of the highest Satisfaction the study of Nature affords' in receiving pleasure 'by our Sense of Beauty arising from Unity of Design, or Uniformity amidst Diversity'.[38]

The aesthetic writings of the Scots Hutcheson and Turnbull were shaped by the increasing cultural importance of science and its pendant, the design argument in natural theology: the philosophy of art is subsumed within the aesthetic appreciation of nature. By contrast, Edmund Burke's influential *A Philosophical Enquiry into the Origin of Our Ideas of the Sublime and Beautiful* (1757, with a second edition in 1759) looks to 'Longinus'. In the preface to the first edition of his treatise Burke states that 'ideas of the sublime and beautiful were frequently confounded ... even [by] Longinus, in his incomparable discourse'. Burke's argument came to be celebrated for discussion of the 'sublime', and he explains his concept of beauty by comparison: 'For sublime objects are vast in their dimensions, beautiful ones comparatively small; beauty should be smooth, and polished; the great, rugged and negligent; ... the great ought to be dark and gloomy; beauty should be light and delicate; ... one being founded on pain, the other on pleasure'. His notion of beautiful objects as 'smooth' and 'polished' was no doubt derived from Hogarth's 'line of beauty', the graceful serpentine curve illustrated in his *Analysis of Beauty* (1753). Burke follows Hogarth in supposing that there was an essence of beauty, that the 'real cause of beauty' was an inherent property of objects, 'some quality in bodies, acting mechanically upon the human mind by the intervention of the senses'. In associating the sublime with greatness Burke draws upon 'Longinus' and Addison; and Burke enlarges upon Addison's discussion of greatness and the stupendous, introducing further criteria of sublimity: 'greatness of dimension', 'vastness of extent', 'infinity', 'magnifi-cence', 'dark and gloomy colours', 'some modification of power', 'delightful horror'; and his most famous definition, that 'terror is ... the ruling principle of the sublime'. Burke's notion of the sublime as arousing emotions of awe, horror and terror in the beholder was the most celebrated and influential feature of his treatise. Ultimately the sublime lies outside human control: 'Look at ... [an] animal of prodigious strength, and what is your idea before reflection? It is that this strength will be subservient to you? ... No; the emotion you feel is, lest this enormous strength be employed to the purposes of rapine and destruction ..... The sublime ... comes upon us in the gloomy forest, and in the howling wilderness, in the form of the lion, the tiger, the panther, or rhinoceros'.[39]

Burke places the emotions generated by nature at the heart of his theory of beauty and the sublime. An additional aesthetic category, the 'picturesque', became important in shaping taste in the latter part of the eighteenth century. The aesthetics of the picturesque view was made popular in the travel writings of William Gilpin from the 1770s, and became important in discussions of the aesthetics of gardening and of landscape parks; the 'picturesque' played a central role in late eighteenth-century discussions of the aesthetics of nature. The landowner and connoisseur Richard Payne Knight was the most philosophically acute of these writers in urging that the 'picturesque' was an aesthetic category distinct from the 'beautiful' and the 'sublime', and in contesting the claim (by Uvedale Price) that the 'picturesque' was a quality to be found in 'distinctions in external objects'. In his *An Analytical Inquiry into the Principles of Taste* (1805) he espoused the common opinion that good taste is only accessible to a cultivated elite; this was especially so in the case of appreciating the 'pleasing effects of colour, light, and shadow' characteristic of the picturesque, which would 'afford no pleasure, but to persons conversant with the art of painting'. Knight claims that the picturesque style of painting had been invented by Giorgione and perfected by Titian: in the work of these Venetian artists tints were 'blended and melted together', and were 'happily broken and blended, and irregular masses of light and shadow harmoniously melted into each other'. The 'picturesque' denoted an aesthetic category associated with a specific style of painting. To elucidate his meaning Knight stressed the Italian derivation of 'picturesque': '*pittoresco* must mean, *after the manner of painters*'. The relation to painting implied that the appreciation of landscape as 'picturesque' can 'only be felt by persons who have correspondent ideas to associate; that is, by persons in certain degree conversant with that art'. The aesthetic appreciation of a landscape painting, and of a landscape itself, is therefore a product of connoisseurship: 'By thus comparing nature and art, both the eye and the intellect acquire a higher relish for the production of each'.[40] As with Turnbull, the aesthetic appreciation of nature is intensified by the study of painting, and the converse.

Archibald Alison and Dugald Stewart were friends from their student days at Glasgow University in 1771–2; and Stewart, appointed to the chair of moral philosophy at Edinburgh in 1785, was the dedicatee of Alison's *Essays on the Nature and Principles of Taste* (1790). Alison and Stewart rejected Hutcheson's notion that the perception of the beautiful is innate, an internal aesthetic sense; to understand the aesthetics of beauty and the sublime they looked to psychology, to the science of human nature developed by David Hartley in his *Observations on Man, his Frame, his Duty, and his Expectations* (1749). Hartley's psychology rested on the extension of the Newtonian natural philosophy of particles and forces to represent the excitation of vibrations and signals in the nerves and brain by sensory impulses; the complex impressions of different sensory signals lead to a neurological process of the association of 'ideas' – the association of visual and auditory sensations. In discussing the pleasures of the imagination, Hartley considered Hutcheson's aesthetic principle of beauty as the conjunction of uniformity amidst variety, arguing that the source of the pleasures of beauty arise from the association of uniformity and variety with the beauties of nature and with works of art, and the associations linking works of nature and works of art. In addition he emphasised aesthetic pleasure in relation to what he termed 'theopathy', the association of beauty with divine order, power and goodness. Alison and Stewart developed this approach to aesthetics based on the association of ideas and natural theology. Writing within the intellectual tradition of the Scottish Enlightenment, they historicised human values and culture. Adam Smith, John Millar and Adam Ferguson saw history in terms of cultural and social development, outlining a theory of society in which social structures were held to progress from hunting, pastorage and agriculture to commerce. Dugald Stewart emphasised that the growth and spread of knowledge altered moral relationships and the basis for political and social institutions. For Alison and Stewart cultural values were a product of civilised society, for the educated mind was susceptible to a higher degree of generalisation and more able to achieve happiness, refinement and manners, and to be susceptible to aesthetic pleasure.

In developing a theory of aesthetics based on the association of ideas, Alison maintains that there is no innate aesthetic sense and objects have no intrinsic aesthetic quality, but that all aesthetic judgements derive from trains of association: 'the Qualities of Matter are not to be considered as sublime or beautiful in themselves, but as either sublime or beautiful from their being the Signs or Expressions of qualities capable of producing Emotion'. A sensory stimulus sets a train of associations in motion, an exercise of the imagination excites the emotions of beauty or sublimity: 'Matter is not beautiful in itself, but derives its Beauty from the Expression of Mind.' The capacity to respond to beauty is dependent on the cultivation of the range of necessary associations, and is shaped by education and habits of life: 'the more that our ideas are increased . . . the greater the number of associations we connect . . . [and] the stronger is the emotion of sublimity or beauty we receive'. Discussing Hogarth's famous winding line of beauty, Alison maintains that the 'Serpentine Form is beautiful not of itself, and originally, but in consequence of the Associations we connect with it'. The aesthetic response to colour provides an important illustration of his argument that judgements about beauty arise from different associations. He points out that the 'different sentiments of Mankind, with regard to the Beauty of Colours, are inconsistent with the opinion that such qualities are beautiful in themselves'. Different cultures have different responses to colour, and this depends on the associations of different colours. 'White is beautiful to us ... as emblematical both of Innocence and Cheerfulness. In China, on the other hand, it is the Colour appropriated to Mourning, and consequently, very far from being generally beautiful' is considered to be 'extremely disagreeable'. Colours are judged beautiful because of their associations with particular qualities, so when 'the particular Associations we have with such Colours are destroyed, their Beauty is destroyed at the same time'.

Alison illustrates his aesthetic theory by considering the colours of natural bodies. He maintains that while the natural colours of trees, rocks and water have no intrinsic beauty, in a landscape painting 'no Colours, but the natural, could possibly be beautiful, in the imitation of such scenes ... of rural scenery' because 'no other Colours could be expressive to us of those qualities which are the sources of our Emotion from such objects in Nature'. There is therefore a necessary correspondence between nature and its representation in painting. But the aim of the painter is not the representation or 'imitation' of 'real scenery'; this is the limitation of 'the mere copiers of nature'. But 'the great masters of the art [of landscape painting] ... Salvator [Rosa] and Claude Lorrain' have achieved 'purity and simplicity of composition' to elicit 'one pure and unmingled character . . . one full and harmonious effect'. Alison considers that this 'unity of expression' attained in great landscape painting is 'the great secret of its power; the superiority which it at last assumes over the scenery of Nature'. Nature is subordinate to the imagination through the imaginative power of the gardener and the painter who can achieve unity of composition and hence can 'inspire some peculiar emotion', giving the capacity 'to realize whatever the fancy of the Painter has imagined, and to create a scenery, more pure, more harmonious, and more expressive, than any that is to be found in Nature itself'. To illustrate Hutcheson's theme of variety amidst uniformity Alison appeals to the development of the art of gardening in the English landscape parks, which has supplemented the 'mere design' of regularity and uniformity of the French style: 'Regularity or Uniformity ... tend immediately to the introduction of Variety'. Alison applies the aesthetic principle of variety amidst uniformity in considering design in nature. He considers that natural objects such as the leaves of a tree are not beautiful in themselves, but that the 'uniformity of the whole number of Leaves is a very beautiful consideration' because it awakens in the mind 'a very powerful conviction of Wisdom and Design'. His aesthetic appreciation of nature is grounded on natural theology; he sees 'Beauty of Regularity and Uniformity, as arising from the Expression of Design', enlarging the concept of design in nature to embrace the (by now commonplace) notion of variety amidst unity: 'the Forms ... that are beautiful in Nature are, in general, such as are distinguished by Variety'. For Alison 'nature' provides the elements that may be contrived, transformed and rendered aesthetically superior in a work of art; the aesthetic appreciation of nature, manifest in design, variety and uniformity, is subordinated to the imaginative control of nature in landscape painting and gardening.[41]

In his essays 'On the Beautiful' and 'On the Sublime' published in *Philosophical Essays* (1810), Dugald Stewart maintained that notions of the 'sublime' and the 'beautiful' acquire their meaning by being applied to a variety of diverse objects. As with Alison, Stewart does not suppose that these aesthetic categories are innate in the objects that excite aesthetic emotions: there is no 'common idea of essence which the word Beauty denotes'. For Stewart beautiful objects do not resemble each other in possessing a common essence of beauty but receive their aesthetic significance from linguistic rather than essential or inherent relationships:

> I shall begin with supposing that the letters A, B, C, D, E, denote a series of objects; that A possesses some one quality in common with B; B a quality in common with C . . . no quality can be found which belongs in common to any *three* objects in the series. Is it not conceivable, that the affinity between A and B may produce a transference of the name of the first to the second . . . [and] pass in succession from B . . . to E . . . a common appellation will arise between A and E, although the two objects may, in their nature and properties, be so widely distant from each other . . ..

Aesthetic association is therefore linguistic and conventional, not inherent in material objects.

Stewart considers that the primitive association of beauty is with objects of sight, for the numerous '*transitive* applications of the word *beauty*' can be attributed to the multiplicity of visual perceptions. He maintains that 'the first ideas of *beauty* formed by the mind are, in all probability, derived from *colours*', citing Joseph Addison and the poet Mark Akenside in support of this contention. He suggests that from the admiration of colours the eye rests on form, and then on motion, and that the word beauty 'gradually and insensibly' acquires a 'more extensive meaning'. Turning to the aesthetic of the picturesque, he is critical of the opinions of Uvedale Price and William Gilpin in holding that the 'picturesque' is an aesthetic property manifest in certain natural scenes. By contrast, Stewart associates the picturesque with beauty, arguing that it is 'only when the Beautiful and the Picturesque are united, that landscape-painting produces its highest effect', and follows Payne Knight in declaring that the 'picturesque properly means what is done in the style, and with the spirit of a painter'. He rejects any claim that the aesthetic of the picturesque can provide the essential criterion for landscape improvement. He concedes that knowledge acquired from the study of painting may suggest '*hints*' for the improvement of landscape, but warns that 'if recognised as the standard . . . it would infallibly cover the face of the country with a new and systematical species of affectation, not less remote than that of Brown', here making allusion to Payne Knight's critique of the aesthetic of the landscape parks designed by 'Capability' Brown. In an implicit criticism of Payne Knight, Stewart warns that the aesthetic of the picturesque carries the danger of valorising painting over nature: 'in laying out grounds . . . the primary object of a good taste is, not to please the connoisseur, but to please the enlightened admirer and lover of nature'. Landscape art may suggest land-scape improvement, but nature cannot be subordinated to painting: 'let Painting be allowed its due praise in quickening our attention to the beauties of Nature . . . but let our Taste for the beauties be *chiefly* formed on the study of Nature herself'. Stewart's discussion marks a significant development in the aesthetic appreciation of nature. While he holds to the conventional natural theology of design, asserting that the works of nature are artefacts created by the 'Unfathomable Design' of 'Almighty Power', he argues that nature transcends the productions of the artist and the aesthetic appreciation cannot therefore be comprehended by categories derived from the language of painting. Narrowly human criteria of design and beauty were not to be expected in the works of nature, where a 'deviation from uniformity . . . appears perfectly suited to that *infinity* which is associated, in our conceptions, with all her operations'.[42]

Turning to the sublime, Stewart is specifically concerned with the aesthetic appreciation of nature in relation to design and natural theology. He begins by considering the opinions of other authors on the sublime, citing Burke's famous assertion that 'terror is . . . the ruling principle of the sublime', Knight's view of the sublime as expressing '*mental energy*', and the view of 'Longinus' that 'it fills the reader with a glorying, and sense of inward great-ness'. Following the principles of his aesthetic theory, Stewart maintains that sublimity does not derive from the 'metaphysical essence of things' but is derived 'from the tie of Habitual Association'. His concern is therefore to unravel these linguistic associations, and he pinpoints the associations of elevation and religion, which he terms 'the *literal* and the *religious* sublime'. The sublime is associated with elevation and 'altitude' and hence, he main-tains, with religion: the 'idea of Sublimity . . . [is] a tendency which the religious sentiments of men, in every age and country, have had to carry their thoughts *upwards*, towards the objects of their worship'. Stewart expounds the range of these associations: the sublime expresses the elevation of mountains, the immensity of the ocean and the universe, and these are associated with the religious aspirations of humanity. Sublimity is associated with divine creativity: the 'sublime effect of rocks and of cataracts; of huge ridges of mountains; of gloomy forests; or immense and impetuous rivers; of the boundless ocean; and, in general, of everything which forces on the attention the idea of Creative Power, is owing, in part, to the irresistible tendency which that idea has to raise the thoughts towards Heaven'. The sublime is therefore fundamentally religious in its associations, hence the 'application of the word *Sublimity* to Eternity, to Immensity, to Omnipresence, to Omniscience . . . to all the various qualities which enter into our conceptions of the Divine Attributes'. The aesthetics of sublimity in nature, like the aesthetics of beauty, is grounded in natural theology. Stewart therefore reinterprets Burke's definition in terms of this exegesis of the associations of sublimity: 'instead of considering, with Mr Burke, Terror as the ruling principle of the *religious sublime*, it would be nearer the truth to say, that the Terrible derives whatever character of Sublimity belongs to it from religious associations'. This leads him to consider the religious associations of the sublime in relation to the design of the universe. The infinity of the universe has associations with divine omnipotence, for its 'sublime effect is much increased by the mathematical regularity of its form; suggesting the image of a vast *Rotundo*, having its circumference nowhere; – a circumstance, which forces irresistibly on the mind the idea of something analogous to architectural design, carried into execution by Omnipotence itself'. Stewart's philosophical analysis, his exposition of the associations of sublimity, thus establishes the connection between the sublime and wonder at the immensity of the universe in eighteenth-century discourse: the 'various associations connected with Sublimity become thus incorporated . . . with the Language of Nature'.[43]

Samuel Taylor Coleridge is often seen as a poet whose early interest in external nature and landscape, fostered by his friendship and poetic association with Wordsworth, faltered, and was ultimately displaced by an engagement with the metaphysics of nature shaped by the aesthetic theory of German transcendental philosophers. Following 'Dejection: An Ode' (1802) Coleridge's evocation of nature in his poetry ceased; but his notebooks show his continuing engagement with and response to nature and landscape. Thus in September 1803 he recorded his response to Glen Nevis, complaining that though the task of depiction would be 'simple for a Painter but in how many words & how laboriously – in what dim similitudes & slow & dragging Circumlocutions must I give it'. Coleridge's description seeks to emulate the pictorial; and he subscribed to the aesthetics of the picturesque, commenting that 'Those who hold it undignified to illustrate Nature by Art – how little would the truly dignified say so – how else can we bring the forms of Nature within our voluntary memory'. Walking in Borrowdale in the Lake District the following month, he responded to the atmosphere and colours of the Lakeland landscape: 'A drisling Rain. Heavy masses of shapeless Vapour upon the mountains . . . yet it is no unbroken Tale of dull Sadness – slanting Pillars travel across the

Lake, at long Intervals – the vaporous mass whitens, in large Stains of Light . . ..
The woody Castle Crag between me & Lowdore is a rich Flower-Garden of
Colours, the brightest yellows with the deepest Crimsons and the infinite
Shades of Brown & Green the *infinite* diversity of which blends the whole – so
that the brighter colours seem as *colors* upon a ground, not coloured Things.'
This is the language of the picturesque; unlike Constable and Wordsworth he
subscribed to the cardinal principle of the picturesque aesthetic, that viewing
nature mediated through representation in works of art is crucial to its aesthetic
appreciation: 'Painting & Engravings send us back with new Eyes to Nature'.

In April 1804, two months after making this notebook entry, Coleridge was
at sea bound for Malta, and recorded this account of the picturesque effect of
ships under sail: 'Every one of these Sails is *known* by the Intellect to have a
strict & necessary action & reaction on all the rest, & that the whole is made
up of parts, each part referring at once to each & to the whole – and nothing
more administers to the Picturesque than this phantom of complete visual
wholeness in an object, which visually does not form a whole, by the influence
ab intra of the sense of its perfect Intellectual Beauty or Wholeness.' Coleridge
finds the picturesque in diversity and variety amidst unity, and in the play
between perception and the inner sense of understanding. The perception of
the picturesque arises in observation and contemplation, from the tension
between the visual impression of the diversity of sails and understanding the
unity and harmony of their uniformity of action. He finds harmony and
variety in the contrast between the hull of the ship and its sails, pointing to the
'harmony of the Lines – the ellipses & semicircles of the bellying Sails & of the
Hull, with the variety from the permanence of the one & the contingency of
the other'.[44] Nature is intelligible to reason, and can be understood as law-like
and uniform in its action; the observation of variety within this uniformity, of
contingency set against the necessity of the laws of nature, engenders the
perception of nature as picturesque.

Coleridge also gave attention to the relation between the beautiful and the
sublime; here his departure from the language of natural theology and from
the terms of British writing on aesthetics is striking. A notebook entry written
in Malta in December 1804 indicates that he conceived beauty as occasioned
by the perception of objects, the experience of their form and colour; while he
considered the sublime to be a faculty of the mind, the experience of unity
and immensity, which he terms 'omneity in unity': 'O that Sky, that soft blue
mighty Arch, resting on the mountains or solid Sea-like plain / what an aweful
adorable omneity in unity. I know of no other perfect union of the sublime
with the beautiful, that is, so that they should both be felt at the same moment
tho' by different faculties, yet each faculty predisposed by itself to receive the
specific modification from the other. To the eye it is an inverted Goblet . . .
perfect Beauty in shape and colour; to the mind it is immensity'. This

distinction between the beautiful and the sublime suggests his reading of Kant's aesthetic theory set out in the *Kritik der Urteilskraft* (*Critique of the Power of Judgment*) (1790), that beauty is found in the objects of nature whereas the sublime is absolutely great, demonstrating a faculty of mind surpassing the senses. For Coleridge the sublime has a relation to the mind rather than to external objects: 'the difference of the Sublime and the Beautiful is a *diversity* . . . I meet, I *find* the Beautiful – but I give, contribute, or rather attribute the Sublime. No object of Sense is sublime in itself; but only so far as I make it a symbol of some Idea. The circle is a beautiful figure in itself; it becomes sublime, when I contemplate eternity under that figure'.[45] Whereas Stewart located the sublime in relation to the immensity of the universe and divine omnipotence, Coleridge cuts the link between the aesthetics of nature and the language of design of natural theology: the sublime is a faculty of mind integrated within the transcendence of the unity and eternity of nature, of 'omneity in unity'.

In the eighteenth century philosophical reflection on the aesthetic appreciation of nature was shaped by appeal to the language of design. The works of nature, like works of art, were considered to be artefacts: the human craftsmanship manifest in the production of a work of art had its counterpart in the order of nature created and designed by God. The natural theologians were concerned to demonstrate the attributes as well as the existence of the deity from design in nature: they appealed to the aesthetics of nature to demonstrate divine benevolence and power. Dugald Stewart contrasted the finite capacities of humanity with God's infinite power; while the creative imagination of the artist was determined and limited by human faculties, and works of art were contrived on a human scale, the works of nature are products of a Being endowed with infinite power and creativity. Nature necessarily transcends art, for human criteria of design and beauty, necessarily restricted in compass, were not to be expected in the works of nature. The language and assumptions of natural theology, braced by Newtonian natural philosophy and astronomy, shaped the terms of discussion of the aesthetics of nature. But whereas Stewart located the sublime in relation to the immensity of the universe and divine omnipotence, Coleridge severed the link between the aesthetics of nature and the language of design: he judged that, unlike beauty, the sublime was not occasioned by the experience of material objects but is a faculty of mind. The language of natural theology faltered: the *Bridgewater Treatises* of the 1830s subordinated the claims of demonstrative natural theology to the exposition of authoritative surveys of the natural world viewed in terms of divine order and contrivance. While science was rendered intellectually safe by the illustration of its religious tendency, the demonstrative claims of natural theology were muted. But natural theology continued to shape and unify scientific theorising in serving to counteract claims that science posed a challenge to cultural orthodoxy. Thus for Whewell, design could not be deduced from the order of nature but was a conviction conse- quent on the appreciation of nature's fecundity; natural theology served an illustrative rather than a demonstrative function. The fragmentation of demonstrative natural theology has its counterpart in the aesthetics of nature of Romanticism: the assertion of the primacy and immediacy of the order of nature over metaphors of design and mechanism.

Visiting South America during the voyage of the *Beagle* between 1831 and 1836, the young Charles Darwin was overawed by the fecundity and 'sublimity [of] the primeval forests, undefaced by the hand of man',[46] using terms derived from his reading of Alexander von Humboldt; his appeal to a holistic aesthetics of nature contrasts with the language of contrivance and mechanism deployed in Paley's *Natural Theology*. But metaphors of contrivance, order and mechanism also played a role in shaping Darwin's outlook. He declared, on the publication of the *Origin of Species* in November 1859, that Paley's *Natural Theology* was a book that he 'admired' and 'could almost formerly have said it by heart'.[47] Metaphors of holistic sublimity, and of contrivance, order and mechanism, helped shape his theory of evolution.

CHAPTER 3

✳

Exploration

IN 1807 ALEXANDER VON HUMBOLDT and Aimé Bonpland launched the scientific narrative of their voyage to the Americas between 1799 and 1804 with an *Essai sur la géographie des plantes, accompagné d'un tableau physique des régions équinoxiales* (*Essay on the Geography of Plants, accompanied by a Physical Portrait of the Tropics*) (1807). Its frontispiece, the *Tableau Physique des Andes*, provided a spectacular graphical physical portrait of the topography of the Andes, a representation of geography, climate and vegetation based on a drawing Humboldt had made during their famous ascent of Mount Chimborazo in Ecuador (Fig. 3). In this pictorial representation of scientific ideas and information, Andean topography is framed by Humboldt's comprehensive tabulation of scientific data, listing the range of magnetic, electrical, meteorological, thermal, tidal and barometric observations which he considered to have bearing on the variations in vegetation encountered during the ascent of the mountain; only when placed within their physical environments would a scientific understanding of flora be possible. The physical data, compiled by a vast effort of exact measurement, and drawing upon the advances in instrumentation achieved in the eighteenth century, provided the evidence for Humboldt's theory of climates as layered like geological strata, where the physical characteristics of a geographical region are correlated with the changes in vegetation due to the increase in altitude. The data, set out in layered columns, provides a complement to the visual display, which shows the succession of climatic layers in a striking graphical representation. Humboldt's illustration of the slopes of Chimborazo displays the ascent from the rainforest through coniferous forests and grasslands, with lichens and bare rock at the summit, a succession of altitudinal zones. The series of floral belts, typical of the tropics, temperate regions and arctic latitudes provides a graphical physical portrait displaying the physical and botanical diversity of the continent. The framing of the panorama of the Andes by the scientific data provides an aesthetic as well as a metrological vision of the natural world.[1]

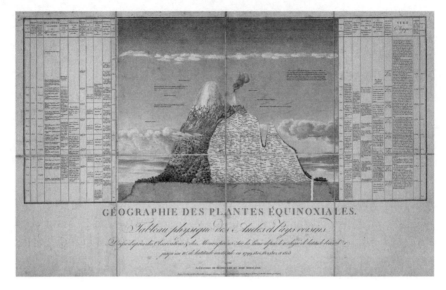

GÉOGRAPHIE DES PLANTES ÉQUINOXIALES.

3   Alexander von Humboldt and Aimé Bonpland, *Tableau Physique des Andes*.

Humboldt's graphical representation of the relation between vegetation and climate had a profound impression on the study of the geographic distributions of plants shaping Charles Darwin's natural history in the *Origin of Species* (1859);[2] while Humboldt's emphasis on the holistic unity of forces aroused Darwin's aesthetic sensibility to the power and fecundity of nature.[3] Indeed, reading Humboldt's *Personal Narrative* of his voyage stimulated Darwin's imagination and led him to follow Humboldt to the tropics; he recalled Humboldt's 'unparalleled' and 'glorious descriptions' of tropical scenery and vegetation when his ship the *Beagle* first made landing in Brazil in February 1832.[4] Humboldt made clear that his urge to undertake a voyage of exploration to the tropics was shaped by his friendship and early association with Georg Forster, who (with his father Johann Reinhold Forster) had travelled as a naturalist on the *Resolution* with Captain James Cook during his second voyage to the Pacific (1772–5); Cook's three voyages to the Pacific in the 1760s and 1770s had become emblematic of scientific exploration. Humboldt's voyage, closely (but not exclusively) focused on scientific interests and shaped by a distinct programme of research, had links to the great tradition of European voyages of geographical discovery and imperial and commercial expansion.

Exploration, Empire and Travel

The understanding and representation of the natural world in eighteenth-century Britain was transformed by voyages of exploration and the burgeoning literature of travel. The encouragement of exploration and commerce, science and power over nature was consequent on the worldwide and imperial expansion of Britain in the eighteenth century. Since the Renaissance European civilisation had been invigorated and transformed by voyages of discovery that began as the exploration of the Atlantic littoral and the quest for the spices of the East, prized since antiquity. The discovery of the Americas, of a sea route around Africa, of the Pacific Ocean and the circumnavigation of the globe, led to the maritime expansion of Europe and to colonisation and the creation of empires. The age of geographical discovery was the age of the scientific revolution; the creation of world geography consequent on the voyages of Vasco da Gama, Christopher Columbus and Ferdinand Magellan had their counterpart in the new astronomy of Nicolaus Copernicus, Johannes Kepler and Galileo Galilei in which the conception of the cosmos and of man's place in nature was dramatically transformed. The bounds of the hierarchical, geocentric, closed world of the Aristotelian cosmos were expanded; the earth was now a planet and the heavens were robbed of their immutability and perfection, and the plurality of worlds in infinite space threatened conventional assumptions about the uniqueness of man. The culture of exploration, of colonial expansion, of maritime endeavour and commerce, led to the discovery of new landscapes and environments and an explosion in the range of natural history. The new cosmography and geography destroyed established canons of knowledge, shaping new understandings of the cosmos and the terrestrial environment alike, challenging assumptions about the nature of humanity: in a universe of a plurality of worlds, the earth was populated by primitives, perceived either as cannibalistic savages or as living in a state of pristine innocence.

The problem of geography became the relation between the earth's universal geography and the special geography of its regions, classified in terms of latitude (in its effect on the weather), boundaries and topography, and their human inhabitants. The new geography stimulated a range of questions, including the charting of coasts; the accurate determination of latitude and longitude; the attention to latitudinal zones; the relation of the old to the new world; variations in the climate and fertility of land masses; the relation of universal physical forces such as the central heat of the earth and the tides to local configurations such as volcanoes and variations in the coastlines. Newton's associate the astronomer Edmond Halley served as a naval captain on voyages of exploration between 1698 and 1700, charting the Atlantic littoral and searching for the *terra australis incognita*, the land to the south that since antiquity had been supposed necessary to balance the known northern world; he made important studies of the tides and variations in the earth's magnetism, and of the atmosphere, winds and ocean currents. The investigation of the relations between environment and vegetation became an important feature in geography. Johann Reinhold Forster, the naturalist on Cook's second voyage to the Pacific, studied the environment, and skies, climates and winds in considering how they shaped vegetation. This ecological outlook was developed by Alexander von Humboldt, who (as noted) had travelled with Forster's son Georg, seeing the distinctive character of different regions of the earth in terms of a combination of the outline of mountains and hills, the physiognomy of plants and animals, the azure of the sky, the forms of the clouds and the transparency of the atmosphere.[5]

By 1800 geographical exploration and mapping had been transformed. The coastal outlines of Australia (thus named by Matthew Flinders in 1814) and New Zealand had been mapped and Antarctica probed by James Cook in his second voyage. Meriwether Lewis and William Clark, commissioned by Thomas Jefferson to cross the North American continent, made pioneering studies of the animals, plants and topography encountered as they travelled to the Pacific Northwest in 1804–6. Humboldt developed a wide range of innovative techniques for the study of the sciences of the earth, taking numerous precision instruments on his journey to Central and South America between 1799 and 1804, during which he established the topographic associations of the physical and organic worlds, providing a unified vision of the terraqueous globe. Climate, rivers, earthquakes, volcanoes, glaciers, geomagnetism, minerals and crystals, fossils and the figure of the earth were all investigated and their relationships charted. Geographical maps and charts were enlarged, and the landscape was coming to be understood in terms of its underlying geological structure through the tracing of geological strata.

In his *Novum Organum* (1620) Francis Bacon had associated the advancement of learning with the exploration of the world and the expansion of trade. His stress on maritime and commercial expansion and the cultivation of knowledge was sanctioned by the appeal, which became familiar in the rhetoric of puritan intellectuals, to the divine injunction to tame the wilderness at the expulsion of Adam and Eve from the paradisiacal garden in Genesis. Colonisation and the dispossession of indigenous peoples came to be justified by God's command to replenish the earth by the productive cultivation of land. In the seventeenth century the English Crown claimed dominion over the sea, a doctrine that provided the basis for later claims for a pan-Atlantic British empire defined in terms of maritime hegemony and commercial enterprise, an empire that contrasted with military monarchies and their territorial dominions. This concept of maritime empire was promoted by a coalescence of different political interests in the 1730s and received expression in James Thomson's poem 'Rule, Britannia' (1740), which evokes the divinely ordained island destined to rule the waves in freedom.[6] British imperial ideology blended maritime, commercial, scientific and religious themes, which shaped the most notable voyages of discovery in the eighteenth century

– the exploration and exploitation of the Pacific. The interests of government and science were both represented in the most famous and productive of these enterprises, the three voyages of James Cook undertaken between 1768 and 1779.

Ever since the first great age of European maritime discovery and expansion in the sixteenth century ideas of nature, shaped by biblical and classical themes, were highlighted by the exploration of the colonial periphery: the Garden of Eden was envisioned in colonised tropical islands and in the pristine landscapes of Africa and the Americas; and in the eighteenth century 'wilderness' was found in the alien and disturbing landscapes and ecology of Australia and Antarctica. These ideas are manifest in literature: in *The Tempest* (1611), evidently suggested by a shipwreck in the Bermudas, William Shakespeare reflects on Prospero's island as an Eden, with its prospects for rebirth and redemption, and as a colonised and degraded territory, a physical environment with problematic indigenous inhabitants and manifesting risks of climate and disease. The religious imagery of the destruction of paradise yielded, in the process of geographical study, to an awareness of the realities of the physical environment. Columbus believed that he had discovered the site of the Garden of Eden and the mines from which Solomon had taken gold to build the Temple at Jerusalem, ideas that withered in the face of the reality of exploration and geography. The discovery of medicinal herbs, new plant species, the promotion of agricultural improvement rather than the discovery of the site of the earthly paradise, came to be seen as the key to amelioration of the human condition. In the seventeenth century botanical gardens incorporating newly discovered species from the Americas were created to provide the basis for the achievement of invigorated cultivation and economic progress. As noted in Chapter 1, Virgil's *Georgics* provided a basis in classical literature and culture for the motif of husbandry and the cultivation of rural virtues.

The Royal Society made agriculture and forestry central concerns of the virtuosi. John Evelyn's *Sylva; or a Discourse of Forest-Trees* (1664) published by the Society, written out of concern for the loss of tree cover and the shortage of timber and fuel, placed arboriculture in the context of practical estate management and the faith in science as a means to control the natural world, a theme prominent in the writings of Francis Bacon that shaped the outlook of the virtuosi of the Royal Society. The arts and sciences formed part of the eighteenth-century ideal of the virtuous gentleman farmer as a landowner familiar with the *Georgics* and alert to modern learning and the improvement and benevolent use of the landscape: draining the land, managing the crops, planting trees, and pursuing yield and utility through manure, turnips and the breeding of livestock. The Swedish botanist Linnaeus argued that botany had economic implications and would provide the scientific basis for the survey

of resources to achieve the most profitable uses of plants. Linnaeus urged his
students (his pupil Daniel Solander served as a naturalist on James Cook's first
voyage on the *Endeavour*) to use the opportunities afforded by exploration
and travel to discover new botanical species and to investigate the profitable
exploitation of plants. Botanists became responsible for the transportation of
plants and their acclimatisation and cultivation in gardens and plantations, an
opportunity eagerly grasped by Joseph Banks, who was a member of Cook's
first expedition.

The three voyages of James Cook have become emblematic of the cultural,
scientific, commercial and imperial elements of eighteenth-century exploration and travel. While the Admiralty had sponsored voyages to the Pacific,
there was no coherent official strategy of Pacific exploration, and the original
objective of Cook's first voyage in the *Endeavour* (1768–71), undertaken at
the request of the Royal Society and supported by King George III, was astronomical, to observe the transit of Venus across the Sun in 1769 and calculate
the scale of the solar system in terms of the radius of the earth. Some of the
transits of Venus occur in pairs at an interval of eight years; the observations
of the transit of 1761 organised by the Royal Society had proved inconclusive,
and to observe the transit of June 1769 the Society organised four expeditions
to different parts of the globe, necessary for the accurate determination of the
values. The Admiralty agreed to provide a ship for travel to the required low
latitude (but undetermined) site in the Pacific. The fortuitous return to
London in May 1768 of Captain Samuel Wallis on the *Dolphin*, with an official report of the discovery of Tahiti and news of the possible sighting of an
unknown continent to the south, provided a suitable site for the observations,
and also prompted the enlargement of Cook's instructions to include considerations of trade and navigation, and to sail south where 'there is reason to
imagine that a Continent or Land of great extent, may be found', to investigate
the legendary southern continental *terra incognita*.[7] Cook's voyages successfully joined scientific investigation, naval cartography and geographical exploration, a conjunction of interests that fostered the incorporation of the
concerns of science within the imperial and naval objectives of the voyages of
discovery.

The most significant scientific achievement of the *Endeavour* voyage was
the treasure trove of botanical specimens collected by Joseph Banks and his
associate Daniel Solander (the Swedish pupil of Linnaeus), who engaged in
studies of the nature of soils, vegetation, fauna and marine life. Linnaeus'
botanical classification, developed in the mid-eighteenth century, made
taxonomy fundamental to natural history. Despite criticism from some
contemporaries (notably the Comte de Buffon) who were concerned at the
inherent limitations of a system of botanical classification based on fructification alone, this was a taxonomy based on the 'artificial' classification of plants

through the sexual system of stamens and pistils rather than a more ambitious 'natural' classification which would encompass all the natural features of plants. But Linnaeus' taxonomy became standard, providing a basis for the ordering of botany whereby newly discovered species could be assigned within the Linnaean system of classification. Solander, who had been especially close to Linnaeus, was one of twenty of his students who travelled on voyages of discovery, but he cut his links with the master, never returning to Uppsala or sending promised specimens while portraying Banks disparagingly to Linnaeus as a wealthy amateur who did not complete his studies of natural history.[8]

Banks had already participated in a voyage to Newfoundland in 1766 and had established himself as a competent botanist, but he owed his position on the *Endeavour* and later in London scientific circles to his wealth and social origins as a landed gentleman in Lincolnshire and his willingness to use his fortune, as in the voyage of the *Endeavour*, to foster scientific work. A landowner of many thousands of acres, he had strong interests in the countryside, in land management, landscapes and improvements in farming, and he shaped the country pursuits of the English gentlemanly elite to include scientific purposes. His objectives were shaped by the culture of the virtuoso as a collector and traveller, with interests that traditionally embraced the study of antiquities and natural history; the Royal Society embraced both pursuits. For men of Banks' class, wealth and education, travel and the ideal of the virtuoso as a collector were cultivated through the Grand Tour, the journey from the cold North to the warm South, the Alps providing the symbolic and geographical transition, and the cultural climax being Rome. Banks portrayed his voyage on the *Endeavour* as a transformation of the leisured cultural cosmopolitanism of the Grand Tour into an exploration of the natural world – 'my Grand Tour shall be one round the whole globe' was his reported response to a query about his plans, promoting the idea of science as a new culture – and he described himself as a 'man of science' in 1768 when writing about his role on the voyage.[9] He envisaged the transformation of gentlemanly science, from the virtuoso collector to the systematic natural historian, and though Solander proved to be correct in judging that he would not publish his botanical specimens, Banks ensured that his collections from the voyage were ordered systematically and made available to other botanists. But his reported interest in indigenous customs and flirtations with Tahitian women made it easy for satirists to portray him as a wealthy amateur seeking amusement and to question the authenticity of his scientific commitment; writing in September 1772 Horace Walpole commented disparagingly on the pretensions of 'that wild man Banks, who is poaching in every ocean for the fry of little islands that have escaped the drag-net of Spain'.[10] But at the time Banks was on a voyage to Iceland rather than the Pacific, having alienated the navy with ambitious demands for an expanded role for himself and his scientific team on Cook's second voyage, aboard the *Resolution* (1772–5), and so had been obliged to withdraw.

As noted, for the voyage of the *Resolution* Johann Reinhold Forster, accompanied by his son Georg, was appointed naturalist, making extensive studies in physical geography, natural history and anthropology. The elder Forster's *Observations Made During a Voyage Round the World* (1778) discussed ocean currents, coral reefs, volcanoes, botany and especially ethnography, and reported a variety of experiments undertaken during the voyage. But Cook still collected specimens for Banks, who continued to shape the objectives of the natural history undertaken on Cook's voyages. Banks became president of the Royal Society in 1778, serving until his death in 1820, but his ascendancy and dominance remained controversial. In a dispute in 1783–4 Banks was viewed by his critics as a leisured virtuoso, being described as a 'mere *amateur*' by Samuel Horsley, the editor of Newton's works; he was accused of promoting natural history and antiquities, fostering the collection and display of 'trifling curiosities', polite interests that contrasted with the work of true 'men of science' pursuing the mathematical sciences in the tradition of Newton, who had once occupied the chair at the Royal Society now filled by Banks.[11] But Banks wished to present himself as a 'man of science', and as his career progressed he stressed that the collection of specimens must be informed by scientific principles, by the spirit of Enlightenment inquiry rather than accumulation in the manner of the virtuoso and antiquary. Using political connections to secure his creation as a baronet in 1781, he also used his position at the Royal Society to shape the framework in which botany was to be pursued, his influence flourishing with his management and expansion of the Royal Botanic Gardens at Kew from 1772 until 1820, where he encouraged plant collection and exploration across the range of the emergent colonial empire. From his research collections in his house in Soho Square he became a focal figure in London science and an adviser to the government, and, also, the butt of satire. James Gillray's 1795 cartoon of Banks as 'The great South Sea Caterpillar, transform'd into a Bath Butterfly', incorporating themes of natural history, Pacific voyaging and social preferment, portrays Banks as a court scientist wearing the red ribbon of a Knight of the Bath gazing into the sun emblazoned with the crown of royal patronage.

It was in his management of the Royal Botanic Gardens at Kew that Banks was able to exercise his most potent influence. Botanical gardens became important in the seventeenth century as resources, collections of known plants providing a source of herbal medicines from across the (newly enlarged) world. The roots of botanical gardens lie in the Renaissance urge to recreate the Edenic paradise, to restore the pristine collection of plants and trees granted to Adam in Genesis. In the work of writers and artists the biblical paradise became associated with the garden of King Alcinous of the Phaeacians in the *Odyssey*, with the pastoral life of Arcadian shepherds derived from Virgil's *Eclogues* and with Ovid's golden age of everlasting spring described in *Metamorphoses*. Links were explored between the classical themes of the loss and restitution of the mythical golden age of classical antiquity and Judaeo-Christian doctrines of the fall and redemption of mankind. Gardens and the cultivation of crops, important in agricultural economies, became associated with profound cultural motifs of fall and redemption, and the cultivation of the garden was seen as an allegory of Christian life. By the early seventeenth century the belief that paradise was to be found in America had faltered, but the discovery of America provided the means to recreate paradise, and the profusion of new plant species collected by the early explorers offered hope to provide remedies for all illnesses. The design of the new botanical gardens of the sixteenth and seventeenth centuries envisaged the re-creation of paradise as a circle or square with four segments or quarters, each intended to contain all the plants of one of the continents, Europe, Asia, Africa and America, each of these being subdivided into parterres. Plants gathered from the continents were put in allotted places, so that the botanical garden served as an encyclopaedia of the natural world. The botanical garden recapitulated God's original creation. According to the Catalogue of the Oxford Botanic Garden of 1658, 'as all creatures were gathered into the Ark, comprehended as in an epitome, so you have the plants of this world in microcosm in our garden'. The voyages of exploration and colonial expansion led to an awareness of the immense diversity of the world's plants, the bewildering variety of nature prompting a reassessment of botanical classification by arrangement in parterres or reference to medicinal human uses.

By the mid-eighteenth century the dominance of the botanical taxonomy of Linnaeus, despite its inherent limitations, signalled a shift from the view of botanical gardens as embracing the world as a 'natural' paradise, a re-creation of Eden, in encompassing the plants of the world according to their geographical distribution, in favour of the Enlightenment vision of order found in the classification itself, in the arbitrary power of taxonomy. The pursuit of natural history created a system of knowledge, botanical taxonomy. The growing British empire brought exotic nature into the compass of learning, imperial expansion enlarging the register of species and fostering the collection and comparison of natural species by the methods of rational science. The botanical garden provided a resource for the classification of plants that could become instruments for agricultural improvement, an economic dimension to botany emphasised by Linnaeus who sought to acclimatise and cultivate in Sweden plants from the tropics such as tea and rice, encouraging his students to travel on voyages of discovery. Less ambitiously, Banks envisioned Kew as 'a great botanical exchange house for the empire', as he put it in 1787, and he used the resources of Kew and satellite botanical gardens throughout the empire to promote the transfer, improvement and reorganisation of cultivation within the empire.[12]

The agricultural improvements Banks made on his Lincolnshire estate were echoed and expanded in the objectives pursued through the policies he instituted at Kew to advance national wealth and power. The creation of the formal botanical garden at Kew incorporated the plant riches of the American colonies, and Banks used his position to turn botanical exploration to imperial advantage. He sought the transplantation of economically important plants within the empire, a policy that required the recruitment of men with the necessary expertise. Gardeners were sent out to collect for Kew, from Australia to India and China, and from Brazil to the Cape Colony, all at the Crown's expense. Between 1770 and 1820 more than 120 plant collectors working outside Europe sent specimens to Banks or to Kew: horticulturalists, gardeners and botanists; physicians, surgeons and apothecaries; civil servants and army officers; naval and merchant officers, navigators and explorers. Erasmus Darwin captured the imperial theme of Banks' botanical collection in his poem *The Economy of Vegetation* (1791), portraying botany as the emblem of the prosperity of England: 'So sits enthron'd in vegetable pride / Imperial Kew by Thames's glittering side / . . . Sweet blooms the Rose, the towering oak expands, / The Grace and Guard of Britain's golden lands.'[13] Botanical gardens were established as outposts of Kew in Calcutta, St Helena, Bombay, Madras and the West Indies. India and Southeast Asia were the most active areas for collection, followed by the West Indies, Central America, the South Pacific and Australasia.

William Bligh's voyages transplanting breadfruit from Tahiti to the West Indies (as food for the slaves working the sugar plantations) were shaped by Banks' stress on plant exchange. Writing in 1787, alluding to the voyage of the *Bounty*, Banks informed the president of the Linnaean Society that 'the ship which we are sending to Otaheite [Tahiti] to bring home the breadfruit to the West Indies will be bringing plants from thence, the Garden at St Vincent flourishes a new one is established at Bengall & an intervening proposed . . . & probably another will soon be starting at Madras'. As is well known, this voyage ended in mutiny and disaster, but in 1791 Bligh undertook a second and successful voyage from Tahiti to the West Indies, and Banks told a Jamaican correspondent that this mission, in its transplantation of breadfruit was 'replete with . . . benevolence' in 'transporting useful vegetables from one part of the earth to another where they do not exist'. Banks instructed his collectors to assess the viability of plant transfers, to judge whether European grains and fruits would survive in new environments, and ultimately the project generated career opportunities for prospective natural historians. Writing in 1813 to William Jackson Hooker, subsequently director of the

Royal Botanic Gardens at Kew, encouraging him to undertake a voyage to Java, Banks suggested that had he himself not joined Cook in 1768 he would have been 'ignorant of a multitude of matters I am now acquainted with & probably have attained to no higher rank in Life than that of a countrey Justice of the Peace'.[14]

Colonial officials had major impact. The Admiralty, the War Office, the Hydrographer's Office, the Board of Longitude, the Ordnance Survey, the Geological Survey, the East India Company, the Royal Naval College, the Greenwich Observatory, the Royal Dockyards, the Royal Military Academy at Woolwich, the Royal Engineers' Institution at Chatham – the august list of government bodies is formidable and they all encouraged an interest in science and natural history. The voyages of exploration fostered by the Admiralty in the wake of Cook's voyages joined a colonial and imperial adventure with an emphasis on natural history: Robert Brown, his blossoming career as a botanist fostered by Banks' patronage, served on the *Resolution* under Matthew Flinders on an expedition (1801–5) seeking to establish the British presence in Australia; Charles Darwin accompanied Robert FitzRoy on the *Beagle* (1831–6), a voyage whose purpose was to assess the commercial and strategic potential of the east coast of South America and to reclaim the Falkland Islands from Argentina; and Joseph Dalton Hooker served on the *Erebus* as assistant surgeon and botanist to James Clark Ross, on an imperial exploration of Australasia and Antarctica (1839–43). For Charles Darwin and Joseph Hooker these voyages had a major impact on their scientific careers – and on the progress of science.

After 1820, with the deaths of George III who had fostered Kew and of Banks who had managed the gardens, the status of Kew and of other scientific offices came under attack as a result of pressure for reduced government expenditure. Although private support remained important for science, government funding was needed. The new community of botanists established by Banks' patronage portrayed botany as necessary to public interest, stressing its role in agricultural improvement. In its report the Treasury Commission emphasised the imperial and economic dimension to the establishment of a 'national garden' as 'the centre round which all minor establishments of the same nature should be arranged ... receiving their supplies and aiding the Mother Country in everything that is useful in the vegetable kingdom', so that 'Government would be able to obtain authentic and official information on points connected with the founding of new colonies'.[15]

As a result of this report, in 1841 ownership of Kew passed from the Crown to the government. The appointment not of a gardener but a botanist, William Jackson Hooker, as the first director, was an example of the impact of the increasingly vocational and professional character of British science that had become especially evident in the 1830s. Charles Babbage's accusation of the 'decline' of science in England, drawing a contrast with the professional organisation of French science, led to the foundation in 1831 of the British Association for the Advancement of Science, a broadly based society of men of science; and William Whewell coined the term 'scientist', prompted by a discussion at the third meeting of the Association. The Royal Gardens at Kew became a national garden, with its professional botanical science sustained by an imperial role. Sir William Hooker, and his successor as director, his son Joseph Dalton Hooker, not only fostered the promotion of botanical research but by communicating with planters and colonial administrators sought to encourage colonial agriculture and metropolitan trade. Banks' imperial vision of botany was maintained and enlarged. Joseph Hooker surveyed in the Himalayas, collecting forty-three species of rhododendrons in 1847–51; and Sir William planted the Rhododendron Dell at Kew. Colonial workers were encouraged to send plants to Kew, which became the hub of the colonial scientific network.[16]

Tropical Forests and Polar Ice

As a naturalist on the *Resolution* on Cook's second voyage to the Pacific from 1772 to 1775, Johann Reinhold Forster was led to reflect on the ecology of the tropics. Before embarking on the voyage he and his son Georg had translated Louis-Antoine de Bougainville's *Voyage Around the World Performed in the Years 1766–1769* (1772) with its glowing account of Tahiti as a pristine and exuberant landscape, its inhabitants living in idyllic innocence. In his journal Forster recorded his initial impressions on landing at Tahiti in August 1773, no doubt shaped by prior expectations of circumstances of happy tranquillity. He was struck by the paradisiacal harmony between the indigenous inhabitants of the island and the fecundity and variety of its unique vegetation and produce: the 'fine shady plantations, the agreeable walks, the fine rivulets, the powerful sun, the queer vegetation, the delicious and salubrious fruit, the summer breezes blowing constantly to cool the air . . . and every other circumstance contributing towards the happiness of its inhabitants'. Like Bougainville he began to consider the conjunction of factors that produce the profusion of the tropical forests, arguing – as had others before him – that the moist atmosphere of the island was related to its high mountains. Forster focused on the significance of the hydrological cycle in maintaining the profusion of the vegetation, associating the moisture of the islands with the water-retaining agency of the tree cover on the mountains. In the published text of his *Observations Made During a Voyage Round the World* (1778) he suggests that the mountains 'attract by their situation, all the vapours and clouds that pass near them . . . the very tops were covered by lofty trees' and that 'the surrounding valleys collect in their bosom the salutary humidity which is not absorbed by the plants'. The foliage of fruit trees shaded 'green turf below, which the rays of a tropical sun would otherwise scorch and destroy', maintaining the island as a 'flourishing and well-kept garden'.

Forster had first begun to consider the links between mountains, trees and rainfall several months earlier. On the outward voyage the *Resolution* had taken on provisions at the Cape of Good Hope, and shortly afterwards Forster recalled his observations, remarking in his journal that 'fogs are nothing but dense vapours . . . it is natural for them to be attracted by land, especially if somewhat elevated', adding that 'when we were at the Cape we had frequent opportunities of seeing this confirmed'.[17] Forster's observations of the clouds swirling around the Cape are consonant with the *View of the Cape of Good Hope, taken on the spot, from on board the Resolution* (1772) by the expedition's artist, William Hodges, recording the turbulent weather at the Cape with dark clouds covering Table Mountain. Uniquely among the artists on Cook's voyages, Hodges painted directly in oils rather than working from sketches drawn in the field, very likely painting this scene in the security of Cook's great cabin. As expedition artist it was his task to contribute to the accurate records to be accumulated during the voyage, here giving a realistic rendering of the meteorological conditions, the turbulent sky dominating the Cape. In this work and in his paintings of Tahiti and New Zealand made later in the voyage, he was concerned to achieve a naturalistic and faithful portrayal, blending the immediacy of the response to nature of landscape sketches with the traditional style of landscape composition – the grandest models being the classical, pastoral landscapes of Claude Lorrain, and the 'sublime' mountainous landscapes of Salvator Rosa evocative of inhospitable wilderness. Hodges' *View of the Cape of Good Hope* is a naturalistic representation of a landscape of sea, mountains and sky, an empirical rendition of topography incorporated within a framework of aesthetic perceptions.[18] When during the return voyage the *Resolution* called at St Helena and Ascension Island in May–June 1775, Forster was struck by the contrast between the barren and desiccated landscape of Ascension Island and the impact of the recent extensive colonial planting on St Helena, reflecting that 'the more the surface of the Earth is covered with plants, the more would they not only evaporate but even attract the moisture of the air, and keep it within the soil and consequently if there are any springs in the soil, they would soon increase their water and perpetuate their supplies'.[19] Deforestation led to the desiccation of the landscape.

In linking deforestation to the decline of rainfall with consequent climatic and environmental changes, Forster's comments were consonant with contemporary natural philosophy. Desiccation theories linking deforestation with rainfall decline have antecedents in classical antiquity in the botanical writings of Theophrastus (a pupil of Aristotle) and the elder Pliny. Following the colonisation of the Canary Islands and Madeira in the fifteenth and sixteenth centuries, the luxuriant native forests were replaced by fields of sugar cane; as the plantation economy flourished, more timber was needed to provide fuel to boil the sugar fluid from the cane; and the water supply on the islands was disrupted. Columbus seemingly made the connection between deforestation and the reduction of rainfall, and colonisation came to be associated with an awareness of the vulnerability of the colonised territories to plantation crops. John Evelyn reported the effect of the clearance of forests and their replacement by plantations on the rainfall on Barbados: 'Every year it becomes more torrid'. In the 1690s Edmond Halley published an account of 'the circulation of the watery vapours of the sea', based on observations at St Helena, work followed by John Woodward's 'thoughts and experiments concerning vegetation', a study of plant transpiration, making a connection between rainfall and forestation. These ideas on the relation between the hydrological cycle and environmental conditions, suggesting a connection between deforestation and the cessation of rainfall, were developed by Stephen Hales, who published a series of papers on the relationship between vegetation and the atmosphere culminating in his *Vegetable Staticks* (1727), a work belonging to the emergent tradition of Newtonian experimental physics. Hales studied the transport of liquids from the earth through plants and leaves into the atmosphere, a process he considered analogous to the rise of liquids in fine tubes (known as capillary action), a topic studied at this time by other natural philosophers in Newton's circle. Hales' investigation of 'the effect of the sun's warmth in raising the sap in trees', inverted and satirised by Swift as experiments on the extraction of sunbeams from cucumbers, ascribed the cause of the ascent of sap to the attractive forces of capillary action in the fine tubes of plants. He drew on Newton's ideas, set out in Query 31 of the 1717 edition of the *Opticks*, on the motion of particles under the action of forces and his hints about the explanation of capillary action. Hales emphasised the role of leaves in the transpiration of 'air' and the effect of sunlight in sustaining the growth of vegetation; and his work on the process and effects of transpiration in plants became influential. Buffon translated *Vegetable Staticks* in 1735 and applied Hales' ideas on the relations between vegetation and air to study the effects of deforestation, and in his *Histoire naturelle* he emphasised the effect of climate on the distribution of species.

Between 1767 and 1772 Pierre Poivre, appointed by the French government as the civil governor of the island of Mauritius, succeeded in transporting nutmeg and clove seeds and seedlings from the Moluccas to Mauritius. Poivre had earlier travelled in China and acquired knowledge of Chinese methods of forestry and agriculture, and of Chinese writings on denudation, erosion, as well as knowledge of the culture of spice trees. In Mauritius he pursued an active policy of environmental management, arguing that the soil was vulnerable to erosion and dehydration after deforestation; to stabilise the climate he pursued a policy of planting trees, seeking the conservation of forests and soils, and discouraging cash crops such as coffee and cotton in favour of planting food crops. Poivre pursued a policy of restoration and protection of the environment through the management of forestry and the hydrological cycle.[20]

By the 1770s the environmental factors connecting tropical forests, rainfall and erosion were being voiced, a conjunction of ecological issues that had a significant impact on Alexander von Humboldt who travelled to England with Georg Forster in 1790. The younger Forster, who had published his own account of the voyage of the *Resolution* in 1777, played an important role in shaping Humboldt's scientific travel writing. Humboldt praised Forster's outlook, his way of philosophising about natural history, which helped to shape the ecological perspective of his own investigations during his journey to the tropics between 1799 and 1804. For his travels Humboldt assembled an array of instruments to measure the earth's magnetism, meteorology, the electrical charges and the chemical composition of the atmosphere, their use to provide exact measurements intended to tabulate the environments in which different forms of vegetation flourished, and in this way to open the way to the creation of a new 'physical geography' or 'terrestrial physics' in place of mere taxonomy and collecting. As noted earlier, he described Mount Chimborazo in terms of an ascent through a series of floral belts, of tree ferns and palms at the base of the mountain, with deciduous woodlands and then coniferous forests and grasslands higher up, and alpine plants and lichens leading to bare rock at the summit; vegetation typical of the tropics, the temperate regions and arctic latitudes.

The description of altitudinal zones each with its own characteristic vegetation may well have been familiar to indigenous inhabitants of mountain regions. In his report of his ascent of Mount Etna in Sicily in late June 1769, Sir William Hamilton, British ambassador to Naples, represented his climb in terms of an ascent through three distinct altitudinal zones. Hamilton described his climb of Etna in the fourth (dated 17 October 1769) of his series of letters to the Royal Society reporting his observations of the volcanoes of the Naples region; first published in the *Philosophical Transactions*, these reports were reprinted in Hamilton's *Observations on Mount Vesuvius, Mount Etna and Other Volcanos* (1772) and in his magnificent illustrated text *Campi Phlegraei. Observations on the Volcanos of the Two Sicilies* (1776). Using the descriptive terms current among the Sicilians, and noting the fall in temperature he encountered during the ascent, Hamilton recorded his climb through the 'inferior district called . . . La Regione Piemontese . . . [which is] exceedingly fertile, and abounding with vines'; then through the 'middle Region of Etna called la Selvosa, *the woody* ... [containing the] largest oak, chestnut and firr trees I ever saw'; and finally to the 'third Region, called la Netta, or Scoperta, *clean* or *uncovered* ... [with a] decrease of vegetation ... [with] small shrubs and plants of the northern climates'.[21] Hamilton made no claim of originality for this botanical description, and specifically attributed the terms used to distinguish the three different altitudinal and botanical zones to the local inhabitants, innocent as he was of scientific knowledge of physical geography; and while he noted the fall in temperature during the ascent, he made no measurements. With Humboldt, however, there is a pronounced shift from descriptive natural history to quantitative 'terrestrial physics'. His representation of the climatic layers is much more complex and stratified; and he integrates the geography of the ascent of Mount Chimborazo through successive floral belts with a scientific description incorporating an enormous compilation of data produced by exact measurement, encompassing the full range of the physical, meteorological and geological characteristics of mountains that are correlated with the changes in vegetation due to the eleva-tion. Humboldt's approach to natural history, based on observation, measure-ment and the recording of data, was consistent with the norms and was indeed emblematic of advances in scientific practice in the early nineteenth century.

The search for a navigable North-West Passage, to reach the spice islands of the Orient by finding a sea route around North America, had been a dream of seamen and merchants since Elizabethan times. The search for an open strait from Hudson's Bay penetrating the Arctic archipelago was always frustrated by the icebound shores and seas. The quest was continued in the eighteenth century, but no saltwater strait or navigable river was found in Hudson's Bay and by the early 1770s it had become apparent that the American continent was much wider than had been generally supposed. Interest turned to the discovery of a passage from the coastline of northwest America, a prospect fuelled by claims of Spanish discoveries made north of California and by rumours about the results of Russian exploration in the region. On returning in 1775 from his second voyage to the Pacific, Cook had signalled his intended retirement from the sea; yet he was induced to undertake a third voyage, again on the *Resolution*, tempted by the prospective discovery of the North-West Passage. For his third voyage to the Pacific, which was curtailed by his death at Kealakekua Bay, Tahiti, on 14 February 1779, Cook effectively wrote his own instructions, to include the investigation of a passage from the Bering Strait. While he was successful in charting the outline of the Alaskan peninsula, on 17–18 August 1778 he encountered a 'large field' of Arctic pack ice and was forced to retreat from any further investigation of a route to the Atlantic from the northwest coast of America. In his journal he reported that 'the ice was quite impenetrable, and extended . . . as far as the eye could reach . . . the edge of the ice . . . was as compact as a wall'.

This was not Cook's first encounter with pack ice. On his second voyage to the Pacific, the first of his two voyages on *Resolution,* he had investigated the legendary southern continent, the hypothetical *terra australis incognita* of the ancients supposed as the counterpart of the land masses of the northern hemisphere. While Cook had confirmed the existence of lands (Australia and New Zealand) that had been conjectured as outliers of the southern continent, on proceeding south and crossing the Antarctic Circle (the first to do so) in January 1773 he had first encountered 'thirty-eight ice islands great and small', and his progress was halted by the pack ice 'entirely closed to the south', an 'immense field . . . of such extent that I could see no end to it from the mast-head', and he was obliged to retreat to the north. Cook's account of the Antarctic ice in his *A Voyage towards the South Pole, and Round the World* (1777) was illustrated by engravings of 'ice islands' and coastal scenes of Tierra del Fuego from paintings by the expedition's artist, William Hodges. Icebergs dominate the human figures, Hodges' depiction of icebound landscapes of sublime horror having aesthetic counterpart in Cook's account of his second attempt to locate the southern continent early in 1775, when he was again forced to abandon the quest before the massed field of pack ice in 'a country doomed by Nature never once to feel the warmth of the sun's rays, but to lie buried in everlasting snow and ice'. Cook found the landscape perilous and horrendous: 'thick fogs, snow storms, intense cold, and every other thing that can render navigation dangerous, must be encountered; and these difficulties are greatly heightened by the inexpressibly horrid aspect of the country'. While he believed that there was land to the south responsible for the ice, he defended his prudent retreat: 'The risk one runs in exploring a coast in these unknown and icy seas is so very great that I can be bold enough to say that no man will ever venture further than I have done; and that the lands which may lie to the south will never be explored.' Further investigation 'would have answered no end whatever, or have been of the least use either to navigation or geography', and would have put at risk all that had been achieved on the voyage. He continued, however, to search for evidence of a southern conti-nent, reporting: 'I had now made the circuit of the Southern Ocean in a high Latitude, and traversed it in such a manner as to leave not the least room for the possibility of there being a continent, unless near the pole and out of the reach of navigation.' He concluded that although it was likely that there was 'a continent or large tract of land near the pole', it would be icebound, not the 'fertile' southern continent supposed by 'geographers of all ages'; his voyage had therefore put 'a final end . . . to the searching after a southern continent'.[22] Cook's account of the wholly alien landscape of frozen horror joined realistic description appropriate to the scientific objectives of the voyage to the portrayal of the ice pack of the Antarctic Circle in terms of the aesthetics of the sublime.

In his *Life of Captain James Cook* (1788) Andrew Kippis remarked that Cook's discoveries 'have opened new scenes for a poetical fancy to range in, and presented new images to the selection of genius and taste'.[23] The icebound landscape of the sublime made familiar by Cook and Hodges shaped Coleridge's 'The Rime of the Ancyent Marinere', first published in Wordsworth and Coleridge's *Lyrical Ballads* (1798), a founding document of Romanticism. The drama is set in the Antarctic, and drew upon Cook's account and upon other narratives of the expedition. The 'argument' of the poem, given in its original version in 1798, describes how a ship was 'driven by Storms to the cold Country towards the South Pole' and then sailed 'to the Tropical Latitude of the Great Pacific Ocean'; this clearly suggests the itinerary of Cook's second voyage to the Pacific. Coleridge certainly drew on the published accounts of the voyage by Cook and the Forsters; and a fascination with the symbolism of the alien landscape of the ice field may have been aroused in his schooldays. William Wales, the mathematics master at his Sussex school Christ's Hospital, which was a training ground for navigators, served as astronomer and meteorologist on the voyage on the *Resolution*, and kept an (unpublished) journal giving an account of his observations.[24] Echoing the language used by Cook and the Forsters, and the experiences recounted by Wales in his journal, Coleridge gives a vivid representation of the mist, snow and ice: '. . . Mist and Snow, / And it grew wond'rous cauld: / And Ice, mast-high, came floating by / As green as Emerauld.' The sound of the pack ice evokes terror: 'The ice was all around: / It crack'd and growl'd, and roar'd and howl'd / . . . The ice did split with a Thunder-fit.' The ice evokes fear; the mariner is a voyager in a landscape of the sublime, a human inter-loper in 'the land of ice, and of fearful sounds where no living thing was to be seen', as Coleridge put it in his prose gloss on these passages of the poem on its revision for republication in his *Sibylline Leaves* (1817).[25] The ice repre-sents the sublime and implacable power of nature; nature is conceived as a brute material reality, not as the product of design, and as indifferent to human habitation, interests and moral or religious improvement.

In his poem 'The Eolian Harp' (1796) Coleridge had written that 'all of animated nature / Be but organic Harps diversely fram'd', lines indicative of his early pantheistic musings. This outlook is echoed in a contemporary notebook entry where he wrote of 'blind Nature ruled by a fatal necessity', and in a letter of January 1796 where he referred to the doctrine that 'we be the outcasts of a blind idiot called nature', ideas given poetic form in his representation of the power of the ice in the 'Ancyent Marinere'.[26] The mist, snow and ice arouse emotions of dread and fear and threaten human interests, but nature is 'blind' and indifferent to (outcast) mankind, and is a self-contained material totality.

In the poem the alienation of nature and the disruption of design is further symbolised in the killing of the albatross, a violation of the harmony between nature and humanity. This conception of nature, as shaped by necessity rather than creation and design, and blind to human concerns, contrasts with the argument and language of the natural theologians who emphasised the contingency of the laws of nature and the benevolence of design.

The imagery of polar ice was applied to the realm of ice and glaciers in the Alps, a region becoming increasingly accessible to travellers in the Romantic period; Chamonix became a tourist site. In Percy Bysshe Shelley's poem 'Mont Blanc' (1817) glaciers form a landscape of the sublime:

> The glaciers creep
> Like snakes that watch their prey, from their far fountains,
> Slow rolling on; there many a precipice,
> Frost and the Sun in scorn of mortal power
> Have piled: dome, pyramid, and pinnacle,
> A city of death, distinct with many a tower
> And wall impregnable of beaming ice.

The glaciers menace humanity:

> So much of life and joy is lost. The race
> Of man flies far in dread; his work and dwelling
> Vanish, like smoke before the tempest's stream,
> And their place is not known.

Describing his impressions of the mountain in letters written in July 1816 to his friend, the satirical novelist Thomas Love Peacock, Shelley reported that he found the glacier to be 'the most vivid image of desolation', and he was struck by the dynamic power of the 'mass of undulating ice': 'the enormous pinnacles of ice perpetually fall, & are perpetually reproduced'. Shelley was familiar with the writings of geologists, including the recent account of Mont Blanc by 'Saussure the naturalist' who had claimed that the glaciers 'have their periods of increase & decay' – noting that 'the people of the country hold an opinion entirely different, but, as I judge, more probable'. The glaciers seemed to be perpetually restored and renewed in a process of continuous rather than episodic regeneration, and he concludes that the 'glaciers must augment & will subsist at least until they have overflowed this vale'. But he adds that 'I will not pursue Buffons sublime but gloomy theory, that this earth which we inhabit will at some future period be changed into a mass of frost'.

The endless creeping flow of glacier ice did not prompt Shelley to speculate about future global geology; the immediacy of the undulating ice sparked his imaginative response to the stony power of the mountain. The glacier appeared to manifest dynamic vitality, an inherent power of regeneration that endowed the mountain itself with a vivifying energy, a process that Shelley illustrated by invoking the analogy of the continuous circulation of the blood in animals: 'This vast mass of ice has one general process which ceases neither day nor night. It breaks & rises forever; its undulations sink whilst other rise . . .. One would think that Mont Blanc was a living being & that the frozen blood forever circulated slowly thro' his stony veins.' His representation of the regenerative powers of the glacier may echo the theory of geological cycles advanced by James Hutton in his *Theory of the Earth* (1795), supposing that the earth was sustained by a cycle of decay and renovation, an unending process fuelled by the power of heat. The final lines of the poem muse on the inherent power of the mountain: 'The secret strength of things / Which governs thought, and to the infinite dome / Of heaven is as a law, inhabits thee!' Writing to Peacock he reflects on 'these palaces of death & frost, sculptured in this their terrible magnificence by the unsparing hand of necessity'; the glaciers suggest the innate regenerative power of nature, of the inevitability of nature's inherent laws.[27]

The conception of nature advanced in 'Mont Blanc' stands in sharp contrast to the design arguments of the natural theologians. The poem is a response to Coleridge's 'Hymn before Sun-rise, in the Vale of Chamouni' (1802), where the mountain proclaims God as its creator and is taken as a symbol of the subordination of humanity to divine power. On the visit to Chamouni (Chamonix) Shelley publicly and famously distanced himself from the pious conventions of the English tourist, signing himself in Greek as 'democrat, philanthropist and atheist' in hotel registers; and his rejection of Christianity is made explicit in his poem, 'Hymn to Intellectual Beauty' (1816), written shortly before the visit to Chamonix. Art, music and nature give 'grace and truth to life's unquiet dream', for 'the name of God, and ghosts, and Heaven, / Remain the records of their vain endeavour, / Frail spells . . .'. The sublimity of nature does not reveal the design of a benevolent deity: the lesson of 'the truth of nature' is to 'love all human kind'.[28]

In Mary Shelley's *Frankenstein* (1818), another product of the Shelleys' visit to Geneva and its environs in 1816, the monster met his creator in a climactic scene set in the 'vast river of ice', the glacier of the Mer de Glace above which towers 'Mont Blanc, in awful majesty'. Mary Shelley sets the story within an icy polar frame, beginning the book with Frankenstein's final pursuit of the monster and encounter with the explorer Captain Walton in the Arctic, a region devoid of humanity. In the second edition of 1831 she emphasises the imagery of the Arctic sublime in providing the context for Frankenstein's ambition to attain power over nature. Where the original text of 1818 quotes the line 'the land of mist and snow' from Coleridge's *Ancyent Marinere* and has

Walton writing to his sister that 'I shall kill no albatross', she here added a passage to the text of the second edition to have Walton explicitly refer to himself as the 'Ancient Mariner' and to confess that 'a love for the marvellous' was 'intertwined in all my projects, which hurries me out of the common pathways of men'. This urge for the control of the polar region sets the scene for the telling of Frankenstein's more ambitious and dangerous project. In the revision of 1831 another passage in this framing section of the novel is amended and enlarged to give the reader a preliminary awareness of the meaning of *Frankenstein*. The polar explorer Walton declares to Frankenstein that he would sacrifice everything for the success of his expedition: 'One man's life or death were but a small price to pay for the acquirement of the knowledge which I sought; for the dominion I should acquire and transmit over the elemental foes of our race.' This declaration of exuberant and untrammelled ambition for the domination of nature does not have its anticipated effect: 'As I spoke, a dark gloom spread over my listener's countenance'. Walton's hubris in seeking dominion over the ice and snow of the Arctic prompts Frankenstein to tell the story of his disastrous attempt to mimic the powers of nature.[29]

The polar ice symbolised human limitations in the face of nature's inherent energy and unfathomable power. Humboldt's environmental vision encouraged the assimilation of the environment of the arctic latitudes to the high altitudes of mountains. By the 1830s the notion of an 'ice age', the product of a glacial advance, was being put forward by geologists. Glaciers became the subject of scientific debate, their motion interpreted by some geologists in terms of their plasticity and flow. The metaphors used to describe glaciers in the scientific literature were human, often drawn from literary tropes, with glaciers seen as shaped like a 'glove' and their crevasses likened to 'jaws'. In his *Glaciers of the Alps* (1860) John Tyndall, Alpine climber and protagonist in the current scientific controversy on glacier motion, amplified the metaphor: 'the glacier resembles a vast gauntlet, of which the gorge represents the wrist; while the lower glacier, cleft by its fissures into finger-like ridges, is typified by the hand'. The glacier could be seen as an animated being, feminised, as in Wordsworth's poem 'The Jung-Frau' (1820) where the mountain is portrayed as an ice-queen: 'The Virgin-Mountain, wearing like a queen, / A brilliant crown of everlasting snow, / Sheds ruin from her sides; and men below / Wonder that aught of aspect so serene / Can link with desolation.' Writing to Effie Gray in 1847 shortly before their marriage, John Ruskin, familiar with Mont Blanc and glaciers, drew upon the metaphor of the feminised glacier: 'You are like the bright – soft – swelling – lovely fields of a high glacier covered with fresh morning snow – which is heavenly to the eye – and soft and winning on the foot – but beneath, there are winding clefts and dark places in its cold – cold ice – where men fall, and rise not again'. This was hardly an encouraging image for their impending marriage.[30]

Polar exploration exerted a similar fascination. The expeditions of William Edward Parry (1819–25) in search of the North-West Passage were especially important in fostering scientific investigation. Edward Sabine, an army officer who had engaged in scientific studies on the Arctic expedition of John Ross in 1818, was appointed to serve on the first of Parry's three voyages. Parry's *Journal of a Voyage for the Discovery of a Northwest Passage from the Atlantic to the Pacific* (1821) gave an account of Sabine's observations of magnetic dip, the effect on magnets of the north magnetic pole; and included an appendix detailing magnetic, pendulum, tidal and lunar observations made on the voyage. The Arctic explorers studied the optical phenomena generated by ice crystals, parhelia ('mock suns' or 'sun dogs'), paraselenae ('moon dogs'), the 'Parry arc' (an arc above the sun, first described by Parry), the aurora borealis and the dazzling light of summer and the darkness of winter. Parry's book, despite his generally dry and dispassionate prose, created a powerful image of the strange, vast and empty landscape of the far north, drawing the contrast between the smiling landscape of agricultural cultivation and the sublime dehumanised landscape of the wilderness in his description of the Arctic winter: 'Not an object was to be seen on which the eye could long rest with pleasure', and he was struck by 'the silence that reigned around us, a silence far different from the peaceable composure which characterizes the landscape of a cultivated country; it was the deathlike stillness of the most dreary desolation, and the total absence of animated existence'.

As a child Emily Brontë admired Parry and was fascinated by Thomas Bewick's description of the northern haunts of seabirds in his *History of British Birds*, first published in 1797, and Parry's description of the Arctic may have shaped the opening passages of Charlotte Brontë's *Jane Eyre* (1847). Jane as the narrator quotes Bewick's text: ' "the vast sweep of the Arctic Zone, and those forlorn regions of dreary space – that reservoir of frost and snow, where firm fields of ice, the accumulation of centuries of winters, glazed in Alpine heights above heights, surround the pole, and concentre the multiplied rigours of extreme cold" '. For Jane these are 'death-white realms . . . shadowy . . . but strangely impressive'.[31] The French translation of Parry's book may have stimulated Caspar David Friedrich's painting of an Arctic scene of ship-wreck, *The Shattered Hope* (1824), a powerful evocation of the Romantic sublime, a contemplation of the majesty and mystery of creation. The painting does not seek to describe the observations of Arctic explorers but to communicate the lifelessness of the Arctic ice and the emotional disquiet of an environment indifferent and hostile to intruding humanity. The diagonal slabs of ice mount to a pyramid of icy death, the majesty of nature being proclaimed triumphant over the puny aspirations of mankind; and an upright triangular plate stands as a memorial stone for the ship disappearing under the slabs of ice. The arrangement of the plates of ice balances symmetry with

asymmetry, creating a dynamic tension within the frozen immobility, drama-
tising the sublime power of nature's inherent energy. The horror of the Arctic
symbolised in Friedrich's painting was, for the Victorians, made real by the
disappearance of Sir John Franklin's expedition on the *Erebus* and *Terror*
(1845–8), and the subsequent search for Franklin and his men. As the search
proceeded there were reports that the survivors had been driven to canni-
balism, (true) rumours that were fiercely contested by Charles Dickens. The
image of the Arctic generated by the fate of the Franklin expedition is
captured in Edwin Landseer's painting *Man Proposes, God Disposes* (1864),
where the terror of the Arctic is evoked by ravening polar bears devouring
human remains. In this painting Friedrich's Arctic sublime is displaced by the
brute unrelenting force of 'Nature, red in tooth and claw', as Alfred Lord
Tennyson (who in 1877 wrote a poem for Franklin's cenotaph) had expressed
it in his poem *In Memoriam* (1850).[32]

Scientific Travel Narratives: Alexander von Humboldt

In an 1801 autobiographical fragment, not intended for publication,
Humboldt traced his yearning to experience 'the Torrid Zone' to his early
study of botany and to his travels through the Low Countries to France and
England in 1790 with Georg Forster, who had died in miserable circumstances
in 1794, a victim of his political radicalism and commitment to the French
revolutionary cause. Humboldt recollected him as a man of 'many-sided
intellect and genius', the kind of man 'who knows a little about everything'; he
considered that 'what was great and rare in young Forster was his way of
philosophising about nature'.[33] Humboldt had read Jean-Jacques Rousseau,
who admired Daniel Defoe's *Robinson Crusoe* (1719) and associated the purity
and virtue of the natural condition of mankind with a tropical island.
Humboldt took the novel *Paul et Virginie* (1787) by Rousseau's disciple
Bernadin de Saint-Pierre with him on his journey to the tropics, praising the
novel 'for the wonderful truth with which [it] paints the power of nature in
the tropical zone'.[34] Writing from Rio de Janeiro in 1832 Charles Darwin paid
similar tribute to Humboldt: 'he alone gives any notion, of the feelings which
are raised in the mind on first entering the Tropics'.[35] Forster published an
account of their journey that was enthusiastically received in literary circles
and led to his friendship with Goethe; his text joined scientific description to
an aesthetic response to nature and helped to shape Humboldt's objectives as
scientist and writer, to convey the richness, complexity and unity of nature
through exact scientific description combined with a celebration of the beauties of the terrestrial environment. Humboldt associated briefly with the Jena
circle of writers and philosophers – Goethe, Friedrich Schiller, August
Wilhelm von Schlegel and his brother Friedrich, and Friedrich Schelling –

and he developed an aesthetic view of nature that links him to German Romanticism, but his vision of science was nevertheless firmly based on exact description and measurement.

The awareness of the relationship between landscape and vegetation, the depiction of the distribution of plant life within geographical regions, the emphasis on biogeography, all were basic to Humboldt's scientific outlook. In an essay 'Ideas for a Physiognomy of Nature', published in his collection *Ansichten der Natur* [*Views of Nature*] (1808), he emphasised the role of vegetation in shaping the physical environment as viewed by man: 'However much the character of different regions of the earth may depend upon a combination of all these external phenomena . . . the outline of mountains and hills, the physiognomy of plants and animals, the azure of the sky, the forms of the clouds, and the transparency of the atmosphere, still it cannot be denied that it is the vegetable covering of the earth's surface which chiefly conduces to the effect.'[36] For Humboldt the new science that he termed *physique du monde* (terrestrial physics) was to be achieved through the study of the distribution of vegetation. He outlined his ambitions in a letter to a friend in April 1799, shortly before leaving Spain on his journey with Aimé Bonpland to Ecuador, Colombia, Venezuela, Mexico and Cuba between 1799 and 1804, following which his achievements brought about a revolution in scientific travel: 'I will collect flora and fauna; I will investigate the heat, elasticity, and magnetic and electrical charge of the atmosphere, and chemically analyse it; I will determine latitudes and longitudes, and measure mountains. But this is not the aim of my voyage. My sole true object is to investigate the confluence and interweaving of all physical forces, and the influence of dead nature on the animate animal and plant creation.' Humboldt knew that this was a very ambitious undertaking, and to be carried through it would require disciplined study and application: 'To this end I have had to instruct myself in every empirical discipline. . .. We have botanists, we have mineralogists, but no physicists, as [Bacon] called for in the *Sylva Sylvarum*.'[37] The reference to Bacon is significant, emphasising that the project would involve the systematic collection of data.

Humboldt came from a family of ennobled Prussian public servants; like his brother Wilhelm, who became celebrated as a philologist and reforming statesman, he had the benefit of a broad cultivated education, dedicated to future state service. He attended a commercial academy in Hamburg, where he learnt how to handle government statistics, and studied geology, mineralogy, surveying and mathematics under Abraham Werner at the Freiberg School of Mines, becoming a mining inspector in Bayreuth in 1792 and undertaking work on geology, geomagnetism, topography and climate. He also pursued botanical interests, publishing an account of the plant distribution in the Freiberg region, *Florae Fribergensis Specimen* (1793). His approach to botanical science was shaped by the argument of the second part of Kant's *Kritik der Urteilskraft* (*Critique of the Power of Judgement*) (1790) which was concerned with principles of teleological natural science. In contrast to the descriptive taxonomy of the Linnaean system, Kant emphasises that living beings must be understood in terms of the purposes organising the unity of which they form a part. Humboldt argues for a programme of botanical science that he terms 'plant geography', to transcend mere description and taxonomy by charting the complex organisation of nature: 'Observations of individual parts of trees or grass is by no means to be considered plant geography . . . [which] traces the connections and relations by which all plants are bound together among themselves, designates in what lands they are found, in what atmospheric conditions they live . . . and describes the surface of the earth in which humus is prepared. This is what distinguishes geography from nature study, falsely called natural history . . .'. As a trained and practising geologist Humboldt conceived the geographical distribution of plants in their relation to geological formations; he maintains that geography is concerned with 'animate and inanimate nature . . . both organic and inorganic bodies', and includes the study of 'solid rock geography . . . zoological geography . . . and the geography of plants', this last being the special science that he aimed to pursue.[38] But the study of plant geography through a search for organic unity would necessitate the widest scientific investigation; in a letter to Marc-Auguste Pictet in 1796, which was read to the *Institut National de France*, Humboldt declared that he was seeking a *physique du monde*, a 'terrestrial physics' which would demand 'considering nature under the most various aspects'. Goethe, who had already published a book on the growth and development of plants, came to know Humboldt at this time and admired him as a 'regular cornucopia of the sciences . . . you could not learn in a week from books what he tells you in an hour's lecture'.[39]

Humboldt's holistic approach to nature, resonating with Goethe, shaped his style in his account of his journey, the *Relation historique du voyage* issued in three large volumes (1814–25). It was immediately translated into English by Helen Maria Williams as the *Personal Narrative*, published in seven volumes between 1814 and 1829, and was the work that excited Charles Darwin's enthusiasm. Humboldt did not complete the book, destroying the manuscript of its fourth volume, and the published narrative ends in April 1801, well before the most spectacular moment in the journey, the ascent almost to the summit of Mount Chimborazo in the Andes, then believed to be the highest peak in the world. Having come into his inheritance on the death of his mother in 1797, Humboldt resigned his official post and dedicated his career and fortune to fulfil his scientific ambition to follow Georg Forster and travel in the tropics. Although he travelled in a private capacity and his scientific researches were ultimately presented to the international public audience of science, his journey traversed a part of the Spanish empire and he was formally authorised by the Spanish Crown to take measurements and to accumulate collections. During his travels he collaborated with officials and was commissioned by the viceroy of New Spain (Mexico) to assemble statistical tables, producing a monumental work (published in two volumes, 1807–11) on the physical geography, population, cities, mining, agriculture, trade and administration of Mexico – with an especially expert account of the silver mines. His journey was framed by the collaboration of the colonial administration, interests that he served.[40]

In the *Personal Narrative* Humboldt explained that he had tended to ignore recording 'the ordinary details of life' encountered on the journey, impressed rather by the 'overwhelming majesty of Nature', and including in his account only those incidents that might contain information useful to future travellers. The scientific tone and purpose is emphatic, and he avoided the emotional language of a travelogue, not wishing to risk a traveller's 'danger of fatiguing his readers with the monotonous expression of his admiration'. But the style of the *Personal Narrative* differed from the tone of his scientific treatises; he had first had the 'firm intention of not writing . . . the historical narrative of a journey', and he had arranged 'the facts not in the order in which they excessively presented themselves, but according to the relation they bore to each other'. But in turning to narrate his itinerary he interpolated descriptions of the phenomena as first observed with reflections on their wider relations: 'I first describe the phaenomena in the order in which they appeared; and I afterward consider them in the whole of their individual relations'. The discursive style of his narrative of travel incorporates reflections on matters of scientific interest, observations shaped by his concern to draw general conclusions through comparisons rather than by focusing on the curiosities of nature: 'we exhibit with more clearness the physiognomy of the landscape, in proportion as we endeavour to sketch its individual features, to compare them with each other, and discover by this kind of analysis the sources of those enjoyments which are offered us by the great picture of nature'.

In explaining the scientific objectives of the voyage, Humboldt emphasised that description, discovery and taxonomy were to yield to measurements and instrument readings. He was not especially interested in discovering new, isolated facts, 'preferring the connection of facts, which have long been observed, to the knowledge of insulated facts, although they were new', claiming that this method 'appears to me more conformable to the plan, which I have proposed to myself in this narrative, to indicate the peculiar character that distinguishes each zone'. Thus botanical classification was merely the necessary preliminary to formulating 'the geography of plants' just as 'descriptive mineralogy' was the basis of the science that provided 'the indication of the rocks which constitute the exterior crust of the earth'. It was because 'the natural sciences are connected by the same ties that link all the phaenomena of nature' that 'the discovery of an unknown genus seemed to me far less interesting than an observation on the geographical relations of the vegetable world'; his scientific investigations had therefore been focused on geographical distribution of plants, on 'the migration of the *social* plants and the limit of the height which their different tribes attain on the flanks of the Cordilleras'. But his vaulting ambition transcended the creation of a science of plant geography from the rudiments of botanical and mineralogical classification, from which it appears that 'every being considered apart is impressed with a particular type'; he sought to comprehend the diversity of nature through its inherent unity. The introduction to the *Personal Narrative* gave emphatic expression to his philosophical outlook: 'We find the same impression in the arrangement of brute matter organised in rocks, in the distribution and mutual relations of plants and animals. The great problem of the physical description of the globe, is the determination of the form of these types, the laws of their relations with each other, and the eternal ties which link the phaenomena of life and those of inanimate matter'.[41]

Nature's narrative, a vast compendium of data, was to be recorded by instruments that would provide the exact physical descriptions and correlations of phenomena necessary to the creation of Humboldt's 'terrestrial physics'. His scientific practice was rigorous and fully conversant with the best contemporary models. If his holistic philosophical outlook was rooted in his native Germany, his emphasis on precision instruments and exact measurement embodied the finest achievements of current French chemistry and physics. Antoine Lavoisier's revolution in chemical theory and nomenclature was based on the systematic application of the chemical balance to the measurement of gases; in their work on specific heats Lavoisier and Pierre Simon Laplace devised an 'ice-calorimeter', a notable illustration of precise experimentation used to achieve the numerical measures of physical quantities; and most striking of all, Charles-Augustin de Coulomb's work on electrostatics employed exceptionally minute measurement as a means to establish the law of electrostatic force, work that came to be seen as providing a paradigm of the value of exact quantitative experiments. By the 1790s precise experimentation and measurement were the norms in physics and chemistry, and a range of precision instruments became available to purchase. Humboldt summarised his aims and methods in a lecture to the Berlin Academy in 1806, emphasising his transformation of the scope of scientific travel: 'travelling naturalists . . . are concerned almost exclusively with the descriptive sciences and with collecting, and have neglected to track the great and constant laws of nature manifested in the rapid flux of phenomena'. Humboldt pointed out that while he too had been 'passionately occupied with botany', he had focused his investigation on the 'physics of the globe'; to this end he had

measured the 'intensity of magnetism . . . in different zones and elevations . . .
hourly changes of the magnetic meridian . . . meteorological phenomena . . .
the mean decrease in temperature in the upper layers of the atmosphere
. . . changes of the barometer . . . the influence of the angle of the sun and
mountain elevations on the electrical charge of the air'. As he told Pictet, he
aimed to chart this flux of nature through the compilation and integration of
physical measurements, to chart and unite all physical forces: 'to conceive the
connection of all phenomena – a connection we call nature – it is necessary
first to discern the parts, and then to reunite them, organically, under the same
point of view'.[42]

In listing his range of magnetic, electrical, meteorological, thermal, tidal and
barometric observations, Humboldt drew upon the advances in instrumentation in the eighteenth century: eudiometers to measure the oxygen content of
the atmosphere; hydrometers to measure humidity; a cyanometer to gauge the
blueness of the sky; thermometers; chronometers; barometers; a theodolite and
sextants; telescopes; an electrometer to measure the electrical charge of the
atmosphere; and magnetic instruments to determine variations in declination
and dip. This was a voyage of instruments; he informed the reader of the
Personal Narrative that he had embarked with instruments: 'I was provided
with instruments of easy and convenient use', reporting of the colonial
authorities that 'I was authorised to make free use of my instruments'.[43]

Humboldt's frontispiece engraving, a graphical physical portrait of the
topography of the Andes based on a drawing he had made at Chimborazo,
forms the most spectacular part of the *Essai sur la géographie des plantes,
accompagné d'un tableau physique des régions équinoxiales* (1807), the work
in which Humboldt expounded his distinctive approach to biogeography,
explaining the connection between botany and climate. 'Botanical geography',
Humboldt explained, 'is a science which considers vegetation under local
conditions in different climates', and he lists the measurements necessary for
a scientific account of the tropical flora.[44] In this pictorial representation
Andean topography is framed by his tabulation of scientific data, showing
how 'the various climates succeed one another, layered one on top of the next
like strata', the data correlating each climatic layer displaying 'all the
phenomena that the surface of our planet and the surrounding atmosphere
present to the observer'. The scientific description incorporates an enormous
compilation of data produced by exact measurement, encompassing the full
range of the physical, meteorological and the geological characteristics of
mountains, correlated with the changes in vegetation due to the elevation.
This extraordinary graphical description embraced 'the general results of five
years in the tropics'.[45]

Humboldt's representation of the slopes of Chimborazo displays the ascent
from the rainforest of tree ferns and palms, through deciduous woodlands,

coniferous forests and grasslands, with lichens and bare rock at the summit. The succession of altitudinal zones shows a series of floral belts typical of the tropics, the temperate regions and of arctic latitudes, displaying the physical and botanical diversity of the continent, a hemisphere in miniature. The framing of the panorama of the Andes by the scientific data offers a holistic view of nature, intended to illustrate the way in which the co-operation of forces provides equilibrium and balance in nature. This is an aesthetic as well as a metrological vision: the floral belts and the azure of the sky were to be appreciated aesthetically, but also measured: 'the man who is sensitive to the beauties of nature will . . . find there the influence exerted by the appearance of vegetation over Man's taste and imagination . . .. What a marked contrast between forests in temperate zones and those of the Equator, where the bare slender trunks of the palms soar above the flowered mahogany trees and create majestical portico arches in the sky'. Humboldt evokes the power and prospect of his conception of global physics, *la physique générale*, 'this science, which without doubt is one of the most beautiful fields of human knowledge, can only progress . . . by the bringing together of all the phenomena and creations which the earth has to offer'.

But Humboldt's ambitions transcended the accumulation and correlation of physical data and scientific description: 'in this great sequence of cause and effect, nothing can be considered in isolation. The general equilibrium, which reigns amongst disturbances and apparent turmoil, is the result of an infinity of mechanical forces and chemical attractions balancing each other out'. In outlining these ambitious objectives and in looking to a science of the earth based on fundamental physical principles, Humboldt echoes the objectives of the unified physics and chemistry of molecular forces fostered by Laplace and Claude Berthollet, his scientific associates in Paris. If the creation of such a universal explanatory theory remained a scientific dream, Humboldt maintained that his descriptive correlation of exact data was an essential preliminary to its attainment: 'Even if each series of facts must be considered separately to identify a particular law, the study of nature, which is the greatest problem of *la physique générale*, requires the bringing together of all the forms of knowledge which deal with the modification of matter.'[46]

The unique character of the *Personal Narrative* is shaped by its style and its place as a narrative counterpart to Humboldt's specialised and systematic scientific publications. It is emphatically the work of a traveller engaged in a scientific quest, concerned to record observations in a systematic and indeed innovatory manner, aiming to transcend the limitations of traditional systems of classification and to raise broad issues of scientific explanation; the work of a natural historian who, in constructing the project of *la physique générale*, initiated a new framework of scientific problems. But the form of Humboldt's narrative is shaped by its purpose, the personal journal of a voyage lasting from 1799 until 1804, the record of an individual's experience and thoughts.[47] In recounting the origins of the voyage as arising from the 'ardent desire' of his 'earliest youth', he explains that his personal interest in undertaking the voyage derived from his aesthetic appreciation of nature: 'Devoted from my earliest youth to the study of nature, feeling with enthusiasm the savage beauties of a country guarded by mountains, and shaded by ancient forests'. Georg Forster had aroused in him the desire to travel to the 'torrid zone', no longer in a spirit of adventure; the urge 'to contemplate nature in all its variety of wild and stupendous scenery; and the hope of collecting some facts useful to the advancement of science incessantly impelled my wishes towards the luxuriant regions spread under the torrid zone'. This aesthetic response to the power of nature and the prospect of achieving scientific understanding shape Humboldt's outlook. While he curbed emotional flourishes in his writing, later in the book he powerfully expressed his response to the fecundity of the tropical environment: 'When a traveller newly arrived from Europe penetrates for the first time into the forests of South America, nature presents herself to him in an unexpected aspect. The objects that surround him recall but feebly those pictures which celebrated writers have traced ... in other temperate regions of the world. He feels at every step, that he is not on the confines, but in the centre of the torrid zone ... on a vast continent, where everything is gigantic, mountains, the rivers, and the mass of vegetation'. The traveller is shocked by 'the deep silence of those solitudes, the individual beauty and contrast of forms, or that vigour and freshness of vegetable life, which characterize the climate of the tropics. It might be said that the earth, overloaded with plants, does not allow them space enough to unfold themselves.'[48] Humboldt's 'glowing accounts of tropical scenery' aroused Charles Darwin's enthusiasm for scientific travel.

On the way to the Americas Humboldt's ship the *Pizarro* stopped at Tenerife in the Canaries, and his account captures in brief compass the form and style of the *Personal Narrative*; his 'sublime descriptions' of Tenerife inspired in Darwin the desire to follow in his footsteps. Humboldt represents the geology, vegetation and environment of Tenerife as illustrative in miniature of his theory of plant geography, based on the linking of latitudinal to altitudinal vegetation zones: the environment of Tenerife 'presents simultaneously, as in Peru and Mexico, the temperature of every climate, from the heats of Africa to the cold of the higher Alps'. He gave a detailed account of the geology of the island, and described the geology and vegetation encountered on his expedition to the highest peak on the island, the Pico de Teide, noting volcanic rock strata, thermal vents and the differences in the vegetation covering the mountain slopes. He describes the panorama of geology and botany spread out to the observer at the summit, in an account that joins aesthetic appreciation and scientific description: 'From the summit of the solitary regions our eyes hovered over an inhabited world; we enjoyed the striking contrast between the bare sides of the Peak, its steep declivities covered with scoriae, its elevated plains destitute of vegetation, and the smiling aspect of the cultivated country beneath; we beheld the plants divided by zones, as the temperature of the atmosphere diminished with the height of the site. Below the Piton, lichens begin to cover the scorious lava with lustered surface; a violet ... rises on the slope of the volcano ... tufts of retama [broom], loaded with flowers, make gay the vallies hollowed out by the torrents ... below ... lies the region of ferns, bordered by the tract of the arborescent heaths. Forests of laurel ... divide the ericas [scrub] from the rising grounds planted with vines and fruit trees. A rich carpet of verdure extends ... even to the group of date trees and the musa [banana]; at the foot of which the ocean appears to roll'.

This account of the succession of floral belts in altitudinal zones encapsulates Humboldt's construction of botanical geography; the scientific authority and significance of this representation was supported by the prior publication of the *Essai sur la Géographie des Plantes*. Observing the landscape from the mountain he noted the clarity of the air, characteristically drawing a comparison with his (yet to be described) experience of the tropics: 'This transparency may be regarded as one of the chief causes of the beauty of the landscape under the torrid zone; it is this which heightens the splendour of the vegetable colouring and contributes to the magical effects of their harmonies and their contrasts.' He was alert to features of special interest such as the 'dragon tree', 'one of the oldest inhabitants of our globe', being 'struck with its enormous magnitude' – characteristically recording measurements of its height and girth.[49]

Scientific Travel Narratives: Charles Darwin

In a letter of February 1845 to Joseph Hooker, who had just met Humboldt in Paris, Charles Darwin wrote that 'my whole course of life is due to have read & reread as a Youth his Personal Narrative', sparking his desire to travel to the tropics and leading to his voyage on the *Beagle* (1831–6). But it was only after his return from the voyage, reflecting on his observations in the Galápagos Islands, that he was led to develop his theory of evolution by natural selection; and he signalled the central importance to his theory of Hooker's field of expertise, the study of botanical geography – 'that grand subject, that almost key-stone of the laws of creation, Geographical Distribution', the science whose scope had been outlined by Humboldt.[50] Darwin's entry in the *Diary* he kept during the voyage, written on the day he landed in Brazil on 28 February 1832, captures the intensity of emotion aroused by the *Personal Narrative*. His delight in the tropical scenery led him to recall the 'rare union of poetry with science' in Humboldt's 'unparalleled' and 'glorious descriptions', adding that 'Humboldt . . . like another Sun illumines everything I behold'.[51] But Humboldt's influence on Darwin went beyond landscape aesthetics. The integrative, holistic style of Humboldt's 'terrestrial physics' and botanical geography, concerned with the interrelations and synthesis of biological, geological and meteorological phenomena, helped to shape Darwin's development as a 'philosophical naturalist'. He used this term in the published account of the voyage, his *Journal of Researches* (1839),[52] to denote a scientific student of natural history concerned with explanatory theories, not merely with observing, collecting and classifying, an outlook that shaped his scientific career. Charles Lyell's *Principles of Geology* (1830–3) was to provide Darwin with a general causal and explanatory theory supplementing the holistic and synthetic view of nature he had imbibed from Humboldt.[53]

Darwin was born in 1809 and it was intended that he would follow his father and grandfather, the celebrated Erasmus Darwin, in a medical career; he studied at Edinburgh University from 1825 to 1827 with the intention of training for a career as a physician. It became clear that this was not to his taste, but Edinburgh offered a range of opportunities for the cultivation of interests in natural history and geology, and Darwin took full advantage. He roamed the shore of the Firth of Forth collecting invertebrate specimens with the young anatomist Robert Grant, who introduced him to the controversial recent work of Jean Baptiste de Lamarck and Étienne Geoffroy Saint-Hilaire on the transmutation of species – speculations that resembled the ideas on evolution proposed by Erasmus Darwin in his *Zoonomia* 1794–6. Charles Darwin participated in meetings of the student Plinian Natural History Society where he presented his first scientific paper on a marine invertebrate, a topic encouraged by Grant's interest in microscopic life. On the more formal side Darwin followed the university syllabus, attending the exciting chemistry lectures of Thomas Charles Hope, whose course included the science of heat, an Edinburgh speciality since the work of Joseph Black. The scope of Hope's popular course extended to geology, where he expounded the dynamic geological theory of Black's friend James Hutton, who supposed that subterranean heat was the cause of geological change; according to Hutton granites and basalts were formed as cooled crystals from an igneous melt of lava. Darwin also attended the more sober systematic course on natural history, geology and mineralogy offered by Robert Jameson, who emphasised the importance of taxonomy. Jameson gave his pupils the experience of working in his museum and on trips in the field; and in contrast to Hope's advocacy of Hutton and the role of subterranean heat in geological history, Jameson presented the theory of his teacher Abraham Werner, that the geological strata were sedimentary precipitates from the ocean.

This early instruction in geology was to prove valuable to the budding philosophical naturalist,[54] who abandoned his medical studies and left Edinburgh in
April 1827 without a degree. Darwin entered Christ's College, Cambridge, in
January 1828 to read for the ordinary degree as a preliminary to a clerical
career; his father, though a disbeliever, was anxious that he should follow a
profession. The study of science, natural history and natural philosophy did
not fall within the syllabus of study for a pass degree, and while mathematics
was the core subject for candidates for honours, scientific pursuits were
fostered through more informal networks. At Cambridge Darwin met his
cousin William Darwin Fox who introduced him to beetle collecting in the
fens, and he was drawn into the circle of scientific Cambridge, being taken
under the wing of the professor of botany John Stevens Henslow with whom
he formed a close relationship. In the final examination in January 1831 he was
ranked tenth in the pass list, a solid achievement, and remained in Cambridge
to complete the residence requirements for graduation.

Darwin now looked forward to a 'very pleasant Spring term', he told his
cousin Fox in April 1831, 'walking & botanising with Henslow'; and he read
Humboldt's *Personal Narrative*, copying out long passages about Tenerife: 'I
talk, think, & dream of a scheme I have almost hatched of going to the Canary
Islands'. In a letter to his sister Caroline written later that month he reported
that he was attending Henslow's lectures on botany, and that 'my head is
running about the Tropics: in the morning I go and gaze at Palm trees in the
hot-house and come home and read Humboldt: my enthusiasm is so great
that I cannot hardly sit still on my chair . . . I will never be easy till I see the
peak of Teneriffe and the great Dragon tree; sandy, dazzling, plains, and
gloomy silent forest are alternately uppermost in my mind'. Studying Spanish
in preparation, he planned to travel to the Canary Islands with Henslow to
whom he wrote from his home in Shrewsbury in July 1831: 'I hope you
continue to fan your Canary ardour: I read & reread Humboldt, do you the
same, & I am sure nothing will prevent us seeing the Great Dragon tree'.[55]

It was at this time that he read William Paley's *Natural Theology* (1802) as
a standard exposition of the design argument; he told John Lubbock in
November 1859, on the publication of the *Origin of Species*, that 'I do not
think I hardly ever admired a book more than Paley's Natural Theology; I
could almost formerly have said it by heart'. But Paley's mechanistic approach
to nature is remote from Darwin's language in the *Diary* that he kept during
the voyage, later developed into the published *Journal of Researches* (1839), or
in the tone of his letters. Darwin followed Humboldt in communicating a
holistic and personal experience of nature, a tone consonant with the Romantic
sensibility that is so strong in Humboldt, the assertion of the primacy of the
power and truth of nature that contrasts with the appeal to the metaphors of
design and mechanism that shaped the aesthetics and language of natural

theology. Darwin's voyage coincided with the publication of the *Bridgewater Treatises*; his language differs utterly from the traditional philosophical and theological pieties of natural theology to be found in these works. In his auto-biography, written late in life and only published complete in 1958, he wrote that this personal experience of nature was 'intimately connected with a belief in God, [and] did not essentially differ from that which is often called the sense of sublimity'.[56] Darwin's religious sense at this time was bound up with an aesthetic sensibility to the fecundity and power of nature, an outlook remote from formal claims of order and design. As the *Beagle* returned to Plymouth in September 1836, he singled out two particular experiences: 'Among the scenes which are deeply impressed on my mind, none exceed in sublimity the primeval forests, undefaced by the hand of man, whether those of Brazil, where the powers of life are predominant, or those of Tierra del Fuego, where death & decay prevail. Both are temples filled with the varied productions of the God of nature:- No one can stand unmoved in these solitudes, without feeling that there is more in man than the mere breath of his body.' Darwin found God in the sublimity of nature, an outlook shaped by the 'rare union of poetry with science' that he found in 'Humboldts glorious descriptions'. His phraseology – 'temples . . . productions of the God of nature' – may echo the title of the scientific poem by his grand-father Erasmus, *The Temple of Nature* (1803), which presents a holistic vision of nature as shaped by immanent active powers. Like his grandfather, he here voices a sensibility quite different from the abstract demonstrative arguments of the natural theologians who claimed to deduce God's existence and attributes from order, design and law; this passage in the *Diary* was transferred almost unchanged to the *Journal of Researches*.[57]

At Cambridge Henslow had introduced Darwin to Adam Sedgwick, the professor of geology and a leading figure in British science; having attended Sedgwick's lectures and made some private geological excursions, and still planning to travel to Tenerife, in August 1831 Darwin undertook a field trip with Sedgwick in North Wales. Sedgwick taught him the essentials of geolog-ical fieldwork, how to recognise rock formations by vegetation and surface features, and how to make drawings of stratification and sections. On this field trip Sedgwick was commencing his important work on the geological formations of North Wales that were to lead to his identification of ancient 'silurian' strata (and into a long controversy on the subject), and was specifi-cally interested in the contact of limestone cliffs with the underlying red sand-stone in the Vale of Clwyd. He sent Darwin on an independent traverse to investigate whether the red soil in the area gave evidence of sandstone. Darwin did not find sandstone, and nor did Sedgwick, who was satisfied with this result and expressed confidence in Darwin's work; he attributed the red soil to 'ferruginous clay', which implied that the Vale of Clwyd was not a complex geological structure (as had been supposed on the current geological map) but that the strata had been stretched. This trip gave Darwin training in the skills of the geologist and the confidence to make judgements in the field, expertise that was to prove invaluable on the voyage of the *Beagle*: 'Tell Prof: Sedgwick', Darwin wrote to Henslow from Rio de Janeiro the following May, 'he does not know how much I am indebted to him for the Welch expedition'.[58] Darwin's early scientific reputation, following his return from the voyage of the *Beagle* in the 1830s, was built on the geological inquiries undertaken during the voyage.[59]

The invitation to undertake the voyage came shortly afterwards; this was not to be an official appointment but a private arrangement with the captain, Robert FitzRoy, whose inquiry to find a gentleman with scientific interests was passed to Henslow by Francis Beaufort, hydrographer to the British navy. Darwin finally gained the approval – and necessary financial support – of his father to accompany the *Beagle* on a surveying expedition to South America. This support was significant: the journey stretched to five years, and while naval courtesy was extended to transporting Darwin's considerable collections of specimens, skins, rocks and dried plants back to Henslow in Cambridge, he was not a member of the official ship's company and travelled in a private capacity as FitzRoy's companion. FitzRoy was a man of mercurial temper, and the two young men disagreed over politics. They clashed especially over Darwin's passionate objection to slavery; but FitzRoy had significant scientific interests, especially in meteorology, and the ship was equipped with a wide range of instruments. Darwin gathered a collection of suitable books for which FitzRoy assured him there would be '*plenty* of room': 'Humboldts personal narative you will of course get' wrote Sedgwick, and FitzRoy assured him that he was 'of course welcome to take your Humboldt – as well as any other books you like'.[60] Henslow presented Darwin with a set of the *Personal Narrative* while FitzRoy gave him a copy of the first volume of Charles Lyell's *Principles of Geology* (1830), although Henslow warned him against accepting Lyell's theory.

Henslow's warning fell on stony ground. Reading Lyell's *Principles* was to be a formative experience for Darwin – he received the second two volumes of the work during the course of the voyage – for Lyell provided a causal and explanatory theory that supplemented the descriptive, geographical and holistic view of nature presented by Humboldt. Writing to Lyell's father-in-law Leonard Horner in August 1844, Darwin confessed that 'I have always thought that the great merit of the Principles was that it altered the whole tone of one's mind & therefore that when seeing a thing never seen by Lyell, one yet saw it partially through his eyes – it would have been in some respects better if I had done this less'.[61] This tribute, couched in more sober terms than his emotional paeans to Humboldt, acknowledged the intellectual grip of Lyell's approach. The conventional geology of the period, that of William Buckland and Sedgwick (both men being clerics as well as geologists), while not framed in biblical terms had nevertheless sought accommodation with Genesis. Lyell's approach was different, insisting that the language of geology should be secularised and that secondary causes were alone to be considered in unravelling the fundamental laws that shaped geological history. He maintained that the causes of geological change that had operated in the past were identical with the causes observed acting at the present. This was not in itself radical; but Lyell made an additional philosophical assumption, that past and present geological causes operated at the same intensity, a principle that came to be termed 'uniformitarianism'. This implied that geological change had been very gradual, having taken place over an immense stretch of time, and had not been punctuated by the periodic and drastic actions of volcanoes, floods and earthquakes lying outside the regular pattern of geological processes. He looked in particular for evidence of the gradual elevation and subsidence of land in support of his theory and method.

The *Beagle* voyage had barely commenced when, as Darwin recalled in the *Journal of Researches*, at St Jago in the St Verde Islands he observed 'a perfectly horizontal white band, in the face of the sea cliff . . . running for some miles along the coast, and at the height of about 45 feet above the water . . . this white stratum is found to consist of calcareous matter, with numerous shells embedded, such as now exist on the neighbouring coast. It rests on ancient volcanic rocks, and has been covered by a stream of basalt, which must have entered by the sea, when the white shelly bed was lying at the bottom'.[62] Darwin was suggesting that the elevation of the calcareous band, formed of similar materials to the shells found on the shore, had been a regular and gradual process and a quite recent event in geological terms. Sedgwick and Henslow would have proffered an explanation in terms of the fall in the level of the ocean, an interpretation supposing the gradual elevation of the land was consonant with the argument of Lyell's *Principles of Geology*.

This initial success sparked Darwin's enthusiasm and confidence in pursuing geological investigations. 'Geology is a capital science to begin', he told his cousin Fox three years later, 'as it requires nothing but a little reading, thinking & hammering'. Writing from Valparaíso in April 1835, Darwin had felt confident enough to offer Henslow a Lyellian interpretation of the gradual elevation of the Andes, but he was hesitant and politely apologetic: 'I am quite afraid of the only conclusion which I can draw'. He suggested that a range of the Andes was composed of the same tertiary rocks as the coastal plain. He had found 'a small wood of petrified trees in a vertical position . . . they consist of snow white columns like Lots wife of coarsely crytall. Carb. of Lime . . . and resemble the dicotyledonous wood' that he had noticed on the plain. Darwin's interpretation invoked the Lyellian theory of gradual depression and elevation. The petrified trees had grown on the plain, and had been sunk beneath the sea and covered with sedimentary deposits; the strata formed had been elevated to form the chain of mountains, and through weathering 'the trees now changed into silex were exposed projecting from the volcanic soil now changed into rock, whence formerly in a green and budding state they had raised their lofty heads', as he put it in his *Journal of Researches*. High in the Andes, he reported, 'I saw the spot where a cluster of fine trees had once waved their branches on the shores of the Atlantic, when that ocean (now driven back 700 miles) approached the base of the Andes.' There is no surprise in finding him affirming to his cousin Fox, four months after reporting this scene to Henslow, that 'I am become a zealous disciple of Mr Lyells views, as known in his admirable book. – Geologizing in S. America, I am tempted to carry parts to a greater extent, even than he does'.[63]

The argument for the elevation of the Andes was bold, but Darwin's subsequent explanation of the formation of coral reefs by the subsidence of the ocean floor and the upward growth of coral did indeed go beyond Lyell.[64] Darwin used Lyell's own form of argument to contradict his view, as set out in the second volume of the *Principles of Geology*, that coral reefs were formed on the crests of submarine volcanoes. If Sedgwick had provided Darwin with the essential tools of geology, Lyell supplied its conceptual framework.

As the *Beagle* returned to Plymouth in September 1836, Darwin reflected on his experiences as recorded in his *Diary* during the five years of the voyage, and attested to Humboldt's formative impact on his outlook: 'As the force of impression frequently depends on preconceived ideas, I may add that all mine were taken from the vivid descriptions in the Personal Narrative which far exceed in merit anything I have ever read on the subject'. This tribute, first entered in his *Diary*, was transferred almost unchanged to the text of the published *Journal of Researches*.[65] Writing in Rio de Janeiro in May 1832, reflecting on his initial impressions of the tropics, he had mused on the significance of Humboldt's narrative: 'Few things give me so much pleasure as reading the Personal Narrative; I know not the reason why a thought which has passed through the mind, when we see it embodied in words, immediately assumes a more substantial & true air.'[66] Darwin's narrative of his experiences, as recorded in the *Diary* sent in installments to his family and in the letters written during the course of the voyage, was shaped and made vivid and real by Humboldt's evocative descriptions.

On the outward voyage as the *Beagle* approached Tenerife, Darwin was enduring seasickness and 'reading Humboldts glowing accounts of tropical scenery'; on 6 January 1832 he recorded that the ship was 'in sight of Tenerife . . .. Everything has a beautiful appearance: the colours are so rich & soft . . . I must have another gaze at this long wished for object of my ambition'; and then 'Oh misery, misery', a quarantine of twelve days prevented landfall and 'we have left perhaps one of the most interesting places in the world'; but he found consolation in nature and Humboldt, for the 'night does its best to smooth our sorrow – the air is still & deliciously warm . . ... Already I can understand Humboldts enthusiasm about the tropical night, the sky is so clear & lofty'. The following May in Rio de Janeiro he again recollected Humboldt's remarks on the clarity of the air in the tropics (prompted by the observations from the Pico de Teide in Tenerife): 'that hills in a Tropical country seen from a distance are of a uniform blue tint, but that contrary to what generally is the case the outline is defined with the clearest edge'. He told Henslow that on approaching Tenerife he had been 'repeating to myself Humboldts sublime descriptions'; but he had now experienced a 'Tropical forest in all its sublime grandeur. – Nothing, but the reality can give any idea, how wonderful, how magnificent the scene is . . . I never experienced such intense delight. – I formerly admired Humboldt, I now almost adore him; he alone gives any notion, of the feelings which are raised in the mind on first entering the Tropics'. Darwin's narrative moves smoothly from recording his experiences to evoking Humboldt: in his imagination they were intertwined. He gave an account of his impressions of the tropical forest to his cousin Fox, describing how he wandered in 'the sublime forests, surrounded by views more gorgeous than even Claude ever imagined, I enjoy a delight which none but those who have experienced it can understand – If it is to be done, it must be by studying Humboldt'. Using the language of the picturesque he compares nature to a painting by Claude Lorrain, and for Darwin (with the Romantics) nature takes precedence over art; though, he adds, Humboldt alone can communicate the immediacy of the experience.[67]

Reflecting on his experiences as the *Beagle* returned to Plymouth, Darwin recalled that of the scenes he had witnessed 'none exceed in sublimity the primeval forests, undefaced by the hand of man, whether those of Brazil, where the powers of life are predominant, or those of Tierra del Fuego, where death & decay prevail'. When he had first described his impressions of the primeval forests his language was suitably evocative. On 29 February 1832 he had recorded in his *Diary* his first impressions of the tropical forest: 'amongst the multitude it is hard to say what set of objects is most striking; the general luxuriance of the vegetation bears the victory, the elegance of the grasses, the novelty of the parasitical plants, the beauty of the flowers – the glossy green of the foliage, all tend to this end. – A most paradoxical mixture of sound & silence pervades the shady parts of the wood'. Even the landscape art of Claude Lorrain could not capture the beauty and tranquillity of such a scene, which transcended the power of painting. A later entry on 11 June enlarged on these impressions in emphasising the sublimity of the forests: 'A profound gloom reigns everywhere; it would be impossible to tell the sun was shining, if it was not for an occasional gleam of light shooting, as it were through a shutter, on

the ground beneath . . .. The air is motionless & has a peculiar chilling damp-
ness. – Whilst seated on the trunk of a decaying tree amidst such scenes, one
feels an inexpressible delight'. These contrasting impressions of the fecundity
of the tropical forests evoked in Darwin a delight in the power of life. The
following December he recorded the contrasting ecology of death in Tierra
del Fuego: 'The gloomy depth of the ravine well accorded with the universal
signs of violence – in every direction were irregular masses of rock & uptorn
trees, others decayed & others ready to fall. – To have made the scene perfect,
there ought to have been a group of Banditti . . . the number of decaying &
fallen trees reminded me of the Tropical forest. – But in this still solitude,
death instead of life is the predominant spirit.' On this occasion, struck by the
impression of death and decay, he alludes to the pictorial imagery of sublime
terror evoked by the craggy mountain scenes and (Italian) bandits in the
paintings of Salvator Rosa.[68]

Darwin's language here is at its most Humboldtian, and it may have been
these passages to which his sister Caroline alluded when she wrote on 28
October 1833 that she had been reading his journal but was concerned with
the lushness of his style: 'I thought . . . that you had, probably from reading so
much Humboldt, got his phraseology, & occasionly made use of the kind of
flowery French expressions which he uses, instead of your own simple straight
forward & far more agreeable style. I have no doubt you have without
perceiving it got to embody your ideas in his poetical language & from his
being a foreigner it does not sound unnatural in him.'[69] But conscious that he
was writing a 'personal narrative', in which like Humboldt he would incorporate solid and sober descriptions and interpretations of geology, landscape,
flora and fauna, Darwin retained two of these passages in the published text
of the *Journal of Researches*.[70] But on his return to Brazil, a chance landing in
August 1836 on the return voyage of the *Beagle* to England, he told his sister
Susan that 'It has been almost painful to find how much, good enthusiasm has
been evaporated during the last four years. I can now walk soberly through a
Brazilian forest; not but what it is exquisitely beautiful, but now, instead of
seeking for splendid contrasts; I compare the stately Mango trees with the
Horse Chestnuts of England.' Thoughts of home and the comfortable and
familiar Shropshire landscape had dissipated his Humboldtian enthusiasm for
the fecundity of the tropics. A month earlier he had written to his sister
Caroline that he was looking forward to the 'green fields & oak woods of
England . . . I am determined & feel sure, that the scenery of England is ten
times more beautiful than any we have seen'.[71]

Exploration, commerce and science were products of the worldwide expansion of Britain in the eighteenth century. European civilisation had been
transformed by the voyages of discovery that began with the exploration of

the Atlantic littoral and the quest for the spices of the East, prized since antiquity. The discovery of the Americas, of a sea route around Africa, of the Pacific Ocean and the circumnavigation of the globe, led to the maritime expansion of Europe and to colonisation and the creation of empire. Captain James Cook explored the Pacific islands and penetrated the Arctic and Antarctic pack ice; geographical and climatic extremes were open to exploration. Climate, rivers, earthquakes, volcanoes, glaciers, geomagnetism, minerals and crystals, fossils, and the figure of the earth were investigated and mapped, opening the way to understanding the landscape in terms of its underlying structure, charted through the tracing of geological strata. Landscape came to be represented both in aesthetic terms and in relation to its geological structure. In the scientific narratives of Cook's voyages the polar ice came to symbolise human limitations in the face of nature's inherent energy and unfathomable power; the frozen horror of the alien and icy landscape was envisioned in terms of the aesthetics of the sublime – shaping the aesthetics of Coleridge's 'The Rime of the Ancyent Marinere', Percy Shelley's 'Mont Blanc' and Mary Shelley's *Frankenstein*.

Building on the work of the Forsters, Cook's scientific associates, Humboldt depicted the relations between geography, climate and the distribution of plants; and his evocative narrative of his travels inspired the young Charles Darwin to follow his lead. Darwin's geological reports were couched in terms dependent on Charles Lyell's theory that geological change occurred through the cumulative effect of gradual processes; he proposed a Lyellian interpretation of the gradual elevation of the Andes and of the formation of coral reefs. In Darwin's *Origin of Species* Lyellian gradualism is balanced by evocation of Humboldt's description of the fecundity and sublimity of tropical forests, evident in the concluding metaphor of nature's fecundity where the natural world is envisaged as an 'entangled bank, clothed with many plants of many kinds'.[72]

CHAPTER 4

Landscape, Georgic and Picturesque

Around 1747 Thomas Gainsborough painted *Wooded Landscape with a Peasant Resting* (Fig. 4), the scene evocative of the countryside of his native Suffolk. It depicts a landscape in which the tonality of greens, yellows and browns gives the impression of a summer's day, and the setting is bathed in a light deployed and varied so as to balance the composition rather than to display the effects of a real light source. This is not a specific view of an actual location – unlike his portrait of *Mr and Mrs Andrews* (*c.* 1748–50), a celebration of landownership. The intention in *Wooded Landscape with a Peasant Resting* is to evoke a sense of timelessness and harmony, not to render the transient colours and quality of light at a particular place at a particular moment.[1] Gainsborough's painting shows an aesthetic that contrasts with John Ruskin's (Romantic) admonition to the painter to 'go to nature trustingly, rejecting nothing, and selecting nothing', to fully and accurately depict the brazen 'real world of nature'.[2] Gainsborough's idealised representation of landscape had its source in the 'classical' landscapes depicted by Claude Lorrain and Nicolas Poussin, shaped by the vision of landscape and use of the land portrayed by Virgil in the *Georgics*. The *Georgics* in turn had an aesthetic counterpart in the landscapes described by Homer, made familiar in Alexander Pope's translations.

In the third volume of *Modern Painters* (1856), in a chapter on 'classical landscape', Ruskin argued that the veneration of wilderness, of nature sanctified as untouched by human hand – a sensibility central to the Romantic aesthetic espoused by Wordsworth and by Ruskin himself – contrasts with the Homeric view of landscape. Ruskin claims that for Homer pleasant landscapes are gentle and humanised, and cultivated ground, tilled fields and vineyards are beautiful. He writes that 'every Homeric landscape, intended to be beautiful, is composed of a fountain, a meadow, and a shady grove', making reference to the description of Calypso's cave in the fifth book of the *Odyssey*.[3] In Alexander Pope's translation the passage reads:

4   Thomas Gainsborough, *Wooded Landscape with a Peasant Resting.*

The cave was brighten'd with a rising blaze:
Cedar and frankincense, an Od'rous pile,
Flam'd on the hearth, and wide perfum'd the Isle;
. . . Without the grot a various sylvan scene
Appear'd around, and groves of living green;
Poplars and alder ever quiv'ring play'd,
And nodding cypress form'd a fragrant shade;
On whose high branches, waving with the storm,
The birds of broadest wing their mansion form,
The chough, the sea-mew, the loquacious crow,
And scream aloft, and skim the deeps below.
Depending vines the shelving cavern screen,
With purple clusters blushing thro' the green.
Four limpid fountains from the clefts distill,
And ev'ry foundtain pours a sev'ral rill,
In mazy windings wand'ring down the hill:
Where bloomy meads with vivid green were crown'd,
And glowing violets threw odors round.[4]

In Ruskin's reading, the pleasant Homeric landscape is shaped by man and suited to human needs and convenience – the cultivated landscape is regarded as beautiful. 'If we glance through the references to pleasant landscape which occur in other parts of the *Odyssey*, we shall always be struck by this quiet subjection of their every feature to human service, and by the excessive similarity in the scenes. Perhaps the spot intended, after this, to be most perfect, may be the garden of Alcinous, where the principal ideas are, still more definitely, order, symmetry, and fruitfulness'.[5] With its orchards and vines and springs the garden of Alcinous exemplifies order, enclosure and usefulness, a magical and paradisiacal garden in which fruits grow all year round:

Close to the gates a spacious garden lies,
From storms defended, and inclement skies:
Four acres was th'allotted space of ground,
Fenc'd with a green enclosure all around.
Tall thriving trees confess'd the fruitful mold;
The red'ning apple ripens here to gold.
Here the blue fig with luscious juice o'erflo ws,
With deeper red the full pomegranate glows.
The branch here bends beneath the weighty pear,
And verdant olives flourish round the year.
The balmy spirits of the western gale
Eternal breathes on fruits untaught to fail:
Each dropping pear a following pear supplies,
On apples apples, figs on figs arise:
The same mild season gives the blooms to blow,
The buds to harden, and the fruits to grow.
Here order'd vines in equal ranks appear
With all th'united labours of the year;
. . . Here are the vines in early flow'r descry'd,
Here grapes discolour'd on the sunny side,
And there in autumn's richest purple dy'd,
Beds of all various herbs, for every green,
In beauteous order terminate the scene.
Two plenteous fountains the whole prospect crown'd;
This thro' the gardens leads its streams around,
Visits each plant, and waters all the ground:
While that in pipes beneath the palace flows,
And then its current on the town bestows;
. . . Such were the glories which the Gods ordain'd
To grace *Alcinous*, and his happy land.[6]

This contrasts with the modern sensibility, which delights in wilderness and the inhospitable, nature devoid of human cultivation and order: 'Precipices, mountains, torrents, wolves, rumblings, Salvator Rosa', Horace Walpole exclaimed when crossing the Alps in 1739,[7] signalling a shift in sensibility. The shift in power from a social order based on landownership and aristocratic patronage to institutions of a commercial society fuelled by technological innovations, the power of finance and the optimism of 'improvement' brought a new emphasis in the control, use and aesthetic appreciation of the landscape. In the eighteenth century the new commercial class absorbed and transformed the values of the aristocracy, creating landscape parks where the countryside was construed in aesthetic categories and exercising landowner-ship by enclosing land for agrarian profit, moulding landscape to human convenience through new methods of cultivation and new criteria of aesthetic appreciation. With the enthusiasm among the emergent middle class for 'picturesque' tours to the mountainous landscapes of the Alps and the English Lake District, 'nature' came to be conceived in terms of the aesthetic categories of the picturesque and the sublime. The new aesthetic can be seen in the interest and depiction of geological formations; rocky and mountainous land-scapes and volcanoes became objects of awed admiration in the aesthetics of the sublime; the golden glow of the classical landscape had been displaced by the aesthetics of the picturesque and the sublime.

Golden Landscape: Pastoral and Georgic

In *An Apology for Poetry* (1595) Sir Philip Sidney drew the contrast between the landscape of nature and the landscape depicted in poetry: 'Nature never set forth the earth in so rich tapestry as diverse poets have done, neither with pleasant rivers, fruitful trees, sweet smelling flowers, nor whatsoever else may make the too much loved earth more lovely. Her world is brazen, the poets only deliver a golden.'[8] Sidney celebrates the capacity of poetry to cast a golden glow over nature; this idealisation of nature was characteristic of eighteenth-century British landscape paintings, which project a sense of the timeless past and the harmony between man and nature, depicting a generalised environ-ment where features are rendered indistinct and indeterminate, and where the landscape details are not intended to show a specific locale. Gainsborough's *Wooded Landscape with a Peasant Resting* depicts such a setting.

Since the revival of classical antiquity in the Renaissance the representation of nature, of landscape and the countryside, under a golden veneer of celebra-tion and nostalgia, had been profoundly shaped by readings of Virgil's pastoral and agricultural poems: the *Eclogues* published *c.* 39–38 BC and the *Georgics* in 29 BC. The *Eclogues* (*eclogae* means 'selections') comprise ten short poems whose original title *Bucolica* ('cowherd songs') alludes to the pastoral idiom, a poetic form created in the *Idylls* of Theocritus, a Greek poet of the third century BC, whose poems are concerned with the loves and songs of idealised rustics. The simplicity of the setting of the *Eclogues*, where nymphs and swains inhabit a verdant landscape in which reality is subsumed in a world of symbolism and disguise, belies the sophisticated and elusive character of the poems: Virgil creates a 'small universe that is at once real and artificial, strange and familiar, ordinary and magical'.[9] In this poetic world, as Erwin Panofsky put it, 'human suffering and super-humanly perfect surroundings create a dissonance . . . resolved in that vespertinal mixture of sadness and tranquillity which is perhaps Virgil's most personal contribution to poetry'.[10] In the *Eclogues* Virgil introduced the theme of social tensions in the Italian countryside, and in the *Georgics* (the title taken from the Greek word for farming) he is concerned with the Italian landscape and the habitation and use of the land; it is a descriptive and didactic poem, its four books concerned in turn with the management of field crops, trees (especially the vine), livestock and bees. The rustic piety of the *Georgics* makes allusion to the *Works and Days* of the archaic Greek poet Hesiod (*c.* 700 BC), its rational spirit to the recent didactic poem of Lucretius (*c.* 94–*c.* 55 BC), *De Rerum Natura* (*On the Nature of Things*). Transcending these sources, Virgil's pastoral and georgic poetic idioms established literary genres for the representation of the harmony of man and nature.

But 'pastoral' is not to be identified as the literature of nature, or as celebrating rural themes, certainly not as a representation of the 'real world of nature'.[11] In the Renaissance the genre flourished in works as varied as Edmund Spenser's *The Shepheardes Calendar* (1579), Sidney's *Arcadia* (1580s), Shakespeare's *As You Like It* (1599/1600) and John Milton's *Lycidas* (1638), and its definition has proved elusive. Seeking generality, William Empson famously described pastoral as a process of 'putting the complex into the simple'; while Renato Poggioli characterised the 'psychological root of the pastoral' as 'a double longing after innocence and happiness, to be recovered not through conversion or regeneration but merely through a retreat', adding that 'pastoral longing is but the wishful dream of a happiness to be gained without effort, of an erotic bliss made absolute by its own irresponsibility'.[12] These evocative descriptions indicate the literary power and sophistication of pastoral, but do not delineate its landscape setting and its significance for the representation of nature in European art and literature. The tradition of pastoral came to embody several connected elements (though not necessarily all of them at the same time): as a literary idiom pertaining to herdsmen, caring for animals, playing music and making love; an idiom in which the values of rustic simplicity are contrasted with the world of civilisation, power and ordered society; a literary consciousness in which the confusions and conflicts of reality are depicted as meaningful and harmonious.[13]

The genre of pastoral is not discussed in Horace's *Ars Poetica* (*c.* 19 BC), and for the Renaissance an important characterisation was drawn from the fourth-century commentary on Virgil by Servius, a commentary generally set alongside the text in printed editions of Virgil's poems. Servius claimed that as a poet Virgil followed a natural sequence, beginning with the lowly pastoral in the *Eclogues*, proceeding to the more superior genre of didactic in the *Georgics* and achieving the crowning glory of epic in the *Aeneid*. In this hierarchy of genres Servius emphasised the lowliness of the subject of pastoral rather than the elegance of Virgil's *Eclogues*, and presented an image of Virgilian pastoral as moral allegory; pastoral came to be seen as lowly in style and allegorical in content. In his *Apology for Poetry* Sidney presents pastoral as an idiom in which 'under the pretty tales of wolves and sheep, can include the whole considerations of wrong doing and patience'.[14] In the fourth Eclogue (not in fact a pastoral poem) Virgil tells of the coming of a child who will restore the golden age; seen as a prophecy of the birth of Christ, it formed the basis for the assimilation of pastoral with Christian imagery. In Milton's *Lycidas* the Christian and pastoral visions merge; Lycidas is portrayed as a shepherd and singer who died a cruel death, and in his apotheosis finds consolation in heaven: 'Weep no more, woful Shepherds, weep no more / For *Lycidas* your sorrow is not dead, / Sunk though he be beneath the watry floar'.[15] In pastoral, Christian imagery came to incorporate the classical myth of the golden age, the imagined period in early human history marked by the spontaneous supply of food and when humanity lived a life of ease, a myth first found in Hesiod's *Works and Days* and especially familiar in the Renaissance from the account in the first book of Ovid's *Metamorphoses* (*c.* AD 2–8), This is the classical equivalent of the Garden of Eden in Genesis, where paradisiacal nature provides food in abundance and labour is unnecessary. Pastoral came to symbolise both a contrast to reality and an elegiac nostalgia, a melancholy yearning and a happy idyll.

In the Renaissance pastoral became elided to 'Arcadia', a trope that came to predominate in post-Renaissance culture. 'Arcadia' is the setting of Virgil's tenth Eclogue – where the poet Gallus perishes of love – and is cold, rocky and remote, like the region of Arcadia in the Peloponnese; but in the Arcadia of Renaissance pastoral romances nymphs and shepherds populate an idyllic landscape suffused with the golden haze of unreality. This post-classical notion of 'Arcadia', though having its source in Virgil, was largely due to the *Arcadia* (1504) of Jacopo Sannazaro who developed themes from the *Eclogues*, also perhaps drawing on an episode in the eighth book of the *Aeneid* where Aeneas visits the site of the future Rome and finds Greek exiles from Arcadia under their king Evander.[16] This is the subject of Claude Lorrain's *Landscape with the Arrival of Aeneas at Pallanteum* (1675), where the picture contrasts the woods, fields, shepherds and recumbent sheep of pastoral landscape with the heroic presence of Aeneas by his ships; the vision of the future imperial splendour of Rome is contrasted with ancient ruins, suggestive of the ruins of Troy from which Aeneas has fled and the lost golden age of the god Saturn as described by Evander.[17] Claude presents a remote idealised landscape redolent of history, myth and epic, embracing the pastoral golden age and the prospect of the foundation and future glory of Rome. The sense of a nostalgic longing for a lost golden age pervades Claude's pastoral landscapes of the 1630s and 1640s, images that shaped the 'picturesque' aesthetic of Richard Payne Knight in the late eighteenth century.

Claude's complex, dreamlike Arcadian pastorals echo the world of Renaissance pastoral poetry, the sensuously beautiful landscape lit by the summer sun and embellished by temples and tombs, evoking a lost golden age lamented by shepherds. Claude developed the pastoral theme to incorporate the mythic landscape pervaded by memories of gods of the countryside as described in Ovid's *Metamorphoses*. In *Landscape with a Temple of Bacchus* (1644) and the *Landscape with Narcissus and Echo* (1644), both probably painted as pendants and the latter much admired by Payne Knight, and in the *Landscape with Dancing Figures* (*The Marriage of Isaac and Rebekah* or *The Mill*) of 1648, Claude suggests the Arcadia of the Renaissance idyll.[18] This 'Arcadia' is the 'spiritual landscape' described by Bruno Snell as the 'land of shepherds and shepherdesses, the land of poetry and love . . . a far-away land overlaid with the golden haze of unreality'.[19] The landscapes of Claude evoked Virgil's description in the fourth Eclogue of the renewal of a golden age of plenty: 'molli paulatim flavescet campus arista . . .' ('the fields shall gradually grow yellow with the soft ear of corn, the reddening grape shall hang from wild brambles, and hard oaks shall sweat the dew of honey').[20] The high view-point, the opening up of the horizon with dazzling sun to which the eye is drawn, gives a sense of remoteness; the eye turns to the foreground's mythical figures, evocative of the golden age. In the *Landscape with Dancing Figures* the setting is unspecific, incorporating motifs suggestive of Rome and its environs including the Falls of Tivoli, forming an assembly of pastoral motifs that incorporate topographical studies. In this picture Claude elides Arcadia, the myth of the golden age and the Italian landscape of the *laus Italiae* (praise of Italy) of the second Georgic: 'hic ver adsiduum atque alienis mensibus aestas . . .' ('here are constant spring and summer in months that are not its own: twice the cattle breed, twice the tree affords its fruits').[21] The real world of Italy is coloured with the lustre of Arcadia and the fecundity of the golden age.

In his course of lectures in 1811 at the Royal Academy J.M.W. Turner expressed his fervent admiration for Claude's landscapes, emulated in his own work: 'Pure as Italian air, calm, beautiful and serene . . . .. The golden orient or the amber-coloured ether, the mid-day ethereal vault and fleecy skies, resplendent valleys . . . replete with all the aerial qualities of distance, aerial lights, aerial colour'.[22] Claude was praised for the naturalism with which he portrayed nature, but in his finished paintings the landscape is idealised, and as Joshua Reynolds noted, his 'pictures are a composition of the various draughts which he had previously made from various beautiful scenes and prospects'.[23] John Ruskin, who did not share the admiration for Claude of his hero Turner, forthrightly criticised the aesthetic of the *Landscape with Dancing Figures* in the preface to the second edition of the first volume of *Modern Painters* (1844): 'This is, I believe, a fair example of what is commonly called an "ideal" landscape; *i.e.* a group of the artist's studies from Nature, individually spoiled, selected with such opposition of character as may insure their neutralizing each other's effect, and united with sufficient unnaturalness and violence of association to insure their producing a general sensation of the impossible'. In contrast to the aesthetic of Claude's painting, its golden glaze of unreality characteristic of the pastoral landscape of Arcadia, Ruskin affirmed the moral and aesthetic dignity of 'an earnest, faithful, loving study of nature as she is' in promoting 'the love of what is simple, earnest, and pure'.[24]

The new interpretation of pastoral and 'Arcadia', of melancholy and nostalgia for a land of idyllic beauty, is summed up in the words 'Et in Arcadia ego', a motto invented in the seventeenth century in the course of which its meaning changed (as shown by Panofsky).[25] This Latin tag was first used in a painting by Guercino (*c.* 1622) of two shepherds looking at a skull resting on decaying masonry on which the words are incised. Poussin produced the first of his two paintings of the *Arcadian Shepherds* (*Et in Arcadia, ego c.* 1630), and in this painting (now at Chatsworth) the skull, greatly reduced in size from that in Guercino's painting, rests on an inscribed sarcophagus. In these paintings it is death that speaks, conveying a warning: 'Even in Arcadia, there am I.' Poussin's more famous version of the theme is in his second painting of the *Arcadian Shepherds* from *c.* 1638 (and now in the Louvre); here four Arcadians are arranged on either side of a sepulchral monument, suggestive of the tomb of Daphnis in Virgil's fifth Eclogue and the tomb of the shepherdess Phyllis in the *Arcadia* of Sannozaro. In Poussin's second painting there is no death's head and the tomb is inscribed *Et in Arcadia ego*; the dead shepherd is now the speaker, and his meaning is the evocative 'I too was once in Arcadia' (for which the Latin should be 'et ego in Arcadia' or 'in Arcadia et ego').[26] Death's warning now becomes elegiac nostalgia, a contemplative reflection on the consequences of mortality, the melancholy of pastoral.

The change in meaning of 'Arcadia' and the invention of the motto 'Et in Arcadia ego', with its change in meaning from death's warning to elegiac melancholy, illustrate the development and broadening of the genre of pastoral in the Renaissance. In the eighteenth century the pastoral theme was generalised and transformed, evoked in painting, landscape gardening and music; as expressed by Alexander Pope in 'A Discourse on Pastoral Poetry' (1717), its meaning had become simplified: 'pastoral is an image of what they call the Golden age'.[27]

In the dedication of his 1697 translation John Dryden described the *Georgics* as 'the best Poem of the best Poet';[28] with its description of farming and rural life and celebration of the cultivated countryside of Italy, the *Georgics* shaped conceptions of nature, landscape and the countryside in the eighteenth century. The engravings by Wenceslaus Hollar after Cleyn that illustrate Dryden's translation, already used in John Ogilby's editions of Virgil of 1654 and 1658, mediate between Roman and English landscape. In Dryden's version the engravings are stripped of the accompanying Latin text found in Ogilby's 1654 translation; the landscape and buildings, and the husbandry and dress of the farm labourers depicted in the engravings, become historically and topographically fluid and ambiguous, encouraging the accommodation of the classical to the English georgic.[29] In his introductory essay to Dryden's translation Joseph Addison explained that the agricultural poetry of the *Georgics* 'addresses it self wholly to the Imagination', and he considered its subject-matter, '*some part of the Science of Husbandry put into a pleasing Dress, and set off with all the Beauties and Embellishments of Poetry*', to be of both aesthetic and didactic interest: 'It is altogether Conversant among the Fields and Woods, and has the most delightful part of Nature for its Province. It raises in our Minds a pleasing variety of Scenes and Landskips, whilst it teaches us: and makes the driest of its Precepts look like a Description.'[30] Addison's usage illustrates the origin of the word 'landscape' as deriving from 'landskip' from the Dutch *landschap*, its root the German *Landschaft*, denoting a geographical region defined by political boundaries rather than natural scenery.[31]

Addison's georgic vision of 'landscape' as cultivated fields and managed woodland conforms to the view, later condemned by Ruskin, of nature as the 'servant of all work in the hands of the agriculturalist ... subdued to the furrow, and cicatrised to the pollard, [and] persuaded into proprieties', not the pristine nature that he valorised as 'nature in her liberty ... the pure wild volition and energy of the creation'.[32] The georgic landscape was tamed, cultivated and rationally ordered; natural forms were imitated and harmoniously moulded to human needs. This landscape vision pervades the painting and poetry of eighteenth-century England, in Gainsborough's *Wooded Landscape with a Peasant Resting* (c. 1747) and *Mr and Mrs Andrews* (1748), and James Thomson's *The Seasons* (1726–46) and Mark Akenside's *The Pleasures of the Imagination* (1744). These works evoke the harmony between man and nature, echoing the rational spirit of the Enlightenment and the ordered landscape of the *Georgics*, which was shaped by the naturalistic outlook of Lucretius' philosophical poem *De Rerum Natura*. In a celebrated passage in the second Georgic, much quoted in the eighteenth century, Virgil applauds the rational understanding of nature: 'felix qui potuit rerum cognoscere causas' ('happy he who has been able to learn the causes of things'). He goes on to contrast and complement the scientific knowledge of nature with the traditional values of the countryside: 'fortunatus et ille deos qui novit agrestos' ('fortunate too he who has known the country gods').[33] He evokes a combination of rationality and emotion, philosophy and traditional culture; the values of the philosopher and the farmer, while juxtaposed, are seen as complementary.

In the eighteenth century the *Georgics* was viewed as a poeticised agricultural treatise, and its portrayal of the cultivation of crops and vines, the management of livestock and the shaping of nature to human ends was set alongside the pastoral vision of the *Eclogues*. The representation of landscape in the *Georgics* is more realistic than in the *Eclogues*; Virgil's concern is with husbandry as a means of achieving agrarian bounty, a landscape of rural labour rather than the golden age abundance of the pastoral idyll. Whereas the *Eclogues* presents a landscape that is at once real and artificial, in the *Georgics* Virgil describes the real, physical landscape of Italy infused and blended into the landscape of imagination. The four books of the *Georgics* divide the work of the farm: ploughing and field crops; trees and vines; livestock; and bees. But across this didactic, agricultural structure Virgil addresses wider moral themes concerned with agricultural effort and achievement, with the virtues of agricultural labour and the farmer's diligence in caring for his animals, set against the destructive potential of war and human passions.[34] Virgil celebrates the landscape and countryside of farms and cultivated fields, the landscape of human habitation, worked and managed for human needs. Virgil's phrase 'divini gloria ruris' ('the glory the divine country offers'), much quoted in the eighteenth century, hints at the association of sacral and military values with the agricultural labour of the countryside.[35] But while Virgil recoils from the harsh and destructive powers of flood, famine and earthquakes, and fears the unvanquished wilderness with its ravening tigers and savage lions, he portrays the various pests, from the tiny mouse ('exiguus mus') to the deadly viper, and the diseases and storms with which the farmer has to contend, as part of the universal natural order.

Eighteenth-century readers found the famous rhetoric of the praise of country life, with which Virgil concludes the second Georgic, in tune with the georgic rural idyll: 'o fortunatos nimium, sua si bona norint, / agricolas, . . .' ('Oh too happy, if they recognize their own blessings, the farmers for whom far from the clash of arms the earth herself, most fairly, pours from the soil an easy sustenance!'). The pleasures of the landscape and the simplicity and moral order of country life are contrasted with the luxuries of the city where doors were inlaid with tortoiseshell and clothes were tricked with gold.

In his introductory essay to Dryden's translation Addison observed that 'He who reads over the Pleasures of a Country Life, as they are describ'd by *Virgil* in the latter end of this Book, can scarce be of *Virgil*'s mind, in preferring even the Life of a Philosopher to it.' Virgil valorises the country but without directly condemning urban life, and if he intended to convey any irony it was not perceived by eighteenth-century readers.[36] This passage in praise of country life was commonly set alongside the catalogue of country pleasures listed by Horace in his second Epode 'Beatus ille . . .' ('Blessed is the rustic who ploughs his land in peace remote from towns'), a poem famously translated by Ben Jonson as 'The Praises of a Countrie Life'. The satirical twist at the end of Horace's poem, where it is revealed that the encomium of the virtues of rural over urban life is uttered by Alfius the moneylender, imparts a mocking note to the glorification of the farmer's life. Horace voices nostalgic longing for the countryside with the sophistication of ironic detachment; and his imitators often suppressed the final stanza of the poem, detaching the irony from the nostalgia.[37]

Landscape paintings of the English countryside emerged as a major genre during the second half of the eighteenth century. This was a period of considerable agrarian change, marked by the process of parliamentary enclosure and the introduction of new agricultural techniques, and by the creation of aristocratic landscape parks; it was also the period in which the newly enriched middle class acquired estates and began a cultural and aesthetic appropriation of the countryside. The agrarian changes – the enclosure of fields, the loss of common land, the creation of new farms, reclaimed heaths and newly introduced crops – were not depicted in the work of English landscape painters. Nor did landscape art directly portray the social conflicts and environmental changes that transformed the agrarian landscape; there is a contrast between the reality of agrarian life and the aesthetic representation of the countryside. Agricultural innovations and the depiction of farming practice were subordinated to the representation of English agrarian life by adapting and enlarging traditional pastoral and georgic themes, portraying the social hierarchy in the order of the landscape, and evoking the harmony of man and nature in the classical golden age.

The countryside of southern England was naturalised in the aesthetics of nostalgia, assimilating rural reality to the motifs of a timeless past. Landscape painters portrayed agrarian continuity and change through symbolic depictions of social relations and landscape, but did not directly focus on the social and agricultural transformations in the countryside. In *Mr and Mrs Andrews* (1748) Thomas Gainsborough departs from the convention of setting the couple in a landscape garden; the painting emphasises the possession of cultivated farmland, the ownership of the well-managed Suffolk estate, and while the farm shows signs of modern agricultural improvements the labour of the farm is hinted at rather than depicted. The focus of the painting is on landownership in a parkland setting and the civilised pleasures of rural life rather than the process of agrarian cultivation. The surrounding farmland smoothly elides into a park landscape; the erosion of the boundary between the garden and cultivated farmland is a major theme in the development of the eighteenth-century landscape park. This is an idealised, georgic vision of the countryside, evoking the harmony between man and nature rather than the labour of husbandry, the continuity of rural life rather than social conflict in the countryside. Other early landscapes, *Gainsborough's Forest* (1748) and *Wooded Landscape with a Peasant Resting* (1747), portray the countryside of his native East Suffolk where enclosure had occurred as early as the sixteenth century and the landscape had retained its patchwork pattern of fields and woodland. In drawing upon pastoral and georgic idioms, the anonymity of the landscape scenes and their nostalgic depiction presents this established and familiar agrarian landscape as the timeless pattern of nature, as the 'natural' form of the harmonious English countryside.[38]

The Aesthetics of the Earth

In a letter of January 1681 to Thomas Burnet, a former fellow of Christ's College, Cambridge, who became master of Charterhouse School in 1685, Isaac Newton expressed the opinion that 'as to Moses I do not think his description of the creation either Philosophical or feigned, but that he described realities in a language artificially adapted to the sense of the vulgar'. Drawn into speculation concerning the physical interpretation of the biblical narrative of creation and the flood in Genesis, Newton's correspondence with Burnet was prompted by the imminent publication of the first volume of Burnet's *Telluris Theoria Sacra* (*The Sacred Theory of the Earth*, 1681). In this work where natural philosophy is mixed with biblical exegesis, Burnet advanced an interpretation of the creation and history of the earth: its most striking feature was his claim that the earth as first created, the paradisiacal earth, was smooth and without mountains and was destroyed in the deluge, its dissolution leading to the formation of the earth in its present form. His second volume, published in 1689, was concerned with the conflagration of the world and the emergence of a new heaven and a new earth; English versions were issued in 1684 and 1690. Burnet believed that Moses (as the author of Genesis) had done more than modify his language to suit the comprehension of the primitive Israelites; he had not only simplified but had falsified his narrative of the creation.

Burnet suggested to Newton that the biblical account of creation gave only 'a description of the present forme of the Earth, which was its forme alsoe then when Moses writ, and not of the primaeval Earth, which was gone out of

being long before'. He maintained that Moses knew of the creation and dissolution of the primitive earth, the cosmogony set out in *The Sacred Theory of
the Earth*, but that he had chosen to describe the creation of the earth directly
into its present form from the original chaos: 'if Moses had given the Theory
it would have been a thing altogether inaccommodate to the people & a
useless distracting amusement and therefore instead of it hee gives a short
ideal draught of a Terraqueous Earth riseing from a Chaos', the narrative
of Genesis. This line of argument (which has its origins in the writings of
St Augustine and was also deployed by Galileo in defending his reading
of scripture), that Moses had simplified both the language and concepts of
Genesis, proved to be one of the most controversial elements of Burnet's
work; to his critics, Burnet had proffered no more than a useless, distracting
(and impious) amusement. Writing to Burnet before the publication of *The
Sacred Theory of the Earth,* Newton signalled his dissent, maintaining that
Moses had merely simplified his language to avoid making 'the narration
tedious & confused', and had not falsified his account of the 'process of
creation'. It was not the purpose of Moses to 'become a Philosopher more
than a Prophet', and he had exercised discretion in 'accommodating his words
to the gross conceptions of the vulgar'. Moses was popularising, not allegorising:
'the things signified by such figurative expressions [in Genesis] are not Ideall
or moral but true'.[39]

In compelling prose Burnet addressed the subject of the history and future
of the earth; his theory of its past destruction and future demise through
conflagration was 'sacred' in that its terms were drawn from the providential
and historical books of the Bible, from Genesis and the second letter of Peter.
Burnet's work was informed by the millenarian tradition flowing from Joseph
Mede's *Clavis Apocalyptica* (1627), translated as the *Key to the Revelation* in
1643, a work that became important in the ferment of apocalyptic ideas that
flourished during the Commonwealth (1649–53). Mede's millenarian ideas
were promoted by the 'Platonist' philosopher Henry More at Cambridge, who
argued that the anticipated transformation of the earth could be understood
in terms of the operation of physical laws. Millenarian themes were evoked in
the influential writings of Robert Boyle, joining natural philosophy and
natural theology, in declaring that after the millennium 'in the great renovation of the world, and the future state of things' our 'faculties will be elevated
and enlarged and probably made thereby capable of attaining degrees and
kinds of knowledge, to which we are here but strangers'. The statement of
Jewish apocalyptic ideas in the second letter of Peter was a major millenarian
text: 'by the word of God the heavens were of old, and the earth standing
out of the water and in the water: Whereby the world that then was, being
overflowed with water, perished: But the heavens and the earth, which are
now, by the same word are kept in store, reserved unto fire against the day of

judgment and perdition of ungodly men'. This biblical text lay at the core of the argument of Burnet's *Sacred Theory of the Earth*.[40] In Burnet's millenarian cosmogony human destiny and history are conceived in terms of the providential historical and prophetic books of the Bible, and had their counterpart in the natural history of the earth; the Fall of man, the degeneration of mankind from pristine perfection, was paralleled by the decay of the natural world. Burnet's physical history of the earth is construed in terms of the major events of the Christian scheme of history, viewed as a history of the earth from creation to the final judgement. This physical and historical scheme is set out in the frontispiece of *The Sacred Theory of the Earth*, depicting a seven-stage historical process: the creation of the earth; the primeval, paradisiacal earth; the deluge; the present earth; the future conflagration; the new heavens and the new earth; and the consummation of all things.

In asserting the role of providence in nature Burnet made a densely learned and argumentative appeal to ancient sources, sacred and profane; to current scientific theorising, especially Descartes' cosmogony; and he defended his scheme of geological and sacred history by affirming the harmony of natural philosophy and religion. 'Reason is to be our first Guide; and where that falls short ... we may receive further light and confirmation from the Sacred writings.' The assertion of the harmony and mutual support of reason and revelation was characteristic of Restoration natural theology and natural philosophy, prominent in the writings of 'latitudinarian' divines and Cambridge 'Platonist' philosophers, including those of his tutors John Tillotson (later Archbishop of Canterbury) and Ralph Cudworth. Burnet cites rabbinical and patristic authorities, echoed by Bede and Abelard, for the claim that the biblical text implied that the primitive earth was oviform and smooth, unlike the present earth, and that mountains were the result of the dissolution of this primeval earth: the 'notion of the *Mundane Egg*, or that the World was *Oviform*, hath been the Sense and Language of all Antiquity'. He found the scientific basis for his cosmogony in the fourth part of Descartes' *Principia Philosophiae* (1644), 'On the earth'. Descartes describes a physical theory of the origin of the earth emerging from the vortex of matter from which the solar system formed. The planetary matter separated from the vortex and cooled, particles of crust settling from the liquid mass, the outer shell separating into layers; mountains and valleys were formed when the earthy exterior crust of the earth fell under its own weight, oceans forming when the ruptured surface allowed water under the crust to escape. The glowing core was the source of gases erupting in volcanoes and causing earthquakes. Burnet adapted for his own purposes Descartes' theory of the solid crust of the earth enveloping a liquid mass, deploying the causal, scientific explanations of the mechanical philosophy in expanding understanding of the biblical account of the history and future prospect of the earth: 'We are almost the last Posterity of the First

Man and fall'n into the dying age of the World; by what footsteps, or by what guide can we trace back our way to those first Ages and the first Order of Things? . . .. We are the inhabitants of the Earth, the Lords and Masters of it; and we are endow'd with Reason and Understanding; doth it not then properly belong to us to examine and unfold the works of God?'

Burnet portrays the stages in the physical history of the earth as a counterpart to the moral history of mankind: the antediluvian earth perished in the flood, corresponding to the fall of mankind; while the present earth will be consumed and perish in the conflagration leading to a new heaven and a new earth, a prelude to the consummation of all things. He argues that the antediluvian earth arose from a fluid chaos: 'we must now return to the Beginning of the World, and look upon the first rudiments of Nature, and that dark but fruitful womb out of which all things sprang, I mean the *Chaos*'. This mass formed an oviform shape, smooth and unwrinkled, the earthy eggshell enclosing the yolk of subterranean water: the 'Globe of the Water vaulted over, and the Exteriour Earth hanging above the Deep . . . a Building without foundation or corner-stone . . . a piece of Divine Geometry or Architecture'. He maintains that 'this Structure is so marvellous, that it ought rather to be considered as a particular effect of the Divine Art, than as the Work of Nature'; the pristine earth was directly created, a manifestation of divine providence. The paradisiacal earth had an unbroken surface, and its axis was so aligned that there was a perpetual spring: 'In this smooth Earth were the first scenes of the world, and the first Generations of Mankind; it had the beauty of Youth and blooming Nature, fresh and fruitful, and not a wrinkle, Scar or Fracture in all its body; no rocks nor Mountains, no hollow caves, nor gaping Chanels, but even and uniform all over. And the smoothness of the Earth made the face of the Heavens so too; the air was calm and serene; none of those tumultuary Motions and conflicts of Vapours, which the Mountains and Winds cause in ours: 'Twas suited to a golden Age, and to the first innocency of Nature.'

Turning to the deluge, Noah's flood, Burnet argues that its universality – attested by biblical authority and other ancient testimony – could not be explained by supposing forty days of rain, 'there not being Water sufficient in Nature to make a Deluge of that kind'. In support of this contention he claims that '*Moses* imputed the Deluge to the Disruption of the Abysse', and he declares that he seeks therefore to make 'the Deluge fairly intelligible, and accountable without the creation of new waters'. It is here that he introduces insights drawn from natural philosophy. The antediluvian earth was perfect, a paradise, but contained within its structure the seeds of its own destruction. At a time appointed by divine providence the earth was brought closer to the sun, which dried and cracked its surface: 'all the revolutions of Nature are under his Conduct and Providence'. Burnet interprets the deluge as the result of the cracking of the shell of the mundane egg and the release of the contained waters: 'the *opening and shutting of the Abysse* is the great hinge upon which Nature turns in this Earth: This brings another face of things, other Scenes, and a new World upon the Stage'. He is at pains to emphasise the intertwining of scientific means with the ends of divine providence that had shaped the correspondence of the physical and moral worlds: 'This seems to me to be the great Art of Divine Providence, so as to adjust the two Worlds, Humane and Natural, Material and Intellectual ... [so] they should all along correspond and fit one another, and especially in their great Crises and Periods.'

Burnet uses Boyle's metaphor of the clock to explain that the mechanism of the earth had been contrived by divine providence to operate by its 'Springs and Wheels'; thus at a 'time being come, upon a signal given, or a Spring toucht, it should of its own accord fall all to pieces'. The mechanism of the earth did not exclude the control and intervention of providence, but was contrived to be subject to it; therefore the greater transformations in the physical structure of the earth, the deluge and the conflagration, would require a 'signal' to be given or the touching of a 'spring' in its clockwork. Indeed, this operation of providence, activating natural causes through a signal or the mere touch of a spring, was a more perfect manifestation of the divine will than the direct suspension of the laws of nature: 'would not this be look'd upon as a piece of greater Art, than if the [divine] Workman came at that time prefixt, and with a great Hammer beat it [the primeval earth] into pieces?' Burnet sees the workings of divine purpose in the destruction of the antediluvian paradisiacal earth, a transformation that he equates to the moral degradation of mankind. The outer crust fell into the abyss and its uneven fall caused the mountains and oceans of the present earth, which is no more than the ruins of a broken world. In a powerful passage he expresses moral and aesthetic distaste for the earth in its present state as disrupted and broken apart by the deluge: '[A] broken and confus'd heap of bodies, plac'd in no order to one another, nor with any correspondency of regularity of parts: and such a body as the Moon appears to us, when 'tis look'd upon with a good Glass, rude and ragged; as it is also represented in modern Maps of the Moon; such a thing would the Earth appear if it was seen from the Moon ... the image or picture of a great Ruine, and have the true aspect of a World lying in its Rubbish.'[41]

In the second volume of *The Sacred Theory of the Earth* Burnet turned to consider the conflagration, which he explains by reference to the natural central fire of the earth and the intervention of providence. He finds the natural sources of the conflagration in the volcanoes of Sicily and Italy, Etna and Vesuvius, and concludes that 'the Conflagration will begin at the City of Rome' sparked by the 'sulphureousness of its Soil, and its fiery Mountains and

Caverns'. He again seeks to establish the correspondence between the natural and moral worlds: 'seeing *Mystical Babylon,* the Seat of Antichrist, is the same as *Rome* . . . both our lines meet in this point'. He echoes Protestant apologetics arising from the Papist scare of 1680, and the millenarian and providential associations given to the events of the Glorious Revolution. In its final form the earth will be like the paradisiacal, antediluvial earth: 'all the Varieties of Nature, all the Works of Art, all the labours of Men, are reduc'd to nothing . . . obliterated or vanished . . . another form and face of things, plain, simple and every where the same, overspreads the whole Earth.' The conflagration will consume the entire globe and habitation of mankind: 'the everlasting Hills, the Mountains and Rocks of the Earth, are melted as Wax before the Sun; and *their place is nowhere found.* Here stood the Alps, a prodigious Range of Stone . . . there was frozen *Caucasus* . . . all these are vanished, dropped away as the Snow upon their Heads, and swallowed up in a red Sea of fire.'[42]

The Sacred Theory of the Earth generated a large and polemical response to its Cartesian mechanical philosophy, its evidential basis, its aesthetics of mountains and its natural theology; and Burnet's work became embroiled in controversies over deism and the encroachment of rational upon revealed religion, leading to a notoriety that hindered his further preferment. These themes are intertwined. Burnet had concerned himself with the grand mechanisms of earth history rather than with geological details, and made no mention of the origin and distribution of fossils; but these were questions germane to the cogency of the argument of *The Sacred Theory of the Earth* and received discussion by John Ray, John Woodward and Edward Lhwyd.[43] In his letter to Burnet, Newton had expressed cautious sympathy with the broad cast of Burnet's physical speculations, but demurred over the interpretation of the text of Genesis and (narrowly) 'with your argument about the oval figure of the earth . . . I am inclined to beleive it spherical or not much oval'.[44] At the time of this correspondence Newton was only in the preliminary stages of the process that was to lead to his theory of gravity: the writing and publication of *Principia Mathematica* (1687) established a new framework. Newton's theory of the attractive force of gravity offered an alternative to the Cartesian mechanism of the solar vortex; and (among other results) he demonstrated that the earth was a spheroid flattened at the poles.

William Whiston, who was to succeed Newton as Lucasian professor of mathematics at Cambridge, joined the debate in publishing his *New Theory of the Earth* in 1696, utilising Newton's new physics of gravitation. In place of Burnet's (to him outdated and refuted) Cartesian mechanisms for the formation of the earth and the destruction of its crust at the deluge, Whiston looked to the periodic reappearance of comets and to their gravitational effect on the earth. Appealing to some ancient authorities, he suggested that the chaos described in Genesis was the atmosphere of a comet and that the earth was created from a comet. The deluge was caused by the near miss of Halley's comet (seen in 1680) that had a period of 575 years, suggesting that there had since been seven revolutions of this comet. The gravitational force of the comet deformed the spherical primeval earth into an oblate spheroid, fissuring the earth's crust; the weight of rainfall from the comet's tail and the tides in the fluid of the Abyss cracked the crust, releasing the 'fountains of the great deep' as recounted in Genesis.[45] According to Whiston's theory the conflagration would be produced by the close approach of a comet with a huge atmosphere. He joined Newtonian science with a reading of the Genesis text, affirming the agency of divine providence. Whiston became notorious subsequently as an avowed Arian (denying the doctrine of the Trinity), and his ideas in the *New Theory of the Earth* were satirised by Jonathan Swift in *Gulliver's Travels* (1726): the rational and mathematical Laputans have a superstitious fear of comets, and through them (and Whiston) Swift ridicules the natural theology and rational religion of the 'moderns', affirming the values of traditional authority and religion. Indeed, William Temple's 'Essay upon Ancient and Modern Learning' was in part inspired as a response to Burnet's *Sacred Theory of the Earth*. Temple was impressed but irritated by Burnet 'who could not end his learned Treatise without a panegyric of modern learning and knowledge in comparison of the ancient'; in integrating his commentary on scripture with modishly fashionable scientific speculation, Burnet epitomised the pretensions of the 'moderns'.[46]

Burnet's aesthetics raised a special difficulty in (implicitly) offering a challenge to the natural theology of design, though this was not of course his intention. Burnet (inadvertently) drew attention to the issue in writing an appreciation of mountain scenery. He had travelled in the Alps and had been impressed by the mountain landscape: 'The greatest objects of Nature are, methinks, the most pleasing to behold; and next to the great Concave of the Heavens, and those boundless Regions where the stars inhabit, there is nothing that I look upon with more pleasure than the wide Sea and the Mountains of the Earth . . . they fill and over-bear the mind with their Excess, and cast it into a pleasing kind of stupor and admiration.' But Burnet's response to the glory and majesty of mountains did not prompt him to argue for the evidence of design in their creation. For Burnet the primeval earth, smooth and oviform, was characterised by 'the beauty of Youth and blooming Nature, fresh and fruitful' and was undoubtedly 'a particular effect of the Divine Art'. This primitive earth did manifest beauty and design, being 'a piece of Divine Geometry or Architecture'; but according to Burnet's *Sacred Theory of the Earth* mountains were formed when the 'golden age' of the primitive earth was brought to an end with the deluge, and the capacity of mountains to inspire awe concealed their true aesthetic status. 'And yet these Mountains we are speaking of, to confess the truth, are nothing but great ruines; but such as show a certain magnificence in Nature'; they are in truth no more than 'heaps of Stones and Rubbish'. Surveying mountain ranges across the globe, he concluded that 'the Globe of the Earth is a more rude and indigested Body than 'tis commonly imagin'd', hardly an object of beauty or the product of design by a divine architect or geometer.[47]

Richard Bentley succinctly addressed the implications of Burnet's natural theology in concluding the last of his series of *Boyle Lectures* delivered in 1692. Having reviewed the way in which the earth as presently constituted with its 'rugged and irregular Surface' did indeed manifest beauty and the wisdom and beneficence of its designer, Bentley scornfully turned to the view of 'some men' who are 'out of Love with the features and meen of our Earth' in finding it to be a 'Deformity, and rather carries the face of a Ruin or a rude and indigested Lump of Atoms that casually convened so, than a Work of Divine Artifice'. Damning (the unnamed) Burnet by association, in invoking the materialist philosophy of the ancient atomists, Bentley rejects his natural theology and aesthetics: 'all Bodies are truly and physically beautifull under all possible Shapes and Proportions; that are good in their Kind, that are fit for their proper uses and ends of their Natures.' And he dismisses the claim that the present earth is anything other than fit for the purpose for which it was designed, this being 'another Argument of the Divine Wisdom & Goodness'.[48] The theory of the primeval earth disrupted and broken in Noah's flood, with the present earth portrayed as an object of deformity and ruin rather than beauty, was contrary to sound natural theology, aesthetics and the understanding of the divine dispensation for mankind.

Despite the controversy surrounding his mechanical philosophy and natural theology Burnet did, however, have his admirers. Joseph Addison wrote a Latin ode in praise of his style; and in the *Spectator* in 1711 Richard Steele extolled Burnet's stylistic and philosophical achievement: 'He has, according to the Lights of Reason and Revelation, which seem'd to him clearest, traced the Steps of Omnipotence. He has, with a Caelestial Ambition, as far as it is consistent with Humility and Devotion, examined the Ways of Providence, from the Creation to the Dissolution of the visible World.'[49] In his discussion of mountain scenery in *The Sacred Theory of the Earth* Burnet indicated that mountain landscape could be considered in terms of two different aesthetics. He regarded mountains as mere 'heaps of Stones and Rubbish', as 'great ruines', and this is the prevailing and overwhelming aesthetic theme of his text; but he also acknowledged his sense of awe, of the sublime (as it came to be termed) before the 'magnificence' and glory of mountains that 'fill and over-bear the mind with their Excess, and cast it into a pleasing kind of stupor and admiration'. Burnet's sense of the sublime was echoed by Addison, in his essays on the 'Pleasures of the Imagination' published in the *Spectator* in 1712, describing the feeling of awe induced by 'that rude kind of magnificence which appears in these stupendous works of nature' such as 'huge heaps of mountains, high rocks and precipices'.[50] Addison was expressing a new aesthetics of the earth and of landscape, partly shaped by *The Sacred Theory of the Earth*, where mountains were found to be awesome, magnificent and aesthetically ennobled. This new sensibility to rocky landscape was famously characterised by the third Earl of Shaftesbury in his philosophical dialogue 'The Moralists' (1709), where the neophyte Philocles responds to the impassioned paean to nature voiced by the sage Theocles: 'I shall no longer resist the Passion growing in me for Things of a *natural* kind: where neither *Art* nor the *Conceit* or *Caprice* of Man has spoil'd their *genuine Order*, by breaking in upon that *primitive State*. Even the rude *Rocks*, the mossy *Caverns*, the irregular unwrought *Grotto's*, and broken *Falls* of Waters, with all the horrid Graces of the *Wilderness* itself, as representing NATURE more, will be the more engaging, and appear with a Magnificence beyond the formal Mockery of Princely Gardens.'[51]

This aesthetic, a new taste for wilderness, rocky landscapes and towering mountains, was succinctly captured by Horace Walpole on writing to his friend Richard West when crossing the Alps with the poet Thomas Gray in September 1739: 'Precipices, mountains, torrents, wolves, rumblings, Salvator Rosa – the pomp of our park and the meekness of our palace! Here we are the lonely lords of glorious desolate prospects.'[52] Mere mention of Salvator Rosa communicated immediately the character of the landscapes depicted in his paintings, the wild beauty and terror of rocky, inhospitable wilderness peopled with the *banditti* of the mountains of his native Abruzzi: 'expressive horror', as Walpole put it in 1755, an aesthetics of nature mediated by art. In his catalogue of his father Sir Robert's art collection, containing four of the paintings of the 'great Salvator Rosa', Horace Walpole paid tribute to the artist's 'masterly management of Horror and Distress', the aesthetics of the sublime.[53] One of Salvator Rosa's paintings, depicting the legend of Empedocles testing his presumption of divinity by leaping into Etna (as reported in the third-century compendium of the lives of the philosophers by Diogenes Laertius), was frequently engraved, and shaped the contemporary vogue for the danger, terror and looming horror of mountains. This was the landscape aesthetic evoked by Horace Walpole in his letter to West: 'But the road, West, the road! Winding round a prodigious mountain, and surrounded with others, all shagged with hanging woods, obscured with pines or lost in clouds! Below, a torrent breaking through cliffs, and tumbling through fragments of rocks! Sheets of cascades forcing their silver speed down channelled precipices, and hasting into the roughened river at the bottom! Now and then an old foot-bridge, with a broken rail, a leaning cross, a cottage, or the ruin of an hermitage! This sounds too bombast and too romantic to one that has not seen it, too cold for one that has.'[54] Mountains became objects of aesthetic appreciation with the development of the language of the sublime.[55]

'Artificial Rudeness': Landscape Gardens

In the passage from 'The Moralists' (1709) where he expressed a passion for 'things of a *natural* kind', Shaftesbury drew the contrast between the magnificence of nature represented by 'the rude *Rocks*, the mossy *Caverns* . . . the horrid Graces of the *Wilderness* itself' and 'the formal Mockery of Princely Gardens', alluding to the topiary gardens popular in the period, by 'formal mockery' he meant the imposition of a style inappropriate to the inherent character of nature. The passage forms part of a rhapsody on the search for truth in uncorrupted nature, a panegyric celebrating the order and beauty of created beings; his text illustrates contemporary interest in charting the relations between the artificial world of the garden and the inherent structure of natural forms.[56] In the early eighteenth century there was a shift in aesthetic preference from enclosed topiary gardens (often identified as a Dutch style of gardening) to a more informal (French) style of gardening based on the extensive planting of trees, a garden design seen as being consonant with nature. The issue was discussed by Alexander Pope in his essay 'On Gardens' published in the *Guardian* in 1713, where he expressed a preference for 'the amiable simplicity of unadorned nature' that he considered to be the 'Taste of the Ancients in their Gardens'; he cited Homer's account of the mythical garden of Alcinous in the *Odyssey* as listing 'all the justest Rules and provisions which can go towards composing the best Gardens'. This appeal to classical authority led him to deprecate the 'modern practice of Gardening', which receded from nature with 'the various tonsure of Greens into the most regular and formal Shapes' and the 'monstrous' effects of topiary where 'we run into Sculpture, and are yet better pleas'd to have our trees in the most awkward Figures of Men and Animals, than in the most regular of their own', the simplicity of their natural forms.[57]

Joseph Addison promoted this taste in garden design, and a broader aesthetics of landscape, in his essays on the 'Pleasures of the Imagination' published in the *Spectator* in 1712. He contrasted the formal, geometric garden designs (derived from Dutch models) found in England with a style of gardening that he had found cultivated in France and Italy, 'where we see a large extent of ground covered over with an agreeable mixture of garden and forest, which represents every where an artificial rudeness, much more charming than that neatness and elegancy which we meet with in our own country'. He disliked the Dutch topiary style with trees shaped into 'cones, globes, and pyramids', the work of gardeners who 'instead of humouring nature, love to deviate from it as much as possible'. Addison preferred to 'look upon a tree in all its luxuriancy and a diffusion of boughs and branches, than when it is thus cut and trimmed into a mathematical figure'. He argued that gardeners should follow rather than distort natural forms; trees should be shaped by human art into a contrived and artificial informality. His preferred aesthetic was for 'artificial rudeness', nature contrived, controlled and shaped through 'variety or regularity as may seem the effect of design', explaining that he took 'delight in a prospect which is well laid out, and diversified with field and meadows'. While he appreciated the splendour of mountain scenery and acknowledged that 'there is something more bold and masterly in the rough careless strokes of Nature, than in the nice touches and embellishments of Art', he considered 'the works of nature still more pleasant, the more they resemble those of art', works of human design. Addison enlarged his discussion of gardens to encompass the design of the surrounding landscape, and looked to the way in which an estate may be 'thrown into a kind of garden by frequent plantations', creating a landscape in which the 'natural embroidery of the meadows' would be 'improved by small additions of art' with 'hedges set off by trees and flowers'.[58] In this vision of the rural garden, garden and landscape were blended, the garden expanded to incorporate the cultivated agricultural landscape of the countryside; and the aesthetic ideal was 'artificial rudeness', the works of nature became pleasant when ordered and subjected to the contrivances of art, to a pattern of controlling design, the theme of contemporary natural philosophy and natural theology.

The evolution in conception and design of pleasure grounds had been shaped by the needs of agriculture and medicine, and by biblical and classical themes. Medieval gardens were enclosed to exclude animals from the surrounding parkland, and allegorised as the Garden of Eden and the enclosed garden of the *Song of Solomon*. In the Renaissance the vision of gardens as the recreation of the Edenic paradise became assimilated to the mythical golden age of perpetual spring in classical literature, to Homer's garden of Alcinous in the *Odyssey* and to Virgilian pastoral. The botanical gardens created in the Renaissance were developed to display the encyclopaedia of creation and to fulfil the needs of medicine, and were divided into quarters containing the flora of the four continents arranged into their allotted places in parterres.[59] In urging the expansion of husbandry, seventeenth-century utopian texts portrayed cultivated land as having the potential to be transformed into a garden.

The puritan writer Gabriel Plattes' utopian *Description of the Famous Kingdome of Macaria* (1641) envisioned a council of husbandry to supervise systematic innovation and the improvement of cultivated lands, 'by which means the whole Kingdome is become like to a fruitfull Garden', drawing on the paradisiacal associations of the garden.[60] His influential associate Samuel Hartlib sought the cultivation of orchards on waste land, views echoed after the Restoration of 1660 by John Evelyn in his *Sylva; or a Discourse of Forest-Trees* (1664), where he urged that fruit trees be planted every 100 feet throughout the country and that London be surrounded with enclosures filled with sweet-scented flowers. In his promotion of silviculture Evelyn showed interest both in native trees (fir, elm and ash) and in recent imports (lime), and he sought out exotic trees such as the cork oak and the white pine. In a letter to Sir Thomas Browne in 1660 he had explained that he saw the garden as a restored arcadia, as the restoration of lost paradise, as sacred and divinised: 'a noble, princely and universall Elysium, capable of all the amoenities, that can naturally be introduced into Gardens of Pleasure ... Rem Sacrum et divinam'. For Evelyn practical husbandry and the creation of gardens were sanctified as the realisation of the divine purpose. In the second edition of *Sylva* (1670) he took up the theme of 'the Sacrednesse and Use of Standing Groves', arguing that sacred groves were seen as sites of spiritual regeneration in biblical and classical texts. '*Paradise* itself', he states, 'was but a kind of *Nemorous* Temple, or Sacred *Grove*, planted by *God* himself.' Evelyn's idea of expanding the garden by planting trees was realised for the Capel family at Cassiobury in Hertfordshire by the gardener Moses Cook. At Cassiobury the pleasure grounds were extended beyond the enclosed parterre garden by planting trees across the estate, creating an enlarged garden with straight paths radiating through the woodland, a formal, rigid and geometrical layout, the radiating avenues demonstrating the landowner's control over his estate, power reaching to the surrounding countryside.[61]

The erosion of the boundary between the garden and cultivated farmland was promoted as the 'Extensive Way of Gard'ning' by the influential gardener Stephen Switzer in his *Ichnographia: The Nobleman, Gentleman and Gardener's Recreation* (1718). Switzer's term the 'extensive way', drawing the country into the garden, was drawn from Virgil's 'ingentia rura' (large estates) in the second Georgic, the text concerned with the management of trees and vines. Switzer argued that the cultivation of flowers and use of walls should be confined to the limited space of town gardens, while country gardens should contain plantations of dense groves of trees threaded by sinuous paths. 'By *Ingentia Rura* (apply'd to Gard'ning) we may understand that Extensive Way of Gard'ning'. Country gardens are georgic, drawing agriculture into the garden: 'Woods, Coppices, Groves, and the busie and laborious Employs of Agriculture, with which *Gardening* is unavoidably as well as pleasantly mix'd'.[62]

Contemporary garden practice in estates encouraged the disappearance of the boundary between the garden and the surrounding fields with the introduction in the 1690s of the sunken ditch, or ha-ha, at Levens Hall (near Kendal) by William Beaumont and at Stowe by Charles Bridgeman. This innovation was deemed so astonishing, according to Horace Walpole, 'that the common people called them Ha! Ha's! to express their surprise'. In his *History of the Modern Taste in Gardening* of 1771 Horace Walpole looked back at these developments, which he attributed (inaccurately but influentially) to the efforts of the painter, architect and garden designer William Kent: 'The contiguous ground of the park without the sunk fence was to be harmonized with the lawn within; and the garden in its turn was to be set free from its prim regularity, that it might assort with the wilder country without . . .. He leaped the fence, and saw that all nature was a garden.' Walpole claimed that the imitation of nature in gardens was a new, original and uniquely English contribution to gardening, achieving a 'point of perfection' by using 'no other art than that of softening nature's harshnesses and copying her graceful touch'. In this landscape vision, 'dealing in none but the colours of nature', gardens and surrounding parkland were aesthetically joined, and in the garden the 'living landscape was chastened or polished, not transformed'. Between 1700 and 1751, 61 new trees were imported and introduced in garden plantings, a development that Walpole considered as 'contributing essentially to the richness of colouring so peculiar to our modern landscape'.[63] In his 'Epistle to Burlington' (1731), commenting on laying out grounds, Alexander Pope expressed the aesthetics of nature that was embodied in the imitation of natural forms: 'In all, let Nature never be forgot . . .. Consult the Genius of the Place in all' (quoting Virgil, 'genius loci', the spirit of the place).[64]

On a visit in 1753 Horace Walpole described Hagley in Worcestershire in exalted and exuberant terms: 'You might draw, but I can't describe the enchanting scenes of the park: it is a hill of three miles, but broke into all manner of beauty; such lawns, such wood, rills, cascades, and a thickness of verdure quite to the summit of the hill, and commanding such a vale of lawns and meadows, and woods . . . there is a ruined castle . . . there is a scene of a small lake with cascades falling down such a Parnassus! With a circular temple on the distant eminence; and there is such a fairy dale, with more cascades gushing out of rocks! and there is hermitage . . . and there is such a pretty well under the wood', which he likens to a well in a picture by Nicolas Poussin.[65] In shaping the design of English landscape gardens the appeal to nature was allied to the imitation of the classical world and its evocation in landscape art. At the Earl of Burlington's Palladian villa at Chiswick, William Kent, who had met his future patron while painting in Rome, stripped away the geometric patterns and introduced winding paths and a serpentine canal, a cascade within a constructed ruin, and a lawn with a circular hedge and classical statues in niches, a landscape garden arranged to suggest the Italian classical landscapes of Poussin and Claude Lorrain. Kent pursued the classical theme more vigorously for Lord Cobham at Stowe, laying out a garden complete with Elysian Fields, the River Styx and temples of virtue; and at Rousham near Oxford he introduced a Vale of Venus with a cascade and pond. At Stourhead in Wiltshire the banker Henry Hoare constructed a Virgilian walk with scenes arranged to evoke episodes in the *Aeneid*; he constructed a miniature Pantheon containing statues and a descent through a rocky passage to the Grotto of the Nymph. More modest in scale, at The Leasowes in Shropshire William Shenstone laid out 'Virgil's Grove' in imitation of the sacred groves of antiquity, and constructed seats and monuments displaying quotations from Virgil. The aesthetic assimilation of the classical and English landscapes was reduced to whimsy.[66]

In the second half of the eighteenth century there was a transformation of landscape architecture, especially due to the work of Lancelot ('Capability') Brown, who was the head gardener at Stowe from 1741, becomimg an independent designer with his own business in 1751, and who had worked on 170 commissions by his death in 1783. Rejecting the integration of the landscape garden with the management of an agricultural estate, Brown created extensive landscape parks, with a house standing in an open landscape of grass and irregularly scattered trees. He avoided geometric planting, cutting down avenues of trees at Stowe to create an irregular vista; in his designs he removed walled, geometric gardens from abutting the house, so that the mansion stood powerfully dominant in the open turf of the park where animals grazed on the lawns. Woodland was used in small ovoid clumps arranged in contrived but irregular patterns spread throughout the park, and belts of woodland were placed on the periphery, sometimes forming the boundary of the park. Serpentine carriage drives were laid out, often through woodland; and Brown often constructed a lake of irregular form placed to appear in the middle distance when viewed from the house, providing earth to construct an artificial hill, as at Berrington Hall in Herefordshire. Pleasure gardens were moved to a subsidiary position placed apart from the house, so as not to interfere with the primacy of the mansion standing solitary, detached and unconnected in the middle of the parkland.

Brown aimed to assess the 'capability' (a favourite term, which became his nickname) of the existing features of the grounds as being suitable for 'improvement', utilising and incorporating appropriate features of the existing topography but intervening, modifying and constructing where judged appropriate, to create a vista that enhanced the 'natural' features of the landscape. The landscape parks affirmed the prerogative of their owners, the position and dominance of the parks reinforcing the values and power of landowners, emphasising the maintenance of a traditional social hierarchy. The parkland could incorporate the agricultural, sporting and recreational interests of the landowners, the presence of grazing sheep and cattle showing aristocratic interest in the selective breeding of livestock. The park grassland was in origin an aristocratic environment, often created from existing deer parks; horses, riding and hunting were central to aristocratic country recreation, and the stables (as at Wimpole in Cambridgeshire) were sometimes magnificent and prominent. The parkland turf served as an economic resource and as an environment for aristocratic diversion. In his only extant statement of his intentions, written in 1770, Brown maintained that in providing an amenity for the selective breeding of livestock, riding, shooting, hunting and forestry, the landscape parks 'when rightly understood will supply all the elegance and all the comforts which mankind wants in the Country and (I will add) if right, be exactly fit for the owner, the Poet and the Painter'. To realise this aim required 'a good plan, good execution, a perfect knowledge of the country and the objects in it, whether natural or artificial, and infinite delicacy in the planting &c'.[67] Brown had an enormous reputation in his lifetime; alluding to Milton's *Paradise Lost* and evoking the Edenic ideal of the landscapes that Brown was held by his patrons to have designed, Horace Walpole wrote an epitaph in the year of his death: 'With one lost Paradise the name / Of our first ancestor is stained; / Brown shall enjoy unsullied fame / For many a Paradise regained.'[68]

In smoothing the landscape, clearing terrain and creating new landscape features, Brown had his critics, who accused him of producing a bland uniform product showing scant regard for local topography and for inherent 'natural' forms, a condemnation given further prominence in the critiques of Uvedale Price and Richard Payne Knight in the 'picturesque' controversy in the 1790s. To its opponents, the landscape park had become the embodiment of the rational control and manipulation of nature, a correlative to the zeal for the 'improvement' of the agricultural landscape of the countryside and manifesting the political, financial and imperial aggrandisement of the Whig aristocracy. The enclosure of common lands, especially as sanctioned by parliament from the mid-eighteenth century, had transformed the agrarian economy and the landscape of the countryside, removing common rights over the use of land. Enclosure was a precondition of aristocratic landscaping, but in seeking greater agricultural productivity through enclosure the great landowners invested in the improvement of the land, transforming the agrarian economy. Enclosure could be presented as the embodiment of progressive ideas of improvement, where self-interest was allied to public benefits; and the improvement of the fertility of the land could be viewed as enhancing the beauty of the landscape, the georgic vision of the countryside. But while transforming the agrarian economy and facilitating farming inno-vations, enclosure also led to the depopulation of the countryside and to the creation of a class of labouring poor. The creation of a landscape park could have a major impact on existing rural settlements, as villages were cleared and moved to different locations, roads terminated or diverted and the rural population stripped of customary rights, a process of depopulation and human decay described in Oliver Goldsmith's poem 'The Deserted Village' (1770). In Goldsmith's fictional village of Auburn its 'bold peasantry, their country's pride', is destroyed by the creation of a landscape park and by the culture of self-interest and avarice and its 'baneful arts' which 'pamper luxury and thin mankind'. Far from leading to the greater aesthetic appreciation of the landscape, the pursuit of profit destroys the 'spontaneous joys' of nature that should lie 'unenvied, unmolested, unconfined'.[69]

Writing the history of gardening in the 1770s Horace Walpole offered a different evaluation of the effects of landscaping, offering a Whig apologetic. He places the development of the landscaping aesthetic within a social and political context, portraying different styles of gardening, ancient and modern, in relation to prevailing patterns of political organisation and power; the 'happy combinations' of the contemporary social and political system had produced the glory of the English landscape garden. His father Sir Robert Walpole had cleared villages in constructing Houghton in Norfolk in the 1720s. Ignoring sentiment, Horace Walpole affirmed the Whig view in arguing that landscape parks were integrated into the life and agricultural work of the countryside, and that the agrarian economy was dependent on the productive and progressive use of wealth: 'Let it be considered that the Composition of our Gardens depends on wealth, or extended possession, on the beauties & animation of Agriculture, Farming, and Navigation. Walls are thrown down to admit the prospect of inclosures, villages, great roads & moving life.' Looking back to antiquity he maintains that Roman villas manifested the 'luxury and apprehension' of the empire and that the 'giant aqueducts & superb public roads' took precedence while the 'amenities of the country were not culti-vated'; moreover the roads were not 'calculated for the intercourse of Trade, but to facilitate the march of legions'. This is the Whig imperial theme, contrasting military monarchies ruling territorial dominions with the British empire based on maritime hegemony and fostering commercial enterprise. Turning to the contemporary world, Horace Walpole associates the formal geometry of French gardens with the dictates of 'arbitrary monarchy' where wealth was not employed for the improvement of the rural economy. The French style of gardening and its aesthetic was the product of an absolutist political system, for 'in the hands of ostentatious wealth, it became the means of opposing nature; and the more it traversed the march of the latter, the more nobility thought its power was demonstrated'. The view of the countryside from a French nobleman's garden would be of 'Desolation, poverty, misery; barren rocks, & plains covered with thistles'. This absolutist landscape contrasts with Walpole's georgic vision of the English agrarian economy, and he concludes that 'The English Taste in Gardening is thus the growth of the English Constitution & must perish with it'.[70]

Walpole was a strong defender of Brown's style of landscaping. Brown's successor as Britain's leading landscape designer was a man of educated back-ground, Humphry Repton, who softened the simplicity and rigidity of pattern of Brown's work but whose proposals were nevertheless criticised in the 'picturesque' controversy. Repton began work as a landscape gardener in 1788 and by 1795 he had worked on 50 commissions. Each client purchased a specially prepared 'Red Book' of the property, its text discussing the site under various categories of 'improvement': the character of the property, its situation, the approach, the house, the walks and drives, and the kitchen garden. Watercolour drawings were intended to give an immediate impression of the effect of the improvements, having a slide or overlay which, when laid flat, shows the present appearance of property and, when lifted, the results of the proposed improvements. Repton was a designer, not a contractor, but he would supervise the work if the client proceeded with the project. His clients ranged from great landowners to wealthy merchants with newly acquired small estates, and he was concerned to establish the owner's 'appropriation' of the landscape, making visible signs of ownership spread throughout the estate. In the 'Red Book' for Tatton Park in Cheshire Repton emphasised the imposition of symbols of ownership: 'The first essential of greatness in a place, is the appearance of united and uninterrupted property . . . the church may be decorated in a style that shall in some degree correspond with that of the mansion; – the market-house, or other public edifice, an obelisk, or even a *mere* stone, with distances, may be made an ornament to the town, and bear the arms of the family.'[71] By the careful placing of belts and plantations he could make a property seem larger, and he went beyond Brown in the manipulation of landscape illusion and symbols of ownership.

The Picturesque Aesthetic

Unlike Brown, Repton expressed his ideas in print and entered into public discussion of the aesthetics of landscape; in his *Sketches and Hints on Landscape Gardening* (1795) he drew upon the plans and approach to landscape design set out in his Red Books. But he delayed publication because of a pre-emptive attack on the practice of professional landscape gardeners by Richard Payne Knight in *The Landscape: A Didactic Poem* (1794) and Uvedale Price in his *Essay on the Picturesque* (1794). Price and Knight owned estates (Foxley and Downton) in Herefordshire and had encountered Repton when he worked in the county. Their critique of professional landscape gardening made reference to the aesthetic of 'picturesque' views set out in the travel guides of the Reverend William Gilpin; to values exercised in the management of their estates in Herefordshire; to an appeal to traditional constitutional principles of liberty and freedom that they perceived to be threatened by the anti-social effects of landscape parks; and to the connoisseurship of painting and Italian landscape acquired on the Grand Tour.[72] In their aesthetics of landscape Price and Knight drew upon local sentiment that presented

Herefordshire as the home of the English georgic, as a county of woodlands, pasture, orchards and cornfields, of gentry with small estates. In his agricultural report of 1794, commissioned by the Board of Agriculture, John Clark, land agent to Lord Hereford, described the county as a district blessed by nature, as being 'clothed in nature's fairest robes, and enriched by a profusion of her most chosen gifts', claiming that 'the ancients, with much propriety, complimented this favourable district as the garden of England'. The cartouche to Isaac Taylor's map of the county of 1786 displays the georgic iconography of apple orchard, cider press, hop yard, a sack of wool, netted salmon (from the River Wye), a sailing barge and a river god.[73] Price was committed to agricultural improvement in the management of his estate at Foxley, situated in a tributary valley of the Wye with wooded slopes encircling the house. In the 1770s he employed Nathaniel Kent, a leading land agent, who emphasised the 'connection' between landlord, tenant and labourer as a central doctrine of estate management. As a result of his survey Kent remodelled Foxley to encourage smallholders, consolidating land holdings and amalgamating farms and fields to support more tenants and increase rentals; he also gave Price control of the woodland by the management of ancient woods, plantations and coppices, creating texture and variety as well as an economic return from the land.[74]

Price's argument in his *Essay on the Picturesque* was shaped by usage that had been introduced by Gilpin in his series of travel guides, which promoted the appreciation of 'picturesque' landscape scenery as 'expressive of that peculiar kind of beauty, which is agreeable in a picture'. Whereas Price directed his discussion to shape gentlemanly improvement of a landscape park, Gilpin was concerned with expanding the pleasures of tourism and amateur sketching. In the first of his published guides, *Observations on the River Wye* (1782), Gilpin explained his object, 'that of not barely examining the face of a country; but of examining it by the rules of picturesque beauty: of not merely describing; but of adapting the description of natural scenery to the principles of artificial landscape'. He gave no precise definition of what he meant by 'picturesque' in this guide, but offered a more formal statement in his *Three Essays: On Picturesque Beauty; On Picturesque Travel; and on Sketching Landscape* (1792). There he explained his distinction between the 'beautiful' and the 'picturesque' as between scenes 'which please the eye in their *natural state*; and those, which please from some quality, capable of being *illustrated in painting*'. He amplified this by explaining that the roughness or ruggedness of a scene or object rendered it a suitable subject for the painter. Smoothness was one of the most essential properties of beauty, but ruggedness (as in a tree or rocky mountain) was the characteristic of the picturesque: '*roughness* forms the most essential point of difference between the *beautiful*, and the *picturesque*; as it seems to be that particular quality, which makes objects chiefly pleasing in painting'. Gilpin expresses a preference for desolate scenery over a land-scape of agricultural improvement, 'from scenes indeed of the *picturesque kind* we exclude the appendages of tillage'. The 'picturesque' is not to be equated with the grandeur of the sublime: '*sublimity alone* cannot make an object *picturesque*' – the immensity of the ocean does not make it picturesque. He finds the picturesque in the ruggedness, variety, harmony and form of natural objects and scenes that arouse the imagination, so that 'picturesque composi-tion consists in uniting in one whole a variety of parts; and these parts can only be obtained from rough objects'.[75]

In his travel guides Gilpin aimed to arouse the sensibility of the tourist to 'picturesque' scenery; he was criticised as an inadequate theorist by Price and Knight, authors concerned to establish a philosophical basis for the aesthetic. They considered 'picturesque' to denote an aesthetic category derived from the manner and method of painters rather than from features of natural scenery; but while Price maintained that objects could be inherently pictur-esque, Knight considered 'picturesque' to be an action of the mind. Turning attention away from the objects depicted to the outlook of the artists who painted them, they rejected the elegant lines of Capability Brown's landscapes, associated with the neatness and smoothness of Edmund Burke's category of 'beauty', in favour of a 'picturesque' style of gardening associated (as with Gilpin) with ruggedness and the intrinsic harmony of unimproved nature. They maintained that roughness and variety should be prominent in the design of landscape gardens, which should be structured by principles of composition derived from the pictures of Nicolas Poussin and Claude Lorrain, the painters of Italian classical landscapes, with views designed to reveal the painter's arrangement of foreground, middle ground and far distance.

Uvedale Price's father had befriended Thomas Gainsborough who sketched a *Study of Beech Trees near Foxley* (1760), and in his landscaping Price favoured the retention of sunken lanes as depicted by Gainsborough, seeking to retain features that seemed intrinsic to the landscape. In his *Essay on the Picturesque* Price launched a critique of Brown and, by implication, Repton, constructing the aesthetic category of 'picturesque' landscape as a bulwark against 'despotic' improvement. He compared Brown's landscaping to a mili-tary invasion of the countryside, a style of 'blind unrelenting power' ignorant of human needs and feelings. Whereas Walpole considered that Brown's land-scaping expressed the 'happy combinations' of the English constitution, Price argued the opposite. Writing during the political anxieties and repression of the 1790s he was concerned, as a Whig and follower of Charles James Fox, with the threat to the political order of despotism; but his aesthetics of landscape shows a conservative outlook in emphasising the importance of traditional forms and of customary conventions to be maintained by a cultivated class.[76]

In Price's opinion landscaping should express the political virtues of the British constitution, 'neither fond of destroying old, nor of creating new systems'. Human habitation, liberty and needs should form the essential features of the improvement of landscape, and he argued that landscape painting provides the appropriate model for ordering the countryside, finding examples in Dutch and Flemish landscapes and in Gainsborough's cottage scenes: 'the lover of painting, considers the dwellings, the inhabitants, and the marks of their intercourse, as ornaments to the landscape'. He sought a land-scape pattern that would harmoniously join landscape to its human habita-tion, Kent's principle of 'connection' expressing the relations between 'the local geography and history of an extensive prospect'. This objective was disrupted by 'improvement', where uniformity erased the natural roughness and variety of nature. Price advocated the preservation of ancient woodland, 'the intricacy of oaks, beeches, and thorns' and the 'fantastic roots of trees'; the maintenance of the agrarian economy of square meadows surrounded by neat hedges and the 'winding paths of sheep'; the retention of old neglected roads and hollows, 'every deep recess' overgrown with 'wild roses, with honey-suckles' allowing glimpses of husbandry through woodland glades, a land-scape populated by wildlife and shaped by weathering and mellowed by time. He wished to preserve 'all the beautiful varieties of form, tint, and light and shade' that 'time only, and a thousand lucky incidents can mature', a land-scape that would remain suitable for the admiration and study of Jacob van Ruïsdael or Gainsborough. Price sought to preserve the harmonious variety of the 'natural and picturesque' landscape, a harmony produced by nature and human use that cannot be created or manufactured by design, arguing that its aesthetic and utility would be destroyed by the mechanistic intervention of landscape gardeners and their rigid patterns of improvement. As noted, Price conceived the aesthetic category of the 'picturesque', characterised by rough-ness, intricacy and variety, as distinct from Burke's categories of the 'beautiful' and the 'sublime'. The picturesque landscape would display 'the coquetry of nature; it makes beauty more amusing, more varied, more playful'. The way to present the intrinsic 'connection' between the human and natural worlds is revealed by the study of painting, which would 'humanise the mind'. The art of the landscape designer was to reveal the pictures that lay hidden in the landscape, to cultivate the mind by following the methods of painters rather than by emulating the structure of finished pictures, by making 'reference to the turn of mind common to painters, who . . . are struck with numberless circumstances . . . to which an unpractised eye pays little or no attention'.[77] The cultivation of the 'picturesque' aesthetic was predicated on a patrician cultural education, a familiarity with the landscape paintings of Italian, French and Dutch masters, knowledge gained through the Grand Tour and by access to English aristocratic collections.

These were not new aesthetic principles, though they were shaped into a new form. Pope had urged that 'in laying out a garden, the first thing to be considered is the genius of the place', that the 'first simplicity' of nature was to be preferred to 'vain efforts for improvements'; and he considered that 'all gardening is landscape painting', like a picture hung up.[78] The picturesque aesthetic has its origins in debates over the relation between painting and poetry, and in their representation of nature. For Walpole, the process of softening rude landscape into a landscape garden was allied to poetry and painting; expanding Horace's famous doctrine *ut pictura poesis* ('as in painting so in poetry') to include the shaping of landscape, he invoked the classical myth of the three 'Graces', goddesses personifying charm, grace and beauty: 'Poetry, Painting & Gardening, or the science of Landscape, will forever by men of Taste be deemed Three Sisters, or *the Three New Graces* who dress and adorn nature.'[79] In this aesthetic, nature was the common theme uniting poetry, painting and landscape gardening.

Richard Payne Knight's *The Landscape, a Didactic Poem* belongs, in its lyrical description of landscape, to the georgic tradition valorising rural life; and like Virgil's *Georgics*, Knight's poem incorporates stylistic and philosophical attitudes drawn from Lucretius.[80] Like Price's *Essay on the Picturesque*, Knight's poem was concerned with issues about the aesthetics of landscape and with the design of landscape gardens. The discussion of garden design was heightened by Thomas Hearne's two contrasting illustrations, to which constant reference is made in the text: the first 'dressed in the modern style' shows a house set in tidy grounds as laid out by Brown, with mown lawns and paths, a stream and undulating ground; this is contrasted with an 'undressed' scene of the same elements with overgrown woodland and rocks in irregular forms (Fig. 5). Knight asserts the superiority of this 'undressed' style of landscaping, the picturesque landscape. The 'dressed' or Brownian style 'shews poor Nature, shaven and defac'd, / To gratify the jaundic'd eye of Taste', a false and corrupted taste. By contrast, for landscape to 'charm the eye and captivate the soul' Knight urges that there was need to follow the practice of painters: 'To make the Landscape grateful to the sight, / Three points of distance always should unite; / And howsoe'er the view may be confin'd, / Three mark'd divisions we shall always find: / Not more, where Claude extends his prospect wide . . .'. Landscape should be shaped by a painterly vision. The landscapes of Claude Lorrain – himself described as 'Nature's own pupil, fav'rite child of Taste!' – are taken as the prime model. Knight urges that in the picturesque landscape 'Wood, water, lawn, in just gradation joins, / And each with artful negligence combines'. Knight rejects the conventional claim that Lakeland scenery, 'Keswick's favour'd pool', Derwentwater (much admired by Gilpin), is sublime, for ''Tis not the giant of unwieldy size, / Piling up hills on hills to scale the skies, / That gives an image of the true sublime'. In preference to the

5 Thomas Hearne, engravings of a park 'dressed in the modern style' and an 'undressed' landscape.

monumental landscape he urges that the true sublime is to be found in 'nature's common works, by genius dress'd, / With art selected, and with taste express'd', in natural forms arranged with a painter's eye. Garden design should be shaped by adherence to the harmony of natural forms: 'teach proud man his labour to employ / To form and decorate, and not destroy'. The introduction of features to enhance landscape should be resisted, and only elements should be employed that are familiar and 'naturalised' through use and in harmony with the natural environment: 'No decoration should we introduce, / That has not first been nat'raliz'd by use, / And at the present, or some distant time, / Become familiar to the soil and clime'.

Like Walpole, Knight takes a broad historical perspective, valorising the achievements of the Greeks in reaching harmony between nature and human art: 'O happy days, when art to nature true, / No tricks of dress, or whim of fashion knew! ... When taste was sense, embellish'd and refin'd / By fancy's charms, and reason's force combin'd'. By contrast, the power of Rome exercised a 'benumbing influence'; and in Knight's Enlightenment perspective the succeeding age of Christianity was the age of 'fierce bigots' with 'Faith in their mouths, and fury in their eyes', with 'creeds obscure to puzzle and confound'. Christianity stood in opposition to the arts and sciences and the cultivation of taste: 'Touch'd by their breath, meek Science melts away; / Art drooping, sinks and moulds to decay; / Books blaze in piles, and statues shiver'd fall, / And one dark cloud of ruin covers all.' Despite his valorisation of Claude Lorrain and the landscape of Italy, and his idealisation of ancient Greek society and culture, it is the scenery of rural England that excites his enthusiasm: 'Hail native streams, that full yet limpid glide! / Hail native woods, creation's boast and pride! / Your native graces let the painter's art, / And planter's skill, endeavour to impart; / Nor vainly after distant beauties roam, / Neglectful of the charms they leave at home.' In this paean to English nature Knight expresses his aesthetic of picturesque landscape: landscape shaped by the painter's eye.[81]

Knight dedicated his poem to Price, whose *Essay on the Picturesque* was published later the same year, but *The Landscape* created a greater impact. Knight was well known as a member of parliament and, like Price, a Foxite Whig; as a connoisseur of painting and ancient artefacts; as openly contemptuous of religion and the author of *A Discourse on the Worship of Priapus* (1786), a notorious treatise on ancient phallic cults; and as a man who expressed his opinions forcibly, fluently and without constraint. He directed his comments on landscape design against Brown and Repton. In defence of his professional practice and business Repton responded in his *Sketches and Hints on Landscape Gardening* (1795), leading Knight to retaliate by issuing a riposte in an enlarged second edition of his poem, published that year. Knight had earlier become disenchanted with Repton's taste in landscape design, and chancing upon the (unpublished) 'Red Book' for Tatton Park in Cheshire when it was displayed in a London bookshop (and mistakenly thinking it was to form part of Repton's advertised *Sketches and Hints*), his indignation and contempt prompted him to write and publish his poem in 1794, pre-empting the publication of Price's *Essay on the Picturesque*. Knight ridiculed Repton's proposals that the ownership of an estate be emphasised by placing the family's arms on neighbouring milestones, and that a sweeping gravel road should lead to the house, winding its leisurely way through the estate to amply display the owner's expansive possession of land; this was no more than a vain parade of wealth and power. Repton's vain defensive reply was satirised by Thomas Love Peacock in *Headlong Hall* (1816). But Repton's more practical response can be seen in his 'Red Book' for Attingham in Shropshire, an estate situated to the north of Price's Foxley and Knight's Downton, a commission undertaken in 1798. He set out the principles on which he would base his improvements, presented as the practical methods of the landscape gardener, which contrasted with the 'picturesque' theories airily proposed by connoisseurs. He illustrated the 'absurdity' and 'futility' of 'making pictures our models for natural improvement' by referring to a landscape by Claude in the Attingham collection. To provide a model for landscaping, it would have to be extended: 'instead of a picture, it would have resembled a panorama'. He argued that it was necessary to improve the course of the River Terne, smoothing the existing channels: 'the landscape gardener ... must secure a constant and permanent display of water ... an ample river majestically flowing through the park'. Repton triumphed on the ground at Attingham, his proposals for improving the course of the river, new woodland planting and creating new approaches to the house being put into effect, and he confidently quoted these passages from his 'Red Book' in his *Observations on the Theory and Practice of Landscape Gardening* (1803).[82]

In *The Landscape* Payne Knight did not use the term 'picturesque' to describe his aesthetics of landscape; but he did so, with a clear definition of its meaning, in *An Analytical Inquiry into the Principles of Taste* (1805). He contested Price's notion that the 'picturesque' was a quality to be found in 'distinctions in external objects', arguing instead that 'picturesque' denoted an aesthetic category associated with a specific style of painting. To elucidate his meaning Knight stressed the Italian derivation of 'picturesque': '*pittoresco* must mean, *after the manner of painters*'. The relation to painting implied that the appreciation of landscape as 'picturesque' can 'only be felt by persons who have correspondent ideas to associate; that is, by persons in certain degree conversant with that art'. The aesthetic appreciation of a landscape painting, and of a landscape itself, is therefore a product of connoisseurship: 'By thus comparing nature and art, both the eye and the intellect acquire a higher relish for the production of each'.[83] Knight's aesthetics of nature can be illustrated by his dismissal of the conventional view that Lakeland scenery provides 'an image of the true sublime'. The Lake District had become a major site for the picturesque tourist, encouraged by the writings of the poet Thomas Gray and by a succession of travel guides.[84]

In his famous *Guide to the Lakes* (1778) Thomas West gave an ecstatic account of the view of Derwentwater from one of his famous 'stations' or viewpoints, Cockshot Hill on its north-eastern shore (above Friar's Crag, later the scene of John Ruskin's first recollection of nature as a young boy): 'On the floor of a spacious amphitheatre, of the most picturesque mountains imaginable, an elegant sheet of water is spread out before you, shining like a mirror, and transparent as chrystal; variegated with islands, that rise in the most pleasing forms above the watery plane, dressed in wood, or clothed with forest verdure, the water shining round them.' This is the landscape of picturesque tourism. William Gilpin was more discriminating in his selection of viewpoints, preferring the beauties of bays and mountains glimpsed when walking around the lake to the more famous views, but he is emphatic in endorsing the picturesque beauty of Derwentwater: 'Of all the lakes in these romantic regions . . . [it is] the most admired . . .. Nothing conveys an idea of *beauty* more strongly, than the lake; nor of *horrour*, than the mountains; and the former *lying in the lap* of the latter, expresses in a strong manner the mode of their combination.'[85] In his *A Guide through the District of the Lakes* Wordsworth agreed that 'Derwent is distinguished from all the other Lakes by being *surrounded* with sublimity'. But the view of the lake framed by the ring of distant mountains did not satisfy Knight's criterion of the picturesque landscape, which he found in 'nature's common works, by genius dress'd, / With art selected, and with taste express'd', natural forms arranged with a painter's eye for a balanced landscape; and he demurred from the more customary opinion that the Lakeland mountains 'of unwieldy size' were to be considered 'an image of the true sublime'.[86]

In his *Observations on the Theory and Practice of Landscape Gardening* (1803) Repton disparaged the theory of picturesque landscaping advanced by Price and Knight, writing with the authority of an expert practitioner on the futility of taking pictures as the model for landscape improvement. 'Pictures may imitate Nature', he declared, 'but Nature is not to copy Pictures'. But he was more conciliatory in reflecting on the implications and method of landscape improvement: 'the highest perfection of landscape gardening', he now declared, was 'to imitate nature so judiciously, that the interference of art shall never be detected'. And he now advised that the management of woodland should not be 'guided by the levelling principles or sudden innovations of former fashion' – that of improvement, which he had followed – but should take due account and 'reverence the glory of former ages, while he cherishes and admires the ornament of the present'[87]; these remarks were akin to the sentiments espoused by Price. And in his last work, *Fragments on the Theory and Practice of Landscape Gardening* (1816), Repton parodied Brown's and his own technique in showing two prints that offered contrasting views of a public road before and after 'Improvements'; these images recall Thomas Hearne's illustrations of modern and picturesque landscape parks (see Fig. 5) drawn for Knight's *The Landscape*. The change from comfortable, humanised natural disorder, where the foreground of woodland dominates the view of a winding lane and venerable beech hedges leading to a deer park – a dignified and harmonious scene suggestive of Price's landscape of 'connection' – to the new levelled road marked out by fencing enclosing plantation firs and poplars – a scene dedicated to the service of utility and the assertion of private ownership – illustrates the ugliness, degeneracy and destructive potential of improvement. In Repton's account the estate had passed from an aristocratic 'ancient proprietor' to a (newly) 'very rich man' who was detached from the cultural values and aesthetics of rural, traditional England, and who had enclosed the land and doubled the rents – a man for whom 'money supersedes every other consideration'. Repton's bitter portrayal was perhaps a response to the change in the class of his clients during the latter part of his career, from the aristocracy to the newly enriched commercial class.[88] He deploys an image of disenchanted rural sentiment, the politics of nostalgia in the face of industrialisation and the revolution in the agrarian economy, prefigured in Swift's espousal of the merits of the traditions of the 'ancients' over the innovations of the 'moderns' in *Gulliver's Travels* (1726).

A much more sophisticated version of these sentiments is voiced in Jane Austen's novel *Mansfield Park* (1814), where the issues of improvement are presented in terms made familiar by Price's *Essay on the Picturesque* and Repton's *Observations on the Theory and Practice of Landscape Gardening*. The aesthetics of nature and the moral economy of connection are contrasted with the effects of destructive improvement, the traditional virtues of the countryside with showy London manners, the propriety of traditional mores with flighty fashion. Fanny Price, the heroine of the novel (with whom Austen identifies), has a marginal status as a poor relation of the family of Sir Thomas Bertram, the owner of Mansfield Park, with whom she lives; she has the critical and independent outlook of the partial outsider. Fanny articulates the traditional values of cultivation, duty and benevolence from which the family have become estranged but to which they should aspire. Her name may not be accidental; and the name of the estate, its wealth produced by slave labour on sugar plantations in the West Indies, recalls the judge Lord Mansfield, who had declared slavery to be illegal in England; Austen subtly signposts aesthetic and moral concerns. In *Mansfield Park* the vacuous and fashionable brother and sister Henry and Maria Crawford, transient residents newly arrived from London, and the weak and stupid local landowner Mr Rushworth who marries (disastrously) into the Bertram family, yearn for 'improvement'. The Crawfords prove to be guilty of impropriety of manners and morals, while the foolish Rushworth plans to cut down old oak trees and destroy his estate. The traditional rural and moral virtues are embodied in Fanny, and it is through her honesty and her marriage to the intelligent and responsible younger son Edmund Bertram, that 'improvement' is repudiated and the natural and moral equilibrium re-established.[89]

Landforms and Rocks: From the Picturesque to Naturalism

Landscapes are shaped by the geology of their underlying rocks, and the popularity of picturesque tourism in the mountain regions of Britain was accompanied by interest in the geological formations shaping these land-scapes and in the rocks and mineral specimens of the underlying geological strata. The occurrence of rock outcrops and mineral resources in moun-tainous regions made these hard rocks, termed 'primary', of especial interest in the nascent earth sciences. In the seventeenth and eighteenth centuries the term 'mineralogy' encompassed the sciences of the earth: the identification and classification of 'minerals', all the naturally occurring, nonliving objects found on the earth; 'mineral geography', the distribution of rocks and minerals; and 'geognosy', the formation and history of rocks and minerals. Between 1770 and 1830 there was a transformation in the scope of earth science from 'mineralogy' to 'geology' (as the terrestrial counterpart of cosmology); from a concern with the identification, distribution and forma-tion of minerals and rocks to a new engagement with the causal and historical processes of earth science, newly stripped of the speculative connotations associated with theories of earth history, as demonstrated by contrasting Thomas Burnet's earlier *Sacred Theory of the Earth* from the 1680s with James Hutton's (non-providential) *Theory of the Earth*, first published in 1788 (enlarged into book form in 1795).[90] Burnet's *Sacred Theory of the Earth* had destabilised the familiar assumptions about the design and permanence of the earth's surface. Burnet portrayed the surface of the earth, its mountains, valleys and seas, as impermanent, the product of cataclysmic disruption and change from a terrestrial state of pristine perfection, and subject to future disruption by geological forces and the ends of providence. His view of the earth in its present form as an object of deformity and ruin rather than beauty and harmonious design for human needs was dismissed by his critics as contrary to sound theology, aesthetics and science; but he acknowledged that mountains 'fill and over-bear the mind with their Excess, and cast it into a pleasing kind of stupor and admiration', and Joseph Addison recognised the 'rude kind of magnificence which appears in these stupendous works of nature'. Mountains became objects of awed appreciation with the development of the aesthetics of the sublime, and the fashion for 'sublime' landscapes and 'picturesque' tours in the eighteenth century fostered interest in the geological features of mountain landscapes and in the underlying processes that resulted in their formation.

Tourist fascination with the Lake District effectively began in the 1770s, fostered by Thomas West's *Guide to the Lakes* and the publication of the letters of the poet Thomas Gray; but the Peak District of Derbyshire had long been the focus of tourist interest, its geological formation of millstone grit and limestone producing a rocky and barren landscape; crags, caverns and rivers, and cave systems containing the curious forms of stalactites and stalagmites and minerals such as the fluorspar Blue John. In *An Inquiry into the Original State and Formation of the Earth* (1778) John Whitehurst supplemented his speculative discussion of the broader themes of earth history with an empirical 'Appendix . . . on the Strata of Derbyshire' based on close study of the geology of his native region. He made deductions about the underlying geological formations of the Peak District on the basis of the evidence provided by examining the rocks exposed at the surface, from the topography of the landscape. Joining description of the landscape to its underlying geological formations, his language evoked the sublime ('romantic') scenery of the Peak District: 'The mountains in Derbyshire, and the moorlands of Staffordshire appear to be so many heaps of ruins . . . the strata lie in the utmost confusion and disorder . . . and their interior parts are no less rude and romantic; for they universally abound with subterranean caverns'.[91]

The seven 'wonders' of the Peak District were celebrated in topographical poems, and included the sublime horror of the Peak Cavern at Castleton (known locally as the 'Devil's Arse') and the cultivated beauties of the Duke of Devonshire's 'palace' of Chatsworth near Bakewell. The unique mineral formations of the region aroused the interest of the scientist, the manufacturer and the tourist. John Whitehurst accompanied his friend and fellow member of the Lunar Society of Birmingham, Erasmus Darwin, in a descent into the Blue John Cavern near Castleton in July 1767, after which Darwin wrote enthusiastically to the Birmingham manufacturer and fellow Lunar Society member Matthew Boulton that 'I have been into the Bowels of old Mother Earth, and seen Wonders, and learnt much curious knowledge . . . am going to make numerous Experiments on aquaeous, sulphureous, metallic and saline Vapours'.[92] The mining of Blue John only began at around this time, and specimens were sold locally as natural curiosities and polished into ornaments; and Boulton was quick to incorporate Blue John into his range of ormolu vases made for the luxury market. Elizabeth Bennet in Jane Austen's *Pride and Prejudice* (1813), disappointed at having to forgo the trip to the Lakes on which she had set her heart, consoled herself with the prospect of Derbyshire and the 'celebrated beauties' of Matlock, Chatsworth, Dovedale and the Peaks, and the chance of acquiring 'a few petrified spars'. The beauty, horror and immensity of the sublime landscape of the picturesque tour elided into interest in geological formations, mineral specimens and natural curiosities.[93] The norms of the aesthetics of nature came to be established by the appreciation of mountain scenery rather than by the contrivance of landscape parks; and the picturesque aesthetics utilised by Gilpin and West in their tour guides to the mountain regions of Britain yielded to a naturalistic aesthetics asserting the primacy of the landscape as an environment shaped by natural forces.

Erasmus Darwin's list of the materials he had retrieved from the 'bowels of the earth', and on which he intended to experiment, comprised the four mineral classes that were then believed to compose the outer portion of the earth, and which were thought to have originally been fluid and then solidified – like crystals – by the effects of heat or desiccation. Mineralogy was pursued as a special branch of natural history; mineral specimens were extracted and collected from mines, cliffs, fields and the beds of streams, and then described and classified, and displayed in cabinets alongside botanical and zoological specimens. As in other branches of natural history the aim was to describe minerals in terms of their natural 'species', such as quartz and feldspar; and as minerals were understood to be chemical substances, their classification was accomplished by chemical analysis. In his *Systema Naturae* (1736) Linnaeus applied his method of botanical classification to minerals, and gave a classification of crystalline minerals in terms of their geometrical form; as in botany, the question of the origins of natural mineral species could be avoided in favour of description and classification, but the origin of minerals and rocks began to be discussed. Rocks were understood to be composed of minerals, granite being composed of crystals of quartz, feldspar and mica, and limestone as composed of calcite. Rocks such as granite and marble were composed of crystalline minerals and supposed to be formed by crystallisation from an aqueous solution or from a volcanic melt; as the chemistry of salts was widely investigated, the aqueous origin of crystalline minerals was widely assumed by chemists and mineralogists.

The controversy over the origin of basalt, a dark fine-grained rock that often occurs embedded with stratified rocks, was of especial significance in shaping the development of the earth sciences in the late eighteenth century, for the question could not be resolved by chemical analysis of the rocks in the laboratory and evidence was sought in the field relations of the rocks. The major outcome of the controversy was in establishing fieldwork as an essential part of the practice of the emergent science of geology, shifting the science from its basis in mineralogy and laboratory investigation. Some basalts seemed to be similar to lava samples or were sited close to present or former volcanoes, and therefore must originally have been molten lavas; other basalts were found in regions remote from volcanoes and present in sedimentary rocks such as sandstone, and therefore seemed likely to have been formed from sediments. The debate broadened into a wider disagreement, between those geologists who favoured the agency of heat in geological change (known as 'Vulcanists', such as James Hutton) and those who favoured the agency of water ('Neptunists', such as Abraham Gottlob Werner). Although the evidence turned in favour of the volcanic origin of basalt (the modern view), most rocks were thought to be of aqueous origin and volcanoes were judged to be of relatively minor importance in shaping the earth's geology.

The controversy had an important aspect in the 1770s: the geological descriptions of the recent eruptions of Vesuvius near Naples and of the basalt columns of Fingal's Cave on the Hebridean island of Staffa were accompanied by artists' representations which portrayed the geological formations in terms of the aesthetics of the sublime and the picturesque. The prismatic columns of basalt on Staffa in the Western Isles were of major interest to geologists because of the debate over their origin, whether volcanic or aqueous. Buffon had advanced the view that volcanoes were eruptions from a heat source close to the volcanic cone, but many geologists thought volcanoes to be caused by local fires produced by the burning of coal beneath the earth's surface; and the large pyramidal basaltic columns, in the Giant's Causeway in Ireland and Fingal's Cave on Staffa, seemed to indicate to mineralogists that basalt columns were of aqueous origin, produced either by crystallisation or through contraction by desiccation. This was the received opinion among mineralogists in the 1770s and 1780s, summarised by the French geologist Jean-Étienne Guettard in 1770 in describing basalt as formed by crystallisation in an aqueous fluid and rejecting the claim that basalt was due to igneous fusion of a volcanic melt. But the volcanic view was given forcible expression by the leading field geologist Nicolas Desmarest, who studied basalt outcrops in the Auvergne close to mountains of volcanic origin, and identified these basalts as similar to samples from Vesuvius and as cooled lava. In the 1770s the issue remained open.[94]

When William Hamilton arrived in Naples in November 1764 as British ambassador he found himself, quite fortuitously, in a position to establish his career as a collector, connoisseur and virtuoso. The grandson of the third Duke of Hamilton, he had followed a career in the army and in parliament, with marriage to an heiress in 1758; it was his wife's frail health in the damp English climate that prompted him to use his connections to secure the diplomatic appointment as Envoy Extraordinary in Naples, but a move to Italy would have seemed agreeable to a man already known for collecting and selling pictures. Horace Walpole gave Horace Mann, the British minister in Florence, notice of the imminent arrival of a 'new neighbour', his friend Hamilton who 'is picture-mad, and will ruin himself in virtu-land'.[95] Hamilton spent nearly 40 years in Italy proving a capable diplomat and receiving some preferment – he was appointed a Knight of the Bath in 1772 – and he did collect pictures; but the circumstances of his residence in Naples gave him opportunity to become an accomplished connoisseur and virtuoso, and to fulfil Walpole's prediction about his likely financial plight. In later life (and in subsequent reputation) he became an object of public derision because of his second wife Emma's affair with Lord Nelson; the acquiescence of the elderly collector of objects of *virtu* seemed especially ridiculous. Hamilton's report of the contemporary (Catholic) rites of the votive phalli at Isernia in Abruzzo, which he believed to be a survival of an ancient cult of Priapus, was included in Richard Payne Knight's *Discourse on the Worship of Priapus* (1786); its frontispiece displays the wax phalli known as the 'toes of Isernia', which Hamilton donated to the British Museum. The book was issued privately by the Society of Dilettanti, but had given rise to scandal. Notoriety shadowed the latter part of his life, but Hamilton had earlier become famous as a connoisseur for his collections of Greek vases and as a virtuoso for his reports on his observations of the eruptions of Mount Vesuvius.

Hamilton's interest in vases and volcanoes was shaped by the history and geology of the Bay of Naples, by the destruction of Pompeii and Herculaneum in 79 AD following the eruption of Vesuvius. The archaeological investigation of the ancient sites had only begun a few years before Hamilton's arrival in Naples, and with his interest aroused he was well placed to make purchases – he later bought the 'Portland Vase' from the Barberini family. He assembled two separate collections of vases, the first collection being acquired by the British Museum in 1772 with a grant voted by parliament, and advanced scholarship by sponsoring the publication of lavish catalogues of his collections. At the time these ancient vases were considered to be Etruscan, but Hamilton very soon voiced the opinion that the vases were made by Greek and Roman artists; and he subsequently affirmed the (modern) view based on the evidence of Greek inscriptions and promoted by Neapolitan scholars and by the German art historian Johann Joachim Winckelmann, that the painted vases were of Greek origin, an attribution made emphatic in the title of the catalogue of his second collection where these vases are described as being 'mostly of pure Greek workmanship'.[96]

Hamilton was well placed to observe the series of eruptions of Vesuvius that began in September 1765 and continued for two years. He spent days on the mountain recording the flows of lava, the changing shapes of the cone and crater, the clouds of ash and smoke, and the flashes of lightning through the ash cloud which he observed in October 1767. These observations were first reported in two letters sent to the Royal Society and which were published in the *Philosophical Transactions*, leading to Hamilton's election as a fellow. Encouraged, he followed this with a third letter accompanied by sketches, and by a painting in transparent colours of the mountain in eruption, to be illu-minated by lamps placed behind it; and he dispatched crates of rocks and lava to the British Museum. In these first brief letters Hamilton was careful to avoid theoretical speculation and to confine himself to description of his observations; his reports were well received, encouraging him to undertake a visit to Sicily and Mount Etna in the spring of 1769 and to report further eruptions of Vesuvius; he also began to offer some views of his own by way of interpretation. These letters were first collected in his *Observations on Mount Vesuvius, Mount Etna, and other Volcanos* (1772), illustrated with engravings; but having sponsored the lavish publication of the catalogue of his first collec-tion of vases, Hamilton was inclined to produce a more sumptuous edition of his volcanic reports, with illustrations that would fully capture the detail of his observations and the overwhelming dramatic power and horror of the volcano in eruption, geological description being expressed in the aesthetics of the sublime. *Campi Phlegraei* (1776), its title 'Fields of Fire' taken from the term applied to the region surrounding the volcano, is a bilingual edition with the English and French texts in facing columns, and is based on his five letters to the Royal Society published in the *Philosophical Transactions*; and it was followed by the *Supplement to the Campi Phlegraei* (1779) containing the text of a further letter of October 1779 addressed to Joseph Banks.[97]

In *Campi Phlegraei* and its *Supplement* Hamilton's text is copiously and lavishly illustrated with 59 superb hand-coloured engravings from gouache drawings by Peter Fabris, an English artist resident in Naples.[98] Hamilton declared that 'accurate and faithful observations on the operations of nature, related with simplicity and truth, are not to be met with often'; he claimed that his reports achieved such descriptive accuracy, but 'being still sensible of the great difficulty of conveying a true idea of the curious country I have described, by words alone ... I employed Mr Peter Fabris, a most ingenious and able artist ... to take Drawings ... in which each stratum is represented in its proper colours'.[99] Fabris depicted the volcanic activity of Vesuvius in spectacular pictures of the eruptions, with drawings of lava spec-imens and of views of the interior of the crater; he illustrated the volcanic rocks of the environs of the mountain, including pumice and tuff excavated at Pompeii; and he portrayed scenes of the landscape of the region of the Bay of Naples, showing rock formations and topography. There was no established artistic tradition for the geological illustration of rock forma-tions and the interior of a volcanic crater,[100] and Fabris achieved his greatest success in the observational detail of his dramatic depictions of eruptions, where he follows the tradition of the 'sublime' associations of volcanoes established by Salvator Rosa with *Empedocles Leaping into Etna* (late 1660s), an icon of the admiration of the horror and terror of sublime landscapes.

Visiting Naples in 1774, Joseph Wright of Derby followed this pictorial theme in his gouache *Vesuvius in Eruption* (1774), the vivid colour and light of the picture evoking the frightening power of the volcano, an image framed in terms of the aesthetics of the sublime. Unlike Fabris (who was following Hamilton's directions and purposes), Wright did not attempt a naturalistic study of the eruption; and he expressed discontent with the capacity of painting to capture the significance of the scene, considering that only a scientific study could reveal the inner workings of the volcano that generated the eruption. Writing to his brother Richard on this 'most wonderful sight in nature' he alludes to the geological studies of his friend John Whitehurst: 'I wished for his company when on Mount Vesuvius, his thoughts would have center'd in the bowels of the mountain, mine skimmed over the surface only; there was a very considerable eruption at the time, of which I am going to make a picture. 'Tis the most wonderful sight in nature.'[101] Wright subsequently painted more than 30 images of Vesuvius; and in his portrait of *John Whitehurst F.R.S.* (*c.* 1782) he depicted Whitehurst's concern to understand the 'system of Subterraneous Geography' determining the 'subterraneous convulsions' and 'fires' of volcanic eruptions, as established by Hamilton. He portrayed Whitehurst drawing his 'Section of the Strata at Matlock High Tor', showing the interleaving of toadstone (a form of basalt) with beds of limestone, for his *Inquiry into the Original State and Formation of the Earth*; the background landscape features a volcano in eruption, indicating his comparison of toadstone with lava and deduction of the igneous formation of Derbyshire toadstone.[102]

Hamilton made 'accurate and faithful observations' of the eruptions of Vesuvius 'related with simplicity and truth', a central objective of his reports; his immediate purpose was to convey naturalistic detail rather than to engage in wider speculations about the causes of the eruptions. The illustrative plates in *Campi Phlegraei* are accompanied by his clear descriptions: 'the streams of lava that run down the steep flanks of the volcano, always cut regular and narrow channels, so regular as to appear the work of art'. In describing the lava flow as a 'beautiful Cascade of fire', Hamilton couches empirical description in language that captures the aesthetic power of the scene: 'the lava had the appearance of a river of red hot and liquid metal, such as we see in the glass houses, on which were large floating cinders, half lighted, and rolling over one another with great precipitation down the side of the mountain, forming a most beautiful and uncommon cascade', descriptions made vivid by the illustrations, interpreting the eruptions of Vesuvius in terms of the aesthetics of the sublime. His argument was empirical, his investigations thorough and fearless: 'After an Eruption, I have walked in some of those subterraneous, or cover'd galleries, which were exceedingly curious; the sides, top, and bottom being worn perfectly smooth, and even in most parts, by the violence of the currents of the red hot Lavas, which they had convey'd for many weeks successively; in others the Lava had incrusted the sides of those channels with some very extraordinary Scoriae beautifully ramified'. In his fourth letter to the Royal Society, dated 17 October 1769, Hamilton recorded his wider geographical study, including his ascent of Mount Etna in Sicily, the largest volcano in the region. Using the descriptive terms current among the Sicilians to describe the zones of vegetation encountered during the ascent of Etna, Hamilton represented his climb of Etna in terms of an ascent through three distinct altitudinal zones, each with its own characteristic vegetation (the lower 'fertile' region abounding with vines, the '*woody*' region of deciduous trees, and the '*clean* or *uncovered*' region of small shrubs and plants of the 'northern climates'); this representation resembles Humboldt's later and famous depiction of altitudinal and geographical botanical zones (see Fig. 3).[103]

Hamilton was especially intrigued by one feature of volcanic eruptions. He noticed that the great eruption of Vesuvius on 19 October 1767 was accompanied by the emission of ashes 'from the crater of the Volcano, and formed a vast column, as black as the mountain itself'. But he was 'much pleased' and fascinated by the sight of 'continual flashes of forked or zig-zag lightning shot from this black column, the thunder of which was heard in the neighbourhood of the mountain but not in Naples', the 'lightning and balls of fire' making a 'crackling noise'. He concluded that 'the smoak of Volcanoes contains always a portion of electrical matter'. The lightning accompanying this eruption is illustrated in a plate in *Campi Phlegraei* showing the view of Vesuvius from the Mole of Naples. This interest in the lightning associated with the eruptions is continued in his report in the *Supplement* of the eruption of 8 August 1779, where forked lightning is displayed in one of the most striking and dramatic of Fabris' plates, showing the eruption as viewed from Posillipo with figures in the foreground standing in amazement, seemingly almost worshipping this demonstration of nature's inherent power (Fig. 6). Describing the volcanic scene as a 'sublime view', Hamilton drew specific attention to the lightning, noting that 'within these puffs of smoke at the very moment of their emission from the crater I could perceive a bright, but pale electrical fire briskly playing about in zig zag lines'. He adds that he had highlighted this observation 'to prove, that the electrical matter so manifest during this eruption, actually proceeded from the bowels of the Volcano'.

To reinforce the significance of lightning in the volcanic eruption Hamilton cites a letter of the younger Pliny, who observed the famous eruption in 79 AD, reporting to Tacitus on seeing 'flashes of zig zag fire, like lightning, but stronger' bursting from the mountain in 'the great eruption of Vesuvius, that proved fatal to his uncle', the author of the *Natural History*. Hamilton concluded that the 'bright zig zags' of 'Volcanic lightening' reported by Pliny were 'evidently the same electrical fire, and with which I am convinced that

6   Peter Fabris, coloured etching of the eruption of Vesuvius on 8 August 1779 as seen from Posillipo.

the smoak of all Volcanoes is pregnant'. The lightning accompanying the eruption is not merely a secondary effect but is generated in the source of the eruption, deep below the surface of the earth, in the bowels of the volcano.[104] These speculations concerning lightning were entirely consonant with the fashion in contemporary natural philosophy, where electricity was the focus of study as a potent agent in nature. At the time some natural philosophers considered that electricity – termed 'electrical matter', 'electrical fire' – was the cause of earthquakes, and its role in volcanic eruptions had been suggested by the physicist Giambatista Beccaria; and Hamilton reported that Beccaria was 'greatly pleased' with his observations 'as coinciding perfectly with several of his electrical experiments'. Hamilton's interest in the fashionable topic of electricity led him to purchase an apparatus for generating electrical sparks.[105] He placed volcanic science firmly within the spectrum of contemporary natural philosophy and the aesthetics of the sublime.

Hamilton felt growing confidence in his scientific powers, and in the fifth letter of the series written for the Royal Society – and in his introduction to *Campi Phlegraei* – he was emboldened to venture into generalisation and theoretical speculation. He contested the general assumption that volcanic regions were 'merely a country torn to pieces by subterraneous fires'. His argument combines study of the geology of the region around Vesuvius with reference to the historical records of eruptions. He argued that confining attention to the observation and study of Vesuvius alone would give a limited and false interpretation of the significance of the effects of volcanic activity: 'we are apt to judge of the great operations of Nature on too confined a plan'. He explained that he rested his broader conjectures on the observation of the 'nature of the soil that covers the antient Towns of Herculaneum and Pompeii, and the interior and exterior form of the new mountain near Puzzole, [and] with the sort of materials of which it is composed'. From these observations he concluded that the geology of the entire Naples region is volcanic, being formed of 'lava . . . .. Tufa and strata of loose pumice', pointing to the succession of strata of pumice, lava and the very fertile soil formed from lava, and speculating that it might be possible to calculate the age of volcanoes from these strata. 'I imagine the subterraneous fires to have worked in this country, under the bottom of the sea as Moles in a field, throwing up here and there a hillock', and using another image, he likened the 'subterraneous fire' to a 'great plough . . . which Nature makes use of to turn up the bowels of the earth'. According to this view of nature, the 'explosions of Volcanos . . . will now be consider'd in a CREATIVE rather than a DESTRUCTIVE light'. He believed that the region around Vesuvius, 'whose beauties have been celebrated by so many Poets . . . all have been produced, and owe the beauty, and variety of their scenery to such a seeming destruction'. Volcanic eruption was not to be attributed to providential intervention; though unpredictable it was wholly determined by natural causes: 'Nature, though varied, is certainly in general uniform in her operations'. While he allowed that 'such wonderful operations of Nature are certainly intended by all-wise Providence for some great purpose', he did not consider what this purpose might be or otherwise allude to issues of natural theology.

In arguing that the landscape of the region had been formed by volcanic activity, Hamilton points to the Monte Nuovo at Pozzuoli, formed in 48 hours in an eruption in 1538, which is illustrated in *Campi Phlegraei*; the plate shows the 'Temple of Serapis', which Charles Lyell used as the frontispiece to the first volume of his *Principles of Geology* (1830). Hamilton notes that the new mountain at Pozzuoli, 'being of so very late a formation, preserves its conical shape entire, and produces as yet but a very slender vegetation', still displaying the form of its volcanic origin. As a result, he confidently asserts the 'Volcanick origin of this country'. He cites contemporary accounts of the formation of the Monte Nuovo, which establish that it was 'formed in a plain by meer explosion, in the space of forty-eight hours', arguing that the occurrence of earthquakes at a distance from Pozzuoli during the formation of the mountain 'proves clearly that the subterraneous fire was at a great depth below the surface of the plains'. From this conclusion he was led to his most confident ventures into the controversies of geological theory, contesting Buffon's view that 'the furnase of the Volcano is ever . . . in the top'; this he believed was contradicted by the great size of Vesuvius and Etna, 'evidently formed by a series of eruptions of Volcanick explosions'. His demonstration of the role of volcanoes in shaping the landscape of the region led him to formulate a broader claim about the geological history of the earth, to declare that 'subterraneous fires . . . have had a greater share in the formation of mountains, Islands, and even great tracts of land, than has hitherto been suspected', and to contest the (current) view of geologists who 'have attributed the formation of all Mountains, to the operations of water alone', though he conceded that it might be equally untenable to hold 'that every Mountain has been formed by explosion from subterraneous fires'.[106]

This assertion of the fundamental role of volcanoes led Hamilton to enter the controversy over basalt. The first plate of *Campi Phlegraei* shows the island of Castel-a-mare 'composed of columns of BASALTE . . . at the foot of Mount ETNA', forming 'part of a great lava that ran from that volcano into the sea'; having established the volcanic geology of the region he was able to urge the view that basalt was of volcanic origin, concluding more broadly that 'wherever Basaltic columns, of the nature of the Giants Causeway in Ireland are found, there have Volcanos existed, for they are meerly LAVA'.[107] This opinion was currently controversial in scientific circles, and seemed contrary to common-sense observation. Horace Walpole had remarked to Hamilton in 1773 that 'I have a little difficulty in believing that volcanoes produce regular columns like those in the giant's causey'. And as a connoisseur of art and antiquities, Walpole was more comfortable with Hamilton in the role of a collector of ancient vases and the purchaser of a painting *Venus Disarming Cupid*, then believed to be by Correggio (now attributed to Luca Cambiaso), and gently mocked his interest in volcanoes: 'Ransack Herculaneum, sift Pompeii, give us charming vases, bring us Corregios and all Etruria, but do not dive into the caverns of Aetna and Vesuvius.' Alluding to Hamilton's recent appointment as a Knight of the Bath, he joked that 'you are a knight of water not of the opposite element; and it is better to be an antiquary of taste, than a salamander that had passed a thousand ordeals'.[108]

But Hamilton was not to be deflected, considering that the study of volcanoes was by no means beneath the dignity of the antiquarian and connoisseur; and he was in a good position to display the scientific expertise strenuously acquired on the slopes of Vesuvius, to make the case for the igneous origin of basalt and to argue that 'subterraneous fires' had shaped the geological history of the earth. Writing to Horace Mann in August 1783, Walpole reported that Hamilton had arrived in London where he 'will not be quite out of his element, for we have had pigmy earthquakes, much havoc by lightning, and some very respectable meteors'.[109]

Hamilton had given the Royal Society a long and detailed account of the great Calabrian earthquakes which had occurred earlier that year, reporting his own observations and collecting eyewitness accounts of exhalations of fire from the earth; and in recounting that the sea off Messina had been seen to boil he speculated that the seabed had been elevated by volcanic action, that 'the present earthquakes are occasioned by the operation of a volcano, the seat of which seems to lye deep, either under the bottom of the sea . . . or under the parts of the plain'.[110] There had also been volcanic eruptions and earth-quakes in Iceland that year, 1783, causing great devastation and loss of life, and the two events seemed to be linked. One hundred years after Burnet's speculations about the biblical deluge and conflagration in *The Sacred Theory of the Earth*, fiery volcanoes were again a focus of interest, but in a trans-formed intellectual milieu. In *Campi Phlegraei* the emphasis is on the natura-listic description of volcanic eruptions: the terror and destructive power of volcanoes is tempered by their rendition in terms of the aesthetics of the sublime; while their eruptions are unpredictable and conceived as wholly determined by natural causes; and volcanoes are regarded as creative and constructive agents, forming the landscape gradually and over an immense period of time. But Walpole was little engaged by speculations concerning subterraneous fires, and the contemporary interest led him to a weary reflec-tion on intellectual vanity and changes in fashion: 'In my youth, philosophers were eager to ascribe every uncommon discovery to the deluge – now it is the fashion to solve every appearance by conflagrations. If there was such an inundation upon the earth, and such a furnace under it, I am amazed that Noah and company were not boiled to death.' He was dismissive of the capacity of 'poor silly animals' living 'for an instant upon a particle of a boundless universe' to resolve such questions effectively: 'Indeed I am a great sceptic about human reasonings. They predominate only for a time, like other mortal fashions, and are so often exploded after the mode is passed, that I hold them little more serious, though they call themselves wisdom. How many have I seen established and confuted!'[111]

In 1769, having studied basalt columns near Kassel in Hesse, Rudolph Erich Raspe reported to the Royal Society that he considered basalts to be of volcanic origin.[112] With Hamilton's studies of Vesuvius and Etna, first collected in his *Observations on Mount Vesuvius, Mount Etna, and other Volcanos* (1772), the origin of basalt columns was on the scientific agenda. When Joseph Banks sailed for Iceland in 1772, having alienated the navy and been obliged to withdraw from James Cook's second voyage to the Pacific, he went in part to observe the volcanoes on the island. The voyage also took in a visit to the Hebrides, including the island of Staffa. Banks published a short account of the basalt columns of Fingal's Cave and Staffa in 1772, judging the sights of Staffa to be 'the greatest natural curiosities in the world'.[113] He wrote a more detailed report which was published by Thomas Pennant in his *A Tour in Scotland, and Voyage to the Hebrides* (1774): 'each hill, which hung over the columns below, forming an ample pediment . . . almost into the shape of those used in architecture . . . Compared to this what are the cathedrals or the palaces built by men!' Banks contrasted the works of man unfavourably with the works of nature, as 'mere models or playthings, imitations as diminutive as his works will always be when compared to those of nature'. The geometrical designs of the architect were seen to be puny when compared with the productions of nature, for 'regularity the only part in which he fancied himself to exceed his mistress, Nature, is here found in her possession, and here it has been for ages undescribed'. Banks had found compensation from having his ambitions thwarted by the navy; and the engraving of *Fingal's Cave in Staffa* published in Pennant's *A Tour in Scotland*, which was prepared by one of Banks' professional draughtsmen following Banks' verbal description, portrayed the geometrical structure of the natural formations of the basalt columns as echoing those of a cathedral. Nature is here depicted in terms of the conventions and patterns of architecture; the 'picturesque' image of Fingal's Cave represents and shapes natural phenomena to conform to the tropes of the visual arts, the aesthetics of nature is subordinated to the aesthetics of architecture. 'The mind can hardly form an idea more magnificent than such a space, supported on each side by ranges of columns; and roofed by the bottoms of those, which have been broke off in order to form it

... the whole is lighted from without'.[114] In *Campi Phlegraei* Hamilton was quick to point to the similarity between the basalt formations of Staffa and those of the island of Castel-a-mare, formed by a current of lava flowing into the sea from Mount Etna, and consisting of 'distinct columns of Basalte in every direction, perpendicular, horizontal, and inclining, like those of Staffa, described by Mr Pennant in his Voyage to the Hebrides'.[115]

The representation of Fingal's Cave as a cathedral-like natural formation was followed in William Daniell's print *The Cave of Fingal* (1807), which shows the entrance to the cave as if the viewer were looking into the nave of a cathedral, with a massive vault-like accumulation of earth forming its roof that rests on regular, closely-connected basalt columns forming its walls and pillars.[116] Daniell subsequently published eight volumes of *A Voyage Round Great Britain* (1814–25); the third volume included an aquatint printed in colour of the *Entrance to Fingal's Cave, Staffa* (1817), in which the 'picturesque' imagery of a cathedral, with nature viewed in mimicry of a work of art, is abandoned (Fig. 7). The basalt columns are reduced in size and are shown as naturally occurring formations rather than architectural structures; the cap of rock and earth forming the roof of the cave is no longer depicted to suggest the vault of a cathedral; nature no longer seems to possess features evocative

7   William Daniell, *Entrance to Fingal's Cave, Staffa.*

of the curious or bizarre inventions of human art. Daniell stated that earlier representations of Staffa, including his own, were 'inadequate to the subject, and in many ways utterly erroneous', hardly surprising since 'it has long been the fashion, in describing any natural curiosity in which regularity is apparent, to contrast it with a work of art'; in these representations the 'optics of a poet's fancy must be requisite to convert the scene before them into the end of an immense cathedral, whose massy roof is supported by stupendous pillars formed with all the regularity of art'.[117]

Daniell linked his new style of landscape drawing to the influence of the fieldwork approach being developed in geology. He cited a paper by the chemist John MacCulloch, 'On Staffa', published in the *Transactions of the Geological Society of London* in 1814, as fostering his new approach, a style of landscape art informed by geology rather than by the conventions of the picturesque: 'Dr MacCulloch observes that the drawings of this cave, which have been engraved, give it an aspect which it is very far from possessing'.[118] The newly founded Geological Society of London advocated fieldwork as the means to resolve disputes such as the question of the aqueous or igneous origin of basalt, and encouraged the development of a visual language for geology. The methodological precept for the new science of geology was stated in the introduction to the first volume of the Society's *Transactions* (1811). Causal hypotheses about geological origins were to be restricted to the discussion of particular formations and were not to be generalised to create a broader natural philosophy: 'it cannot be supposed that the Society should attempt to decide upon the merits of the different theories of the earth that have been proposed'; the Geological Society advocated the pursuit of 'inquiries . . . to serve as a guide to the geological traveller, by pointing out some of the various objects, which it is his province to examine'. Fieldwork rather than speculation and theorising should be the method of geology.[119] While Daniell's aquatint of the *Entrance to Fingal's Cave, Staffa* is more accomplished, even more realistic and topographically accurate than the engraving of the *Entrance to Fingal's Cave, Staffa* that John MacCulloch included in his *A Description of the Western Islands of Scotland* (1819),[120] their intentions were different. Like Daniell, MacCulloch aimed to provide a guide for the traveller and to avoid picturesque exaggeration; but he was concerned to highlight the geology of the island and the cave, and to promote geological understanding. By the time of MacCulloch's study of Staffa the theory of the igneous origin of basalt had been adopted by a number of geologists, and accorded with James Hutton's theory of igneous geology in his *Theory of the Earth* (1788, 1795). But basalt was viewed as a precipitation from water or mud by Robert Jameson in his *A Mineralogy of the Scottish Isles* (1800), following the influential 'Neptunist' theory of Abraham Gottlob Werner in his *Short Classification and Description of the Various Rocks* (1786), which supposed that stratified rocks arose from precipitation into a primeval ocean. Arguing that basalt was a stratified rock, Jameson concluded that basalts were aqueous in origin. Because MacCulloch was by profession a chemist he was, unsurprisingly, broadly sympathetic to the Wernerian theory of aqueous deposition; in his paper 'On Staffa' he emphasised the mineralogical character of the basalt of Staffa as 'more crystalline, and less earthy than that of basalt in general'.

MacCulloch highlighted a new and, he believed, significant observation that he had made of the geology of the island, in finding a 'bed of alluvial matter on some parts of its surface . . . a circumstance before unnoticed'. On the basis of this observation he speculated that it was possible that 'the island of Staffa was elevated from the bottom of the sea in its present detached form, and retaining on its summit a portion of the bed of loose matter deposited under the present waters', the 'ponderous cap . . . which crowns the summit of the grand *façade*' of the cave. But he did not pursue such theoretical issues; in the preface to his *Description of the Western Islands of Scotland* he espoused the objectives of the Geological Society in emphasising that he was concerned to record observations rather than to formulate a theory, for which his observations would however be a necessary preliminary. This was an empirical programme of research and description of nature: 'Such as the facts are, I have however attempted . . . to place them in such a light as to render them useful to those who may possess greater inclination or greater power to arrange them under some general theory'. This professed concern with observational fidelity is manifest in MacCulloch's intention that his drawings should be naturalistic. In his paper 'On Staffa' he comments on the inadequacy of the engraved drawings of Fingal's Cave with which he was familiar – seemingly having the engraving in Pennant's *A Tour in Scotland* and Daniell's *The Cave of Fingal* in mind; these representations give the cave 'an aspect of geometrical regularity which it is far from possessing'.[121]

MacCulloch developed this critique in his *Description of the Western Islands of Scotland*, where he prints topographical sketches. As in his paper 'On Staffa', he disparaged the 'geometrical aspect' with which the basalt columns have been 'commonly represented in drawings . . . that air of architectural regularity which I have censured in the published representations'. His drawing of the *Entrance to Fingal's Cave, Staffa* avoids false geometrical regularity and architectural allusion, and succeeds in its purpose, in showing the geological detail of the basalt formations; in particular, the depiction of the ponderous cap which crowns the summit of the cave complements his description of the 'three distinct beds' of basalt forming the structure of the island's geology, 'the uppermost an irregular mixture of small implicated and bent columns with an amorphous basalt'. He confesses the inadequacy of his drawings of Staffa – 'I dare not illustrate it by engravings as finished and as numerous as it merits'

– and admits that it 'would be no less presumptuous than useless to attempt a description of the picturesque effect of that to which the pencil itself is inadequate'. Reference to the 'picturesque' is an echo of the language of the tourist guidebooks of Pennant, Gilpin and West; in his *A Description of the Western Isles of Scotland* MacCulloch was writing for the traveller 'with a taste for the grand and the beautiful', as well as serving the needs of the geologist. His verbal depiction of landscape scenes utilises the terms of picturesque description, the association of landscape with the conventions of works of art. He draws explicit parallels between landscape and architecture in his account of the geology of the island: the aperture of Fingal's Cave 'terminates above in . . . [a] species of Gothic arch'. He deploys the conventional language of the sublime to convey his impressions to the prospective visitor to the island: 'if this cave were even destitute of that order and symmetry, that richness arising from multiplicity of parts combined with greatness of dimension and simplicity of style, which it possesses; still . . . the profound and fairy solitude of the whole scene, could not fail strongly to impress a mind gifted with any sense of beauty in art or in nature'.

Appealing to the association of ideas, the theory of aesthetics promoted in Archibald Alison's *Essays on the Nature and Principles of Taste* (1790), MacCulloch conceives the aesthetics of landscape as deriving from trains of association, derived in turn from the aesthetic experience of art. Using the language and argument of contemporary aesthetics, he appeals to the analogy between the natural forms of geology and the man-made structures of architecture in his description of the basaltic columnar promontory on the isle of Egg, the 'Scuir of Egg'. He likens the towering pinnacle of the 'huge and black mass' of the rock to 'the castle of some Arabian enchanter built on the clouds and suspended in the air', and finds the 'resemblance to architecture . . . much increased by the columnar structure'. He suggests that the 'association in the mind of the efforts of art with the magnitude of nature' generated the impression of the 'sublimity' of the Scuir; on viewing the rock, the mind generates the 'sense of power', which is 'a fertile source of the sublime', by 'insensibly transferring the operations of nature to the efforts of art'.[122] Whereas the verbal descriptions in MacCulloch's *Description of the Western Islands of Scotland* portray landscape through the imagery of art, his drawings follow the prescription that he had urged in his paper 'On Staffa' addressed to an audience of scientists, and avoid this picturesque aesthetics of nature: consonant with the development of a visual language appropriate to the science of geology, he rejects the images of 'geometrical' and 'architectural regularity' that had portrayed Fingal's Cave in terms of the conventions of picturesque description, and seeks geological accuracy. The changes in landscape art used in topographical illustration between 1770 and 1830 show a shift from an emphasis on a striking or bizarre 'picturesque' feature in the landscape to a decentralised and naturalistic depiction emphasising geological processes, with the rocks shown as part of an environment shaped by natural history.[123]

As a counterpart to the shift in power from a social order based on land-ownership and aristocratic patronage, to institutions of a commercial society fuelled by technological innovations, the power of finance and the optimism of 'improvement', emphasis came to be placed on the appreciation of the land-scape through its control and use. The new commercial class transformed the values of the aristocracy, creating landscape parks and exercising power by enclosing common land for their own agrarian profit. Enclosure moulded the agrarian economy and facilitated farming innovations, but led to the depopulation of the countryside and to the creation of a class of labouring poor. Landscapes were shaped to human convenience through new methods of cultivation and criteria of aesthetic appreciation, with a shift in preference from enclosed gardens to a more informal style of gardening based on the extensive planting of trees, a design seen as being consonant with 'nature'. In smoothing the landscape, clearing terrain and creating new landscape features, the professional landscape gardeners Brown and Repton created a style of gardening, which, while espousing an aesthetic closer to the ebullience of nature, was criticised by the 'picturesque' theorists Price and Knight for its truncation and distortion of nature. Knight based his aesthetics of nature and prescription for garden design on a painter's vision of the landscape: the contemplation of paintings, especially those of Claude Lorrain, would show that only the incorporation of familiar forms in harmony with the natural environment would shape aesthetic order.

The picturesque aesthetic was consonant with the growing fashion for 'sublime' landscapes and 'picturesque' tours in the late eighteenth century. This aesthetic fostered interest in the geological features of landscapes, and in understanding the processes shaping the formation and sublimity of volcanoes, mountain landscapes and the craggy Hebridean islands. With the enthusiasm among the emergent middle class for wilderness, rocky land-scapes and towering mountains, 'picturesque' tours to the mountainous landscapes of the Alps, Scotland and the English Lake District became popular; 'nature' was conceived in terms of the aesthetic categories of the picturesque and the sublime. The new aesthetic is manifest in the depiction of the mountains and volcanoes of Italy in shaping these sublime landscapes. The golden glow of the classical landscape was displaced by awed admiration for the aesthetics of the picturesque and the sublime, which ultimately gave way to naturalistic depiction emphasising the effect of geological processes, with the rocks shown as part of an environment shaped by natural history and geology.

CHAPTER 5

✳

Landscape, 'Truth of Nature'

In 1854 JOHN RUSKIN made his first extended visit to the Alps following his encounter with the Pre-Raphaelite artists, after spending the summer of 1853 having his portrait painted by John Everett Millais at Glenfinlas in Scotland (with disastrous consequences for Ruskin's marriage when his wife Effie left him for Millais). Having given his main attention in previous years to the art and architecture of Venice, Ruskin spent two summer months in Chamonix where he worked on the drawing *Chamonix: Rocks and Vegetation* (1854) (Fig. 8). Ruskin had watched Millais at work on the landscape background to the portrait, encouraging painstaking attention to the minute details of the rocks, vegetation and flowing water in the scene, and had concluded that the application of Pre-Raphaelite principles would preclude the depiction of large Alpine vistas. These painters, he told an Edinburgh audience in 1853, would be led to depict 'mere foreground work' (the drawing of natural objects singly or in groups, rather than to shape an elaborate composition), as against the portrayal of 'evanescent effects and distant sublimities which nothing but the memory can arrest'. But Turner, he declared, 'has done it already'.[1] As Ruskin explained in the third volume of *Modern Painters* (1856), it was the ability to invoke the power of memory that distinguished Turner's capacity to achieve truth and transcend mere mimetic representation in his imaginative response to nature; for Turner was 'the first poet who has, in all their range, understood the grounds of noble emotion which exist in landscape'.[2] Ruskin's own emphasis in his drawings changed from seeking to achieve wide and imaginative compositions to factual studies of nature and architecture, with a meticulous depiction of naturalistic landscape detail.[3] This is apparent in the drawing of the rocks and vegetation in his drawing *Chamonix*, where he records the lichens and the markings on the stone surface of the rock, and indicates the presence of glacial ice, a feature of the Chamonix landscape.[4]

The question of how best to represent the truth of nature became a central issue in landscape aesthetics in the nineteenth century, and involved a reappraisal and critique of picturesque theory. In Wordsworth's Romantic aesthetic the construal of the natural world – of lakes, mountains and trees –

8   John Ruskin, *Chamonix: Rocks and Vegetation*. This may be the drawing Ruskin exhibited in 1878
as 'Old Sketch of Gneiss, with its weeds, in colour (Chamouni)' (*The Works of John Ruskin*, Library
Edition, ed. E.T. Cook and Alexander Wedderburn, 39 vols (London, 1903–12), vol. 13, p. 524, no. 46);
see *Pre-Raphaelite Vision: Truth to Nature*, ed. Allen Staley and Christopher Newall, exh. cat. Tate
Gallery (London, 2004), p. 148.

as analogous to a work of art was displaced by an aesthetic based on the
primacy of nature as unfettered by the artificial structures of human culture.
For Wordsworth and Constable the immediacy of nature transcended the artificial aesthetic categories of the picturesque; the natural world was not to be
represented in terms of the categories of art; rather art was to be rooted in the
contemplation of nature. The Romantic landscape painter (Turner pre-
eminently) came to be valorised for transfiguring the natural world into a
sublime image of the terror and grandeur of nature. In the representation of
nature by the painter, emphasis came to be placed on the portrayal of visual
impressions of colour and the effects of light and shade rather than on the
traditional academic virtues of composition and drawing.[5] As Ruskin drew
upon the work of two of his major heroes, Wordsworth (of whose outlook, as

he represented it, he became critical), and Turner (the outright hero of *Modern Painters*), he integrated the perceptions of poet and painter. He commended them for their clarity of vision in comprehending and communicating the true reality of natural phenomena; but their representation of the truth of nature is seen in aesthetic terms, and Turner has the status of a 'poet' because of his power of imaginative sympathy and engagement. The development of this new aesthetic outlook made the relation between the representation of landscapes in the natural sciences and their depiction in art the focus of debate. Constable pointed to the analogy between painting and natural philosophy; Wordsworth described the Lake District landscape in terms of the lithology, natural history and geology of the mountains; and Ruskin described mountains in terms of his own (idiosyncratic) understanding of geology, envisioning the mountain landscape as a geological and aesthetic unity. For Ruskin, the representation of the truth of nature was to embrace the scientific study of phenomena (which he terms the 'science of *Essence*') and the imaginative grasp necessary to capture reality (the 'science of *Aspects*').[6] An emphasis on 'naturalism' in the sense of fidelity to nature denoted the aesthetic appreciation of landscape.

Naturalism and Landscape Aesthetics: John Constable

As noted in Chapter 2 (p. 47), the picturesque aesthetic came under philosophical critique from Dugald Stewart in his essay 'On the Beautiful' published in his *Philosophical Essays* (1810). Taking issue with Uvedale Price on the design of landscape gardens, he recognises that knowledge acquired from the study of painting may suggest '*hints*' for the improvement of landscape, but warns that 'if recognised as the standard . . . it would infallibly cover the face of the country with a new and systematical species of affectation, not less remote than that of Brown'. Stewart considers that the aesthetic of the picturesque carries the danger of valorising painting over nature: 'in laying out grounds . . . the primary object of a good taste is, not to please the connoisseur, but to please the enlightened admirer and lover of nature'. Landscape painting may suggest landscape improvement, but nature cannot be subordinated to painting: 'let Painting be allowed its due praise in quickening our attention to the beauties of Nature . . . but let our Taste for the beauties be *chiefly* formed on the study of Nature herself'. Nature is simply too immense and various to be subject to the picturesque aesthetic, and he rejects the subordination of the aesthetic appreciation of nature to the aesthetics of painting. For Stewart this follows from the natural theology of design, because a painting as a human artefact cannot match the richness and complexity of created nature. He drives a wedge between nature as a designed artefact and the aesthetics of the picturesque. He asserts that the works of nature are 'impressed . . . with the signatures of Almighty Power, and of Unfathomable Design', and therefore transcend the productions of the artist; and that narrowly human criteria of beauty, unity and simplicity which determine the aesthetic effect of a landscape painting were not to be expected in nature, where variety and diversity, a 'deviation from uniformity', were features consequent upon unlimited creative power. The infinity and variety of nature could not therefore be subsumed under the aesthetics of the painter constrained by inherent human limitations; the aesthetic appreciation of nature can only be found in nature, viewed as the product of design.[7]

Around the turn of the nineteenth century the status of British landscape art was subject to debate over its place in the hierarchy of genres: history painting, portraiture and landscape painting. In his 'Discourses on Art' (1769–90) delivered at the Royal Academy, Joshua Reynolds had placed history painting at the summit of artistic endeavour, while allowing the inferior genres some merit. Writing in 1814 in a review of a biography of Reynolds, Richard Payne Knight contested Reynolds' theory of genres as based on the moral value of history painting, rejecting the traditional supremacy of history over landscape painting. He set out a doctrine of the empirical basis of painting, concerned with the imitation of visual effects rather than the arousal of moral responses: 'Painting is an imitation of nature, as seen by the eye, and not, as known, or perceived by the aid of other senses',[8] giving emphasis to visual impressions of colour and the effects of light and shade in the representation of nature by the painter. But while Knight placed emphasis on sense impressions and visual effects, he did not deny that landscape art embodied a cultural heritage and could arouse emotional responses.[9] The landscape paintings of Nicolas Poussin and Claude Lorrain had placed landscape art within the rich cultural context of classical antiquity, with a range of religious and moral associations. The writings on the 'picturesque' encompassing readings of scenic views, the design of landscape gardens, and the aesthetics of landscape and landscape painting, continued and enlarged these cultural associations in the context of the aesthetic and political concerns of the period, permitting landscape art to engage with a serious moral and political content. In *Pope's Villa at Twickenham* (1808) Turner used imagery drawn from Poussin's *Arcadian Shepherds* of the 1630s to associate the Thames valley with the pastoral melancholy of the classical tradition and to link pictorial beauty and moral virtue. In *The Stour Valley and Dedham Village* (1814), painted for the marriage of the daughter of the squire of his native village, Constable documented agricultural practice – foregrounding a dunghill – while he adjusted the composition to echo the layout of trees in Claude's *Landscape with Dancing Figures* (*The Mill*; 1648). He assimilated the familiar

Suffolk scene to the landscape of classical antiquity, while the prominence of Dedham Church tower in the painting provides associations of piety and Christian iconography.[10]

The relation between the landscape of nature and the power of composition open to the landscape painter is discussed by Archibald Alison in his *Essays on the Nature and Principles of Taste* (1790), which was widely read and ran to six editions by 1825. Alison considers the relation between nature, its manipulation in gardening, and its representation in painting, issues central to 'naturalism' in art. He was concerned to characterise the aesthetic scope of gardening and landscape painting, maintaining that 'nature' provides elements that can be contrived, transformed and rendered aesthetically superior in a work of art. The gardener had the power to execute the dreams of the imagination, to achieve a 'purity and harmony' of composition and 'remove from his landscape whatever is hostile to its effect'; this was 'the great source of the superiority of its productions to the original scenes in nature'. Alison emphasises the importance of design, the gardener's power to shape natural forms into a pattern, 'to awaken an emotion more full, more simple, and more harmonious than any we can receive from the scenes of Nature itself'. But while gardening is aesthetically superior to unimproved nature, the 'art of Landscape painting is yet superior in its effect'. This is because the painter can call upon a range of images as extensive as his imagination will yield, and is not restricted by the limitations imposed by the contingent and intractable materials available to the gardener. 'In gardening, the materials of the scene are few, and these few unwieldy . . . the scanty and intractable materials of Nature. In a landscape, on the contrary, the whole range of scenery is before the eye of the painter. He may . . . unite into one expression, the scattered features with which Nature has feebly marked a thousand situations . . . to improve the expression of real scenery'. The gardener, working with materials to hand, and even more the painter, drawing upon the products of the imagination, have the capacity to excite 'emotion' through 'purity and simplicity of composition', to impose a plan, a design, that can transform the inchoate features of nature into a harmonious composition. It is this power of composition to achieve 'unity of expression' that is the 'great secret' of the power of painting: 'the superiority which it at last assumes over the scenery of Nature, is found to arise in one important respect, from the greater purity and simplicity which its composition can attain'. Alison affirms 'the genius of the Painter' to shape the unity of composition of a painting and arouse 'Emotions of Sublimity and Beauty'.[11] The imposition of design, shown through the purity, simplicity and unity of the scene depicted in a landscape painting, establishes the aesthetic superiority of a scene in a landscape painting to the raw 'scenes in nature'.

Constable read Alison's *Essay* in 1814, writing that 'I am delighted with Alison's book on the nature and principles of Taste'.[12] Constable was a professional artist and did not publish a general theory of aesthetics, but expressed his opinions on the principles of painting in scattered but pithy maxims. Although he rejects Alison's key claim that 'nature' is aesthetically inferior to its depiction in a landscape painting, Alison's philosophical criticism may have helped shape his view of the relation between nature and its representation in works of art.[13] At the core of Constable's aesthetics is his view that nature transcends art in beauty, fecundity and variety, and that the painter should only paint landscape scenes after close study of nature rather than attempt to imitate the work of other painters; but that the power of composition possessed by the artist can have the capacity to heighten the viewer's understanding and appreciation of the natural world. In a letter to his friend John Fisher in 1827, he wrote of the landscape painter Richard Wilson that he 'showed the world, what existed in nature, but which it had never seen before'.[14]

Constable developed this line of argument in the introduction to his issue of mezzotints in *English Landscape* (1833), firmly locating the representation of nature by art, and the power of art to illuminate nature, in the close study of the works of nature rather than 'on the study of departed excellence ... the study of pictures, or the art alone'. By seeking 'perfection at its PRIMITIVE SOURCE, NATURE' the painter could find 'innumerable sources of study, hitherto unexplored, fertile in beauty, and by attempting to display them for the first time, forms a style which is original; thus adding to the Art, qualities of Nature unknown to it before'. Here he seems to echo Alison in arguing for the capacity of the artist to shape features of nature into a new and heightened form; the painter is not a mere copyist or imitator, of nature or of the pictures produced by eminent predecessors. Constable developed this argument in his lectures on landscape painting delivered between 1833 and 1836, where he was concerned to contest the implications of the picturesque aesthetic: 'It appears to me that pictures have been over-valued; held up by a blind admiration as ideal things, and almost as standards by which nature is to be judged rather than the reverse.' Although pictures have the capacity to reveal hitherto unknown features of the natural world, the artist can only draw his power of composition from the study of nature, not from the study of paintings. Constable maintained that 'mere copies of the productions of Nature ... can never be more than servile imitations'; the true artist's relation to nature lies in a capacity for 'selection and combination', and this could only be 'learned from nature herself'. The artist is not a passive and unresponsive observer, nor is art the mirror of nature. The painter's understanding of nature is consequent on his place in a designed universe: 'man is the sole intellectual inhabitant of one vast natural landscape ... he cannot but sympathize with its features'. But the fecundity of nature transcends the human imagination and 'the most sublime productions of the pencil [are] but selections of the forms of nature'. Despite the power of art to awaken a new perception and understanding of the glories of nature, nature provides an inexhaustible fount of images whereas art is confined by the limitations of human imagination and invention. Constable urged painters to look to 'nature herself, who constantly presents us with compositions of her own, far more beautiful than the happiest arranged by human skill'. It was from careful study of nature that the painter could derive the knowledge, to be embodied in works of art, that would awaken the clouded and dormant perceptions of the viewer: '*We see nothing till we truly understand it.*'[15]

In these lectures on landscape painting Constable declared that 'Painting is a science, and should be pursued as an inquiry into the laws of nature. Why, then may not landscapes be considered as a branch of natural philosophy, of which pictures are but the experiments?'[16] In 1836 he delivered his lectures at the Royal Institution, the centre for scientific research and lecturing in London first made famous by Humphry Davy, and subsequently by Michael Faraday (who attended Constable's lectures), which may have prompted him to appeal to the authority of natural philosophy and to make reference to 'experiments' in painting. But Constable rigorously followed his own maxims of seeing through understanding and experiment. His naturalistic portrayal of clouds in pictures such as *The Hay Wain* (1821) and *Hampstead Heath* (1821–2) was based on a thorough study of meteorological science and by painterly experimentation in numerous sketches. Between 1820 and 1822 he made more than 100 studies of sky and clouds at Hampstead Heath, working in oils and in the open air. His sky studies may well be described as experiments in lighting, colour and cloud form, capturing the transient appearance of meteorological phenomena; his dated and timed sketches match the contemporary weather records, and show that his sky studies were undertaken in preparation for his major landscape pictures. Constable possessed a copy of the second edition of Thomas Forster's *Researches about Atmospheric Phaenomena* (1815), 'corrected and enlarged with a series of engravings, illustrative of the modifications of the clouds, etc', which offered descriptions and explanations of meteorological phenomena. The first chapter of Forster's text gave an account of Luke Howard's system for the classification of clouds as set out in the *Essay on the Modification of Clouds* (1804), where Howard introduced terms such as 'stratus' and 'cumulus'. Constable's annotations to Forster's book suggest that he only studied the parts of the text that related to Howard's classification; and while it is unclear when he read and annotated Forster's *Atmospheric Phaenomena*, or whether he subsequently read Howard's *Essay* itself, his scientific interest is clear, and his engagement with meteorology was significant.[17]

Writing to John Fisher on 23 October 1821, Constable set out the scope of this interest:

> I have done a great deal of skying – I am determined to conquer all the difficulties and that most arduous one among the rest . . .. That Landscape painter who does not make his skies a very material part of his composition – neglects to avail himself of one of his greatest aids . . .. Certainly if the Sky is *obtrusive* – (as mine are) it is bad, but if they are *evaded* (as mine are not) it is worse, they must and always shall with me make an effectual part of the composition. It will be difficult to name a class of Landscape – in which the sky is not the '*key note*', the *standard of* '*scale*' – and the chief '*Organ of sentiment* '. . .. The sky is the '*source of light*' in nature – and governs every thing.[18]

In his introduction to *English Landscape* he declared that the light and shade of 'the summer skies and autumnal clouds' expressed the drama and emotion of the English landscape, where 'the Student of Nature may daily watch her endless varieties of effect'. In his portrayal of the sky and clouds, and the play and balance of light and shade, he aimed to display 'the CHIAR'OSCURO OF NATURE, to mark the influence of light and shadow upon Landscape . . . to show its use and power as a medium of expression, so as to note "the day, the hour, the sunshine, and the shade"'. The landscape painter could only portray the realism, and express the emotional power of nature, by understanding the phenomena of the natural world. Constable sought to capture the transient and evanescent in nature, 'to give "to one brief moment caught from fleeting time", a lasting and sober existence'.[19] Writing to his friend (and future biographer) the painter C.R. Leslie in 1833, he spoke of the qualities that he aimed to achieve in his pictures, to capture the momentary flickering of 'light – dews – breezes – bloom – and freshness; not any one of which has yet been perfected on the canvas of any painter in the world'.[20]

In his letter to Fisher on 'skying', Constable turns from expressing his concern to capture the grand shaping influence of the sky on the landscape to reflect on his love for the mundane details of the humanised landscape in the region of his childhood around East Bergholt and the Stour Valley in Suffolk, 'the sound of water escaping from Mill dams . . .. Willows, Old rotten Banks, slimy posts, & brickwork . . . I shall never cease to paint such places'. He adds that 'I should paint my own places best – Painting is but another word for feeling . . .. They made me a painter'.[21] Constable's evocation of landscape, in awakening feeling by the recovery of the emotions embedded in the memory of features in the landscape, has often been portrayed as the pictorial counterpart of Wordsworth's poetry, and as displaying a Romantic sensibility in affirming the primacy and immanent unity of nature, and the harmony between man and nature.[22]

Constable's favoured landscape (already known during his life as 'Constable's country')[23] was very different from Wordsworth's Lakeland of slate and mountain. In striking contrast to his contemporary Turner, who sought out picturesque views in Britain and sublime Alpine scenery as subjects for his paintings, Constable painted scenes that were immediately familiar to him: the Stour Valley, Hampstead Heath, Brighton and Salisbury. In a letter to Fisher in 1824 he declared that 'grand & affecting natural landscape' was 'a scene most unsuitable for a picture'; to try to represent magnificent scenery would be to 'contend with nature', and nature could not be matched. It was the 'business of a painter' rather to shape a work of art from humbler scenes of nature so as 'to make something out of nothing, in attempting which he must almost of necessity become poetical'.[24] Commenting on the drawings and watercolours Constable made while on a picturesque tour to the Lake District in 1806, when he applauded the magnificence of the Lakeland scenery,[25] Leslie judged that they 'abound in grand and solemn effects of light, shade, and colour, but from these studies he never painted any considerable picture, for his mind was formed for a different class of landscape . . . he required villages, churches, farmhouses, and cottages'. Leslie reported that 'I have heard him say that the solitude of mountains oppressed his spirits.'[26] Though Constable was commissioned to paint landscape parks, as in *Wivenhoe Park, Essex* (1816), he disliked the artificiality of contrived landscape: 'I never had a desire to see sights', he told Fisher in 1822, 'and a gentleman's park – is my aversion. It is not beauty because it is not nature.' [27]

'Nature' for Constable was the smiling landscape of pasture, hedges, woodland, rivers and canals, especially the agrarian and social landscape of East Anglia. His landscape paintings portray scenes of the familiar, quotidian countryside, paintings that reveal numerous topographical and human details, of 'Willows, Old rotten Banks, slimy posts, & brickwork', fragmentary elements that form part of a convincing whole because these are real landscapes not an assemblage of disparate elements artfully joined to form an unreal if harmoniously contrived scene. These landscapes seem connected and unified, because they are inhabited and worked – his 'own places'. A comparison of Gainsborough's *Wooded Landscape with a Peasant Resting* (c. 1747) with Constable's *The Stour Valley and Dedham Village* (1814) and *Flatford Mill* (1816–17) shows that Gainsborough does not portray an actual location and does no more than make generic distinctions between trees, and deploys light to shape the composition and evoke a sense of timelessness and harmony; whereas Constable depicts specific scenes in Suffolk with natural features individualised in faithful detail, and light and colour are not organised to direct the viewer's gaze to highlight specific features of the composition. With

Constable there is no ordered shaping of the viewer's response to the scene, no sense of an imposed unifying principle of design, but rather the artist's representation of a real scene at an actual moment and place, a timeless order being portrayed by the cultivated beauty and realism of the scene depicted.[28]

But Constable's paintings are pictures, not mirrors of nature, and are shaped by artistic practice, by the composition of the scenes depicted and in particular by the balance of light and shade across the landscape, 'the chiar'oscuro of nature'. He strove to escape from the visual convention of the brown tonal gradation of eighteenth-century landscape painting, using lighter tones, greens rather than browns, to render the play of sunlight on pasture, as in *Wivenhoe Park, Essex*. In his lectures on landscape painting Constable observed that 'I have endeavoured to draw a line between genuine art and mannerism, but even the greatest painters have never been wholly untainted by manner', the tradition of painting to which every artist is heir; but he sees this as a taint, to be contested (and overcome) by the artist's 'selection and combination . . . learned from nature herself'.[29] He was aware of the tension between the weight of artistic tradition and the direct observation of nature from the outset of his career. In a letter of 1799 (written from Gainsborough's home town of Ipswich) he declared that Suffolk 'is a most delightful country for a landscape painter, I fancy I see Gainsborough in every hedge and hollow tree'. Three years later he declared that while the study of 'the Great Masters' was important to the aspirant painter, 'still Nature is the fountain's head, the source from whence all originality must spring'. He looked to make 'laborious studies of nature' to create a 'natural painture'.[30]

The term 'naturalism' was not generally used to denote a style of painting (concerned with fidelity to nature) in the early nineteenth century. 'Picturesque' had wide, encompassing connotations, but a distinction between 'picturesque' and 'natural' was drawn by William Hazlitt in his *Table Talk* (1821–2): 'natural in visible objects' is that which is 'ordinarily presented to the senses', while the picturesque is 'that which stands out, and catches the attention by some striking peculiarity'.[31] This sense of 'natural' characterises Constable's aim to make 'something out of nothing' in his landscape paintings; but he was also concerned with pictorial naturalism in the sense of fidelity to nature.

In seeking to characterise the means through which Constable achieved the naturalism of his landscape paintings, Ernst Gombrich notes that although 'Constable saw the English landscape in terms of Gainsborough's paintings' he made advances in grasping that 'only experimentation can show the artist a way out of the prison of style toward a greater truth'. He concludes that for Constable experimentation opened the door to understanding: 'Only through trying out new effects never seen before in paint could he learn about nature.

Making still comes before matching.' Gombrich discusses the sketches that Constable carefully copied from the drawing book by Alexander Cozens, the eighteenth-century landscape painter who published a series of schemata for clouds. Through working over a variety of combinations and permutations of cloud forms, Constable was alerted to a schema, a visual classification that helped to increase his awareness of the possible ways in which the sky and clouds could be represented.[32] Constable copied these sketches from Cozens shortly after his own direct studies of clouds and sky at Hampstead Heath. To improve the pictorial effectiveness of the skies in his paintings, he joined the study of nature, advances in the science of meteorology and the practical guidance in technique offered by a fellow painter. His sketches of skies and clouds are experiments in which various possibilities of representation are explored, and he draws upon direct observation and study of technique to accomplish his end. He conceives painting to be a science, an inquiry into the laws of nature, and pictures to be forms of experiment; and he invokes the norms and intellectual authority of natural philosophy to establish the fidelity to nature of the landscape painter. His studies of skies and clouds had made clear the transient and evanescent features of the natural world; just as natural philosophy seeks, as with Luke Howard, to classify and understand meteorological phenomena, Constable sought to bring such transient phenomena within the compass of painting; and (in his view) this can only be done by the close study of nature and through 'experiments'.

The allegorical cloud paintings of a (younger) contemporary English landscape artist, Samuel Palmer, which express a religious and visionary aesthetics of nature, bear a striking contrast with the naturalism of Constable's clouds and skies. The crucial difference in their aesthetics of nature can be located in Constable's analogy between landscape painting and natural philosophy; in other respects Constable and Palmer held some values in common. They were both political and ecclesiastical conservatives; religious and political allegorical meanings can be read into many of Constable's paintings; and when Constable read Alison's *Essays on the Nature and Principles of Taste* he expressed approval because he found an aesthetics conceived in terms of design and natural theology, judging that Alison 'considers us as endowed with minds capable of comprehending the "beauty and sublimity of the material world" only as the means of leading us to *religious sentiment*'.[33] As a boy Palmer had made a careful study of Cozens' drawings of cloud compositions, and in 1828 he expressed admiration for Constable's representation of clouds; but in Palmer's paintings such as *The Valley with a Bright Cloud* (1825), *The White Cloud* and *The Bright Cloud* (both painted c.1833–4), the billowing and massive cumulus clouds are not portrayed realistically but symbolically in expressing a religious vision of providential plenitude, the manifestation of the divine in nature.[34] This is a visionary aesthetics of nature remote from the naturalism through which Constable appeals to the world view of natural philosophy in seeking to make landscape art 'become poetical'.

The Language of Landscape: William Wordsworth

William Wordsworth's *A Guide through the District of the Lakes* (to use the title it was finally given in 1835) has its origins in a short text written to accompany the engravings of Lakeland scenery issued by Joseph Wilkinson in his *Select Views in Cumberland, Westmoreland, and Lancashire* (1810). In 1820 Wordsworth supplemented his brief guide for the tourist with a topographical description of the region, enlarging and revising this work in three further editions by 1835. In the original publication in the *Select Views* Wordsworth described a tour through the region, making reference to Wilkinson's drawings to which his letterpress was a complement; in his enlarged text, detached from the drawings, he naturally eliminated these references. But it is a striking feature of the *Guide* that Wordsworth does not seek to communicate his impressions of the mountains and lakes by the customary evocation of paintings and appeal to the picturesque aesthetic, the style typified by the guides of his predecessors Thomas West and William Gilpin. In his *Guide to the Lakes* West describes the approach to the Lakes from the south across Morecambe Bay, beginning the visit with Coniston, in the following terms: 'By this course the lakes lie in an order more pleasing to the eye, and grateful to the imagination. The change of scenes is from what is pleasing, to what is surprising, from the delicate and elegant touches of CLAUDE, to the noble scenes of POUSSIN, and, from these, to the stupendous, romantic ideas of SALVATOR ROSA.'[35] The aesthetic appreciation of the scenery is communicated by the evocation of landscape art.

Wordsworth, by contrast, avoids any reference to paintings or painters and the terms of the picturesque aesthetic in describing the same journey across the Sands from Lancaster towards Coniston: 'The Stranger, from the moment he sets foot upon those Sands, seems to leave the turmoil and traffic of the world behind him; and, crossing from the majestic plain whence the sea has retired, he beholds, rising apparently from its base, the cluster of mountains among which he is going to wander, and towards whose recesses, by the Vale of Coniston, he is gradually and peacefully led.'[36] In his *Guide* Wordsworth lays emphasis on the traveller's emotions in approaching the Lakes, and on the forms of landscape anticipated and observed; his descriptions of the scenery are naturalistic and are couched in clear and direct language, presenting the landscape as it is encountered; by promoting 'habits of more exact and considerate observation' he aimed to awaken and shape the emotional and aesthetic experience of the attentive traveller.

In giving an outline of the region Wordsworth places emphasis on the character of the landscape rather than simply offering a route for tourists to observe a series of picturesque views. He begins his description of the scenery of the Lakes by portraying the unity of the 'country as formed by nature', and to describe the topography of the region he finds a point of observation that he describes as a 'station', using West's term for a viewpoint overlooking a picturesque scene. But Wordsworth's 'station' is imaginary and geographical, permitting a panoramic view of the topography of the entire region. He asks the reader 'to place himself with me, in imagination, upon some given point ... let us suppose our station to be a cloud hanging midway' between the mountains of Great Gable and Scafell, from which he sees the valleys of the region radiating out 'like spokes from the nave of a wheel'. From this vantage point he finds 'in the forms and surfaces, first of the swelling grounds, next of the hills and rocks, and lastly of the mountains – an ascent of almost regular gradation, from elegance and richness, to their highest point of grandeur and sublimity', presenting to the observer 'every possible embellishment of beauty, dignity, and splendour, which light and shadow can bestow upon objects so diversified'.[37] Wordsworth's aesthetic division of the landscape as gradually rising to the mountains (in a sequence of elegance, richness and grandeur) corresponds to West's evocation of landscapes held to be characteristic in turn of the paintings of Claude, Poussin and Rosa (described in turn as elegant, noble and stupendous); but Wordsworth deliberately avoids the customary reference to painters characteristic of the vocabulary of picturesque aesthetics. His aesthetics of landscape is based on fidelity to nature unmediated by the categories of art.

Although Wordsworth eschews allusion to paintings as a means of characterising the scenery, his naturalistic descriptions of the landscape in the *Guide* are enhanced with literary illustrations, drawing freely on his own poetry including extracts from the (unpublished) text of *The Prelude*. In the Preface to the 1802 edition of *Lyrical Ballads* Wordsworth explained that the poet 'considers man and nature as essentially adapted to each other, and the mind of man as naturally the mirror of the fairest and most interesting properties of nature'.[38] In the *Guide* he draws on poetry and the capacity of the poet to converse with nature in place of the painterly vocabulary of the picturesque, and uses the power of language to convey the majesty of mountains: 'in the combinations which they make, towering above each other, or lifting themselves in ridges like the waves of a tumultuous sea, and in the beauty and variety of their surfaces and colours, they are surpassed by none'. His language makes full use of the terms of eighteenth-century discourse on the aesthetics of nature: the beautiful and the sublime, beauty defined (with Hutcheson) as uniformity amidst variety; but he transforms this language into a naturalistic aesthetics. The mountains, valleys and lakes provide a 'variegated landscape', in which the effect of the 'awful and sublime' mountains is softened by the 'beauty' of the valleys where rivers shape the variety of the landscape forms, so mountains and valleys meld to form a unity. 'Sublimity is the result of Nature's first dealings with the superficies of the earth; but the general tendency of her subsequent operations is towards the production of beauty, by a multiplicity of symmetrical parts uniting in a consistent whole.'

Wordsworth conceives mountains as the primitive 'mould in which things were originally cast' in the formation of the earth; and following the categories of eighteenth-century aesthetics he judges the mountains as 'awful and sublime'. But this pristine landscape has been transformed from its stark majesty by the '*secondary* agents of nature, ever at work', which have moulded the 'primitive frame' of the mountains into a pleasing variety of softer land-scape forms. By secondary agents he means rocks falling from cliffs into the valleys, and the effect of rivers, lakes and woods in shaping the landscape. Rocky shapes lie like 'stranded ships' in the lakes, peninsulas are 'crested with native wood', rivers deposit gravel and are gradually shaped into curves, a promontory forms a 'sweeping outline that contrasts boldly with the longi-tudinal base of the steeps on the opposite shore', introducing 'into the midst of desolation and barrenness, the elements of fertility'. These secondary agents of nature, which soften and shape into a harmonious unity the variety of elements that form the Lakeland landscape, are subsumed under the aesthetic category of 'beauty'. Wordsworth melds a geological with an aesthetic reading of the landscape, the primitive sublimity of the mountains being overlaid by the contours of beauty.[39] His descriptions of Lakeland scenery and his aesthetics of landscape are permeated by geological imagery.[40]

To mitigate the rigid, geometrical image of the valleys as likened to the spokes of a wheel, Wordsworth emphasises that they are generally winding (a feature associated, since Hogarth's graceful serpentine curve of the 'line of beauty', with the aesthetics of beauty), 'the windings of many being abrupt and intricate'. He observes that the Lakeland valleys differ from Welsh valleys in not being formed by the juxtaposition of the bases of the mountains, but that instead they form a level plain that he likens to the 'surface of a lake'. He perceptively describes a feature of Lake District valleys – Great Langdale is a striking example, with its flat floor and steep rocky sides forming a U-shaped profile – which came to be understood as the effect of glaciation. He describes the rocks and hills in these valleys, carved into basins by glaciers, as rising 'up like islands from the plain'; the moraines and rocks (like the Bowder Stone in Borrowdale) were deposited in the valleys by glacier ice. He describes the 'bottom of these vallies' as forming 'mostly a spacious and gently declining area, apparently level as the floor of a temple'. Wordsworth's language here suggests that in his imagination the Lakeland landscape has become sancti-fied, that the mountains and valleys form a 'temple' of nature. He does not make further use of religious imagery or language; nature is sanctified in its immanence, and he conveys the intensity of its impact through precise and naturalistic descriptions of the landscape. He characterises the mountains by an exact description of their lithology, natural history and geology, beginning with their overall appearance: 'the general *surface* of the mountains is turf, rendered rich and green by the moisture of the climate'. He then turns to describe their underlying geological structure: 'the mountains are for the most part composed of the stone by mineralogists called schist'. Having explained the substance of the rocks forming the mountains, he can then describe their appearance: 'the predominant *colour* of their *rocky* parts is bluish, or hoary grey – the general tint of the lichens with which the bare stone is encrusted'. Finally he draws attention to a distinctive feature of the lithology of the rocks of these mountains, that 'with this blue or grey colour is frequently intermixed a red tinge, proceeding from the iron that interveins the stone, and impregnates the soil'.

With these descriptions Wordsworth aimed to promote 'habits of more exact and considerate observation than, as far as the writer knows, have hitherto been applied to local scenery'. He is especially alert to the influence of the landscape of mountains, valleys and lakes on the climate, finding that the evanescent effects of mist and dew render a mysterious quality to the landscape scenery: 'the effect indeed of mist or haze, in a country of this character, is like that of magic', and the 'vapours exhaling from the lakes and meadows after sun-rise, in a hot season, or, in moist weather, brooding upon the heights, or descending towards the valleys with inaudible motion, give a visionary character to everything around them'. Like Constable, he celebrates the interplay of light and shadow on the landscape, finding this especially manifest in the Lake District and as characteristic of the scenic pleasures of the region: 'I do not indeed know any tract of country in which, within so narrow a compass, may be found an equal variety in the influences of light and shadow upon the sublime or beautiful features of landscape'. And like Constable he is struck by the appearance of the clouds above the mountains 'lifting up suddenly their glittering heads from behind rocky barriers'; he found the effect to be 'not easily managed in a picture', but 'how glorious are they in nature'; the forms of 'fleecy clouds resting upon the hill-tops' are 'pregnant with imagination for the poet'.[41] Nature takes precedence over its pictorial representation. The clouds, skies, the play and balance of light and shade, reveal the drama and emotional power of the landscape.

In the displacement from West's 'picturesque' to his own panoramic, topographical and naturalistic view of the Lakeland landscape, Wordsworth incorporates a further element, exploring the relationship between the landscape and its inhabitants, showing how 'the hand of man has acted upon the surface of the inner regions of this mountainous country, as incorporated with and subservient to the powers and processes of nature'. He considers that the traditional cottages of the region, which are constructed from unhewn stone and slates, seem to have 'risen, by an instinct of their own, out of the native rock', and 'in their very form call to mind the processes of nature' and 'appear to be received into the bosom of living principles of things'. But he sees innovation as the enemy of the traditional landscape, pointing to the planting of larch as a cash crop and the building of an Italianate house on Belle Isle in Windermere, and cites Thomas Gray's description of the peace and rusticity of Grasmere of the 1760s as the 'unsuspected paradise . . . in its neatest and most becoming attire'. Wordsworth comments adversely on the developments of the last fifty years: 'It was well for the undisturbed pleasure of the Poet that he had no forebodings of the change which was soon to take place; and it might have been hoped that these words . . . would have secured scenes so consecrated from profanation.'

Wordsworth concludes that the harmony between the landscape and its inhabitants is threatened by the incursion of new settlers, following the decline of cottage industry; and that the way of life of the Lakeland farmers is threatened by the 'invention and universal application of machinery', for mechanisation and the growth of the factory system had halted the profit that farmers had gained from spinning wool in their own houses, threatening the Lakeland economy. He predicts as a consequence the decline of farming and the purchase of land by 'gentry, either strangers or natives'. He expresses the hope that a 'better taste should prevail among these new proprietors', that 'skill and knowledge' should be deployed to assist the settlers to adhere to the 'path of simplicity and beauty along which, without design and unconsciously, their humble predecessors have moved'. He appeals to a wider constituency to join him in promoting this wish, 'persons of pure taste throughout the whole island', who by their visits 'to the Lakes in the North of England testify that they deem the district a sort of national property, in which every man has a right and interest who has an eye to perceive and a heart to enjoy'.[42]

In promoting a pattern of landscape improvement that would harmoniously join the landscape to its human habitation, Wordsworth's approach shows similarities to the social attitudes voiced by Uvedale Price.[43] This concern with the embodiment of cultural identity in the landscape is apparent in the poem 'Home at Grasmere', composed between 1800 and 1806 but not published until 1888. In this poem Wordsworth describes his arrival with his sister Dorothy in Grasmere in December 1799, and evokes a profound sense of harmony between the natural world and humankind. He sanctifies the valley, which embraces him in guardianship:

Embrace me then, ye Hills, and close me in;
Now in the clear and open day I feel
Your guardianship; I take it to my heart;
'Tis like the solemn shelter of the night.

There is unity between poet and landscape; in returning to nature the poet is enclosed by his environment.[44] His perception of the landscape of the valley is emotional and environmental, remote from the picturesque aesthetics espoused by Price; Wordsworth's concern is with his place in the landscape, and with the cultural identity of the village community in its relation to the natural environment. He extends this sense of community to the wild creatures that share the landscape with its human inhabitants, lamenting the disappearance of two swans and fearing human betrayal of the wild creatures that inhabit the shared environment.[45]

In the poems of his early maturity in *Lyrical Ballads* (1798) Wordsworth does not describe nature in the sense of recording detailed observations of the natural world, but evokes the experience of nature as mediated by memory. In the Preface to the second edition of 1800, the edition where he first stated his authorship on the title page, Wordsworth famously maintains that 'Poetry is the spontaneous overflow of powerful feelings: it takes its origin from emotion recollected in tranquillity'.[46] In his poem 'Lines Written a Few Miles above Tintern Abbey' (1798) he revisits the scene of a tour to the Wye that he had made five years earlier. The 'picturesque' tour of the Wye Valley and the ruins of Tintern Abbey had formed the subject of the first of William Gilpin's published guides, *Observations on the River Wye* (1782). Gilpin found the abbey to be 'a very inchanting piece of scenery', finding that 'Nature has now made it her own'. But he recorded a sense of disappointment, for the view would have been 'more picturesque' if the 'area, unadorned, had been left with all its rough fragments of ruin scattered round', and he even envisaged – if only in the imagination – judiciously wielding a mallet to mitigate the 'vulgarity' of the shape of the surviving walls.[47] Wordsworth's imaginative response was very different, as he described his early sensual response to nature and the loss of his youthful ability to feel 'aching joys' and 'dizzy raptures' in the pleasure of nature:

For I have learned
To look on nature, not as in the hour
Of thoughtless youth, but hearing oftentimes
The still, sad music of humanity,
Not harsh nor grating, though of ample power
To chasten and subdue.

The natural and human landscapes are intertwined, prompting his awareness of an agency that permeates and integrates the natural and human worlds, a unifying 'presence that disturbs me with the joy / Of elevated thoughts; a sense sublime / Of something far more deeply interfused'. He finds this inherent power permeating all natural things in the features of the natural world associated with the sense of the sublime, in the vastness of the ocean and the immensity of the sky and the heavens, and it infuses and enervates both mind and matter. Its dwelling

> . . . is the light of setting suns,
> And the round ocean, and the living air,
> And the blue sky, and in the mind of man,
> A motion and a spirit, that impels
> All thinking things, all objects of all thought,
> And rolls through all things.

His awareness of this power in nature means that he is still a 'lover of the meadows and the woods, / And mountains; and of all that we behold / From this green earth'; and he now recognises 'In nature and the language of the sense, / The anchor of my purest thoughts, the nurse, / The guide, the guardian of my heart, and soul / Of all my moral being'. This leads him to an affirmation, a 'prayer' addressed to his 'dear, dear sister' Dorothy:

> Nature never did betray
> The heart that loved her; 'tis her privilege,
> Through all the years of this our life, to lead
> From joy to joy.[48]

This is not a picturesque vision of the ruins of the abbey, but a meditation of individual feeling and consciousness, leading from personal memory and reflection to the evocation of the universal, found in nature. In the poem written in 1804 and known after 1815 as 'Ode: Intimations of Immortality', Wordsworth again recollects his youthful perceptions of the glories of nature:

> There was a time when meadow, grove, and stream,
> The earth, and every common sight,
> To me did seem
> Apparelled in celestial light,
> The glory and the freshness of a dream.
> It is not now as it has been of yore; – . . .
> The things which I have seen I can now see no more.

He claims his youthful delight in nature and landscape arose from 'intimations of immortality', recreating his emotions through memory and spiritualising the material world in a concluding paean to nature:

> And oh ye Fountains, Meadows, Hills, and Groves,
> Think not of any severing of our loves!
> Yet in my heart of hearts I feel your might;
> I only have relinquished one delight
> To live beneath your more habitual sway.

The final lines of the poem express the sensibility that, for his Victorian readers, identified Wordsworth as a nature poet: 'To me the meanest flower that blows can give / Thoughts that do often lie too deep for tears.'[49]

The work now considered to be Wordsworth's masterpiece, his autobiographical poem *The Prelude*, was completed in 1805 but not published; it was conceived as a preliminary to a greater philosophical poem which was never finished, and the poem was issued after extensive reworking and revision in July 1850, three months after his death. In Book VIII of the 1805 *Prelude*, 'Retrospect – love of nature leading to love of mankind', Wordsworth transposes the pastoral from 'Arcadia' to the 'hoary grey' rocks and green turf of the Lakeland hills. In placing the way of life of Lakeland shepherds in the high cultural tradition of classical and Renaissance pastoral, Wordsworth enlarges his poetic project in *Lyrical Ballads*. As he explained in the Preface to the second edition of 1800, it was his aim 'to make the incidents of common life interesting by tracing in them . . . the primary laws of our nature', and he had chosen low and rustic life 'because in that situation the essential passions of the heart find a better soil . . . [and] are incorporated with the beautiful and permanent forms of nature'. The simple language of men arises 'out of repeated experience and regular feelings [and] is a more permanent and a far more philosophical language' than the customary discourse of poetry.[50] There are echoes of Wordsworth's earlier political commitments in this manifesto for a new poetic voice. The 'still, sad music of humanity' evoked in 'Tintern Abbey' is embodied in universal values which Wordsworth finds in nature; and in 'Home in Grasmere' and in the *Guide through the District of the Lakes* he integrates the landscape and rural life, finding social life and community in nature and the habitation of the landscape, transferring to nature the revolutionary ideals for humanity which had withered following his political disillusion with the revolution in France.[51]

In *The Prelude* Wordsworth valorises Lakeland landscape and the lives of the shepherds who work its hill farms by appropriating and transforming the tradition of pastoral poetry to assimilate the familiar landscape of his childhood and the occupations of its rustic inhabitants. In 'A Discourse on Pastoral

Poetry' (1717) Alexander Pope had observed that in the pastoral idiom 'we are not to describe our shepherds as shepherds at this day really are, but as they may be conceiv'd then to have been', and to enter an 'illusion . . . in exposing the best side only of a shepherd's life, and in concealing its miseries'.[52] Wordsworth allows no illusions about the realities of rural life; but he dignifies and gives cultural resonance to these severities by invoking the tradition of pastoral poetry. He contrasts the lives of the shepherds with the pastoral imagery of the golden age of Arcadia: 'And Shepherds were the men who pleased me first; / Not such as, in Arcadian fastnesses / Sequestered, handed down among themselves, / So ancient poets sing, the golden age'. This is the Arcadia of Virgil's tenth Eclogue, and Wordsworth also draws the contrast with the golden landscape of the Arcadia of Renaissance pastoral: 'Nor such, a second race, allied to these, / As Shakespeare in the wood of Arden placed / . . . Nor such as Spenser fabled.'

By contrast, Wordsworth's shepherds inhabit the real landscape of his childhood in the Lake District: 'the rural custom / And manners which it was my chance to see / In childhood were severe and unadorned, / The unluxuriant produce of a life / Intent on little but substantial needs, / Yet beautiful, and beauty that was felt.' This is not an image of the golden age; but Wordsworth uses classical and Renaissance pastoral as a basis for the cultural assimilation of the realities and values of rural life. He fosters the cultural enlargement of the inhabited and worked landscape of Lakeland by developing the pastoral theme to incorporate the husbandry and landscape of farming depicted in Virgil's *Georgics*:

> Smooth life had flock and shepherd in old time,
> Long springs and tepid winters on the banks
> Of delicate Galesus; and no less
> Those scattered along Adria's myrtle shores:
> Smooth life the herdsman, and his snow-white herd
> To triumphs and to sacrificial rites
> Devoted, on the inviolable stream
> Of rich Clitumnus.

The Galesus and Clitumnus are rivers mentioned in the *Georgics*, the Clitumnus celebrated for the 'milk-white herds' of cattle on its banks, the Galesus where the poet recalls a farmer struggling with a patch of land unsuited for pasturage, ploughing, or the vine, yet his happiness in his simple banquet 'equalled the wealth of kings'. Wordsworth's northern shepherds and farmers do not enjoy the 'smooth life' of their Italian forbears; yet like the farmer on the banks of the Galesus, their happiness is worth a royal treasury in their struggle to eke out a living in the harsh and unforgiving northern landscape:

Yet, hail to you,
Your rocks and precipices! Ye that seize
The heart with firmer grasp! Your snows and streams
Ungovernable, and your terrifying winds,
That howled so dismally when I have been
Companionless among your solitudes!
There 'tis the shepherd's task the winter long
To wait upon the storms: of their approach
Sagacious, from the height he drives his flock
Down into sheltering coves, and feeds them there
Through the hard time.[53]

Wordsworth here creates a pastoral poetry of the sublime.[54]

In the opinion of Wordsworth's readers during the latter part of his life, *The Excursion* (1814) was his most substantial achievement. The poem was influential – despite Francis Jeffrey's (in)famous summary dismissal in the *Edinburgh Review*, 'This will never do'[55] – because it seemed to be the most sustained and complete statement of his philosophy of nature, and it was for its spiritual power that Wordsworth's poetry came to be valued.[56] In this poem Wordsworth gave voice to his philosophy of the unity and harmony of man and nature:

What soul was his, when, from the naked top
Of some bold headland, he beheld the sun
. . . his spirit drank
The spectacle: sensation, soul, and form,
All melted into him; they swallowed up
His animal being; in them did he live,
And by them did he live; they were his life.

And he powerfully expressed a doctrine of the immanence of a spirit of nature as permeating all reality:

To every form of being is assigned . . .
An *active* Principle: – howe'er removed
From sense and observation, it subsists
In all things, in all natures; in the stars
Of azure heaven, the unenduring clouds,
In flower and tree, in every pebbly stone
That paves the brooks, the stationary rocks,
The moving waters, and the invisible air.[57]

But Wordsworth's rhapsodies on the active powers immanent in the fabric of nature troubled some commentators, because he could be understood to be expressing pantheism and seemed to disregard Christian doctrine. This unease was expressed by an early reviewer of *The Excursion*, the poet James Montgomery: 'We do not mean to infer that Mr Wordsworth excludes from his system the salvation of man, as revealed in the Scriptures, but it is evident that he has not made "Jesus Christ the chief corner-stone" of it'. The acerbic John Wilson (Christopher North) asserted that Wordsworth 'certainly cannot be called a Christian poet', and that *The Excursion* 'would puzzle the most ingenious to detect much, or any, Christian religion'. The diarist Henry Crabb Robinson noted that 'Wordsworth's own religion . . . would not satisfy either a religionist or a sceptic', and that Wordsworth had 'no need of a Redeemer'.[58] Coleridge, writing in 1820 with the advantage of their early intimacy, commented adversely that 'the vague misty, rather than mystic, Confusion of God with the World & the accompanying Nature-worship . . . is the trait in Wordsworth's poetic works that I most dislike'. More absurd and irritating was 'the odd introduction of the popular, almost the vulgar, Religion in his later publications', which Coleridge's son Hartley had likened to 'the popping in . . . of the old man with a beard'.[59] In 1803 Coleridge recorded a conversation in which Wordsworth 'spoke so irreverently so malignantly of the Divine Wisdom, that it overset me', and he questioned whether natural theologians such as William Paley would have 'spoken of God' as Wordsworth 'spoke of Nature',[60] a telling anecdote dating from Wordsworth's most productive period.

Encouraged by Coleridge, Wordsworth found philosophical aspiration to be formative in shaping his vocation as a poet,[61] and in making nature's transcendent reality (in place of design and divine wisdom) central to his poetic vision he broke the link between the aesthetics of nature and the language of natural theology, asserting in its place an aesthetics of the sublime immediacy and immanence of the active powers permeating nature. Wordsworth (like Coleridge) was averse to the mechanistic structures of design and natural theology, but Coleridge, whose intellectual voyage had led him away from pantheism, found that his friend's philosophy of nature confused 'God with the World' and embodied 'Nature-worship' which, according to this charge, was pantheistic. But if *The Excursion* was found by some critics to be not truly compatible with Christian doctrine, the theology of the poem was sufficiently ambiguous and embracing to accommodate it, and by the 1830s Wordsworth became publicly identified with Anglican orthodoxy.

In the *Guide through the District of the Lakes* Wordsworth had defended the landscape and the integrity of the way of life of its inhabitants against the invasions of settlers; and in a passage in *The Excursion* he extended this concern to pour scorn on the incursions of geologists into the mountains. In the *Guide* he used geological rather than picturesque imagery in promoting the appreciation of the topography of the Lakeland landscape. But in *The Excursion* he was dismissive of the interests of botanists and geologists; their activities could be physically intrusive, and he implied that scientific investigation was destructive of the imaginative power of the mountain landscape. While a 'wandering Herbalist', who 'peeps round / for some rare floweret of the hills, or plant / Of craggy fountain' was merely 'harmless', the geologist was more destructive, for 'you may trace him oft / By scars which his activity has left', damaging the rocks in pursuit of rock specimens and scientific knowledge:

> He who with pocket-hammer smites the edge
> Of luckless rock or prominent stone, disguised
> In weather-stains or crusted o'er by Nature
> With her first growths, detaching by the stroke
> A chip or splinter – to resolve his doubts.[62]

The 1842 edition of the *Guide through the District of the Lakes* includes an appendix on the geology of the Lake District in the form of three letters addressed to Wordsworth by Adam Sedgwick, Woodwardian Professor of Geology at Cambridge, with whom he had established a friendship. In these letters Sedgwick directly confronted the issue that 'one of your greatest works seems to contain a poetic ban against my brethren of the hammer'. To mitigate the sense of a conflict between imagination and science, for 'no one has put forth nobler views of nature's kingdom than yourself', Sedgwick advanced an elevated portrayal of the scope of geology, a conception of scientific inquiry intended to harmonise with Wordsworth's sense of nature's immanence, affirming that 'All nature bears the impress of one great Creative Mind'. Sedgwick sought to meet the charge that geological investigation might destroy the imaginative mystery of the mountains while penetrating their scientific depths: 'there is another "mighty voice" muttered in the dark recesses of the earth . . . of wisdom, of inspiration, and of gladness; telling us of things unseen by vulgar eyes – of the mysteries of creation . . . of laws as unchangeable as the oracles of nature'. He explained to the readers of the *Guide* that understanding the geology of the Lakeland rocks would illuminate the appreciation of the landscape, and he outlined the techniques that were used to enable underlying geological structures to be inferred from surface topography. By undertaking a series of parallel traverses at right angles to the outcrops of the strata, the tilt and direction ('dip' and 'strike') of strata could be marked and given visual representation in traverse and columnar sections, setting out the horizontal structure and sequence of formations of the strata in a given area. Geological maps could then be drawn 'to explain the features of the country', charting the sequence and thickness of rock formations rather than the geographical details of the surface topography, and these formations could be correlated with equivalents in other regions to widen geological understanding.

Sedgwick emphasised that the study of geology would enlarge and was in harmony with the appreciation of the beauty and sublimity of the Lakeland landscape. Addressing Wordsworth, he declared that 'You believe however and I subscribe to the same creed, that material science is only so far truly good, as it tends to elevate the mind of man.'[63] This affirmation by a leading geologist and man of science who was also a pillar of clerical orthodoxy encouraged the assimilation of Wordsworth's philosophy of nature within conventional religious and scientific norms. But the charge of pantheism lingered and was repeated, and in the 1853 edition of the enlarged *Guide*, published after Wordsworth's death, Sedgwick found it necessary to draw the contrast between those who became 'idolators of Nature to the verge of Pantheism' and Wordsworth, who was 'pure from the influence of a principle that soared above any motives which he drew from his communion with Nature.'[64]

Landscape and Geology: Charles Lyell

For the frontispiece of the first volume of his *Principles of Geology* (1830) Charles Lyell printed an engraving, 'carefully reduced' from a contemporary Italian archaeological work, of the 'Present State of the Temple of Serapis in Puzzuoli'. In taking the region of Hamilton's *Campi Phlegraei* and the eruption of Monte Nuovo as emblematic of his theory, Lyell was pointing to the importance of fundamental igneous causes, earthquakes and volcanoes in shaping geological change; indicating that fluctuations in physical geography have been steady-state, temporally non-directional, even over the span of recorded history; and integrating geological and human history by using a work of art, a human monument, as material evidence of the operation of geological forces. While travelling in Italy and Sicily in 1828–9, studying the active volcanoes of Vesuvius and Etna,[65] he became convinced that in the most recent era of the earth's history (in the tertiary formations) the elevation of the earth's crust was consequent on volcanic activity and earthquakes, and that these formations, while recent in geological time, were ancient in relation to human records of eruptions. This implied that an immense time scale would be necessary for geological explanation, and Lyell was convinced that modern processes acting at their present intensities could explain the record of the rocks. He planned to compose a treatise on the principles of geology, and writing from Naples in January 1829 he set out the objectives of his book in a letter to his friend the geologist Roderick Murchison: 'it will endeavour to establish the *principle of reasoning* in the science; and all my geology will come in as illustration of my views of those principles, and as evidence strengthening the system necessarily arising out of such principles . . . that *no causes whatever* have from the earliest time to which we can look back, to the present, ever acted, but those *now acting*, and that they never acted with different degrees of energy from that which they now exert'.[66]

Lyell's discussion of the 'Temple of Serapis' in Chapter 25 of the first volume of the *Principles of Geology* provides a crucial illustration of his theory of geological processes. It is important for Lyell's argument that he give a description of the 'celebrated monument of antiquity' so as to establish its history, and he uses its customary name but points to recent scholarly discussion concluding that the building could not have been a temple. The three remaining pillars of the monument had been partly covered by marine deposits and hidden by bushes; and the soil was only removed in 1750 revealing 'part of the remains of a splendid edifice', which was assumed to have been dedicated to a deity, Serapis. In promoting their rule the Macedonian conquerors of Egypt had used the cult of the god Serapis (in Latin, from *Sarapis*, the Greek form of the Egyptian Osiris) as a divine Graeco-Egyptian patron of the royal power of the Ptolemies, and established a temple complex at Alexandria, *Sarapis* becoming identified with various Greek gods in the process of cultural assimilation. The cult of Serapis, identified as Jupiter, became established in Italy with Serapis as the guarantor of imperial power (his name is invoked in texts bearing on Vespasian and Hadrian), and the building carries inscriptions relating to Marcus Aurelius and Septimius Severus. These inscriptions establish that the monument was constructed as far back as the third century; for Lyell this dating is important when he presents conclusions about the geological history of Pozzuoli deduced from the physical state of the monument.

Lyell begins with a survey of the physical geography of the region around Pozzuoli, noting that there are new sedimentary deposits along the shore rising to a height of about 20 feet (6 metres) above the sea, and that historical records attest that there has been no significant variation in the level of the sea since antiquity. He concludes, 'without the aid of the celebrated temple', that the recent marine deposit 'was upraised in modern times above the level of the sea'. Turning to examine the monument itself, its salient features clearly depicted in the frontispiece of the volume, he considers 'the memorials of physical changes, inscribed on the three standing columns in most legible characters by the hand of nature' (Fig. 9). He records that the pillars are 42 feet (12.8 metres) in height, and their 'surface is smooth and uninjured' to a height of 12 feet (3.65 metres) above the pedestals. Above this is a further zone of 12 feet (3.65 metres) where the columns are disfigured by pear-shaped holes with shells in the cavities showing that 'the marble has been pierced by a species of marine perforating bivalve', the perforations being so considerable

T. Bradley, Sc.

Present State of the Temple of Serapis at Puzzuoli.

9 'Present State of the Temple of Serapis at Puzzuoli', engraving from Charles Lyell, *Principles of Geology.*

that they must have been made over a long period of time; the upper parts of the columns were found to be weathered but otherwise undamaged. He concludes that the columns must have been subjected to 'a long continued immersion of the pillars in sea-water'. During this time the central parts of the columns had been exposed to the sea and the destructive perforations of the bivalves, and he suggests that the lower parts had been protected by being covered up by other building and rocks; and after 'remaining for many years submerged' the columns must then have been raised up above the level of the sea.

In the meticulous form in which Lyell presents his case, thus far he has established that examination of the physical condition of the standing columns of the monument corroborates the information obtained from study of the new marine deposits around Pozzuoli, that the submerged marine deposit and columns had been raised up in modern times. But the evidence of the monument provides grounds for an additional and significant conclusion, that there had been alternate depression and elevation: 'as the temple could not have been built originally at the bottom of the sea, it must first have sunk down below the waves, and afterwards been elevated', back to its modern position at sea level. Turning to discussion of the era in which these geological events took place, he points out that the inscriptions in the monument estab-lish that the building 'existed at least down to the third century of our era in its original position'; and he notes that a historical account attested both that the marine deposit on the shore 'was still covered by the sea in the year 1530, or just eight years anterior to the tremendous explosion of Monte Nuovo', and that 'the re-elevation of the low tract' of shore had occurred between 1530 and 1580. The subsidence of the ground on which the columns of the monument stand must therefore have occurred between the third and sixteenth centuries, and 'the only two events which are recorded in the imperfect annals of the dark ages' were a volcanic eruption 'very near the Temple' in 1198 and an earthquake in 1488 'by which Puzzuoli was ruined'. Lyell judges it to be 'at least highly probable' that the earthquakes, which preceded the volcanic eruption of 1198, 'caused a subsidence'. This leads him to 'confidently conclude' that the subsequent elevation of the land 'happened in the year 1538 when Monte Nuovo was formed'; but he is able to assert that 'fortunately we are not left in the slightest doubt that such was the date of this remarkable event' because of the testimony of two contemporary accounts describing the eruption of 1538, the formation of Monte Nuovo and the emergence of the ancient ruins with the elevation of the land.[67] His source for these documents, which he quotes at length, is Hamilton's *Campi Phlegraei*.[68]

This meticulous assembly of evidence and carefully ordered statement of inferences to be drawn is characteristic of Lyell's style; he had been called to the bar in 1822 and practised as a barrister, and contemporaries judged that he used the 'language of the advocate' throughout the *Principles of Geology*, and the structure of the book is carefully designed.[69] In discussing the geological history of the volcanic region around Pozzuoli, he provides a striking illustration of his temporally non-directional, steady-state theory of earth history. Although the ultimate causes of earthquakes and volcanoes – perhaps the result of seawater leaking into the earth's molten core – remained a speculative matter,[70] Lyell is here concerned with their effects; and the force of his inferences derives from his integration of the geological argument with a narrative drawn from historical records. The form of argument follows a pattern that William Whewell was shortly to term, in his *Philosophy of the Inductive Sciences* (1840), the '*Consilience of Inductions*', the joining of different classes of facts (here geological and historical) leading to a convergence of a theory towards simplicity and unity.[71]

Lyell's discussion provides support for his theory that a long succession of small-scale changes could produce the elevation of mountains and the subsidence of tracts of land. He planned the *Principles of Geology* as a treatise on natural philosophy, a search for the true causes of geology rather as Newton had sought to uncover the cause of gravity, and he assumes that geological laws are unchanged over time, and that the operation of these causes could be observed. The epigraph to the *Principles*, drawn from John Playfair's *Illustrations of the Huttonian Theory of the Earth* (1802), highlights Lyell's philosophical assumption of the uniformity of nature's laws and his commitment to geological explanation in terms of natural processes alone: 'Amid all the revolutions of the globe the economy of Nature has been uniform, and her laws are the only things that have resisted the general movement. The rivers and the rocks, the seas and the continents have been changed in all their parts, but the laws which direct those changes, and the rules to which they are subject, have remained invariably the same.'[72] In his text Lyell declares that the assumption of the 'permanency of the laws of nature' and of their 'immutable constancy' lies at the basis of geological reasoning.[73] In his discussion of the 'Temple of Serapis' Lyell illustrates his principles of explanation: that no causes other than those that we can now see acting should be employed in explanations; and that these causes had not varied in degree.

This latter principle was termed 'uniformitarianism' by Whewell in a review of the *Principles* in 1831, where he contrasted Lyell's outlook with 'catastrophism', the view of the senior geologists William Buckland and Adam Sedgwick (and himself), that past geological change had occurred through massive geological paroxysms;[74] in his *Reliquiae Diluvianae* (1823) Buckland had used the word 'catastrophe', and the term stuck.[75] This was derived from the view, promoted by the leading French naturalist Georges Cuvier, that there had been major 'revolutions' in earth history, and that the disappearance of fossil genera and species was to be attributed to their extinction rather than to their transformation into forms now known to be alive.[76] The distinction was not Lyell's, but in the *Principles of Geology* he takes the assumption of these principles – the uniformity of geological laws, that causes observable in the present day are of the same kind and degree of intensity as those operative in the past – as regulative, as necessary to create a true science of geology.[77] In maintaining that the causes of geological change operative in the past were identical in kind with the causes observed acting at the present, Lyell was not making a radical claim; this principle was taken as regulative of geological theory by Buckland and Sedgwick also.

But Lyell's additional assumption, that past and present geological causes operated at the same degree of intensity ('uniformitarianism'), was more controversial, and remained contested, for it implied that geological change had not been punctuated by the periodic actions of volcanoes, floods and earthquakes acting on a drastically vaster scale than was visible in the present day, but had been very gradual and had taken place over an immense stretch of time. In the *Principles* he described the eruption of a volcano in Iceland in 1783, and ridiculed the assumption that a volcano of a past epoch could have 'poured forth lavas at a single eruption, a hundred times more voluminous', for the river of lava would 'stretch out to the length of nine thousand miles'.[78] In responding to the *Principles*, Sedgwick rejected Lyell's theoretical claim that geological causes had not varied in degree of intensity over time; for Sedgwick this was a 'gratuitous hypothesis', and he pointed to the violently twisted mountain strata and erratic boulders as evidence for episodes of 'feverish spasmodic energy', arguing that 'long periods of comparative repose' had been punctuated by 'periods of extraordinary volcanic energy'.[79]

The received geology of the period, that of Buckland and Sedgwick – both men being clerics as well as leading geologists – while not framed in biblical terms had nevertheless sought accommodation with Genesis. Lyell had attended Buckland's famous geology lectures at Oxford University and was familiar with his outlook, but his approach in the *Principles* is very different, in insisting that the language of geology should be secularised and that natural causes were alone to be invoked in unravelling geological history. In *Reliquiae Diluvianae* Buckland had argued that there was a 'perfect harmony and consistency' between his scientific findings and the biblical narrative, finding evidence for Noah's flood in the wide dispersal of gravels which had been produced by a 'catastrophe', a 'universal inundation of the earth' dating from a 'period not more ancient than that which our received chronologies assign to the deluge'.[80] Lyell did not by any means reject religion, but he was critical of clerical domination of intellectual life; and he sought to redefine the boundary between geology and Genesis that had been blurred in the tradition of theological commentary on earth history flowing from Burnet's *Sacred Theory of the Earth*. Lyell wished to 'free the science from Moses', as he put it in a letter to the political economist George Poulett Scrope; he aimed to sever geology from its purported relation to scripture.[81] His main antagonists were 'scriptural' geological writers such as Andrew Ure, the author of a recent literalist book urging that geology be based on the biblical cosmogony; for such works, as devoid of scientific integrity, Lyell had contempt.[82] But Lyell also scorned Buckland's sophisticated accommodation between geology and the Bible in *Reliquiae Diluvianae,* where he had claimed that there was physical evidence for the biblical deluge, interpreted as a universal geological inundation.[83] Reporting on a discussion at the Geological Society in May 1829, prompted by a paper from William Conybeare attributing the physical geography of the Thames Valley to diluvial erosion rather than to erosion by rain and rivers over much longer periods of time, Lyell mocked the claim of Buckland and his followers, that the geological inundation could be identified with the biblical flood: 'Conybeare admits 3 deluges before the Noachian! and Buckland adds god knows how many *catastrophes* besides, so we have driven them out of the Mosaic record fairly'.[84]

While the interpretation of Genesis was not central to the concerns of geologists, Lyell's *Principles of Geology* set out a marker for secularist science. In the *Principles* Lyell proceeded cautiously, but he succeeded in convincing his colleagues in the Geological Society to abjure incorporating the biblical flood within geology. Responding to the publication of the *Principles* in his formal address as the Society's president in 1831, Sedgwick admitted that it was now untenable for geologists to make use of the biblical flood and thereby link Genesis with the science of geology: the 'double testimony' of the Bible and of physical remains of diluvial action had led him to an 'erroneous induction'; and he confessed that having 'myself been a believer, and to the best of my power, a propagator of what I now regard as a philosophic heresy', he wished to retract 'opinions I do not now maintain' and to 'publicly read my recantation'.[85]

Lyell had originally planned just one further volume of the *Principles of Geology,* and this intention retained its trace in the frontispiece of the second volume, an engraving of his own drawing of the Val del Bove of Mount Etna in Sicily. This indicates the central importance he attached to his observations of Etna and the Plain of Catania in giving an impression of the magnitude of the time scale of the history of the earth. But he greatly expanded his treatment of the organic world, and these chapters filled the second volume of the *Principles.* The crucial discussion of Etna appeared in the third and final volume of the *Principles,* published in 1833. His account of the volcanic processes that had produced Etna was based on his first-hand experience and study of the volcano in 1828, and was decisive in the formation of his geological theory.[86] The narrative of his ascent of Etna and view of the Val del Bove drew from Lyell his most evocative piece of descriptive writing in the *Principles,* a Humboldtian account of the mountain landscape powerfully suggesting the imaginative impact of the ascent:

Let the reader picture to himself a large amphitheatre, five miles in diameter, and surrounded on three sides by precipices ... the magnificent
circle of precipitous rocks which inclose, on three sides, the great plain of
the Val del Bove. This plain has been deluged by repeated streams of lava
... the stern and severe grandeur of the scenery which they adorn is not
such as would be selected by a poet for a vale of enchantment. ...

The face of the precipices ... is broken in the most picturesque
manner by the vertical walls of lava which traverse them. These masses
usually stand out in relief, are exceedingly diversified in form, and
often of immense height. In the autumn their black outline may often be
seen relieved by clouds of fleecy vapour which settle behind them, and
do not disperse until midday, continuing to fill the valley while the
sun is shining on every other part of Sicily, and on the higher regions of
Etna. ...

An unusual silence prevails, for there are no torrents dashing from the
rocks, nor any movement of running water in this valley, such as may
almost invariably be heard in mountainous regions. Every drop of water
that falls from the heavens, or flows from the melting ice or snow, is
instantly absorbed by the porous lava; and such is the dearth of springs,
that the herdsman is compelled to supply his flocks, during the hot
season, from stores of snow laid up in hollows of the mountains during
winter.

The strips of green herbage and forest-land, which have here and there
escaped the burning lavas, serve, by contrast, to heighten the desolation
of the scene. When I visited the valley, nine years after the eruption of
1819, I saw hundreds of trees, or rather the white skeletons of trees, on
the borders of the black lava, the trunks and branches being all leafless,
and deprived of their bark by the scorching heat emitted from the melted
rock; an image recalling those beautiful lines – 'As when heaven's fire /
Hath scath'd the forest oaks, or mountain pines, / With singed top their
stately growth, though bare, / Stands on the blasted heath'.

These lines are from Book I of John Milton's *Paradise Lost*, and Lyell
illustrates the scene with an engraving from his own drawing of the 'View
from the summit of Etna into the Val del Bove'.[87] Lyell was very familiar
with Humboldt's writings. He made especial use of Humboldt's concept of
isothermal lines in expounding his theory of climate in terms of the continual
fluctuation around a mean; and his picturesque description of the Val del
Bove recalls Humboldt's account of the ascent of the Pico de Teide on Tenerife
in the *Personal Narrative*. Lyell's description of the view of Etna has the same
Humboldtian style as Darwin's almost contemporary and independent
reports, set out in his *Diary* in June and December 1832, of his contrasting

impressions of the luxuriance of a tropical forest in Brazil and the barren landscape of Tierra del Fuego. Lyell's drawing of the Val del Bove shows the geological feature that he notes as being especially striking, the vertical basalt dykes projecting from the far cliffs, and that he regarded as significant for understanding the geological history of the volcano. The cliffs show a series of lava flows and layers of volcanic tuff which are cut by the basalt dykes; Lyell considered that the basalt dykes had formed channels for the eruptions of lava, and that the layered structure of lava and tuff indicated that the mountain had been formed in a process of gradual growth from successive flows of lava.[88]

As in his reconstruction of the history of the 'Temple of Serapis' at Pozzuoli, Lyell deployed historical records of the eruptions of Etna and analysis of the physical geography to establish that an immense time had been required to produce a mountain of 10,000 feet (3,048 metres) by lava flows; yet there were tertiary fossil-bearing rocks, geologically recent, beneath the mountain. He concludes that 'we cannot fail to form the most exalted conception of the antiquity of this mountain', which 'must have required an immense series of ages anterior to our historical periods for its growth'; yet Etna is merely 'the product of a modern portion' of the most recent tertiary epoch.[89] Lyell concludes his *Principles of Geology* with a triumphant illustration of his strictly naturalistic method and vindication of his enlarged time scale of geological history.

As a contribution to natural philosophy that set out the principles of reasoning for the science of geology, Lyell's *Principles of Geology* stands out as a major development, but his leading senior contemporaries Sedgwick and Buckland remained unconvinced by the principle of 'uniformitarianism'. The concerns of geologists in the 1830s were directed to more practical matters, the pursuit of fieldwork to unravel the record of the rocks and the construction of geological maps under the auspices of the Geological Survey; the broader causal problems of geology discussed by Lyell were marginal to these interests. Fossils were found to be characteristic of different formations and were increasingly used to chart correlations and as evidence of historical change and environmental conditions in past geological epochs. The delineation of strata became central to the practice of geologists, and in the 1830s two debates preoccupied the world of British geology, concerning the sequence of strata in North Wales (where Sedgwick was pitted against Lyell's friend, Roderick Murchison) and the seemingly anomalous discovery of fossils in rock formations in Devon. Both the 'Silurian' and 'Devonian' controversies were resolved by the charting of strata and the resolution of the fossil evidence.[90] Sedgwick, incongruously, regaled the readers of the 1853 edition of Wordsworth's *Guide through the District of the Lakes* with an angry account of the continuing controversy over the Welsh formations, in a supplement to his letters on the geology of the Lake District first published in the 1842 edition.[91]

The religious commitments of geologists were of marginal importance in this pattern of geological practice. But clerical geologists such as Buckland and Sedgwick were committed to the theistic implications of geology, which remained significant elements in their engagement with the wider public in communicating geological discovery and in seeking to enlarge the evidential base of natural theology. The publication of the *Principles of Geology*, deliberately secularist in style, was closely followed by the issuing of the *Bridgewater Treatises*, works that sought to establish the accommodation and conformity of scientific studies with religion. William Buckland's treatise on *Geology and Mineralogy* (1836) displays marked contrast with Lyell's *Principles*, which excluded the biblical frame of reference from geological reasoning. But for Buckland natural theology provided norms of cultural orthodoxy within which science could be confidently made public, and as Canon of Christ Church and Reader in Geology at Oxford University Buckland reassured his readers that there was no reason to fear any discrepancy between the biblical texts and the results of discoveries in geology. But his introductory chapter purporting to show the 'consistency of geological discoveries with sacred history', and his concluding assertions claiming to have established that the facts of geology proved 'the existence of multifarious examples of Design', serve as a wrapping for the geological detail of his work. His apologetic claims are overwhelmed by the exhaustive survey of geological science that forms the substance of the book and that established its value as a text; Buckland's apologetics served to provide a vehicle for the safe communication of geology.[92]

Buckland himself wrote under the pressure of clerical ignorance and the prejudices of orthodoxy; his wife Mary told William Whewell in May 1833 that in Oxford Buckland was obliged to listen to discourses 'on the heresies of geologists, denouncing all who assert that the world was not made in 6 days as obstinate unbelievers . . .. Alas! My poor husband. Could he be carried back a century, fire and faggot would have been his fate'. The consistency that Buckland strove for, as geologist and theologian, was hard to achieve in the contentious worlds of geological science and religious controversy of the 1830s, and his different audiences were difficult to satisfy and reconcile.[93] His text shows the strains to which the mediating and apologetic functions of natural theology had become subject. As an undergraduate at Christ Church, Oxford, in the late 1830s, John Ruskin had become acquainted with Buckland, who encouraged his geological interests; but scientific engagement had its perils. Writing to his Oxford friend Henry Acland in May 1851 on the present 'flimsiness' of his faith, John Ruskin attested to the impact of the developments flowing from the enlarged time scale of geological history, which had inexorably weakened his old certainties: 'If only the Geologists would let me alone, I could do very well, but those dreadful Hammers! I hear the clink of them at the end of every cadence of the Bible verses'.[94]

'Truth of Nature': John Ruskin

In a letter to Walter Lucas Brown, his former tutor at Christ Church, written in December 1843 after the publication of the first volume of *Modern Painters*, Ruskin paid tribute to Wordsworth's poetic power and spiritual influence: 'Wordsworth may be trusted as a guide in everything, he feels nothing but what we all ought to feel . . . what we all ought to believe – what all strong intellects *must* believe'. Of Wordsworth's poetry he considered 'the magnificent comprehension – faultless majesty of "The Excursion", to crown all'.[95] Ruskin's veneration of Wordsworth, and of the philosophy of nature espoused in *The Excursion*, was made prominently public in the epigraph from Book IV of the poem which he printed in each of the five volumes of *Modern Painters*:

> Accuse me not
> Of arrogance, [unknown Wanderer as I am,]
> If, having walked with Nature [threescore years],
> And offered, far as frailty would allow,
> My heart a daily sacrifice to Truth,
> I now affirm of Nature and of Truth,
> Whom I have served, that their Divinity
> Revolts, offended at the ways of men, . . .
> Philosophers, who, though the human soul
> Be of a thousand faculties composed,
> And twice ten thousand interests, do yet prize
> This soul, and the transcendent universe
> No more than as a mirror that reflects
> The proud Self-love her own intelligence.[96]

Ruskin had planned to write a pamphlet to contest criticism in the periodicals that the paintings of J.M.W. Turner were not true to life: 'To every observation on their power, sublimity, or beauty, there has been but one reply: They are not like nature.' Ruskin determined to show 'that Turner *is* like nature, and paints more of nature than any man who ever lived'. The pamphlet defending Turner became *Modern Painters* (1843), published anonymously by a 'Graduate of Oxford', where Ruskin outlined a theory of art as a basis for lauding Turner as the greatest of landscape painters; but he did not then envisage that the work would stretch to five volumes to be completed only by

1860, nor that he was commencing a career as a cultural critic and author of treatises on art and architecture.

As *Modern Painters* progressed, its publication interrupted by other projects, Ruskin's objectives were enlarged, moving away from the polemical defence of Turner to develop a more complete theory of art and aesthetics, an argument unique in scope and vision based on an acquaintance with writings on aesthetics and an extensive knowledge of works of art. *Modern Painters* encompasses a theocentric system of aesthetics; the discussion of early Italian art and painters such as Titian and Tintoretto (whose work he had come to admire); a treatment of landscape art in different periods; an account of mountain topography; and it turns finally to applaud Turner's capacity for pictorial composition. Ruskin had first met Turner in 1840, and he and his father commissioned watercolours from the artist in 1842; and Ruskin's own drawing style was developing towards naturalism. His theme was Turner's adherence to 'truth, as applied to art', which meant 'the faithful statement . . . of any fact of nature'. But Ruskin's conception of 'ideas of truth' went beyond the accurate representation of naturalistic detail in landscape: 'There is a moral as well as material truth, – a truth of impression as well as of form, – of thought as well as of matter'.[97] He found this adherence to higher truth in Wordsworth and especially in Turner. Describing Turner as a poet, using 'the words painter and poet quite indifferently', and aware of Turner's use of poetic epigraphs for his paintings, he associates Turner with Wordsworth as romantic poets, both being concerned with the expression of 'personal feeling' for the 'noblest purposes'; he enlarges the tradition of poetry and painting as sister arts, *ut pictora poesis*. Ruskin later noted that in the full title of Turner's painting *Snowstorm: Steam Boat off a Harbour's Mouth* (1842), one of the paintings he had sought to defend, Turner had described himself as the 'author' of the painting 'instead of "artist"'.[98]

In the preface to the second edition of the first volume of *Modern Painters* Ruskin explains that the meticulous observation and reproduction of the distinguishing details of the natural world are basic to the realisation of truth to nature in a work of art. A painting of a landscape scene that ignores the specifics of geology and botany would be false to nature: 'a rock must be either one rock, or another rock; it cannot be a general rock, or it is no rock'. He rejects the claim that the painter of landscape can neglect the particular in favour of the evocation of the general: 'Every attempt to produce that which shall be *any* rock, ends in the production of that which is *no* rock'. To achieve the rendition of specific detail the painter must follow the meticulous habits of observation and classification cultivated by the scientist: 'every class of rock, earth, and cloud, must be known by the painter, with geologic and meteorologic accuracy'. But he denies that mimetic accuracy or scientific fidelity is sufficient for the painter concerned with the realisation and expression of 'truth' in a work of art: 'it does not follow that, because such accurate knowledge is *necessary* to the painter, it should constitute the painter; nor that such knowledge is valuable in itself, and without reference to high ends'. The scientist is concerned with accurate description and understanding of the world of nature, which the painter must master, but this is a mere preliminary to his endeavour. There is a difference between the botanist's knowledge of plants and the artist's knowledge, for the artist is concerned to 'render them vehicles of expression and emotion'. The botanist counts the stamens and assigns the plant a place and name in the Linnaean classification, whereas the poet and painter 'observes every character of the plant's colour and form; considering each of its attributes as an element of expression', and 'seizes on its lines of grace or energy, rigidity or repose' and notes the 'feebleness or the vigour, the serenity or tremulousness of its hues'. Truth to nature is built upon keen perception, but its realisation in painting or poetry transcends the methods and objectives of scientific naturalism.

He develops his argument by a discussion of Claude Lorrain's *Landscape with Dancing Figures* (*The Mill*; 1648). He describes the foreground of the painting as 'a piece of very lovely and perfect forest scenery', which would be quite sufficient as a subject 'to form, in the hands of a master, an impressive and complete picture'. But in Claude's painting this forms part of 'an "ideal" landscape, *i.e.* a group of the artist's studies from Nature, individually spoiled, selected with such opposition of character as may insure their neutralizing each other's effect, and united with sufficient unnaturalness and violence of association to insure their producing a general sensation of the impossible'. Claude's painting purports to be a depiction of the Roman Campagna, and to establish the basis of his critique Ruskin gives a description of this landscape sensitive to its topographical particulars and human history. Then, 'with Claude', he makes a 'few "ideal" alterations in the landscape' conforming to the elements introduced into the painting itself: reducing the precipices of the Apennines 'to four sugar loaves', knocking down aqueducts and ruins and substituting an arch and some trees, and for the 'purple mist and declining sun we will substitute a bright blue sky, with round white clouds'; and to cap it all 'we will send for some fiddlers, and get up a dance, and a pic-nic party'. This caricature, nullifying the aesthetic impact of Claude's painting, is intended to drive home Ruskin's claim that with Claude, landscape painting has become a 'manufacture', altered and modified to suit the ambitions of the artist. In Ruskin's rendition Claude's landscape is seen as unnatural. Given Ruskin's conception of 'truth' to nature as embracing moral as well as material elements, it is unsurprising that his critique of Claude's painting leads him to make a moral judgement: 'It cannot, I think, be expected, that landscapes like this should have any effect on the human heart, except to harden or to degrade it' and 'to lead it from the love of what is simple, earnest, and pure'. For his own part he insists on 'the necessity, as well as the dignity, of an earnest, faithful, loving, study of nature as she is, rejecting with abhorrence all that man has done to alter and modify her'.[99]

In a letter to W.L. Brown written in November 1843, Ruskin made explicit the contrast between Claude and Turner that is implicit in his line of argument. According to Ruskin, Claude is concerned with 'ideal beauty', and to this end he takes 'some rocks, and some water, and some trees, and some houses' and combines them in a 'recipe . . . as straightforward and simple as can be, and the result certain, provided the power of manipulation be tolerable'. But this combination of natural features, however aesthetically charming and pleasing, is false to nature: 'this is *not* what nature does'. Each landscape has its own individual character, 'and all her details are thrown in with reference to the particular influence or spirit of the place', and these features cannot be combined arbitrarily in an attempt to produce a harmonious arrangement. This would be to make nature subservient to painting. By contrast Turner is true to nature and faithful to the spirit of the landscapes he paints, drawing together their disparate elements into a convincing unity that seems to the viewer to be a true representation of reality: 'Turner takes it for granted that more is to be learned by taking her lessons individually and working out their separate intents, and thus bringing together a mass of various impressions which may all work together as a great whole'; he does not pick and choose those elements of the landscape that he likes and then discount those he dislikes: 'I am aware of *nothing* in nature which Turner has not *earnestly* painted. Nothing on the surface of the earth has either been rejected by him as too little or shrunk from as too great.'[100]

As the writing of *Modern Painters* proceeded, Ruskin developed a theory of art to encompass this enlarged conception of 'truth' as transcending mimetic representation. In the second volume, published in 1846, he argues that the beauty of nature is to be understood in sacramental terms. In a draft discarded from publication in the text he recalled a formative experience leading him to grasp the spiritual efficacy of nature, an epiphany he experienced one stormy evening in July 1842 when, lying on the Brévent, he saw the Aiguilles of Chamonix break through the clouds: 'Spire of ice – dome of snow – edge of rock – *all* fire in the light of the sunset, sank into the hollows of the crags – and pierced through the prisms of the glaciers, and dwelt within them – as it does in clouds . . . the mighty pyramids stood calmly – in the very heart of the high heaven – a celestial city with walls of amethyst and gates of gold – filled with the light and clothed with the Peace of God. And then I learned – what till then I had not known – the real meaning of the word Beautiful . . . how thought itself may become ignoble and energy itself become base – when compared with the absorption of all power – and the cessation of all will – before, and in the Presence of, the manifested Deity'. The exaltation of this vision of nature established the spiritual efficacy of beauty, an argument pervading the second volume of *Modern Painters* where he developed a theology of nature which is both sacramental and Romantic, arguing that the beauty of the natural world is made manifest by unveiling its spiritual power.[101]

To reveal this beauty the artist required the capacity for an enhanced perception of nature, a breadth of visual and imaginative sympathy to be conveyed through mastery of detail, and Ruskin found this power in Wordsworth as well as in Turner. He expressed this in a famous passage in the third volume of *Modern Painters* (1856): 'I find this conclusion more impressed upon me, – that the greatest thing a human soul ever does in this world is to *see* something, and tell what it *saw* in a plain way. Hundreds of people can talk for one who can think, but thousands can think for one who can see. To see clearly is poetry, prophecy, and religion, – all in one.' In the same volume he declared that the primary endeavour of the landscape painter was 'faithfulness in representing nature'. Assessing landscape art in terms of the aesthetic categories of the 'beautiful, or sublime, or imaginative' should be ignored in favour of 'truth; bare, clear, downright statement of facts', a study that would establish the 'truth of nature'. This would be aesthetically pleasing 'because every truth of nature is more or less beautiful: and if there be just and right selection of the more important of these truths ... the facts so selected must, in some degree, be delightful to all, and their value appreciable by all'. Observation of the facts of nature harmonised with aesthetic valuation and spiritual efficacy, science with art and religion. Ruskin maintained that the careful observation and faithful description of nature was a task and obligation common to the scientist and the landscape painter, a necessary (if preliminary) accomplishment for an artist seeking the 'truth of nature'; but he affirmed the doctrine that art could and should achieve a higher moral 'truth' which transcended the concerns and objectives of the scientist.

In the seminal chapter on 'The moral of landscape' in the third volume of *Modern Painters*, Ruskin draws a distinction between the scientific understanding of natural objects, 'that they are made up of certain atoms or vibrations of matter', and their capacity to excite the imagination, to 'produce such and such an effect upon the eye or heart'. As noted on page 150, he distinguished between natural science which he terms 'the science of *Essence*', and the form of science pursued by the artist which he terms 'the science of *Aspects*', this being an enhanced perception, an instinctive power of achieving and communicating a unifying vision which will clothe natural facts in the language of the human mind and emotion. Thus he declares that 'there is a science of the aspects of things as well as of their nature'. And it is here that Ruskin locates the power of Turner's imaginative vision, his capacity of truth to nature that transcends natural science (limited to the study of 'essence', the material structure of reality), and shows his supremacy over other painters: 'It is as the master of this science of *Aspects*, that . . . Turner must eventually be named always with Bacon, the master of the science of *Essence*. As the first poet who has, in all their range, understood the grounds of noble emotion which exist in landscape, his future influence will be of a still more subtle and important character.' The science of 'aspects' rests on a process of critical perception, a breadth of visual and imaginative sympathy conveyed through mastery of detail.[102]

In the first volume of *Modern Painters*, Ruskin took as an example of truth to nature the portrayal of the sky and clouds by Turner and Wordsworth. In a section headed 'Of truth of skies' he celebrates the aesthetic impact of the open sky, for in the sky 'there is not a moment of any day of our lives, when nature is not producing scene after scene, picture after picture, glory after glory, and working still upon such exquisite and constant principles of the most perfect beauty'. The sky 'is not a flat dead colour, but a deep, quivering, transparent body of penetrable air', and he argues that Turner had successfully captured this quality of the sky by applying blue colour in 'breaking, mingling, melting hues' so the sky is rendered as '*spacious*, still infinite and immeasurable in depth', a true 'painting of the air'. He finds that Wordsworth has also perceived and communicated this sense of the true quality of the sky, and he quotes a passage from *The Excursion* in illustration:

> – the chasm of sky above my head
> Is heaven's profoundest azure; no domain
> For fickle, short-lived clouds to occupy,
> Or to pass through; but rather an abyss
> In which the everlasting stars abide.[103]

Ruskin celebrates Wordsworth's poetic vision in perceiving and communicating the truth of nature, and he elevates Turner's capacities as a painter by the association.

In the first of his three chapters comprising 'Of truth of clouds', on cirrus clouds, Ruskin describes the 'sweeping lines mingled and interwoven . . . melting into banks of sand-like ripple and flakes of drifted and irregular foam', the colours of cirrus being 'more pure and vivid, and their white less sullied than those of any other clouds'. In illustration of his description he quotes a passage from *The Excursion*:

> rays of light . . ..
> – Shot upwards to the crown
> Of the blue firmament – aloft, and wide:
> And multitudes of little floating clouds, . . .

– had become
Vivid as fire . . .
. . . with unity sublime.

Ruskin again maintains that Turner is the 'one master whose works we can think of while we read this; one alone has taken notice of the neglected upper sky'.[104] He enlarges his naturalistic description by drawing on religious imagery, describing these clouds as providing 'fifty aisles penetrating through angelic chapels to the Shechinah of the blue', the visible symbol of the temple of God.[105] On rain clouds, Turner's representation of 'the tumultuous separate existence of every wreath of writhing vapour, yet swept away and overpowered by one omnipotence of storm' is paired with Wordsworth's passage, 'while the mists/Flying, and rainy vapours, call out shapes/And phantoms from the crags and solid earth' from *The Excursion*.[106] He follows the same procedure in the chapter 'Of truth of chiaroscuro'. He claims that it is in his 'clear and exquisite drawings of the *shadows*' that Turner had attained 'brilliancy of light', by throwing shadows 'one after another like transparent veils, along the earth and upon the air, till the whole picture palpitates with them'. Once again Ruskin finds that 'Wordsworth, the keenest-eyed of all modern poets for what is deep and essential in nature, illustrates Turner', and again quotes from *The Excursion*:

Almost at the root
Of that tall pine, the shadow of whose bare
And slender stem, while I sit at eve,
Oft stretches toward me, like a long straight path
Traced faintly in the greensward.[107]

Ruskin emphasises that Wordsworth and Turner possessed clarity of vision in comprehending nature, and the power to communicate this capacity of understanding the truth of nature in their poetry and painting.

Ruskin develops his appreciation of Turner in the fourth volume of *Modern Painters* (1856), concerned with 'mountain beauty', and he begins the book with a discussion of the 'Turnerian picturesque'. He again proceeds by contrasting Turner with Claude Lorrain, continuing his critique of the paintings of Claude and the aesthetics of the 'modern feeling of the picturesque'; this he defines as 'a sublimity not inherent in the nature of the thing, but caused by something external to it'. He gives as an example the way in which the 'ruggedness of a cottage roof possesses something of a mountain aspect, not belonging to the cottage as such'; this picturesque character is therefore false, not true to the nature of the object. He associates this aesthetic with Claude and considers it a sign of the degeneracy of art in the seventeenth century. Ruskin argues that an unlimited sympathy for nature, a concern with the truth of nature and the mastery of the science of 'aspects' kept Turner 'from delighting too much in shattered stones and stunted trees', the familiar features of a picturesque landscape. The aesthetic category that Ruskin terms the 'Turnerian picturesque' is very different, achieving an overarching vision of sublimity that is true to nature. In the next chapter, 'Of Turnerian topography', he provides further discussion of what he means by Turner's faithfulness to nature. This is not to be understood as a literal representation of a landscape scene, but the exercise of a visionary faculty, an imaginative sympathy to the 'spirit of the place', to the 'great whole'.

Ruskin illustrates the point by comparing Turner's imaginative representation of the Alpine Pass of St Gotthard near Faido, which he declares to be 'true to nature', with his own drawing of the scene, which however he shows to be a more accurate depiction of the Alpine topography. Soon after publication of the first volume of *Modern Painters* Ruskin had acquired a watercolour, commissioned from Turner, of *The Pass of Faido, St Gotthard*. Turner had worked from memory, using a sketch he had made at the scene; and from his own recollections of St Gotthard, Ruskin recognised that Turner's watercolour is not topographically accurate and is therefore 'totally useless to engineers or geographers'. But Ruskin maintains that in this watercolour Turner has achieved a truth to nature that transcends a superficial concern with topographical accuracy. To provide the basis for discussion of this point, crucial to his representation of Turner as the artist who portrayed the truth of nature, Ruskin returned to St Gotthard in 1845, recording the scene in two drawings of the Pass of Faido in which he paid close attention to an accurate portrayal of the topography, so as to enable a comparison to be made between the scene and Turner's composition. In the fourth volume of *Modern Painters* he illustrates the chapter 'Of Turnerian topography' with two etchings (Fig. 10a, b), one made from his own drawings and the other from the Turner drawing in his possession: *Pass of Faido* (*1st Simple Topography*) and *Pass of Faido* (*2nd Turnerian Topography*). Ruskin describes the scene at St Gotthard, which he then compares with the etching of Turner's watercolour.

In the discussion that follows Ruskin places emphasis on Turner's mental vision in transforming the scene and thereby being 'true to nature'. Ruskin declares that: ' "It is always wrong to draw what you don't see." This law is inviolable . . . [but] the only harm is when people try to draw non-apparent things . . . but think they can calculate or compose into existence what is to them evermore invisible'. The representation of what is *seen* is fundamental to achieving truth to nature: but what *is* seen? In his topographical pictures Turner does not 'arouse in the beholder those sensations which would be caused by the facts themselves, seen in their natural relations'; but he aims to give 'the far higher and deeper truth of mental vision, rather than of the

20. Pass of Faido. (1st Simple Topography.)

21. Pass of Faido. (2nd Turnerian Topography.)

10a, b John Ruskin, *Pass of Faido (1st Simple Topography)* and J.M.W. Turner, *Pass of Faido (2nd Turnerian Topography)*.

physical facts'. His representation of the landscape could be 'totally unlike the place', but it would evoke 'precisely the impression which the reality would have produced' on the beholder's mind. Turner is praised for arousing a power of sympathy in the viewer by incorporating, transcending and universalising the representation of detail. To achieve this symbolic or emblematic representation of reality, exemplifying his mastery of the science of 'aspects', Turner brought to his pictures a lifetime's knowledge of landscape and nature: 'he only did right in a kind of passive obedience to his . . . strong memory of the place itself which he had to draw' and of 'memories of other places (whether recognized as such by himself or not I cannot tell), associated in a harmonious and helpful way'. The 'Turnerian picturesque' is achieved through a 'kind of mental chemistry', by the 'involuntary remembrance' of images seen in the past and stored in his memory; it is an imaginative representation of landscape and nature, achieved through an 'act of dream-vision', which is true to nature even if useless to engineers or geographers.[108]

The fourth volume of *Modern Painters* interweaves mountain landscape, painting and geology. In the final chapter, on 'The mountain glory', Ruskin declared that 'to myself, mountains are the beginning and the end of all natural scenery'. He portrays the colour and variety of the mountain landscape as transcending the aspect of mountains, as inert, unyielding and inhospitable to man as discussed in the previous chapter on 'The mountain gloom'. The book contains a famous example of Ruskin's purple prose, where he envisions the mountains as animated and imagines the '*undulation*' of the rocks as being internally energised, flowing and rippling like rivers, trembling as the strings of an Eolian harp are stirred into vibration and music by the wind. He evokes this throbbing energy and pulse of the mountain landscape in describing rocks that he termed 'slaty crystallines' (the 'primary' rocks of the geologist):

all that is necessary . . . to know or remember, is this broad fact of the *undulation* of their whole substance. For there is something, it seems to me, inexpressibly marvellous in this phenomenon, largely looked at . . . one adamantine dominion and rigid authority of rock . . . as we look further into it, it is all touched and troubled, like waves by a summer breeze; rippled, far more delicately than seas or lakes are rippled: *they* only undulate along their surfaces – this rock trembles through its every fibre, like the chords of an Eolian harp – like the stillest air of spring with the echoes of a child's voice. Into the heart of all those great mountains, through every tossing of their boundless crests, and deep beneath all their unfathomable defiles, flows that strange quivering of their substance. Other and weaker things seem to express their subjection to an Infinite power only by momentary terrors: as the weeds bow down before the feverish wind, and the sound of the going in the tops of the taller trees passes on before the clouds, and the fitful opening of pale spaces on the dark water, as if some invisible hand were casting dust abroad upon it, gives warning of the anger that is to come, we may well imagine that there is indeed a fear passing upon the grass, and leaves, and waters, at the presence of some great spirit commissioned to let the tempest loose; but the terror passes, and their sweet rest is perpetually restored to the pastures and the waves. Not so to the mountains. They, which at first seemed strengthened beyond the dread of any violence or change, are yet, also ordained to bear upon them the symbol of a perpetual Fear: the tremor which fades from the soft lake and gliding river is sealed, to all eternity, upon the rock; and while things that pass visibly from birth to death may sometimes forget their feebleness, the mountains are made to possess a perpetual memorial of their infancy.[109]

There is a pictorial counterpart to this passage in Ruskin's drawing *Gneiss Rock, Glenfinlas* (1853), which shows his fascination with the swirling pattern of the rock produced by the undulating ripples of the igneous flow as the rock had cooled. This drawing evokes the energy and vitality that he attributed to inorganic nature. He made this drawing at the same time that John Everett Millais was painting his portrait, *John Ruskin* (1853–4), working from a slightly different vantage point and focusing minutely on the rocks and the flowing water. As noted earlier, the portrait was painted during a time of emotional crisis – Ruskin's wife Effie left him for Millais. Making his drawing and watching Millais at work led Ruskin to declare that the Pre-Raphaelite artists' principles of naturalistic precision and truth to nature 'must, in great part, confine them to mere foreground work.' Ruskin regarded Millais' painting as a landscape rather than a portrait, predicting that it would 'make a revolution in landscape painting', and he sought to ensure that Millais kept 'up to the Pre-Raphaelite degree of finish' and truth to nature in recording the precise observation of geological detail, with 'maps of all the lichens on the rocks, and *bubbles* painted in the foam' of the descending stream. In his discussion of rocks in the fourth volume of *Modern Painters* Ruskin described a stone as a 'mountain in miniature', claiming that geological processes were expressed in single rocks as much as in a mountain range. The artist, moreover, seeking truth to nature, should appreciate that the 'beauty of the stone surface is in so great a degree dependent on the moss and lichens which root themselves upon it'. His drawing *Chamonix: Rocks and Vegetation* (1854), displays a rock foreground that again shows the influence of Pre-Raphaelitism on his drawings, and where he strove to record the pattern of the rocks and the detail of the surface vegetation.[110]

In the climactic chapter on 'The moral of landscape' in the third volume of *Modern Painters* Ruskin's appreciation of Wordsworth took a critical turn. Alluding to the passage in *The Excursion* where Wordsworth criticises the meddling botanist and the geologist for destroying the rocks with his hammer, Ruskin now questions this prejudice: 'This was the chief narrowness of Wordsworth's mind; he could not understand that to break a rock with a hammer in search of crystal may sometimes be an act not disgraceful to human nature, and that to dissect a flower may sometimes be as proper as to dream over it . . . the most useful members of society are the dissectors, not the dreamers. It is not that they love nature or beauty less, but that they love result, effect, and progress more.' Ruskin now considers Wordsworth's 'distinctive work' (perhaps having the poems of *Lyrical Ballads* in mind) to have been 'a war with pomp and pretence, and a display of the majesty of simple feelings and humble hearts'; without this central pinnacle of his poetic achievement his 'love of nature would have been comparatively worthless'.[111]

In this third volume Ruskin sets out a systematic and profound analysis of the poetry and painting of landscapes, suggesting that in antiquity mankind took 'very little interest in anything but what belonged to humanity; caring in nowise for the external world, except as it influenced his own destiny'. In a famous chapter, 'Of the pathetic fallacy', he discusses the practice of attributing feeling (*pathos*) to inanimate nature, which he considers to be a characteristic of the modern poetic sensibility. He takes as an example a poem by Charles Kingsley, 'The Sands of Dee' published in his novel *Alton Locke* (1850), where the sea is described as 'cruel, crawling foam'. Ruskin responds that 'the foam is not cruel, neither does it crawl'; the imagery of feeling in nature does not ring true. He terms this form of language the 'pathetic fallacy' and he argues that it is 'eminently characteristic of the modern mind', for the modern landscape painter and poet endeavour to 'express something which he, as a living creature, imagines in the lifeless object'. By contrast classical poets and medieval painters expressed the 'unimaginary and actual qualities of the object itself'. Ruskin declares that Homer would not have used such language: 'he could not by any possibility have lost sight of the great fact that the wave . . . do what it might, was still nothing else than salt water'. Homer calls the waves 'monstrous', 'compact-black' and 'wine-coloured'; but 'every one of these epithets is descriptive of pure physical nature'. Ruskin attributes this change to a loss of belief in gods or spirits of nature: to the modern mind the landscape is no longer filled with spiritual presences, so sentience is attributed to the trees and water, to nature itself. He alludes to a passage in *The*

Excursion where the goddess Diana, described as 'a beaming Goddess with her Nymphs, / Across the lawn and through the darksome grove', is envisioned as hunting at night. Whereas Wordsworth, in a manner characteristic of the moderns, uses this image 'figuratively', for the Greeks there is 'a living spirit, to which the light of the moon is a body; which takes delight in glancing between the clouds and following the wild beasts as they wander through the night; and that this spirit sometimes assumes a perfect human form' while retaining its godlike status, 'its power and being in the moonlight, and all else that it rules'. For the modern mind the 'pathetic fallacy' is a substitute for religious belief. In Ruskin's new estimation Wordsworth is diminished in exemplifying the modern sensibility of 'ineffective dreaming and moralizing' over nature, his poetry illustrating 'the satisfaction made to our modern consciences for the want of a sincere acknowledgment of God in nature'. In the chapter on 'The moral of landscape' Ruskin expounds his view that 'nature-worship' is the means by which 'sacred truths' can now be uniquely communicated: 'the love of nature, wherever it has existed, has been a faithful and sacred element of human feeling ... nature-worship will be found to bring with it such a sense of the presence and power of a Great Spirit as no mere reasoning can either induce or controvert; and where that nature-worship is innocently pursued ... it becomes the channel of certain sacred truths, which by no other means can be conveyed'. Religious belief is transformed into the worship of nature.[112]

In his later writings Ruskin distanced himself further from his former enthusiasm for Wordsworth's poetry; and at the same time – in his hostility to the establishment of Darwin's theory of evolution in the 1860s – his sympathy hardened against the scientific 'dissectors' of nature with whom he had compared Wordsworth so dismissively in his chapter on 'The moral of landscape'. He contrasted Wordsworth's poetic contemplation of nature in *The Excursion* unfavourably with the investigative spirit of scientific travel he found displayed in Humboldt's *Personal Narrative*, a work he admired for its empiricism and rich vision of nature and landscape, and for Humboldt's sympathy for the social condition of the indigenous peoples he encountered on his travels. In Ruskin's collection of geological writings, *Deucalion* (1875–83) – one of three late works, with *Proserpina* (1875–86) on flowers and *Love's Meinie* (1873–81) on birds, shaped by the 'imaginative power' of Greek and biblical mythology and personal symbolism set against the 'materialistic theory' of science – he refers to Humboldt as one of 'the most careful and logical geologists', praising him for his 'universal and serene philanthropy and sagacity'. When commenting in *Fiction, Fair and Foul* (1880) on Matthew Arnold's recent edition of Wordsworth's poems, Ruskin makes allusion to the proximity of the Arnold family home Fox How and Wordsworth's final residence Rydal Mount. He also contrasts the charm of the Lakeland fell of Silver How overlooking Wordsworth's nearby Grasmere with the sublimity and grandeur of Humboldt's landscape of the Andes: 'though it is very proper that Silver How should clearly understand and brightly praise its fraternal Rydal Mount, we must not forget that, over yonder, are the Andes, all the while'. Just as the Lakeland landscape celebrated by Wordsworth is dwarfed by the grand topography of the Andes described by Humboldt, so the poet himself – now regarded as 'simply a Westmoreland peasant' with a capacity for loquacity – when compared with the 'great masters of the Muse's teaching' (Ruskin alludes to Byron), is found to be no more than a 'pleasant fingerer of his pastoral flute among the reeds of Rydal'.[113]

The representation of the truth of nature became central to geology and landscape aesthetics in the nineteenth century and involved a critique of picturesque representation, which gave way to naturalistic depiction emphasising geological processes; rocks were seen in relation to an environment shaped by natural history and geology. In Wordsworth's Romantic aesthetic the picturesque construal of lakes, mountains and trees in relation to works of art was displaced by an aesthetic based on the primacy of nature as unfettered by the artificial structures of human culture. For Wordsworth and Constable, the immediacy of nature transcended the artificial aesthetic categories of the picturesque; the natural world was to be depicted by the direct contemplation of nature rather than through the mediation of terms of art. Turner was valorised for representing sublime nature by vivid impressions of colour and the effects of light and shade; and Ruskin commended Wordsworth and Turner for their clarity of vision in comprehending and communicating the true reality of natural phenomena, an aesthetic achieved through their power of imaginative sympathy and engagement.

The relation between the representation of landscapes in the natural sciences and their depiction in art became the focus of discussion. Wordsworth described the aesthetics of the Lake District landscape in relation to the natural history and geology of the mountains, and Ruskin envisioned the mountain landscape in terms of the throbbing energy and pulse of swirling patterns of flowing rock. For Ruskin, landscape was to be regarded as a geological and aesthetic unity; the representation of the truth of nature was to embrace the scientific study of phenomena (the 'science of *Essence*') and the imaginative grasp necessary to capture reality (the 'science of *Aspects*'). The aesthetics of 'naturalism' in the sense of fidelity to nature, embracing Ruskin's 'aspects' and 'essence', became the motif of the aesthetic appreciation of landscape. In his formative *Principles of Geology* Charles Lyell deliberately avoided any attempt to seek an accommodation between natural theology and geology, renouncing the objectives of the contemporary *Bridgewater Treatises*.

He envisaged his work as a contribution to natural philosophy, to set out the principles of reasoning for the science, establishing a naturalistic method based purely on the regularity, intensity and constancy of geological processes. His style of reasoning, with natural processes acting gradually, regularly and over immense periods of time, established the parameters within which Charles Darwin articulated his theory in *On the Origin of Species.*

CHAPTER 6

Flora and Fauna, the 'Tree of Life'

O<small>N</small> 21 A<small>PRIL</small> 1837, as John Ruskin reported to his father, he had met and 'talked all the evening' with Charles Darwin at the Oxford house of the geologist William Buckland.[1] Recently returned to England from the voyage of the *Beagle* (1831–6), Darwin was at the time in the midst of his first private speculations on the transformation of species – the chronological succession, localisation and mutability of species. Around July 1837, in the first of his notebooks dedicated exclusively to the emergence and extinction of species, he sketched a diagram illustrating the evolutionary basis for understanding the classification of species and the extinction and emergence of life forms through branching development (Fig. 11). His diagram gives an abstract schematic illustration of the familiar image of the branching tree of life, showing 'between A & B immens[e] gap of relation', between 'C & B the finest gradation' and between 'B & D rather greater distinction' between species; when classification is understood in terms of the transformation of species, this branching of species showed how 'genera would be formed – bearing relation to ancient types – with several extinct forms'.[2] Recording these jottings marked an important early stage in Darwin's development of his theory of evolution by natural selection, not to be made public until *On the Origin of Species by Means of Natural Selection* was published in 1859, in which the image of the 'Tree of Life' is developed in an elaborate abstract schematic diagram illustrating the classification, descent, variation and extinction of species in evolutionary terms.[3]

Darwin's theory excited Ruskin's contempt and hostility – despite his private respect for its author. He was especially aroused by the implication that the aesthetic appreciation of nature could be comprehended in evolutionary terms. In his chapter on 'The moral of landscape' in the third volume of *Modern Painters* (1856), Ruskin drew a contrast between two modes of knowledge about nature, the sciences of 'the aspects of things as well as of their nature', either conceiving the 'sky as a blue dome' and the 'cloud as a golden throne' or (with the natural sciences) representing the sky as 'a dark cavity' and clouds as 'a sleety mist'. His preference was for understanding

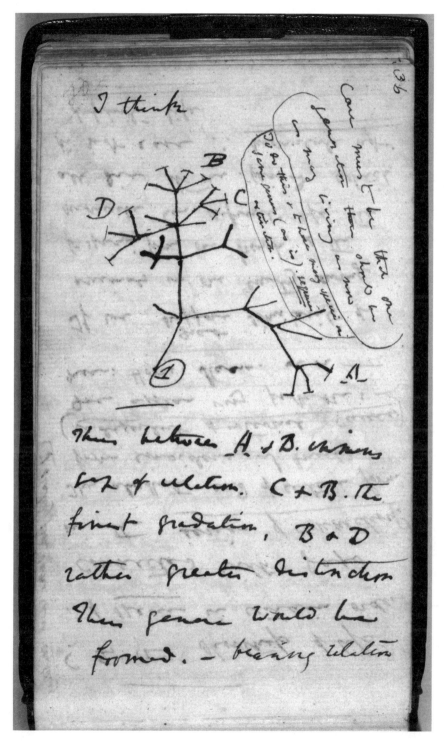

11 Charles Darwin, 'Notebook B'.

nature through aesthetic appreciation and human values rather than through study of the 'laws of material nature', promoting the science of 'aspects' of which Turner was the master: 'We cannot fathom the mystery of a single flower, nor is it intended that we should; but that the pursuit of science should constantly be stayed by the love of beauty, and accuracy of knowledge by tenderness of emotion.'[4]

In his late collection of writings on flowers and botany, *Proserpina* (1875–86), Ruskin further developed and enlarged his view of the inherent limitations of the natural sciences as capable of forming a system of knowledge of nature, now more firmly rejecting the abstractions of botanical science in favour of the 'aesthetic relations of species'. His aim was to recover the innocent enjoyment of the 'wayside flowers' of the book's subtitle from the alienating sophistication of scientific classification, which by the 1870s meant for Ruskin the natural history of the *Origin of Species* and Darwin's subsequent studies of birds and flowers, work that became increasingly offensive to his sensibility. In *Proserpina* Ruskin's primary concern was with questions of nomenclature and classification. But Ruskin did not engage with the work of Linnaeus, whose botanical classification based on fructification (which had brought stability to a subject that had seemed inherently inchoate) he described as one of the 'permanent classical treasures of the world'. Ruskin recognised that 'no single classification can possibly be perfect or anything *like* perfect', for even if 'the arrangement of plants could, with respect to their flowers and fruits, be made approximately complete, they must instantly be broken and reformed by comparison of their stems and leaves', and he discarded the abstractions of botanical morphology. In its place he suggested a botanical nomenclature based on the immediately observable, on what is perceptible to the naked eye and to the place where a flower was likely to be seen by the wayfarer, and 'rather by reference to mythological associations than to botanical structure'. This was to be a botanical science of 'aspects', Ruskin's own 'Systema Proserpinae' in place of the *Systema Naturae* of Linnaeus – the reference to Proserpina the daughter of Ceres and queen of the underworld making explicit the mythological allusions that shaped his endeavour. Ruskin looked to a botanical classification based on human values and the aesthetic judgement of the 'ugliness and beauty absolute' of flowers; his classification was not founded on the qualities of plants as defined by the botanical 'properties' discovered by scientists. In emphasising that 'the flower is the end or proper object of the seed, not the seed of the flower', he rejects Darwin's form of botany based on the survival of plant species, the supposition (as Ruskin phrases it) that the object of life was the 'bequeathing of itself' in the mere 'continuance' and propagation of plants through their seeds.[5]

For Ruskin, the study of botany expressed the culture of flowers. *Proserpina* embodies his private language of the naming and classification of flowers, expressing his belief in the enduring and universal values of myth and embracing his personal symbolism of flowers.[6] In taking aesthetic and human values as the basis of his nomenclature Ruskin turned from the language and concerns of contemporary natural history, which he associated with Darwin (rather than Linnaeus); and he discarded the developments in botanical classification and nomenclature that had been achieved since the seventeenth century.

Wonders and Classification

In Renaissance and seventeenth-century natural philosophy the classification of animals, plants and 'stones' (a large and anomalous group) was shaped by the theological categories of the natural and the miraculous, and by philosophical principles such as the correspondences linking the animate and the inanimate, and the material and the nonmaterial worlds. Lines of demarcation were recognised between three categories of reality, the natural, the preternatural and the supernatural; but these boundaries were unstable and subject to controversy, debate and adjustment.[7] In the Renaissance, natural philosophers envisaged a cosmology in which the terrestrial and celestial realms are linked in a web of affinities and correspondences, and where matter is impregnated with planetary influences; this was a natural order encompassing a hierarchy of visible and invisible agents where analogies and links between planets, metals and gemstones could be activated. This world picture defined the realm of the natural; and its breadth and elasticity readily accommodated 'wonders' – the preternatural, the unusual, chance events, marvels and wonderful occurrences which could be embedded in the vocabulary of natural causes – including traditions of secret knowledge such as alchemy. The supernatural, by contrast, was manifest in divine intervention in effecting miracles, events falling outside the natural order (and therefore distinct from preternatural wonders). The philosophical revolution engendered by Descartes and the mechanical philosophers meant that the range of the natural was restricted to the interactions of matter, its motion determined by laws of nature acting under God's ordinary providence. Preternatural wonders were viewed as the product of natural causes and although they remained of interest their occurrence was regarded with greater scepticism; but as miracles were supposed as being performed by divine intervention, their occurrence required God's suspension of the laws of nature by acts of special providence.

With the scientific revolution the boundaries between these categories shifted. Natural philosophers saw nature as following divinely established laws; wonders came to be seen as marking the boundaries of current scientific explanation; and the enlightened regarded claims for supernatural intervention with scepticism and as superstitious, miracles being confined to the biblical era. For the mechanical philosophers the boundary between the natural and supernatural was marked by the laws of nature; they claimed that metaphors of law and mechanism enriched the range of divine providence, that concepts of order, design and natural laws enlarged the dominion of divine sovereignty rather than contracted or diminished it. The definition of the boundary between the natural and the preternatural became shaky. It could depend upon the unusualness of the occurrence of wonders; monstrous births and other naturally occurring oddities, marvels and monsters were avidly reported and persisted in the discourse of learned academies such as the Royal Society. The rarity of such encounters – the salamander immune to fire, the monstrous races of Cyclops, tailed Sciopods (men with only one leg) and Blemmyes (men with faces on their torso) – made these traditional legends of the marvels of geography and anthropology still intriguing in their retelling in the age of exploration. But as the notion of laws of nature became securely embedded, marvels were often dismissed as imaginary, believed in only by the ignorant and superstitious, their reports laughed at by the educated. Wonders were also seen as marking the boundaries of current scientific explanation: in early 1672 Isaac Newton trailed his experiments with the prism to the Royal Society by claiming the extraordinary oddity of his discoveries, declaring that he had made 'in my Judgment the oddest if not the most considerable detection wch hath hitherto beene made in the operations of Nature'.[8]

The collections of natural objects displayed in cabinets of curiosity illustrate the problems of anomaly and classification. These cabinets offered a display of both natural and artificial oddities, exotica and antiquities, shells, crystals, corals and gems, gatherings that blurred the distinction between the categories of art and nature. The analogy between works of art and the works of nature lay deep in traditional philosophical argument. Aristotle, whose writings remained a dominant intellectual force, had considered that the forms of artefacts derive from nature, and he had represented natural processes (such as the growth of plants) as analogous to the creation of a work of art. There was an interest in hybrid objects, natural objects transformed by human craft and ingenuity, their manufacture exploiting the analogies of form between objects of nature and works of art. Bacon and Descartes perceived an affinity between the works of nature and the creations of art. Bacon urged the collection of rare and unusual facts as a preliminary to the reform of natural philosophy, and considered monsters and marvels to be emblematic of the correspondence between the works of nature and works of art. Descartes maintained that the mechanical philosophy could explain all marvels, offering the prospect of subsuming the class of wonders under the class of the natural. With the establishment of scientific methods, and of academies of the learned such as the Royal Society, came the demand that agreement over the veracity of matters of fact could only be achieved if contested facts were witnessed and testified, a demand applicable to accounts of marvels as well as to reports of scientific experiments. While the disinterested autonomy of witnesses and the reliability of their documented testimony could be contested, this procedure became established within the domain of science, and a model for rational enquiry.[9]

The philosophers of the Enlightenment were sceptical and even contemptuous of reports of marvels; the rejection of a class of wonders in favour of scientific forms of classification came to be seen as defining the enlightened state of mind.[10] In the essay on miracles published in his volume of *Philosophical Essays Concerning Human Understanding* in 1748, David Hume treated reports of wonders with characteristic irony, not least in directing his argument against the claim that the miracles reported in the Bible could provide a convincing foundation for religion: 'consider a book, presented to us by a barbarous and ignorant people ... corroborated by no concurring testimony ... full of prodigies and miracles ... I desire any one to ... declare, whether he thinks that the falsehood of such a book, supported by such a testimony, would be more extraordinary and miraculous than all the miracles it relates'.[11] Nature was viewed as being shaped by immutable laws, natural phenomena were perceived as regular and uniform, and the class of 'wonders' was subsumed under classes of the natural. Buffon, the leading natural historian of the eighteenth century, allocated monsters only three pages in his *Histoire Naturelle*, considering that marvels did not belong to the ordinary facts of nature and should therefore be pushed to the margins of science. Claims of divergence from the 'natural' were ignored, the anomalous and extraordinary interpreted as natural; just as philosophers questioned belief in hell and demons, the category of marvels was displaced from natural philosophy.[12]

The classification of 'fossils' illustrates these developments.[13] Conrad Gesner's *A Book on Fossil Objects, Chiefly Stones and Gems, Their Shapes and Appearances* (1565) is one of the earliest Renaissance treatises on natural history. As his title indicates, Gesner considered 'fossils' (*fossa*) to be any distinctive objects dug up from the earth or lying on its surface, embracing gemstones, crystals, marble and 'fossils' resembling objects of organic origin – but such resemblance did not signify organic descent. He followed the presentation adopted in the treatises by Leonhart Fuchs on the *History of Plants* (1542) and Andreas Vesalius on the *Human Body* (1543), using illustrations to assist precise identification of the 'fossils' collected in cabinets of curiosities. The study of 'fossils' was shaped by the prevailing philosophical doctrine of analogies and correspondences; affinities between celestial and terrestrial objects suggested a basis for the exploitation of planetary influences on terrestrial phenomena, the colour, lucidity and brilliance of gemstones manifesting the luminosity of heavenly bodies. The frontispiece of Gesner's treatise displays the twelve stones of the breastplate of the High Priests of the Temple of Jerusalem engraved with the names of the twelve tribes of Israel. He illustrated these stones as cut gems displayed like a necklace arranged around two rings, one ring set with a cut diamond, another ring with a stone engraved with a scarab beetle, an image associated with hieroglyphs believed to record the pristine source of natural magic. The 'stoniness' of fossils suggested that they arose, like crystals and stalactites, from a petrifying fluid, in a process of growth where the earth was conceived as analogous to a living organism. The variety in the forms of fossils led to a classification according to their resemblance to other objects in nature, in a hierarchy ranging from geometrical figures down to terrestrial objects. The isolation of a class of 'fossils' bearing a resemblance to natural objects of organic origin would have been problematic, because of the fortuitous resemblance of rocks and minerals to organic structures, and the occurrence of fossils of unfamiliar organisms belonging to extinct groups such as belemnites and ammonites. Where Gesner does identify fossils in the modern sense – in *glossopetrae* ('tongue-stones'), which resemble the teeth of sharks – it is likely that he construed tongue-stones as marking affinities, or as stones that had grown in a process analogous to the growth of organisms, rather than in terms of their origins (in the modern sense) as the fossilised remains of sharks' teeth. The theory of organic origin required the assumption of historical, geographical and geological change, and the rejection of traditions of astrological influences and natural magic.

In 1666 Nicolas Steno, a Danish anatomist working in Italy, examined the teeth of a giant shark brought ashore near Livorno, which he compared with tongue-stones found embedded in rocks, concluding that tongue-stones were the teeth of sharks deposited during the sedimentation of the rocks. His style of empirical argument echoed wider developments in scientific explanation, avoiding discussion of the purposes, associations in natural magic and the medical virtues of such 'fossils', and abandoning the encyclopaedic assembly of opinions, a style inherited from Pliny the Elder's *Natural History*, which had characterised compilations such as Gesner's. Steno's presentation of the case for the similarity between *glossopetrae* and living shark's teeth strongly suggested that they were the teeth of fossil sharks. But this was a specific case, and he sought to establish criteria to distinguish fossils of organic origin from crystals, to establish distinctions within the broad category of 'fossils'. He used a corpuscular theory of matter to establish that quartz and pyrite crystals were accretions of particles precipitated from fluids, concluding that naturally occurring crystals did not differ from those produced in the laboratory. These crystals were unlike fossil shells, which resembled the shells of living molluscs that varied in form because their growth was due to the growth of an organism. This established criteria to distinguish crystals from objects similar to living organisms or of organic origin, and led to the theory that the stratification of the rocks was due to precipitation from a fluid, enclosing 'fossils', the petrified remains of organisms. In the wake of Burnet's *Sacred Theory of the Earth* (1681–9), a theory of the deluge that could not provide an organic interpretation of the marine fossils found in mountain strata, in the 1690s John Ray, John Woodward and Edward Lhwyd discussed the problems and implications of accepting that organic resemblances implied the organic origin of fossils, and the consequences for the conventional biblical chronology of the history of the earth. It was not until Buffon's *Epochs of Nature* (1778) that an adequate time scale for this process began to be developed. Buffon argued that, just as in the study of human history it was necessary to investigate archives and inscriptions 'to determine the epochs of human revolutions and to fix the dates of human events', similarly in natural history 'it is necessary to excavate the world's archives, to extract ancient monuments from the earth's entrails'.[14] He suggested that there had been seven stages or 'epochs' of earth history, using the occurrence of fossils in the rocks to reconstruct the sequence of strata and to indicate the history of life on earth. The 'primary' mountains were relics of the earth's condition before the appearance of life, the 'secondary' mountains included limestone and their fossils showed the abundance and variety of life, while the 'tertiary' rocks gave evidence of more recent biological history.

Buffon's imaginative, but speculative, style of argument was transformed by Georges Cuvier writing in the mid-1790s. Cuvier, a naturalist of genius, established that the methods of comparative anatomy could distinguish and identify fossil bones, opening the way to a reconstruction of the history of the earth before the advent of human history. Reporting to the Paris *Institut* on engravings of a fossil skeleton of a 'Paraguay animal' (real bones were not available to him), he concluded that the rhinoceros-sized animal which he termed 'megatherium' (great beast) had anatomical affinities to living sloths, and was an extinct inhabitant of a vanished former world, distinct from living species: 'there is no perfect analogy whatever between the bones found in the earth's interior and the same parts of the animals that are known to us [alive]'. In a paper on the jaws and teeth of living and fossil elephants he concluded that the elephant remains found in Siberia belonged neither to the African nor the Indian species (which he had been able to distinguish), but to a third and unknown species which, like the megatherium, 'belonged to a world previous to ours, destroyed by some kind of catastrophe'.[15] He saw no reason to suppose that there had been a process of modification or evolution from ancient to modern species of sloth and elephant, and concluded that these ancient species had become extinct, and that the sloth and elephant should be considered as new rather than as modified species. The organic and historical origin of 'fossils' was now firmly established, with important consequences for the subsequent history of geology and earth history: fossils were understood as organic residues belonging to extinct species; the characteristic fossils of various geological formations were considered as unique to these strata and as defining distinct geological epochs; and fossils could provide indices of historical change and environmental conditions. The classification of fossils as natural objects of organic origin required, and helped to shape, the development of a broad understanding of the history of the earth and the emergence of a science of geology.

Classification and the Culture of Flowers: Carl Linnaeus, Erasmus Darwin and Horace Walpole

The most decisive and influential achievement of classification in natural history came with the system of plant classification proposed by the Swedish botanist Carl Linnaeus in his *Systema Naturae* (1735); this work appeared in many subsequent editions, enormously enlarged from the original eleven-page pamphlet, establishing a system of floral classification that became widely used during the eighteenth century, though ultimately abandoned by botanists. Linnaeus set out a hierarchy of classes, orders, genera, species and varieties; plants were divided into 23 classes according to their stamens, with a twenty-fourth class of fungi and mosses; and these plant classes were divided into orders, according to their pistils. This system of plant classification could be used as a practical field guide and was especially suited to recording unknown plants from foreign floras; by counting the number, arrangement and characteristics of stamens and pistils, plants could be allocated to the appropriate group. Linnaeus made botany widely accessible, open to the leisured amateur as well as to the expert horticulturalist; for this achievement an English magazine described him in 1750 as 'the greatest Botanist that the world ever did or probably ever will know'.[16] His taxonomy of plants was based on the notion that the fertilisation of plants was analogous to the reproduction of animals, an analogy that implied that plants had sexual features; this was the essential feature of the Linnaean classification. The terms 'stamen' and 'pistil' had been introduced in the Renaissance, 'stamen' meaning the warp of a fabric, 'pistil' denoting the resemblance to pestle, but without the sexual connotation (of male and female parts) as suggested by Linnaeus. But in conceiving plants as sexual beings Linnaeus personified the fertilisation of plants as a 'marriage' and the male and female organs as 'husbands' and 'wives'; and in his tiered taxonomy where class stands above order, the social order of the gender hierarchy is echoed in the priority of class, determined by the male parts (stamens) over the female parts (pistils).[17] The reproductive parts of plants were given explicitly sexual interpretations; in Hugh Rose's *Elements of Botany* (1775), an English translation of Linnaeus' *Philosophia Botanica* (1751), the 'calyx then is the marriage bed, the corolla the curtains, the filaments the spermatic vessels, the antherae the testicles, the dust the male sperm, the stigma the extremity of the female organ, the style the vagina . . . the seeds, the ovula or eggs'. Taxonomic classes were humanised in terms of various relationships between the 'husbands' and 'wives', with the mosses ('cryptogamia' in Linnaeus' taxonomy) having secret lovers in 'clandestine marriages'. These vivid and direct expressions, plant taxonomy expressed in terms of human relationships, aroused incredulity and censure, a commentator immediately disparaging this 'lewd method' of classification; the entry on 'Botany' in the first edition of the *Encyclopaedia Britannica* (1771) declared that 'obscenity is the very basis of the Linnean system'.[18]

In Linnaeus' system of plant taxonomy a single characteristic, the flowering parts of plants, was taken for the systematic foundation of botany. He was obliged to acknowledge that his system of classifying plants by the quantitative procedure of counting stamens and pistils was 'artificial', being based on the external characteristics of plants, rather than 'natural', a taxonomy based on features that would accurately reflect the characteristics determining the natural relations of plants. Fructification had been used as the basis for the classification of plants by Andrea Cesalpino in the sixteenth century, and plant sexuality had been suggested by Nehemiah Grew in his *The Anatomy of Plants* (1682), where stamens and pistils are given male and female connotations; but, while Joseph Pitton de Tournefort used the flowers and fruits of plants as the basis for classification, the leading botanist of the late seventeenth century, John Ray, had argued that no single characteristic of plants could provide the basis for a natural system, and that the external characteristics of plants could do no more than indicate the structure of the natural order. Among Linnaeus' own contemporaries the leading naturalist Buffon adopted the same attitude, arguing that the Linnaean floral system was inherently artificial and limited, and did not have a true basis in nature because it did not embody the natural relations of plants. Michel Adanson declared that any botanical classification such as that of Linnaeus, which only considered one part or a small number of parts of the plants, was arbitrary and abstract and could not be a satisfactory basis for taxonomy. The Oxford professor of botany Johann Jakob Dillenius told Linnaeus that 'every scheme of classification offers violence to nature', but offered the consoling thought that 'I do not doubt that you yourself will, one day, overthrow your own system'.[19]

Although Linnaeus shared the prevailing goal of a 'natural' taxonomy, he considered its attainment – even by himself – as unlikely, but he had aimed to create a useful, stable and practical method of classification. Stamens and pistils were easily identified and their number and characteristics could be charted in the field, yet they showed a sufficiently diverse pattern in plants to provide a working system of classification. He accepted that his system of classification was 'artificial' and even provisional but denied that it was arbitrary; it was internally consistent and practical, and he believed that the fructification structure of plants did reflect the natural order and that stamens and pistils did embody the essence of plants, however difficult it was to understand the true basis of the relations between botanical families. His emphasis was on bringing unity to the practice of botany, ever more complex with the discovery of new species, and on facilitating ease of identification and description. Linnaeus first introduced his binomial system of nomenclature, where each species of flora and fauna is designated by the name of its genus and species, in works of economic botany where simplicity and rapid identification were of paramount importance; and he developed the method in his more systematic treatises, initially in his *Philosophia Botanica*. This stable and standardised reference system became his enduring scientific contribution, establishing the basis for the modern codes of nomenclature for plants and animals, and subsequently for bacteria and viruses.[20]

Linnaeus' taxonomy assumed a static conception of natural history. In his essay *Oeconomia Naturae* (1749), translated as 'The oeconomy of nature' in 1759, he drew upon the natural theology of John Ray's *Wisdom of God Manifested in the Works of Creation* (1691); as a naturalist and classifier Ray was a hero to Linnaeus. The word 'oeconomy' derives from Xenophon's *Oeconomicus* of the fourth century BC, a work concerned with agriculture and household management; and in the seventeenth century it came to be used to denote the divine organisation of nature. Arguing for a divine economy of nature, Linnaeus conceived the natural world as a cyclical and self-regulating system manifesting circulating patterns of renewal, pointing to natural equilibria such as the hydrological cycle as an example of this process. Reviewing the interactions between vegetables and animals, he argued that nature shows an endless process of propagation, preservation and destruction, manifesting a continuous series of universal warfare through which the natural world dissolves and is replenished according to the divine plan. Every creature has its allotted place in the economy of nature bound together in the order established by God. Nature is fecund, beneficent and purposive, its integrated order providing the basis of the broader analogy that he drew between his system of classification in botany, in five tiers of classes, orders, genera, species and varieties, and the order of political geography in the state, organised into the kingdom, region, province, territory and district. The natural world was ordered but complex, a labyrinth to be negotiated by Linnaeus' taxonomy, its inherent rationality and capacity to be ordered being based on its design – and science was the means to penetrate its mysteries.[21]

Because of its link between sex and taxonomy Linnaeus' system aroused controversy, as well as the interest of expert botanists. The most striking of the works addressed to the literary public written to support and elaborate the Linnaean system is the poem *The Loves of the Plants*. It was published anonymously in 1789 by Erasmus Darwin who practised as a physician in Lichfield and Derby, was a member of the Lunar Society of Birmingham and the friend of Josiah Wedgwood, Joseph Priestley and John Whitehurst, and who had already published translations of two of Linnaeus' systematic plant catalogues. In *The Loves of the Plants* he presents a humanised and personified account of the fertilisation of plants; the poem was enthusiastically received, bringing the Linnaean system to wide attention. It encouraged Darwin to publish its companion, *The Economy of Vegetation* (1791), a more ambitious treatment of nature and society, the two poems forming Darwin's *The Botanic Garden*. Initially impressing Wordsworth and Coleridge among others, he established a reputation, temporarily at least, for poetic achievement. As he explained in the preface to *The Temple of Nature* (1803), the most ambitious of his scientific poems, it was his aim to bring 'distinctly to the imagination the beautiful and sublime images of the operations of nature'.[22] This language is significant in expounding his aesthetic outlook, of poetry evoking beautiful and sublime pictures. In a notebook entry in 1796 Coleridge accurately commented that 'Dr Darwin's Poetry [is] a succession of Landscapes or Paintings', adding that it 'makes the great little'.[23] Whereas Coleridge nursed ambitions for a form of philosophical poetry shaped by an aesthetics that would transcend the Horatian doctrine of *ut pictura poesis*, Darwin likened poetic imagery to sketching pictures in a landscape. In *The Loves of the Plants* he explains that when nature is interpreted by art, 'in the playhouse or picture room', it is represented by images shaped by the aesthetic criteria of beauty and the sublime: 'The further the artist recedes from nature, the greater novelty he is likely to produce; if he rises above nature he produces the sublime; and beauty is probably a selection and new combination of her more agreeable parts'. Darwin separated his poem, with the fanciful pictures evoked by 'the imagery of poetry', from his scientific comments, the 'strict analogies of philosophy', which he placed in supplementary prose footnotes, interludes and appendices. He explains that he aimed to transmute trees and flowers into men and women, 'to restore some of them to their original animality, after having remained prisoners so long in their respective vegetable mansions', to be contemplated by the reader as 'diverse little pictures'. Darwin illustrates Linnaeus' taxonomic classes through a series of anecdotes personifying plant taxonomy in imaginative vignettes analogous to a painter's landscape sketches, where he affirms the unity of nature – human, animal, plants – in portraying the relations of plants by evoking human sexual patterns.

In a footnote in *The Loves of the Plants* Erasmus Darwin signalled his philosophical difference from Linnaeus' static economy of nature, emphasising that the fertilisation of plants drove a process of progressive development in nature: 'Perhaps all the products of nature are in their progress to greater perfection? An idea countenanced by the modern discoveries and deductions concerning the progressive formation of the solid parts of the terraqueous globe.'[24] Appealing here to the analogy of the temporal and progressive development of strata in forming the earth's crust, he later elaborated his notorious evolutionary ideas in *Zoonomia* (1794–6).

In his verses Erasmus Darwin sought botanical accuracy, even advancing on Linnaeus' numerical system by representing the structure of each plant and its means of fertilisation. Whereas Linnaeus had given stamens (determining taxonomic classes), as the males in his system, primacy over the pistils (determining order), as the females, Darwin gave the plant-women of his verses priority in shaping the character and narrative of his floral anecdotes, as presented by a 'Botanic Muse' presiding in his botanical garden.[25] Darwin's poetic narrative aimed to explain the Linnaean taxonomy of classes and orders based on stamens and pistils and the reproductive processes of plants; he offered amused and suggestive comments on contemporary morals and social patterns; and he gave hints of a wider naturalistic meaning to his humanised descriptions of plants, implying that nature's laws were universal in encompassing humanity. He begins with a series of anecdotes based on the sexual relationships of plants with one stamen and one pistil. His first poem about the canna lily – described as 'virtuous' in plighting the 'nuptial vow', with the male stamen protectively clasping 'the timorous beauty to his breast' – is very much the idealised marriage. But as the poem unfolds the relationships between stamens and pistils become more complicated, and Darwin's language becomes teasing and suggestive, making full use of the blunt and direct Linnaean terminology. With one pistil for every five stamens Meadia, the American cowslip, is seen as a wanton flirt:

> Meadia's soft chains five suppliant beaux confess,
> And hand in hand the laughing Belle addresses;
> Alike to all, she bows with wanton air,
> Rolls her dark eye, and waves her golden hair.

With the Linnaean class of Polyandria, many stamens being in the same flower with the pistil, Darwin describes the Arum (or cuckoopint) who 'trails her long lance, and nods her shadowy plumes', here evoking an image of female divinity or sorcery as 'grinning Satyrs tremble as she moves'.

Erasmus Darwin concludes his series of poetic anecdotes with the reproductive strategy of the plant genus Adonis, which has multiple stamens and pistils; and here he evokes an idealised picture of the easy sexual relations of the Tahitians described by Joseph Banks and James Cook in their travel narratives of the 1770s – noble savages following nature's way rather than the conventions of supposedly civilised society and the repressive dictates of clerics:

A hundred virgins join a hundred swains
And fond Adonis leads the sprightly trains; . . .
Licentious Hymen joins their mingled hands,
And loosely twines the meretricious bands.
Thus where pleased Venus, in the southern main,
Sheds all her smiles on Otaheite's plain,
Wide o'er the isle her silken net she draws,
And the Loves laugh at all, but Nature's laws.[26]

The moral of the poem was not lost on Horace Walpole who wrote to two young women friends on the publication of *The Loves of the Plants*, finding it 'strange . . . that a man should have been inspired with such enthusiasm of poetry by . . . peeping through the keyholes of all the seraglios of all the flowers in the universe! I hope his discoveries may leave any impression but of the universal polygamy going on in the vegetable world, where however, it is more *galant* than amongst [the] human race, for you will find that they are the botanic *ladies* who keep harems, and not the *gentlemen*'.[27] Darwin gave the flowers of traditional verse a new range of associations and meanings. Bridging the gap between nature and humanity by his personalised botanical stories, he suggested that the laws of nature were universal, bringing humanity under the framework of laws of organic nature. Plants were seen to represent the diversity of natural and human relationships; the botanic garden described in the poem envisioned the order of nature as an independent, autonomous and diverse self-contained natural system, an image consonant with Darwin's sceptical, deistic outlook.

Erasmus Darwin's volumes of scientific poems were illustrated by William Blake and Henry Fuseli; and his poem *The Loves of the Plants* inspired a pictorial complement, Robert Thornton's *The Temple of Flora: Or, Garden of Nature* (1807), its title making allusion to Darwin's *The Temple of Nature* (1803) and *The Botanic Garden* (1791). Thornton's *The Temple of Flora* forms the third part of his *A New Illustration of the Sexual System of Carolus von Linnaeus* (1799–1807); its hand-coloured prints of plants providing a pictorial equivalent of Darwin's verse, its paintings prepared by Philip Reinagle and Peter Henderson and by specialised botanical draughtsmen. Thornton's text engages with the cultural, religious and political issues of the day. The work is dedicated to Queen Charlotte, and he used the botanical diversity of the world to urge the virtues of peace against the evils of warfare and conquest, giving free rein to his patriotic anti-Napoleonic fulminations. The allegorical painting by Reinagle, *Cupid Inspiring the Plants with Love* (1805), forms one of the frontispieces to *The Temple of Flora*, showing Cupid and the 'bird of paradise' plant from the Cape of Good Hope, the mythological personification prompted by the style of Darwin's botanical verse. Darwin praised engravings sent to him by Thornton, assuring him that 'all my acquaintances, to whom I have shown the prints you have been so good to send me, greatly admire them ... the coloured print of the tulip quite astonishes them'.[28] In these illustrations the plants are shown in landscape settings, and although the backgrounds may make some allusion to the environments where the plants were found to flourish, the landscape settings follow the aesthetic canons of eighteenth-century art in utilising themes and motifs characteristic of the depiction of beautiful, sublime and picturesque landscapes, transcending the terms of Linnaean botany.[29] In 1800 Reinagle had shown *The Night-Blowing Cereus* (the moon cactus) at the Royal Academy, and Thornton commissioned a second version with a landscape background painted by Abraham Pether. Known for painting moonlight scenes, for a hothouse flower native to the Caribbean Pether provided a background of an English churchyard with a tower showing the clock at midnight and a moonlit wood, a collection of sublime motifs capped by the ghostly churchyard barn owl glimpsed perching on the tower. In his 'Explanation of the Picturesque Plates' Thornton noted that 'each scenery is appropriated to the subject ... in the night-blowing Cereus you have the moon playing on the dimpled water, and the turret-clock points to XII, the hour at night when this flower is in its full expanse'. By contrast Pether's painting of *The Snowdrop* (1804) has a naturalistic land-scape setting, utilising the artist's expertise in painting snow scenes, incorporating picturesque motifs of a snow-covered cottage and a bare tree with a distant village and church, set in a hilly landscape at sunset. In Peter Henderson's painting of *The Dragon Arum* (1801) the violent purple of the plant is set in an artificial landscape evocative of the sublime, a darkly looming and threatening background of mountains and sky suggestive of the erotic associations of the Arum presented in Darwin's *The Loves of the Plants*. Thornton commented that 'the clouds are disturbed, and every thing looks wild and sombre about the *dragon* ARUM, a plant equally poisonous as foetid'. Linnaeus' taxonomy, interpreted through the personifications of Darwin's botanical verse, is illustrated in *The Temple of Flora* by using the customary aesthetic conventions of landscape painting; the background land-scape against which the flowers are depicted, sublime, beautiful, or pictur-esque, is shaped to correspond to the cultural associations evoked by the flowers, though the appropriate naturalistic environment is represented where culture and ecology coalesce.

Horace Walpole's response to Darwin's botanic poem manifests his own interest in the creation of flower gardens within landscape parks. In January 1750 he had written to Horace Mann with the news that he was 'going to build a little Gothic castle at Strawberry Hill', the house with a fine view over the Thames that he had acquired at Twickenham. He built battlements and arched windows with the result, he told Mann in 1753, that 'the house is so monastic that I have a little hall decked with long saints in lean arched windows and with taper columns'; the design was completed with a library containing a chimney piece derived from medieval tombs. Mann had thought that the garden too was to be in Gothic style, prompting Walpole to explain that 'Gothic is merely architecture; and as one has a satisfaction in imprinting the gloomth of abbeys and cathedrals on one's house, so one's garden on the contrary is to be nothing but *riant*, and the gaiety of nature'. He sent Mann his own sketch of the 'enchanted little landscape' and described the view of the castle as depicted in Johann Heinrich Müntz's painting *Strawberry Hill from the South* (*c.* 1759): 'Directly before it is an open grove, through which you see a field which is bounded by a serpentine wood of all kind of trees and flowering shrubs and flowers. The lawn before the house is situated on the top of a small hill, from whence to the left you see the town and church of Twickenham encircling a turn of the river, that looks exactly like a seaport in miniature.'[30]

In his garden Walpole gave full scope to the eighteenth-century taste for the creation of landscape views through the planting of trees, shrubs and flowers. Müntz's painting of Strawberry Hill shows the contrasts of texture and form that Walpole made the basis of his design for the shrubbery. In creating a pleasure ground of shrubberies and flower gardens, Walpole's design exemplified the scope of eighteenth-century taste: landscape gardens were created around the landscape park, a composition of lawns, clumps of trees and groves in the classical style, and were complemented by the ornamental planting of shrubberies and flower gardens to form pleasure grounds. Shrubberies could be used as screens or to frame a view by creating perspectives and prospects, being used to form a decorative display, to mimic favoured views, or to recall (in the picturesque mode) paintings by Claude Lorrain or Nicolas Poussin. In planting flower gardens the aim was to create a graduated array of flowers; in the words of the influential gardener Batty Langley in his *New Principles of Gardening* (1728), the gardener should create 'a perfect Slope of beautiful Flowers'.[31] A graduated arrangement of shrubs and flowers offered a departure from earlier geometrical or serpentine forms of planting, following the order of nature in effecting a graduated transition from flowers to shrubs to trees, and permitting the display of exotic species acquired from North America and the Orient. In his garden at Strawberry Hill, Walpole propagated the 'New England or Lord Weymouth's pine', which was favoured for evergreen shrubberies, and 'Carolina cherries', and he planted 'roses, pinks, orange-flowers, and . . . acacias'. He described the sensuous and theatrical effect of the garden in a letter to George Montagu in June 1765: 'I am just come out of the garden in the most oriental of all evenings, and from breathing odours beyond those of Araby. The acacias . . . are covered with blossoms, the honey-suckles dangle from every tree in festoons, the seringas are thickets of sweets, and the new-cut hay of the field in the garden tempers the balmy gales with simple freshness'; the garden was a 'paradise'.[32] At Nuneham Courtenay in Oxfordshire, Walpole's friend the poet and gardener William Mason created a famous flower garden for another friend of Walpole's, Viscount Nuneham. The design (in which Lord Nuneham and his gardener Walter Clarke may have had a hand) was recorded in two watercolours painted by Paul Sandby in 1777; they show views of the flower garden and the Temple of Flora, architectural features with their mythological associations being integral to the overall plan of the garden. These paintings show an orangery, shrubbery clumps and perimeter shrubbery, and circular and kidney-shaped flower beds planted with sunflowers and hollyhocks. The garden had a circuit walk, a lawn with clumps of shrubs, and a temple and grotto, joining horticultural and architectural features; the triangular garden was located close to the house in a landscape park planned by 'Capability' Brown. Humphry Repton was later struck by the design of the garden and the arrangement of the flower beds at Nuneham, where the temples and statues 'being works of art, beautifully harmonize with that profusion of flowers and curious plants which distinguish the flower garden from natural landscapes'.[33] The garden at Nuneham was the culmination of an eighteenth-century style featuring a graduated array of plants of diversified colours, arranged like 'seats in the Theatre'.[34]

'Natural Selection': Charles Darwin

When the *Beagle* berthed in Montevideo in November 1832, almost a year into its voyage, Charles Darwin received his copy of the second volume of Charles Lyell's *Principles of Geology* published that year. It was in this volume that Lyell directly, and at length, contested the theory of transmutation of species that had been promoted by Jean Baptiste de Lamarck in his *Philosophie Zoologique* (1809). Lamarck's theory of transformation and flux in the natural world – the claim that organisms had an intrinsic tendency towards development and transmutation, that the environment had a direct influence on organisms, and that species were mutable rather than fixed – was directed against Cuvier's theory that the extinction of species had occurred during the revolutions or catastrophes that had shaped the earth's surface. Lyell argues that there are limits to the degree to which species vary, and that although species have the capacity to 'accommodate themselves, to a certain extent, to a change of external circumstances', there was no evidence for the 'notion of the gradual transmutation of one species into another', so that contrary to Lamarck's claim, 'species have a real existence in nature'. He argues that an ecological balance maintains the survival of species, and their extinction is determined by fluctuations in physical geography disturbing the ecological equilibrium. Although 'species cannot be immortal, but must perish one after the other', extinction is matched by the introduction of new species which serve 'for the repair of these losses'; but Lyell offers no explanation of the means by which the production of new species is effected, suggesting that the span of human history had been too short for such introductions to have come to 'the attention of naturalists'.[35] Lyell's challenge to the tenability of Lamarck's theory was forthright and detailed, and at the time seemed conclusive. But on writing to Darwin in March 1863, after the publication of the *Origin of Species* (1859), he confessed that when he 'came to the conclusion that after all Lamarck was going to be shown to be right, that we must "go the whole orang", I re-read his book, and remembering when it was written, I felt I had done him injustice'. Lyell's challenge to Lamarck was fuelled by his fear that the theory of the transmutation of species would allow the closeness of the human species to the orang-utan, the anthropoid ape of Borneo, shaking the doctrine of the uniqueness of man: 'I remember that it was the conclusion he came to about man that fortified me thirty years ago against the great impression which his arguments at first made on my mind'.[36]

But Lyell had left the question of the introduction of new species open and unanswered. It was on this issue that the astronomer and natural philosopher Sir John Herschel wrote to him in February 1836 offering comment on a new edition of the *Principles of Geology*, in particular complimenting him on his success in 'exposing to view the immense extent and complication of the problems' to be addressed: 'I allude to that mystery of mysteries, the replacement of extinct species by others ... I cannot but think it an inadequate conception of the Creator, to assume it as granted that his combinations are exhausted upon any one of the theatres of their former exercise ... we are led, by all analogy, to suppose that he operates through a series of intermediate causes ... the origination of fresh species, should it ever come under our cognizance, would be found to be a natural in contradiction to a miraculous process'. Herschel affirmed that the origin of species would fall under the same principles of naturalistic explanation that Lyell had established for geology, agreeing that scientific language should be secularised, and declaring that the introduction of new species was not to be attributed to a 'miraculous process'. Herschel's letter was published in Charles Babbage's *Ninth Bridgewater Treatise* (1837) and Darwin recorded reading the passage (in the second edition of the book) in December 1838, at a time when he was immersed in formulating his theory of evolution (or 'descent', as he termed it). His response was immediate and fervent: 'Herschel calls the appearance of new species the mystery of mysteries & has grand passage upon problem! Hurrah – "intermediate causes".[37] Herschel placed the question of the origin of species firmly within the boundary of science, judging that it should be understood as a 'natural' process intelligible in terms of natural laws, 'intermediate causes'. By 1838 this had become Darwin's aim, and he made reference to evolution as the 'mystery of mysteries, as it has been called by one of our greatest philosophers' in the opening passage of the *Origin of Species*, alluding to Herschel's letter and strategically invoking his authority.

Darwin had read his grandfather Erasmus Darwin's book *Zoonomia* (1794–6) on the transmutation of species, and during Darwin's time in Edinburgh Robert Grant had introduced him to more recent ideas on evolution; but Lyell's assault on Lamarck would have only confirmed him in the view, promoted by his Cambridge teachers, that these speculations were unorthodox and untenable. Darwin's visit to the Galápagos Islands on the *Beagle* in September and October 1835 was to prove crucial in leading him to question the fixity of species, but during the visit the significance of observations, which in retrospect were found to be seminal, passed him by; taxonomic issues bearing on the origin of species lay beyond the range of his scientific inquiries. He had pursued a broad range of collecting in natural history on the voyage, but his scientific interest had engaged most enthusiastically with geology where he had gained in confidence and authority, his outlook shaped by Lyell's *Principles of Geology*. Writing to his cousin W.D. Fox from Lima, Peru in August 1835, he declared that he found geology 'so much larger a field for thought than in other branches of Nat: History', adding that 'I am become a zealous disciple of Mr Lyells views, as known in his admirable book',[38] hardly suggesting that he dissented from Lyell's reasoning on the species question. The *Beagle* reached the Galápagos Islands a month later, and Darwin was to regret being unprepared for making the systematic observations and collections which, on his return to England, he came to realise were necessary; but he was fortunate to bring back sufficient evidence, when supplemented by the collections of other members of the *Beagle*'s company, of the diversification of mockingbirds, finches and tortoises on the separate islands, which was to prove crucial in suggesting common ancestry and the possibility of evolution. In his diary he made a single reference to seeing 'Doves & Finches',[39] but he paid them little attention and did not trouble to separate his collections of finch skins taken from the different islands. He noticed that the mockingbirds differed from island to island, and it was mentioned to him that the inhabitants claimed to be able to tell from which island any giant tortoise was from, but he did not at the time consider the differences between the mockingbird and tortoise populations of the separate islands to be significant. But in June 1836, while *Beagle* was approaching England, Darwin began to reflect on the possible implications that could be drawn from his experiences on the Galápagos islands, tentatively raising the possibility of evolution. He recollected 'the fact that from the form of the body, shape of scales & general size, the Spaniards can at once pronounce, from which Island any Tortoise may have been brought'. Ruminating on the mockingbirds he noted that the islands of the archipelago were 'in sight of each other, & possessed of but a scanty stock of animals, tenanted by these birds, but slightly differing in structure & filling the same place in Nature', but he judged that these differences did not mark out separate species, rather 'I must suspect they are only varieties'. But if the mockingbirds were found to be separate species, 'such facts would undermine the stability of Species'.[40] He did not affirm this conclusion because he considered that the mockingbirds were different varieties within a single species; but he had broached the thought, though ambiguously and tentatively, that if birds on the different islands were separate species having a common ancestry, then the fixity of species would be in doubt.

On the return of the *Beagle* to England in October 1836, Darwin allocated specimens accumulated on the voyage to various scientific experts; John Gould undertaking the work on the birds, Richard Owen the fossils. Gould had begun his career as a gardener, and was subsequently employed as a taxidermist by the Zoological Society; by the 1830s he was an established ornithologist, with the publication of hand-coloured lithographs of the birds of the *Himalaya Mountains* (1830–2) and *The Birds of Europe* (1832–7), each in five volumes. These were collective enterprises. Gould was the collector and taxonomist: he wrote the texts and designed the arrangement of the birds on the plates, and made 'rough sketches' from which a team of artists, including his wife Elizabeth and Edward Lear, painted the finished drawings. By early 1837 Gould had recognised that three of Darwin's four Galápagos mockingbirds were separate species; Darwin had labelled them by island and it became clear that the different species lived on separate islands. Suggesting that the finches formed a new group, Gould distinguished 13 species divided into four genera, a classification made primarily (and unusually) on the basis of the gradation from thick to thin beaks; and after Robert FitzRoy's labelled finch specimens were examined, Darwin confirmed that the finches were island-specific. The localisation of the mockingbird and finch species was capped by Gould's examination of the 'ostrich' specimens that Darwin had brought back from Patagonia, distinguishing between two rhea species occupying overlapping territories (and naming one *Rhea Darwinii*); for Darwin this highlighted questions about common ancestry, localisation and adaptation.

In February 1837 Lyell, with whom Darwin had already established a close friendship, made public Richard Owen's conclusion that Darwin's South American fossil mammals, including an extinct species of llama, were related to existing species. The immediacy of these developments is apparent in

Darwin's notebook jottings in March 1837, where he floated speculations about the chronological succession, localisation and mutability of species. He suggested that the geographical distribution of the rheas had its counterpart in the chronological succession of extinct and existing llamas: 'The same kind of relation that common ostrich bears to [Darwin's rhea]' is that of 'extinct Guanaco [Llama] to recent: in former case position, in latter time'. A comment on the possible mutability of species took up the query he had raised in his note of June 1836, and was prompted by Gould's conclusion that the localised mockingbirds were not mere varieties, as Darwin had then judged, but were distinct species: 'if one species does change into another it must be per saltum [by degrees] – or species may perish'.[41] He later made an entry in his 'Journal' which, as Janet Browne emphasises, highlights his own assessment of this turning point in his intellectual development: 'Had been greatly struck from about month of . . . March [1837] – on character of S. American fossils – & species on Galapagos Archipelago. – These facts origin (especially latter) of all my views'.[42] In the first edition of his *Journal of Researches* (1839), the narrative of his voyage on the *Beagle*, Darwin commented on the differentiation of the species of Galápagos finches: 'a nearly perfect gradation may be traced, from a beak extraordinarily thick, to one so fine, that it may be compared to that of a warbler. I very much suspect, that certain members of the series are confined to different islands . . .. But there is not space in this work, to enter on this curious subject'. In Darwin's view, this gradation in the thickness of the beaks of the finches was indicative of diversification through geographical isolation and adaptation in feeding on the different islands. He expanded this brief, unrevealing comment with a striking statement in the second edition of *Journal of Researches* (1845), where the four genera of Galápagos finches are illustrated: 'Seeing this gradation and diversity of structure in one small, intimately related group of birds, one might really fancy that from an original paucity of birds in this archipelago, one species had been taken and modified for different ends'.[43] By 1845, when he published this second edition, Darwin had developed his theory of evolution, and he had the confidence to hint at the significance of the diversification of species on the different islands: the possibility of the common ancestry and descent by modification of the finches (along with that of the mockingbirds and tortoises) on the separate islands led him to question the fixity of species. But the evidence for the localisation of the finches on the different islands was fragmentary, and Darwin did not discuss these birds in the *Origin of Species*.[44]

Around July 1837 Darwin began making entries in the first of a series of notebooks on the species question. The first notebook bears his heading of '*Zoonomia*', the title of the book on transmutation by his grandfather Erasmus. As implied by this title, his first jottings circulate around Lamarck's theory of the progressive development of organisms; at the time these ideas

were espoused by political radicals and dissident anatomists, seeing trans-
formism in nature as supporting political and social change.[45] Darwin turned
from such notions of inherent development, to consider the 'Galápagos
Tortoises, Mocking birds' that had prompted his speculation that 'species
vary'; and he then began to formulate a scheme of life as a branching tree. To
encompass the extinction as well as the emergence of life he incorporates an
image, suggested by his work on coral reefs, in which he had used Lyell's
uniformitarian geology to suggest that the continual subsidence of the reefs
was accompanied by the gradual growth of coral: 'The tree of life should
perhaps be called the coral of life, base of branches dead; so that passages
cannot be seen'. He then sketches a schematic diagram of the branching tree
of life, illustrating the process of evolution through the branching development of species, representing an 'immens[e] gap of relation', 'the finest
gradation' and 'rather greater distinction' between species. Significantly, he is
critical of a human-centred theory of life, rejecting the supposition that
evolutionary change had a single path of development, that there is a
preordained pattern of ascent culminating in human beings: 'It is absurd to
talk of one animal being higher than another. – *We* consider those, where the
cerebral structure/intellectual faculties most developed, as highest', but a
bee would measure highness 'when the instincts were [developed]'. Human
valuation, which singles out the intellectual development of man as the criterion of highness and uniqueness, contradicts Darwin's Humboldtian sense of
the fecundity and holistic unity of nature: 'When we talk of higher order, we
should always say intellectually higher. – But who with the face of the earth
covered with the most beautiful savannahs & forests dare to say that intellec-
tuality is only aim in this world'. Turning away from a human-centred view of
life he questioned the uniqueness of man in raising the issue of a simian
ancestry, with a barb directed at conventional pieties: 'If all men were dead
then monkeys make men. – Men make angels'.[46]

Darwin pursued these thoughts further in 1838–9, filling three more notebooks on transmutation and two notebooks devoted to the human implications of evolution. Observing an orang-utan in London Zoo, with its
'expressive whine . . . intelligence . . . affection . . . passion & rage', led him to
draw analogies between the emotions of apes and humans, and to see human
instincts and thoughts as products of evolutionary development: 'Why is
thought being a secretion of brain, more wonderful than gravity a property of
matter? It is our arrogance'. He took this line of speculation to its furthest
extent in considering religious belief to be an instinct: 'love of the deity [an]
effect of organization. oh you Materialist!' he exclaimed. While being perfectly
clear in these private musings about the naturalistic, even materialistic implications of his evolutionary speculations, which from the outset he envisaged
to encompass humankind, he was fully aware of the scientific difficulties that

stood in his way. His argument rested on the assumption, derived from Lyell's natural philosophy, that large changes could be explained by a long sequence of incremental events, but he conceded that it was hard to envisage how a long sequence of seemingly organised and directive changes could occur: 'We never may be able to trace the steps by which the organization of the eye, passed from simpler stage to more perfect, preserving its relations – the wonderful power of adaptation given to organization. – This really perhaps greatest difficulty to whole theory.'[47] These remarks were entered into a species notebook kept between March and July 1838. At this preliminary stage the theory posited some assumptions about the variation and adaptation of species that were to be abandoned or transformed in the *Origin of Species*. Darwin assumed that organisms produced variations in response to changes in external environmental circumstances, caused by geological or climatic changes; that this variation is episodic, for only when environmental changes occur does transmutation adjust organisms to meet external conditions; this intermittent variation is a response to external changes, and only when these changes occur do some organisms become poorly adapted to their environments; transmutation is envisaged as occurring within a Lyellian scheme of the balance and equilibrium in nature; and the process of variation, through which organisms become adapted to changing environments, is the means of maintaining harmony in nature.[48]

But Darwin lacked a causal basis for this process of evolution – a principle shaping the variation, preservation and adaptation of organisms within their environments, the principle 'of being preserved in the struggle for life' that, in the *Origin of Species*, he 'called, for the sake of brevity, Natural Selection'.[49] A sequence of reading in philosophical texts and the periodical literature, following lines of inquiry prompted by his speculations on species, led him to the *Essay on the Principle of Population* by Robert Malthus, first issued in 1798 and published in expanded form in 1803 with several subsequent editions.[50] It is likely that Darwin had been familiar with the general cast of the *Essay on Population*; its doctrines on the relation between food supply and the size of the population had been very widely discussed in the context of William Paley's natural theology and utilitarian moral philosophy, had generated vociferous intellectual debate, and Malthusian political economy had become politically controversial in its association with the Poor Law Amendment Act of 1834 which curtailed support for the destitute. Notions of competition for survival had become familiar in natural history. In the *Principles of Geology* Lyell had discussed the struggle of organisms to survive within their environments, drawing the parallel with humans obtaining possession of the earth by conquest, and he had cited the botanist Augustin de Candolle: '"All the plants of a given country," says de Candolle in his usual spirited style, "are at war one with another".'[51] In the *Essay on Population* Malthus began by invoking the analogy with the 'prolific nature of plants and animals' which was only controlled 'by their crowding and interfering with each other's means of subsistence'; he argued that the human 'population has this constant tendency to increase beyond the means of subsistence' and that 'the population when unchecked goes on doubling itself every twenty-five years or increases in a geometrical ratio', vastly outstripping any possible increase in agricultural production. While the fecundity of plants and animals is checked by natural ('positive') causes, he suggested that in the case of the human population there would need to be 'preventive checks' to preserve the balance between the size of the population and the amount of available food; it was therefore necessary to direct the charitable support of the poor to encourage social responsibility, including late marriage.[52] Darwin did not record his views about Malthusian social policy, but in his *Autobiography* he later explained that he now encountered Malthus 'being well prepared to appreciate the struggle for existence', and turned the theory of population pressure from political economy back to discussion of the fecundity of plants and animals, finding that he 'had at last got a theory by which to work'.[53] He recorded his reading of Malthus in a notebook entry dated 28 September 1838: 'Even the energetic language of Malthus [and] Decandoelle does not convey the warring of the species as inference from Malthus . . . in Nature production does not increase, whilst no checks prevail, but the positive check of famine & consequently death . . . yet until the one sentence of Malthus no one clearly perceived the great check amongst men.' Darwin's reading of Malthus on checks to the population, in the context of his appreciation of the significance of the struggle for existence and warfare among species, suggested a metaphor for the process of variation and adaptation: 'One may say that there is a force like a hundred thousand wedges trying [to] force every kind of adapted structure into the gaps in the oeconomy of Nature, or rather forming gaps by thrusting out weaker ones. The final cause of all this wedgings, must be to sort out proper structure & adapt it to change'.[54]

In this first formulation of what became the principle of natural selection Darwin appeals to the metaphor of warfare in nature, derived from de Candolle and Malthus, which he was to blend with the holistic concepts of fecundity and harmony that he had imbibed from Humboldt and which in his *Autobiography* he described as embodying a 'sense of sublimity'. The mechanistic metaphor of 'wedging', by contrast – unsurprisingly given that it was prompted by reading Malthus – suggests the aesthetics and language of natural theology, with an emphasis on order, design and mechanism, with nature now being represented as a selector.[55] Darwin was familiar with works of natural theology, especially Paley's *Natural Theology* (1802) where he may first have encountered discussion of Malthus; he told John Lubbock in November 1859, on the publication of the *Origin of Species*, that 'I do not think I hardly ever admired a book more than Paley's Natural Theology; I could almost formerly have said it by heart'.[56] In the natural theology tradition the design and adaptation of organisms to their function and environment was discussed in terms of design, in terms of the perfect contrivance with which they had been created. Darwin had conceded that understanding the complex pathway through which the 'power of adaptation' could give rise to the 'organization of the eye' was the 'greatest difficulty' his theory had to surmount; by contrast, Paley pointed to the eye as being 'decisive of contrivance' and design, through which 'the existence, the agency, the wisdom of the Deity, *could* be testified to his rational creatures'.[57] For Paley contrivance is demonstrated by the perfection of design and adaptation to function; and Darwin conceived selection as a wedging force shaping variations into perfectly adapted forms.

Over the next few months Darwin developed his initial insight, prompted by reading Malthus, into the theory of natural selection.[58] In a notebook entry made some time after October 1838 he commented on the relation between variation and adaptation: 'Species are innumerable variations. Every structure is capable of innumerable variations, as long as each shall be *perfectly* adapted to circumstances of times'. But he considers that this perfect adaptation is produced by the operation of natural laws (the Malthusian wedging force of natural selection) rather than being the result of divine contrivance and design. In the following notebook entry he succinctly summarises his theory: 'Three principles will account for all (1) Grandchildren like grandfathers (2) Tendency to small change ... (3) Great fertility in proportion to support of parents'; the theory rests on heredity, variation and Malthusian population pressure (Darwin's wedging force), not on a divine plan. This lapidary statement is followed in the notebook by his enthusiastic response on reading Herschel's affirmation, in his letter to Lyell, that the introduction of new species should be understood in terms of natural laws: 'Hurrah – "intermediate causes".' This repudiation of the natural theology of design and contrivance is confirmed in a subsequent entry, which cuts to the heart of the aesthetics of design of the natural theologians: 'Seeing the beautiful seed of a Bull Rush I thought, surely no "fortuitous" growth could have produced these innumerable seeds – yet if a seed were produced with infinitesimal advantage it would have better chance of being propagated & so &c.' The introduction of new species through variation, natural selection and adaptation to their organic and inorganic environments, promoting the preservation of advantaged variations, was to be understood as a wholly naturalistic process.[59]

By 1839 Darwin had formulated the basic principles of his theory of evolution by natural selection. But he made no plans to publish his work, and when he did so 20 years later in the *Origin of Species* he had transformed the theory in subtle but significant ways: the concept of relative adaptation superseded his earlier acceptance of the notion, deriving from the natural theology of design, of perfect adaptation to an environment; he supposed variation to be continuous rather than episodic; and with his 'principle of divergence' he succeeded in clarifying the relation between variation and adaptation. Work on the species theory was impeded by his professional commitments and by bouts of illness; he married his cousin Emma Wedgwood in January 1839, and there is evidence that he was concerned to exercise caution in fully revealing his ideas to his wife. But before moving his family to Down in Kent in September 1842, Darwin wrote out a preliminary 'Sketch' of his theory. He introduced the structure of argument that he was to follow in subsequent presentations, including the *Origin of Species*, beginning with a discussion of the origin of domesticated varieties and drawing the analogy to natural processes, stating the argument for natural selection and then applying the concept to the solution of core problems in natural history. In this document he begins to integrate his notion of the sublimity of nature with the mechanistic and selective concept of the 'wedging' force. In line with his Humboldtian holistic view of nature he personifies 'selection': 'if a being infinitely more sagacious than man (not an omniscient creator) during thousands and thousands of years were to select all the variations which tended towards certain ends'. Following his reading of Malthus he conceives this process as the 'natural means of selection', which he associates with 'De Candolle's war of nature' and 'Malthus on man'. In early 1844 Darwin transformed this preliminary 'Sketch' into an enlarged 'Essay' of 230 pages, where he again integrates the two conceptions of nature, holistic and selective. He supposes a 'Being with penetration sufficient to perceive differences in the outer and innermost organization quite imperceptible to man, and with foresight extending over future centuries to watch with unerring care and select for any object the offspring of an organism', working through '*secondary* means in the economy of nature by which the process of selection could go on adapting, nicely and wonderfully, organisms, if in every so small a degree plastic, to diverse ends'. This was envisaged as a process working through natural laws, immediate or secondary causes; and he firmly declares that 'I believe such secondary means do exist'. He still considered variation in nature to be episodic rather than continuous and he invokes the metaphor of wedging to explain how natural selection, personified as a 'being', scrutinises and adapts the organism to fit its environment: 'Nature may be compared to a surface, on which rest ten thousand sharp wedges touching each other and driven inwards by incessant blows'; but let the 'external conditions of a country change' then 'the original inhabitants must cease to be so perfectly adapted to the conditions as they originally were'. He maintains his view that variations are intermittent and episodic, and adaptation is perfect; perfectly adapted forms only vary when there is a change in external conditions.[60]

Darwin had the 'Essay' copied out in 1844, but not with a view for its immediate issue; he left instructions with Emma for its publication in the event of
his death, suggesting Lyell as the editor. The theory was beset with internal
problems seeking resolution, on the formation of the branching taxonomic
tree and why natural selection acted to produce such high level of diversity.
Darwin also had a sense of trepidation that his Cambridge mentors Henslow
and Sedgwick, and even Lyell for whom he was a scientific disciple, would be
appalled and contemptuous of his speculations. He took courage while
writing the 'Essay' to broach the subject tentatively with his new friend, the
botanist Joseph Dalton Hooker, in January 1844: 'I am almost convinced
(quite contrary to the opinion I started with) that species are not (it is like
confessing a murder) immutable'; his parentheses show the anxiety he had to
overcome.[61] These difficulties were heightened, later the same year, with the
anonymous publication by the Edinburgh publisher Robert Chambers of a
sensational book, the *Vestiges of the Natural History of Creation* (1844). In his
astonishing exposition and popularisation of an evolutionary cosmology,
going far beyond Darwin's engagement with natural history, Chambers drew
upon a wide range of scientific writing in describing a universal process of
continuous generation from the swirling 'fire-mist' of creation to nebulae,
solar systems and planets, showing how the earth's strata display a progressive
history of increasingly complex organisms from invertebrates, fish, reptiles
and mammals, to man, and promoting the hypothesis of the transmutation of
species. Hooker told Darwin that he was 'delighted with *Vestiges*' though he
did not agree with the conclusions, considering the book 'more like a 9 days
wonder than a lasting work'; Darwin rather stiffly responded that he was 'less
amused at it, than you appear to have been', finding the writing 'admirable' but
'his geology strikes me as bad, & his zoology far worse'. There was much speculation over the authorship, and Darwin told his cousin W.D. Fox that he was
alarmed to find that the 'strange unphilosophical, but capitally-written book'
had been 'by some attributed to me – at which I ought to be much flattered
and unflattered'. The response from Darwin's scientific mentors was immediate and unremittingly hostile, notably an assault and demolition of the
geology of *Vestiges* by Adam Sedgwick in the *Edinburgh Review* of July 1845,
in which the natural philosophy advocated by the book '*annulled all distinction between physical and moral*', a criticism he later pressed on Darwin after
reading the *Origin of Species*. Darwin read Sedgwick's review with alarm, telling
Lyell that 'some passages savour of the dogmatism of the pulpit, rather than of
the philosophy of the Professor', but he allowed that it was 'a grand piece of
argument against mutability of species; & I read it with fear & trembling, but
was well pleased to find, that I had not overlooked any of the arguments'.[62]

Despite Darwin's sense of private confidence, the response to *Vestiges* hardly
encouraged publication of a theory on the transmutation of species; and he

felt the need to provide overwhelming evidence before he ventured to bring his theory before his scientific peers. A chance remark by Hooker led him to undertake a project in taxonomy, the field of Hooker's expertise and where Darwin felt his own lack of credentials: 'How painfully (to me) true is your remark that no one has hardly a right to examine the question of species who has not minutely described many.' He had a ready specimen to hand, an anomalous species of barnacle that he had found off the coast of Chile, initiating a study that expanded to a description of all living and fossil species of barnacle and that fully established his credentials as a taxonomist. His investigation highlighted the problem of explaining the origin of apparently bizarre and diverse barnacles, to understand how natural selection had produced so much diversity; and he was able to establish that the separate barnacle sexes had descended from a hermaphrodite ancestor, strengthening his argument for the descent and modification of species. 'I never should have made this out, had not my species theory convinced me', he told Hooker in May 1848, exuberantly declaring that 'I don't care what you say, my species theory is all gospel'. When Darwin was finally able to return to the transmutation theory in late 1854, it was the problem of diversity and the branching tree that engaged his intention, to show, as he wrote in a note, 'that there is a tendency to diverge . . . in offspring of every class; & so to give the diverging tree-like appearance to the natural genealogy of the organised world'.[63]

Darwin formulated his 'principle of divergence' in the light of statistical studies of the relative proportions of botanical species and genera in defined geographical locations, and investigated the maximum number of individual plants a plot of land could support. 'I have been trying from land productions to take a very general view of the world', he told Hooker, whose expertise and current work on biogeography were to prove invaluable to him in carrying though this study; and he began corresponding with a network of botanists, including the Harvard professor Asa Gray, endlessly seeking data which he would file and assimilate. Darwin established that resources would be distributed to support more life forms if an area was occupied by diverse species. Specialisation would be an adaptive advantage, for natural selection would favour new varieties exploiting new opportunities, filling evolutionary niches. In June 1855 he asked Gray for data on a point that 'can at present interest no one but myself', so that he could 'compare in *different* Floras whether the same genera have "close species"'. Armed with such information Darwin was able to establish that small genera occupied restricted localities while large genera were widely distributed. He finally explained his interest and reasoning to Gray in a letter of September 1857, outlining his theory of natural selection and including a statement of the 'principle of divergence': 'The same spot will support more life if occupied by very diverse forms: we see this in the many generic forms in a square yard of turf (I have counted

20 species belonging to 18 genera) . . . the varying offspring of each species will try (only few will succeed) to seize on as many and as diverse places in the economy of nature, as possible. Each new variety or species, when formed will generally take the place of and so exterminate its less well-fitted parent. This, I believe, to be the origin of the classification of all organic beings at all times'.[64]

In May 1856, encouraged by Lyell, Darwin began writing a book to which he gave the title 'Natural Selection'. The 'principle of divergence' impacted on his earlier assumption that variations are intermittent and episodic, and that adaptation would be perfect. 'No country can be named', he now wrote, 'in which all the inhabitants are perfectly adapted to its conditions of existence', so that 'in the course of time, natural selection might modify some few of the inhabitants & adapt them better to their place in the great scheme of nature'. He now maintained that the slight difference that separates two varieties of a species is augmented into the greater difference that separates two species, and this process 'must on our theory be continually occurring in nature, if varieties are converted into good species . . . to fill as many, as new & as widely different places in nature as possible'. He concludes that 'our principle of Divergence . . . regulates the natural Selection of variations, & causes the Extinction of intermediate & less favoured forms'.[65] He now considers that variation is continuous and adaptation to be relative to environmental circumstances, the better adapted species surviving. In a letter of 8 June 1858 he reaffirmed the strategy of his argument to Hooker: 'I discuss the "principle of Divergence", which with "Natural Selection" is the key-stone of my Book & I have great confidence it is sound'.[66]

Darwin's confident plans for completing his manuscript were disrupted ten days later on 18 June 1858, on the receipt of a letter and manuscript of a paper from Alfred Russel Wallace, an established correspondent. The deflation of his spirits and confidence is apparent in a letter to Lyell written that day: 'Wallace . . . has today sent me the enclosed & asked to forward it to you. It seems to me well worth reading. Your words have come true with a vengeance that I should be forestalled. You said this when I explained to you here very briefly my views of "Natural Selection" depending on the Struggle for existence. . . . I never saw a more striking coincidence. . . . Even his terms now stand as Heads of my Chapters. . . . So all my originality, whatever it may amount to, will be smashed'. Lyell and Hooker read Wallace's paper and decided that the joint announcement of the theories of the two men would be the appropriate solution. Darwin was ill and worried over the sickness of his infant son (who died on 28 June), and he left the arrangements to Lyell and Hooker, who formally presented Wallace's paper, together with extracts from Darwin's 1844 'Essay' and a copy of the letter he had sent to Asa Gray in September 1857, to the Linnaean Society on 1 July 1858. This first public presentation of the theory of natural selection caused no stir; but urged on by Hooker to quickly publish a more structured account of his theory, Darwin agreed that he could 'easily prepare an abstract of my whole work'.[67] He initially planned to write a journal article, but his text expanded to become the *Origin of Species*, published in November 1859; he discarded the references and detail of his uncompleted manuscript on 'Natural Selection', and the book was aimed at the wider reading public.

The title page of the *Origin of Species* is prefaced with two epigraphs, a passage from Francis Bacon's *Advancement of Learning* (1805) on the study of the book of God's works (nature) and the book of God's word (the Bible), and a philosophical assertion of the domain of laws of nature quoted from William Whewell's *Bridgewater Treatise* of 1833, the claim that 'with regard to the material world . . . we can perceive that events are brought about not by insulated interpositions of Divine power exerted in each particular case, but by the establishment of general laws'.[68] The appeal to these authorities gave the reader assurance that the origin of species fell within the appropriate study of God's works and should be understood in terms of natural laws rather than miraculous interventions. In quoting Whewell, an opponent of the transmutation of species, Darwin sought to use the citation to place discussion of the origin of species firmly within the boundary of science as marked out by natural theology, but as intelligible in terms of natural laws. The point is reinforced by his reference, in the opening passage of the *Origin of Species*, to the introduction of new species as the 'mystery of mysteries, as it has been called by one of our greatest philosophers', making allusion to Herschel's letter to Lyell and strategically invoking Herschel's authority for discussion of the origin of species as a natural process. Darwin stated that 'this whole volume is one long argument', the exposition of his theory of 'descent with modification through natural selection'. In setting out his carefully structured argument 'on the origin of species by means of natural selection', he aimed to establish the more fundamental doctrine of the 'descent' (evolution) of species. In May 1863 he remarked to Asa Gray that the '*change of species by descent* . . . seems to me the turning point', though 'Personally, of course, I care much about Natural Selection . . . that seems to me utterly unimportant compared to [the] question of *Creation* **or** *Modification*'.[69]

Darwin structured his argument in three groups of chapters: the exposition of the theory of natural selection, beginning with the analogy between variation under domestication and variation under nature; a review of the various objections that he anticipates might be offered; and finally a discussion of a range of problems that can be explained by the theory of natural selection and descent by adaptation.[70] Darwin presents his account of the 'struggle for existence' as the 'doctrine of Malthus applied with manifold force to the whole animal and vegetable kingdoms', and he invokes the metaphor of wedging that he had first used, on responding to Malthus, in September 1838: 'the face of Nature may be compared to a yielding surface, with ten thousand sharp wedges packed close together and driven inwards by incessant blows'. He declares that 'plants and animals, most remote in the scale of nature, are bound together by a web of complex relations', and mitigates his dark vision of life forms as beset by struggle and warfare with a more elevated view of nature, a moral vision to which he returns at the end of the book: 'we may console ourselves with the full belief, that the war of nature is not incessant, that no fear is felt, that death is generally prompt, and that the vigorous, the healthy, and the happy survive and multiply'. The principle of 'natural selection' is described as leading to the 'preservation of favourable variations and the rejections of injurious variations', and is presented as a doctrine of improvement and progress: 'natural selection is daily and hourly scrutinising, throughout the world, every variation . . . rejecting that which is bad, preserving and adding up all that is good; silently and insensibly working . . . at the improvement of each organic being in relation to its organic and inorganic conditions of life'.

Drawing the parallel with Lyell's theory of geology, Darwin argues that natural selection proceeds 'by the preservation and accumulation of infinitesimally small inherited modifications, each profitable to the preserved being'. He cites Paley's view of benevolence, stripped of its theological reference, to support his view that 'natural selection acts solely by and for the good of each' species so that if any part becomes injurious to its possessor 'the being will become extinct'. But whereas the natural theologians appealed to perfect adaptation as evidence of design, Darwin declares that perfect adaptation is illusory. The 'degree of perfection attained under nature' is that which will be sufficient to give competitive advantage to an organism in its struggle for existence. Thus the plants and animals endemic to New Zealand are 'perfect one compared with another' but were now yielding under the impact of species imported from Europe. 'Natural selection will not produce absolute perfection, nor do we always meet, as far as we can judge, with this high standard under nature.' This process of selection occurs through diversification, enabling species to 'seize on many and widely diversified places in the polity of nature, and so be enabled to increase in numbers'. In accordance with this 'principle of divergence' Darwin finds numerous instances showing that 'the greatest amount of life can be supported by great diversification of structure'. He explains the processes of selection and divergence by the simile of a tree, its green and budding twigs representing living species and the decayed branches as species now extinct and only known as fossils: 'As buds give rise by growth to fresh buds, and these if vigorous branch out and overtop on all sides many a feebler branch, so by generation it has been with the great Tree of Life, which fills with its dead and broken branches the crust of the earth, and covers the surface with its ever branching and beautiful ramifications.' His concept of nature remains infused with anthropomorphic imagery; in comparing selection under domestication and in nature he writes that 'Man selects only for his own good; Nature only for that of the being which she tends.'[71]

Natural selection is a description of a process, a metaphor in which nature is personified; and the analogy between selection under domestication and selection by nature fostered this personification. This feature of the argument caused problems with some readers, including Adam Sedgwick, who made immediate comments on receipt of a copy of the book in November 1859: 'You write of "natural selection" as if it were done consciously by the selecting agent. – 'Tis but a consequence of the pre*supposed* development, and the subsequent battle for life', and was no more than a description of 'supposed, or known, primary facts'.[72] Darwin responded to these complaints in the third edition of the *Origin of Species* issued in 1861. 'It has been said that I speak of natural selection as an active power or Deity; but who objects to an author speaking of the attraction of gravity as ruling the movements of the planets? ... So again it is difficult to avoid personifying the word Nature, but I mean by Nature, only the aggregate action and product of many natural laws'. Darwin did not have a mechanism for selection, and understood 'natural selection' as a 'metaphorical expression ... almost necessary for brevity'.[73] This metaphorical language about nature pervades the text of the *Origin of Species*, and is especially prominent in the concluding recapitulation of the argument. Darwin was concerned to make it clear that his was a theory about the descent and modification of species, not a theory of the origin of life itself. The distinction lies behind his statement that 'probably all the organic beings which have ever lived on this earth have descended from some one primordial form, into which life was first breathed'. In response to Richard Owen's sarcastic reference to his phrase 'into which life was first breathed' as being 'Pentateuchal', Darwin commented to Hooker in March 1863 that 'I have long regretted that I truckled to public opinion & used Pentateuchal term of creation, by which I really meant "appeared" by some wholly unknown process. – It is mere rubbish thinking, at present, of origin of life; one might as well think of origin of matter'. But in referring to 'the laws impressed on matter by the Creator', Darwin sought to present the argument of the *Origin of Species* as congruent with accepted cultural norms, and his final peroration in the book utilises the aesthetic language of design and natural theology but stripped of its providential associations: 'There is grandeur in this view of life ... having been originally breathed into a few forms or into one; and that, whilst this planet has gone cycling on according to the fixed law of gravity, from so simple a beginning endless forms most beautiful and most wonderful have been, and are being, evolved.'

This statement suggests a parallel between the familiar and unassailable Newtonian law of gravity in the physical cosmos and the status of Darwinian natural selection in the world of terrestrial life; and in the third edition of 1861 Darwin invoked the comparison with gravity in defending his metaphor of natural selection. But Adam Sedgwick responded furiously and immediately to Darwin's notion of a non-providential 'grandeur' in nature: 'There is a moral or metaphysical part of nature as well as a physical. A man who denies this is deep in the mire of folly. Tis the crown & glory of organic science that it *does* thro' *final cause* link material to moral . . .. You have ignored this link, &, if I do not mistake your meaning, you have done your best in one or two pregnant cases to break it. Were it possible (which thank God it is not) to break it, humanity in my mind might suffer a damage that might brutalize it'. Darwin had been careful to restrict reference to human origins to one sentence in the final pages of his book – 'Light will be thrown on the origin of man and his history' – but Sedgwick's despairing response to the *Origin of Species*, addressed to Darwin by 'a son of a monkey & an old friend of yours', encapsulated the reaction that he had always feared, but could now endure, and underlines the naturalistic thrust of his argument. Darwin's teleology is non-providential and is expressed in terms of the naturalistic and Humboldtian ecology of the 'entangled bank' of the final paragraph of the book: 'It is interesting to contemplate an entangled bank, clothed with many plants of many kinds, with birds singing on the bushes, with various insects flitting about, and with worms crawling through the damp earth, and to reflect that the elaborately constructed forms, so different from each other, and dependent on each other in so complex a manner, have all been produced by laws acting around us.'[74]

The Aesthetics of Natural History: John Ruskin

On 3 April 1860 Darwin told Asa Gray 'that I remember well [the] time when the thought of the eye made me cold all over, but I have got over this stage of the complaint, & now small trifling particulars of structure often make me very uncomfortable'. As an instance of his discomfort he declared that the 'sight of a feather in a peacock's tail, whenever I gaze at it, makes me sick!'.[75] In the *Origin of Species* Darwin argued that the eye was formed by 'numerous, successive, slight, modifications' through a sequence of 'transitional gradations';[76] but unlike the eye, the feathers in a peacock's tail seemed extravagantly decorative – even burdensome – rather than functional and advantageous, and the basis for their evolutionary development obscure. Darwin's later development of his theory from its first statement in the *Origin of Species* (1859), to explain the colouration and beauty of orchids and the variegated display of the plumage of birds, formed a body of argument that Ruskin became determined to contest and ridicule, and to replace by his own natural history based on human values and the aesthetic appreciation of the natural world. Indeed, it was the claim that Darwin's evolutionary theory could be enlarged to explain ornamentation – the feathers in the peacock's tail – in terms of the aesthetic appreciation of nature by birds that Ruskin found especially offensive.

Darwin confronted the issue of the plumage of birds in *The Descent of Man, and Selection in Relation to Sex* (1871) with a lengthy discussion of ornamentation and sexual selection in birds (enlarged in the second edition of 1874), emphasising the role of sexual selection in promoting evolution. Darwin argued that male ornamentation – the feathers in a peacock's tail – had evolved because of female choice, favouring the decorative plumage colours and elaborate display rituals of males. Darwin's theory of sexual selection posited reproductive competition between individuals of the same species and members of the same sex: ornamentation and combat among males would generate female choice and reproductive success.[77] He argued that 'the strongest and most vigorous males, or those provided with the best weapons, have prevailed under nature'; by analogy, man could improve the breed of poultry by the selection of individual male birds. This had aesthetic as well as practical implications in the state of nature: 'just as man can give beauty, according to his standard of taste, to his male poultry . . . so it appears that female birds in a state of nature, have by a long selection of the more attractive males, added to their beauty or other attractive qualities' by manifesting 'powers of discrimination and taste'. He acknowledged that attributing aesthetic choice to birds 'will at first appear extremely improbable', but declared that he aimed to establish 'that the females actually have these powers'.[78] Darwin's naturalistic theory explained the acquisition of the ornamental plumage of birds by positing continuity between the aesthetic sense of mankind and that of animals.[79] He pointed to the display by male birds of 'graceful plumes or splendid colours before the female' as showing that the female 'admires the beauty of her male partner'; and 'as women everywhere deck themselves with these plumes, the beauty of such ornaments cannot be disputed'. Just as human aesthetic choice shows 'capricious changes of customs and fashions', the 'lower animals are . . . capricious in their . . . sense of beauty', and 'love novelty, for its own sake'.[80]

Courtship display had as its purpose sexual selection. Darwin explained that the complex and beautiful decorative plumage of the male Argus pheasant is not 'exhibited in full perfection, until the male assumes the attitude of courtship'; these 'beautiful ornaments are hidden until the male shows himself off before the female'. The mating success of the male 'appears to depend on the great size of his plumes, and the elaboration of the most elegant patterns'. This implied that 'a female bird should be able to appreciate fine shading and exquisite patterns' in the male bird's plumage, demonstrating an 'almost human degree of taste' in the aesthetic appreciation of 'the wonderful beauty of his plumage'.[81] Darwin gave illustrations of the ocelli (the coloured spots surrounded by rings of different colours) in the wing feathers of the male Argus pheasant. Examining the patterns of markings he argued that 'a gradation is possible', maintaining that 'a perfect series can be followed from simple spots to the wonderful ball-and-socket ornaments', giving a 'clue' to the 'steps passed through by the extinct progenitors of the species' as the ornamental plumage had developed through sexual selection. Noting the care with which the male Argus pheasant displayed his plumes in advantageous fashion before the female during courtship, Darwin concluded that it was 'probable that female birds prefer the more attractive males', arguing that sexual selection was fostered through the aesthetic appreciation of ornamentation by the female birds.[82]

In *Proserpina* (1875–86) Ruskin expressed his contempt for Darwin's claims for the aesthetic sense and discrimination of birds, rejecting Darwin's connection of the human aesthetic sense to that of animals: 'the perception of beauty and the power of defining physical character, are based on moral instinct, and on the power of defining animal or human character'. He made scathing reference to Darwin's 'vespertilian treatise on the ocelli of the Argus pheasant which he imagines to be artistically gradated and perfectly imitative of a ball and socket'; this was a form of materialistic analogy that was 'essentially the work of human bats' in its 'one-sided intensity', blind to the true perception of colour and beauty in the natural world. In reducing the human aesthetic sense to the physical sensations of animals Darwin had, according to Ruskin, trivialised and degraded in 'unclean stupidity' the humanistic and moral status of the aesthetic appreciation of nature.[83] For Ruskin, Darwinian naturalism represented a fundamental challenge to human values expressed in art and the appreciation of the truth of nature, the focus of *Modern Painters*.[84]

Concerned with the classification and nomenclature of flowers, *Proserpina* provided a uniquely Ruskinian alternative form of botany, in striking contrast to Darwin's books published in the 1860s and 1870s. Darwin commented that his book on the fertilisation of *Orchids* (1862) 'will, *perhaps*, serve [to] illustrate how natural History may be worked under the belief of the modification of Species'.[85] His late books on orchids, the forms of flowers, fertilisation, insectivorous plants and climbing plants form a considerable body of influential work – though Darwin modestly and wholly characteristically disclaimed botanical expertise. As with his emphasis on analogical reasoning in his discussion of the decorative plumage and display rituals of male birds and sexual selection by females, where his argument is structured by positing the continuity between the aesthetic sense of mankind and birds, Darwin argued for continuity between the behaviour of animals and plants – insectivorous plants captured insects as prey, while climbing plants manifested movement. As with his discussion of the feathers in the peacock's tail, when considering orchids he explained their elaborate structure and the gorgeous colours of their flowers as arising from the process of natural selection, by attracting insects through contrivances of structure by which cross-fertilisation is best assured. The complexity and beauty of orchids may suggest 'the direct inter-position of the Creator', Darwin explained in the introduction to his book on the fertilisation of *Orchids*, but it was his aim to show 'that the structure of each is due to secondary laws', that the beauty of orchids was the product of natural selection. The provision of illustrations to assist the presentation of his argument was important to the exposition, and the figures combine portraits of the flower and more detailed depictions of their pollination and reproductive systems, focusing especially on their structure through which the form and colours – and in consequence the beauty – of orchids would facilitate their cross-fertilisation by insects.[86]

Ruskin had discussed botanical issues – in terms of the 'truth of vegeta-tion' and 'leaf beauty' – in the first and fifth volumes of *Modern Painters*; but *Proserpina* formed a new departure in scope and outlook, its subtitle 'Studies of wayside flowers while the air was yet pure among the Alps, and in the Scotland and England which my father knew' giving indication of the eccentricity of his argument. Unlike Darwin, who was concerned to display the reproductive parts of flowers in the illustrations in his botanical books, Ruskin discreetly avoided matters of fertilisation; in his 'four stages in the young life of a primrose' his drawings show the growth of the flower without revealing its structure, depicting the primrose flower as it would be seen 'by the wayside'. He poured scorn on botanical dissection and the 'microscopic malice of botanists' as insensitive to the beauty of flowers, in his view the true end of the study of botany; and his obsession with the innocence of young girls gave rise to an alarmed warning to 'my girl-readers against all study of floral genesis and digestion'.[87] His outlook in *Proserpina* was shaped by his personal symbolism of flowers, fostered by his relationship with Rose La Touche, the young girl with whom he became infatuated in 1858 after the collapse of his marriage; he associated Rose with the goddess Proserpine, shared with Rose a language of flowers, and her personal tragedy filled his thoughts.[88] In a passage, 'The Stem', written and published in 1876 but dated 25 May 1875, the day of Rose's death, he wrote that 'there is no question but that all nice people like hawthorn blossom'. Of a hawthorn branch he writes that 'the lovely thing is more like the spring frock of some prudent little maid of fourteen, than a flower', continuing in a flight of fancy that the blossom was 'going to be a Rose, some day soon'. The book may well have been written as a memorial to his love for Rose.[89]

Ruskin did not consider flowers in terms of the scientific botany set out by Linnaeus and Darwin, in relation to a reproductive taxonomy or to structures for facilitating fertilisation, but rather placed emphasis on aesthetic judgement, the appreciation of the colour and form of flowers, maintaining that 'the flower is the end of the seed – not the seed of the flower' and that 'the glory is in the purity, the serenity, the radiance' of flowers. Botany was to be pursued in its relation to human perception of beauty and was dependent on 'moral instinct'. These values shaped Ruskin's proposed revision of botanical nomenclature. In place of the conventional Linnaean nomenclature based on fructification, especially alarming to Ruskin because of Darwin's emphasis on the connection between fertilisation and the forms, colours and beauty of flowers, he suggested a botanical nomenclature based on the immediately observable, on what is perceptible to the naked eye and to the place where a flower was likely to be seen by the wayfarer. This nomenclature was shaped 'rather by reference to mythological associations than to botanical structure'. In Ruskin's system of nomenclature he grouped plants in orders of 12, and noted the conformity with the 'most beautiful parts of Greek mythology, leading on to early Christian tradition' – the 12 Olympian gods and the 12 disciples.[90]

Despite Ruskin's strictures against Darwinian science and his harsh comments about Darwin's outlook, the two men preserved the occasional personal acquaintance that had begun in Oxford in April 1837. In August 1879 Ruskin wrote to Darwin's son-in-law R.B. Litchfield (who had been a Cambridge friend of James Clerk Maxwell in the 1850s),[91] following a visit by Darwin to Ruskin's home 'Brantwood', near Coniston, assuring him that 'you must not think that I did not before recognize in him all that you speak of so affectionately'. Ruskin claimed that 'there is no word in any of my books of disrespect towards *him*', but regretted that the 'simplicity and humility of Darwin's character' had prevented him separating 'accurately observed truth' from the 'wild and impious foolishness' of the age. Following this cordial visit, Ruskin sent Darwin a drawing of the decorative plumage of the peacock, as if to underline their differences in outlook.[92]

Darwin's 1837 schematic diagram illustrating the descent of species through branching development became the basis for understanding the classification of species and the emergence and extinction of life forms. Acceptance of the principle of the descent and modification of species was in his view the 'turning point';[93] and it was in 1838, prompted by reading Malthus on checks to population, that he formulated his theory of natural selection as the causal basis of this process of the change of species by descent (evolution). In the argument of the *Origin of Species*, the uniformitarian natural philosophy of Lyell's *Principles of Geology* established the basis for the immense time span and gradualism of this process of modification from primordial forms. The metaphor of location on the branches of the 'Tree of Life' signalled the descent and extinction of species in terms of the process of natural selection. In the *Origin of Species*, natural selection is a description of a process, a metaphor in which nature is personified; and the analogy between selection by man under domestication and selection by nature – fundamental to Darwin's presentation of his argument – fostered this interpretation. But it was not until May 1856, when encouraged by Lyell, that Darwin began writing a book to which he gave the title 'Natural Selection'. He revised his earlier assumption that variation of species would be intermittent and episodic, now arguing that variation is continuous and adaptation is relative to environmental circumstances; according to his 'principle of divergence', natural selection would favour new varieties exploiting new opportunities in filling evolutionary niches, with the continuous variation and descent of species represented by the branching 'Tree of Life'; Darwin declared that divergence and natural selection together established the 'key-stone' of his argument. Interrupted by Wallace's intervention in June 1858, he proceeded to write the *Origin of Species*. On its publication in November 1859 it received a furious response from Sedgwick, who lambasted Darwin for ignoring the claims of natural theology, the 'moral or metaphysical part of nature'. But Darwin's appeal to non-providential grandeur in nature was a tactic crucial to the naturalistic, secular argument of the book.[94]

Classification was fundamental to natural history, as pursued by Linnaeus, Darwin and Ruskin. In Linnaeus' plant taxonomy the flowering parts of plants were taken as the systematic foundation of botany, an 'artificial' system of classifying plants by the quantitative procedure of counting their stamens and pistils. While Ruskin applauded the Linnaean system of classification as based on observation of the external characteristics of plants, his private language of the naming and classification of flowers expressed his belief in the enduring and universal values of myth, and embraced his personal symbolism of the culture of flowers. The appreciation of floral beauty was to be understood in relation to aesthetic and human values, which were taken as the basis of nomenclature and botanical classification. Ruskin combated Darwin's theory of natural selection and appeal to sexual selection to explain the ornamental plumage of birds, expressing contempt for Darwin's appeal to aesthetic discrimination by birds. In the face of Darwinian naturalism Ruskin asserted the primacy and uniqueness of human judgement in the aesthetic appreciation of nature, an outlook also evident in his discussion of the moral and aesthetic associations of colours, where he claims that colourists have 'nature and life on their side'.[95]

✳

CHAPTER 7

Colour

In 1852 WILLIAM HOLMAN HUNT, a member of the Pre-Raphaelite group, painted *Our English Coasts* (Fig. 12), which was exhibited the following year at the Royal Academy. Under the title *Strayed Sheep* the painting was shown in Paris in 1855, where it excited the admiration of Eugène Delacroix. In his attempt to give a realistic portrayal of the effects of sunlight and colour, Hunt drew upon the writings of artists, colourists and natural philosophers. The foundational text for the theory of colour, Newton's *Opticks* (1704), had been subject to many critiques since its publication – famously by Goethe, but also by Hunt's contemporaries the colourist George Field, the Edinburgh-based Scottish decorative artist David Ramsay Hay and the Scottish physicist David Brewster, whose works were familiar to Hunt. Brewster in particular had offered a trenchant and influential critique of Newton's theory of the spectrum of sunlight as displaying the gradation of irreducible colours, claiming to have established that red, yellow and blue were the primary colours distributed through the entire spectrum, and that the mixture of these rays, in various proportions, produces the colours of the Newtonian spectrum. Field and Hay agreed with Brewster in rejecting the Newtonian theory of the spectrum of sunlight and in affirming that red, yellow and blue were primaries that could not be further decomposed by a prism, a theory of spectral lights that was compatible with the experience of painters in using the triad of primary colourants, red, yellow and blue. Artists and theorists discussed the visual effect of the admixture of white and black in modifying tints, of the juxtaposition of contrasting colours, and the effect and depiction of coloured shadows. Hunt drew upon the ideas advanced in these works; and he used Field's new bright pigments to give dazzling effect in his paintings.[1]

In *Our English Coasts* Hunt sought to depict colour as it really appears in nature; the colours of the pigments are juxtaposed so that the illumination of the landscape by sunlight is rendered as polychromatic and intensified. The glimmering fleece of the sheep is represented by the juxtaposition of (Brewster's and artists') primaries of red, yellow and blue; use is made of the effects of coloured shadows and of contrasting colours in order to highlight

12   William Holman Hunt, *Our English Coasts (Strayed Sheep)*, 1852.

the visual representation of natural effects.[2] In a fully self-conscious way the painting draws upon the theoretical treatment of colours and their mode of representation in art as current in the 1840s. According to John Ruskin in a lecture in 1883, *Our English Coasts* was an attempt, 'for the first time in the history of art', to show 'the absolutely faithful balances of colour and shade by which actual sunshine might be transposed into a key in which the harmonies possible with material pigments should yet produce the same impressions upon the mind which were caused by the light itself'.[3] Hunt's painting exemplifies, in a new and innovative way, the effect of discussions about the relation between Newton's colours (the colours of spectral lights) and artists' pigments (the painters' triad of primary colourants); this relationship had shaped the treatment of colour in art and natural philosophy since the seventeenth century.

Colour in Nature and Art

Writing in 1870, the physicist James Clerk Maxwell, who played a seminal role in establishing a new understanding of colours in the 1850s, discussed the 'aesthetic beauty' of the 'new forms of splendour' displayed in the chromatic effects of polarised light on crystals, an investigation made possible in consequence of 'the perfection with which the phenomena may be seen by means of modern instruments'; he described the chromatic patterns as 'gorgeous entanglements of colour'.[4] Maxwell signalled that the aesthetic appreciation of colours was enlarged by new discoveries in colour science. Since antiquity, the theories of colours held by natural philosophers and the practices and aesthetic judgements of painters had interweaved; but the discoveries to which Maxwell made allusion formed part of a tradition of scientific investigation that flowed from Isaac Newton's theory of the spectral colours, first made public two centuries earlier. Newton's experiments with glass prisms established the style and conceptual framework for the investigation of the colour fringes generated by the transmission of light through transparent bodies, and became emblematic of experimental procedure in natural philosophy. Making his discoveries more widely available in the *Opticks*, Newton established a new language for the description and understanding of colour, a mode of representation that shaped discussion of the aesthetics of colours in nature and in paintings.

Newton had from the outset been convinced of the magnitude of his achievement, writing in January 1672 to Henry Oldenburg, the Secretary of the Royal Society, with the claim that he had made a 'Philosophicall discovery' which was 'in my Judgment the oddest if not the most considerable detection wch hath hitherto beene made in the operations of Nature'. Early the following February Newton wrote again to 'perform my late promise to you', giving an account of his experiments on the 'celebrated *Phaenomena* of *Colours*', a sequence of experiments and reasoning arising from his display of the 'coloured *Spectrum*', as he termed the band of coloured rays emerging from a glass prism.[5] The prismatic rainbow colours were familiar, as Newton implied; but his carefully structured sequence of experiments on the prism led him to novel conclusions, which to contemporaries did indeed seem odd, if not justifying the hyperbole of his claim that his work was 'the most considerable detection' yet made in natural philosophy.

In his *Opticks* Newton presented his theory of spectral colours in terms that were consonant with, and incorporated, the painters' triad of red, yellow and blue as the three primary pigment colours, facilitating the elision of discussion of the colours of nature to the use of colour pigments in works of art. The aesthetic appreciation of colours in nature and in painting came to be framed in terms of a common language, derived from Newton's theory of the sun's 'white' light being differentially refracted into heterogeneous coloured rays by a prism. In one of his essays on the 'Pleasures of the Imagination' published in the *Spectator* in 1712, Joseph Addison discussed the association of beauty with the 'delight in colours'. Taking sunrise and sunset as examples of the vivid appearance of colours, Addison found that there is no 'more glorious or pleasing show in nature, than . . . the rising and setting of the Sun, which is wholly made up of those different strains of light that shew themselves in

clouds of a different situation', making allusion to Newton's theory of the
dispersion of the sun's light by the prism into the colours of the spectrum.[6]
Beauty was found to reside in the pleasing form of bodies and in the vibrant
colours found in nature. In his poem *The Pleasures of Imagination* (1744)
Mark Akenside found beauty in the play of colours in nature: 'in th' effusive
warmth / Of colours mingling with a random blaze, / Doth beauty dwell', and
he made explicit appeal to the Newtonian theory of the spectrum of colours
in his poetic evocation of the beauty of the rainbow.[7] In his essay 'On the
Beautiful' (1810) Dugald Stewart associated beauty with the visual perception
of colours in giving 'pleasure to the eye', citing Addison and Akenside in
support of his contention that 'the first ideas of *beauty* formed by the mind
are, in all probability, derived from *colours*'.[8] If beauty is apprehended through
vision, then the Newtonian theory of light as a mixture of coloured rays sanctioned the aesthetic primacy of colour in nature. In his *Treatise on Ancient
Painting* (1740) George Turnbull took the Newtonian laws of light and colour
to illustrate his claim that painting is a language conveying scientific information about nature. It is through the operation of the laws of light and colour
that the 'Phaenomena of the visible World' are made manifest, and paintings
present examples of the operation of these laws and may be considered as
analogous to experiments in natural philosophy in fostering scientific understanding: 'Pictures which represent visible Beauties, or the Effects of Nature in
the visible World, by the different Modifications of Light and Colours, in
Consequence of the Laws which relate to Light, are Samples of what these
Laws do or may produce.'[9]

    Newton's theory of colours assumed that colour is a sensation produced in
the eye by light, an idea derived from the emergent mechanical philosophy of
Descartes and Boyle, but which was wholly at variance with traditional modes
of thinking about the nature of light and colour, which held that colour was a
real property of material bodies. The classic ancient source was Aristotle's
treatise *On Sense and Sensible Objects*, where the theory of light and colour is
based on the notion of the four elements, earth, water, air and fire. According
to Aristotle light arises when the element fire is present in a transparent
medium such as air or water; when the element fire generates light within
bodies, colours arise in their bounding surfaces, colours being transmitted to
the eye by light. White and black are regarded as the fundamental colours and
are due to the presence or absence of fire in bodies; the chromatic colours
arise from the mixture of white and black in differing degrees. In discussing
colour mixtures he introduces an important theme, which was to have an
enduring influence, claiming that if the proportions of white and black are
simple ratios then the most pleasant colours will arise, as in musical
harmonies. Following the analogy with the musical scale Aristotle suggests
that there are seven species of colour – the sequence of chromatic colours,

yellow, red, violet, green and blue spread between the extremes of white and black – and he supposes that all other colours are derived from combining these colours. Colour mixtures can be obtained by mixing coloured bodies or by the overlay or superimposition of different colours. Colours are classified on a linear scale between white and black: yellow is bright and contains mostly white, and is placed next to white; blue is dark and contains little white and is placed closest to black. Lightness and darkness, or whiteness or blackness, with yellow and blue as similarly juxtaposed colours, are fundamental concepts in Aristotle's colour theory. In opposing Newton's theory of light and colours, Goethe was to invoke a modification theory of colour based on a similar Aristotelian duality between light and dark, yellow and blue, sunlight and darkness.

This representation of colours and colour mixing was maintained in scholastic treatises in the seventeenth century, with white and black regarded as the extreme colours and the intermediate colours derived from their mixture, some colours inclining more to black, others to white. Scholastic formulations of colour theory continued to use the theory of the four elements, with fire as the luminous element generating colours at the surface of bodies; and as all substances were thought to be composed of the four elemental principles, colours were regarded as essential qualities of bodies. Aristotle considered the rainbow to be a transient phenomenon, and his explanation of its colours differed fundamentally from his account of the colours of natural bodies. In his *Meteorology* he identified three colours, red, green and violet, in the rainbow; however, these colours were not real and inherent colours but were held to arise from the modification of pure, uniform sunlight. The weakening and darkening of light by distant, dark, black clouds would generate the three colours of the bow, the upper band being red because it is the largest and the reflections from it are least weakened, the lower band being violet because it is the most darkened. This representation provided the basis for a three-colour scheme of rainbow colours. Whereas the real or true colours are regarded as inherent qualities of natural bodies, their colour being brought to the eye and disclosed by light, the apparent and transient rainbow and prismatic colours appear without a coloured body and are considered to be produced as modifications of incident light.

The mechanical philosophers of the seventeenth century rejected the Aristotelian theory of bodies as formed of the four elements, the theory of colour based on light and fire, and the distinction between the real and inherent colours of bodies and the transient coloured phenomena generated by modifications of light. Supposing that all natural bodies consist of particles of matter defined by size, shape and motion, and that all knowledge derives from sensations propagated from the nerves to the brain, in his *Meteores*

(1637) Descartes rejects the distinction between colours supposed to be true and inherent and others regarded as false or apparent. For Descartes, all colours are regarded as visual sensations, so the true nature of colours consists only in their appearance, known through sensory experience as light falls on the eye. He explains the colours of the rainbow and prism in terms of his concept of an aether filling space. The globules of aether are supposed to rotate uniformly when transmitting a direct beam of sunlight, and when the beam is refracted (by water drops in the rainbow, or by the glass of the prism) the rate of rotation of the globules changes. At the edges of the beam, at the boundary of light and shadow, the balls of aether rotate more swiftly or more slowly with the generation of different colours being ascribed to the different rotations. The more vigorous rotations produce the colour red, those that rotate a little slower make the colour yellow, while green appears where the balls rotate at around their usual rate, and blue when they rotate very much slower.

Descartes supposes that colour arises from a modification of sunlight, not from the mixture (or modification) of white and black, or light and shadow. He applies an analogous form of explanation when considering the colours of natural bodies. On the supposition that bodies do not possess colours as essential qualities, merely a disposition to excite sensations, the globules of aether are held to acquire different rotations when reflected from the textured surfaces of bodies, the differences in texture generating different colour sensations. In his *Meteores* Descartes provided the basis for a unitary theory of colour, inverting Aristotelian assumptions: as modifications of light, the transient rainbow and prism colours now have a privileged explanatory status in providing the basis for understanding the colours of natural bodies. In his *Experiments and Considerations Touching Colours* (1664) Robert Boyle also rejects the Aristotelian distinction between real and apparent colours, for both are equally colour sensations; the transient prismatic and rainbow colours are held to affect the eye 'as Truly and as Powerfully as other Colours'. All colours, of natural bodies and of the transient rainbow, are alike in being sensations excited by light in the brain, different colours being held to arise from different properties of light: 'Light it self produces the sensation of a Colour'. This had the consequence that the investigation of coloured lights could yield knowledge of the nature of colour, a conclusion drawn by Newton. From his reading of Descartes and Boyle he undertook an investigation of the effects of transient prismatic colours, leading to the proposal of a general theory of colour, including a theory of coloured bodies.[10]

The shift away from white and black, and light and dark, as the basis for understanding the colours of the rainbow and prism by the mechanical philosophers, followed the discovery by artists, early in the seventeenth century, that white and black are not true colours, and that their mixture cannot generate chromatic colours. Colour mixing by artists only became commonplace in the Renaissance. In his *Natural History* Pliny the elder reported that Apelles and other artists of the fourth century BC had used only four colours, white, yellow, red and black. Alexander of Aphrodisias argued that painters could not imitate the rainbow and that the artificial colours produced by mixing pigments were inferior to natural colours. Plutarch condemned mixing colour pigments as producing conflict and a form of putrefaction, and in practice the mixing of pigments was uncommon in the absence of a painters' palette. Medieval painters infrequently mixed pigments, except with white or black, but by 1400 pigment mixing was more common, the painters' palette first being used at this time. In his treatise *On Painting* (*c*.1435) Leon Battista Alberti made a significant break with Aristotelian colour theory in maintaining that white and black are not true colours but the moderators of colours, and were to be used for introducing the effects of light and shadow. He distinguished four chromatic primary colours of red, blue, green and an ash colour, associating these colours with the four Aristotelian elements of fire, air, water and earth.

Early in the seventeenth century several scholars announced the discovery of the painters' three primaries of red, yellow and blue, which could not be obtained by the mixture of any other colours and from which (together with white and black) all other colours could be derived. The Flemish mathematician and architect François d'Aguilon described a colour-mixing diagram in his *Optics* (1613), ordering the colours in a sequence in the Aristotelian manner between white and black, but arguing that white and black might not be true colours and that mixing white and black with the chromatic colours only changed the intensity, not the variety, of the colour. In d'Aguilon's scheme yellow, red and blue are the 'simple' colours, which can be mixed to form the 'composites' of orange, purple and green. He was a friend of the painter Peter Paul Rubens, who provided vignette designs for his treatise and whose use of colour in his *Juno and Argus* (1611) suggests the adoption of the scheme of the three primary colours. In this painting Rubens adds the figure of Iris with her rainbow to Ovid's story of Juno sprinkling Argus' hundred eyes on a peacock's tail, with the red of Juno's costume, the blue of Iris' robe, and the yellow of Juno's chariot utilising the three primaries. In Iris' rainbow the red, yellow and blue primaries, or simple colours, are interspersed with the composites orange and green. By the early seventeenth century colour mixing had become common in artistic practice. It was becoming understood among artists that white and black are not chromatic colours, and that their mixture would only produce grey and could not generate the chromatic colours. This theory of the colours of the pigments used in paintings had its counterpart in the new theory of light proposed by the mechanical philosophers Descartes and Boyle, that colours were to be understood as

visual sensations arising from the modification of sunlight, not from combinations or modifications of black and white; and at this time it was assumed
that the same rules determined the mixing of coloured lights and the mixing
of pigments. These developments, in the discoveries of artists and the
theories of natural philosophers, prompted Newton's study of the prismatic
spectrum and shaped the conclusions he advanced in his 'New theory about
light and colours'.[11]

Casting Light on Colours

Newton's engagement with colours can be dated from the onset of his career
as a natural philosopher on his graduation at Cambridge. In a notebook entry
'Of Colours' dating from 1664–5 he records viewing colours through a prism,
observing the boundaries of a bicoloured thread and a bicoloured card
through the prism and noticing the divided images, which he explained in
terms of the unequal refraction of the two colours, an insight that was to form
a crucial element in his theory of colour.[12] Early in 1666, as he recounted in
his letter to Henry Oldenburg of 6 February 1672 forming his 'New theory
about light and colours', he 'procured me a Triangular glass-Prisme, to try
therewith the celebrated *Phaenomena* of *Colours*'. Darkening his room and
making a small hole in the shutter to let in a 'convenient quantity of the Suns
light', he transmitted a narrow beam of sunlight symmetrically through the
prism and cast its refracted image on the opposite wall. At first taking pleasure
with this 'very pleasing divertissement, to view the vivid and intense colours
produced', he soon reverted to the role of the natural philosopher, 'after a
while applying myself to consider them more circumspectly', and noticed a
curious feature. He had expected that the refracted coloured image would be
'*circular*' but was 'surprised to see . . . [the colours] in an *oblong* form', and on
comparing the length of this 'coloured *Spectrum*' (as he termed the image)
with its breadth 'I found it about five times greater; a disproportion so extrav-
agant that it excited me to a more than ordinary curiosity of examining, from
whence it might proceed'.[13] The word 'spectrum' is a relatively uncommon
Latin word, its contemporary usage referring to images, ghosts and visions,
and to the transient colours of the rainbow; Newton used 'spectrum' to mean
the solar image but more generally the coloured band produced by the
prism.[14]

Newton then proceeds to describe his famous '*Experimentum Crucis*', the
crucial experiment, a term used in Robert Hooke's *Micrographia* (1665), a
work that had shaped his optical studies. Using an arrangement of two prisms
he selected different portions of the coloured spectrum to be again refracted
by the second prism. He found that the light most refracted in the first prism
was most refracted in the second prism: 'And so the true cause of the length of

that Image was detected to be no other, then that *Light* consists of *Rays differently refrangible*. This is all that Newton claims to prove by the *experimentum crucis*, that 'Light it self is a *Heterogeneous mixture of differently refrangible Rays*'. But the outcome of the experiment with two prisms suggested conclusions about the '*Origin of Colours*', and he makes the strong claim that his theory of colours, which he presents as a 'Doctrine' of 13 propositions, though not directly proved by the *experimentum crucis*, follows as a 'most rigid consequence ... evinced by the mediation of experiments'. Turning from the 'historicall narration' of his experimental procedure, Newton proceeds to 'lay down the *Doctrine*' of his theory of colours, that the colours of the spectrum are not modifications of light produced by the prism, as supposed by Descartes, but that colour is an innate property of different rays (more strictly, that the rays have the power or disposition to cause the perception of colour); that there is a direct correspondence between colours and the degree of refrangibility of the rays; and that the original and simple colours of the spectrum are immutable and could not be altered by further refraction. He states this theory in the first three propositions of his 'Doctrine': '1. As the Rays of Light differ in degrees of refrangibility, so they also differ in their disposition to exhibit this or that particular colour. Colours are not *Qualifications of Light*, derived from Refractions ... but *Original* and *connate properties*, which in divers Rays are divers'; '2. To the same degree of Refrangibility ever belongs the same colour, and to the same colour ever belongs the same degree of refrangibility'; and '3. The species of colour, and degree of Refrangibility proper to any particular sorts of Rays, is not mutable by Refraction, nor by Reflection from natural bodies, nor by any other cause'.[15]

Newton then lists the 'original and simple' spectral colours that are immutable and cannot be altered by further refraction by a prism. 'The Original or primary colours are, *Red, Yellow, Green, Blew*, and a *Violet-purple*, together with Orange, Indico, and an indefinite variety of Intermediate gradations.'[16] The form in which Newton lists the seven spectral colours is revealing, for he had initially judged that there were five principal colours (red, yellow, green, blue and violet) in the spectrum. He added the two additional colours to his original list in the revision of his *Optical Lectures* delivered at Cambridge in 1671–2 (which remained unpublished in his lifetime), to introduce an analogy between seven principal colours of the spectrum and the seven notes of the musical scale, setting out a musical division of the spectrum: 'in order to divide the image into parts more elegantly proportioned to one another, it is appropriate to admit to the five prominent colours two others – namely, orange between red and yellow, and indigo between blue and violet'.[17]

As Newton explained in the 'New theory about light and colours', these five, now seven colours are the most prominent colours, not the only ones; at this stage (a feature muted in his presentation in the *Opticks*) he emphasises that the spectrum contains innumerable colours and that rays correspond not only to 'the more eminent colours, but even to all their intermediate gradations'. The spectrum is continuous, and 'to all the intermediate colours in a continued series belong intermediate degrees of refrangibility'. Having set out the list of simple spectral colours, which cannot be altered by refraction, Newton explains that there are also compound colours, formed 'by composition' of the simple colours and which can be resolved by refraction into the simple spectral colours. 'For, a mixture of *Yellow* and *Blew* makes *Green*; of *Red* and *Yellow* makes *Orange*'. The test of decomposition, passing rays through a prism to see whether they are refracted alike, would determine whether a colour is simple or compound. The theory has an important and striking implication, that '*Whiteness*', the 'usual colour of *Light*', was formed in a 'most surprising and wonderful composition' as a 'confused aggregate of Rays imbued with all sorts of Colors'. He declares that 'There is no one sort of Rays which alone can exhibit this. 'Tis ever compounded, and to its composition are requisite all the aforesaid primary Colours, mixed in a due proportion'. According to Newton's theory of light and colours, the spectral colours are not modifications or 'qualifications' of light but are 'original' and immutable; sunlight is a heterogeneous and compound mixture of the 'original' and 'simple' coloured rays of the spectrum, mixed in due proportion.[18]

Newton's conclusions were found to be problematic by his contemporaries Robert Hooke and the Dutch mathematician and astronomer Christiaan Huygens. Their criticisms were expressed in immediate and to Newton annoying correspondence, but the issues raised led him to modify his presentation and argument in his *Opticks*, the work that established and made widely public his new language for the representation and aesthetic appreciation of colours. A central issue was Newton's claim, in the 'New theory about light and colours', to have established as a 'most rigid consequence' of the *experimentum crucis* the doctrine that colours are immutable and are innate to the light of the sun. The validity of this claim seemed to depend on the prior assumption (to which Newton in fact held) that light consists of a stream of corpuscles differing in size, and that these light corpuscles correspond to different coloured rays which were separated by the prism; but Newton had firmly disavowed asserting 'an Hypothesis' about the nature of light. He conceded that although he had suggested that light was corpuscular, this was a secondary element in his theory, a consequence of the theory rather than a prior assumption: ''Tis true that from my Theory I argue the corporeity of light, but I doe it without any absolute positivenesse . . . & make it at most but a very plausible consequence of the Doctrine, & not a fundamentall supposition'. His presentation in the 'New theory about light and colours' is casual, but he did not explicitly make the claim that the *experimentum crucis* proved that colours are innate to white light before any refraction, merely that the experiment established that light consists of differently refrangible rays. This conclusion was preliminary to the statement of his 'Doctrine' about colours, the theory that colours are immutable and innate to white light, where he had proceeded to 'lay down the *Doctrine* first, and then, for its examination, give ... an instance or two of the *Experiments*, as a specimen of the rest'.[19] As Alan Shapiro notes, his presentation is ambiguous, for he did wish to prove that the colours are immutable and innate to the sun's light, and over the years tried various stratagems to achieve this end. But by the time he came to publish the *Opticks* he finally abandoned his attempt to prove this theory as a 'most rigid consequence' of his experiments. Expanding and loosening his argument, he no longer uses the term *experimentum crucis*; the experiment with two prisms is presented in the *Opticks* as one among a series purporting to prove that '*The Light of the Sun consists of Rays differently Refrangible*', the proposition that he had explicitly claimed to have established in 1672.[20]

On considering the mixtures of the 'simple' colours, in the 'New theory about light and colours' Newton drew a direct analogy between processes involved in the mixing of pigments and in the mixing of coloured lights. On discussing the mixture of blue and yellow spectral colours, he advances the claim that 'by composition . . . a mixture of *Yellow* and *Blew* makes *Green*' just as '*Blew* and *Yellow* powders, when finely mixed, appear to the naked eye *Green*'. Just as compound spectral colours can be resolved into component simple colours by the prism, the colours of component corpuscles of pigments are not 'transmuted, but only blended', for when viewed with a microscope 'they still appear *Blew* and *Yellow* interspersedly'.[21] Like his contemporaries, Newton assumed the equivalence of mixing pigments and mixing coloured lights; it took two centuries for it to be established that different rules apply to the mixing of pigments and lights, and that mixing yellow and blue spectral lights does not yield green. Robert Boyle, whose *Experiments and Considerations Touching Colours* (1664) Newton studied, had obtained green on mixing yellow and blue spectral lights, the same result that he had found on mixing yellow and blue pigments. The delicacy of performing experiments with spectral lights may account for the persistence of a well-attested but fallacious result, but one contrary contemporary opinion stands out. Huygens suggested to Newton that mixing yellow and blue lights might be 'sufficient' for the composition of white. This claim is striking, indeed extraordinary, because Huygens contradicts all other contemporary reports that mixing spectral yellow and blue produced green, and his assertion stands in opposition to the doctrine of colour mixing, of the equivalence of mixing pigments and spectral lights, as generally held in the seventeenth century: as blue and yellow pigments when mixed give green, the mixture of spectral blue and yellow should also yield green.[22] It was only in 1852 that the German physiologist and physicist Hermann Helmholtz, mixing yellow and blue lights using greatly improved instruments and under meticulous experimental procedures, found that 'yellow and blue do not furnish green', noting that this 'contradicts in the most decided manner the experience of all painters during the last thousand years' in mixing blue and yellow pigments. Helmholtz argued that whereas the mixture of coloured lights is an additive process, pigment mixing is subtractive; pigments act as filters to light reflected from interior layers below the surface; and he found that 'yellow and indigo-blue' when combined together produced 'pure white'.[23]

In his 'New theory about light and colours' and the last of the propositions of his 'Doctrine' of colours, Newton made only passing mention of the explanation of the colours of natural bodies, the question to which natural philosophers from Aristotle onward had devoted primary attention. He remarks that 'the Colours of all natural Bodies have no other origin than this, that they are variously qualified to reflect one sort of light in greater plenty then another'. He gives a brief report of 'illuminating those bodies with uncompounded light of divers colours' to prove his claim that coloured bodies reflect coloured light, and that they 'are most brisk and vivid in the light of their own day-light colour'.[24] According to the mechanical philosophers all colours were sensations excited by light, so experiments on radiant colours could establish knowledge of the true nature of colours; and for Newton the transient rainbow and prism colours (considered merely as apparent colours in scholastic natural philosophy) had a privileged explanatory status in providing the basis for understanding the colours of natural bodies. His explanation of the origin of the permanent colours of natural bodies rests on understanding the relation between the particles of matter forming all bodies and their illumination by light; in his theory of the colour of natural bodies, the size of the particles of the bodies determines the mode in which light is reflected from them and is the source of the sensation of colour as perceived by the eye.

When Newton presents a discussion of the colours of natural bodies – of vegetation, the sky and fabrics – in Book II of the *Opticks*, his argument rests on establishing a measure of these particles, and in charting the correspondence between their size and the colours they generate. To do so he utilises a study he had undertaken of another transient phenomenon, the periodic colours of thin films, which he had encountered on reading Robert Hooke's *Micrographia* (1665) and which he first discussed in a manuscript 'Of Colours' written in 1666. He placed a glass lens on a flat plate of glass, generating rings of periodic colours (which became known as 'Newton's rings'), and measured the diameters of the rings; by using a formula drawn from Euclid's *Elements* he calculated the thickness of the film producing a given ring.[25] He observed the rings in light reflected by and transmitted through the film, finding that the colours of the reflected and transmitted rings were complementary (a term that subsequently came into use to denote the two colours that compose white when added together). As he later explained in the *Opticks*, he found that the colours of the rings change in successive orders beyond the central spot 'made by the contact of the Glasses', which for the reflected rings appeared black and in the case of the transmitted rings was white. Comparing the coloured rings produced by reflection with those produced by transmission, Newton found that 'white was opposite to black, red to blue, yellow to violet, and green to a Compound of red and violet'.[26] He had presented his observations of thin films to the Royal Society in 1675, introducing a graphical method to represent the relation between the thickness of the films and the colours of white light reflected at any thickness. Newton's nomograph, described in the *Opticks*, enables the colour composition of a thin film to be correlated with the thickness of the film generating the colour. And he provides a table listing the orders of colours in the rings and the thickness (in millionths of an inch) of thin films of air, water and glass producing the coloured rings. This measure of the thickness of the films producing the coloured rings provides a method of determining the sizes of the component particles generating the colours of natural bodies.[27]

Newton assumed that there was a close causal relation between the optical properties of thin films and the colours of natural bodies: 'Having given my Observations of these Colours [of thin films]', he declares in the *Opticks*, 'I make use of them to unfold the Causes of the Colours of natural Bodies'. He argues that bodies acquire their colour by selectively reflecting the colours in the light falling on them; the colours of bodies are produced by the sizes of their corpuscles, just as the colours of thin films are determined by the thickness of the film. To deduce the sizes of the corpuscles, he reasons from the analogy with the thickness of a film producing a given colour, comparing the colours of bodies with the colours observed in Newton's rings; and assuming that there is a correspondence between the sizes of the corpuscles of coloured bodies and the thickness of the films generating rings of a similar colour, he asserts that the sizes of the corpuscles of bodies can be determined by calculating the thickness of the corresponding film. 'The bigness of the component parts of natural Bodies may be conjectured by their Colours' Newton declares, and this can be achieved by reference to the table listing the colours of the rings where the 'thickness of Water or glass exhibiting any Colour is expressed'.

The colours of bodies are therefore explained purely in terms of the sizes and densities of their corpuscles, reducing the optical properties of bodies to mechanical properties and processes. Newton devoted special attention to the green of vegetables, the most common colour in nature. He noted that in the sequence of Newton's rings the 'purest' greens were those of the third order of the rings, and suggested that 'of this Order the green of all Vegetables seems to be'. To determine 'the diameter of a Corpuscle, which being of equal density with Glass shall reflect green of the third Order', he refers to his table which gives the order of colours in the rings and the thickness of films producing the colours in given rings. From this table he reads off the thickness of a film of glass that would generate the green ring of the third order of Newton's rings, a measure equal to the diameter of corpuscles, of equal density to glass; this ring produces 'the green of all Vegetables'.[28]

Newton's theory of coloured bodies rests on the assumption that there is a close relation between the properties of thin films and coloured bodies; that the colours of natural bodies are explicable purely in terms of the size and density of its corpuscles, as in thin films; and that the possible effect of the chemical composition of bodies on their colour is to be ignored. These are problematic assumptions about the nature of matter, but the theory was widely accepted in the eighteenth century. The understanding of colour, the colours experienced in everyday life and the handling of colours by artists, was shaped by the terms of Newton's theory of the seven spectral colours, and the extension of this theory from the transient phenomena of the rainbow and prism to the representation of coloured bodies. In a paper presented to the Royal Society in 1765 Edward Hussey Delaval, a natural philosopher inter-ested in exploring Newtonian themes in electricity, chemistry and optics, confirmed that the colours of opaque bodies varied in proportion to their density; and in his *Experimental Inquiry into the Cause of the Changes of Colours in Opake and Coloured Bodies* (1777), a forceful statement in favour of Newton's theory of coloured bodies, he found that the colours of permanently coloured bodies do vary with the size of their corpuscles.

But in the 1770s, prompted by contemporary work on photosynthesis, photochemistry and the chemistry of dyestuffs, some French chemists advanced the unorthodox opinion that light was a chemically active substance interacting with matter. This led to the development of a chemical theory of colour, that light entered into chemical combination with ordinary matter and that the colours of bodies arise from the selective absorption of the various component particles of light, challenging Newton's mechanical theory that the colour of a body is determined only by the size and density of its corpuscles. In the eighteenth century chemical combination was understood in terms of the theory of chemical affinities between reagents, a theory often expressed in terms of forces, analogous to Newton's force of gravity, between the particles of matter. Following the terms of the Newtonian theory of the heterogeneity of the corpuscles of light as correspon-ding to differently coloured rays, the chemical theory of light supposed that the component particles of bodies had different affinities for different corpuscles of light, and that the colours of natural bodies were determined by a process of the selective absorption of light according to the different chemical affinities.[29]

In 1785 Delaval, who as noted had formerly been a strong supporter and advocate of Newton's theory of coloured bodies, published a paper questioning its central assumption; that coloured bodies reflect coloured light, and the requirement that bodies are of one colour by reflection and its complement by transmission. In place of Newton's mechanical theory Delaval embraced a chemical theory of colours. In his 'An experimental inquiry into the cause of the permanent colours of opake bodies', published in the *Memoirs* of the Manchester Literary and Philosophical Society, he took a sceptical line on the seeming success of Newton's examination of 'the properties of Permanently Coloured Bodies, and their operations on the rays of light'. To remedy this newly identified deficiency Delaval undertook a test of Newton's theory that '*all Coloured Matter reflects* the rays of light', setting up a careful experiment to determine whether transparent coloured liquids reflect coloured light. As a result he was led to conclude emphatically, against Newton, that 'Transparent Coloured Liquors do not yield any Colour by reflection, but by transmission only'. He emphasised, contrary to Newton's theory of coloured bodies, that 'the Colouring Matter *does not reflect any light*', arguing that coloured light is not reflected from the surface of a coloured body but is transmitted within it prior to reflection. Finding that plants consist of colouring matter and a white substance, he suggested that it was this substance, not the colouring matter, that reflected light: the 'Colouring Matter is transparent . . . it does not reflect colours, but exhibits them by transmission only . . . the reflecting power does not consist in colouring matter, but in Opake White Substances only'. He concludes that contrary to Newton's theory, the colour of bodies cannot be attributed to the mechanical properties of their particles, and suggests that colour is to be explained chemically, by the presence of phlogiston (the chemical principle of inflammability) in the colouring matter: 'the matter of light acts upon coloured bodies in the same manner as the phlogistic vapours'.[30]

Delaval applied his theory of coloured bodies, that 'Opake coloured Bodies consist of transparent matter, which cover opake white particles, and transmits the light, which is reflected from them', to consider the methods employed in dyeing and the use of pigments by painters. He added a comment on the vexed question of the techniques employed by the celebrated Venetian colourists Titian, Tintoretto and Veronese, suggesting that they had achieved the vibrancy of their colours by laying colours over a white ground, adopting a practice that (according to his theory) mimicked the process of colouration in nature. Sir Joshua Reynolds had striven to rediscover the Venetian techniques, and it was no doubt his opinion to which Delaval alluded in reporting

that 'One of our most eminent Painters has observed, from a minute examination of some of the most capital pictures of Titian, Tintoret, Paul Veronese',
that they had 'painted with transparent colours, upon a white ground', and
that this was a 'practice carried to the highest degree of perfection by
Correggio ... [who] gave to his compositions a peculiar force and relief, and
a near resemblance of nature'.[31] This technique was to be employed by the
Pre-Raphaelite painters around 1850, achieving an extraordinary brilliance of
hue by covering white-lead grounds with thin glazes of pure and transparent
colours.[32]

By the 1820s a new experimental procedure had been developed, the observation of the absorption spectra of coloured substances, which led debate on
the colours of bodies to turn from the concern with chemical affinities back
to the discussion of colouration as a physical process. When a beam of
sunlight was transmitted through a transparent coloured body, its spectrum
observed through a prism was found to consist of a sequence of coloured and
dark bands; as John Herschel described the phenomenon in 1822, the spectrum consists of 'an assemblage of more or less sharply defined streaks of
different breadths and colours, separated by intervals, in some cases absolutely
black, – in others only feebly illuminated'. In an effort to understand the
chemical composition of substances Herschel and the Scottish physicist David
Brewster pursued the investigation of absorption spectra, and were led to
contest and refute Newton's theory of colouration. They established selective
absorption (though without reference to the theory of chemical affinities) as
the cause of the colours of bodies. Writing in 1833, Herschel concluded that
Newton's 'analogy of the colours of thin plates to those of natural bodies is
limited to a comparatively narrow range', appealing rather to 'the phenomena
of absorption, to which I consider the great majority of natural colour to be
referrible', for the explanation of the colours of natural bodies. The questions
posed by Newton's theory of coloured bodies were resolved by the application
of the concept of absorption and the new exact experimental techniques and
measurements deployed by natural philosophers in the 1820s.[33]

Colour Harmonies, Circles and Triangles

In January 1673 Christiaan Huygens had queried Newton's claim, expressed in
the 'New theory about light and colours', that it was necessary for white to be
composed from the mixture of all the spectral colours, suggesting that spectral 'yellow and blue might also be sufficient for that'. As already noted,
Huygens contradicts all other contemporary reports that mixing spectral
yellow and blue produced green, and his assertion is at variance with the
doctrine of colour mixing as generally held in the seventeenth century, that
mixing pigments and spectral lights was equivalent. The matter was not

clarified until 1852 when Helmholtz obtained 'pure white' from the mixture of spectral 'yellow and indigo-blue', and established that whereas the mixture of coloured lights is an additive process, pigment mixing is subtractive. Newton responded to Huygens in the terms set by his theory of light and colours, qualifying his claim that the composition of white necessarily required the mixture of all the primary colours mixed in due proportion; he now restricted this doctrine to the composition of the sun's light. Were white to be compounded from 'two uncompounded colours', as Huygens had claimed was possible, then 'such a White, (were there any such) would have different properties from the White which I had respect to, when I described my Theory, that is, from the white of the Sun's immediate light'. Newton therefore introduces two kinds of white into his theory of light and colours, the white of the sun's light and a white produced by a given mixture of colours with 'different properties [which] would evince it to be of a different constitution'.[34]

When Newton discussed colour mixing in the *Opticks* in terms of his colour-mixing circle, he incorporated his concession to Huygens' criticism, and gave his account of colour mixing an extended range of application. The colour circle illustrates the composition of white from a mixture of spectral lights, showing that sunlight, composed from all the spectral colours and their intermediate gradations mixed in due proportion, differs from a white, which could be sensibly identical to the light of the sun, compounded from a given mixture of colours; the two kinds of white differ in refrangibility. In his major paper 'On the theory of compound colours, and the relations of the colours of the spectrum' (1860), concerned with the mixture of spectral colours, James Clerk Maxwell explained this distinction between 'the optical constitution, as revealed by the prism' and the '*chromatical* properties' of a mixture of colours. He echoed Newton, who uses differences in refrangibility determined by passing the rays through a prism, to differentiate physically between colour mixtures that may be sensibly identical. He crisply expounded Newton's distinction between the sun's white light and white compounded from a given mixture of colours: 'Newton is always careful, however, not to call any mixture white, unless it agrees with common white light in its optical as well as its chromatical properties, and is a mixture of *all* the homogeneal colours.'[35]

As noted earlier, in setting out the proportions of his colour-mixing circle Newton drew upon his musical division of the spectrum into seven segments proportional to a string sounding the seven notes of the octave in the musical scale (Fig. 13). Having suggested that there are five principal colours of the spectrum (red, yellow, green, blue and violet), he added orange and indigo in the revision of his *Optical Lectures* (1671–2), introducing a musical division of the spectrum in order to divide the image into elegantly proportioned parts. In his division of the spectrum according to the proportions of a diatonic

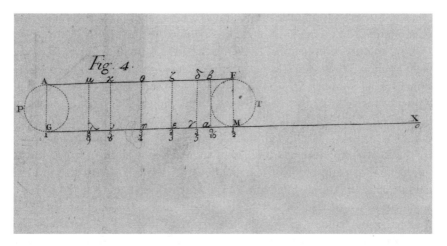

13   Isaac Newton, the 'musical division' of the spectrum, in *Opticks*. 'Let GM be produced to X, that MX may be equal to GM, and conceive GX, λX, ιX, ηX, εX, γX, αX, MX, to be in proportion to one another, as the Numbers 1, 8/9, 5/6, 3/4, 2/3, 3/5, 9/16, 1/2, and so to represent the Chords of the Key, and of a Tone, a third Minor, a fourth, a fifth, a sixth Major, a seventh and an eighth above that Key: And the Intervals Mα, αγ, γε, εη, ηι, ιλ, and λG, will be the Spaces which the several Colours (red, orange, yellow, green, blue, indigo, violet) take up.'

scale 'everything appeared just as if the parts of the image occupied by the colours were proportional to a string divided so it would cause the individual degrees of the octave to sound'. He conceded that he could not 'so precisely observe and define' the boundaries of the colours and that the spectrum could be 'constituted somewhat differently', but declared his preference for a musical division rather than one based on geometrical proportions 'because it perhaps involves something about the harmonies of colours (such as painters are not altogether unacquainted with, but which I myself have not yet sufficiently studied) perhaps analogous to the concordance of sounds'.[36] The musical analogy was familiar in colour theory, François d'Aguilon having based the colour scale in his *Optics* on a diagram of Pythagorean musical consonances that had been discussed in Renaissance texts. Newton's colour circle in the *Opticks* was perhaps adapted from the diagram of the octave as a circle of major and minor tones published by Descartes in 1650.[37] In the *Opticks* Newton drew dividing lines between the seven colour bands in the prismatic spectrum, 'the Spaces which the several Colours (red, orange, yellow, green, blue, indigo, violet) take up', identifying 'after the manner of a Musical Chord' a series of proportions 'to represent the Chords of the Key, and of a Tone, a third Minor, a fourth, a fifth, a sixth Major, a seventh and an eighth above that Key'.[38]

When Newton explains his colour-mixing rules in the *Opticks* – 'In a mixture of Primary Colours, the Quantity and Quality of each being given, to know the Colour of the Compound' – he applies the musical division of the spectrum in establishing the proportions of his colour circle. He divides the circumference of a circle into arcs proportional to the lengths of the seven spectral colours, 'proportional to the seven Musical Tones or Intervals of the eight Sounds, *Sol, la, fa, sol, la, mi, fa, sol*, contained in an eight, that is proportional to the Number 1/9, 1/16, 1/10, 1/9, 1/16, 1/16, 1/9', representing in sequence the red, orange, yellow, green, blue, indigo and violet 'Colours of uncompounded Light gradually passing into one another, as they do when made by Prisms'. The circumference represents pure, unsaturated hues (without any admixture of white), each arc containing all the degrees of that hue; and the centre of the circle *O* represents the mixture of the spectral colours as in the sun's white light. At the centre of each arc Newton places a small circle, whose size (or weight) is proportional to the number of rays of that particular colour in any given mixture. The point *Z* represents the common centre of gravity of all the small circles, and indicates the colour compounded from a mixture of any seven 'primary' colours (Fig. 14).

In the example in the figure, *Z* is an unsaturated orange that results from a mixture of seven colours in which red, orange and yellow predominate. The centre of gravity of all the seven colours mixed in due proportion, as in sunlight, falls at the centre of the circle *O* yielding white. But Newton's diagram indicates that if the point *Z*, representing a mixture of colours, were to fall upon the centre *O* then white could be compounded of fewer colours. Newton recognises that if two of the primary colours that are opposite to one another in the circle (the complementary colours) are mixed in an equal proportion, then 'the point *Z* shall fall upon the center *O*, and yet the Colour compounded of those two shall not be perfectly white, but some faint anonymous colour'. Although he declares that he had failed 'by mixing only two primary Colours' to produce a 'perfect white' (as Huygens had suggested might be possible by mixing blue and yellow lights), he allows the possibility of achieving it with 'a mixture of three taken at equal distances in the circumference', while with four or five colours 'I do not much question but it may'. Any 'white' colour thus compounded is, however, to be distinguished optically from sunlight; in consequence he declares that 'these are Curiosities of little or no moment to the understanding of the Phaenomena of nature. For in all whites produced by nature, there uses to be a mixture of all sorts of rays, and by consequence a composition of all Colours'.[39]

Earlier in his text Newton had discussed the mixture of the adjacent spectral colours blue and yellow; these are not complementary colours in the colour circle, and (contrary to Huygens' claim that their mixture produces white) he continues to affirm that a compound green will result: 'the yellow and blue, on either hand, if they are equal in quantity they draw the intermediate green equally towards themselves in Composition'. Newton's colour circle is directed to the mixture of coloured lights but he makes it clear that it

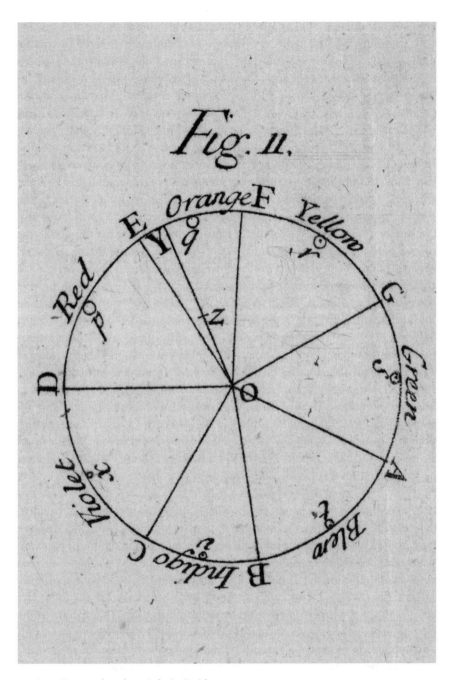

14   Isaac Newton, the colour circle, in *Opticks*.

applies to the mixing of pigments; in the example in the figure he declares that the unsaturated orange marked by the point Z could be imitated by mixing painters' orange and white 'Powders'. This reference to pigments fostered the assimilation of his theory into the artists' tradition of pigment mixing. In his influential *New Principles of Linear Perspective* (1719) the mathematician Brook Taylor described and lauded Newton's colour circle because 'Knowledge of the Theory may be of great use in Painting', though warning the artist that the impurities of pigments meant that perfect correspondence to Newton's principles should not be expected. It was in an effort to reinforce this analogy between the mixing of the 'primary' coloured lights and the mixture of painters' pigments that Newton, in presenting his theory in the *Opticks*, suppressed stating his doctrine that the spectrum is continuous and consists of innumerable degrees or gradations of colours, using this qualifying phrase only once. His term 'primary' for the seven colours of the spectrum evoked painters' primaries, and the analogy between their method of producing a range of colours from coloured powders and his composition of coloured lights. He noted that painters used only a few pigments, and as he found that these 'Colours were severally so compounded of others', even 'a Mixture of all Colours', the plausibility of attributing anomalies in colour mixing to impurities in the colours of pigments led the significance of painters' triad of primaries to be diminished. In similar fashion Newton remarked that the rules of mixing for various combinations of spectral lights, as set out in his exposition of the colour circle, were 'accurate enough for practice, though not mathematically accurate'. Newton used the language of pigment mixing, and in the eighteenth century his doctrine of the seven primary colours of sunlight was understood to be as much about setting out general rules of colour mixing as a statement of a theory of light.[40]

Ever since antiquity the languages of colour and music had been intertwined. The Greeks had termed the musical scale of half-tones 'chromatic', and the musical terms 'tone' and 'harmony' came to be incorporated into the aesthetic vocabulary of painting. The colour circle integrated the analogy between musical and chromatic harmony within the framework of Newton's authoritative theory of light and colours. Newton's presentation of his theory of colours in the *Opticks* emphasised the applicability of the colour circle to the practice of painters, and smoothed away discordance between the properties and mixing of spectral lights and artists' pigments. Bolstered by Newton's scientific authority, and the appeal to universal musical and chromatic harmonies, the colour circle was incorporated into pictorial practice.[41]

In the eighteenth century it was clearly understood that the term 'chromatics' had musical associations, as explained in the article on 'Chromatic' in the third edition of the *Encyclopaedia Britannica* (1797). The term is defined as characterising 'a kind of music which proceeds by several semitones in succession', and as deriving from the Greek χρομα 'which signifies *colour* . . . [and also] perhaps that shade of a colour by which it melts into another'; this interpretation of the term was 'highly applicable to semitones'.[42] The relation between the musical scale and the Newtonian scale of spectral colours prompted interest in the aesthetic possibilities of the analogy. 'Colorific music' is discussed in the substantial article on 'Chromatics', written by the mathematical lecturer and author Charles Hutton, published in the same volume of the *Encyclopaedia Britannica*. Having summarised Newton's exposition of the correspondence between the 'seven primary colours of the spectrum' and the 'seven notes in the diatonic scale of music', Hutton turned to a brief discussion of the speculative genre of 'colorific music', questioning 'how far the analogy supposed by F. Castel really exists'.[43] Hutton was alluding to the project, announced in 1725 by the French Jesuit Louis-Bertrand Castel, of the construction of an 'ocular harpsichord' where the keyboard would play colour sequences rather than melodies, with the claim that this instrument would produce beautiful chromatic harmonies. Hutton's scepticism was entirely consonant with contemporary opinion, but the subject was however sufficiently interesting, as having its origin in Newton's discussion of the harmonic spectrum, for it to be noted in an article largely concerned with discussion of the theory of coloured bodies.

Castel had been inspired by Newton's discussion of the spectrum as a harmonic proportion, based on the musical analogy of the seven spectral colours and the seven tones of the musical scale, and by Athanasius Kircher's *Misurgia Universalis* (1650), in which Kircher had set out a table of precise equivalences for notes and colours in terms of an Aristotelian scale from white to black. In developing his theory of colour mixtures, Castel blended the Newtonian spectral sequence of hues with Kircher's tonal gradations from white to black. He eventually decided that blue was the 'fundamental' note of colour, being the colour of the sky, and that red, yellow and blue were the primary colours that corresponded to the major triad in music. In working out his colour theory he became increasingly anti-Newtonian in outlook; in his *L'Optique des Couleurs* (1740) he rejected Newton's prism experiment and 'its fantastic spectrum . . . as an unfaithful mirror of nature'. Castel considered that Newton's prism and scheme of spectral colours provided an unsatisfactory basis for the construction of a theory of colour, declaring Newton had constructed a theory by 'flights of imagination' from the dispersion of colours by the prism. In place of the 'enchantment' of the band of spectral colours Castel reprised the Aristotelian distinction between real and apparent colours, stating that he preferred to 'concentrate above all on the material and normal colours of painters' rather than the 'accidental colours, like the incorporeal ones of the prism and rainbow'. In his scale of colours he placed primaries of 'celestial or sky blue', the 'red of fire' and 'natural or earthy yellow' between the 'extremes of black and white', with a range of intermediate mixtures interspersed between the colours, giving 12 hues corresponding to the 12 notes of the chromatic musical scale. By incorporating 12 tonal grada-tions from black to white, 144 units of colour could be generated; Castel intro-duced further combinations through mixtures, setting out a cabinet of colours as the basis for constructing a chromatic instrument, the aforesaid 'ocular harpsichord'. He never succeeded in his ambition to create a musical harmony of colours, but in the 1730s he had a simple model of his instrument constructed where the keyboard activated coloured pop-up cards. Various devices were described in the 1750s, using candles or an elaborate system of lamps and coloured glass-filters, the colours being brought into play by the keys of a modified harpsichord, but the evidence of any success is uncertain; and the idea of an ocular harpsichord was widely noticed, but greeted with scepticism.[44]

In one of his more effusive statements on colour music Castel integrated the language of colour harmony with the evocation of the aesthetics of flowers: 'I saw a garden dotted with flowers; a sweet zephyr blew, and singling out that moment, I saw the harpsichord. I saw a meadow strewn with rose drops; the sun rose, I moved my head a little, and my eye said to me: there is the harpsichord.'[45] In Britain, the painters' use of colour harmony and mixing and the gradation of the spectrum discussed in Newton's *Opticks* helped shape discussion of the colour harmonies that could be achieved in planting flower beds; some eighteenth-century designers of pleasure gardens urged utilising the aesthetic effects of the painter's triad of primary colours and the colours of the rainbow to achieve a gradation and harmonious blending of colours in flower beds. In his *Philosophical Enquiry into the Origin of Our Ideas of the Sublime and Beautiful* (1757) Edmund Burke suggested that 'the beauty both of shape and colouring are as nearly related, as we can well suppose for things of such different natures to be'; he pointed to gradation as the basis for the aesthetic pleasure in perceiving colours. He illustrated the point by noting that the 'dubious colour' of a drake's head was perceived as beautiful through the subtle gradation of the colours of its feathers, a similar effect being produced by the 'dubious colours in the necks and tails of peacocks'. Burke found 'beauty in colour' in gradation, and harmonious blending.[46]

In the 1770s the leading garden designer and poet William Mason wrote an essay on the arrangement of flowers to form harmonious colour combina-tions. His theory of the colour arrangement of flowers was based on the appli-cation of painters' practice, with 'Red, yellow, & blue' as the triad of 'primitive, or original colours in nature' and a triad of 'blended colours' produced by combinations of red and yellow (yielding orange) and red and blue (yielding crimson or purple, depending on the prevalence of red or blue in the mixture). Noting that 'Yellow & blue, according to the increase of the one & decrease of the other, give every kind of Green', he pointed out that the gardener had no use for flowers of this blended colour since the leaves were 'constantly Green'. Mason suggested a compositional principle of planting based on the 'trinal combination' of the 'primitive' and 'blended' colours, so that 'wherever a Flower of one of the three primitive hues is planted or sown, two others should be placed nearly contiguous to the first', following the sequence of red, yellow and blue; and a similar arrangement should be used for the blended colours, with the flowers planted in the sequence crimson, orange and purple. In each sequence of colours, yellow and orange flowers, being 'the most vivid of the three' primitive and blended colours, should be planted in the central position in the flower bed, as having 'the gayest effect in the centre'. Mason envisaged that the arrangement of coloured flowers could be managed to accommodate seasonal blooms, so that the 'judicious Planter may so arrange the Flowers, that when one trinal combination of hues fade, another may begin to flow', to produce 'a succession of living Bouquets . . . produced to the eye during the whole summer'. The gardener Joseph Spence commented on the effects of the rainbow spectrum in determining aesthetic pleasure, considering whether it might be possible to 'plant a whole Rainbow' of all seven colours 'in their order, after one another'. He thought that the 'Gradation of the different colors in the Rainbow' from red to violet could be applied in planting flower beds; the flowers would be planted so that their colours would conform to the 'different friendships and enmities of different colours', achieving aesthetic harmony by ensuring that the 'extreames' of red and violet or blue and orange flowers were not planted next to each other. The rainbow theme of the gradation of spectral colours was invoked in an essay written in the 1750s by the gardener Sir John Dalrymple, who advised the gardener to 'make the colours run into and lose themselves in each other, like the dies of the rainbow'.[47]

These were perhaps theoretical discussions rather than practical proposals, but they show how the aesthetics of the colour gradation in the spectrum bore on the design of pleasure gardens. Erasmus Darwin made allusion to this theme of contriving colour harmony in the design of ornamental gardens in his discussion of the 'Melody of Colours', one of the 'philosophical notes' in his *The Temple of Nature* (1803). As a physician and natural philosopher, he sought a physiological cause of the harmony of colour and music in an analogy between the organs of sight and of hearing, finding an explanation in the phenomena of after-images described by Buffon, which he had himself investigated. His argument drew on a paper 'New experiments on the ocular spectra of light and colours' published by his son the physician Robert Waring Darwin (the future father of Charles) in the Royal Society's *Philosophical Transactions* of 1786.[48] Robert Darwin described the after-image generated by looking at a bright object and then withdrawing the gaze, which he termed the 'ocular spectrum of that object'. He classified ocular spectra as falling under four classes; the fourth class, where images 'of a colour contrary to that of their object' were observed, he termed '*reverse ocular spectra*' describing a series of experiments to establish the relationship between these 'contrary' colours. On first viewing coloured silk threads against a background of white paper, the eye was then focused upon another white paper so that 'a spectrum will be seen of the form of the silk thus inspected, but of a colour opposite to it'. By 'opposite' colours Darwin was alluding to the complementary colours in two sequences featured in figures in Newton's *Opticks*: the colours opposite to each another in the colour circle; and the depiction of the colours of Newton's rings, the coloured rings generated when a convex lens is pressed against a flat plate of glass, the figure showing the sequence of concentric circles of complementary colours when the lens and plate are viewed by reflected and transmitted light. Darwin reported that in his experiment the red silk thread produced a green after-image while green silk produced a red after-image; orange silk produced a blue after-image; yellow produced violet. These observations were consistent with the reversal of colours of Newton's rings in reflected and transmitted light: 'those which reflected yellow, transmitted violet, those which reflected red, transmitted a blue-green', Newton's observations being in agreement, Darwin claimed, with his experiments on after-images.[49]

Commenting in *The Temple of Nature*, Erasmus Darwin judged that his son's experiments showed that for aesthetic harmony 'where colours are required to be distinct, those which are opposite to each other should be brought into succession or vicinity; as red and green, orange and blue, yellow and violet'. He suggested that 'certain colours are more agreeable, when they succeed each other; or when they are disposed in each other's vicinity, so as successively to affect the organ of vision'. He illustrates the aesthetics of colour in terms set by Newton's natural philosophy of colour harmony and colour mixing, remarking on how the 'gradations and contrasts of colours' as set out in Newton's colour circle had been 'practically employed both by the painters of landscape and by the planters of ornamental gardens'. He suggested that red and green being 'opposite to each other' in the colour circle would offer contrast 'where colours are required to be distinct', whereas if it was required that colours would 'intermix imperceptibly, or slide into each other' then these colours should not be used as they might 'by contrast appear too glaring or tawdry'.[50]

In the third 'Interlude' of *The Loves of the Plants* (1789), on 'Painting and Music', Erasmus Darwin commented on Newton's musical division of the spectrum, where 'the breadths of the seven primary colours in the Sun's image refracted by a prism are proportional to . . . the intervals of the eight sounds contained in an octave'. From this 'curious coincidence' of a 'mathematical relationship, or perhaps I should have said a metaphysical relationship' between the octave and the seven primary colours of the Newtonian spectrum arose the notion of producing 'luminous music, consisting of successions or combinations of colours, analogous to a tune'. He cited an account of Castel's ocular harpsichord, an instrument designed to 'produce at the same time visible and audible music in unison with each other', given in G.G. Guyot's book of scientific toys and 'recreations' published in 1769, but he noted that Castel's endeavour had not met with success. Darwin found a more convincing illustration of the relation between music and colour in reflecting on the implications of his son's experiments. He pointed to the pleasure experienced when certain colours were viewed in succession, green after red, orange after blue, and yellow after violet, finding the explanation in the phenomenon of after-images. He argued that there was an analogy between the persistence of after-images in 'coinciding with the irritation of the colour now under contemplation', and the 'pleasure we receive from the sensation of melodious notes' as a result of 'our hearing some proportions of sounds after others more easily, distinctly, or agreeably'. He found the 'sisterhood of Music and Painting' in the 'coincidence between the proportions of the primary colours, and the primary sounds if they may be so called'; the same laws govern both phenomena, and music and painting could aptly share the same metaphors and aesthetic language – the 'brilliancy of sounds', the 'light and shade of a concerto' in music, while painters can speak of the 'harmony of colours, and the tone of a picture'.[51] The sisterhood of the arts of music and painting is given scientific explanation, through Newton's colour circle and theory of thin films and in the phenomenon of after-images.

The contemporary investigation of coloured shadows bore on the study of the complementary colours generated in after-images and on the discussion of colour harmony and ocular music. In a paper published in the *Philosophical Transactions* of 1794 the American natural philosopher Benjamin Thompson (Count Rumford) reported the results of his experiments on illuminating a wooden cylinder simultaneously by light from a candle and by daylight, where he found that the different light sources cast differently-coloured shadows. The shadow cast by daylight was yellow, whereas the shadow corresponding to the light of the candle was 'the most beautiful *blue* that it is possible to imagine'; in this pair of coloured shadows 'one shadow may with propriety be said to be the *complement* of the other', and he found that the complementary colours when mixed produce white. He obtained a range of coloured shadows using coloured glass filters and suggested that these experiments on coloured shadows might 'not only lead to a knowledge of the harmony of colours' but prompt the construction of instruments 'for producing that harmony for the entertainment of the eyes, in a manner similar to that in which ears are entertained by musical sounds', raising the possibility of creating ocular music.[52] The topic of coloured shadows was pursued further by the Cambridge natural philosopher Isaac Milner, in a paper on the 'Theory of colours and shadows' published by the landscape gardener Humphry Repton in his *Observations on the Theory and Practice of Landscape Gardening* (1803). Milner reported on his own experiments generating and mixing the complementary colours of shadows, finding that the 'three primary colours *red, yellow,* and *blue*' when mixed 'in certain proportions' could produce 'a sort of white, or any colour may be formed'. Finding that white can be obtained by mixing 'even two colours only', he sought to understand the basis of the 'harmony of colours' by considering 'what is the *other* colour . . . which, joined to a given one . . . will constitute *white*'; he concluded that 'red, requires green; yellow, purple; blue, orange', so that the mixtures of these pairs of colours 'in proper proportion will be white'. Milner acknowledged Newton's statement in the *Opticks* that he could not produce a 'perfect white by the mixture of only two primary colours'; but Newton had disclaimed mathematical accuracy in describing the mixing of colours in terms of his colour circle, and Milner noted that it was 'not easy, even for mathematicians, to put his rules into practice'. He contended that his own argument 'respecting the mixtures of such colours as are called contrasts' to form white is '*so near* the truth' that it could be accepted as such for all practical purposes of colour mixing.[53]

By the early nineteenth century the focus of attention shifted to the generation of colour mixtures from the complementary colours as set out in the colour circle; and Newton's careful distinction between the white of the sun's light and a white produced from a given mixture of colours was discounted. But Newton's emphasis on the harmony of colours continued to exercise influence. In his *Treatise on the Kaleidoscope* (1819) David Brewster gave an account of his invention, an 'Optical Instrument designed for creating and exhibiting beautiful forms'; and as with other contemporary colour theorists he discusses colour mixing and colour harmonies in terms of conjoining colours opposite to one another in the colour circle, listing the 'harmonic colours' as red and blue, orange-yellow and indigo, and green and violet. He terms these colours the '*complementary colours*', and consistent with the practice of other colour theorists he affirms that 'when the two [complementary] colours are mixed, they will always form white by their combination'; by now this had become an accepted doctrine. In a chapter of his book where he advertises the kaleidoscope as an instrument of amusement he makes comparison with 'the formerly chimerical idea of an ocular harpsichord'. By generating a 'combination of fine forms, and every-varying tints' the kaleidoscope will provide 'a pleasure as intense and as permanent as that which the finest ear derives from musical sounds'.[54] The display of 'harmonic colours' had now been realised, but 'ocular music' remained a vain ambition.

In his paper on the theory of colours and shadows Isaac Milner included a colour diagram, a device used by Humphry Repton, 'the gentleman who has consulted me on this subject of shadows', to assist in achieving harmony of colours in painting. This diagram is a triangle of colours, which embodied the scheme of primary and complementary colours that Milner had described in his discussion of shadows and the mixing of colours. The primary colours of red, blue and yellow are placed at the vertices of the triangle, and the complementary colours of green, orange and purple are placed along the sides opposite these primaries.[55] The distinction between these two sequences of colours had been promoted by the entomologist Moses Harris, who around 1770 published his *Natural System of Colours*, setting out two colour wheels with the hues arranged in two separate circles, of 'prismatic' and 'compound' colours. The first circle of the 'principal or primitive' colours is based on red, yellow and blue, set out in a sequence of 18 gradations in hue around the circumference of the circle and 20 gradations of lightness from its centre, a total of 360 'teints'. The second circle of 'mediate' colours is based on orange, green and purple, with a corresponding range of circular and radial gradations, providing a range of 300 further 'teints'. Repton's colour triangle followed the representation of colours by a triangular colour scheme promoted by the German astronomer Tobias Mayer, who had introduced a colour triangle to facilitate colour mixing; his work was first announced in 1758 but was only fully published in 1775. Mayer's colour triangle was also based on red, yellow and blue as the primary constituents of colour, these colours being placed at the vertices of the triangle; and each side of the triangle displays the sequence of 12 transitions between the 2 primary colours at the vertices, a gradation from red to yellow embracing orange, from yellow to blue embracing green, and blue to red embracing purple. Mayer's triangle incorporates a system of 91 colour variations and gradations.[56] Repton's simple triangle of colours lacks the sophistication of the systems of colour classification developed by Harris and Mayer, or the 'colour pyramid' proposed by Johann Heinrich Lambert in 1772, but suggests that a triangular classification, and the relation between the painters' triad of primary colours and their complementary colours, was well established by around 1800.

Reviewing and enlarging upon a century of theory in a major paper 'Hints towards a classification of colours', published in the *Philosophical Magazine* in March 1849, the Edinburgh scientist James David Forbes described Mayer's colour triangle as 'a complete and perfect diagram of mixed colours, starting from red, yellow, and blue, as constituents'. Recognising that Newton had introduced the sequence of seven colours of the spectrum, Forbes argued that in the absence of a 'peculiar respect' for the number seven and a 'fancied analogy' between the breadths of the spectral bands and the musical intervals, 'Newton would not have classed blue and indigo as distinct colours', concluding that 'we may consider that the Newtonian spectrum consists of the three primary colours, red, yellow, and blue, and the three secondary orange, green and purple'. Transforming Newton's spectrum of colours to accommodate Mayer's triangular system of colour classification, Forbes set out his own version of Mayer's scheme. Red, yellow and blue as the primary 'constituents' are 'painted' at the vertices of a triangle, with the 'periphery of the triangle . . . [being] composed of graduating' secondary colours of orange, green and purple placed between the red and yellow, yellow and blue, and blue and red primary colours, so that 'perfect' orange, green and purple are located at the 'centres of the sides of the triangle'. In this triangular scheme 'a point in the triangle may always be found which shall represent *any possible* proportional mixture of the three [primary] colours'. While maintaining, with Newton, the identity of the mixing rule for lights and pigments, he did recognise the 'essential difference' between these two processes, 'of compounding rays of the spectrum and compounding pigments'. Mixing lights is an additive process, but 'by combining pigments we do not add together *lights*'.[57]

Forbes did not however develop this insight to question the assumption of the identity of the mixing rules for lights and pigments, a convention challenged by Helmholtz in 1852. In his paper on colours (which was published, as noted, in March 1849) Forbes had noted that 'Newton was perfectly aware' that combining the primary spectral colours 'yellow and blue together, a green, not distinguishable from that of the spectrum, *except by its refrangibility*, will be formed'. But he had gone some way towards Helmholtz's discovery that mixing yellow and blue spectral colours did not generate green. In January 1849 Forbes had experimented with a rapidly spinning disc fitted with adjustable coloured sectors of tinted papers (supplied by the Edinburgh decorative artist David Ramsay Hay), and on observing the hues generated he found (as he recorded in his laboratory notebook) that 'Yellow and blue only, equal, produce a yellow grey or citrine – *never green*'. Writing to his former pupil James Clerk Maxwell in May 1855, he claimed that 'before Helmholtz, or I believe any one else', he had found that 'the mixture of yellow and blue, under these circumstances at least, does not produce green; you yourself being a witness to what I then tried'.[58] But whereas Helmholtz directly questioned the identity of the mixing rules for pigments and spectral colours, Forbes had not drawn this conclusion; and his experiments with coloured papers on a whirling disc did not prompt him, at the time, to disclaim publicly the conventional view that blue and yellow lights when combined generate green.

Observing Forbes' experiments had aroused Maxwell's interest in colour theory; and in August 1852, independently of Helmholtz's work, he mixed coloured beams of light. His subsequent experiments, using a series of 'colour boxes' that he designed to mix and compare spectral colours so as to make direct measurements, confirmed that in mixing spectral hues 'blue and yellow do *not* make green'. But his first major sequence of experiments, reported in his paper 'Experiments on colour, as perceived by the eye', published in the *Transactions* of the Royal Society of Edinburgh in 1855, involved an improvement of Forbes' use of Hay's adjustable tinted papers fitted to a spinning disc. Maxwell devised a colour top, a 'chromatic teetotum', in which he added a second set of adjustable coloured papers of smaller diameter to the first set, so that colour comparisons could be made between two different sets of colours. The circumference of the top was divided into 100 graduations, so that the proportions of each colour in a given combination could be read off. The sectors of coloured paper were adjusted so that the tints of the outer and inner circles were 'perfectly indistinguishable, when the top has a sufficient velocity of rotation', and he constructed colour equations expressing the equality between the sectors in the two circles.[59]

In preparing this paper Maxwell's interest in the theory of colours broadened to seek a resolution of the dissonance between the Newtonian theory of the innumerable gradations of the colours of the spectrum and the painters' doctrine of three primary colours. The issue was heightened by the work of David Brewster, a leading authority on optics. In his 'New analysis of solar light' read to the Royal Society of Edinburgh in 1831, Brewster had rejected Newton's explanation of the refraction of sunlight and his theory of colour. Brewster maintained that sunlight consists of only three primary colours: red, yellow and blue. He claimed that rays of these colours are not unequally refrangible (as supposed by Newton) but are distributed through the entire spectrum – that '*red*, *yellow* and *blue* light exist at every point of the solar spectrum';[60] and that the mixture of these rays, in various proportions, produces the colours of the Newtonian spectrum. Brewster therefore attacked the core of Newton's account of the prism experiments, that each spectral colour corresponds to a unique degree of refrangibility; and his theory of the triplicity of spectral colours (with red, blue and yellow primary colours) harmonised with the painters' triad of primary colours. The theory was based on experiments on the absorption of light; and though initially (and tentatively) endorsed by John Herschel, the theory was controversial and was decisively refuted by Helmholtz in 1852, demonstrating that Brewster's experiments were vitiated by numerous experimental and observational errors.[61]

Maxwell found the solution to the disagreement between the physical discoveries in optics and the practical experience of colourists in a physiological explanation, the three-receptor theory of colour vision expounded by the physicist and physician Thomas Young in 1807: 'Young . . . saw that, since this triplicity has no foundation in the theory of light, its cause must be looked for in the constitution of the eye; and . . . he attributed it to the existence of three distinct modes of sensation in the retina, each of which he supposed to be produced in different degrees by the different rays'. Young had suggested that the colour receptors in the retina of the eye were sensitive to red, green and violet light, and that these colours should be considered the primary spectral colours; and he set out a colour triangle showing that all other colours, including white, could be generated from combinations of these primaries.[62] In his *Course of Lectures on Natural Philosophy* (1807) Young drew a 'triangular figure' with the 'three simple sensations . . . red, green, and violet' at the vertices (Fig. 15), these colours being 'gradually shaded off towards the opposite sides'.[63] While Young's choice of primary colours was judged 'a singular opinion' by Forbes in 1849, by January 1855 Maxwell had adopted Young's scheme of three colour sensations, but emphasised that the colours chosen as primaries were not uniquely specified: 'Young has called them red, green, and violet; but any other three colours might have been chosen, providing that white resulted from their combination in proper proportion'.[64]

Maxwell was able to give a new and comprehensive account of the classification of colours. He adopted the theory recently proposed by the German mathematician and physicist Hermann Grassmann, that there are three variables of colour vision (spectral colour, intensity of illumination and the

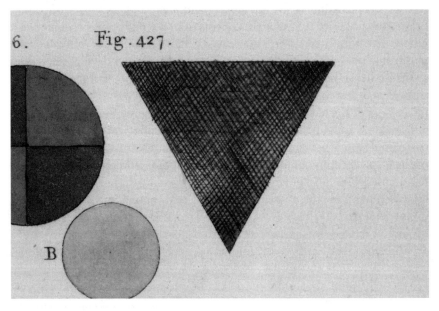

15   Thomas Young, colour triangle, from *A Course of Lectures on Natural Philosophy and the Mechanical Arts*. 'A triangular figure, exhibiting in theory all possible shades of colour, the red, the green, and the violet, are single at their respective angles, and are gradually shaded off towards the opposite sides; a little yellow and blue only are added in their places, in order to supply the want of brilliancy in the colours which ought to compose them. The centre is grey, and the lights of any two colours, which are to be found at equal distances on opposite sides of it, would always very nearly make up together white light, as yellow and violet, greenish blue and red, or blue and orange.'

degree of saturation). Grassmann demonstrated that this method of representing colour could be expressed by the position and magnitude of loaded
points on Newton's colour circle.[65] Maxwell termed these variables 'hue'
(representing the wavelength), 'intensity' (representing brightness) and 'tint'
(representing the gradations of purity). He showed that these colour variables
can be graphically represented on a colour diagram that incorporates Young's
triangular scheme, Newton's colour circle and Grassmann's classification of
colours (Fig. 16). The three colour sensations red, green and violet are placed
at the vertices of a triangle, so that a point within the triangle 'will be the position of the given colour, and the numerical measure of its intensity will be the
sum of the three primitive sensations'. A point W within the triangle denotes
white; the variables 'hue' and 'tint' are represented on the diagram by angular
position with respect to W and distance from W, and the 'intensity' is represented by a coefficient. Grassmann's use of three colour variables and Young's
triangular scheme of colour primaries are brought into 'exact numerical
comparison'; and Maxwell declares that 'the relation between the two
methods of reducing the elements of colour to three becomes a matter of
geometry'.[66] This was an original synthesis of ideas in the theory of colours.[67]
He illustrated Young's theory of three colour sensations by outlining 'a
supposed case taken from the art of photography', indicating how colour
photographs could be projected using red, green and violet filters; and in May
1861 he succeeded – fortuitously, despite the limitations of his materials – in
projecting a photograph of a coloured ribbon to an audience at the Royal
Institution in London.[68]

In the 1850s the study of colour theory was, in Britain, very much within
the Edinburgh experimental tradition of optics, that of Brewster and Forbes.
Maxwell's early papers were published in Edinburgh journals. Yet he wished
to engage the interest of his senior contemporaries in this work, William
Thomson and George Gabriel Stokes, like himself Cambridge-educated
mathematical physicists. But they were initially doubtful about the merit of
pursuing this speculative subject. Responding to a query by Thomson on
the colour theory advanced in Maxwell's paper 'Experiments on colour, as
perceived by the eye', Stokes – who was a leading authority on optics and the
discoverer of fluorescence in 1852 – replied that 'I have not made any experiments on the mixture of colours, nor attended particularly to the subject'. But
by November 1857 Stokes had familiarised himself with Maxwell's work,
complimenting the younger physicist that his 'results afford most remarkable
and important evidence of the theory of 3 primary colour perceptions, a
theory which you and you alone so far as I know have established on an
exact numerical basis'.[69] Stokes applauded Maxwell's introduction of exact
measurements and equations into colour theory; he secured concrete public
approbation by promoting the award of a medal for this work by the Royal

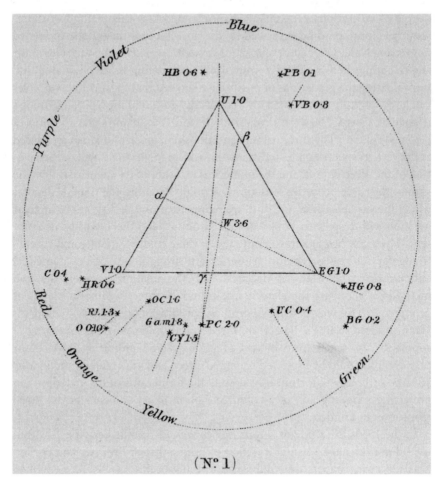

16 James Clerk Maxwell, colour diagram, from 'Experiments on colour, as perceived by the eye'.
Maxwell's colour diagram represents the relations of the coloured papers used in the experiments with
the colour top. Three coloured papers, vermilion (*V*), emerald green (*EG*), and ultramarine (*U*), are
taken as the standard colours, and placed at the vertices of the equilateral triangle. The other coloured
papers – carmine (*C*), red lead (*RL*), orange orpiment (*OO*), orange chrome (*OC*), chrome yellow
(*CY*), gamboge (*Gam*), pale chrome (*PC*), mixed green (*UC*), Brunswick green (*BG*), verditer blue
(*VB*), and Prussian blue (*PB*) – are arranged in their relation to the standard colours. The point *W*
within the triangle denotes the position of white. Lines drawn through *W* to the different colours
establish their sequence, which corresponds to the order of the spectral colours (though the spectrum
is deficient in the purples lying between ultramarine and vermilion). The distance of the colours from
W represents the purity (degree of saturation) of the coloured papers. The numbers are the coefficients
of intensity (brightness) of the colours. The letters *HR*, *HB*, and *HG* denote D.R. Hay's red, blue, and
green papers.

Society; and (as Secretary of the Society), he encouraged Maxwell to submit
to the *Philosophical Transactions* his paper 'On the theory of compound
colours, and the relations of the colours of the spectrum' (1860). In this
paper Maxwell described his method of obtaining accurate quantitative data

on spectral colours using his calibrated 'colour box', which enabled mixtures of spectral colours to be directly compared with white light. Through exact experimental measurements and the formulation of a coherent and systematic theory of colours, Maxwell brought closure to the debates on colour mixing initiated by Newton.

Unweaving the Rainbow

The painter Benjamin Robert Haydon, famous for his historical and religious pictures, recalled hosting an 'immortal dinner' on 28 December 1817 with John Keats, Charles Lamb and William Wordsworth: 'Lamb got exceedingly merry and exquisitely witty . . . he then in a strain of humour beyond description, abused me for putting Newton's head into my picture [*Christ's Entry into Jerusalem*, completed 1820] – "a fellow", said he, "who believed nothing unless it was as clear as three sides of a triangle". And then he and Keats agreed that he had destroyed all the poetry of the rainbow, by reducing it to the prismatic colours. It was impossible to resist him, and we all drank "Newton's health and confusion to mathematics".'[70] But Wordsworth hesitated before joining the toast, perhaps having in mind the lines in his 1805 *Prelude* recollecting the sound of 'Trinity's loquacious clock' and the view, from his 'nook obscure' above the humming college kitchens of St John's, of Trinity College and its 'antechapel, where the statue stood / Of Newton with his prism and silent face'. Two years after the 'immortal dinner' Keats wrote the lines in 'Lamia' that echo Lamb's sentiment:

> Do not all charms fly
> At the mere touch of cold philosophy?
> There was an awful rainbow once in heaven:
> We know her woof, her texture; she is given
> In the dull catalogue of common things,
> Philosophy will clip an Angel's wings,
> Conquer all mysteries by rule and line,
> Empty the haunted air, and gnomed mine –
> Unweave a rainbow.

The spiritual and imaginative associations of the rainbow, evoked in the toast at the 'immortal dinner' and in Keats' lines, have been seen to embody the antithesis between reason and religious symbol, a conflict between the values of rational, exact science and the power of imagination associated with Romanticism. But Percy Bysshe Shelley struck a different note in his allusion to the Newtonian prism and the rainbow in his poetic tribute to the dead Keats in 'Adonais' (1821). In musing on life and death Shelley conjoins the imagery of the prismatic colours and the symbolism of the rainbow. As Adonais 'is made one with Nature' he rose from darkness of the earth's shadows through the light of the rainbow colours, 'Life, like a dome of many-coloured glass, / Stains the white radiance of Eternity, / Until Death tramples it to fragments'.[71]

Shelley's attitude to the prism, as a symbol of the capacity of natural philosophy to provide illumination of the mysteries and enlarge the aesthetic appreciation of nature, shared common ground with the poets of the eighteenth century, characterised by Alexander Pope's 1730 eulogy of Newton in the epitaph 'Nature and Nature's Laws lay hid in Night. / God said, *Let Newton be!* and All was *Light.*' In the *Opticks* Newton noted the views of ancient and recent authors on the rainbow, specifically following Descartes' account in his *Meteores*, in confidently affirming that 'it is now agreed upon, that this Bow is made by Refraction of the Sun's Light in drops of falling rain'. He used the 'discovered properties of light' from his theory of spectral colours to explain the rainbow's colours in terms of the different refrangibility of the rays of each colour; his systematic presentation included an explanation of the characteristics of the higher-order bows.[72] In extending the mechanical philosophy, based on the sizes and motions of particles, to the secondary quality of colour, Newton integrated colour within the framework of the new science; and the beauty of colour, as manifest in the rainbow, came to be celebrated in terms drawn from Newtonian optics. Joseph Addison described the colours of the rising and setting sun in terms of 'strains of light', evoking the language of the Newtonian spectrum. In 'Spring', the first poem of *The Seasons* (1726–46), James Thomson described the rainbow in terms of the Newtonian prismatic colours, celebrating Newton as a scientific sage:

> Mean-time refracted from yon eastern cloud,
> Bestriding earth, the grand ethereal bow
> Shoots up immense; and ev'ry hue unfolds,
> In fair proportion running from the red,
> To where the violet fades into the sky.
> Here, awful Newton, the dissolving clouds
> Form, fronting on the sun, thy show'ry prism;
> And to the sage-instructed eye unfold
> The various twine of light, by thee disclos'd
> From the white mingling maze.

In his long poem *Pleasures of Imagination* (1744) Mark Akenside used the rainbow to illustrate the response of science to the wonders of nature:

Nor ever yet
The melting rainbow's vernal-tinctur'd hues
To me have shone so pleasing, as when first
The hand of science pointed out the path
In which the sun-beams gleaming from the west
Fall on the watry cloud . . .
    . . . and that trickling show'r
Piercing, thro' every crystalline convex
Of clust'ring dew-drops to their flight oppos'd,
Recoil at length where concave all behind
Th' internal surface of each glassy orb
Repells their forward passage into air.[73]

For Akenside the scientific understanding of the rainbow heightened the aesthetic appreciation of the beauty of a natural wonder; rational understanding and scientific knowledge of nature does not diminish but enlarges the aesthetic appreciation of nature's glories. The rainbow has complex cultural meanings in Christian iconography, in the classical tradition and as a transient natural object, with a corresponding range of intertwined moral, aesthetic and scientific meanings. The rainbow was traditionally seen as a natural object interpreted as part of an allegorical, sacramental universe. As a religious metaphor its symbolism was established in God's covenant with Noah after the Deluge: 'I do set my bow in the cloud, and it shall be for a token of a covenant between me and the earth'; while other biblical texts portray the rainbow as a symbol of divine power at the Last Judgement. To the poets of antiquity, Ovid and Virgil, the delicacy of the colour transitions in the rainbow indicated that it contained a 'thousand colours'; more prosaically, Aristotle observed red, green and purple.[74] Colour theorists from antiquity to Newton attributed various numbers of colours to the rainbow. In Rubens' *Juno and Argus* (1611), painted under the influence of d'Aguilon's treatise on optics where the red, blue and green triad of painters' primary colours is introduced, a rainbow is painted with these primaries interspersed with the composite colours of orange and green.

In his lectures on landscape painting, delivered between 1833 and 1836, John Constable commented on two of Rubens' landscapes, *An Autumn Landscape with a View of Het Steen in the Early Morning* (about 1636; National Gallery), and *Rainbow Landscape* (1636/8; Wallace Collection), regretting the separation of these companion pictures, 'two of his finest works'. He remarked that 'Rubens delighted in phenomena; – rainbows upon a stormy sky – bursts of sunshine – moonlight – meteors', and was particularly enthusiastic about Rubens' painting of rainbows. 'By the rainbow of Rubens, I do not allude to a particular picture, for Rubens often introduced it; I mean indeed, more than the rainbow itself, I mean dewy light and freshness, the departing shower, with the exhilaration of the returning sun, effects which Rubens, more than any other painter, has perfected on canvas.'[75] Constable was unconcerned with Rubens' lack of fidelity to the sequence of spectral colours in his representation of the rainbow in the *Rainbow Landscape*, but was struck by his delicacy of treatment of atmospheric effects, an achievement that Constable hoped to excel in capturing the momentary flickering of 'light – dews – breezes – bloom – and freshness; not any one of which has yet been perfected on the canvas of any painter in the world'.[76]

In Constable's letter to John Fisher of 23 October 1821, where he expounded his concern to achieve a realistic painting of the sky as 'an effectual part of the composition' in rendering the play of light and shade in the landscape, he excluded phenomena such as the rainbow from his strictures. Urging that the sky must be 'the *"key note"*, the *standard of "Scale"*, and the chief *"Organ of sentiment"*', emphasising that 'the sky is the *"source of light"* in nature – and governs everything', he excluded the rainbow from his criteria for the naturalistic portrayal of skies: 'these remarks do not apply to *phenomenon* – or what the painters call *accidental Effects of Sky* – because they always attract particularly'.[77] Constable alludes to the traditional disjunction between real colours (the inherent qualities of natural bodies) and the phenomenal, transient colours appearing without a coloured body, as with the rainbow. He implies that such transient and 'accidental' phenomena could be introduced by the painter for decorative or symbolic purposes, as a pictorial device to attract the attention of the viewer to a feature of the landscape, or to awaken awareness of the moral intentions of the painter; the rainbow could be introduced into a landscape without qualifying the primary concern of the painter to capture naturalistically the grand shaping influence of the sky and the mundane details of the humanised environment.

These aspirations shaped the composition of one of Constable's major paintings, *Salisbury Cathedral from the Meadows* (1831), which combines a spectacular and naturalistic treatment of the sky and clouds with optical and meteorological inaccuracy in the depiction of the rainbow; the sun is in the wrong position to produce the rainbow in the picture. Constable introduced the rainbow for symbolic and decorative reasons. Fearing the consequences of parliamentary reform for the Anglican Church, he had originally planned to paint Salisbury Cathedral 'under a cloud', but he added the rainbow to lighten and enhance the composition and to provide a traditional symbol of hope and reconciliation. He contrived the rainbow to terminate on Archdeacon John Fisher's house, and it has a personal as well as universal symbolism. Constable's seeming lack of concern that the rainbow in his painting was inaccurate in its representation of the necessary optical conditions is consistent with his contrast between real and 'accidental' meteorological effects – the rainbow being introduced as a pictorial device without any demand for its naturalistic portrayal – and with his purpose in adding the rainbow to the scene. When the engraver David Lucas reproduced the painting in mezzotint, Constable recognised that the rainbow formed its central visual element rather than a pictorial embellishment. He changed the title to *The Rainbow*: *Salisbury Cathedral*, telling Lucas that the rainbow 'forms the subject of the picture', and in making changes during the process of engraving he strove to improve the accuracy of his representation. His detailed study of meteorology, of clouds, skies and rainbows, is apparent in his contemporary watercolour *London from Hampstead, With a Double Rainbow* (1831) which shows a careful rendition of a rainbow effect, with the primary and secondary bows (a 'double rainbow' is a direct bow with its companion produced by light reflected from water) showing the correct optical reversal of the colour sequence of the secondary arc.[78]

Constable praised Rubens' depiction of rainbows for capturing the delicacy of atmospheric effects, the freshness of departing rain and the exhilaration of the returning sunlight, but Rubens' inaccuracy in lighting and in depicting the band of rainbow colours, of no concern to Constable, was criticised by J.M.W. Turner and by John Ruskin. In notebook entries in 1802 Turner recorded that he found Rubens to be guilty of 'distorting what he was ignorant of – natural effect' in his portrayal of rainbows. He considered Rubens' incorporation of the rainbow into his landscapes to be 'ill-judged and misapplied', to be 'one continual glare of colour and absurdities when investigated by [the] scale of Nature', but nevertheless conceded that Rubens' rainbows were 'captivating' in their visual effect.[79] On viewing the *Rainbow Landscape* at an exhibition in 1872 Ruskin was dismissive, finding that the bow was 'a dull blue, *darker* than the sky, in a scene lighted from the side of the rainbow', and judged that in his failure to achieve a naturalistic representation 'Rubens is not to be blamed for ignorance of optics, but for never having so much as looked at a rainbow carefully'.[80]

Ruskin's criticism of Rubens is consonant with his doctrine 'that the greatest thing a human soul ever does in this world is to *see* something, and tell what it *saw* in a plain way'; the deficiency in Rubens' composition arose from a lack of power of careful observation; and it was in possessing this quality (Ruskin maintained) that Turner reigned supreme over all other landscape painters.[81] Turner's *Buttermere Lake* (1798) was the first rainbow painting that he exhibited, and it departs from the conventional subject. Faithful to his observation of the scene, he chose to depict an unusual and especially evanescent phenomenon requiring great delicacy of technique, the rarely observed white rainbow, also known as a cloud bow or fog bow, produced by very small water droplets; he depicts the diaphanous bow extended into a reflection in the water of the lake. He was less interested in utilising the traditional iconography of the rainbow as a symbol of hope than in portraying his observation of nature, depicting the white rainbow as a purely visual motif. The rainbow remained a significant cultural emblem, but became a more problematic image in consequence of the tension between the representation of the natural order and traditional religious values. In the 1840s Turner did use the rainbow image symbolically, but to suggest a cautionary view of human destiny. In *The Wreck Buoy*, originally painted around 1807 but modified for exhibition in 1849, the picture juxtaposes two contrasting images, a rainbow arching over a buoy warning ships away from sunken hulks. In Turner's image the wreck buoy is a threatening marker of potential hidden disaster, and the rainbow becomes a symbol of pessimism and not of hope, a warning against the spurious illusions of mankind. This outlook was articulated in Turner's poem 'The Fallacies of Hope' from which he drew many of the epigraphs that he attached to his paintings. In his late paintings the rainbow becomes an ambiguous image of man's problematic relationship with nature.[82]

The scientific study of rainbows advanced considerably in the 1830s, with Cambridge mathematicians, notably George Biddell Airy, casting the theory of the rainbow in terms of the complexities of wave-fronts and caustic curves, and devoting mathematical power to resolving the consequent problems of analysis, but this work was accessible and familiar only to an audience of experts.[83] The rainbow retained its power as an exemplar of nature's glory and mystery, as an emblem of transcendence beyond the power of scientific investigation. In line with Keats and the toast at the 'immortal dinner' of 1817, in the chapter on 'The moral of landscape' in the third volume of *Modern Painters* (1856) Ruskin wrote that 'I much question whether any one who knows optics, however religious he may be, can feel in equal degree the pleasure of reverence which an unlettered peasant may feel at the sight of a rainbow'. Scientific knowledge had engendered a loss of perception and understanding, of the awareness of nature as a source of wonder; the rational spirit of cold philosophy was seen as destructive of the transparency and immediacy of the purity of the experience of nature, which can reveal the mystery hidden in natural phenomena. Amplifying this representation of the disjunction between scientific knowledge and the unmediated experience of the beauty and emotional power embodied in nature, Ruskin declares that: 'We cannot fathom the mystery of a single flower, nor is it intended that we should; but that the pursuit of science should constantly be stayed by the love of beauty, and accuracy of knowledge by tenderness of emotion'. It is at this point in his text that Ruskin explains his distinction between the 'science of aspects' and the science of 'essence'. He declares that the love of beauty is not 'in all respects unscientific', for 'there is a science of the aspects of things as well as of their nature' and this can be comprehended and communicated through the power of art; and, he affirms, 'the master of this science of *Aspects*' is Turner.[84]

For Ruskin the mystery of nature is to be approached with reverence, and works of art can illuminate truths that are inaccessible to science. In striking contrast to Turner's secular and pessimistic vision in *The Wreck Buoy*, which by juxtaposing images of hope and of death casts doubt on the promise and prospect of the redemption of humanity, John Everett Millais evoked the traditional optimistic moral and sacramental meanings of the rainbow in his painting *The Blind Girl* (1854–6). By his use of conjoined sacramental images Millais makes it clear that in his painting the rainbow is to be understood symbolically and in religious terms. In introducing a butterfly, the traditional emblem of the soul and in Christian iconography the symbol of the resurrection, he joins the religious symbolism of the rainbow as a perpetual and renewed sign of God's covenant to the promise of Christian redemption; the covenant of the Old Testament is seen to prefigure the Christian dispensation. The picture shows two girls, shabbily clothed and resting by the wayside, enduring poverty and vagrancy. The blind girl sits with her back to the double rainbow, which is portrayed with the correct optical reversal of the colour sequence of the secondary arc, but she is oblivious to its beauty; the younger child looks back at the glorious sight enfolding the landscape in a double arch. With the conjunction of the butterfly on the blind girl's shawl and the double rainbow affirming the divine covenant with mankind, Millais affirms the hope and expectation that in the world to come Christ will raise the blind girl with a new and transcendent vision.[85]

Nature Takes a 'Colouring Fit'

Questions of colour harmonies and combinations were discussed in writings by colour makers and artists, who took for granted the equivalence of spectral and pigment primaries. An important innovator, George Field was led from pigment technology to a concern with colour theory. He began his career as a chemist concerned with dyestuffs, especially the red colourant from the root of the madder plant, an interest that led him to manufacture artists' pigments. His theory of light and colours was outlined in *Chromatography; or a Treatise on Colours and Pigments, and of their Powers in Painting* (1835) and *Chromatics; or, the Analogy, Harmony and Philosophy of Colours* (1845). He embraced the pre-Newtonian idea that colours had their origin in black and white: by 'the latent concurrence of *Light* and *Shade* they become chromatic, and *colours* are produced'. The 'primary' colours blue, red and yellow could not be further decomposed by a prism, and from their combinations the 'secondary' colours were produced: orange from yellow and red, purple from red and blue, and green from yellow and blue. From the combination of these secondary colours the 'tertiary' colours were produced: citrine from orange and green, olive from green and purple, russet from orange and purple. Field set out a '*Definitive Scale* of Colours' ranging from white to black and incorporating these colours, a scale that had an analogy to the 'Fundamental Scale' of music. Field argued that Castel's 'ocular harpsichord' had failed not from 'presuming a false analogy' but from misconceptions about colours. Field claimed that his 'Definitive Scale' of colours established the basis for a '*melody of colours*', the 'gradations and successions' of the colour scale establishing the basis for 'the sweetest effects of colours in nature and in painting'. Variations in colour, or 'Tints', could be produced by mixing any of these colours with white, which Field considered to be 'the inherent active element of all colour'; and from combinations of tints he could produce 'an infinite variety of Hues'. From the combinations of hues and tints with black, 'their inherent passive element', a 'whole infinite variety of Shades' could be generated.[86]

Field rejected Newton's theory of light and colours and the physical doctrines of the physicists, the 'modern corpuscular theory and undulatory doctrines, with all the mathematical and mechanical explanations'; he claimed that these theories – the Newtonian emission theory of particles of light and the theory of light as waves propagated in an ether – were 'entirely incompetent' to explain colours. In place of these physical theories of light he proposed a 'chemistry of light', arguing that light was 'an effect of the concurrence of two elementary powers', the 'active' and the 'passive or re-active' principles of light, which he identified with the chemical elements of oxygen and hydrogen. According to Field's version of a chemical theory of light, 'the sunbeam . . . is a compound of these elements' and consists of a mixture of 'oxidizing or *whitening* rays' and 'hydrogenising or *blackening* rays'; the compounding of these rays produces the range of colours found in nature.[87] Field found support for his rejection of the Newtonian theory of spectral colours in David Brewster's theory that sunlight consists of only three primary colours, red, yellow and blue, and that rays of these colours are not unequally refrangible (as supposed by Newton) but are distributed through the entire spectrum; he supposed that the mixture of these rays, in various proportions, produces the colours of the Newtonian spectrum. Brewster's theory of the triplicity of the primary spectral colours of red, yellow and blue harmonised with the painters' triad of primary colours; as Field put it, Brewster supposed that there were 'three primary colours only', a theory consonant with his own view that the colours '*Blue, Red,* and *Yellow* . . . are *primary*'.[88] But Field's significant impact on art was as a colour maker; he was celebrated for the manufacture of pigments, and having formulated his 'Definitive Scale' of colours he was led to manufacture all the colours in the scale, paying particular attention to his three primary hues, his madders, his lemon yellow and his ultramarine (refined from lapis lazuli). He considered it essential to provide pure and unmixed colours for use by artists. The pure hues of his scale of colours were in great demand and were used around 1850 by Pre-Raphaelite artists such as Millais and Hunt to cover white-lead grounds with thin glazes to achieve astonishing brilliance of hue in their paintings.[89]

The Edinburgh decorative artist David Ramsay Hay, who was familiar with Field's writings, also appealed to Brewster's authority. In *The Principles of Beauty in Colouring Systematized* (1845) he resolutely points out that Newton's theory 'in treating of the transient colours in the phenomena of nature', the colours of the prismatic spectrum, was indeed 'different from that of the practical artist, in treating of the inherent colours of his pigments'; for the painter, red, yellow and blue were 'the only simple elements of chromatics'. Hay resolved this divergence in favour of the colour scheme customary among artists, by reporting the results of his own experiments undertaken in 1828 and which, he believed, served to refute Newton's theory of the seven colours of the prismatic spectrum and established that 'white light consists of the three primary colours, red, yellow, and blue'. This result was in conformity with the experience of painters and contradicted the 'scientific theory of the natural philosopher'. Hay declared that he was now confident in making public his work and conclusions because his experiment on the prismatic colours had been 'afterwards proved . . . by Sir David Brewster', who had established that sunlight consists of the three primary colours red, yellow and blue in consonance with the painters' triad of primaries.[90]

In his *Nomenclature of Colours, Hues, Tints and Shades* (1845) Hay confidently declared the truth of Brewster's theory of the prismatic colours: 'three colours [are] now universally acknowledged to be the primary elements of chromatics'. He was familiar with George Field's *Chromatography* and he set out a theory similar to Field's, based on a chemical theory of light and the antithesis between the 'active principle' of light and the 'passive principle' of darkness with colour as 'an intermediate phenomenon'. According to Hay, white and black were supposed to be the 'representatives' of the 'principles of light and darkness', and were not themselves colours but were the 'modifiers of colours'. He follows Field's list of primary, secondary and tertiary colours, arguing that all other colours could be generated from the 'primary elements of colour' of red, yellow and blue, 'out of which, by commixture and union amongst themselves, every conceivable variety of colour and hue arises'. He adopted Field's terminology of hues, tints and shades, setting out how it was possible to 'reduce the colours and hues to tints and shades by the admixture of white and black'. Hay's understanding of colours is based on the notion of contrasting complementary colours and their relation to principles of light and darkness: 'Red is opposed to green, yellow to purple, and blue to orange. Of these contrasts the most perfect is red and green, the former being equally allied to light and darkness, the latter arising out of the combination of yellow and blue, colours related to the principles of light and darkness in equally opposite ratios'.[91]

The most notable feature of Hay's *Nomenclature of Colours* is his set of 40 colour plates depicting 220 hues, tints and shades; as noted earlier, he supplied the tinted papers for Maxwell's experiments on the spinning colour top, and Maxwell utilised his colour nomenclature.[92] Artists and theorists considered the relation between spectral colours and pigments, the depiction of the colour effects manifest in nature, and the way in which the juxtaposition of the colours of different bodies influence each other in the process of perception. A contemporary article considered the 'power of complementary colours in juxtaposition' in considering the 'mutually modifying powers of colours'. It set out a distinction between 'absolute' and 'relative' colours, 'absolute colours' being defined as those possessed by bodies when seen separately and uninfluenced by others, 'relative' colours being those '*produced to the perception* by the modifying power each has over the other when placed together'.[93] William Holman Hunt read Field, Hay and Brewster, and in his painting *Our English Coasts* of 1852 he sought to depict colour as it really appears in nature; the colours of the pigments, especially red, yellow and blue, are juxtaposed so that the illumination by sunlight – 'this power of true sunshine', as Ruskin described it[94] – is rendered as polychromatic and intensified.

In the famous passage in the first volume of *Modern Painters* (1843), recounting his visit to La Riccia near Albano, John Ruskin described the noonday sunlight 'slanting down the rocky slopes of La Riccia, and their masses of entangled and tall foliage, whose autumnal tints were mixed with the wet verdure of a thousand evergreens, were penetrated with it as with rain'. The visual effect was overwhelming: 'I cannot call it colour, it was conflagration. Purple, and crimson, and scarlet, like the curtains of God's tabernacle, the rejoicing trees sank into the valley in showers of light, every separate leaf quivering with buoyant and burning life; each, as it turned to reflect or to transmit the sunbeam, first a torch and then an emerald.' Ruskin's word painting, which evokes Turner's own manipulation of light and colour, was intended to meet criticism that the vivid colours of Turner's paintings outfaced nature. Ruskin maintained that this complaint was far from the truth, for Turner 'does not, as far as mere vividness of colour goes, one half reach' the colours exhibited in nature, which 'no mortal effort can imitate or approach': 'Not in his most daring and dazzling efforts could Turner himself come near it'. As in Ruskin's portrayal of clouds forming aisles 'penetrating through angelic chapels to the Shechinah of the blue', the temple of God, the description of the purple, crimson and scarlet autumnal tints of the trees at La Riccia blazing in sunlight leads him to evoke comparison with the curtains of 'God's tabernacle' described in Exodus, envisioning the colours of nature in sacramental terms and utilising the language of the religious sublime.[95]

Turning to the rendition of 'subjects which no colours of earth could ever vie with' such as sunsets among the high clouds, Ruskin maintains that Turner 'alone has followed nature in these her highest efforts', but that he again follows nature 'faithfully, but far behind'. He gives as an example Turner's painting *The Fighting 'Temeraire'* (1838). *Blackwood's Magazine* for July–December 1839 had found the picture 'very beautiful – a very poetical conception; here is genius'. But it had wished that the painting had 'been more true'.[96] Ruskin commented that there was 'not one hue in this whole picture which was not far below what nature would have used in the same circumstances', and appealed to the reader, 'why then do you blame Turner because he dazzles you?' Turner's portrayal of the sunset in this painting does not intrude with 'overcharged brilliancy', nor was the artist guilty of 'outstepping nature', for the 'stormy blood-red of the horizon, the scarlet of the breaking sunlight . . . the pure gold and purple of the upper sky . . . all were given with harmony as perfect as their colour was intense'. Turner had striven to depict an extraordinary appearance in nature, which transcended 'the ordinary effects of daylight on ordinary colours'; he describes such sunsets in high clouds as an effect 'when nature herself takes a colouring fit, and does something extraordinary, something really to exhibit her power'.[97] Ruskin's expression 'colouring fit' to describe gorgeous entanglements of colour in natural phenomena is curious, and may well echo the term 'fits' that Newton had used in the *Opticks* when describing the periodic colours exhibited in thin films and thick plates. The term was drawn from contemporary medical language, where it was used to describe the recurrent attacks of a periodic ailment such as malaria (ague), and in Newton's usage it characterises the periodicity of the colour phenomena and the recurring states (fits) that dispose light rays to be easily reflected or transmitted.[98]

For Ruskin colour is essential to the perception and true representation of nature: a world drained of colour suggests the monochrome of photography.[99] In concluding the chapter 'Of Turnerian light' in the fourth volume of *Modern Painters* (1856), he maintains that the 'man who can see all the greys and reds, and purples in a peach, will paint the peach rightly round, and rightly altogether; but the man who has only studied its roundness, may not see its purples and greys, and if he does not, will never get it to look like a peach'. In giving precedence to colourists over the mere depiction of form and of chiaroscuro, he grounds his argument in sacramental and moral terms. He invites the reader to envisage a world denuded of bright colours, to consider 'what sort of a world it would be if all flowers were grey, all leaves black, and the sky *brown*'. For Ruskin this hypothetical world would be bereft of sacred and moral value; he maintains that the world is resplendent with colour, where 'innocent things are bright in colour', and he draws the contrast with an absence of colour that he associates with the malignancy of 'death, night, and pollution of all kinds'. He compares a dove's neck with the 'grey back of a viper', and contrasts rainbows, sunrises, roses, rubies, opals and corals, with alligators, lions, wolves, sharks, slugs, bones and 'corrupting, stinging, destroying things in general'; colour is associated with 'nature and life' and is 'richly bestowed on the highest works of creation, and the eminent sign and seal of perfection in them'. He argues that the 'sanctity of colour' has biblical authority, referring to the 'sacred chord of colour (blue, purple, and scarlet, with white and gold) as appointed in the tabernacle'. This harmony of colours is 'the fixed base of all colouring', found in the work of all 'noble painters', and he alludes to the description by Herodotus of this same sequence of 'colour harmony' being used to colour the concentric battlements of Ecbatana in Media.[100]

In the second volume of *The Stones of Venice* (1853) Ruskin had cited Herodotus' description of these battlements, 'of which one circle was golden like the sun, and another silver like the moon; and then came the great secret chord of colour, blue, purple, and scarlet; and then a circle white like the day, and another dark, like night; so that the city rose like a great mural rainbow, a sign of peace amidst the contending of lawless races, and guarded, with colour and shadow, that seemed to symbolize the great order which rules over Day, and Night, and Time'. Colour has primacy in nature and colours have sacramental and moral meaning, evoking the temple of God, the curtains of the tabernacle, and the duality of good and evil; and the colours of the battlements of Ecbatana seemed to symbolise 'the first organization of the mighty statutes – the law of the Medes and Persians, that altereth not'.[101] In the penultimate chapter of the fifth and final volume of *Modern Painters* (1860), Ruskin reprises his doctrine of colour as the 'sanctifying element of visible beauty, inseparably connected with purity and life'. In his typology, sunlight 'undivided is the type of the wisdom and righteousness of God'; when 'divided', sunlight is 'the type of wisdom of God becoming sanctification and redemption'; so that colour is 'the type of love', the divine attribute of love manifest to humanity in nature.[102]

Turner's colour effects were achieved on the basis of reading and reflecting on the literature of the theory of colours, consulting the writings of Moses Harris, George Field and David Brewster, and (after its partial publication in Charles Eastlake's 1840 translation) Goethe's *Theory of Colours*. Following the convention among artists, Turner adopted a three-colour theory of primaries, but the diagrams he prepared for his lectures at the Royal Academy around 1820 show that he sought to distinguish 'aerial' (spectral) from 'material' colours, using two separate colour circles. In the 'aerial' circle of colours the primaries are arranged to produce white, while in the 'material' circle the primaries overlap to produce a grey: 'white in the prismatic order, in the rainbow, is the union or compound of light, as is daylight', while 'the commixture of our material colours becomes the opposite, darkness'. For Turner light and dark represented the basic polarities of colour, with the chromatic colours as intermediaries: 'Sink the yellow until it light into the red and blue, and hence two only: light and shadow'. When he read Eastlake's translation of Goethe's *Theory of Colours* in the early 1840s he was struck by the table of polarities:

Plus	*Minus*
Yellow	Blue
Action	Negation
Light	Shadow
Brightness	Darkness
Force	Weakness
Warmth	Coldness
Proximity	Distance
Repulsion	Attraction
Affinity with acids	Affinity with alkalis

Against this table, in his own copy, Turner jotted 'Light and Shade'.[103]

Goethe's investigation of colour theory began in 1790–91 when he looked through a prism at a white wall expecting, from his mistaken understanding of Newton's prism experiment, to see the colours of the spectrum; but he saw white, and only at the boundaries of dark objects viewed against the wall did colours appear. While Goethe's expectation (as he later came to understand) was erroneous – being in part derived from garbled accounts of Newton's theory and experiments in contemporary texts, where viewing a wall through a prism was not explained or differentiated from Newton's prism experiment – he nevertheless persisted in his conviction that the Newtonian theory was false. He maintained that Newton's error lay in interposing theory in recounting his experiments, and in using the complicated phenomenon of optical dispersion as the foundation of his interpretation of colours.[104] However, Goethe's approach was not solely determined by science but by aesthetics, shaped by his journey to Italy in 1786–8, which transformed his studies of art and nature. He contrasted the vivid hues of the Italian landscape, 'how harmoniously there the sky is joined to the earth and spreads over it its radiance', with the gloom and sombre colours of his native Germany, where 'in our latitudes we are only rarely reminded of those paradisal moments'. The sky in Italy 'usually displays to us a pure deep blue; the rising and setting sun furnishes us with notions of the most intense red to the palest yellow', while a 'blue distance shows us the most charming transition from heaven to earth and in a pure diffused haze a vivid sheen floats over the land in a myriad playful gleams'.[105] The light and harmony of the Italian atmosphere unites the colours of water, sun and sky, a recollection of sunlight and glowing landscape that established for Goethe the primary importance of brightness and darkness and the duality of yellow and blue as the basis for understanding colours. He proposed a modification theory of colour based on the interaction of light and dark, where colours emerge from their boundaries; the overlap of white on black produces blue, while the overlap of black on white produces yellow, these being the fundamental colours produced by interaction of lightness and darkness; by intensification and mixing, the other colours of the spectrum are produced.

In 1843 Turner used Goethe's scheme to give emotional expression to two episodes from the story of Noah's flood. Drawing upon Goethe's table of colour polarities he painted two counterpart paintings demonstrating the polarities of threatening darkness and radiant light, contrasting the emotions of pessimism and optimism. *Shade and Darkness – the Evening of the Deluge* utilised the terms and colours of the 'minus' side of Goethe's table of polarities, 'shadow' and 'darkness', showing the last families, tarnished by 'negation' and 'weakness', about to be swept away by flood in a shadowy, brooding landscape; the emotional mood is of 'coldness', and the dark and blue colours of the coming flood overcome the bright colours of the dawn. The painting was exhibited with a caption from Turner's poem 'The Fallacies of Hope':

> The morn put forth his sign of woe unheeded;
> But disobedience slept; the dark'ning Deluge closed around,
> And the last token came: the giant framework floated,
> The roused birds forsook their nightly shelters screaming
> And the beasts waded to the ark.

The counterpart painting *Light and Colour (Goethe's Theory) – the Morning after the Deluge – Moses Writing the Book of Genesis* utilised the terms and colours of the 'plus' side of the polarity. The dominant 'yellow' space is full of 'action', 'brightness' and 'force' in the vortex of figures whirling around Moses writing Genesis and around the Brazen Serpent (serving as an analogue for the Crucifixion). The rainbow of Noah's covenant is transformed into an iridescent prismatic bubble, and the emotional mood of the painting is of 'warmth'. The painting was exhibited with a caption from 'The Fallacies of Hope':

> The ark stood firm on Ararat; th' returning sun
> Exhaled the earth's humid bubbles, and emulous of light,
> Reflected her lost forms, each in prismatic guise

Hope's harbinger, ephemeral as the summer fly
Which rises, flits, expands, and dies.

The theme of the painting is hope, evoked in the golden iridescent bubble, but the sense of optimism is constrained by a mood of pessimism; the ephemeral character of human life and hope is suggested by the residual threatening forces of darkness. Turner explained the meaning of the painting to Ruskin as 'Red, blue and yellow', signifying the harmony of the primary triad and the emotional tension between optimism and pessimism which his use of these colours evokes.[106]

The aesthetic appreciation of colours in nature and in painting came to be framed in language derived from Newton's theory of the sun's 'white' light being differentially refracted into heterogeneous coloured rays by a prism. Colour was conceived as a sensation produced in the eye by light, rather than as an inherent and real property of matter. Newton explained the permanent colours of natural bodies in terms of the illumination by light of the particles of matter forming bodies; the size of the corpuscles determines the mode in which light is reflected and is the source of the sensation of colour as perceived by the eye. When he presented his account of the colours of natural bodies – of vegetation, the sky and fabrics – he obtained a measure of the size of the particles generating colours from his study of 'Newton's rings', the periodic colours of thin films. The investigation of spectral lights by the prism enlarged the aesthetic appreciation of nature as portrayed in works of art – the depiction of the rainbow by Constable and Turner, and of striking prismatic colour effects by Holman Hunt. In the *Opticks* Newton presented his theory of spectral colours in terms that fostered the assimilation of his theory into the artists' tradition of pigment mixing; but in the 1850s Helmholtz and Maxwell established that mixing yellow and blue spectral lights does not yield green, thus rejecting the equivalence of the mixing rules for pigments and lights. Promoting Young's triangular classification of spectral colours based on the three colour sensations of red, green and violet, Maxwell's scheme for mixing spectral colours incorporates Young's triangular classification and Newton's colour circle. In setting out the proportions of his colour-mixing circle, Newton drew upon his musical division of the spectrum into seven segments proportional to a string sounding the seven notes of the octave in the musical scale. This analogy divided the spectral image into harmonic proportions, and the colour circle placed the theory of spectral colours and colour mixing within an aesthetic framework of musical and chromatic harmony – shaping discussions of coloured shadows, complementary colours and after-images by Erasmus Darwin and others.

Defending Turner from the charge that the vivid colours of his paintings outface nature, Ruskin urged that Turner followed rather than challenged natural effects. Ruskin emphasised that colour is essential to the perception and representation of nature; that shape alone will not truly represent reality. Ruskin's evocative descriptions of colour effects parallel Turner's own manipulations of light and colour, and in giving precedence to the depiction of colour over form Ruskin framed his argument in sacramental and moral terms. In a world denuded of bright colours, he considers 'what sort of a world it would be if all flowers were grey, all leaves black, and the sky *brown*'.

For Ruskin this imaginary world drained of colour would lack sacred and moral value; he draws a contrast between a world denuded of colour and the resplendent real world where colour marks 'nature and life' and is the seal of its perfection.[107] The appreciation of colours and their representation in painting rests on moral and biblical authority.

Newton's theory of prismatic colours embodied an implicit 'hypothesis' about the nature of light and matter: that light consists of a stream of corpuscles differing in size, and that these light corpuscles correspond to different coloured rays which were separated by the prism. This theory of matter played a fundamental role in shaping his speculations about vital powers.

CHAPTER 8

※

Vital Forces

In the opening lines of the last and most systematic of his scientific poems, *The Temple of Nature*, which was published posthumously in 1803, Erasmus Darwin appeals to love as the power binding the universe; this provides a parallel to the invocation to nurturing ('alma') Venus with which Lucretius opens his didactic poem *De Rerum Natura* (*On the Nature of Things*).[1] In the frontispiece to Darwin's book the personification of 'nature' as a generative and nurturing goddess is made explicit in the engraving by Henry Fuseli (Fig. 17):

> Shrin'd in the midst majestic NATURE stands
> Extends o'er earth and sea her hundred hands,
> Tower upon tower her beamy forehead crests,
> And births unnumber'd milk her hundred breasts.[2]

Darwin uses this image of the unveiling of the secrets of 'nature' to embody the union of the poetic imagination and natural philosophy, an aesthetics of nature that suffuses his book, 'bringing to the imagination the beautiful and sublime images of the operations of nature' as he puts it in the preface. In emphasising the active and generative powers of 'nature' Darwin echoes the breadth of Lucretius' argument, presenting a version of contemporary materialism as a counterpart to Lucretius' Epicurean atomism. Darwin's natural philosophy of immanent active powers parallels the systems of his friends Joseph Priestley and James Hutton, dissolving Newton's dualism of matter and its attendant powers, and placing emphasis on the permanence of matter in the natural world and the self-sufficiency of active ethereal powers. While Samuel Taylor Coleridge came to challenge Darwin's poetic style and his materialistic and deistic natural philosophy, during the period of radical questioning of orthodox doctrines at the outset of his career he was impressed by the scope and vision of Darwin's writings in shaping an enlightened and critical intellectual milieu. The ambition of Darwin's materialistic system,

17   Henry Fuseli, 'The Temple of Nature'.

with its triumphant emphasis on a naturalistic theory of the origin of life
– that life in its simplest form arose through a sequence of chemical reactions
– impressed Percy Bysshe Shelley and left its mark on Mary Shelley's
Frankenstein.

Active Principles and Ethers

In Query 28 of the second English edition of the *Opticks* (1717) Isaac Newton declared that one of the tasks of natural philosophy was 'to unfold the Mechanism of the World'.[3] This had been the burden of his *Philosophiae Naturalis Principia Mathematica* (*Mathematical Principles of Natural Philosophy*), published in 1687. As Newton indicated in the title of his formidable treatise, his concern was with natural philosophy, the science of natural bodies, and his argument was couched in the abstract language of mathematics. In using the expression 'mechanism of the world' in the *Opticks,* Newton did not imply his allegiance to the canonical form of the 'mechanical philosophy' – a term coined by Robert Boyle to describe the theory that all phenomena could be explained in terms of the size, shape and motion of the corpuscles of matter. The framework of *Principia,* based on the concept of 'force' as the causal agent inducing changes in the state of motion of bodies, is evidently richer than the action-by-contact condition by which Descartes had sought to explain the interaction of particles. Newton expressed the explanatory scheme of *Principia* in terms of the espousal of a mathematical way of pursuing natural philosophy: 'I use interchangeably and indiscriminately words signifying attraction, impulse, or any sort of propensity toward a centre, considering these forces not from a physical but only from a mathematical point of view.'[4]

Newton rejected many of the core tenets of Descartes' principles of philosophy, denying the intelligibility of a purely corporeal world regulated by mechanistic necessity and a cosmology based on the supposition of a fluid forming a series of celestial vortices that carry the planets with them as they rotate; and he maintained that Descartes' mechanical philosophy implied materialism. In place of the Cartesian programme of advancing plausible hypotheses based on the arrangement, motion and contact of corpuscles, Newton offered a mathematical and experimental natural philosophy for which he claimed the prospect of certainty. He followed Boyle in his early and permanent commitment to atomism; and in rejecting the ontology of the mechanical philosophy of Descartes he allowed a role for non-material agents along with material causes.[5]

Newton's three laws of motion provide the physical basis for his mathematical theory of the motion of bodies. Adopting a conflict theory of motion, he supposed that by its 'inertia' a body would tend to move in straight lines, but by acting successively in a sequence of impulses 'impressed force' could act upon the body and deflect it from this path. A force is measured by the effect it has in inducing a body to move either from its state of rest or, if in motion, to deviate from a rectilinear path; while 'inertia' denotes the property of the body by which it perseveres in its state of rest or motion. In *Principia* Newton explains that force is external to matter, generating a change in motion: impressed force 'consists solely in the action and does not remain in a body after the action has ceased'. The tendency of a body to resist the action of an impressed force is explained by the 'inertia of matter': 'a body perseveres in any new state solely by the force of inertia'. Newton's designation of the concept of inertia as the 'force of inertia [*vis inertiae*]' is ambiguous but echoes contemporary usage and his own sense of 'inertia' as a 'power of resisting', an 'inherent force of matter' by which bodies persist in the state of motion or rest; he declares that this 'inherent force may also be called by the very significant name of force of inertia'.[6]

But Newton considered 'inertia' to be a property of matter. In the third of the 'rules for the study of natural philosophy' that he appended to the second edition of *Principia* (1713) he lists inertia, together with extension, impenetrability, hardness and mobility as 'qualities of all bodies universally'. These essential or 'universal qualities' of bodies are the necessary and sufficient conditions of the materiality of bodies, so that the 'force of inertia', which explains the perseverance of a body in a state of rest or uniform rectilinear motion, is considered to be a defining property of matter. While the meaning of impressed force is defined by the mathematical formalism of *Principia*, and Newton affirms that he does not offer a physical, merely a mathematical explication of force, he grounds the concept of force on the relation between impressed force as external action producing change and inertia as the fundamental property of matter by which bodies resist change of rest or motion. Newton declares that we have knowledge of inertia, and of the other universal properties of matter, 'only through experiments' and 'through our senses'; in accord with his empiricist outlook he maintains that it is through sensory experience that bodies are known to possess spatial extension, hardness, and to be movable, and to persevere in motion 'by means of certain forces (which we call forces of inertia)'. Although the essential properties of bodies are known only through sensory experience, yet he claims that these properties can be 'ascribed to all bodies universally', to 'bodies beyond the range of these senses'.

To justify this inference from observable bodies to unobservable atoms Newton appeals to the 'analogy of nature', which he justifies by the doctrine that 'nature is always simple and ever consonant with itself'. Newton therefore seeks to establish the ascription of the essential qualities of matter, including inertia, to all material particles, including the fundamental atoms of his natural philosophy, bodies that he acknowledges are imperceptible to the senses: he affirms that 'we conclude that every one of the least parts of all our bodies is extended, hard, impenetrable, movable, and endowed with a force of inertia'. The primordial atoms differ only in size, not in their essential properties, from observable particles; and he justifies this conclusion by appeal to the 'analogy of nature', declaring that this principle is the 'foundation of all natural philosophy'.[7] Newton's argument, ostensibly grounded on the appeal to sensory experience, rests on a metaphysical doctrine, the 'analogy of nature', and the appeal to the uniformity of nature, to justify the ascription of the essential qualities of matter to the imperceptible particles composing natural bodies, corpuscles that lie beyond experience.[8]

Following the expectation of his contemporaries Boyle and Robert Hooke, who expressed the hope that improvements in microscopes would permit the secret workings of nature, including the particles responsible for generating the colours of bodies, to become accessible to observation, Newton affirmed in the *Opticks* (1704) that 'it is not impossible but that Microscopes may at length be improved to the discovery of the Particles of Bodies on which their Colours depend'. But these corpuscles, though small, nevertheless have the physical properties of the bodies of which they form a part – whether of glass or grass. Although the observation of corpuscles of sufficient size to generate colours remained a possibility, this did not apply to the primordial atoms; the particles producing colours were very much larger than atoms, and Newton maintained that there was a limit to the capacity of microscopes to observe the innermost structure of bodies, which could only be conjectured: 'what is really their inward Frame is not yet known to us'. This conclusion was a consequence of his theory of coloured bodies and his assumptions about the nature of matter.

In expounding his theory of the colours of natural bodies in Book II of the *Opticks*, Newton explains that despite their small size the corpuscles responsible for the colours of bodies are not atoms, for these corpuscles are themselves composed of a compound structure of particles. According to Newton's theory, 'Bodies . . . appear of divers Colours, accordingly as they are disposed to reflect most copiously the Rays originally endued with those Colours'; and from study of the colours of thin films he showed how 'the bigness of the component parts of natural Bodies may be conjectured by their Colours'. But the smallest particles composing bodies lay beyond the possibility of such calculation, because these particles are so small as to 'reflect so very little Light as to appear intensely black, and yet may perhaps variously refract it to and fro within themselves so long, until it happen to be stifled and lost'. Hence the primordial atoms are imperceptible, and he judges that it seems impossible 'to see the more secret and noble Works of Nature'. Espousing a theory of matter as composed of a compound structure of particles led him to the conclusion that seemingly solid bodies in fact consist mostly of empty space: 'Bodies are much more rare and porous than is commonly believed'.[9]

In a letter to Newton in 1693 Leibniz applauded his ability to 'handle nature in mathematical terms', but expressed his own belief that gravity was 'caused or regulated by the motion of a fluid medium'.[10] But Newton refused to accept this conclusion. In the *General scholium* with which he concluded the second edition of *Principia* (1713) he distinguishes between the discussion of gravity as physical phenomenon and the problem of determining its cause: 'I have not yet assigned a cause to gravity'. He renounced the possibility of formulating an explanation of gravity by a mechanism of intervening particles pressing on the surfaces of planets, as had been suggested by Descartes. Newton maintains that any such mechanism would fail to meet the condition that 'this force arises from some cause that penetrates as far as the centers of the sun and planets . . . and that acts not in proportion to the quantity of the *surfaces* of the particles on which it acts (as mechanical causes are wont to do)'. A mechanism explaining gravity through the contact of mediating particles would be inconsistent with the law of gravity itself. He draws the contrast with his own achievement, the provision, in place of a hypothetical and inadequate mechanism, of a mathematical theory of gravity based on the concept of the attractive force of gravity: 'it is enough that gravity really exists and acts according to the laws that we have set forth and is sufficient to explain all the motions of the heavenly bodies'. And in a famous statement he declared that 'I do not "feign" hypotheses'.[11]

This tactic became the core of Newton's mathematical philosophy; but he had long given serious thought to the problems raised by seeking a cause of gravity. The four letters that he wrote to Richard Bentley in 1693, which were published in 1756, contain some of his most famous statements on understanding gravity: his denial that gravity is a property of matter, 'innate, inherent and essential to Matter', thereby rejecting a mechanistic interpretation, and his affirmation that 'Gravity must be caused by an Agent acting constantly according to certain Laws', adding that 'whether this Agent be material or immaterial, I have left to the Consideration of my Readers'.[12] To suppose that gravity acts directly at a distance without the mediation of some agent would imply that gravity was an inherent property of matter; but Newton quite explicitly excludes gravity from his list of the 'universal qualities' of matter; and as a force acting on planets gravity was in a different category to 'inertia', which was an 'innate, inherent and essential' property of matter. It was necessary to provide a causal explanation of gravity, though he left open whether this was to be found in the workings of some kind of material substance or to be attributed to the agency of a non-material cause. He explored both of these options.

In Query 31 of the 1717 *Opticks* Newton contrasts inertia, as a 'passive Principle by which Bodies persist in their Motion or Rest' and which is 'accompanied with such passive Laws of motion as naturally result', with certain 'active principles, such as are the cause of Gravity'. He emphasises that matter does not have the capacity to originate motion. Passive principles such as inertia, which explains the power of bodies to persist in their state of rest or motion, could not explain the origin of motion in the world. And because motion is constantly being dissipated, in the collision of inelastic or partially elastic bodies, it was apparent that 'Some other Principle was necessary for putting Bodies into Motion; and now that they are in Motion, some other Principle was necessary for conserving the Motion'. Defining matter in terms of the passive 'universal qualities' such as inertia specifically excluded mention of active powers; the source of the activity of bodies must therefore lie outside the domain of matter and its properties. This fundamental duality of active and passive principles reflects Newton's emphasis on matter as contingent on God's will. To grant matter inherent powers of activity would be to allow matter to have the status of self-sufficiency, a doctrine that for Newton was tantamount to materialism and atheism. He declares that 'the variety of Motion which we find in the world is always decreasing, [and hence] there is a necessity of conserving it and recruiting it by active Principles, such are as the cause of Gravity'.

The motion and activity of bodies is therefore seen in terms of the causal agency of 'active principles'; and in locating the explanation of gravity in terms of the agency of 'active principles', whose operation is held to be distinct from the 'passive' laws of matter, Newton refers to 'active principles' as being both the 'cause of Gravity' and as being 'general Laws of Nature'.[13] The clear implication of this argument, set out in the closing pages of Query 31 of the *Opticks* where he places emphasis on God's creative power, is that 'active' principles were to be considered both as laws of nature (though not 'passive' laws of matter) and as the mediating agents by which God conserved motion and gravity in the cosmos. Newton first made public these comments on gravity and active principles in the Latin edition of the *Opticks* published in 1706, to which Leibniz responded in his correspondence with Samuel Clarke in 1715–16. Leibniz correctly understood Newton to hold that the attractive force of gravity could be conceived as a mathematical construct, unexplained by a mechanism of particles; that gravity was construed as the direct expression of God's continued active presence in the world; and that the solar system would require occasional reformation by divine providence to restore irregularities developing over time. Newton conceived active principles as the manifestation of God's lawful, causal agency in the cosmos; in drafts of the queries to *Opticks* he explicitly referred to God as the cause of the 'force of gravity' acting through 'the mediation of some active principle', establishing the intelligibility of the concept of gravity by appealing to a physico-theological argument.[14]

In seeking to establish the operation of active principles as natural agents whose mode of action was not reducible to the 'passive' laws of matter, Newton linked their agency to chemical phenomena rather than to the laws of motion of *Principia*. Referring to a diversity of 'great and violent' chemical processes, of 'sulphureous Steams in the Bowels of the Earth', 'Fermentations', the 'kindling of Fire by blowing, and the beating of the Heart by means of Respiration', he asserts that in these processes particles 'are put into new Motions by a very potent Principle'. To 'active Principles' he assigns not only the 'cause of Gravity', but 'the cause of Fermentation, by which the Heart and Blood of Animals are kept in perpetual Motion and Heat . . . [and] Mountains take fire, the Caverns of the Earth are blown up, and the Sun continues violently hot and lucid, and warms all things by his Light'.[15] Newton gives clear expression to the concept of a cosmos permeated and replenished by active powers external to matter, their effect manifest in the violent processes of chemistry and their role in sustaining life. The tenor of these remarks suggests that his construction of a duality of active and passive principles has its roots in his enduring concern with the relation between mechanical and chemical processes, in pondering whether the internal structure of substances could be conceived in terms of the interaction between gross particles, or whether a chemistry concerned with the active processes of fermentation and putre-faction (concepts shaped by contemporary alchemy) should be invoked to elucidate the internal structure of matter.[16]

The appeal to vivifying principles is a constant theme in Newton's natural philosophy. His earliest speculations on ether, introduced in his 'Hypothesis explaining the properties of light' read to the Royal Society in 1675 (though not published until 1757) and in a letter to Henry Oldenburg correcting this paper (published in 1744), suggest a cosmology based on the circulation and trans-formation of ethereal spirits. He supposed that 'the whole frame of Nature may be nothing but various Contextures of some certaine aethereall Spirits or vapours condens'd as it were by praecipitation', and speculated that 'perhaps may all things be originated from aether'. He adds that 'nature is a perpetuall circulatory worker, generating fluids out of solids, and solids out of fluids, fixed things out of volatile, & volatile out of fixed' (the word 'circulatory' was omitted from the version of this text as published in 1757); and he conjectures that 'the vast aethereall Spaces between us, & the Stars are for a sufficient repos-itory for this food of the Sunn & Planets'; thus by 'nature makeing a circulation' the activity of the cosmos would be conserved.[17] In stressing that this 'aether' was an underlying first principle from which all things originated in a chemical process, and in supposing that the activity of the cosmos was conserved by circulation, Newton echoed contemporary alchemical writers.[18] In purporting to explain the activity of natural agents, he gave the 'aether' of the 1675 'Hypothesis' the same function in his natural philosophy that he was later to allot to 'active principles', both concepts expressing a chemical cosmology lying outside the framework of the 'passive' laws of motion of *Principia*.

Newton's speculations culminated in the introduction of an ether in queries added to the 1717 edition of the *Opticks*, perhaps intended to answer

Leibniz's charge that his concept of gravity was a 'miracle', an 'occult quality' and a 'fiction'.[19] Newton envisaged the minute particles of ether to have great 'elastick force', its tendency to 'expand it self' enabling it to 'press upon gross Bodies' being explained in terms of the intensity of this force: 'the exceeding smallness of its Particles may contribute to the greatness of the force by which those Particles may recede from one another'.[20] This ether, invoked to explain gravity, did not act through the direct contact of its particles; these particles were separated by void space and acted on one another by their repulsive forces. As a putative explanation of gravity the ether of the 1717 *Opticks* was, by implication, both an active principle, communicating God's lawful, causal agency to matter, and also a physical model establishing the intelligibility of the force of gravity as a legitimate scientific concept.[21]

For eighteenth-century natural philosophers Newton's association between ether and active principles provided the basis for the formulation of a concept of matter as inherently active and of the cosmos as a self-contained system possessing inherent active powers. The ambiguous conceptual status of Newton's ether, as both an 'active' and a material principle, led many eighteenth-century theorists to interpret ether as a substance endowed with inherent activity, conflating the active-passive dualism of Newton's natural philosophy.[22] Newton's ether theory aroused little interest among natural philosophers until the 1740s. A contemporary assessment of the ether of the 1717 *Opticks* as 'something new in the latest edition of his *Opticks* which has surprised his physical and theological disciples'[23] hinted at the reason for this lack of interest. Newtonian natural philosophers and theologians such as John Keill and Samuel Clarke had been schooled to be wary of physical explanations of gravity, and had taken up the cudgels in public defence of Newton's mathematical theory of the attractive force of gravity; and in his recent correspondence with Leibniz, Clarke had defended Newton's thesis that gravity was to be understood as the effect of the divine will. Though making occasional mention of the idea, writers seeking to popularise Newton's world view at first avoided the ether in favour of placing emphasis on his theory of forces.[24]

But the situation changed in the 1740s, with signs of evident interest in the ether of the 1717 *Opticks*. This engagement with Newton's theory of ether among British natural philosophers was related to the burgeoning enthusiasm for electrical studies in the 1740s. As Benjamin Martin noted in his *Philosophia Britannica* (1747), though Newton had discussed ether 'he seem'd not at all delighted with the thought, nor ever laid any stress upon it'; by contrast, contemporary theorists 'are arriv'd at great dexterity since Sir Isaac's time ... [and] can now almost prove the existence of this aether by the phenomena of electricity'.[25]

This shift in focus was fostered by the emergent notion of a balance in the natural order between the forces of attraction and repulsion, each associated with different material substances, which developed into a theory of the balance of powers between attracting matter and repelling ether, and the emphasis on active principles in chemistry. In his *Vegetable Staticks* (1727) the cleric and chemist Stephen Hales followed Newton's suggestion in Query 31 of the *Opticks* that the properties of 'airs' (gases) should be considered in terms of the repulsive forces possessed by their particles, the production and absorption of 'airs' by chemical substances being explained by a balance between their forces of repulsion and the forces of attraction in ordinary matter. Hales maintained that the material world would become 'one inactive cohering lump' if matter were 'only endued with a strongly attracting power'; so intermingled with 'attracting matter' there was 'a due proportion of strongly repelling elastic particles ['airs'], which might enliven the whole mass, by the incessant action between them and the attracting particles'.[26] The *Elementa Chemiae* (1732) of the Dutch chemist and physician Herman Boerhaave introduced another principle of chemical activity, 'fire', as the cause of chemical change. For Boerhaave 'fire' was 'the great changer of all things in the universe, while itself remaining unchanged' and was supposed to exist 'always and everywhere', permeating the cosmos. He claimed that 'fire' was a principle of activity: it was through the agency of the 'active element' of fire that the 'whole universe might continue in perpetual motion'. In the notes to his translation of the treatise, published as Boerhaave's *New Method of Chemistry* in 1741, the chemist Peter Shaw implied a relation between Boerhaave's quasi-material 'fire' and Newton's active principles, emphasising the strongly chemical content of Newton's argument in Query 31 and drawing the conclusion that 'chemistry, in its extent, is scarce less than the whole of natural philosophy'.[27] As a substance possessing inherent activity, the source of the activity of the universe, 'fire' came to be interpreted as analogous to Newton's ether and as an active principle. By the 1740s natural philosophers had incorporated Hales' physical model of a balance of forces, and developed dualistic theories in which '*elementary fire*' was considered to be an ethereal substance 'endowed with active Powers distinct from those of other Matter'.[28]

The interest in electricity in the late 1740s was prompted by the invention in 1746 of the 'Leyden jar', a device capable of delivering electric shocks. Benjamin Franklin, the most influential of the electrical theorists, had read Boerhaave, Hales and Newton's *Opticks*, and he drew upon analogies with 'fire', 'airs' and 'ether' in his explanation of electrification. He suggested that an electrical 'fluid', which he described as 'electrical fire', permeated the interstitial pores of an electrified body. Franklin judged that 'though the particles of electrical matter do repel each other, they are strongly attracted by all other matter'. Echoing Hales' dualism of matter and 'airs' he supposed electrical matter to be held around electrified bodies as an 'electrical atmosphere'; and he considered that fire, ether and electricity were 'different modifications of the same thing'.[29]

A systematic presentation of this theme was offered by a natural philosopher known for his research on magnetism. Gowin Knight's *An Attempt To Demonstrate, That all the Phaenomena in Nature, May be Explained by Two Simple Active Principles, Attraction and Repulsion* (1754) commenced with a paean to Newton's achievement in expounding the theory of attraction, which the author modestly aimed to supplement by giving due regard to the principle of 'Repulsion' which would provide 'a Door to the most secret Mysteries of Nature'. In familiar fashion, he declares that the activity manifest in the natural world implied 'some Active Principle or Principles capable of producing and continuing Motion in the Universe', these being the forces of attraction and repulsion embodied in material substances: 'there are in Nature two kind of Matter, one attracting the other repelling', with the repellent ether clustered around the particles of attracting matter. Light is explained as due to the 'Vibrations in a repellent fluid', as the propagation of a tremor along a chain of the repelling particles, and magnetism as the 'Circulation of the repellent Fluid' between the poles of a magnet.[30] Although Knight envisaged active principles to be manifestations of divine agency, by the 1750s natural philosophers began to argue that it was 'unphilosophical' to ascribe these principles to the effect of divine agency, and that ether was to be construed as an inherently active substance, an 'acting principle' and a 'species of matter' which has 'in itself the power of moving'. The active powers of the natural order were now located in the manifestations of a single ethereal substance, and it was claimed that the 'terms *Fire, Electricity, electrical Aether, aetherial Spirit*' were 'synonymous'.[31] This interpretation of ether was to be fundamental to the development of the unified theory of ether in the second half of the eighteenth century.

The revival of interest in ether in the 1740s led chemists to invoke ether in the explanation of chemical processes. The chemical connotations of ether and active principles, heightened by the strongly chemical ethereal speculations in Newton's 'Hypothesis explaining the properties of light', were strengthened by the assimilation of Boerhaave's concept of 'fire'. Peter Shaw, the translator of Boerhaave's *New Method of Chemistry* (1741), also issued in 1730 a translation of G.E. Stahl's *Philosophical Principles of Universal Chemistry*, a major exposition of the chemical principle of combustion, 'phlogiston'. Shaw's efforts helped to shape the doctrines advanced by William Cullen in his chemistry lectures at Glasgow University in the late 1740s. Cullen followed Newton and Hales in finding 'two great principles, the attractive & repulsive' to be the 'source of motion and change' in the natural order, and echoed Boerhaave and Shaw in his stress on the expansive force of fire as the source of repulsion: 'fire pervades all bodies and keeps their parts asunder', and hence 'attraction & fire were to be considered as the primary causes of motion'. Reflecting contemporary work in natural philosophy, he associated fire with electricity and ether: 'Fire [is] an elastic fluid . . . [we know there is] an aether in bodies from the reflexion &c of light, from electricity. The same with fire & present everywhere.' Lecturing in 1757–8 he developed a dualistic theory, arguing that 'there are only two elements, one of them gravitating matter, the other a subtile aether', going on to note that according to this hypothesis it is 'probable that light and all other phaenomena of Fire depend upon this Subtile Aether in all Bodies'. Cullen explains the chemical phenomenon of combustion by supposing that 'inflammable bodies are of such a particular texture as to recover these particles of Aether' as 'phlogiston'.[32]

Cullen's introduction of Stahl's principle of inflammability, phlogiston, to denote the chemical manifestations of ether broadened the scope of the ether concept, doctrines taken further by his former student Joseph Black in his lectures at Edinburgh University. In 1768 Black argued that the 'inflammable principle' (phlogiston) was a modification of ether, which also produced the 'phenomena of Electricity, magnetism and Gravity'. In a lecture delivered in the 1780s he maintained that 'phlogiston', which he described as 'aether' and as being 'active', is a 'matter [which] is exempted from the laws of gravitation'. Black advanced a cosmology of heat underlying natural processes: 'heat may be considered in nature as the great principle of chemical movement and life'.[33] His followers promoted the idea that phlogiston, fire and electricity were different modifications of the 'Newtonian ether, the electrical aura, material subtilis, fire and light', a vivifying principle sustaining and replenishing the cosmos, 'the chief cause and principle of activity in the universe' which is 'exempted from the common laws of gravitation'.[34]

By the 1790s the theory of the unified active ether was widely held, providing a coherent scheme for representing the essential unity to be found within the diversity observed in natural phenomena. The textbook by the prominent lecturer Adam Walker, A System of Familiar Philosophy, first published in 1799 with an enlarged edition in 1802, provided a full exposition. He asserted the identity of fire, light, electricity and phlogiston as 'modifications of one and the same principle', the ethereal repelling substance. Natural phenomena were determined by a 'balance' of the two 'powers' of attraction and repulsion which were 'opposing or antagonistic principles . . . in a state of unceasing warfare'. Electricity was the 'genuine principle of light and fire', and the emanation of the 'ethereal matter' of electricity from the sun activated the universe; electricity was the 'soul of the material world'. In his Mathematical and Philosophical Dictionary (1795–6), a reliable guide to contemporary views, Charles Hutton reported that 'there was such a strong affinity between the elements of fire, light, and electricity, that we may not only assert their identity upon the most probable grounds, but lay it down as a position against which at present no argument of any weight has an existence'.[35] This was the theory espoused by the young chemist Humphry Davy in an 'Essay on Heat, Light, and the Combinations of Light', which was published by the chemist and political radical Thomas Beddoes in 1799. Davy argued that light and electricity were different forms of ethereal matter: 'the electric fluid is probably light in a condensed state' for 'its chemical activity upon bodies is similar to that of light'; and he supposed that there is a balance in nature between different active powers, declaring that 'the different species [of matter] are continually changing into each other'. In conformity with current thinking about the scope of chemical science he expressed the hope that 'chemistry, in its connection with the laws of life, [will] become the most sublime and important of all sciences', an ambition that he sought to bring to fruition in his subsequent career, first in Beddoes' Pneumatic Institution in Bristol and from 1801 in his lectures and experiments at the Royal Institution in London.[36]

As Benjamin Martin noted in his *Philosophia Britannica* (1747), natural philosophers of the day believed that they could prove the existence of ether 'by the phenomena of electricity'. Electricity offered insight into the active powers of matter and transformed the scope and popular appeal of natural philosophy, providing the means for the display of scientific marvels. 'Electricity became the subject in vogue', reported the *Gentleman's Magazine* in 1745, exciting 'the ladies and the people of quality, who never regard natural philosophy but when it works miracles'; the reporter judged that the 'electrical fire [was] as surprising as a miracle'.[37] Electrical demonstrators capitalised on the popular taste for marvels and public spectacle.[38] One of the most spectacular effects was the '*Apotheosis* or Beatification' performed by Georg Matthias Bose of Wittemberg. It was reported that a man wearing a pointed metal crown sat on an insulated pedestal; that electricity ran from a conductor to a plate above the crown, and 'by continuing the electrification the man's head is surrounded by a Glory', like a halo surrounding the heads of saints in medieval paintings. William Watson, reporting to the Royal Society in 1750, was unable to replicate the spectacle until Bose explained that the subject should wear a pointed metal helmet and a 'suit of armour . . . decked with many bullions of steel'.[39] But the London popular lecturer Benjamin Rackstrow, alert to developments in the study of 'Aethereal or Electrical Fire', claimed to have successfully demonstrated the 'Chair of Beatification' with a suitably capped subject seemingly without armour, to judge from Rackstrow's illustration of the phenomenon. Displaying glass balls revolving under electrical influence Rackstrow suggested that the electrical fire was the cause of planetary motion; and he declared that 'if Sir *Isaac Newton* was alive, to see the experiments we now make in Electricity, he would allow of Elementary Fire himself', making the conventional association in which the 'vivifying spirit' of electricity, fire and aether was viewed as an active principle.[40] Electrical demonstrators extracted sparks from a glass of water and rendered subjects convulsed and paralysed after discharges from the Leyden jar, evoking awe before the powers of nature – this was the 'sublime' as characterised by Edmund Burke in 1757: 'whatever is fitted in any sort to excite the idea of pain, and danger ... whatever is in any sort terrible ... is a source of the *sublime*'.[41]

The natural philosophers fuelled the popular taste for marvels, and no phenomenon was more awesome and sublime than the demonstration of the electrical power of lightning. In 1755 the *Gentleman's Magazine* commented on the death of G.W. Richmann in Russia, who had perished in seeking to draw lightning directly from thunderclouds: 'we are come at last to touch the celestial fire, which, if ... we make too free with, as it is fabled Prometheus did of old, like him we may be brought too late to repent of our temerity'.[42] Lightning had long been associated with electricity – 'the effects of lightning, and those of electricity, appear very similar', commented the electrician William Watson in 1751. But it was Benjamin Franklin who made the connection intimate and spectacular. In 1750 he proposed that a sentry box, fitted with a projecting iron rod, be mounted on a tower; the electricity would run from the clouds to the rod and the sentry would draw off the sparks. Writing to the Royal Society in 1752 he explained how to perform an experiment with his 'electrical kite'. A silk kite should be fitted with sharp-pointed wire, and with twine attached to a key held in the hand. The 'electric fire' will be drawn from the thunder-clouds and the kite and twine 'will be electrified' and 'electric fire ... will stream out plentifully from the key on the approach of your knuckle'. These experiments were problematic in their execution – Richmann was to die performing the sentry box experiment designed by Franklin – but British and French electricians wrote to the Royal Society confirming their 'extraction of electricity from clouds'.[43]

In his *History and Present State of Electricity*, first published in 1767 and reaching its third edition by 1775 (such was the popularity of its subject), the natural philosopher and Unitarian theologian Joseph Priestley testified to the scientific interest and popular appeal of electricity: 'Electricity has one considerable advantage over most other branches of science, as it both furnishes matter of speculation for philosophers, and of entertainment for all persons promiscuously.' Priestley judged that the demonstration of 'the perfect similarity between electricity and lightning' was Benjamin Franklin's most notable discovery. In June 1752, he continued, 'Dr Franklin, astonishing as it must have appeared, contrived actually to bring lightning from the heavens, by means of an electrical kite'. By the time he wrote his treatise on electricity,

Priestley could wonder 'what Newton himself would have said, to see the present race of electricians imitating in miniature all the known effects of that tremendous power'. Led by Franklin, natural philosophers had succeeded in 'disarming the thunder of its power of doing mischief . . . drawing lightning from the clouds' and amusing themselves 'by performing with it all the experiments that are exhibited by electrical machines'.[44] The association of Prometheus, lightning and 'electrical fire' was, and remained, a potent image. Kant called Franklin 'the modern Prometheus', and this designation became the subtitle of Mary Shelley's *Frankenstein*.

Interest in electricity satisfied the contemporary fashion for awe and spectacle in nature, and as an agent of scientific explanation it supplanted gravity in its seeming universal application. As lightning, electricity was invoked to explain the most violent and sublime phenomena of nature; it was proffered as the cause of earthquakes and was associated with the eruption of volcanoes. In 1750 a series of earthquakes in England aroused much concern among the population. The Royal Society published an appendix to the *Philosophical Transactions* containing 57 communications concerning the earthquakes experienced in England that year. In letters to his friend Horace Mann, resident in Florence, Horace Walpole viewed the public response with ironical Enlightenment amusement: 'as far as earthquakes go towards lowering the price of wonderful commodities, to be sure we are overstocked'. He reported that the 'earth had a shivering fit' which he himself experienced, but he saw 'no mischief done'. But such a plethora of wonders, however harmless the effect of the earthquake 'which has done no hurt, in a country where no earthquake ever did any', was proving to be a harvest for the clergy 'who have had no windfalls for a long season'; and he reported that 'all the women in town have taken them upon the foot of *judgments*'. Parsons and bishops had produced a 'shower of sermons and exhortations' asserting that earthquakes were instances of divine retribution, sent by divine wrath to 'punish bawdy prints, bawdy books, gaming . . . and all other sins, natural or not, particularly heretical books'. Cynical about clerical posturing, Walpole's own thoughts were more earthy; he inquired of a female married friend 'if the earthquake had happened at any *critical* time to any married couple', receiving a direct and robust answer in the negative. If earthquakes were grist for the clerical mill, they also gave an opportunity for natural philosophers to show their capacity for scientific explanation. Natural philosophers were often clerics, so earthquakes presented a perfect opportunity to join science and theology, to mix natural philosophy with warnings of divine judgement. Walpole mocked that 'one Stukeley, a parson, has accounted for it, and I think prettily, by electricity – but that is the fashionable cause, and everything is resolved into electrical appearances, as formerly everything was accounted for by Descartes' vortices, and Sir Isaac's gravitation. But they all take care, after accounting for the earthquake systematically, to assure you, that still it was nothing less than a judgment'.[45]

For Walpole, natural philosophy was as much subject to fashion as other products of culture; and the popular astonishment and learned interest in earthquakes prompted human characteristics of superstition and opportunism to come to the fore. William Stukeley, a noted antiquarian and the biographer of Sir Isaac Newton, did indeed mix electrical speculations with clerical moralising in his communications on the subject to the Royal Society. He duly contrasted earthquakes with volcanic eruptions, which were clearly caused by 'vapours, fermentations, rarefactions, and inflammable substances, and actual fires, in the bowels of the earth'. Earthquakes, it was plain to see, were not accompanied by the exhalation of 'sulphureous vapours' from vents in the earth; their origin was therefore different from that of volcanoes, and not hard to pinpoint in the current climate of natural philosophy: 'Electricity has been so much our entertainment, and our amazement . . . hither we turn our thoughts'. But, he did not fail to add, it was important for a 'Christian Philosopher' to remember that the investigation of the 'material causes' of earthquakes should not deflect attention from their significance as 'warnings and judgments'. London, he noted ominously, was 'the place to which the finger of God was pointed' in the recent earthquakes. Stephen Hales agreed that while earthquakes 'are capable of being accounted for by natural causes . . . the Hand of God is not to be overlooked . . .. Natural and Moral agents are all under his direction' and were in harmony. As a famous investigator of the production of 'airs' in chemical and biological processes, Hales was unwilling to discount the role of chemical explosions. He urged that 'the ascending sulphureous vapours in the earth may probably take fire, and thereby cause an earth-lightning', suggesting that 'the explosion of this lightning is the immediate cause of an earthquake'. In a lengthy essay on the 'philosophy of earthquakes' Stukeley reiterated the link that he had forged between science and natural religion. Earthquakes could be explained through the 'rare and wonderful' agency of electricity, in terms of the 'ethereal fire' of 'the subtil fluid of Sir Isaac Newton, pervading all things'. But earthquakes should yet be seen as warnings and judgements, and it was important to understand the conjunction of 'earthly wonders' and 'moral wisdom'. It followed that there was 'a conscious and intelligent Nature, that presides over, and directs all things . . . a divine necessity but a voluntary agent; who gives the commanding nod to what we commonly call Nature'.[46] Walpole accurately pinpointed the intellectual tone of these conventional pieties.

In his *History and Present State of Electricity* Priestley gave a full account of the theory of the relation between lightning and earthquakes developed by the Italian natural philosopher Gianbattista Beccaria, who maintained that electric matter circulated through and around the earth, 'darting from the clouds in one place' and arising 'from places far below the surface of the earth . . . from subterraneous cavities'. Priestley judged that electricity was the cause of rain, hail, snow, meteors, waterspouts, whirlwinds, hurricanes and earth-quakes. According to this theory an earthquake was 'an electrical shock', and was the result of electric matter 'lodged deep in the bowels of the earth . . . bursting its way into the air', so that 'violent concussions may be given to the earth, by the sudden passage of this powerful agent'. In illustration of the elec-trical theory of earthquakes Priestley set up his own tabletop earthquake model, supporting a plate of ice on sticks and 'making an electric flash pass over the surface of the ice', observing the collapse of one of the sticks. He suggested that earthquakes might be prevented by discharging the 'redundant electricity' from the surface by means of 'kites constantly flying very high, with wires in the strings', a reversal of Franklin's method of drawing lightning from the clouds. Whereas Stukeley had differentiated earthquakes (as caused by electricity) from volcanoes (caused by sulphureous exhalations), Beccaria argued that the phenomena were connected. Priestley reported that 'flashes of light, exactly resembling lightning have been seen to rush from the top of Mount Vesuvius, at the same time that ashes and other light matter have been carried out of it into the air'.[47] Writing to the Royal Society with accounts of the eruptions of Vesuvius, Sir William Hamilton had recorded that on 25 October 1767 a vast column of ash issued from the crater of the volcano, and 'continual flashes of forked or zig-zag lightning shot from this black column'. He observed that the 'lightning and balls of fire' made a 'crackling noise'. In his *Campi Phlegraei* (1776) Hamilton reported that Beccaria was 'greatly pleased' with his observations on this species of lightning 'as coinciding perfectly with several of his electrical experiments'. As noted in Chapter 4 (pp. 137–9), Hamilton gave an account of his further observations of volcanic lightning in his report of the eruption of 8 August 1779 in the *Supplement to the Campi Phlegraei* (1779), recording that within the puffs of smoke emitted from the crater 'I could perceive a bright, but pale electrical fire playing about in zig zag lines'. He judged that the 'electrical matter so manifest during this eruption, actually proceeded from the bowels of the volcano'; he found this to be a 'sublime view'.[48]

Problems of Materialism

By the 1770s the tradition of Newtonian natural philosophy had fragmented. Joseph Priestley expressed the mood in his *History and Present State of Electricity*: 'Hitherto, philosophy has been conversant about the more sensible properties of bodies; electricity, together with chymistry, and the doctrine of light and colours, seems to be giving us an inlet into their internal structure, on which all their sensible properties depend. By pursuing this new light, therefore, the bounds of natural science may possibly be extended, beyond what we can now form an idea of.' The problems of understanding the inner structure of matter, set out in the *Opticks*, were now investigated under a new framework of concepts, developments that would transcend Newtonian principles: 'New worlds may open to our view, and the glory of the great Sir Isaac Newton . . . be eclipsed, by a new set of philosophers'.[49] For Priestley, the envisaged transformation in the principles and scope of natural philosophy would lead to a new understanding of the nature of matter and spirit, and this implied reappraisal of Newton's doctrine that matter is an impenetrable substance devoid of inherent activity. Consistent with his theology of rational dissent Priestley affirmed a monism of matter and spirit, rejecting the argument of Andrew Baxter's *An Enquiry into the Nature of the Human Soul* (1733), where the traditional orthodoxy of the duality of matter and spirit is affirmed and the claim that active powers are inherent in matter strongly contested. Baxter used the Newtonian concept of gravity as the 'virtue and power of an immaterial cause, or being, constantly impressed' upon matter to claim the active agency of God in the cosmos and the duality of matter and spirit. If it is established that active powers are not inherent in matter, then the effects ascribed to the operation of these active powers could be seen as being 'immediately produced by the power of an immaterial being'.[50]

But three discoveries in the 1740s seemed to support the possibility, held by materialists, that matter was endowed with inherent activity and was capable of self-organisation. The claim by John Turbeville Needham to have produced microscopic organisms from rotting corn by spontaneous generation; Albrecht von Haller's investigation of the inherent force of 'irritability', finding that muscle tissue when removed from the body would contract when pricked; and Abraham Trembley's discovery that a freshwater polyp, the hydra, could regenerate itself when cut in pieces, called into question the doctrine that matter was inherently inert and did not harbour the active principles of life.[51]

In his *History and Present State of Discoveries Relating to Vision, Light, and Colours* (1772) Priestley outlined the new developments in natural philosophy that held up to question Newton's dichotomy of passive matter and forces, giving prominence to the theory advanced by the Serbo-Croat natural philosopher Roger Joseph Boscovich in his *Theoria Philosophiae Naturalis* (1758, 1763). In Priestley's account Boscovich held 'that matter is not impenetrable . . . [and] consists of physical points only endued with powers of attraction and repulsion . . . surrounded with various spheres of attraction and repulsion, in the same manner as solid matter is generally supposed to be'. But Priestley reported that the doctrine of the '*immateriality of matter . . .* or rather the *mutual penetration of matter*' had been formulated, independently of Boscovich's work, by John Michell, the Cambridge natural philosopher.

Michell's reflections had been prompted by 'reading Baxter *on the immateriality of the soul*', leading him to question Baxter's advocacy of the notion of matter as formed of corpuscular 'bricks cemented together by an immaterial mortar'. Michell had reasoned that the sense of touch gave evidence of the relative rather than the absolute impenetrability of matter, and he had concluded that if matter did not possess the property of impenetrability ascribed to it by Newton then 'he might as well admit of *penetrable material* as well as *penetrable immaterial substance*', and had therefore been led to abandon the doctrine of the dualism of passive, inert, impenetrable matter and non-material agents.[52]

Priestley presented Boscovich and Michell as working in the context of the established and familiar Newtonian theory of the forces of attractiom and repulsion. Newton's early followers, such as Stephen Hales, had placed emphasis on his discussion, in Query 31 of the 1717 *Opticks*, of the envelopes of interstitial attraction and repulsion surrounding particles of matter, these forces being held to determine the optical and chemical properties of substances. This model of matter and its attendant forces had inspired Boscovich's theory of alternating zones of attraction and repulsion surrounding points of matter, and had been espoused by Newtonians in dismissing Descartes' mechanical philosophy. The theory was elaborated in the text by the Cambridge-educated natural philosopher John Rowning, *A Compendious System of Natural Philosophy*, which went through seven editions between 1735 and 1772 and was familiar to Priestley (who adopted his phraseology). Rowning envisaged Newton's successive zones of repulsion and attraction surrounding the particles as 'three Spheres of Attraction and Repulsion, one within another'. He found a lapidary expression for Newton's doctrine of the paucity of matter in the cosmos, suggesting that Newton's theory 'shews that the whole Globe of Earth, nay all the known Bodies of the Universe, for any thing that appears to us to the contrary, may be composed of no greater Quantity of Matter than what might be reduced into a Globe of an Inch diameter, or into a *Nut-shell*'; the source for the nutshell image is very likely Hamlet, who declares 'I could be bounded in a nutshell and count myself a king of infinite space'.[53]

But Priestley gave the nutshell image – which became a 'walnut' for Adam Walker in 1799[54] – special meaning in his *Disquisitions Relating to Matter and Spirit*, published in 1777 and in an enlarged second edition in 1782:

> The principles of the Newtonian philosophy were no sooner known, than it was seen how few, in comparison, of the phenomena of Nature were owing to solid matter, and how much to powers, which were only supposed to accompany and surround the solid parts of matter. It has been asserted . . . that for any thing we know to the contrary, all the solid

matter in the solar system might be contained within a nut-shell, there is so great a proportion of *void space* within the substance of the most solid bodies. Now, when solidity had apparently so very little to do in the system, it is really a wonder that it did not occur to philosophers sooner, that perhaps there might be nothing for it to do at all, and that there might be no such thing in Nature.

Priestley collapses the distinction between matter and its attendant forces, rejecting the Newtonian theory of impenetrable atoms in favour of matter as a causal nexus of active powers. Matter is defined by categories traditionally applied to the non-material: he supposes that 'matter is not that *inert* substance that it has been supposed to be; that powers of *attraction* or *repulsion* are necessary to its very being, and that no part of it appears to be impenetrable to other parts'. God operated uniformly through powers of matter that were neither material nor immaterial as traditionally understood.

Drawing on this theory of active powers being immanent in matter, the dualisms of Newton's natural philosophy – of atoms and space, of passive and active principles, and of matter and spirit – are rejected in favour of a monism of matter, defined in terms of the powers of attraction and repulsion: 'Whatever *solidity* any body has, it is possessed of it only in consequence of being endued with certain *powers*'. These powers, rather than solidity and impenetrability, which are construed as relational not absolute properties of matter, define the essential qualities of matter: 'take away attraction and repulsion', he declares, 'and matter vanishes'. Priestley maintained that his monism provided a theologically satisfactory explanation of the dependency of matter on divine agency: 'the common hypothesis', of the dualism of God and nature, 'is much less favourable to piety, in that it supposes something to be *independent* of the *Divine Power*'. Priestley denied the dualism of matter and mind, for if matter was 'properly *immaterial*' then 'we have no reason to suppose that there are in man two substances so distinct from each other'.[55] But his rejection of the dualism of matter and spirit ran counter to conventional theological argument, which asserted the potency of divine agency in the activation of inert matter. His monism made the *Disquisitions Relating to Matter and Spirit* a highly controversial text and its author the object of abuse in a political milieu where, with the advent of the revolution in France, the espousal of radical doctrines threatening the orthodox consensus became equated with sedition.

Joseph Black's associate James Hutton, whose interests included agriculture and (famously) geology, provided a full and systematic statement of the dualistic theory of ordinary matter and the modifications of ether in his massive *Dissertations on Different Subjects in Natural Philosophy* (1792), where his argument ranges over topics in meteorology, chemistry and natural philosophy. In his biography of Hutton, published in 1805, the Edinburgh professor of natural philosophy John Playfair noted that in Hutton's system of natural philosophy 'the chemist, indeed, is flattered more than anyone else with the hopes of discovering in what the essence of matter consists; and Nature, while she keeps the astronomer and mechanician at a great distance, seems to admit him to a more familiar converse, and to a more intimate acquaintance with her secrets'.[56]

Hutton's natural philosophy places emphasis on the irreducibly chemical associations of phlogiston, viewed as a modification of ether. His system is based on the interaction and balance of material powers in the cosmos: 'Whether we conceive this world as a mechanical machine . . . or as a chymical process . . . there are necessarily required powers in order to actuate that moving system in which we live'. He represents these powers in terms of a dualism of gravitational (attractive) matter and the 'emanation of [repelling] matter from the sun'; these two kinds of matter maintained the operations of the material world, 'the opposite powers . . . continually balancing one another, or alternately prevailing'. If the gravitational matter were to prevail then 'gravitation would soon bring all the matter of this machine [the universe] to rest, and would lock up every body in a state of the most absolute inactivity'. But these 'opposing powers conspire to form a systematic order in material things', and it is in the 'just combination of those two different powers' that the universe is 'properly disposed in a great and connected system'. According to Hutton's system of natural philosophy 'Light, heat, and electricity appear to be three different modifications of the same matter', which he describes as the 'emanation of matter from the sun [and which] may be considered as one of the prime movers of the machine'. The 'circulation' of the solar substance, counteracting the passivity of gravitational matter, is regarded as the 'necessary cause of vital motion' in the universe: 'without the influence of the sun this world would remain an useless mass of inert matter'. The solar substance is envisaged as the active principle of generation and renewal in the material world.

Biological processes are basic to this scheme, for plants 'compose phlogistic matter in growing, as animals in breathing decompose the same substance', thus securing the 'order of life and circulation' in the natural world. In this process the matter of light and heat is 'fixed in the bodies of growing plants, and may be stored in the constitution of this world'. Chemical reactions, especially combustion, are central to Hutton's scheme: he supposes that the solar substance is 'arrested and detained in a certain modification' within bodies to form a 'phlogistic substance', from which phlogiston is released in combustion and the solar substance would then 'resume its former character of light'. The breathing of animals, the growth of plants and the chemical process of combustion are connected in a grand system of 'circulation' and conservation, where the 'decay', 'waste' and 'dissolution' of 'phlogistic substance' are balanced by a process of 'regeneration'. The material world is conceived as a circulating system of processes and transformations, with the different modifications of the ethereal solar substance serving as sources for regeneration, a 'reproductive power', by which the constitution of this world, necessarily decaying, is renewed'. In this system of the 'oeconomy of nature' there was 'admirable contrivance' of design, manifesting 'beauty of order and contrivance . . . in the oeconomy of animal and vegetable bodies, sustaining themselves in forming a certain circulation of matter'.

Hutton's system has analogies with Newton's speculation of 1675 that 'nature is a perpetual worker' (a description made public in these words in 1757), where ether is held to maintain the activity of the cosmos by its circulation; but Hutton rejects Newton's dichotomy between active principles and passive matter, and providential interpretation of 'active principles', urging that 'Matter may . . . be considered as acting powers', as an inherently active substance. Like Priestley, he considered impenetrability to be a relational or 'conditional' property of matter, not a defining and essential property as supposed by Newton: 'instead then of saying that matter, of which natural bodies are composed, is perfectly hard and impenetrable, which is the received position of philosophers, we would affirm, that there were no permanent properties of this kind in a material thing: but that there were certain resisting powers in bodies, by which their volume and figure are presented to us'.[57]

In his biography Playfair summarised Hutton's theory, which dissolves the duality of matter and its attendant powers: 'in the material world every phenomenon can be explained by the existence of power, [and] the supposition of extended particles as a *substratum* or residence for such power, is a mere hypothesis . . . power is the essence of matter'. According to this system, matter is conceived as being 'indefinitely extended' through space, and gravity 'is the action of certain powers, diffused through all space'.[58] In Hutton's natural philosophy Newton's emphasis on the regenerative agency of the divine will in sustaining the order of nature through active principles is replaced by a deistic scheme of the contrivance of design, the 'wisdom of nature' manifest in the self-sufficiency of the powers that maintain natural processes: 'There would also appear to be in the system of this globe, a reproductive power, by which the constitution of this world, necessarily decaying, is renewed; consequently the future duration of this world, as well as what is past, is protracted for a space of time which is at least unmeasurable.'[59] Hutton's natural philosophy shaped the eternalism of his 'Theory of the Earth' (1788), where the wisdom of the terrestrial system is manifest in its enduring stability and where, as stated in the paper's famous conclusion, 'we find no vestige of a beginning, – no prospect of an end'.[60] He conceives the material world as a self-regenerating system of circulating active powers, its self-sufficiency maintained by the inherent activity of matter and the balance of the forces of attraction and repulsion. For Hutton the material world is inherently active, its 'oeconomy' and 'wisdom' apparent in the regeneration of the circulating ethereal solar substance.[61]

Joseph Priestley's fellow member of the Lunar Society of Birmingham, Erasmus Darwin, applied the theory of active powers inherent in matter to explain the vital force of organisms, deliberately departing from religious orthodoxy. In *The Economy of Vegetation* (published in 1791 as Part I of his didactic poem *The Botanic Garden*) he portrays the vital power of organisms in terms of the active powers of the ether:

> Starts the quick Ether through the fibre-trains
> Of dancing arteries, and of tingling veins,
> Goads each fine nerve with new sensation thrill'd,
> Bends the reluctant limbs with power unwill'd.

The inherent powers embodied in the ether are self-sufficient to the natural order and act without the exercise of the will of a deity. Darwin's natural philosophy shows strong affinities to that of his friend and correspondent James Hutton in emphasising that the material world is self-contained, and maintained and energised by the circulation of immanent active powers. In a note on the power of the 'Sun's Rays' he remarks that 'Some modern philosophers are of the opinion that the sun is the great foundation from which the earth and other planets derive all the phlogiston which they possess'; according to this theory phlogiston 'is formed by the combinations of the solar rays with all opake bodies, but particularly with the leaves of vegetables'. In his *Dissertations*, published the following year, Hutton expounded his detailed speculations on the circulation of the phlogistic substance through plants.

Darwin gave electricity pride of place as an energising principle, its power visible in lightning. 'Nature' is seen to draw Benjamin Franklin into the clouds where he 'Snatch'd the raised lightning from the arm of JOVE', in mimicry of Prometheus who challenged Olympian Zeus and brought fire to humankind:

> You led your FRANKLIN to your glazed retreats,
> Your air-built castles, and your silken feats;
> Bade his bold arm invade the lowering sky,
> And seize the tiptoe lightnings, ere they fly;
> O'er the young Sage your mystic mantle spread,
> And wreath'd the crown electric round his head.

The association between electricity and fire, commonplace in the unified ether theory, is made explicit in a later passage:

> Led by the phosphor-light, with daring tread
> Immortal FRANKLIN sought the fiery bed;
> Where, nursed in night, incumbent tempest shrouds
> The seeds of Thunder in circumfluent clouds,
> Besieged with iron points his airy cell,
> And pierced the monster slumbering in the shell.

Franklin confronted lightning with the iron lance of his lightning conductor, taming the savage and monstrous powers of nature, just as Prometheus brought fire for humanity.[62] The passage continues with a vision of electricity as a symbol of liberty and revolution, evoking Franklin as the statesman who had led the American colonies to independence from Britain, again deploying the association of fire and electricity: 'When Tyrant-Power had built his eagle nest;/ . . . Immortal FRANKLIN watch'd the callow crew,/ And stabb'd the struggling Vampires, ere they flew./ The patriot-flame with quick contagion ran, /Hill lighted hill, and man electrified man'. The hill-top warning fires of the revolutionaries are envisioned as a chain of electricity, like the popular demonstrations of electric charges leaping across a conductor formed of a human chain; electricity energised the revolutionary spirit of the colonists.[63]

In Darwin's poetry 'nature' is personified, and natural processes are allegorised in the figures of the gods of Graeco-Roman mythology. In the eighteenth century two main categories for the interpretation of myth flourished. The first was the historical interpretation, that the stories of the Greek gods concealed a national political history which could be unravelled by patient scholarship; the second was the psychological interpretation, given elegant expression in David Hume's *Natural History of Religion* (1757), where the origin of religion is found in human nature, in the combination of hope and fear. But in the 1780s there was a revival of the allegorical interpretation of myth, interest focusing on sexual imagery; in his *Discourse on the Worship of Priapus*, published by the Society of Dilettanti in 1786, Richard Payne Knight viewed myths as a symbolic language.[64]

Erasmus Darwin explained myths as hieroglyphs, as symbolic emblems through which the ancients communicated knowledge about natural processes. In the *Economy of Vegetation* he offered an interpretation of the scenes depicted on the Portland Vase, acquired by Sir William Hamilton from the Barberini family, reproducing these scenes in engravings by William Blake. Darwin interpreted the scene depicted in the 'first compartment' of the vase as a mourning for human mortality, and the scene in the 'second compartment' as representing the entry of the soul into the underworld, supposing the imagery to have been drawn from the Eleusinian mysteries, by tradition derived from Egypt and preserving ancient wisdom concerning the immortality of life. In this scene a male figure, which Darwin interprets to be a human soul entering Hades, is shown being guided by Cupid (Love) and welcomed by a seated woman holding a serpent, which Darwin interprets as a symbol of immortal life:

There the pale GHOST through Death's wide portal bends
His timid feet, the dusky steep descends;
. . . IMMORTAL LIFE, her hand expanding, courts
The lingering form, his tottering step supports.

In a note Darwin explains that the scene 'represents . . . a part of the Eleusinian mysteries . . . [the] expectation of a future life after death'. Following his emphasis on the natural processes of regeneration, he gives pride of place to myths of resurrection, seeing the death and rebirth of Adonis as 'a story explaining some hieroglyphic figures representing the decomposition and resuscitation of animal matter'. He interprets the story of the phoenix arising from the fire as 'an ancient hieroglyphic emblem of the destruction and resuscitation of all things', a symbol of the regeneration of nature:

Till o'er the wreck, emerging from the storm,
IMMORTAL NATURE lifts her changeful form,
Mounts from her funeral pyre on wings of flame,
And soars and shines, and another and the same.[65]

Darwin develops these themes more fully in the most systematic of his scientific poems, *The Temple of Nature* (1803). As noted earlier, the influence of Lucretius' *De Rerum Natura* (*On the Nature of Things*) in shaping his outlook is most explicit in this didactic poem. The four parts of *The Temple of Nature* are titled 'The Production of Life', 'Reproduction of Life', 'Progress of the Mind' and 'Of Good and Evil', and Darwin echoes Lucretius in his breadth of argument in the description of a world deprived of providence and regulated by the properties of matter. As a counterpart to Epicurean atomism, a philosophical outlook through which Lucretius contested fear of the gods and of death, Darwin's materialism is expressed through the self-sufficiency of active ethereal powers; immortality is viewed not in the prospect of eternal life granted to the soul but in terms of the permanence of matter as secured in its perpetual circulation in natural processes; and divine wisdom is limited to the role of a first cause. Immortal matter is endowed with immanent active powers, its circulation energising and regenerating natural processes; the natural order does not require the sustenance of divine agency to mitigate its dissipation. In the first lines of the poem he refers to the 'firm immutable immortal laws/Impress'd on Nature by the GREAT FIRST CAUSE', and he espouses a deistic outlook, declaring that 'there is more dignity in our idea of the supreme author of all things, when we conceive him to be the cause of causes, than the cause simply of the events, which we see'.[66] Darwin was indeed accused of materialism: the 'grand fault' of his work, according to the *Critical Review*, was its 'unrestrained and constant tendency to subvert the first principles and most important precepts of revelation'.[67]

In a parallel to the invocation to Venus with which Lucretius opens *De Rerum Natura*, Darwin appeals in *The Temple of Nature* to 'IMMORTAL LOVE' as the power binding the universe, 'who ere the morn of Time / . . . Warm'd into life the bursting egg of Night, / And gave young Nature to admiring light!' As noted, the personification of nature as a goddess is made explicit in the frontispiece of the book, an engraving by Henry Fuseli (see Fig. 17).[68] In the preface Darwin declares his intention of 'bringing to the imagination the beautiful and sublime images of the operations of nature', and in the philosophical notes appended to the poem he discusses questions of taste and the aesthetics of nature. His discussion ranges over the aesthetics of 'wavy lawns' and the 'sublime' crests of the 'high summits' of mountains. Appealing to the philosophical principle of the association of ideas, he justified the aesthetics of William Hogarth's serpentine line, that beauty 'consists of curved lines and smooth surfaces', in terms of the recollection of infant experience of the mother's breast; he suggests that 'when any object is presented to us, which by its waving or spiral lines bears any similitude to the form of the female bosom', as in 'a landscape with soft gradations of rising and descending surface', we 'feel a general flow of delight' occasioned by the pleasurable associations. The 'idea of sublimity' is occasioned by 'any object larger than usual, as a very large temple or a very large mountain', while he associates the picturesque with objects that by their 'variety and intricacy joined with a due degree of regularity or uniformity convey to the mind an agreeable sentiment of novelty'. He voiced approval for the 'modern' taste in gardening, the aesthetics of the picturesque expressed by Richard Payne Knight in his didactic poem *The Landscape* (1794): 'While Taste with pleasure bends his eye surprised / In modern days at Nature unchastised'. He elaborates his meaning in a footnote, explaining that 'an uncultivated forest' leaves us 'amazed with greater variety of form' and 'at the same time enchanted by the charm of novelty'.[69]

The materialism of Darwin's system is emphasised in his representation of life as generated by the agency of heat and renewed through the circulation of matter. He describes the regeneration of decayed vegetable matter, emphasising processes of conservation and renewal:

Awhile extinct the organic matter lies;
But, as a few short hours or years revolve,
Alchemic powers the changing mass dissolve;
Born to new life unnumber'd insects pant,
New buds surround the microscopic plant.

This is a process of death and rebirth, where plants perish but their regeneration and immortality are secured:

While Nature sinks in Time's destructive storms,
The wrecks of Death are but a change of forms;
Emerging matter from the grave returns,
Feels new desires, with new sensations burns;
With youth's first bloom a finer sense acquires,
And Loves and Pleasure fan the rising fires.

This renewal of natural powers is maintained by a chemical process:

Organic forms with chemic changes strive,
Live but to die, and die but to revive!
Immortal matter braves the transient storm,
Mounts from the wreck, unchanging but in form.[70]

In Darwin's materialist system the circulation of matter renews the death and decay of organisms; matter is permanent and in its permanence is immortal. He explains the origin of life in terms of the operations of the active ether, and the effects of the forces of attraction and repulsion in shaping material processes:

First Heat from chemic dissolution springs,
And gives to matter its eccentric wings;
With strong Repulsion parts the exploding mass,
Melts into lymph, or kindles into gas.
Attraction next, as earth or air subsides,
The ponderous atoms from the light divides,
Approaching parts with quick embrace combines,
Swells into spheres, and lengthens into lines.
Last, as fire goads the gluten-threads excite,
Cords grapple cords, and webs with webs unite;
And quick Contraction with ethereal flame
Lights into life the fibre-woven frame.

Hence without parent by spontaneous birth
Rise the first specks of animated earth;
From Nature's womb the plant or insect swims,
And buds or breathes, with microscopic limbs.[71]

In his 'Additional Note' on the 'Spontaneous Vitality of Microscopic Animals' in *The Temple of Nature*, Darwin made it clear that such 'spontaneous birth' is 'only to be looked for in the simplest organic beings, as in the smallest animalcules'. In support of his theory of the spontaneous generation of organisms he refers to the generation of microscopic 'eels', first announced by John Needham. He reports that in the 'experiments of Buffon, Reaumur . . . Ingenhousz and others, microscopic animals are produced in three or four days, according to the warmth of the season, in the infusions of all vegetable or animal matter'. He describes how 'in paste composed of flour and water, which has been suffered to become acescent [turning sour], the animalcules called eels, vibrio anguillula, are seen in great abundance; their motions are rapid and strong; they are viviparous, and produce at intervals a numerous progeny . . .. These eels were probably at first as minute as other animalcules; but by frequent, perhaps hourly reproduction, have gradually become the large animals above described, possessing wonderful strength and activity'. This process of generation of the primitive forms of life is chemical: the 'simplest animations were spontaneously produced like chemical combinations'.[72]

While Charles Darwin was to limit his work carefully to the *Origin of Species*, telling J.D. Hooker in March 1863 that it 'is mere rubbish thinking, at present, of origin of life; one might as well think of the origin of matter',[73] his grandfather Erasmus explicitly and triumphantly espoused a theory of the origin of life, maintaining that through 'elemental strife' the 'first spark' was 'lighten'd into Life' by the power of 'Heat, pervading oceans, airs, and lands'. Life arose through chemical reactions and the agency of heat, processes maintained by the forces of attraction and repulsion. He caps his account of the spontaneous generation of the 'simplest organic beings' with the assertion of the evolution of species. Whereas he considered that life in its simplest form had arisen spontaneously through a chemical process, he made it clear that he judged that the generation of the 'larger or more complicated animals' could not be explained in this way; he declared that they 'have acquired their present perfection by successive generations during an uncounted series of ages'.[74] Erasmus Darwin's famous statement on evolution, which he had first made public in *The Loves of the Plants* in 1789, was marked by his grandson Charles in his personal copy of *The Temple of Nature*: 'Perhaps all the productions of nature are in their progress to greater perfection'.[75]

The Temple of Nature was published posthumously in 1803, its subtitle (Erasmus Darwin's original title) *The Origin of Society* making explicit his concern to place human aspirations within the framework of his materialist science of life. In the opening lines of the poem he set out his intention to show:

> ... how rose from elemental strife
> Organic forms, and kindled into life;
> How Love and Sympathy with potent charm
> Warm the cold heart ...
> And bind Society in golden chains.

Darwin locates the organic unity of mind and matter, and the origins of society, in the science of life.[76] On (anonymously) reviewing *The Temple of Nature* in the *Edinburgh Review* in July 1803, the prominent Scottish chemist Thomas Thomson singled out Darwin's materialism for criticism, as 'constantly blending and confounding together the two distinct sciences of matter and mind', judging that he had 'lost himself in that gulph which will probably for ever separate the sciences of matter and of mind'. Thomson found Darwin's 'presumptuous contempt, or perhaps gross ignorance, of the legitimate bounds of philosophical inquiry' to be especially unacceptable, ridiculing Darwin's scientific argument as showing a 'strange incapacity for strict inductive reasoning' in 'ever aiming at the construction of a vast and comprehensive system'. Although he recognised Darwin's 'claims to the praise of genius', as a poet he found his style, relying solely on 'metaphors, personifications and allegories', and the evocation of '*picturesque*' visual effects, to be limited in imaginative range in being addressed 'directly and solely to the eye'.[77]

Thomson's criticisms were telling, indicative of the tone of an emergent scientific style hostile to deism and materialism and to the construction of systems. Initially impressed, Coleridge and Wordsworth rejected Darwin's philosophical outlook and cast his thumping verse into literary oblivion. In a notebook entry written in 1796, Coleridge criticised Darwin's poetry for its repetitive visual imagery: 'Dr Darwin's Poetry, a succession of Landscapes or Paintings – it arrests the attention too often, and so prevents the rapidity necessary to pathos – it makes the great little'.[78] Some years later he defined philosophical poetry in terms remote from the aspirations of Darwin's didactic verse: Wordsworth would 'hereafter be admitted as the first & greatest philosophical Poet – the only man who has effected a compleat and constant synthesis of Thought & Feeling and combined them with Poetic Forms'.[79] The materialistic natural philosophies of Hutton, Priestley and Darwin were controversial, yet significant in the formation of an enlightened intellectual milieu in Britain in the late eighteenth century; but their influence waned in the reaffirmation of philosophical, theological and scientific orthodoxies in the train of the government's repressive political policy during the protracted war with France.[80] Scientific knowledge became fragmented and codified into specialised divisions; the *Bridgewater Treatises* of the 1830s embodied this shift in sensibility, in seeking to expunge speculative materialistic systems by reaffirming the hegemony of traditional forms of knowledge as shaped by natural theology.

The Philosophy of Nature: Samuel Taylor Coleridge

Samuel Taylor Coleridge, the collaborator of William Wordsworth and the friend of Humphry Davy, sought to construct a comprehensive scheme encompassing the harmony of the natural world and the self, the reality of the external material world and the subjectivity of human free will, seeking a philosophical system grounded on Christianity and (ultimately) the doctrine of the Trinity which became for him the unifying and 'primary Idea, out of which all other Ideas are evolved'.[81] He first worked within the framework of Newton's natural philosophy, Locke's empiricism and David Hartley's theory of the human mind in the *Observations of Man* (1749); and he studied the contemporary natural philosophy of Priestley, Erasmus Darwin and Hutton. From the outset of his intellectual career Coleridge was concerned with the relation between matter and spirit, and he became critical of the empiricists Locke and Newton with their emphasis on knowledge as gained through sensory experience. But he became uneasy with the determinism and materialism that he judged to be implied by these systems; doctrines that stood opposed to his own developing philosophical vision and ambition.

For Coleridge, an understanding of the order of nature would transcend scientific theorising and required explication of the metaphysical principles that formed the foundation of any system of natural philosophy: 'Learning without philosophy a *Cyclops*', he asserted some time after his return from Germany in 1799.[82] He rejected his early engagement with determinism, materialism and pantheism; his change of tone in favour of orthodox doctrines is implicit in his response to 'a most unpleasant Dispute' in October 1803 with 'dearest Wordsworth' and William Hazlitt on the design argument as developed by John Ray, William Derham and William Paley, recording that 'they spoke so irreverently so malignantly of the Divine Wisdom . . .. O dearest William! Would Ray, or Durham have spoken of God as you spoke of Nature?'[83] Subsequently he incorporated his reading of contemporary German 'nature philosophers' into his critique of empiricist philosophy and science. The philosophical movement of *Naturphilosophie* stressed the unity of the spiritual processes pervading the natural world and the self, seeking to reintegrate a spontaneity of feeling with the discipline of reason; aesthetic principles were held to shape the imaginative contemplation of nature and the philosophical concepts regulating science.[84] Coleridge adopted the philosophical terms of this school in seeking to integrate nature as both an object of imaginative and aesthetic contemplation. In a notebook entry written in 1818 he explained his concern to explicate 'a Form, that answers to the notion of Beauty, namely, the many seen as one' with an understanding of the inner constitution and development of nature, its '*essence*', a mode of thinking which 'presupposes *a bond* between *Nature* in this higher sense and the Soul of Man'.[85]

Coleridge began his intellectual life as a political radical and Unitarian, and was strongly influenced by the writings of Joseph Priestley. After his precipitous departure from Cambridge without a degree, Coleridge moved to Bristol in 1795 where he was drawn into the circle of Thomas Beddoes, a radical, a chemist, a reviewer of German philosophy and a friend of Erasmus Darwin whose works were admired by Coleridge at the time. His attention became engaged by issues of scientific materialism, especially Hartley's extension of the Newtonian natural philosophy of atoms, forces and ether to mental processes, which supposed that sensory impulses stimulate vibrations and signals in the nerves and brain so that thoughts are transmitted by the vibrations of nerve fibres, the impressions of different sensory signals leading to the association of ideas in the mind. Coleridge's questioning was directed at Newton's dualistic natural philosophy, viewed in the light of his reading of Priestley's monism of matter and spirit in the *Disquisitions Relating to Matter and Spirit* (1777, 1782). Like Priestley, he constructed his argument in response to reading Andrew Baxter's *An Enquiry into the Nature of the Human Soul* (1733). Using the Newtonian idea of forces as the manifestation of God's power and gravity construed as an immaterial cause constantly impressed upon matter, Baxter had asserted the central importance of maintaining the distinction between mind and matter. But in alluding to the ether of the 1717 edition of Newton's *Opticks* he denied that gravity could be explained in terms of the action of any material ether, for the cause of the motion of ether must itself be referred to an immaterial cause.[86]

This was the burden of Newton's own critique of Descartes in insisting that gravity lay outside the explanatory framework of the interactions of matter; and Priestley had also judged that ether could not 'produce the effects that are ascribed to it'. Coleridge echoed Baxter's exposure of the implications of the ether in Newton's *Opticks* and extended this line of argument to incorporate Hartley's theory of the mind. He considered the very existence of matter to be problematic if, as with Newton, matter is defined by the inherent properties of solidity and impenetrability, and is considered to have a separate existence from spirit; and Hartley's theory of the mind seemed to imply that thoughts were generated by matter. In a note written in 1795 Coleridge pondered the issues: 'It has been asserted that Sir Isaac Newton's philosophy leads in its consequences to Atheism: perhaps not without reason. For if matter, by any power or properties *given* to it, can produce the order of the visible world and even generate thought; why may it not have possessed such properties by inherent *right*? and where is the necessity of a God?'[87] Newtonian dualism was insufficient to establish the necessity of divine agency in the natural order, and the doctrines of Newton and Hartley seemed to imply atheism and materialism.

Priestley's monism of matter and spirit, his doctrine of the '*immaterialisty of matter*', offered an alternative to the Newtonian system of supposing matter as 'bricks cemented together by an immaterial mortar' and Baxter's dualism of matter and spirit. Priestley had aimed to reinterpret the relationship between matter and man, stating in the *Disquisitions* that his principal object was 'to prove the uniform composition of man, or that what we call *mind*, or the principle of perception and thought, is not a substance distinct from the body'. According to Priestley's materialism, the human mind is 'nothing more than a modification' of matter, and the 'corporeal and mental faculties, inhering in the same substance, grow, ripen, and decay together'. Man and mind flow both from a single substance, a monism that implied materialism and determinism: 'the doctrine of necessity is a direct inference from materialism', he declared.[88] In December 1794, at the time of his high enthusiasm for Priestley's political and theological radicalism, Coleridge wrote to Robert Southey declaring agreement with the abolition of the separate categories of matter and spirit, and affirmed that 'I am a compleat Necessitarian . . . but I go further than Hartley and believe the corporeality of *thought*'.[89] This was not to prove a permanent commitment for Coleridge's restless and inquiring intellect, but he pondered Priestley's implicit pantheism (as he construed it), the identification of God and nature and the notion that divine agency is subsumed within the operations of matter; these doctrines, Coleridge judged, implied that man is 'an outcast of blind Nature ruled by a fatal Necessity'.[90]

Nevertheless, the natural philosophies of Priestley, Hutton and Erasmus Darwin, which affirmed the activity of the material world through the operation of inherent regenerative active powers, helped to shape Coleridge's early philosophical thought. The version of his poem 'Effusion XXXV', published in 1796 (which in his *Sibylline Leaves* of 1817 is given the title 'The Eolian Harp'), includes the lines:

Or what if all of animated nature
Be but organic Harps diversely fram'd,
That tremble into thought, as o'er them sweeps
Plastic and vast, one intellectual breeze,
At once the soul of each, and God of all?[91]

He had studied the writings of the Cambridge Platonists, especially Ralph Cudworth's *True Intellectual System of the Universe* (1678), and here makes allusion to Cudworth's notion of the 'plastic nature', conceived as a mediating agent for the divine will; but these lines suggest that, for Coleridge, God's activating power is to be conceived as immanent in the fabric of nature. At this time he studied the writings of Erasmus Darwin and Hutton, including Hutton's massive *Investigation of the Principles of Knowledge* (1794). He visited Darwin in January 1796 but formed an unfavourable impression of the depth of his engagement with the philosophical issues that for Coleridge had prime importance over scientific inquiries. In a letter written after their meeting he reported that while 'Dr Darwin would have been ashamed to have rejected Hutton's theory of the earth without having minutely examined it', he was not so circumspect in passing judgement on the most profound issues: '*all at once he makes up his mind* on such important subjects, as whether we be the outcastes of a blind idiot called Nature, or the children of an all-wise and infinitely good God'. The scope of his reading and the tenor of his interests at this time can be judged from a letter of June 1696 to the radical John Thelwall, in which he reported that 'I was told that Hutton was an atheist & procured his three massy Quartos on the principles of Knowledge in the hopes of finding some arguments in favour of atheism – but lo! I discovered him to be a profoundly pious Deist'.[92]

Responding to Beddoes' high opinion of current German philosophy and science, Coleridge studied at Göttingen in 1799. His reading in German philosophy led him to denounce pantheism, materialism and Unitarianism, and he became more confident in rejecting empiricist philosophy. Writing to his friend Thomas Poole in March 1801 he declared that he had 'overthrown the doctrine of Association, as taught by Hartley, and with it all the irreligious metaphysics of modern Infidels – especially, the doctrine of Necessity'.[93] In a notebook entry of February 1805 Coleridge declared 'Unitarianism' to be 'the Religion of a man, whose Reason would make him an Atheist but whose Heart and Common sense will not permit him to be so'. This pungent characterisation of Priestley's theology – which he had once shown an inclination to embrace – was followed some months later by a renunciation of monism and materialism, and the materiality of the soul, with the affirmation of a non-material explanation of gravity: 'Gravitation, all in all / nothing in any one part, as fluid, ether, or such like / – analogy of this to *Soul*, to Consciousness / that nothing-something, something-nothing'.[94] He began a critique of Locke and Newton and studied the *Opticks*, leading him to tell Thomas Poole in 1802 that 'Newton was a mere materialist – *Mind* in his system is always passive'; and while he declared delight in the 'beauty & neatness of his experiments, & with the accuracy of his *immediate* Deductions from them', he found 'his whole Theory . . . exceedingly superficial as without impropriety to be deemed false'. He found the problem to lie in Newton's empiricist theory of knowledge, concluding that 'any system built on the passiveness of the mind must be false'.[95]

Coleridge had returned to Bristol in 1799 to find the young Humphry Davy working in the chemical laboratory of Thomas Beddoes' Pneumatic Institution, engaged in researching the medical properties of nitrous oxide, and Davy soon established friendships with both Coleridge and Wordsworth. Davy subsequently moved to the new Royal Institution founded in 1799 in London, where he entertained a huge and fashionable audience with his famous lectures and commenced the sequence of researches on electro-chemistry that led to his theory of the identity of chemical and electrical forces. Coleridge attended the lectures delivered in 1802, pursuing an interest in chemistry which he admitted might be 'but *Davyism!*'[96] For Coleridge the structures implied by chemical metaphors – of combination and affinity, concepts expounded in Davy's lectures – came to embody the harmony between the powers and forms of mind and the powers and forms of nature. Davy's explication of the electrical basis of chemical affinity helped to shape Coleridge's concept of the opposition of a dynamical to the mechanical philosophy of nature, an opposition between a system based on the unity of forces (of electricity and chemistry) and a system based on the arrangement of atoms of brute matter. Writing to Dorothy Wordsworth in 1807 he stated that he believed Davy had established 'the identity of electricity and chemical attractions . . . [and] proved that by a practicable increase of electric energy all *ponderable* compounds (in opposition to *light* & *Heat*, magnetic fluid, &c) may be decomposed, & presented simple – & recomposed thro' an infinity of new combinations'. Building on Davy's emphasis on the unity of the natural order, a doctrine derived from natural philosophers such as Hutton, Coleridge looked 'to resolve this into some Law of vital Intellect – and all human Knowledge will be Science and Metaphysics the only Science'.[97]

But Coleridge soon renounced Davy's version of the theory of active powers. He came to interpret Davy's chemistry as being grounded on a natural philosophy of matter rather than on the metaphysics of mind; by 1812 he was describing Davy (inaccurately) as 'an *Atomist*'.[98] Coleridge intended this term to denote a philosophical outlook, the world view of a natural philosopher rather than a scientific hypothesis, and he used it pejoratively in its association with materialism and empiricism. 'A system of Science *presupposes* – a system of Philosophy', he declared in 1820; but atomism was inextricably bound up with the empiricist philosophy of Locke and Newton that supposed knowledge to be derived from sensory experience, an outlook that Coleridge equated with materialism. As late as 1826 he returned to this subject, setting out the boundaries and consequences of any system of natural philosophy based on the principles of atomism: 'The System of Epicurus, that a finite

Universe composed of Atoms, is *notionally* true. But it expresses the limits and necessities of the human imagination and understanding, not the truth of Nature.'[99]

The atomism of Epicurus and his modern disciple Newton would only be acceptable in so far as it might provide a method and model for purposes of scientific explanation, but atomism could not stand as the foundational principle of natural philosophy. 'Materialists ... reduce all Perceptions to mere modes of *Sensation* ... the whole Philosophy of the modern Epicurists resting on the term', Coleridge noted in April 1819. He continued with a lengthy disquisition on the philosophical implications of 'Atoms', explaining that they would be acceptable if interpreted as mere symbols: if 'understood as xyz in Algebra, and for the purpose of scientific Calculus, as in elemental Chemistry, I see no objection to the Fiction not over-weighted by its technical utility'. But, he continued, 'if they are asserted as real and existent ... [this] is such and so fruitful an absurdity' and could only result in an infinite regress: 'when the Theorist has got his Atoms, he must then make a new set of Atoms still less in order to compose his subtlest fluid, by which they are to be dilated, attracted, repelled and generally put in motion'. Atomism was acceptable if invoked as a hypothetical instrument for purposes of scientific explanation, as a method of calculation in chemistry; but atoms must not be judged real and existent, and ultimately they explained nothing. But Coleridge had grand aims for the scope of natural philosophy, not limited to the formulation of a system of rules for ordering experience: 'Physics must be confined to Phaenomena, and yet must not be grounded on a mere fiction. How can these two equal claims be reconciled? – Only by taking some result of metaphysical Dynamics, as the prior Science'.[100] The natural philosophy of atomism, resting on the empiricist theory of knowledge, would only generate a 'fiction', and could not be accommodated with the desired metaphysical principles.

Beginning in 1806, and especially after 1813, Coleridge began to draw systematically upon German Romantic *Naturphilosophie* in explicating the basis of his rejection of 'materialism'.[101] Repudiating the empiricist theory of knowledge as derived from sensory experience, he gave primacy to unravelling the relation between self and the material world. The *Naturphilosophen* urged the uniqueness of experience; the singularity, individuality and distinctness of a person, a work of art and of a scene in nature. They supposed that the understanding of the natural world was to be achieved by an immediate engagement with experience through a multiplicity of interpretations, where aesthetic appreciation was seen to provide the basis of reunion with nature. Coleridge studied the writings of the leading figures of the German school, Friedrich Schelling and Henrik Steffens. They invoked the potency of vital powers, of growth, development and decay in supplanting the foundational status of the mechanical world view of inert matter in motion; they placed emphasis on 'dynamism' – a theory partly derived from Kant, ultimately from Leibniz – which meant a focus on the interplay and conflict between forces rather than on the interactions of matter.

Schelling represented natural phenomena in terms of the transformations of two fundamental forces, described as the opposing or polar forces of attraction and repulsion. He considered that Newtonian atomism was insufficient to explain the phenomena of physics and chemistry, and saw this as manifest in contemporary developments in the sciences of electricity and magnetism. In seeking to demonstrate philosophical foundations to establish that matter should be conceived as a dynamic equilibrium of forces of attraction and repulsion, he incorporated, and transformed, Kant's discussion of the links between the critical philosophy and the conceptual foundations of physics. But whereas Kant had sought to demonstrate the metaphysical foundations of Newtonian science, including the laws of motion, from the explication of matter in terms of two fundamental forces of attraction and repulsion, Schelling's aim was thoroughly anti-Newtonian, the creation of a truly dynamical science, not a physics based on Newtonian atomistic concepts. He conceived the objects of experience to be manifestations of the polarity and balance of the fundamental forces, attraction and repulsion, and placed emphasis on the interaction between the 'productivity' of nature and the 'limitation' of this productivity: 'these opposite tendencies must concur', and when 'they meet they will annihilate each other'. His model of physical processes highlights their fluidity and transience, and he refuses to construe the operations of hard, impenetrable, permanent atoms as fundamental to the natural order; in explaining his notion of physical reality he appeals to the analogy of eddies in fluid motion, where an 'eddy is not an object at rest, but with each moment it disappears and then re-establishes itself'. The productivity of nature is like the flow of a river in which eddies are transformed in a process of dynamic tension. Schelling conceived the system of nature as a conflict between a productive and a limiting power, envisaging a developmental history of the earth and cosmos.[102]

Schelling followed Johann Gottlob Fichte rather than Kant in emphasising the creative role of the mind in constructing the world: he identified the system of nature with the system of the mind, and conceives nature as a product of the self. In conceiving the physical world and the self as conjoined Schelling rejects the dualism of thought and things: 'The sum of all that is purely objective in our knowledge we may call nature; while the sum of all that is subjective may be designated the self, or intelligence . . .. In knowledge itself, in my knowing, the two are so united that it is impossible to assign priority to one or the other'. This philosophical project entailed the investigation of the self to interpret the signs in which the physical world is encoded, to discuss the 'inner' structure of nature which is inaccessible to empirical science as conventionally conceived, seeking an understanding that is to be gained through intellectual intuition. Schelling's dynamical concept of the natural world as active, as maintained by a balance of forces, has a (superficial) analogy with the natural philosophy of active powers of Priestley, Hutton and Erasmus Darwin. But Coleridge considered that Priestley's monism of matter endowed with inherent active powers reduced mind to matter and implied materialism and atheism, and he rejected this natural philosophy of powers as defining matter along with Newton's dualism of passive matter and active principles; he judged that in both systems powers are effectively superadded to matter, which is considered to have an objective reality independent of mind. By contrast Schelling's system, in Coleridge's view, 'Instead of considering the powers of bodies to have been miraculously stuck into a prepared and pre-existing matter, as pins in a pin-cushion, conceives the powers as the productive factors, and the body or phenomenon as the fact, product, or fixture.'[103]

In his *Biographia Literaria* (1817) Coleridge set out 'a sketch of the *subjective* Pole of the Dynamic Philosophy' where he rejects empiricist philosophy in favour of the subjective idealism of Schelling, in whose work he found 'a genial coincidence with much that I had toiled out for myself, and a powerful assistance in what I had yet to do'. Schelling had set out the goal of philosophy in a form consonant with his own unified vision of man, mind and the imagination, the natural order being rendered intelligible through the operation of the laws of mind. Even so, Coleridge came to the conclusion that in making the system of nature absolute Schelling's system implied pantheism; but as he explained in 1818, he recognised that 'as far as the attack on the mechanic and corpuscular Philosophy extends, his works possess a permanent value'.[104] The transformation in Coleridge's philosophical outlook from 1795 to 1817 can be illustrated by changes he made to the text of his poem 'The Eolian Harp'. In the revision of the poem published in *Sibylline Leaves* (1817) he added a reference to the analogy between sound and light which he explored in *Biographia Literaria* and other works, an idea originating with Schelling:

O! the one Life within us and abroad,
Which meets all motion and becomes its soul,
A light in sound, a sound-like power in light,
Rhythm in all thought . . ..[105]

Light and sound reveal the inherent rhythm unifying nature and thought, produced by the balance and interaction of powers. At this time Coleridge wrote that 'Color is Gravitation under the power of Light . . . while Sound on the other hand is Light under the power or paramountcy of Gravitation . . ..

The two poles of the material Universe are Light and Gravitation', emphasising that phenomena were to be understood as generated from the polarity and opposition of fundamental powers.[106]

Coleridge's preferred science was to follow his assimilation of 'Davyism', chemistry. As he explained in his 'Essays on the principles of method' in *The Friend* of 1818, 'the assumed indecomponible substances of the Laboratory . . . are the symbols of elementary powers, and the exponents of a law, which, as the root of all these powers, the chemical philosopher, whatever his theory may be . . . is instinctively labouring to extract'. Chemical substances and reactions reveal the variety, unity and transforming power of nature: 'so water and flame, the diamond, the charcoal, and the mantling champagne, with its ebullient sparkles, are convoked and fraternized by the theory of the chemist'. In this lay 'the first charm of chemistry, and the secret of the almost universal interest excited by its discoveries', and 'the strong hold which in all ages chemistry has had on the imagination'. He drew the contrast between poetry and the study of chemistry: 'in SHAKESPEARE we find nature idealized into poetry, through the creative power of a profound yet observant meditation', so 'through the meditative power of a DAVY . . . we find poetry, as it were, substantiated and realized in nature'. Chemistry symbolises the relations of laws, exemplifying creativity in natural agents: 'nature itself disclosed to us . . . as at once the poet and the poem'.[107] Like Schelling, Coleridge emphasised the productivity of natural processes, of the order of nature viewed as the product of will, as acting with a purpose and producing change with time. In a notebook entry in 1820 he outlined his theory of the productivity, inherent power and development of nature, claiming to avoid pantheism by a distinction between nature and history, necessity and freedom, and thus preserving the distinction between nature and God:

> The proper objects of knowledge and which may be regarded as the Poles of true Learning are Nature and History – or Necessity and Freedom. And these attain their highest perfection, when each reveals the essential character of the other in itself and without loss of its own distinctive form. Nature attains its highest significancy when she appears to us as an inner power . . . that coerces and subordinates to itself the outward – the conquest of Essence over form – when by Life + superinduced Finality she reveals herself as a plastic Will, acting in time and of course finitely . . .. This maintains the necessary distinction of Nature from Deity, and consequently the reality of both. . . . Here there is Process and Succession, in each Plant and Animal as an Individual, and in the whole Planet as at once a System and a Unit – and the Knowledge of Nature becomes Natural History. . . . History reveals herself to us in the form of a necessity of Nature . . . that coerces and takes up into itself the inner

power – the conquest of Form over Essence . . .. But here is *Law*, and the *Ever-present* in the moving Past, the eternal as the Power of the Temporal – and the Historic Science become a higher Physiology . . . a transcendent Nature.[108]

Nature and history, necessity and freedom develop in a dynamic tension; nature is shaped by an inner power unfolding and developing towards a goal. Nature is envisaged as a dynamic, living process, its historical development determined by teleology ('superinduced Finality') imposed by God. Man is conjoined to nature and the laws of science embody nature in history. To explain the development, hierarchy and productivity of natural processes Coleridge introduced an image of an ascending and expanding spiral: 'this is one proof of the essential vitality of nature, that she does not ascend as links in a suspended chain, but as the steps in a ladder'; more accurately, '[nature] at one and the same time *ascends* as by a climax, and expands as the concentric circles on the lake from the point to which the stone in its fall had given the first impulse'.[109]

Matter and Life: Mary Shelley's Frankenstein

In 1809 Johann Wolfgang von Goethe published a novel *Die Wahlverwandschaften* (*Elective Affinities*). Its curious title alludes to the concept of 'affinity' that had been developed by chemists in the eighteenth century, with tables of affinities setting out a classification of the relative powers of reaction of chemical substances. The method of affinities was first developed by French chemists, but the Scottish chemists William Cullen and Joseph Black interpreted 'affinity' as 'attraction', and the concept of 'affinity' became assimilated to Newton's concept of short-range forces of attraction determining chemical reactions as set out in Query 31 of the *Opticks*. The term *attractio electiva* became familiar through the influential text by the Swedish chemist Torbern Bergman, *De Attractionibus Electivis Disquisitio* (*A Dissertation on Elective Attractions*), which was first published in 1775, a subsequent and enlarged version being translated into English, French and German; this work was familiar to Goethe, who used the German translation of the term *attractio electiva*, *Wahlverwandschaft*, in the title of his novel. Bergman gave the laws of affinity a mathematical precision and appealed to the analogy with Newtonian astronomy. This was an important Newtonian theme in eighteenth-century natural philosophy and chemistry, and was given an important restatement and development around the turn of the nineteenth century by the French physicist and mathematician P.S. Laplace. He envisioned a universal programme of scientific explanation, an expression of the unity of nature in Newtonian terms, which he announced in his popular

Exposition du Système du Monde first published in 1796. Laplace held out the hope that chemical combinations would be integrated with all the varieties of attractive forces that are found in nature, a unified science that would bring every phenomenon of physics and astronomy under a single, general law; and his colleague C.L. Berthollet brought the forces of chemical affinity within this programme of explanation, declaring that the force shaping chemical combination derived from the mutual attractions between particles and that it was probable that this was the same force as astronomical attraction. At the time Goethe wrote his novel, Laplacian physics and chemistry gave prospect of a theory of nature based on a unifying law, an outlook promoted by his friend Alexander von Humboldt, who had joined the group around the Parisian scientists, as a central element in his *physique générale*.[110]

Goethe uses the metaphor of affinities in its application to human relationships, confronting human life and free will with the necessity imposed by laws of nature: in his advertisements for the novel he stated that *Elective Affinities* reveals how 'there is everywhere only *one* Nature'.[111] Bringing humanity within the framework of physical laws, the novel contests the separation or alienation of man from nature and offers a unified vision of humanity as embraced within the order of nature. The novel forms a counterpart to Goethe's scientific works on the theory of colours and plant morphology, where his aesthetic language and imagery was intended to free science from abstractions and encourage the reader to envision what the experimenter has observed, using art as a mirror to nature. He reverses the procedure in *Elective Affinities*, bringing natural philosophy to bear upon human life and imagination, exploring the gap between science and human values. The theme of the novel is marriage, the 'elective affinity' between a married couple, Eduard (also Otto) and Charlotte, and their two friends, the Captain (whose name is also Otto) and a young woman Ottilie. The metaphor of 'elective affinity' binds the four main characters, united in sharing the name 'Otto' and its variants, and illuminates the symmetry of the action. The Captain is visiting the married couple, drawing Eduard away from spending time with his wife; subsequently Ottilie is invited to join the party as a companion for Charlotte. The planned affinities do not transpire, for Eduard and Ottilie are attracted to one another, as are the Captain and Charlotte though this relationship remains passive. In a central episode of the novel, the spiritual adultery or adultery in the marriage bed, the 'elective affinity' is actualised in the imagination of Eduard and Charlotte during their marital embrace. 'By lamplight then, in a twilight, the heart's desires and the imagination at once asserted their rights over reality. Eduard held Ottilie in his arms; now closer, now receding, the Captain hovered before Charlotte's soul; and thus absent and present in the queerest fashion were intermingled, in excitement and delight.'[112] The child conceived that night is christened Otto, and has the features of Ottilie and the Captain. The story ends tragically, with Ottilie's turmoil bringing about the death of the child by drowning and with the deaths of Ottilie (effectively a suicide) and finally of Eduard.

The narrator's detachment is signalled in the opening sentence of the novel: 'Eduard – let that be the name we give to a wealthy baron . . .'; and the narrator preserves an irony and remoteness throughout. The characters, dialogue and events have a rigidity and formality with little authorial attempt to secure the reader's emotional involvement. Goethe had original conceived the work as a *Novelle*, a German literary form in which the action is focused on a single theme and the characters and relationships are described only in relation to that theme, with a parsimony of names and little enrichment of characters and plot through a thickening of the description of their wider social life. Walter Benjamin commented on '[Goethe's] refusal to summon the reader's sympathy into the centre of the action itself', remarking that the narrative arranges the characters in a series of formal groups: 'the story's pictorialness is fundamentally unpainterly; it may be called plastic, perhaps stereoscopic'.[113] The formality and symmetry of the characters and plot are suggestive of the theme of 'elective affinity', of actions shaped and determined by scientific laws; but the metaphor of 'chemical affinity' is qualified by the outcome of the plot, for the anticipated combinations of Eduard and the Captain, Charlotte and Ottilie, do not occur. Predicting the outcome of chemical reactions through affinities was found to be difficult. Berthollet exposed 'insurmountable obstacles' that led to the ultimate demise of the theory;[114] but human emotion and imagination function on a different level of complexity. When the theory of 'elective affinities' is first introduced Charlotte and the Captain debate the central philosophical issue of determinism and free will, which would seem to differentiate chemical compounds and human beings. 'These comparisons are very entertaining', concludes Charlotte, 'everyone likes playing with analogies', but even if nature holds up a mirror to life 'a human being is after all superior by several degrees to those natural substances'. To describe chemical combinations in terms of 'choice' and human emotions in terms of 'elective affinity' is a 'lax' use of 'fine words'. If the applicability of the metaphor of 'elective affinity' to complex human relationships is shown to be limited, the metaphor is seen as suggestive of the way fate and death thwart and compromise the volition of the characters, just as chemical substances are constrained to form specific combinations.[115]

The scientific basis of human life and the necessity imposed by laws of nature is explored in another novel of the early nineteenth century, Mary Wollstonecraft Shelley's *Frankenstein; or, The Modern Prometheus*, which was published in 1818 and with a revised edition in 1831. Concerned with the creation of life, *Frankenstein* is suffused with images of death and degeneration, consequences not of the limitations of scientific laws but of human creativity and understanding. Mary Shelley was born in 1797, the daughter of the philosopher and political radical William Godwin, author of the *Enquiry Concerning Political Justice and its Influence on Morals and Happiness* (1793), and Mary Wollstonecraft, author of *A Vindication of the Rights of Woman* (1792), who died ten days after her birth. Brought up in a household where high educational standards were fostered, she received an exceptional schooling, and was intellectually precocious and exposed to a wide circle of authors, philosophers and political reformers. The radical poet Percy Bysshe Shelley became close to Mary Godwin, and she eloped with him in July 1814, giving birth to a daughter in February 1815 who died twelve days later, and a son in January 1816. The couple married in December 1816 after the suicide by drowning of Shelley's first wife Harriet. The themes of life and death pervade *Frankenstein*, which Mary began to write in 1816 in Geneva when the Shelleys were staying with Byron. Members of the party began to compose ghost stories, and *Frankenstein* was Mary Shelley's contribution to the contest; the novel is dedicated to her father, was completed by May 1817 when the couple were back in England, and published anonymously in 1818.

The preface, written by P.B. Shelley, hints at the ideas shaping the theme of the novel: 'The event on which this fiction is founded has been supposed, by Dr Darwin, and some of the physiological writers of Germany, as not of impossible occurrence.' The allusion to Erasmus Darwin's note on the spontaneous vitality of microscopic life published in *The Temple of Nature* (1803) is unmistakable, and the dedication to William Godwin gave the work a radical and materialist edge: Walter Scott, who received a complimentary copy of the novel from P.B. Shelley, assumed that he was the author.[116] For the revised edition of 1831 Mary Shelley wrote an introduction where she gives an account of the genesis of the novel, and provides more complete and explicit indications of its intellectual context:

Many and long were the conversations between Lord Byron and Shelley, to which I was a devout but nearly silent listener. During one of these, various philosophical doctrines were discussed, and among others the nature of the principle of life, and whether there was any probability of its ever being discovered and communicated. They talked of the experiments of Dr Darwin, (I speak not of what the Doctor really did, or said that he did, but . . . of what was then spoken of as having been done by him,) who preserved a piece of vermicelli in a glass case, till by some extraordinary means it began to move with voluntary motion. Not thus, after all, would life be given. Perhaps a corpse would be re-animated; galvanism had given token of such things: perhaps the component parts of a creature might be manufactured, brought together, and endued with vital warmth. . . . I did not sleep, nor could I be said to think. My imagination, unbidden, possessed and guided me . . . I saw the pale student of unhallowed arts kneeling beside the thing he had put together. I saw the hideous phantasm of a man stretched out, and then, on the working of some powerful engine, show signs of life, and stir with an uneasy, half vital motion. Frightful . . . would be the effect of any human endeavour to mock the stupendous mechanism of the Creator of the world. His success would terrify the artist; he would rush away from his odious handywork, horror-stricken.[117]

The explicit reference to Erasmus Darwin's note on the 'Spontaneous Vitality of Microscopic Animals' in *The Temple of Nature*, to which P.B. Shelley had already made allusion in the preface to the 1818 edition of *Frankenstein*, evokes his authority in giving a semblance of scientific credibility to the story, but also invites recall of the controversial character of his doctrines of generation, evolution, vital powers and materialism. While amplifying the reference to Darwin, Mary Shelley qualified these radical associations with the conventional piety of mention of the 'stupendous mechanism of the Creator'. According to her reminiscence, Byron and Shelley had turned from Darwin's discussion of the spontaneous generation of microscopic animals to a process that they judged more plausible for the production of life, for 'galvanism had given token of such things'. In his note on the 'Chemical theory of electricity and magnetism' in *The Temple of Nature* Darwin had mentioned 'the experiments conducted by Galvani' and the phenomenon of 'Galvanism, that animal flesh, and particularly perhaps the nerves of animals, both which are composed of much carbon and water, are the most perfect conductors yet discovered'.[118]

In 1791 Luigi Galvani had discovered that disembodied frog legs twitched in response to electrical excitation, claiming that his experiments gave evidence of a distinct kind of nervous electric fluid in animal tissue, 'animal' electricity. Galvani's interpretation of the experiment, as implying a new and unique form of 'animal' electricity characteristic of living tissue, did not command universal assent. In the 1770s Henry Cavendish had studied an electric fish, the 'torpedo', constructing an artificial torpedo that delivered shocks in similar fashion to the living fish; he concluded that 'there seems nothing in the phenomenon of the torpedo at all incompatible with electricity' as commonly understood. Questioning Galvani's interpretation of his experiment, Alessandro Volta demonstrated that the electricity observed in the frog legs could be attributed to metallic contact in the experiment. His identification of 'animal' with common electricity led him to the invention of the 'voltaic' pile, the generation of electricity by linking pairs of silver and zinc disks separated by pieces of moist cardboard.[119] But Galvani had his supporters, notably his nephew Giovanni Aldini who travelled throughout Europe between 1800 and 1805 repeating the famous experiments and producing evidence of electricity in animal tissues without the use of connective metals. He paid a successful visit to London in 1802–3, giving convincing demonstrations of the existence of animal electricity.[120] Galvani's discovery prompted discussion of the relationship between electricity and life, evidenced by Darwin's reference to his work. Contemporary discussion of the scope of chemistry, the interpretation of 'animal electricity', and the relations between chemical principles and the origins of life are distinctively echoed in Mary Shelley's text.

The subtitle of the novel, *The Modern Prometheus*, makes allusion to the myth of Prometheus who made humankind out of clay and stole fire from the gods; and again it suggests that electricity provided the spark of life, in the allusion to the contemporary association between Promethean fire and Benjamin Franklin, 'the modern Prometheus' as Kant called him. As described by Erasmus Darwin in *The Economy of Vegetation*, Franklin snatched lightning from the clouds:

You led your FRANKLIN to your glazed retreats,
Your air-built castles, and your silken feats;
Bade his bold arm invade the lowering sky,
And seize the tiptoe lightnings, ere they fly;
O'er the young Sage your mystic mantle spread,
And wreath'd the crown electric round his head.

In the 1818 text of the novel explicit mention is made of drawing down lightning, in a passage deleted from the 1831 edition. Victor Frankenstein's childhood astonishment at the 'catastrophe' of an oak tree destroyed by a lightning strike in a 'stream of fire' leads his father to demonstrate some electrical experiments, including Franklin's experiment with the 'kite, with a wire and string, which drew down that fluid from the clouds', as described in Darwin's poem.[121]

The nature of life was the subject of vigorous debate at the time the novel was written. In his preface to the 1818 text P.B. Shelley's allusion to 'physiological writers of Germany' is too vague to pin down, though he may have had in mind the *Bildungstrieb* (formative drive) of J.F. Blumenbach, or the naturalistic laws of *organische Kräfte* (organic forces) suggested by his pupil C.F. Kielmeyer, or the *Lebenskraft* (living force) of J.C. Reil.[122] But Mary Shelley did not elaborate on her husband's allusion in her introduction to the 1831 edition. Nor did she make any reference to a contemporary debate on the relationship between organisms and the principle of life, a controversy in full flow around 1817 when she was writing the novel. William Lawrence, P.B. Shelley's physician, was one of the protagonists in the debate, maintaining that vitality was a property of living matter, while his former teacher John Abernethy adhered to the view, derived from the famous medical author John Hunter, that vitality was a power independent of matter. Abernethy and Lawrence were distinguished medical practitioners and presented their arguments in lectures to the Royal College of Surgeons, focusing their discussion on John Hunter's theory that blood, rather than the organisation of tissue, is the source of life. In a lecture delivered in 1814 Abernethy appealed to the analogy between organisms and physical nature, seeking to explain vitality by a material principle similar to electricity, as a power superadded to the structure of tissue. In 1816 Lawrence responded by rejecting the analogy between the animate and inanimate, finding no evidence for an ethereal vital substance, a special principle of life independent of organised tissue, and maintaining that manifestations of life were dependent on the structure of tissue alone. They continued their disagreement in lectures delivered the following year, when their discussion enlarged to encompass moral and religious issues.[123] Mary Shelley may have had this controversy in mind when writing of Victor Frankenstein pondering 'the principle of life', 'discovering the cause of generation and life' and becoming 'capable of bestowing animation on lifeless matter'. But Frankenstein kept his method 'secret', and the text does not indicate which (if either) of these two theories he adopted or Shelley may have preferred. Frankenstein does not create organic tissue; he reanimates human remains with the power of vitality, the nature of this power being left 'secret'. Both Abernethy and Lawrence held that living beings had unique properties of vitality, a power open to investigation; their disagreement was about the relation between the vital power and the organic tissue. Frankenstein's narrative merely requires the suspension of disbelief, to allow the possibility of the reanimation of human parts.[124]

The novel carries an epigraph from Milton's *Paradise Lost*, Adam's complaint to God: 'Did I request thee, Maker, from my clay / To mould me man? Did I solicit thee / From darkness to promote me? –'.[125] In these lines, his complaint qualified later in Milton's text, Adam bemoans the injustice of the terms of his creation and existence, a remonstrance echoed in the novel by the monster's complaint of rejection by his creator Victor Frankenstein. The monster equates his creation to God's creation of Adam, but his rejection to God's renunciation and punishment of Satan. In their climactic encounter on the 'vast river of ice', the glacier of the Mer de Glace above which towers 'Mont Blanc, in awful majesty', the monster reproaches his creator: 'I am thy creature: I ought to be thy Adam; but I am rather the fallen angel, whom thou drivest from joy for no misdeed'.[126] Is Frankenstein's relation to the creature to be understood as analogous to that of God the creator to Adam (as implied by the epigraph from *Paradise Lost*), or to God's repudiation of the fallen angel (as suggested in the text of the novel)? Frankenstein does not create human tissue, or matter itself, *ex nihilo*; he reanimates created organic tissue that has lost its vital power. The analogy to the God of Genesis is incomplete. In his *Enquiry Concerning Political Justice* William Godwin portrayed Milton's Satan as questioning divine providence and 'that extreme inequality of rank and power, which the creator assumed', and as persisting in his 'spirit of opposition' after the Fall from 'a persuasion that he was hardly and injuriously treated.'[127] For Godwin, Milton's Satan is a heroic rebel against the unreasonable impositions of the divine will, and Shelley's creature presents his own violent actions in similar terms, as the fallen angel raging against his creator's persistent negligence and hostility: 'I was benevolent and good; misery made me a fiend. Make me happy, and I shall again be virtuous', he declares.[128] In his hubris in seeking to usurp divine control of life and death, is Frankenstein mimicking the heroic rebellion of Milton's Satan as interpreted by Godwin?

In the 1831 edition of *Frankenstein* Mary Shelley circumvents the question by omitting the epigraph from *Paradise Lost*; her remark on mocking the 'Creator of the world' in the introduction to this version of the text places emphasis on the religious values that Frankenstein's actions may be seen to transgress, and smoothes over any suggestion of impiety in a narrative untouched by Christian redemption and one that follows the logic of a world bereft of divine providence. But Frankenstein does not present his ambition to achieve power over life and death as an attempt to usurp the divine will; he couches his intentions in secular terms, as an effort to attain knowledge and to be useful to humanity. In giving an account of his ultimate ambitions he expresses the hope 'that if I could bestow animation upon lifeless matter, I might in process of time (although I now found it impossible) renew life where death had apparently devoted the body to corruption'.[129] Is Frankenstein to be understood as a natural philosopher seeking to ameliorate the human condition? As noted earlier, the novel's subtitle *The Modern Prometheus* makes allusion to Benjamin Franklin, electricity and the control of the damaging effects of lightning; but while Frankenstein portrays himself as a natural philosopher seeking knowledge for the future benefit of humanity, he is found to be an unreliable narrator. Mary Shelley presents his secretive style of research as departing from the established norms of open scientific inquiry and as arising from a perverted ambition; death and disaster ensue, human aspirations wither and Frankenstein exists on the fringes of human society, bereft of the moral and scientific authority of a Franklin.

Although the subtitle of the novel hints at electricity as the means of vivification, an association reinforced by Mary Shelley's reference to 'galvanism' in her 1831 introduction, the method by which Frankenstein might have reanimated human remains is veiled in silence and as a result his science remains mysterious and 'secret'. While mention is made of his childhood astonishment at the destructive power of lightning and interest in electricity, as he attains intellectual maturity more specific emphasis is placed on his engagement with the science of chemistry. Frankenstein portrays himself as having been inspired from his childhood by the dreams of Paracelsus and the alchemists, the 'masters of the science' who 'sought immortality and power'. He attends the University of Ingolstadt, famous as the centre of the Illuminati, a branch of freemasonry sympathetic to science and radical politics. There, moved by a 'panegyric upon modern chemistry' in a lecture delivered by the professor of chemistry, Waldman, he grasps that the alchemists 'promised impossibilities, and performed nothing', for 'the elixir of life is a chimera', but 'modern chemistry' would provide him with the means to realise his ambitions. 'Chemistry is that branch of natural philosophy in which the greatest improvements have been and may be made', Waldman assures him, 'and it is on that account that I have made it my peculiar study'.[130]

While writing her novel Mary Shelley noted that she read 'the Introduction to Sir H. Davy's Chemistry'.[131] In his *Elements of Chemical Philosophy* (1812) Humphry Davy collected the results of his research of the previous decade, work initiated by Volta's invention of the electric pile and its application in studying the effects of chemical dissociation by means of electric currents. While Davy concluded that the 'electrical power' was 'apparently connected with the power of chemical combination', he insisted that these were '*distinct* phaenomena' but 'produced by the *same power*'. He dismissed as 'vague speculations' and 'mere associations of words' the appeal to the electric power of the 'torpedo' as the basis for the dependence of the powers of life on electricity: 'The laws of dead and living nature appear to be perfectly distinct'.[132] Davy's circumspect *Chemical Philosophy* would have offered little encouragement to the author of *Frankenstein*; but the argument of his famous *Discourse Introductory* to his course of lectures on chemistry, advertised as an 'important and sublime subject', which was delivered at the Royal Institution in London in January 1802 and published several months later, shows parallels with Mary Shelley's evocation of the interest and power of chemistry and might have been the work to which she made reference.[133]

Davy's introductory lecture, eloquent in style and inspirational in content, was carefully tailored to satisfy the outlook of his audience. He places emphasis on the utility of chemistry in offering the prospect of improvements in the practical arts; many of the founders of the Royal Institution were landowners with an interest in philanthropy and agrarian reform, and his early work there was on tanning and agricultural chemistry. Davy presents the prospects of chemistry in terms of the values of improvement, benevolence and utility, but he mutes the radical implications of these aspirations as avowed by Priestley and his mentor Beddoes.[134] His concluding, conventional appeal to natural theology does not compromise the most striking feature of the lecture, his use of the language of Romantic genius in portraying chemistry as providing aesthetic satisfaction, in being the equal of poetry in giving the man of genius creative powers to satisfy the restlessness of his ambition. At Bristol, Davy had become intimate with Coleridge and friendly with Wordsworth, and had corrected the proofs of the second edition of *Lyrical Ballads* (1800); his *Discourse Introductory* echoes themes in Wordsworth's preface, that poetry (chemistry, for Davy) would ameliorate social progress, improve the human mind and temper the imagination. But shortly after Davy's lecture Wordsworth published a third edition of *Lyrical Ballads* (1802) in which he added to the preface a long disquisition on the character of the poet, drawing comparison between the poet and the man of science. Here Wordsworth seems to echo Davy, declaring that the poet 'converses with general nature, with affections akin to those, which, through labour and length of time, the Man of science has raised up in himself, by conversing with those particular parts of nature which are the objects of his studies'. He offers the prospect that if 'the time should ever come when what is now called science, thus familiarised to men, shall be ready to put on, as it were, a form of flesh and blood, the Poet will lend his divine spirit to aid the transfiguration, and will welcome the Being thus produced, as a dear and genuine inmate of the household of man'.[135]

In his panoramic *Discourse Introductory* Davy strove to portray chemistry as integral to cultural sensibility, as a 'branch of sublime philosophy'. He sought to arouse interest in the subject by emphasising its universal application, claiming that it provides understanding of 'the great changes and convulsions in nature, which, occurring but seldom, excite our curiosity, or awaken our astonishment'. Chemistry, he declares, was fundamental to understanding the operation of the vital forces that determined the 'spirit of life': he affirms that the 'nourishment and growth of organized beings' and their 'death and decomposition' are 'dependent . . . upon chemical processes'. He deploys the language of Romantic genius in portraying chemistry as the equal of poetry, a science giving the 'man of true genius . . . powers which may almost be called creative . . . allaying the restlessness of his desires, or of extending and increasing his power'. The chemist 'in the search of discovery . . . will rather pursue the plans of his own mind than be limited by the artificial divisions of language . . . [and] he will combine together mechanical, chemical, and physiological knowledge', which will enable him 'to interrogate nature with power, not simply as a scholar, passive and seeking only to understand her operations, but rather as a master, active with his own instruments'. Davy argues that chemistry offered the prospect of understanding 'the most profound secrets of nature . . . of ascertaining her hidden operations', and in offering the hope of bridging the disjunction between the animate and the inanimate chemistry would transcend the 'dreams of Alchemy'. He traces the links between chemistry, electricity, lightning, galvanism and the vital powers of life: 'the phenomena of electricity have been developed; the lightnings have been taken from the clouds', and in an allusion to galvanism he points out that 'a new influence has been discovered, which has enabled man to produce from combinations of dead matter effects which were formerly occasioned only by animal organs'.

Davy couched his statement of the scope of chemistry in terms of Enlightenment doctrines of progress and civilisation but he used terms acceptable to his audience at a time of political uncertainty, accepting that inequalities of wealth 'are the sources of power in civilized life' and that his project was above all realistic: 'But we reason by analogy from simple facts. We consider only a state of human progression arising out of its present condition'. Chemistry offered the real and present prospect of wholly trans-forming the present circumstances of human life: 'In this view we do not look to distant ages, or amuse ourselves with brilliant, though delusive dreams, concerning the infinite improveability of man, the annihilation of labour, disease, and even death'.[136] In *Frankenstein* Waldman, the professor of chemistry at Ingolstadt, uses similar language in exalting the power and prospect of chemistry; but in seeking to justify the terms of his scientific and philosophical ambitions, Victor Frankenstein transforms this tempered version of the progress and consequences of chemical research. In engaging in 'secret toil' in a laboratory described as a 'solitary chamber' and as a 'workshop of filthy creation', his endeavour is seen as a form of alchemy, both in its ambitions and practice, rather than in terms of the transparency of modern science, based on public demonstration, experimentation and publication as practised by Davy. In pursuing his perverted version of 'science' Frankenstein is alienated from landscape and the aesthetics of nature, in contrast to the harmony envisaged by Wordsworth and Davy. Encountering the scenes of his childhood on his return to his native Geneva, he weeps 'like a child' on seeing 'the black sides of the Jura, and the bright summit of Mont Blanc'. The sight of the 'beautiful . . . blue and placid' lake led him to wonder whether their welcome to the wanderer was 'to prognos-ticate peace, or to mock at my unhappiness?' A lightning storm, 'so beautiful yet terrific', provides the answer in giving him sight of his monstrous creation, 'the wretch, the filthy daemon to whom I had given life'. Frankenstein's achievement is shown to be a distorted perversion of Davy's evocation of chemistry as a study 'connected with the love of the beautiful and the sublime'.[137]

Newton's atomism, which helped to shape his theory of colours, and his duality of active and passive principles, posited a cosmos permeated and replenished by 'active' principles external to matter, their effect manifest in the violent processes of chemistry. To grant matter inherent powers of activity would allow it self-sufficiency, a doctrine that he saw as tantamount to materialism and atheism; and he invoked a cosmology based on active principles and the circulation and transformation of ether. For his successors James Hutton and Erasmus Darwin, this association between ether and active principles offered insight into the source of the active powers of matter, with electricity given pride of place as an energising principle. The cosmos now came to be conceived as a self-regenerating system of circulating active powers; with its self-sufficiency maintained by the inherent activity of matter, the active-passive dualism of Newton's natural philosophy was conflated. Joseph Priestley collapsed the disjunction between matter and its attendant forces, rejecting the Newtonian theory of impenetrable, passive atoms in favour of conceiving matter as a causal nexus of active powers. The dualisms of Newton's natural philosophy – of atoms and space, of passive and active principles, of matter and spirit – were rejected in favour of a monism of matter, controversially evoking materialism.

Erasmus Darwin's materialism is expressed in his representation of life as generated by the agency of heat and renewed through the circulation of matter. In urging the organic unity of mind and matter, his scientific poetry helped shape Coleridge's early philosophical outlook; but Coleridge and Wordsworth came to criticise his reliance on visual imagery and didactic poetic style. With Coleridge there is a manifest turn from the Enlightenment focus on the effects of matter to the Romantic concern with the relation between nature and the self. Establishing a friendship with Davy, Coleridge used chemical metaphors of combination and affinity (as expounded in Davy's lectures) to embody his notion of the harmony between the powers and forms of mind and of nature. He began to draw upon German Romantic *Naturphilosophie* in formulating his rejection of 'materialism', seeking to unravel the relation between the self and the material world; aesthetic appreciation provided the basis for the union of self and nature. Rejecting atomism, which he regarded as the foundation of materialism, he envisaged nature as a dynamic, living process, its development determined by teleology.

Echoing these debates on the powers of matter in her novel *Frankenstein*, Mary Shelley expounded a theory of the electrical basis of life, a topic of scientific controversy at the time; she drew upon Erasmus Darwin's controversial doctrines of generation, evolution, vital powers and materialism, and on Davy's evocation of the interest and prospective power of chemistry. Mary Shelley conjoined perspectives obtained from science and the literary imagination, echoing Davy in deploying the language of Romantic genius to portray chemistry as endowing the man of true genius with creative powers. In the novel, Victor Frankenstein's achievement in regenerating the powers of life is seen as a distorted perversion of Davy's evocation of chemistry as integral to cultural sensibility – to the love of the beautiful and the sublime – and as diminishing the aesthetic appreciation of nature.

CHAPTER 9

✳

Nature and Culture

IN THE PERIOD SPANNED by Newtonian science and natural theology, and Charles Darwin's *Origin of Species* (1859) and John Ruskin's *Modern Painters* (1843–60), 'nature' came to be central to cultural debate, viewed as the source of moral and religious values, as a repository of sensibility, as the norm for imagination and aesthetic judgement, and as the object of rational scientific analysis and technological control. The culture of nature had diverse roots, in the pursuit of science and in landscape art, both established in the seventeenth century. The scientific revolution accomplished by Francis Bacon, René Descartes and (especially) Isaac Newton established the intellectual authority of the new science: for John Locke and David Hume (as for Gottfried Wilhelm Leibniz and Immanuel Kant) the truth claims of science generated new and compelling problems of philosophy. In his *Essay Concerning Human Understanding* (1690) Locke described himself as 'an under-labourer in clearing the ground a little' around the scientific 'monuments' erected by 'master-builders' such as Robert Boyle and Newton.[1] Landscape art was first denoted as a category of painting in the Renaissance, and the landscapes of Nicolas Poussin, Claude Lorrain and Salvator Rosa established landscape as an independent genre in art: these paintings became emblems of the culture of nature in the eighteenth century. 'Precipices, mountains, torrents, wolves, rumblings, Salvator Rosa' exclaimed Horace Walpole when crossing the Alps in 1739; art was projected into nature, the communication of the experience mediated by art.[2] The poet Thomas Gray, Walpole's travelling companion, reported that they had yet to encounter 'grand and simple works of art' on their Grand Tour, but he found the works of nature stupendous: 'not a precipice, not a torrent, not a cliff, but is pregnant with religion and poetry'; these 'solemn ... romantic, and ... astonishing' scenes of nature evoked religious awe.[3]

The intellectual authority of Newtonian science promoted the valorisation of 'nature' under the banner of modernity, but concepts of 'nature' continued to be interpreted through the lens of traditional cultural forms deriving from the Bible and the classical legacy; Virgil's *Eclogues* and *Georgics* were especially important. The argument that nature manifested the order and design, implanted and then sustained by its creator through laws of nature, blunted the threat to religious orthodoxy posed by the new science. The concept of nature as analogous to a clock, a material artefact designed and constructed by a craftsman, established the aesthetic appreciation of nature as an artefact of God's creative power. The links between the aesthetics of nature and natural theology forged in the era of Newtonian science established a sensibility of 'design', the basis for aesthetic judgement in the arts and the justification of the authenticity of the sciences; this conjunction of natural theology and aesthetics can be traced in ideas on landscape and the natural world, and in the major themes in Newtonian natural philosophy (colour and matter theory, electricity and chemistry).

In the eighteenth and nineteenth centuries 'nature' had a range of over-lapping and nonexclusive meanings, deriving from traditional and modern usages and contexts – meanings that are still current in our contemporary usage. At one level, 'nature' denoted the structure of reality, the essential nature of things, the basis of the physical world and the cause of phenomena. This meaning was not new and had been important since antiquity in the writings of philosophers. The works of Aristotle and Lucretius were especially important and influential in setting out competing world views; the interpre-tation and authority of these texts was debated and contested in the course of the Renaissance and the seventeenth-century 'scientific revolution'. In conse-quence the association of 'nature' and 'science' became especially significant in the eighteenth-century Enlightenment, the era of Newtonian science. 'Science' (commonly termed 'natural philosophy' in this period) derives from the Latin *scientia*, understood as knowledge, demonstrated truths and systematically acquired facts, forming a system of knowledge whereby 'nature' is rendered intelligible in terms of causal and systematic 'laws'; scientific explanation established ordered and structured knowledge of natural phenomena, delimiting the meaning and boundaries of 'nature'. This construction of nature as law-like and open to human comprehension (and manipulation) is a marked and indeed seminal feature of the seventeenth-century scientific revolution, a mode of thinking associated initially with Descartes and (especially for the Enlightenment) with Newton.

The notion of 'mechanism' was enlarged from the analogy with clockwork, with cogs, wheels and pulleys (in the discourse of Newtonians, disparaged as a representation of nature), to embrace the conceptual structure of the Newtonian system; and the notion of 'machine' could function as a metaphor for intertwined concepts of order, system and laws of nature. The painting by Joseph Wright of Derby, *A Philosopher Giving That Lecture on the Orrery, in which a Lamp is Put in Place of the Sun* (1766), captures the sense of system, order, law and the divine light permeating the universe, which characterise the culture of science in the eighteenth century. In his exposition of 'The Principles which lead and direct Philosophical Enquiries' (published in 1795), the philosopher and economist Adam Smith declared that 'Philosophy is the science of the connecting principles of nature . . . [and] by representing the invisible chains which bind together all these disjointed objects, endeavours to introduce order into this chaos of jarring and discordant appearances.' He went on to argue that different 'systems of nature' had been adopted at different times and that these 'systems in many respects resemble machines', a system of nature, being a representation of reality, being an 'imaginary machine'.[4]

But a definition of 'nature' broader than its delimitation by scientific explanation was widely current, a definition (more common in wider cultural, rather than philosophical, usage) that contrasted 'nature' with human culture and civilisation, distinguishing the features and products of the earth with the contrivances of mankind. But both the untamed wilderness and the humanised landscape of cultivated fields were commonly perceived as 'nature'. The distinction between these two senses of 'nature' was already current in the writings of classical antiquity. In *De Natura Deorum* (*On the Nature of the Gods*) the Roman philosopher Cicero distinguished two senses of 'nature', between the untamed 'products of the earth' and a 'second nature' contrived by human effort and ingenuity: 'Total dominion over the products of the earth lies in our hands. We put plains and mountains to good use; rivers and lakes belong to us; we sow cereals and plant trees, we irrigate our lands to fertilize them. We fortify river banks, and straighten or divert the courses of rivers. In short, by the work of our hands we strive to create a sort of second nature within the world of nature.'[5] Although Cicero makes a contrast between untamed wilderness and the cultivated, humanised landscape, both are conceived as 'nature'. Cicero's 'second nature', landscape manipulated for human ends, is therefore 'nature' subjected to cultivation, to civilisation and to 'culture'.[6] The Latin *cultura* denotes both the cultivation of the land and crops, the pastoral and agricultural work of farming, and the refinement of the intellect and the development of the artistic aspects of civilisation. In Cicero's and subsequent usage 'nature' incorporates untamed wilderness and the humanised landscape of human habitation – the 'countryside' cultivated, farmed and managed for human needs.

The modern sensibility, craving and creating a (fictitious) 'nature' devoid of history, venerates 'wilderness' as primordial and sacral; but both 'wilderness' and 'countryside', the humanised landscape of fields, copses and woods, are products of history and are framed and entwined by culture. Landscapes seemingly untamed by human agency, the bleak, bare mountains of the Lake District, Yosemite Valley in California valorised as a pristine wilderness by the Scottish-born American naturalist John Muir, were shaped by centuries of human intervention and management: as Wordsworth pointed out in his *Guide Through the District of the Lakes*, 'formerly the whole country must have been covered with wood to a great height up the mountains', the primeval native forests were stripped from the Lakeland hills; and indigenous peoples created the meadow-floor of Yosemite by fire-clearance. This is not to deny that there has been recent human experience of pristine landscapes: some British moorland has been judged wholly natural, though much of it is the result of interactions between human activity and natural processes; and the southern continent of Antarctica is a wholly alien ecosystem devoid of human habitation and indigenous cultures.[7] But 'wilderness', like 'countryside', is a cultural construct, a product of history.[8] While the antithesis between the country and the city has been a familiar trope since the writings of Horace and the younger Pliny, the aesthetic and moral veneration of wilderness, integral to modern sensibility, has its origins in the writings of the Romantics, though the Romantic poets did not confine the perception and valorisation of nature to wilderness.[9] The perception and representation of landscape and 'nature', of wilderness, countryside and city, are entwined with cultural and aesthetic motifs, drawn from centuries of literature and painting. As Simon Schama puts it: 'For although we are accustomed to separate nature and human perception into two realms, they are, in fact, indivisible. Before it can ever be a repose for the senses, landscape is the work of the mind. Its scenery is built up as much from strata of memory as from layers of rock.'[10] Nature and culture are intermingled.

The contrast between wilderness and the cultivated landscape has been fundamental in shaping attitudes to the aesthetics of nature since the Romantics. Writing on *Forest Scenery, and the Woodland Views* in 1791, the exponent of 'picturesque' travel William Gilpin remarked that 'the idea of a wild country, in a natural state, however picturesque, is to the generality of people but an unpleasing one', for 'there are few, who do not prefer the busy scenes of cultivation to the grandest of nature's rough productions'. Reviewing the second edition of Archibald Alison's *Essays on the Nature and Principles of Taste* (1790, 1811) in the *Edinburgh Review*, Francis Jeffrey made a similar comment: 'There is scarcely any one who does not feel and understand the beauty of smiling fields and comfortable cottages; but the beauty of lakes and mountains is not so universally distinguishable.'[11] These opinions seem surprising, even discordant to the modern sensibility; yet Gilpin and Jeffrey were writing at a crucial cultural moment, evoking the new aesthetic of picturesque landscape – an aesthetic that Jeffrey, like Alison, assumed to be accessible only to the leisured and educated classes. When later concluding the first volume of *Modern Painters* (1843), in a passage offering advice to the prospective landscape painter, Ruskin forthrightly expresses the (Romantic) view in valorising untouched pristine wilderness as embodying the 'real works of nature' unconstrained by human agency, 'nature in her liberty . . . the pure wild volition and energy of the creation . . . not subdued to the furrow, and cicatrized to the pollard, not persuaded into proprieties, nor pampered into diseases'. He urges painters to study 'nature in her liberty, not as servant of all work in the hands of the agriculturist, nor stiffened into court-dress by the landscape-gardener'. He contrasts the 'real works of nature' with 'the diseased results of man's interference with her'.[12]

In the third volume of *Modern Painters* (1856), in a chapter on 'classical landscape', Ruskin evokes a different aesthetic. He argues that the veneration of wilderness, of nature sanctified as untouched by human hand – a sensibility central to the Romantic aesthetic of Wordsworth – contrasts with the Homeric view of landscape. Ruskin claims that for Homer pleasant landscapes are gentle and humanised, and cultivated ground, tilled fields and vineyards are beautiful. He writes that 'every Homeric landscape, intended to be beautiful, is composed of a fountain, a meadow, and a shady grove', making reference to the description of Calypso's cave in the fifth book of the *Odyssey*.[13] In Ruskin's reading, the pleasant Homeric landscape is shaped by man and suited to human needs and convenience; the cultivated landscape is regarded as beautiful. 'If we glance through the references to pleasant land-scape which occur in other parts of the *Odyssey*, we shall always be struck by this quiet subjection of their every feature to human service, and by the exces-sive similarity in the scenes. Perhaps the spot intended, after this, to be most perfect, may be the garden of Alcinous, where the principal ideas are, still more definitely, order, symmetry, and fruitfulness'.[14] With its orchards and vines and springs the garden of Alcinous exemplifies order, enclosure and usefulness, a magical and paradisiacal garden in which fruits grow all year round.[15]

Eighteenth-century readers of Alexander Pope's translation, especially those of Pope's frame of mind disposed to exalt the achievements in manners and literature of the 'ancients' over the 'moderns', considered that the aim of epic poetry was to instruct. For Pope the *Odyssey* was a moral and political work, providing an exemplary account of the universal values regulating civil and domestic life; this work above all portrayed the 'amiable' values of clas-sical civilisation, 'the landscapes of nature, the pleasures of private life, the duties of every station, the hospitality of ancient times'.[16] Homer's portrayal of the cave of Calypso and garden of Alcinous were, for this sensibility, evocative representations of perfected, cultivated nature, images suffused with meaning and value and made emblematic in the landscape paintings of Claude Lorrain. Quoting Pope's translation, Horace Walpole wondered whether there was any 'admirer of Homer who can read his description [of the garden of Alcinous] without rapture'.[17]

The modern sensibility, by contrast, delights in wilderness and the inhos-pitable, nature devoid of human cultivation and order, Walpole's 'precipices, mountains, torrents, wolves, rumblings', 'the lofty characters in which Nature here speaks to the heart and the imagination' as Jeffrey more portentously put it.[18] The Romantic sensibility to unvanquished nature has its origins in the aesthetics of 'sublime' terror and awe; the doctrine that 'terror is in all cases . . . the ruling principle of the sublime' received its classic statement in Edmund Burke's *Philosophical Enquiry into the Origin of Our Ideas of the Sublime and Beautiful* (1757).[19] In 'sublime' landscapes, as in the rocky mountain landscapes captured in the paintings of Salvator Rosa, the dramatic force of inhospitable nature is not subdued by human control and evokes horror and awe. Discourses about 'nature' in eighteenth-century Britain were shaped by discussion of aesthetic categories, debates about beauty, the sublime and the picturesque landscape where landscape was viewed in terms of the norms and practices of painters. Central to these discussions was concern with the new aristocratic taste for landscape parks, and the relation between the ordering of landscape gardens and the craft of the painter. Here cultivated nature, Cicero's 'second nature', Ruskin's 'servant of all work in the hands of the agriculturist', was subjected to further human control and contrivance – 'stiffened into court dress by the landscape-gardener', as Ruskin put it. Landscape parks reshaped the relations between untamed wilderness and uncultivated nature, and the aesthetic of cultivation rooted in classical and biblical sources. In glorifying this aesthetics of nature, Horace Walpole argued that nature was thereby drawn into the garden: 'Thus dealing in none but the colours of nature, and catching its most favourable features, men saw a new creation opening before their eyes. The living landscape was chastened or polished, not transformed.'[20]

In contrast to Ruskin, in his *Essays on the Nature and Principles of Taste* (1790) Archibald Alison found the productions of gardening superior to the 'original scenes in nature' because of the power of the gardener 'to remove from his landscape whatever is hostile to its effect'. Alison finds greater aesthetic merit in nature as shaped, tamed and contrived by human hand, as refined through the power of human control and imagination, over 'the scenes of Nature itself'. The art of composition in landscape painting possessed even greater aesthetic advantage: 'In gardening, the materials of the scene are few, and these few unwieldy. . . the scanty and intractable materials of Nature. In a landscape . . . the whole range of scenery is before the eye of the painter. He may . . . unite into one expression, the scattered features with which Nature has feebly marked . . . to improve the expression of real scenery.'[21] 'Nature' is here judged as aesthetically inferior to its depiction in a painting, as providing elements that may be contrived and aesthetically transformed in a work of art. By contrast, lecturing at the Royal Institution in 1836 and echoing the Romantic aesthetic of William Wordsworth, John Constable rejected the aesthetics of nature according to which 'pictures were over-valued . . . as ideal things, and almost as standards by which nature is to be judged rather than the reverse'.[22]

Scientific language about nature incorporated these modes of thought, utilising motifs of art, design, order and system, in a culture where science
provided public spectacle and entertainments, and where analogies were
constantly drawn between human artefacts and God's creative power. These
associations were made in a formative treatise of eighteenth-century
aesthetics, Francis Hutcheson's *Inquiry into the Original of our Ideas of Beauty
and Virtue* (1725), which utilised discourses of aesthetics and Newtonian
natural philosophy, grounding both in the language of natural theology.
Hutcheson maintains that our sense of the beauty of the works of nature
arises from the 'intention of the Author of Nature'. Our senses have been so
constituted that we find beauty in the 'uniformity, proportion and similitude'
of nature: 'the Great Architect' has adorned 'this vast theatre in a manner
agreeable to the spectators'. Hutcheson sees the harmony, beauty and system
of nature as a mechanism of dynamic conservation, of interacting powers of
heat and gravity. He writes that heat from the sun is the cause of rain, rivers,
winds and vegetation, while gravity preserves the planets in their orbits and
gives cohesion and stability to the earth, and is the cause of tides and rivers;
gravity and heat maintain the circulation of vapours in rain. The mechanism
of nature, secured by the interaction of gravity and the principle of heat,
evidences both 'Wisdom [and] a Sense of Beauty . . . in the administration of
nature'.[23] The order and beauty apparent in nature have their basis in divine
intention and are linked through design. Natural philosophy and aesthetics
are integrated in the language of natural theology. In a seminal text *The
Pleasures of Imagination* (1744) Mark Akenside argued that the 'Powers of
Imagination' intermediate between the bodily senses, and moral perceptions
shape knowledge of nature and aesthetic judgments. He cites Xenophon's
recollection that Socrates had advanced the view that 'the same object is
accounted both beautiful and good, insomuch as it answers the purposes for
which it was designed'; and notes that Hutcheson had shown that this
doctrine that 'truth and good are one . . . holds in the general laws of nature,
in the works of art, and the conduct of the sciences'.[24] Aesthetic judgements,
the powers of imagination, join works of art with works of nature. In his
exposition of 'The Principles which lead and direct Philosophical Enquiries'
(published in 1795), Adam Smith argued that in endeavouring to introduce
order into the 'chaos of jarring and discordant appearances . . . Philosophy
[science] may be regarded as one of those arts which address themselves to the
imagination'.[25] The endeavour to establish principles of uniformity, order and
system is an exercise of the powers of imagination.

Hutcheson's integration of science and aesthetics through natural theology
provides a basis for understanding the urge for system, order and design that
drove eighteenth-century natural philosophy. The world-picture expounded
by James Hutton in his *Dissertations on Different Subjects in Natural Philosophy*

(1792) exemplifies these themes. Drawing upon a rich tradition of natural philosophy and chemistry, he conceives the natural order as a system of processes and transformations manifesting cycles. He supposes an interaction between ordinary or gravitational matter acting by the principle of attraction, and the matter of light and heat emanating from the sun, which acts by the principle of repulsion: these two 'opposite powers are continually balancing one another, or alternately prevailing'. The material world is regenerated and conserved by 'the emanation of matter from the sun'; this emission is 'a necessary cause of vital motion', without which 'this world would remain an useless mass of inert matter'. Vitalised matter is destroyed when bodies burn but is regenerated in plants: there 'would appear to be in the system of this globe, a reproductive power, by which the constitution of this world, necessarily decaying, is renewed'. Hutton uses Hutcheson's imagery of circulation and conservation: the natural order is conceived as an aesthetic and harmonious unity, dynamically active through circulating powers, its operation maintained by chemical and biological processes of consumption and regeneration, continually conserved and renewed. As with Hutcheson, creative order, unity and divine wisdom are emphasised in the balance of powers: there is a 'certain systematic order' in the 'wise economy of nature'. Hutton declares that this order is shaped by 'means properly adapted to the end', showing that 'in every law of nature there is system or design'; he concludes that the system of nature demonstrates 'wisdom' and 'purpose'. The language of natural theology, of order and design in nature, joins the discourses of aesthetics and natural philosophy. In his *Investigation of the Principles of Knowledge* (1794) Hutton remarked that because beauty is 'founded in truth and established in nature . . . its basis is fixed in the nature of things', in 'order' and 'regularity'; thus the study of nature 'opens the taste of man for beauty', the 'beauty of order'.[26]

The roots of the eighteenth-century aesthetics of nature lie in biblical imagery and classical literature. The Garden of Eden in Genesis is termed 'paradise' in the King James Bible (1611): the word *paradeisos* is derived from the Persian and entered the Greek language to mean park, enclosure or pleasure ground, and was used in the Septuagint (the Greek translation of the Hebrew Bible) for Adam and Eve's home in Eden, a pristine state of perfection, a garden planted by God. The biblical Garden of Eden came to be blended with the classical myth of the golden age, the imagined period in early human history marked by the spontaneous supply of food when humanity lived a life of ease, a myth first found in Hesiod's *Works and Days* and especially familiar to Renaissance scholars from the account in the first book of Ovid's *Metamorphoses*. The myth of the golden age of plenty, the biblical notion of a paradisiacal garden, the garden of Alcinous described in the seventh book of the *Odyssey*, blended in forming the medieval *hortus conclusus* (closed garden) enclosed by hedges or walls: the enclosed garden came to be identified with the earthly paradise. The pastoral tradition, inspired by Virgil's *Eclogues* (which became an important literary trope in the Renaissance) along with the *Georgics,* Virgil's poem praising farming and rural life, shaped conceptions of nature. The *laus Italiae* (praise of Italy) in Virgil's *Georgics* celebrates a cultivated landscape, one becoming familiar to the eighteenth-century aristocracy through the Grand Tour that culminated in Rome. In numerous passages in the *Georgics* Virgil recoils from the harsh and destructive powers of flood, famine and earthquake. The farmer is shown as pitted against pests, and Virgil fears unvanquished nature lying beyond the power of human understanding and the control of nature exerted by agriculture. He associates the fecundity of the cultivated land of Italy, its crops, herds, wine and olives, with the golden age of plenty and perpetual spring: '*hic ver adsiduum atque alienis mensibus aestas*' ('here are constant spring and summer in months that are not its own'). Virgil celebrates the civilising work of man: moral virtue, national identity, the historical links of land and people, the essential constancy of rural life, the patriotic associations of land and habitation.[27] In a celebrated passage in the second Georgic he applauds rational, philosophical understanding of nature: '*felix qui potuit rerum cognoscere causas*' ('happy he who has been able to discover the causes of things'), a line often quoted in the eighteenth century. He goes on to contrast scientific knowledge of nature with the traditional values of the countryside: '*fortunatus et ille deos qui novit agrestis*' ('fortunate too he who has known the country gods'); but the values of the philosopher and the farmer, while juxtaposed, are seen as complementary.[28] In John Dryden's 1697 translation of the *Georgics,* which he described as 'the best Poem of the best Poet', a text regularly quoted in the eighteenth century, the passage is rendered:

> Happy the Man, who, studying Nature's Laws,
> Thro' known Effects can trace the secret Cause:
> His Mind possessing, in a quiet state,
> Fearless of Fortune, and resign'd to Fate.
> And happy too is he, who decks the Bow'rs
> Of Sylvans, and adores the Rural Pow'rs . . ..[29]

In his introductory essay to Dryden's translation Joseph Addison commented that the agricultural poetry of the *Georgics* 'addresses it self wholly to the Imagination', and he considered its subject matter, '*some part of the Science of Husbandry put into a pleasing Dress*', where 'the dryest of its Precepts look like a Description'.[30] The laws of nature could be traced in shaping the economy of the agricultural landscape, in celebrating the rural virtues of the farmer. The promotion of agricultural improvement through the application of natural philosophy had Virgilian sanction; and in a modern context this implied the association of the world view of the scientific revolution with agricultural and technological improvement, a theme promoted by Francis Bacon and pursued in the agricultural revolution in the eighteenth and nineteenth centuries.

The most striking example of the natural world as aestheticised in natural philosophy is in the scientific poems of Erasmus Darwin, directly modelled on Lucretius' didactic poem *De Rerum Natura* (*On the Nature of Things*). Darwin followed conventional poetic norms in making his poem dense with allusions to the myths and literature of classical antiquity; but he deployed ancient myths to provide poetic expression for his scientific ideas. In *The Economy of Vegetation* (1791) he discusses the renewal and regeneration in nature in 'the destruction and resuscitation' of plants, suggesting that the mythical 'story of the phoenix' is the 'antient hieroglyphic emblem' of this process. In the *Temple of Nature* (1803) he again personifies nature as a goddess, and he locates natural philosophy within the Virgilian didactic aesthetic by echoing the *Georgics*:

> Blest is the Sage, who learn'd in Nature's laws
> With nice distinction marks effect and cause;
> Who views the insatiate grave with eye sedate,
> Nor fears thy voice, inexorable Fate![31]

In Erasmus Darwin's writings the natural world is conceived aesthetically, as a harmonious and systematic unity.

In eighteenth-century Britain the pursuit of rational knowledge through natural philosophy (science, the search for the causes of things), and the cultivation of rural virtues through management of pasture, agriculture and forest, were not seen as discordant but as complementary elements of a common culture. The expulsion of Adam and Eve from the paradisiacal garden into a wilderness that must be tamed by human effort, and Virgil's association of the cultivated landscape of Italy, linked the control and cultivation of landscape and the taming of the wilderness with the early period of human society, the loss of biblical Eden and the passing of the Hesiodic golden age. Writing in the early years of the seventeenth century, Francis Bacon emphasised ancient achievements in rhetoric, poetry and history as fundamental to public virtue. He called for a study of nature liberated from ancient authority, an experimental philosophy to be prosecuted in terms of theological obligation, which would restore mankind to the knowledge and power over nature that had been lost at the Fall. Bacon presented his ideas in the idioms of classical culture, following tradition in suggesting that the ancient poets had concealed truths in fables. In *De Sapientia Veterum* (*The Wisdom of the Ancients*) of 1609 he expounded his view of nature by tracing the allegorical meaning of classical myths. In 'Pan' (*Pan sive natura*) the god is interpreted as representing the universal frame of nature, his sterility a representation of the self-sufficiency of nature; and the myth of Cupid (*Cupido sive atomus*) is used as an allegory of atomism, the god's nakedness signifying the simplicity of atoms and his arrows the capacity of atoms to act at a distance.[32]

In the late seventeenth century the traditional social order based on land-ownership and aristocratic patronage began to give way to institutions of a commercial and centralised society. There was a shift from power based on landed property to an urbanised world driven by the financial power of the commercial classes. Literary and artistic production moved from court patronage to the new cultural community shaped by commerce. This commercial society was in part the result of technological innovations; contemporary rhetoric associated technology (based on the new science of the seventeenth century) with financial speculation. The arts – literature, painting and music – were part of the cultural values of this new commercial and consumer society, which also fostered cultivation of the aesthetic pleasures of landscape parks and the natural world. The countryside, through the enclosure of land, was brought ever more systematically under agricultural control; landscape became moulded to human convenience, the scenes of nature being transformed and polished in landscape gardens. The construal of 'nature' in terms of aesthetic categories and the glorification of cultivated rural life were responses to the rise of refined urban society; the commercial class incorporated and transformed the values and social mores of the traditional aristocratic elite.[33] Technological control was an important element in the new commercial society, where landscapes were shaped to human ends. In *Gulliver's Travels* (1726) Jonathan Swift polemically argues for the antithesis between science and traditional cultural forms: the culture of science, which he associates with the values of the 'moderns', involved theory, methods, principles and procedures at variance with the traditional techniques and cultural norms of the 'ancients'. He portrays traditional arts, techniques and knowledge as effective because they are consonant with nature's actual inherent processes, to be contrasted with the presumption and ineffectiveness of the abstract and theoretical pretensions of the new science. Swift constructs a nostalgic ideology where 'science' is opposed to 'nature'; 'nature' is interpreted as the embodiment of pristine reality, an analogue of unchanging cultural and religious values.

In the eighteenth century these traditional views were displaced. Science came to be seen as expressing the philosophical counterpart to the ordered nature of the countryside and landscape garden. And science and the culture of nature could be interpreted through the medium of classical culture as well as through the values of modernity: 'happy he who has been able to discover the causes of things. . . fortunate too he who has known the country gods'. The understanding of nature was expressed in terms of order, contrivance and design, and science received philosophical justification by natural theology: nature evidenced order, and the laws of nature were viewed as manifestations of God's design of this natural order. This characteristic theme is struck by James Hutton in concluding his *Dissertations* on natural philosophy: 'It is thus from matter of fact, or strict physical truths, that we have reasoned for the purpose of investigating the wise economy of nature, which it is the business of philosophy to understand . . . we have been led, in examining nature, to perceive a certain systematic order in the course of physical events. We have then considered this order as being probably the design of nature; and that this design had been conceived in wisdom, so far as those means are properly adapted to the ends, which are the objects of our knowledge.'[34]

But by the turn of the nineteenth century Horace Walpole's confident view that the 'living landscape was chastened or polished, not transformed' in the landscape garden no longer commanded general assent: the landscape garden came to be seen as 'stiffened into court dress', as Ruskin later put it, where 'nature' came to be seen as transformed, even violated rather than polished. As the epigraph to his volumes of *Modern Painters*, Ruskin printed a passage equating the 'Divinity' of 'Nature' with 'Truth' from Wordsworth's *The Excursion* (1814). In Wordsworth's Romantic aesthetic the construal of the natural world as analogous to a work of art, to be comprehended by categories derived from the language of painting, yielded to a new aesthetic: the assertion of the primacy of nature as immeasurable and unfettered by the forms of human representation. In Book VIII of the 1805 *Prelude* Wordsworth writes of the 'sanctity of Nature given to man', and in 'Tintern Abbey' (1798) he portrays nature as 'the anchor of my purest thoughts, the nurse . . . of all my moral being'. The Lake Poets Wordsworth and Coleridge conceive nature as primordial and blessed. Walking in Borrowdale in the Lake District in October 1803, Coleridge recorded a passionate, indeed religious response to the power of nature's immediacy: 'I worshipped with deep feeling the grand outline & perpetual Forms, that are the guardians of Borrodale, & the presiding Majesty, yea, the very Soul of Keswick – the Birches were in all their Pride of gold & orange'. On the view of Skiddaw and Derwentwater from Ashness Bridge, Coleridge exclaimed 'O what is there on Earth that can better deserve the name of Divine?'[35] The magnitude and mystery of creation is seen as the source of the aesthetic and moral senses. From the time of the Romantics the immediacy of nature was seen as transcending artificial aesthetic categories and human aims, convenience and material advantage. The Romantics transferred the vision of nature's immediacy to a theory of art as rooted in the contemplation of nature as a living totality; nature was conceived as dynamically evolving, the source of spiritual and artistic illumination, to be contrasted with the artificial productions of human civilisation.

This shift in aesthetic sensibility bore on the interaction of aesthetics and natural philosophy secured by natural theology. The accommodation between the aesthetics of nature and the language of design of natural theology, developed during the eighteenth century, was dissolved; and after 1800 scientific theorising looked askance at the unifying pretensions of speculative systems such as Hutton's, grounded on natural theology and aesthetic unity. In 1797 the *Encyclopaedia Britannica* stated the object of natural philosophy to be 'speculative truth'.[36] The creation of speculative scientific systems such as that of James Hutton, which utilised the aesthetic language of natural theology in appealing to principles of harmony, order, design and beauty in nature, was in consonance with the established practice of natural philosophy. But the re-ordering of the sciences into new and specialised discourses early in the nineteenth century, and the faltering grip of natural theology, led to a repudiation of speculative systems of natural philosophy. By the 1830s the generic natural philosophy and natural history were in the process of being transformed into recognisably modern forms, construed in terms of the pursuit of specialised disciplines, from astronomy to zoology. Each had its distinct boundaries, subject matter, conceptual structure and techniques of investigation, which were pursued by specialised practitioners who increasingly became seen as a clerisy of scientific professionals.[37] In the 1830s the *Bridgewater Treatises* were commissioned to present a wide range of scientific information 'considered with reference to natural theology', and the texts were successful in communicating current scientific knowledge to a wider public in an accurate and intelligible form. The treatises divided the sciences into specialised fields – astronomy and physics, geology and mineralogy, chemistry and meteorology – and the authors had expertise in these disciplines. The tenor of argument tended to mute the (familiar) arguments of natural theology; design was illustrated rather than demonstrated, subordinated to the exposition of authoritative scientific surveys; natural theology established the norms of cultural orthodoxy within which science could be communicated to the public. The *Bridgewater Treatises* show a distinct loss of conviction in the demonstrative power of natural theology, suggesting a shift in intellectual authority.

The challenge of the new science of Boyle and Newton to traditional religious values had been mitigated by interpreting natural philosophy through the rhetoric and culture of natural theology: nature was portrayed as beautiful and systematically ordered. The claims of science were ameliorated as nature was interpreted and presented through the language of design and the aesthetics of nature. But the Romantic theory of art, rooted in the contemplation of the natural world as a living totality, led to the development of 'naturalism' in aesthetics. The primacy of nature as unfettered by forms of human representation, transcending artificial aesthetic categories, led to a shift from the language of nature as a created and designed artefact. The unifying grip of natural theology weakened; the apologetic arguments of natural theology became increasingly vapid intellectual structures for the safe packaging and communication of scientific ideas, even exercises in self-conviction. In painting John Constable sought 'naturalism': in *Wivenhoe Park, Essex* (1816), he painted a real view in its transient light and shade rather than an idealised landscape, painting studies of clouds and skies whose aim was naturalistic realism. In science Charles Lyell created a framework of *Principles of Geology* (1830–33), which aimed to establish the 'true causes' of geological processes and to sever geology from reference to scripture: appeal to natural theology was avoided as an irrelevance, a distortion of the aims and methods of natural philosophy, of proper scientific practice. Lyell's style of presentation and mode of argument was to prove especially influential in shaping the outlook of Charles Darwin's *Origin of Species*. As Darwin explained to Asa Gray in May 1863, his main concern was to defend the naturalistic explanation of the origin and descent of species through successive modifications: 'Natural Selection ... seems to me utterly unimportant compared to [the] question of *Creation* **or** *Modification*.'[38]

✳

Notes

Chapter 1 Themes and Contexts

1. Eric Shanes, *Turner's Picturesque Views in England and Wales 1825–1838* (London, 1979), p. 24 and plate 3; Elizabeth K. Helsinger, *Rural Scenes and National Representation: Britain, 1815–1850* (Princeton, NJ, 1997), pp. 162–74.
2. Hugh Prince, 'Art and agrarian change, 1710–1815', in *The Iconography of Landscape: Essays on the Symbolic Representation, Design and Use of Past Environments*, ed. Denis Cosgrove and Stephen Daniels (Cambridge, 1988), pp. 98–118; John Barrell, *The Dark Side of the Landscape: The Rural Poor in English Painting 1730–1840* (Cambridge, 1980).
3. *The Oxford Companion to J.M.W. Turner*, ed. Evelyn Joll, Martin Butlin and Luke Herrmann (Oxford, 2001), p. 254.
4. Simon Schama, *Landscape and Memory* (London, 1995), pp. 6–7; Roy Porter, '"In England's green and pleasant land": the English enlightenment and the environment', in *Culture, Landscape and the Environment: the Linacre Lectures 1997*, ed. Kate Flint and Howard Morphy (Oxford, 2000), pp. 15–43.
5. Jonathan Topham, 'Science and popular education in the 1830s: the role of the *Bridgewater Treatises*', *The British Journal for the History of Science*, 25 (1992), 397–430.
6. Here and elsewhere I have drawn on my essay 'The scientific revolutions', in *The New Cambridge Modern History. XIII: Companion Volume*, ed. Peter Burke (Cambridge, 1979), pp. 248–70.
7. William Whewell, *The Philosophy of the Inductive Sciences, Founded upon their History*, 2 vols (London, 1840), vol. 1, p. lxxi.
8. John Brewer, *The Pleasures of the Imagination: English Culture in the Eighteenth Century* (London, 1997), pp. 615–61.
9. William Wordsworth, *The Excursion*, Book VIII, lines 129–30, in *The Poetical Works of William Wordsworth*, ed. Ernest de Selincourt and Helen Darbishire, 5 vols (Oxford, 1940–9), vol. 5.
10. Francis Jeffrey in *Edinburgh Review*, 18 (May 1811), 1–46, on p. 15.
11. *The Works of John Ruskin*, Library Edition, ed. E.T. Cook and Alexander Wedderburn, 39 vols (London, 1903–12), vol. 3, p. 627n.
12. Keith Thomas, *Man and the Natural World: Changing Attitudes in England 1500–1800* (London, 1983), pp. 257–63.
13. W.G. Hoskins, *The Making of the English Landscape*, new edn (London, 1977), pp. 138–40.
14. Quoted in Roy Porter, *Enlightenment: Britain and the Creation of the Modern World* (London, 2000), p. 308; and in Mark Overton, *Agricultural Revolution in England: The Transformation of the Agrarian Economy 1500–1850* (Cambridge, 1996), p. 1.
15. Mauro Ambrosoli, *The Wild and the Sown: Botany and Agriculture in Western Europe: 1350–1850*, trans. Mary McCann Salvatorelli (Cambridge, 1997), pp. 337–94.
16. Overton, *Agricultural Revolution in England*, pp. 133–92.

17. Quoted in Porter, *Enlightenment*, pp. 309, 566.
18. E.J. Hobsbawm and George Rudé, *Captain Swing* (Harmondsworth, 1973).
19. Prince, 'Art and agrarian change, 1710–1815', in *The Iconography of Landscape*, ed. Cosgrove and Daniels, pp. 98–118.
20. David S. Landes, *The Unbound Prometheus: Technological Change and Industrial Development in Western Europe from 1750 to the Present* (Cambridge, 1969), esp. p. 1.
21. Peter Mathias, 'Who unbound Prometheus? Science and technical change, 1600–1800', in Mathias, ed., *Science and Society 1600–1900* (Cambridge, 1972), pp. 54–80.
22. A.E. Musson and Eric Robinson, *Science and Technology in the Industrial Revolution* (Manchester, 1969).
23. Arnold Thackray, 'Natural knowledge in a cultural context: the Manchester model', *American Historical Review*, 79 (1974), 672–709.
24. Jeffrey A. Auerbach, *The Great Exhibition of 1851: A Nation on Display* (New Haven, CT/London, 1999).
25. James Winter, *Secure from Rash Assault: Sustaining the Victorian Environment* (Berkeley, CA/Los Angeles/London, 1999); Michael Freeman, *Railways and the Victorian Imagination* (New Haven, CT/London, 1999).
26. Walter Benjamin, *Selected Writings. Volume 1: 1913–1926*, ed. Marcus Bullock and Michael W. Jennings (Cambridge, Mass./London, 1996), p. 487.
27. Thomas Carlyle, 'Signs of the times', *Edinburgh Review*, 49 (1829): 438–59.
28. 'Sonnet on the projected Kendal and Windermere Railway', in *The Prose Works of William Wordsworth*, ed. W.J.B. Owen and Jane Worthington Smyser, 3 vols (Oxford, 1974), vol. 3, p. 339.
29. *The Works of John Ruskin*, vol. 4, pp. 36–7; vol. 36, p. 62; Freeman, *Railways and the Victorian Imagination*, p. 53.
30. Michael Freeman, *Victorians and the Prehistoric: Tracks to a Lost World* (New Haven, CT/London, 2004).
31. *The Correspondence of Charles Darwin*, ed. Frederick Burckhardt, Sydney Smith *et al.* (Cambridge, 1985–), vol. 3, p. 224.
32. Freeman, *Railways and the Victorian Imagination*, pp. 225–7.
33. Joseph M. Levine, *The Battle of the Books: History and Literature in the Augustan Age* (Ithaca, NY/London, 1991), pp. 13–84.
34. 'On False Criticks' [in the *Guardian*, no. 12 (25 March 1713)], in *The Prose Works of Alexander Pope. Vol. I. The Earlier Works, 1711–1720*, ed. Norman Ault (Oxford, 1936), p. 90.
35. *A Tale of a Tub* [5th edn, 1710] in Jonathan Swift, *Gulliver's Travels and Selected Writings in Prose & Verse*, ed. John Hayward (London, 1949), pp. 318–20, 330n.
36. Charles Webster, *The Great Instauration: Science, Medicine and Reform 1626–1660* (London, 1975).
37. Quoted in Larry Stewart, *The Rise of Public Science: Rhetoric, Technology and Natural Philosophy in Newtonian Britain, 1660–1750* (Cambridge, 1992), pp. xxv, 346.
38. Quoted in Isaac Kramnick, *Bolingbroke and His Circle: The Politics of Nostalgia in the Age of Walpole* (Cambridge, MA/London, 1968), pp. 69, 209.
39. Swift, *Gulliver's Travels*, pp. 43, 45, 55, 128.
40. Dennis Todd, 'Laputa, the whore of Babylon, and the idols of science', *Studies in Philology*, 75 (1978): 93–120.
41. Marjorie Nicolson and Nora M. Mohler, 'The scientific background to Swift's *Voyage to Laputa*', *Annals of Science*, 2 (1937): 299–334, in Marjorie Nicolson, *Science and Imagination* (Ithaca, NY, 1956), pp. 110–54.
42. Swift, *Gulliver's Travels*, pp. 172–5.
43. Claude Rawson, *God, Gulliver and Genocide: Barbarism and the European Imagination, 1492–1945* (Oxford, 2001), pp. 2–3.

Chapter 2   Design

1. Alison Smith, catalogue entry in *Pre-Raphaelite Vision: Truth to Nature*, ed. Allen Staley and Christopher Newall, exh. cat., Tate Gallery (London, 2004), pp. 188–9.

2. Marcia Pointon, 'Geology and landscape painting in nineteenth-century England', in *Images of the Earth: Essays in the History of the Environmental Sciences*, ed. Ludmilla Jordanova and Roy Porter, 2nd edn (n.p.,The British Society for the History of Science 1997), pp. 93–123, esp. p. 119.

3. Rebecca Stott, 'Darwin's barnacles: mid-century Victorian natural history and the marine grotesque', in *Transactions and Encounters: Science and Culture in the Nineteenth Century*, ed. Roger Luckhurst and Josephine McDonagh (Manchester/New York, 2002), pp. 151–81.

4. Jonathan Smith, *Charles Darwin and Victorian Visual Culture* (Cambridge, 2006), pp. 44–91, esp. p. 75.

5. *The Leibniz–Clarke Correspondence*, ed. H.G. Alexander (Manchester, 1956), pp. 11, 14, 18, 30, 53.

6. On these and other issues in natural theology see John Hedley Brooke, *Science and Religion: Some Historical Perspectives* (Cambridge, 1991), pp. 117–89.

7. Robert Boyle, *Works*, ed. T. Birch, 5 vols (London, 1744), vol. 4, pp. 367, 372, 400; vol. 5, p. 46; J.E. McGuire, 'Boyle's conception of nature', *Journal of the History of Ideas*, 33 (1972), 523–42.

8. William Whiston, *Astronomical Principles of Religion, Natural and Reveal'd* (London, 1717), pp. 45–6.

9. *Four Letters from Sir Isaac Newton to Doctor Bentley. Containing Some Arguments in Proof of a DEITY* (London, 1756), pp. 25–6, in *Isaac Newton's Papers & Letters on Natural Philosophy*, ed. I. Bernard Cohen (Cambridge, 1958), pp. 302–3.

10. David Hume, *Enquiries Concerning the Human Understanding and Concerning the Principles of Morals*, ed. L.A. Selby-Bigge, 2nd edn (Oxford, 1902), pp. 127, 131, 144–6 (thus titled in 1756).

11. David Hume, *Dialogues Concerning Natural Religion*, ed. Henry D. Aiken (New York/London, 1969), pp. 47, 53–4, 62, 87n, 94.

12. Thomas Chalmers, *Of the Power, Wisdom and Goodness of God as Manifested in the Adaptation of External Nature to the Moral and Intellectual Constitution of Man*, 2 vols (London, 1833), vol. 2, p. 297.

13. Quoted in Asa Briggs, *England in the Age of Improvement*, revised edn, The Folio Society (London, 1999), p. 82.

14. William Paley, *Natural Theology: or, Evidences of the Existence and Attributes of the Deity, Collected from the Appearances of Nature* (London, 1802), pp. 1, 19, 29, 83, 361, 473, 482, 488.

15. *Coleridge's Notebooks: A Selection*, ed. Seamus Perry (Oxford, 2002), p. 2; and see p. 139.

16. Paley, *Natural Theology*, pp. 539ff.

17. *Coleridge's Notebooks*, pp. 44–5.

18. Letter of Coleridge to Thomas Allsop, July 1820, in *The Collected Letters of Samuel Taylor Coleridge*, ed. Earl Leslie Griggs, 6 vols. (Oxford, 1956–71), vol. 1, p. 95.

19. Quoted in the editors' introduction to *Romanticism and the Sciences*, ed. A. Cunningham and N. Jardine (Cambridge, 1990), p. 4.

20. *The Works of John Ruskin*, Library Edition, ed. E.T. Cook and Alexander Wedderburn, 39 vols (London, 1903–12), vol. 25, p. 263. Ruskin cites Darwin's *Descent of Man*, part ii, chap. xiv.

21. Quoted in the introduction to *Romanticism and the Sciences*, p. 4.

22. *The Notebooks of Samuel Taylor Coleridge. Volume 4, 1819–1826*, ed. Kathleen Coburn and Merton Christensen (London, 1990), no. 4,948.

23. Erasmus Darwin, *The Temple of Nature; or, The Origin of Society: A Poem, with Philosophical Notes* (London, 1803), p. 134 (Canto IV, line 66).

24. Brooke, *Science and Religion*, pp. 192–225.
25. William Buckland, *Vindiciae Geologicae* (Oxford, 1820), p. 23.
26. Jonathan Topham, 'Science and popular education in the 1830s: the role of the *Bridgewater Treatises*', *The British Journal for the History of Science*, 25 (1992): 397–430; Topham, 'Beyond the "common context": the production and reading of the *Bridgewater Treatises*', *Isis*, 89 (1998), 233–62.
27. [William Cooke Taylor,] '*Bridgewater Treatises*', *Athenaeum* (1833), no. 282, p. 184; quoted in Topham, 'Science and popular education in the 1830s: the role of the *Bridgewater Treatises*', p. 404.
28. Chalmers, *Moral and Intellectual Constitution of Man*, vol. 2, pp. 289–91.
29. William Kirby, *On the Power, Wisdom and Goodness of God as Manifested in the Creation of Animals and in their History, Habits and Instincts*, 2 vols (London, 1835), vol. 2, p. 526.
30. William Prout, *Chemistry, Meteorology and the Function of Digestion Considered with Reference to Natural Theology*, 2nd edn (London, 1834), pp. 23, 169.
31. William Buckland, *Geology and Mineralogy considered with reference to Natural Theology*, 2 vols (London, 1836), vol. 1, pp. 19, 21, 28, 581, 584, 596.
32. William Whewell, *Astronomy and General Physics Considered with Reference to Natural Theology* (London, 1833), pp. 3, 9, 11, 19–21, 253, 344.
33. Dugald Stewart, *Philosophical Essays*, 3rd edn (Edinburgh, 1818), p. 284.
34. Archibald Alison, *Essays on the Nature and Principles of Taste* (Edinburgh, 1790), pp. 62–3.
35. *The Works of the Right Honourable Joseph Addison, Esq; In Four Volumes* [ed. Thomas Tickell] (London, 1721), vol. 3, pp. 487, 489, 492, 495, 514–15.
36. *The Prose Works of Alexander Pope. Vol. II: The Major Works, 1725–1744*, ed. Rosemary Couler (Oxford, 1986), pp. 186, 191.
37. Francis Hutcheson, *An Inquiry into the Original of our Ideas of Beauty and Virtue*, 2nd edn (London, 1726), pp. 17, 44–6, 69, 92, 103, 105.
38. George Turnbull, *A Treatise on Ancient Painting, containing Observations on the Rise, Progress, and Decline of that Art amongst the Greeks and the Romans* (London, 1740), pp. 130–47.
39. Edmund Burke, *A Philosophical Enquiry into the Origin of Our Ideas of the Sublime and Beautiful*, 2nd edn (1759), ed. J.T. Boulton (London, 1958), pp. 1, 58, 64–6, 72, 78, 82, 112, 124.
40. Richard Payne Knight, *An Analytical Inquiry into the Principles of Taste*, 4th edn (London, 1808), pp. 146–53, 196.
41. Alison, *Essays on the Nature and Principles of Taste*, pp. 25, 88, 91, 215, 217, 240, 269, 305–8, 320, 322, 331, 410–11.
42. Stewart, *Philosophical Essays*, pp. 262, 274, 279, 284, 313, 317, 324–6, 342–3.
43. Stewart, *Philosophical Essays*, pp. 376–8, 394, 396, 400–2, 419, 432, 440.
44. *Coleridge's Notebooks*, pp. 33, 34, 40, 57, 61.
45. Quoted in Raimonda Modiano, *Coleridge and the Concept of Nature* (Tallahassee, FL, 1985), pp. 118, 126.
46. *Charles Darwin's Beagle Diary*, ed. R.D. Keynes (Cambridge, 1988), p. 444.
47. *The Correspondence of Charles Darwin*, ed. Frederick Burckhardt and Sydney Smith et al. (Cambridge, 1985–), vol. 7, p. 388.

Chapter 3   Exploration

1. Al. de Humboldt and A. Bonpland, rédigé par Al. de Humboldt, *Essai sur la Géographie des Plantes, accompagné d'un Tableau Physique des Régions Équinoxiales* (Paris, 1807), frontispiece.
2. Janet Browne, *The Secular Ark: Studies in the History of Biogeography* (New Haven, CT/London, 1983).

3. Robert J. Richards, *The Romantic Conception of Life: Science and Philosophy in the Age of Goethe* (Chicago/London, 2002), pp. 522–6.

4. *Charles Darwin's Beagle Diary*, ed. R.D. Keynes (Cambridge, 1988), p. 42.

5. Margarita Bowen, *Empiricism and Geographical Thought: From Francis Bacon to Alexander von Humboldt* (Cambridge, 1981).

6. David Armitage, *The Ideological Origins of the British Empire* (Cambridge, 2000).

7. Quoted in Glyndwr Williams, 'The Pacific: exploration and exploitation', in *The Oxford History of the British Empire. Volume II. The Eighteenth Century*, ed. P.J. Marshall (Oxford, 1998), pp. 552–75, on p. 558; Rob Iliffe, 'Science and voyages of discovery', in *The Cambridge History of Science. Volume 4. Eighteenth-Century Science*, ed. Roy Porter (Cambridge, 2003), pp. 618–45.

8. Lisbet Koerner, *Linnaeus: Nature and Nation* (Cambridge, MA/London, 1999), p. 155.

9. Quoted in John Gascoigne, *Joseph Banks and the English Enlightenment: Useful Knowledge and Polite Culture* (Cambridge, 1994), pp. 61, 67.

10. Letter to Horace Mann, 20 September 1772, in *The Yale Edition of Horace Walpole's Correspondence*, ed. W.S. Lewis *et al.*, 48 vols (New Haven, CT/London, 1937–83), vol. 23, p. 436.

11. Quoted in Gascoigne, *Joseph Banks and the English Enlightenment*, p. 62.

12. Quoted in Richard Drayton, *Nature's Government: Science, Imperial Britain, and the 'Improvement' of the World* (New Haven, CT/London, 2000), pp. 9, 108.

13. [Erasmus Darwin,] *The Botanic Garden; A Poem, in Two Parts. Part I. Containing The Economy of Vegetation. Part II. The Loves of the Plants. With Philosophical Notes* (London, 1791), Canto IV, lines 561ff, p. 207; and see David Mackay, 'Agents of empire: the Banksian collectors and evaluation of new lands', in *Visions of Empire: Voyages, Botany and Representations of Nature*, ed. D.P. Miller and P.H. Reill (Cambridge, 1996), pp. 38–57.

14. Quoted in Drayton, *Nature's Government*, p. 125; and in Gascoigne, *Joseph Banks and the English Enlightenment*, pp. 19, 204.

15. Quoted in Lucile H. Brockway, *Science and Colonial Expansion: The Role of the British Royal Botanic Gardens* (New York, 1979), p. 80.

16. A long list of staff and institutions (as current in 1889) is printed in Brockway, *Science and Colonial Expansion*, pp. 197–201.

17. *The 'Resolution' Journal of Johann Reinhold Forster, 1772–1795*, ed. M.E. Hoare, 4 vols (London, 1982) and J.R. Forster, *Observations Made During a Voyage Round the World* (London, 1778), quoted in Richard H. Grove, *Green Imperialism: Colonial Expansion, Tropical Island Edens and the Origins of Environmentalism, 1600–1860* (Cambridge, 1995), pp. 323–5.

18. Bernard Smith, *Imagining the Pacific: In the Wake of the Cook Voyages* (New Haven, CT/London, 1992), pp. 111–34; and see Barbara M. Stafford, *Voyage into Substance: Art, Science, Nature and the Illustrated Travel Account 1760–1840* (Cambridge, MA/London, 1984), pp. 51–6, 426.

19. *The 'Resolution' Journal*, quoted in Grove, *Green Imperialism*, p. 326.

20. Grove, *Green Imperialism*, pp. 24–32, 64–7, 156–61, 199–222.

21. Sir William Hamilton, *Campi Phlegraei. Observations on the Volcanos of the Two Sicilies* (Naples, 1776), pp. 38–44; and on native Andean representations see Mary Louise Pratt, *Imperial Eyes: Travel Writing and Transculturation* (London/New York, 1992), p. 143.

22. *Captain Cook's Voyages, 1768–1779*, ed. Glyndwr Williams, The Folio Society (London, 1997), pp. 158, 277–8, 447–8.

23. Quoted in Stephen J. Pyne, *The Ice*, new edn (London, 2003), p. 161.

24. Smith, *Imagining the Pacific*, pp. 135–71.

25. The original 1798 text of 'The Rime of the Ancyent Marinere' is printed in *The New Oxford Book of Romantic Period Verse*, ed. Jerome J. McGann (Oxford, 1993), pp. 144–5

(I, lines 49–52, 57–9, 67); the 1817 text (with the gloss) is printed in *Samuel Taylor Coleridge: Selected Poems*, ed. Richard Holmes, The Folio Society (London, 2003), p. 83.

26. 'The Eolian Harp', in *New Oxford Book of Romantic Period Verse*, p. 120; *Coleridge's Notebooks: A Selection*, ed. Seamus Perry (Oxford, 2002), pp. 5, 146.

27. 'Mont Blanc', in *New Oxford Book of Romantic Period Verse*, pp. 417–18 (lines 100–6, 117–20, 139–41); *The Letters of Percy Bysshe Shelley*, ed. Frederick L. Jones, 2 vols (Oxford, 1964), vol. 1, pp. 499–500; and see Nigel Leask, 'Mont Blanc's mysterious voice: Shelley and Huttonian earth science', in *The Third Culture: Literature and Science*, ed. Elinor S. Shaffer (Berlin/New York, 1998), pp. 182–203.

28. 'Hymn to Intellectual Beauty', in *New Oxford Book of Romantic Verse*, pp. 413–14 (lines 28–30, 78–9, 84); and see Martin Priestman, *Romantic Atheism: Poetry and Freethought, 1780–1830* (Cambridge, 1999), pp. 232–5.

29. Mary Wollstonecraft Shelley, *Frankenstein; or, The Modern Prometheus*, ed. D.L. Macdonald and Kathleen Scherf (Peterborough, Ontario, 1994), pp. 55, 126, 318, 319.

30. Quoted in Kate Flint, *The Victorians and the Visual Imagination* (Cambridge, 2000), pp. 133–5.

31. Chauncey C. Loomis, 'The Arctic sublime', in *Nature and the Victorian Imagination*, ed. U.C. Knoepflmacher and G.B. Tennyson (Berkeley and Los Angeles, CA/London, 1977), pp. 95–112, quotations on pp. 102–3; and see Trevor H. Levere, *Science and the Canadian Arctic: A Century of Exploration 1818–1918* (Cambridge, 1993), pp. 44–84.

32. August Wiedemann, *Romantic Art Theories* (Henley-on-Thames, 1986), pp. 126–8; Loomis, 'The Arctic sublime', pp. 103–11.

33. Quoted in Jason Wilson, 'Introduction' to Alexander von Humboldt, *Personal Narrative of a Journey to the Equinoctial Regions of the New Continent* [1814–25], abridged, translated and with an introduction by Jason Wilson (Harmondsworth, 1995), p. xlvii.

34. Quoted by Wilson from an autobiographical summary of 1806, in 'Introduction' to *Personal Narrative*, p. xlix.

35. *The Correspondence of Charles Darwin*, ed. Frederick Burckhardt and Sydney Smith *et al.* (Cambridge, 1985–), vol. 1, p. 237.

36. Alexander von Humboldt, *Views of Nature or Contemplations on the Sublime Phenomena of Creation*, trans. E.C. Otté and H.G. Bohn (London, 1850), p. 217; quoted in Malcolm Nicolson, 'Alexander von Humboldt and the geography of vegetation', in *Romanticism and the Sciences*, ed. Andrew Cunningham and Nicholas Jardine (Cambridge, 1990), p. 173.

37. *Jugendbriefe Alexander von Humboldts*, ed. Ilse Jahn and Fritz G. Lange (Berlin, 1973), p. 657; quoted in Michael Dettelbach, 'Global physics and aesthetic empire: Humboldt's physical portrait of the tropics', in *Visions of Empire*, ed. Miller and Reill, pp. 266–7.

38. Quoted in Nicolson, 'Humboldt and the geography of vegetation', p. 170.

39. Quoted in Dettelbach, 'Global physics and aesthetic empire', p. 266; and in Nicholas Boyle, *Goethe: The Poet and the Age. Volume II: Revolution and Renunciation (1790–1803)* (Oxford, 2000), pp. 482–3.

40. D.A. Brading, *The First America: The Spanish Monarchy, Creole Patriots and the Liberal State 1492–1867* (Cambridge, 1991), pp. 517, 526–32; Pratt, *Imperial Eyes*, p. 127.

41. Alexander de Humboldt, *Personal Narrative of Travels to the Equinoctial Regions of the New Continent, During the Years 1799–1804. By Alexander de Humboldt and Aimé Bonpland*, trans. Helen Maria Williams, 7 vols (London, 1814–29), vol. 1, pp. iv, viii, xxxviii, xlii, 178.

42. Humboldt in *Annalen der Physik*, 24 (1806): 2–3, and letter to Pictet of 3 January 1806, quoted in Dettelbach, 'Global physics and aesthetic empire', pp. 260, 267.

43. Humboldt, *Personal Narrative*, trans. Williams, vol. 1, pp. ii, 14.

44. Humboldt and Bonpland, *Essai sur la Géographie des Plantes*, pp. 41–2; see Browne, *The Secular Ark*, pp. 47, 230.

45. As translated in Dettelbach, 'Global physics and aesthetic empire', p. 268.

46. Humboldt and Bonpland, *Essai sur la Géographie des Plantes*, pp. 42–3; as translated in Nicolson, 'Humboldt and the geography of vegetation', p. 172.

47. Nigel Leask, *Curiosity and the Aesthetics of Travel Writing 1770–1840: 'From an Antique Land'* (Oxford, 2002), pp. 281–98.

48. Humboldt, *Personal Narrative*, trans. Williams, vol. 1, pp. i, 3, 4; vol. 3, pp. 35–6.

49. Humboldt, *Personal Narrative*, trans. Williams, vol. 1, pp. 126, 142–3, 180–2.

50. *Correspondence of Charles Darwin*, vol. 3, p. 140.

51. *Darwin's Beagle Diary*, p. 42 (entry for 28 February 1832); see Nigel Leask, 'Darwin's "second sun": Alexander von Humboldt and the genesis of *The Voyage of the Beagle*', in *Literature, Science, Psychoanalysis, 1830–1970: Essays in Honour of Gillian Beer*, ed. Helen Small and Trudi Tate (Oxford, 2003), pp. 13–36.

52. *Voyage of the 'Beagle': Charles Darwin's 'Journal of Researches'* (1839 edn), edited with an introduction by Janet Browne and Michael Neve (Harmondsworth, 1989), p. 163.

53. Phillip R. Sloan, 'The making of a philosophical naturalist', in *The Cambridge Companion to Darwin*, ed. Jonathan Hodge and Gregory Radick (Cambridge, 2003), pp. 17–39.

54. James A. Second, 'The discovery of a vocation: Darwin's early geology', *British Journal for the History of Science*, 24 (1991): 133–57.

55. *Correspondence of Charles Darwin*, vol. 1, pp. 120, 122, 125–6.

56. *Correspondence of Charles Darwin*, vol. 7, p. 388; *The Autobiography of Charles Darwin 1809–1882*, ed. Nora Barlow (London, 1958), p. 65; see Sloan, 'The making of a philosophical naturalist', p. 33.

57. *Darwin's Beagle Diary*, pp. 42, 444; *Voyage of the 'Beagle'*, p. 374; and see Richards, *The Romantic Conception of Life*, pp. 522–6.

58. *Correspondence of Charles Darwin*, vol. 1, p. 238. On Darwin's education and the voyage of the *Beagle* see Janet Browne, *Charles Darwin: Voyaging* (London, 1995).

59. Sandra Herbert, *Charles Darwin, Geologist* (Ithaca, New York, 2005); Herbert, 'Charles Darwin as a prospective geological author', in *British Journal for the History of Science*, 24 (1991): 159–92.

60. *Correspondence of Charles Darwin*, vol. 1, pp. 157, 167.

61. *Correspondence of Charles Darwin*, vol. 3, p. 55.

62. *Voyage of the 'Beagle'*, p. 44.

63. *Correspondence of Charles Darwin*, vol. 1, pp. 442, 460; *Voyage of the 'Beagle'*, p. 253.

64. *Voyage of the 'Beagle'*, pp. 345–7.

65. *Darwin's Beagle Diary*, p. 443; *Voyage of the 'Beagle'*, p. 374.

66. *Darwin's Beagle Diary*, p. 67.

67. *Darwin's Beagle Diary*, pp. 18–20, 67; *Correspondence of Charles Darwin*, vol. 1, pp. 233, 236–7.

68. *Darwin's Beagle Diary*, pp. 42, 74, 125–6, 444.

69. *Correspondence of Charles Darwin*, vol. 1, p. 345.

70. *Voyage of the 'Beagle'*, pp. 50, 175.

71. *Correspondence of Charles Darwin*, vol. 1, pp. 501, 503.

72. Charles Darwin, *On the Origin of Species by Means of Natural Selection, or the Preservation of Favoured Races in the Struggle for Life* (London, 1859), p. 489.

Chapter 4   Landscape, Georgic and Picturesque

1. Charlotte Klonk, *Science and the Perception of Nature: British Landscape Art in the Late Eighteenth and Early Nineteenth Centuries* (New Haven, CT/London, 1996), p. 1.

2. *The Works of John Ruskin*, Library Edition, ed. E.T. Cook and Alexander Wedderburn, 39 vols (London, 1903–12), vol. 3, p. 627n.

3. *The Works of John Ruskin*, vol. 5, p. 234.

4. *The Odyssey of Homer*, translated by Alexander Pope, 5 vols (London, 1725–6), vol. 2, pp. 9–12 (Book V, lines 75–94).

5. *The Works of John Ruskin*, vol. 5, p. 235.
6. *The Odyssey of Homer*, translated by Alexander Pope, vol. 2, pp. 105–8 (Book VII, lines 142–77).
7. *The Yale Edition of Horace Walpole's Correspondence*, ed. W.S. Lewis *et al.*, 48 vols (New Haven, CT/London, 1937–83), vol. 13, p. 181.
8. Quoted in Richard Jenkyns, 'Pastoral', in *The Legacy of Rome: A New Appraisal*, ed. Richard Jenkyns (Oxford, 1992), p. 162.
9. Richard Jenkyns, *Virgil's Experience. Nature and History: Times, Names and Places* (Oxford, 1998), p. 199.
10. Erwin Panofsky, *Meaning in the Visual Arts* (Harmondsworth, 1970), p. 346.
11. Paul Alpers, *What is Pastoral?* (Chicago, IL/London, 1996).
12. William Empson, *Some Versions of Pastoral: A Study of the Pastoral Form in Literature* (London, 1935); Renato Poggioli, *The Oaten Flute: Essays on Pastoral Poetry and the Pastoral Ideal* (Cambridge, MA, 1975), pp. 1, 14.
13. David M. Halperin, *Before Pastoral: Theocritus and the Ancient Tradition of Bucolic Poetry* (New Haven, CT/London, 1983), pp. 70–4.
14. Quoted in Jenkyns, 'Pastoral', p. 156.
15. 'Lycidas', lines 165–7, in *The Poems of John Milton*, ed. Helen Darbishire (Oxford, 1958), p. 451; and see Poggioli, *The Oaten Flute*, pp. 83–104.
16. Virgil, *Aeneid*, Book VIII, lines 51–4 in *P. Vergili Maronis Opera*, corrected edition, ed. R.A.B. Mynors (Oxford, 1972); Jenkyns, 'Pastoral', pp. 159–60.
17. Virgil, *Aeneid*, Book VIII, lines 324–5.
18. Helen Langdon, 'The imaginative geographies of Claude Lorrain', in *Transports: Travel, Pleasure and Imaginative Geography, 1600–1830*, ed. Chloe Chard and Helen Langdon (New Haven, CT/London, 1996), pp. 151–78.
19. Bruno Snell, 'Arcadia: the discovery of a spiritual landscape', in his *The Discovery of the Mind*, trans. T.G. Rosenmeyer (Oxford, 1953), pp. 281–2. Jenkyns, *Virgil's Experience*, p. 157, rejects Snell's further statement that the 'discoverer [of Arcadia] is Virgil'.
20. Virgil, *Eclogues*, Book IV, lines 28–30; Jenkyns, *Virgil's Experience*, p. 202.
21. Virgil, *Georgics*, Book II, lines 149–50; Jenkyns, *Virgil's Experience*, p. 359.
22. Quoted in *The Oxford Companion to J.M.W. Turner*, ed. Evelyn Joll, Martin Butlin and Luke Herrmann (Oxford, 2001), p. 48.
23. Joshua Reynolds, 'Discourses on Art', quoted in Malcolm Andrews, *Landscape and Western Art* (Oxford, 1999), p. 97.
24. *The Works of John Ruskin*, vol. 3, pp. 42–4.
25. Panofsky, 'Et in Arcadia Ego' (1936), in his *Meaning in the Visual Arts*, pp. 340–67.
26. Jenkyns, *Virgil's Experience*, p. 158n.
27. 'A Discourse on Pastoral Poetry', in *The Poems of Alexander Pope*, ed. John Butt (London, 1963), p. 120.
28. *The Works of John Dryden*, vol. 5, ed. W. Frost and V.A. Dearing (Berkeley and Los Angeles, CA/London, 1987), p. 137.
29. John Dixon Hunt, '"Gard'ning can speak proper *English*"', in *Culture and Cultivation in Early Modern England: Writing and the Land*, ed. Michael Leslie and Timothy Raylor (Leicester/London, 1992), pp. 195–222.
30. Joseph Addison, 'An Essay on the *Georgics*', in *The Works of John Dryden*, vol. 5, p. 146.
31. Andrews, *Landscape and Western Art*, pp. 28–9.
32. *The Works of John Ruskin*, vol. 3, p. 627n.
33. Virgil, *Georgics*, Book II, lines 490, 493; Jenkyns, *Virgil's Experience*, p. 374.
34. L.P. Wilkinson, *The Georgics of Virgil: A Critical Survey* (Cambridge, 1969).
35. Virgil, *Georgics*, Book I, line 168; Jenkyns, *Virgil's Experience*, pp. 199, 319.
36. Virgil, *Georgics*, Book II, lines 458–60; Jenkyns, *Virgil's Experience*, pp. 372–3; Addison, 'An Essay on the *Georgics*', in *The Works of John Dryden*, vol. 5, p. 151; compare David O. Ross, *Virgil's Elements: Physics and Poetry in the Georgics* (Princeton, NJ, 1987), pp. 109–27.

37. Eduard Fraenkel, *Horace* (Oxford, 1957), pp. 59–61; Charles Martindale, 'Introduction' to *Horace Made New*, ed. Charles Martindale and David Hopkins (Cambridge, 1993), p. 15.

38. Anne Bermingham, *Landscape and Ideology: The English Rustic Tradition, 1740–1860* (London, 1987), pp. 28–40; Hugh Prince, 'Art and agrarian change, 1710–1815', in *The Iconography of Landscape: Essays on the Symbolic Representation, Design and Use of Past Environments*, ed. Denis Cosgrove and Stephen Daniels (Cambridge, 1988), pp. 98–118; John Barrell, *The Dark Side of the Landscape: The Rural Poor in English Painting 1730–1840* (Cambridge, 1980).

39. *The Correspondence of Isaac Newton*, ed. H.W. Turnbull *et al.*, 7 vols (Cambridge, 1959–77), vol. 2, pp. 323, 331, 333; Frank E. Manuel, *A Portrait of Isaac Newton* (Cambridge, MA, 1968), pp. 364–5.

40. Ernest Lee Tuveson, *Millennium and Utopia: A Study in the Background of the Idea of Progress* (Berkeley and Los Angeles, CA, 1949), pp. 100, 103, 113–26.

41. Thomas Burnet, *The Theory of the Earth: Containing an Account of the Original of the Earth, and of all the General Changes Which it hath already undergone or is to undergo Till the Consummation of all Things. The First two Books Concerning The Deluge, and Concerning Paradise* (1684, 2nd edn, 1691), reprinted in *The Sacred Theory of the Earth*, ed. Basil Willey (London, 1965), pp. 26, 27, 34, 41–2, 63, 64, 66, 79, 89, 91; Marjorie Hope Nicolson, *Mountain Gloom and Mountain Glory: The Development of the Aesthetics of the Infinite* (Ithaca, NY, 1959), pp. 184–224.

42. Thomas Burnet, *The Theory of the Earth: Containing an Account of the Original of the Earth, and of all the General Changes Which it hath already undergone or is to undergo Till the Consummation of all Things. The Two Last Books, Concerning the Burning of the World, and Concerning the New Heavens and New Earth* [1690], reprinted in *The Sacred Theory of the Earth*, ed. Willey, pp. 289, 306.

43. Nicolson, *Mountain Gloom and Mountain Glory*, pp. 225–70; Martin J.S. Rudwick, *The Meaning of Fossils: Episodes in the History of Palaeontology*, 2nd edn (New York, 1976), pp. 77–86; Roy Porter, *The Making of Geology: Earth Science in Britain 1660–1815* (Cambridge, 1977), pp. 62–90.

44. *Correspondence of Isaac Newton*, vol. 2, p. 329.

45. James E. Force, *William Whiston: Honest Newtonian* (Cambridge, 1985), pp. 40–60.

46. Quoted in Joseph M. Levine, *The Battle of the Books: History and Literature in the Augustan Age* (Ithaca, NY/London, 1991), p. 20.

47. Burnet, *The Sacred Theory of the Earth*, ed. Willey, pp. 63–4, 109–12; Basil Willey, *The Eighteenth-Century Background* [1940] (Harmondsworth, 1962), pp. 32–9; Nicolson, *Mountain Gloom and Mountain Glory*, pp. 212–16.

48. Richard Bentley, *A Confutation of Atheism from the Origin and Frame of the World. Part II* (London, 1693), pp. 32, 37, 40, in *Isaac Newton's Papers & Letters on Natural Philosophy*, ed. I. Bernard Cohen (Cambridge, 1958), pp. 384, 389, 392.

49. *Spectator*, no. 146, 11 August 1711, quoted in Levine, *The Battle of the Books*, pp. 21–2.

50. *The Works of the Right Honourable Joseph Addison, Esq; In Four Volumes*, ed. Thomas Tickell (London, 1721), vol. 3, p. 489.

51. The third Earl of Shaftesbury, 'The Moralists', in *Characteristicks of Men, Manners, Opinions, Times*, 3 vols (London, 1714), vol. 2, pp. 393–4.

52. *Horace Walpole's Correspondence*, vol. 13, p. 181.

53. *Horace Walpole's Correspondence*, vol. 35, p. 252; Horace Walpole, *Aedes Walpolianae* (London, 1743), p. xxvii, quoted in Simon Schama, *Landscape and Memory* (London, 1995), pp. 447–57, on p. 453.

54. *Horace Walpole's Correspondence*, vol. 13, p. 182.

55. Nicolson, *Mountain Gloom and Mountain Glory*, pp. 271–323; Roy Porter, '"In England's green and pleasant land": the English enlightenment and the environment', in *Culture, Landscape and the Environment*, ed. Kate Flint and Howard Morphy (Oxford, 2000), pp. 15–43.

56. David Leatherbarrow, 'Character, geometry and perspective: the third Earl of Shaftesbury's Principle of Garden Design', *Journal of Garden History*, 4 (1984): 332–58; Douglas D.C. Chambers, *The Planters of the English Landscape Garden: Botany, Trees and the 'Georgics'* (New Haven, CT/London, 1993), pp. 50–3.

57. 'On Gardens' (in the *Guardian*, No. 173, 29 September 1713), in *The Prose Works of Alexander Pope. Vol. I. The Earlier Works 1711–1720*, ed. Norman Ault (Oxford, 1936), pp. 145–8.

58. *The Works of Joseph Addison*, vol. 3, pp. 495–7.

59. John Prest, *The Garden of Eden: The Botanic Garden and the Re-Creation of Paradise* (New Haven, CT/London, 1981).

60. Quoted in Charles Webster, *The Great Instauration: Science, Medicine and Reform 1626–1660* (London, 1975), p. 360.

61. Evelyn to Browne, 28 January 1660 (Christ Church, Oxford); John Evelyn, *Sylva*, 4th edn (London, 1706), p. 329, quoted in Chambers, *The Planters of the English Landscape Garden*, pp. 3, 33, 39, 49.

62. Virgil, *Georgics*, Book II, line 412; Stephen Switzer, *Ichnographia Rustica* (London, 1742), quoted in Chambers, *The Planters of the English Landscape Garden*, pp. 61–2.

63. Horace Walpole, *The History of the Modern Taste in Gardening* (2nd edn 1782), in *Horace Walpole: Gardenist*, ed. I.W.U. Chase (Princeton, NJ, 1943), pp. 25, 27, 35.

64. 'Epistle to Burlington', lines 50, 57, in *Poems of Alexander Pope*, ed. Butt, p. 590; Virgil, *Aeneid*, Book VII, line 136.

65. *Horace Walpole's Correspondence*, vol. 35, pp. 148–9.

66. Timothy Mowl, *Gentlemen & Players: Gardeners of the English Landscape* (Stroud, 2000), pp. 105–48.

67. Quoted in Tom Williamson, *Polite Landscapes: Gardens and Society in Eighteenth-Century England* (Baltimore, MD, 1995), pp. 77–99, on p. 79.

68. Letter to William Mason, 10 February 1783, in *Horace Walpole's Correspondence*, vol. 29, p. 286.

69. Quoted in Nigel Everett, *The Tory View of Landscape* (New Haven, CT/London, 1994), pp. 61–4.

70. Horace Walpole (1779), in *Satirical Poems. Published Anonymously by William Mason. With Notes by Horace Walpole*, ed. Paget Toynbee (Oxford, 1926), pp. 43–5; Chase, ed., *Horace Walpole: Gardenist*, p. 10.

71. Quoted in Williamson, *Polite Landscapes*, p. 147.

72. Stephen Daniels, *Humphry Repton: Landscape Gardening and the Geography of Georgian England* (New Haven, CT/London, 1999), pp. 103–47.

73. Quoted in Stephen Daniels, Suzanne Seymour and Charles Watkins, 'Border Country: the politics of the picturesque in the middle Wye valley', in *Prospects for the Nation: Recent Essays in British Landscape, 1750–1880*, ed. Michael Rosenthal, Christiana Payne and Scott Wilcox (New Haven, CT/London, 1997), pp. 157–81, on p. 160.

74. Stephen Daniels and Charles Watkins, 'Picturesque landscaping and estate management: Uvedale Price and Nathaniel Kent at Foxley', in *The Politics of the Picturesque: Literature, Landscape and Aesthetics since 1770* (Cambridge, 1994), pp. 13–41.

75. William Gilpin, *An Essay upon Prints* (1768) quoted in Malcolm Andrews, *The Search for the Picturesque: Landscape Aesthetics and Tourism in Britain, 1760–1800* (Aldershot, 1989), p. 56; William Gilpin, *Observations on the River Wye, and Several Parts of South Wales, &c, relating chiefly to Picturesque Beauty* (London, 1782), pp. 1–2; Gilpin, *Three Essays: On Picturesque Beauty; On Picturesque Travel; and on Sketching Landscape* (London, 1792), pp. 3, 6, 19, 43.

76. Everett, *The Tory View of Landscape*, pp. 91–122.

77. Uvedale Price, *Essays on the Picturesque as Compared with the Sublime and the Beautiful: and on the Use of Studying Pictures for the Purpose of Improving Real Landscapes*, 3 vols (London, 1810), vol. 1, pp. 22, 24, 31–2, 44–5, 89, 127, 338–9, 374; vol. 2, pp. 147, 248.

78. Bonamy Dobrée, ed., *Anecdotes, Observation and Characters of Books and Men . . . by the Reverend Joseph Spence* (London, 1964), pp. 40, 104.

79. Horace Walpole (1779), in *Satirical Poems . . . With Notes by Horace Walpole*, ed. Paget Toynbee, p. 43; John Dixon Hunt, *The Figure in the Landscape: Poetry, Painting and Gardening during the Eighteenth Century* (Baltimore, MD/London, 1976).

80. Andrew Ballantyne, *Architecture, Landscape and Liberty: Richard Payne Knight and the Picturesque* (Cambridge, 1997), pp. 190–239.

81. Richard Payne Knight, *The Landscape, a Didactic Poem, In Three Books. Addressed to Uvedale Price, Esq.* (London, 1794), Book I, lines 19–20, 196, 227–31; Book II, lines 79–80, 156–61, 284–7, 310–15, 380–91, 424; Book III, lines 295–300.

82. Humphry Repton, the 'Red Book' for Attingham quoted in Repton, *Observations on the Theory and Practice of Landscape Gardening* (London, 1803), pp. 117–19; see Daniels, *Humphry Repton*, pp. 131–4.

83. Richard Payne Knight, *An Analytical Inquiry into the Principles of Taste*, 4th edn (London, 1808), pp. 148, 152–3, 196.

84. Andrews, *The Search for the Picturesque*, pp. 153–95; Ian Ousby, *The Englishman's England: Taste, Travel and the Rise of Tourism* (Cambridge, 1990), pp. 130–94.

85. Thomas West, *A Guide to the Lakes: Dedicated to the Lovers of Landscape Studies . . . [in] the Lakes in Cumberland, Westmorland and Lancashire* (London, 1778), pp. 89–90; William Gilpin, *Observations, Relative Chiefly to Picturesque Beauty . . . [in the] Mountains and Lakes of Cumberland and Westmoreland*, 2 vols (London, 1786), vol. 1, p. 183.

86. *A Guide through the District of the Lakes in the North of England* (1835), in *The Prose Works of William Wordsworth*, ed. W.J.B. Owen and Jane Worthington Smyser, 3 vols (Oxford, 1974), vol. 2, p. 230n; Knight, *The Landscape*, Book II, lines 156–61.

87. Repton, *Observations on the Theory and Practice of Landscape Gardening*, pp. 38, 76, 107.

88. Humphry Repton, *Fragments on the Theory and Practice of Landscape Gardening* (London, 1816), p. 193; Stephen Daniels, 'The political iconography of woodland in later Georgian England', in *The Iconography of Landscape*, ed. Cosgrove and Daniels, pp. 43–83, esp. 70–2.

89. Everett, *The Tory View of Landscape*, pp. 188–94.

90. Rachel Laudan, *From Mineralogy to Geology: The Foundations of a Science, 1650–1830* (Chicago/London, 1978), pp. 21–46; Martin J.S. Rudwick, 'Minerals, strata and fossils', in *Cultures of Natural History*, ed. N. Jardine, J.A. Secord and E.C. Spary (Cambridge, 1996), pp. 266–86.

91. John Whitehurst, *An Inquiry into the Original State and Formation of the Earth; Deduced from the Facts and the Laws of Nature. To which is Added an Appendix, Containing Some General Observations of the Strata in Derbyshire* (London, 1778), p. 63.

92. *The Collected Letters of Erasmus Darwin*, ed. Desmond King-Hele (Cambridge, 2007), p. 79; see Jenny Uglow, *The Lunar Men: The Friends who Made the Future 1730–1810* (London, 2002), pp. 144–5.

93. Jane Austen, *Pride and Prejudice* (1813), ed. R.W. Chapman (Oxford, 1932), p. 239; Ousby, *The Englishman's England*, pp. 131–7; Noah Heringman, *Romantic Rocks, Aesthetic Geology* (Ithaca, NY/London, 2004), pp. 228–66.

94. Laudan, *From Mineralogy to Geology*, pp. 181–5; Rudwick, 'Minerals, strata and fossils', in *Cultures of Natural History*, ed. Jardine, Secord and Spary, pp. 266–71; Richard Hamblyn, 'Private cabinets and popular geology: the British audiences for volcanoes in the eighteenth century', in *Transports*, ed. Chard and Langdon, pp. 179–205.

95. *Horace Walpole's Correspondence*, vol. 22, p. 243.

96. Ian Jenkins and Kim Sloan, *Vases & Volcanoes: Sir William Hamilton and his Collection*, exh. cat. British Museum 1996 (London, 1996); David Constantine, *Fields of Fire: A Life of Sir William Hamilton* (London, 2001).

97. John Thackray, '"The modern Pliny": Hamilton and Vesuvius', in Jenkins and Sloan, *Vases & Volcanoes*, pp. 65–74; Karen Wood, 'Making and circulating knowledge

through Sir William Hamilton's *Campi Phlegraei*, *The British Journal for the History of Science*, 39 (2006): 67–96.

98. Sir William Hamilton, *Campi Phlegraei. Observations on the Volcanos of the Two Sicilies, As they have been Communicated to the Royal Society of London, with 54 Plates illuminated from Drawings taken and colour'd after nature, under the inspection of the Author, by the Editor Mr Peter Fabris*, 2 vols (Naples, 1776); Sir William Hamilton, *Supplement to the Campi Phlegraei being an Account of the Great Eruption of Mount Vesuvius in the month of August 1779. Communicated to the Royal Society* (Naples, 1779).

99. Hamilton, *Campi Phlegraei*, p. 5.

100. Martin J.S. Rudwick, 'The emergence of a visual language for geological science 1760–1840', *History of Science*, 14 (1976): 149–95, esp. 173, 175.

101. Letter from Joseph Wright to Richard Wright, Rome, 11 November 1774, in William Bemrose, *The Life and Works of Joseph Wright, commonly called 'Wright of Derby'* (London/Derby, 1885), pp. 34–5.

102. Whitehurst, *Inquiry into the Original State and Formation of the Earth*, pp. ii, 73–4; David Fraser, '"Fields of radiance": the scientific and industrial scenes of Joseph Wright', in *The Iconography of Landscape*, ed. Cosgrove and Daniels, pp. 119–41, on pp. 124–9; Hamblyn, 'Private cabinets and popular geology', in *Transports*, ed. Chard and Langdon, pp. 196–200.

103. Hamilton, *Campi Phlegraei*, pp. 5, 16, 38–44, letter press accompanying Plates V and XXXVIII; Hamilton, *Supplement*, p. 3.

104. Hamilton, *Campi Phlegraei*, pp. 30–31, 87; Hamilton, *Supplement*, pp. 10–11.

105. Hamilton, *Campi Phlegraei*, p. 31n; Joseph Priestley, *The History and Present State of Electricity, with Original Experiments*, 3rd edn, corrected and enlarged, 2 vols (London, 1775), vol. 1, p. 455; Thackray, '"The modern Pliny": Hamilton and Vesuvius', in Jenkins and Sloan, *Vases & Volcanoes*, p. 69.

106. Hamilton, *Campi Phlegraei*, pp. 4, 6, 13, 53–4, 67, 69, 77, 86.

107. Hamilton, *Campi Phlegraei*, p. 7, letter press accompanying Plate I.

108. *Horace Walpole's Correspondence*, vol. 35, pp. 413, 415.

109. *Horace Walpole's Correspondence*, vol. 25, p. 427.

110. Sir William Hamilton, 'An account of the earthquakes which happened in Italy, from February to May 1783', *Philosophical Transactions of the Royal Society*, 73 (1783): 169–208, on p. 205.

111. *Horace Walpole's Correspondence*, vol. 35, p. 383.

112. R.E. Raspe, 'A letter … containing a short account of some basalt hills in Hessia', *Philosophical Transactions of the Royal Society*, 61 (1771): 580–3.

113. Quoted in Klonk, *Science and the Perception of Nature*, p. 170.

114. Joseph Banks, 'Account of Staffa', in Thomas Pennant, *A Tour in Scotland, and Voyage to the Hebrides; MDCCLXXI I* (Chester, 1774), pp. 262–3.

115. Hamilton, *Campi Phlegraei*, p. 8.

116. See Klonk, *Science and the Perception of Nature*, p. 68.

117. William Daniell, *A Voyage Round Great Britain*, 8 vols (London, 1814–25), vol. 3, p. 37; Klonk, *Science and the Perception of Nature*, p. 68.

118. Daniell, *A Voyage Round Great Britain*, vol. 3, p. 40.

119. *Transactions of the Geological Society of London*, 1 (1811): v, viii–ix; Rudwick, 'The emergence of a visual language for geological science 1760–1840', pp. 158, 181.

120. Klonk, *Science and the Perception of Nature*, pp. 82–6.

121. John MacCulloch, 'On Staffa', *Transactions of the Geological Society of London*, 2 (1814): 501–9; John MacCulloch, *A Description of the Western Islands of Scotland, including the Isle of Man: comprising an Account of their Geological Structure; with Remarks on their Agriculture, Scenery, and Antiquities*, 3 vols (London, 1819), vol. 1, p. xv.

122. MacCulloch, *Description of the Western Islands of Scotland*, vol. 1, pp. 1, 8, 10, 15–16, 18; vol. 2, pp. 508–9.

123. Rudwick, 'The emergence of a visual language for geological science 1760–1840', pp. 172–7; Charlotte Klonk, 'From picturesque travel to scientific observation: artists' and geologists' voyages to Staffa', in *Prospects for the Nation*, ed. Rosenthal, Payne and Wilcox, pp. 205–29.

Chapter 5 Landscape, 'Truth of Nature'

1. *The Works of John Ruskin*, Library Edition, ed. E.T. Cook and Alexander Wedderburn, 39 vols (London, 1903–12), vol. 12, pp. 158–9.
2. *The Works of John Ruskin*, vol. 5, p. 387.
3. Paul H. Walton, *Master Drawings by John Ruskin: Selections from the David Thomson Collection* (London, 2000), pp. 54, 99.
4. Catalogue entry by Allen Staley in *Pre-Raphaelite Vision: Truth to Nature*, ed. Allen Staley and Christopher Newall, exh. cat., Tate Gallery, London, February to May 2004 (London, 2004), p. 148.
5. Kay Dian Kriz, *The Idea of the English Landscape Painter: Genius as Alibi in the Early Nineteenth Century* (New Haven, CT/London, 1997).
6. *The Works of John Ruskin*, vol. 5, p.387.
7. Dugald Stewart, *Philosophical Essays* (1810), 3rd edn (Edinburgh, 1818), pp. 284, 325–6.
8. Richard Payne Knight, *Edinburgh Review*, 23 (1814): 285.
9. Kriz, *The Idea of the English Landscape Painter*, pp. 53–5.
10. Michael Rosenthal, 'Landscape as high art', in *Glorious Nature: British Landscape Painting 1750–1850*, exh. cat., ed. Katharine Baetjer, Denver Art Museum 1993 (London, 1993), pp. 13–30; Rosenthal, *Constable: The Painter and his Landscape* (New Haven, CT/London, 1983), pp. 82–7.
11. Archibald Alison, *Essays on the Nature and Principles of Taste* (Edinburgh, 1790), pp. 85–7, 88, 90–1, 104.
12. *John Constable's Correspondence*, ed. R.B. Beckett, 6 vols (Ipswich, 1962–8), vol. 2, p. 131.
13. Andrew Hemingway, *Landscape Imagery and Urban Culture in Early Nineteenth-Century Britain* (Cambridge, 1992), pp. 65–6.
14. *Constable's Correspondence*, vol. 6, p. 232.
15. *John Constable's Discourses*, comp. and annot. R.B. Beckett (Ipswich, 1970), pp. 10, 57, 64, 68, 72–3.
16. *Constable's Discourses*, p. 69.
17. John E. Thornes, *John Constable's Skies: A Fusion of Art and Science* (Birmingham, 1999); Thornes, 'Constable's meteorological understanding and his painting of skies', in *Constable's Clouds: Paintings and Cloud Studies by John Constable*, ed. Edward Morris, exh. cat., National Gallery of Scotland and National Museums and Galleries on Merseyside, 2000 (Edinburgh/Liverpool, 2000), pp. 151–60.
18. *Constable's Correspondence*, vol. 6, pp. 76–7.
19. *Constable's Discourses*, pp. 9–10; Edward Morris, 'Introduction: Constable's clouds and the chiaroscuro of nature', in *Constable's Clouds*, ed. Morris, pp. 9–11.
20. C.R. Leslie, *Memoirs of the Life of John Constable. Composed Chiefly of His Letters* (2nd edn, 1845), ed. Jonathan Mayne (Oxford, 1951), p. 218.
21. *Constable's Correspondence*, vol. 6, pp. 77–8.
22. Elizabeth K. Helsinger, *Rural Scenes and National Representation: Britain, 1815–1850* (Princeton, NJ, 1997), pp. 52–3; compare John Barrell, *The Dark Side of the Landscape: The Rural Poor in English Painting 1730–1840* (Cambridge, 1980), pp. 138–41, and Rosenthal, *Constable*, pp. 38–41, 147.
23. Stephen Daniels, *Fields of Vision: Landscape Imagery and National Identity in England and the United States* (Cambridge, 1992), pp. 200–42; Helsinger, *Rural Scenes and National Representation*, pp. 41–64.

24. *Constable's Correspondence*, vol. 6, p. 172.

25. *The Solitude of Mountains: Constable and the Lake District*, exh. cat., The Wordsworth Trust, Grasmere, July 2006, ed. Stephen Hebron, Coral Shields and Timothy Wilcox.

26. Leslie, *Memoirs*, p. 18.

27. *Constable's Correspondence*, vol. 6, p. 98.

28. Anne Bermingham, *Landscape and Ideology: The English Rustic Tradition, 1740–1860* (London, 1987), pp. 119–23; Charlotte Klonk, *Science and the Perception of Nature: British Landscape Art in the Late Eighteenth and Early Nineteenth Centuries* (New Haven, CT/London, 1996), pp. 2–3.

29. *Constable's Discourses*, p. 68.

30. *Constable's Correspondence*, vol. 2, pp. 16, 31–2.

31. Quoted in Hemingway, *Landscape Imagery and Urban Culture*, p. 24.

32. E.H. Gombrich, *Art and Illusion: A Study in the Psychology of Pictorial Representation*, 3rd edn (London, 1968), pp. 150–1, 268, 271.

33. *Constable's Correspondence*, vol. 2, p. 131; Rosenthal, *Constable*, pp. 74–87 and *passim*.

34. William Vaughan, Elizabeth E. Barker and Colin Harrison, *Samuel Palmer 1805–1881: Vision and Landscape*, exh. cat., British Museum, London, 2005, and Metropolitan Museum of Art, New York, 2006 (London, 2005), pp. 71, 89, 148–50, 158–9.

35. Thomas West, *A Guide to the Lakes: Dedicated to the Lovers of Landscape Studies . . . [in] the Lakes in Cumberland, Westmorland, and Lancashire* (London, 1778), pp. 13–14.

36. William Wordsworth, *A Guide through the District of the Lakes in the North of England* (1835), in *The Prose Works of William Wordsworth*, ed. W.J.B. Owen and Jane Worthington Smyser, 3 vols (Oxford, 1974), vol. 2, p. 160; Ian Ousby, *The Englishman's England: Taste, Travel and the Rise of Tourism* (Cambridge, 1990), pp. 182–3.

37. *Prose Works of Wordsworth*, ed. Owen and Smyser, vol. 2, pp. 170, 171, 173.

38. *Prose Works of Wordsworth*, ed. Owen and Smyser, vol. 1, p. 140.

39. *Prose Works of Wordsworth*, ed. Owen and Smyser, vol. 2, pp. 175, 181–2.

40. Theresa M. Kelley, *Wordsworth's Revisionary Aesthetics* (Cambridge, 1988), pp. 14–23; John Wyatt, *Wordsworth and the Geologists* (Cambridge, 1995), pp. 17–51.

41. *Prose Works of Wordsworth*, ed. Owen and Smyser, vol. 2, pp. 171, 174–6, 178, 190–1.

42. *Prose Works of Wordsworth*, ed. Owen and Smyser, vol. 2, pp. 108, 202–3, 224–5.

43. Nigel Everett, *The Tory View of Landscape* (New Haven, CT/London, 1994), pp. 156–60.

44. William Wordsworth, *Home at Grasmere*, ed. Beth Darlington (Ithaca, NY/ Hassocks, Sussex, 1977), lines 129–32.

45. James C. McKusick, *Green Writing: Romanticism and Ecology* (Basingstoke, 2000), pp. 69–76.

46. *Prose Works of Wordsworth*, ed. Owen and Smyser, vol. 1, p. 148.

47. William Gilpin, *Observations on the River Wye, and Several Parts of South Wales, &c, relating chiefly to Picturesque Beauty* (London, 1782) , pp. 32–3, 35.

48. Wordsworth, 'Lines Written a Few Miles above Tintern Abbey' (1798), lines 89–111, 122–6, in *The New Oxford Book of Romantic Period Verse*, ed. Jerome J. McGann (Oxford, 1993), p. 180.

49. Wordsworth, 'Ode: Intimations of Immortality' (1807), lines 1–6, 9, 190–5, 205–6, in *New Oxford Book of Romantic Period Verse*, ed. McGann, pp. 269, 273–4.

50. *Prose Works of Wordsworth*, ed. Owen and Smyser, vol. 1, pp. 122, 124.

51. Nicholas Roe, *The Politics of Nature: William Wordsworth and Some Contemporaries*, 2nd edn (Basingstoke, 2002), pp. 159–96; Ralph Pite, 'Wordsworth and the natural world', in *The Cambridge Companion to Wordsworth*, ed. Stephen Gill (Cambridge, 2003), pp. 180–95.

52. Alexander Pope, 'A Discourse on Pastoral Poetry', in *The Poems of Alexander Pope*, ed. John Butt (London, 1963), p. 120.

53. Wordsworth, *The Prelude* (1805), Book VIII, lines 182–91, 205–10, 312–19, 353–63, in *William Wordsworth: Selected Poems*, ed. Nicholas Roe, Folio Society (London, 2002), pp. 328–9, 332–3; Virgil, *Georgics*, Book II, line 146; Book IV, lines 126–33.

54. Jonathan Bate, *Romantic Ecology: Wordsworth and the Environmental Tradition* (London/ New York, 1991), pp. 22–8.
55. *Edinburgh Review,* 24 (1814): 1–31.
56. Stephen Gill, *Wordsworth and the Victorians* (Oxford, 1998), pp. 40–80; Bate, *Romantic Ecology,* pp. 8–10.
57. Wordsworth, *The Excursion* (1814), Book I, lines 198–9, 206–10; Book IX, lines 1–9, in *The Poetical Works of William Wordsworth,* ed. Ernest de Selincourt and Helen Darbishire, 5 vols (Oxford, 1940–9), vol. 5, pp. 14–15, 286.
58. James Montgomery in the *Eclectic Review,* 2nd ser., 3 (1815): 13–39, John Wilson in *Blackwood's Magazine,* 24 (1828): 917–38, and Henry Crabb Robinson, quoted in Gill, *Wordsworth and the Victorians,* pp. 44, 66; Crabb Robinson quoted in Nicola Trott, 'The shape of the poetic career' in *Cambridge Companion to Wordsworth,* ed. Gill, p. 5.
59. Coleridge to Thomas Allsop, July 1820, in *The Collected Letters of Samuel Taylor Coleridge,* ed. Earl Leslie Griggs, 6 vols (Oxford, 1956–71), vol. 5, p. 95; see Thomas McFarland, *Coleridge and the Pantheist Tradition* (Oxford, 1969), p. 271.
60. *Coleridge's Notebooks: A Selection,* ed. Seamus Perry (Oxford, 2002), pp. 44–5.
61. Stephen Gill, 'The philosophic poet', in *Cambridge Companion to Wordsworth,* ed. Gill, pp. 142–60.
62. Wordsworth, *The Excursion,* Book III, lines 161–82, in *Poetical Works of Wordsworth,* ed. de Selincourt and Darbishire, vol. 5, p. 80.
63. *A Complete Guide to the Lakes . . . with Mr Wordsworth's Description of the Scenery of the Country, &c and Three Letters upon the Geology of the Lake District by the Rev. Professor Sedgwick* (Kendal/London, 1842), Appendix, pp. 3, 4, 29, 54.
64. Adam Sedgwick in *A Complete Guide to the Lakes,* 4th edn, ed. J. Hudson (Kendal, 1853), p. 257; Wyatt, *Wordsworth and the Geologists,* p. 204; Gill, *Wordsworth and the Victorians,* pp. 66–9, 280.
65. Leonard G. Wilson, *Charles Lyell. The Years to 1841: The Revolution in Geology* (New Haven, CT/London, 1972), pp. 218–61.
66. Katherine M. Lyell, *Life, Letters and Journals of Sir Charles Lyell, Bart.,* 2 vols (London, 1881), vol. 1, pp. 234–5.
67. Charles Lyell, *Principles of Geology, Being An Attempt to Explain the Former Changes of the Earth's Surface, By Reference to Causes Now in Operation,* 3 vols (London, 1830–3), vol. 1, pp. 449–59.
68. Sir William Hamilton, *Campi Phlegraei. Observations on the Volcanos of the Two Sicilies . . .,* 2 vols (Naples, 1776), pp. 70–77.
69. Martin J.S. Rudwick, 'The strategy of Lyell's *Principles of Geology*', in *Isis,* 61 (1970): 5–33, esp. p. 6, citing Adam Sedgwick and W.H. Fitton.
70. Rachel Laudan, *From Mineralogy to Geology: The Foundations of a Science, 1650–1830* (Chicago/London, 1978), pp. 216–18.
71. William Whewell, *The Philosophy of the Inductive Sciences, Founded upon their History,* 2nd edn, 2 vols (London, 1847), vol. 2, pp. 65–74.
72. John Playfair, *Illustrations of the Huttonian Theory of the Earth* (Edinburgh, 1802), in *The Works of John Playfair,* 4 vols (Edinburgh, 1822), vol. 1, p. 415.
73. Lyell, *Principles of Geology,* vol. 1, p. 165.
74. [William Whewell,] 'Principles of Geology . . . by Charles Lyell', *British Critic, Theological Review, and Ecclesiastical Record,* 9 (1831): 180–206; W.F. Cannon, 'The uniformitarian-catastrophist debate', *Isis,* 51 (1960): 38–55.
75. William Buckland, *Reliquiae Diluvianae; or, Observations on the Organic Remains contained in Caves, Fissures, and Diluvial Gravel, and on other Geological Phenomena attesting the Action of an Universal Deluge* (London, 1823), p. 43.
76. Martin J.S. Rudwick, *Bursting the Limits of Time: The Reconstruction of Geohistory in the Age of Revolution* (Chicago, IL/London, 2005), pp. 585–99.
77. Rudwick, 'The strategy of Lyell's *Principles* of Geology', pp. 7–8; James A. Secord, 'Introduction' to Charles Lyell, *Principles of Geology* (Harmondsworth, 1997), p. xix.

78. Lyell, *Principles of Geology*, vol. 1, p. 375.
79. Adam Sedgwick, 'Address to the Geological Society, delivered on the evening of 18th of February 1831', *Proceedings of the Geological Society of London*, 1 (1831): 281–316.
80. William Buckland, *Reliquiae Diluvianae*, pp. 43, 226, 228.
81. Katherin M. Lyell, *Life, Letters and Journals*, vol. 1, p. 268.
82. Martin J.S. Rudwick, *Worlds Before Adam: The Reconstruction of Geohistory in the Age of Reform* (Chicago/London, 2008), pp. 288–96.
83. Secord, 'Introduction' to Lyell, *Principles of Geology*, pp. xxiv–xxv.
84. Rudwick, *Worlds Before Adam*, p. 290; Katherine M. Lyell, *Life, Letters and Journals*, vol. 1, p. 253.
85. Sedgwick, 'Address to the Geological Society . . . February 1831', p. 313.
86. Martin J.S. Rudwick, 'Lyell on Etna, and the antiquity of the earth', in *Towards a History of Geology*, ed. Cecil J. Schneer (Cambridge, MA, 1969), pp. 288–304.
87. Lyell, *Principles of Geology*, vol. 3, pp. 88–90, 93; John Milton, *Paradise Lost*, Book I, lines 612–15.
88. Rudwick, 'Lyell on Etna', p. 292.
89. Lyell, *Principles of Geology*, vol. 3, pp. 99, 101.
90. Martin J.S. Rudwick, *The Great Devonian Controversy: The Shaping of Scientific Knowledge Among Gentlemanly Specialists* (Chicago/London, 1985); James A. Secord, *Controversy in Victorian Geology: The Cambrian-Silurian Dispute* (Princeton, NJ, 1986).
91. Adam Sedgwick, 'Letter II – (5th of the series)', in *A Complete Guide to the Lakes*, 4th edn, ed. J. Hudson, pp. 236–58; Secord, *Controversy in Victorian Geology*, p. 264.
92. William Buckland, *Geology and Mineralogy considered with reference to Natural Theology*, 2 vols (London, 1836), vol. 1, p. 582; Jonathan Topham, 'Science and popular education in the 1830s: the role of the *Bridgewater Treatises*', *British Journal for the History of Science*, 25 (1992): 397–430.
93. Mary Buckland to William Whewell, 12 May 1833, in Jack Morrell and Arnold Thackray, ed., *Gentlemen of Science: Early Correspondence of the British Association for the Advancement of Science*, Royal Historical Society, Camden Fourth Series, Vol. 30 (London, 1984), p. 168; John Hedley Brooke, 'The natural theology of the geologists: some theological strata', in *Images of the Earth: Essays on the History of the Environmental Sciences*, ed. Ludmilla Jordanova and Roy Porter, British Society for the History of Science Monograph, 2nd edn (n.p., 1997), pp. 53–74.
94. *The Works of John Ruskin*, vol. 36, p. 115.
95. *The Works of John Ruskin*, vol. 4, pp. 392–3.
96. *The Works of John Ruskin*, vol. 3, p. vii; Wordsworth, *The Excursion*, Book IV, lines 978–92 (with Ruskin's elision and text), in *Poetical Works of Wordsworth*, ed. de Selincourt and Darbishire, vol. 5, p. 140.
97. *The Works of John Ruskin*, vol. 3, pp. 51–2, 104.
98. *The Works of John Ruskin*, vol. 5, pp. 31–2, 221; vol. 13, p. 161n; George P. Landow, *The Aesthetic and Critical Theories of John Ruskin* (Princeton, NJ, 1971), pp. 3–53.
99. *The Works of John Ruskin*, vol. 3, pp. 36–44.
100. *The Works of John Ruskin*, vol. 36, p. 34.
101. *The Works of John Ruskin*, vol. 4, p. 364; Michael Wheeler, *Ruskin's God* (Cambridge, 1999), pp. 29–72; C. Stephen Finley, *Nature's Covenant: Figures of Landscape in Ruskin* (University Park, PA, 1992), pp. 161–225.
102. *The Works of John Ruskin*, vol. 5, pp. 135, 138, 333, 387; Elizabeth K. Helsinger, *Ruskin and the Art of the Beholder* (Cambridge, MA/London, 1982), pp. 41–110.
103. *The Works of John Ruskin*, vol. 3, pp. 343–8; Wordsworth, *The Excursion*, Book III, lines 94–8, in *Poetical Works of Wordsworth*, ed. de Selincourt and Darbishire, vol. 5, p. 78.
104. *The Works of John Ruskin*, vol. 3, pp. 361–3; Wordsworth, *The Excursion*, Book IX, lines 592–608, in *Poetical Works of Wordsworth*, ed. de Selincourt and Darbishire, vol. 5, p. 306.

105. *The Works of John Ruskin*, vol. 3, p. 381; Wheeler, *Ruskin's God*, pp. 29–30.
106. *The Works of John Ruskin*, vol. 3, pp. 404–5; Wordsworth, *The Excursion*, Book IV, lines 520–5, in *Poetical Works of Wordsworth*, ed. de Selincourt and Darbishire, vol. 5, p. 125.
107. *The Works of John Ruskin*, vol. 3, pp. 306–7; Wordsworth, *The Excursion*, Book VII, lines 395–9, in *Poetical Works of Wordsworth*, ed. de Selincourt and Darbishire, vol. 5, p. 244.
108. *The Works of John Ruskin*, vol. 6, pp. 10, 25, 27–8, 35, 41–2; Walton, *Master Drawings by John Ruskin*, pp. 44–53.
109. *The Works of John Ruskin*, vol. 6, pp. 150–2, 418.
110. *The Works of John Ruskin*, vol. 12, pp. xxiv, 158; vol. 6, pp. 368–9; catalogue entries by Allen Staley in *Pre-Raphaelite Vision: Truth to Nature*, ed. Staley and Newall, exh. cat., Tate Gallery, 2004, pp. 145–8.
111. *The Works of John Ruskin*, vol. 5, pp. 359, 362; Wordsworth, *The Excursion*, Book III, lines 161–82, in *Poetical Works of Wordsworth*, ed. de Selincourt and Darbishire, vol. 5, p. 80.
112. *The Works of John Ruskin*, vol. 5, pp. 197, 205, 221–2, 226–7, 352, 378; Wordsworth, *The Excursion*, Book IV, lines 861–71, in *Poetical Works of Wordsworth*, ed. de Selincourt and Darbishire, vol. 5, p. 136; Bate, *Romantic Ecology*, pp. 62–84.
113. *The Works of John Ruskin*, vol. 26, pp. 281, 336, 343; vol. 34, p. 318; Robert Hewison, '"Paradise lost": Ruskin and science' and Paul Wilson, '"Over yonder are the Andes": reading Ruskin reading Humboldt', in *Time and Tide: Ruskin and Science*, ed. Michael Wheeler (London, 1996), pp. 29–44, 65–84.

Chapter 6   Flora and Fauna, the 'Tree of Life'

1. *The Works of John Ruskin*, Library Edition, ed. E.T. Cook and Alexander Wedderburn, 39 vols (London, 1903–12), vol. 36, p. 14 (letter of 22 April 1837 to his father).
2. *Charles Darwin's Notebooks, 1836–1844. Geology, Transmutation of Species, Metaphysical Enquiries*, transcr. and ed. Paul H. Barrett, Peter J. Gautrey, Sandra Herbert, David Kohn and Sydney Smith (Cambridge/Ithaca, NY, 1987), p. 180 ('Notebook B, p. 36') ; see Jonathan Hodge, 'The notebook programmes and projects of Darwin's London years', in *The Cambridge Companion to Darwin*, ed. Jonathan Hodge and Gregory Radick (Cambridge, 2003), pp. 40–68, esp. p. 49.
3. Charles Darwin, *On the Origin of Species by Means of Natural Selection, or the Preservation of Favoured Races in the Struggle for Life* (London, 1859), between pp. 116 and 117, and p. 130.
4. *The Works of Ruskin*, vol. 5, p. 387.
5. *The Works of Ruskin*, vol. 19, pp. 357–8; vol. 25, pp. 200, 250, 268, 340, 353, 359–60, 473.
6. Frederick Kirchhoff, 'A science against sciences: Ruskin's floral mythology', in *Nature and the Victorian Imagination*, ed. U.C. Knoepflmacher and G.B. Tennyson (Berkeley & Los Angeles, CA/London, 1977), pp. 246–58.
7. Lorraine Daston and Katharine Park, *Wonders and the Order of Nature 1150–1750* (New York, 1998).
8. *The Correspondence of Isaac Newton*, ed. H.W. Turnbull *et al.*, 7 vols (Cambridge, 1959–77), vol. 1, pp. 82–3.
9. Steven Shapin and Simon Schaffer, *Leviathan and the Air-Pump: Hobbes, Boyle and the Experimental Life* (Princeton, NJ, 1985).
10. Daston and Park, *Wonders and the Order of Nature*, pp. 329–63; Michel Foucault, *The Order of Things: An Archaeology of the Human Sciences* (1966) (London, 1970), pp. 125–65.
11. David Hume, *Enquiries Concerning the Human Understanding and Concerning the Principles of Morals*, ed. L.A. Selby-Bigge, 2nd edn (Oxford, 1902), p. 130.

12. D.P. Walker, *The Decline of Hell: Seventeenth-Century Discussions of Eternal Torment* (Chicago, IL/London, 1964).

13. Martin J. S. Rudwick, *The Meaning of Fossils: Episodes in the History of Palaeontology*, 2nd edn (New York, 1976), chapters 1–3.

14. Quoted and translated in Martin J.S. Rudwick, *Bursting the Limits of Time: The Reconstruction of Geohistory in the Age of Revolutions* (Chicago, IL/London, 2005), p. 230.

15. Quoted and translated in Rudwick, *Bursting the Limits of Time*, pp. 359, 363.

16. Quoted in Lisbet Koerner, *Linnaeus: Nature and Nation* (Cambridge, MA/London, 1999), p. 26.

17. Londa Schiebinger, 'Gender and natural history', in *Cultures of Natural History*, ed. N. Jardine, J.A. Secord and E.C. Spary (Cambridge, 1996), pp. 163–77.

18. Quoted in Janet Browne, 'Botany in the boudoir and garden: the Banksian context', in *Visions of Empire: Voyages, Botany and Representations of Nature*, ed. D.P. Miller and P.H. Reill (Cambridge, 1996), pp. 153–72, on pp. 155–7.

19. Quoted in Koerner, *Linnaeus*, p. 28.

20. Koerner, *Linnaeus*, pp. 14–55; James Larson, *Reason and Experience: The Representation of Natural Order in the Work of Carl Linné* (Berkeley & Los Angeles, CA/London, 1971).

21. Donald Worster, *Nature's Economy: A History of Ecological Ideas*, reprint edn (Cambridge, 1985), pp. 31–9.

22. Erasmus Darwin, *The Temple of Nature; or, The Origins of Society: A Poem, with Philosophical Notes* (London, 1803), preface.

23. *Coleridge's Notebooks: A Selection*, ed. Seamus Perry (Oxford, 2002), p. 3.

24. [Erasmus Darwin,] *The Botanic Garden, Part II. Containing The Loves of the Plants, A Poem: With Philosophical Notes* (Lichfield, 1789), pp. i, vi, 7n, 49.

25. Janet Browne, 'Botany for gentlemen: Erasmus Darwin and *The Loves of the Plants*', *Isis*, 80 (1989): 593–621.

26. [Erasmus Darwin,] *The Loves of the Plants*, pp. 4, 6, 148–9, 164–5 (Canto I, lines 39–44, 61–4; Canto IV, lines 190, 206, 387–8, 401–6).

27. *The Yale Edition of Horace Walpole's Correspondence*, ed. W.S. Lewis *et al.*, 48 vols (New Haven, CT/London, 1937–83), vol. 11, p. 11.

28. *The Collected Letters of Erasmus Darwin*, ed. Desmond King-Hele (Cambridge, 2007), p. 525.

29. Charlotte Klonk, *Science and the Perception of Nature: British Landscape Art in the Late Eighteenth and Early Nineteenth Centuries* (New Haven, CT/London, 1996), pp. 37–65.

30. *Horace Walpole's Correspondence*, vol. 20, pp. 111, 372, 380.

31. Batty Langley, *New Principles of Gardening* (London, 1728), p. 182.

32. *Horace Walpole's Correspondence*, vol. 9, p. 176; vol. 10, pp. 127, 156.

33. Humphry Repton, *Observations on the Theory and Practice of Landscape Gardening* (London, 1803), p. 102.

34. Mark Laird, *The Flowering of the Landscape Garden: English Pleasure Grounds 1720–1800* (Philadelphia, PA, 1999), pp. 12–17, 163–72, 350–60; quotation from Nathaniel Swinden, *The Beauties of Flora Display'd* (London, 1778) on p. 331.

35. Charles Lyell, *Principles of Geology, Being an Attempt to Explain the Former Changes of the Earth's Surface, By Reference to Causes Now in Operation*, 3 vols (London, 1830–3), vol. 2, pp. 65, 169, 179; Martin J.S Rudwick, 'The strategy of Lyell's *Principles of Geology*', *Isis*, 61 (1970): 5–33, esp. pp. 18–21.

36. *The Correspondence of Charles Darwin*, ed. Frederick Burckhardt and Sydney Smith *et al.* (Cambridge, 1985–), vol. 11, pp. 230–1.

37. *Charles Darwin's Notebooks*, p. 413 ('Notebook E', p. 59) and footnote.

38. *Correspondence of Charles Darwin*, vol. 1, p. 460.

39. *Charles Darwin's Beagle Diary*, ed. R.D. Keynes (Cambridge, 1988), p. 359.

40. [Charles] Darwin, *On Evolution: The Development of the Theory of Natural Selection*, ed. Thomas F. Glick and David Kohn (Indianapolis, IN/Cambridge, 1996), p. 49.

41. *Charles Darwin's Notebooks*, pp. 62–3 ('Red Notebook', p. 130).

42. *Correspondence of Charles Darwin*, vol. 2, p. 431; Janet Browne, *Charles Darwin: Voyaging* (London, 1995), pp. 358–61.

43. *Voyage of the 'Beagle': Charles Darwin's 'Journal of Researches'* [1839 edn], ed. Janet Browne and Michael Neve (Harmondsworth, 1989), pp. 287–8; *Darwin's Beagle Diary*, p. 360; Darwin, *On Evolution*, p. 29.

44. Frank J. Sulloway, 'Darwin and his finches: the evolution of a legend' and 'Darwin's conversion: the *Beagle* voyage and its aftermath', *Journal of the History of Biology*, 15 (1982): 1–53, 325–96.

45. Adrian Desmond, *The Politics of Evolution: Morphology, Medicine, and Reform in Radical London* (Chicago, IL/London, 1989), pp. 398–414.

46. *Charles Darwin's Notebooks*, pp. 172, 177, 180, 189, 213, 233 ('Notebook B', pp. 7, 8, 25, 36, 74, 169, 252).

47. *Charles Darwin's Notebooks*, pp. 264, 291, 293 ('Notebook C', pp. 79, 166, 175).

48. Dov Ospovat, *The Development of Darwin's Theory: Natural History, Natural Theology and Natural Selection, 1838–1859* (Cambridge, 1981), pp. 39–59.

49. Darwin, *Origin of Species*, p. 127.

50. Silvan S. Schweber, 'The origin of the *Origin* revisited', *Journal of the History of Biology*, 10 (1977): 229–316.

51. Lyell, *Principles of Geology*, vol. 2, p. 131.

52. T.R. Malthus, *An Essay on the Principle of Population*, ed. Donald Winch (Cambridge, 1992), pp. 14, 17, 21.

53. *The Autobiography of Charles Darwin 1809–1882*, ed. Nora Barlow (London, 1958), p. 120.

54. *Charles Darwin's Notebooks*, pp. 375–6 ('Notebook D', pp. 134e–5e).

55. *Autobiography of Charles Darwin*, p. 65; Philip R. Sloan, ' "The sense of sublimity": Darwin on nature and divinity', *Osiris*, 16 (2001): 251–69.

56. *Correspondence of Charles Darwin*, vol. 7, p. 388.

57. *Charles Darwin's Notebooks*, p. 293 ('Notebook C', p. 175); William Paley, *Natural Theology: or, Evidence of the Existence and Attributes of the Deity, Collected from the Appearances of Nature* (London, 1802), pp. 29, 42.

58. M.J.S. Hodge and David Kohn, 'The immediate origins of natural selection', in *The Darwinian Heritage*, ed. David Kohn (Princeton, NJ, 1985), pp. 185–206.

59. *Charles Darwin's Notebooks*, pp. 412–13, 436 ('Notebook E', pp. 57–9, 137); Ospovat, *The Development of Darwin's Theory*, pp. 60–73.

60. Darwin, *On Evolution*, pp. 91–2, 101, 103, 104–5; Sloan, '"The sense of sublimity"', p. 264; Ospovat, *The Development of Darwin's Theory*, pp. 73–86.

61. *Correspondence of Charles Darwin*, vol. 3, p. 2.

62. *Correspondence of Charles Darwin*, vol. 3, pp. 103, 108, 181, 258; [Adam Sedgwick,] 'Vestiges of the natural history of creation', *Edinburgh Review*, 82 (1845), 1–85, on p. 3; James A. Secord, *Victorian Sensation: The Extraordinary Publication, Reception and Secret Authorship of 'Vestiges of the Natural History of Creation'* (Chicago, IL/London, 2000), pp. 231–47, 429–33.

63. *Correspondence of Charles Darwin*, vol. 3, p. 253; vol. 4, p. 140; Darwin's note quoted in Ospovat, *The Development of Darwin's Theory*, p. 176.

64. *Correspondence of Charles Darwin*, vol. 5, pp. 233, 348; vol. 6, pp. 447–9; Janet Browne, *The Secular Ark: Studies in the History of Biogeography* (New Haven, CT/London, 1983), pp. 195–220.

65. R.C. Stauffer, ed., *Charles Darwin's Natural Selection: Being the Second Part of His Big Species Book Written from 1856 to 1858* (Cambridge, 1975), pp. 218–19, 243–4, 249.

66. *Correspondence of Charles Darwin*, vol. 7, p. 102. Ospovat, *The Development of Darwin's Theory*, pp. 170–209.

67. *Correspondence of Charles Darwin*, vol. 7, pp. 107, 127.

68. William Whewell, *Astronomy and General Physics considered with reference to Natural Theology* (London, 1833), p. 356.

69. Darwin, *Origin of Species*, pp. 1, 459; *Correspondence of Charles Darwin*, vol. 11, pp. 402–3.

70. C. Kenneth Waters, 'The arguments in the *Origin of Species*', in *The Cambridge Companion to Darwin*, ed. Hodge and Radick, pp. 116–39.

71. Darwin, *Origin of Species*, pp. 63, 67, 73, 79, 81, 83–4, 95, 112, 114, 130, 201–2.

72. *Correspondence of Charles Darwin*, vol. 7, p. 397.

73. Morse Peckham, ed., '*The Origin of Species*' by Charles Darwin: a Variorum Text (Philadelphia, PA, 1959), p. 165; Robert M. Young, 'Darwin's metaphor: does nature select?', *The Monist*, 55 (1971): 442–503; Gillian Beer, *Darwin's Plots: Evolutionary Narrative in Darwin, George Eliot and Nineteenth-Century Fiction*, 2nd edn (Cambridge, 2000), pp. 62–6.

74. Darwin, *Origin of Species*, pp. 484, 488–90; *Correspondence of Charles Darwin*, vol. 7, p. 397; vol. 11, p. 278; David Kohn, 'Darwin's ambiguity: the secularization of biological meaning', *British Journal for the History of Science*, 22 (1989): 215–39.

75. *Correspondence of Charles Darwin*, vol. 8, p. 140.

76. Darwin, *Origin of Species*, pp. 189–90.

77. Helena Cronin, *The Ant and the Peacock: Altruism and Sexual Selection from Darwin to Today* (Cambridge, 1991).

78. Charles Darwin, *The Descent of Man, and Selection in Relation to Sex*, reprint of the revised 2nd edn of 1874 (New York, 1974), p. 207.

79. John R. Durant, 'The ascent of nature in Darwin's *Descent of Man*', in *The Darwinian Heritage*, ed. Kohn, pp. 283–306.

80. Darwin, *The Descent of Man, and Selection in Relation to Sex*, pp. 89–91.

81. Darwin, *The Descent of Man, and Selection in Relation to Sex*, pp. 392, 394.

82. Darwin, *The Descent of Man, and Selection in Relation to Sex*, p. 435.

83. *The Works of Ruskin*, vol. 25, pp. 263, 268.

84. Jonathan Smith, *Charles Darwin and Victorian Visual Culture* (Cambridge, 2006), pp. 134–6.

85. *Correspondence of Charles Darwin*, vol. 9, p. 279.

86. Smith, *Darwin and Victorian Visual Culture*, pp. 138–43, 152–5.

87. *The Works of Ruskin*, vol. 25, pp. 189, 260–1, 391, 413; Smith, *Darwin and Victorian Visual Culture*, pp. 167–8, 173–5.

88. Dinah Birch, 'Ruskin and the science of *Proserpina*', in *New Approaches to Ruskin*, ed. Robert Hewison (London, 1982), pp. 142–56.

89. *The Works of Ruskin*, vol. 25, pp. 300–1; Tim Hilton, *John Ruskin* (New Haven, CT/London, 2002), p. 593.

90. *The Works of Ruskin*, vol. 25, pp. 250, 268, 340, 352, 353.

91. [Henrietta Litchfield,] *Richard Buckley Litchfield. A Memoir written for his Friends by his Wife* (Cambridge, 1910); *The Scientific Letters and Papers of James Clerk Maxwell*, ed. P.M. Harman, 3 vols (Cambridge, 1990–2002), vol. 1.

92. *The Works of Ruskin*, vol. 38, p. 334; vol. 15, p. 411; Smith, *Darwin and Victorian Visual Culture*, pp. 133–4, 278.

93. *Correspondence of Charles Darwin*, vol. 11, p. 403.

94. *Correspondence of Charles Darwin*, vol. 7, pp. 102, 397.

95. *The Works of Ruskin*, vol. 6, p. 69.

Chapter 7 Colour

1. John Gage, *George Field and His Circle: From Romanticism to the Pre-Raphaelite Brotherhood*, exh. cat., Fitzwilliam Museum 1982 (Cambridge, 1982), p. 65; Alison Smith, '"The enfranchised eye"' and catalogue entry, in *Pre-Raphaelite Vision: Truth to Nature*, ed. Allen Staley and Christopher Newall, exh. cat., Tate Britain 2004 (London, 2004), pp. 17, 34–5.

2. Martin Kemp, *The Science of Art: Optical Themes in Western Art from Brunelleschi to Seurat* (New Haven, CT/London, 1990), pp. 304–5.
3. *The Works of John Ruskin*, Library Edition, ed. E.T. Cook and Alexander Wedderburn, 39 vols (London, 1903–12), vol. 33, pp. 272–3.
4. *The Scientific Letters and Papers of James Clerk Maxwell*, ed. P.M. Harman, 3 vols (Cambridge, 1990–2002), vol. 2, pp. 559, 563.
5. *The Correspondence of Isaac Newton*, ed. H.W. Turnbull *et al.*, 7 vols (Cambridge, 1959–77), vol. 1, pp. 82–3, 92.
6. *The Works of the Right Honourable Joseph Addison, Esq; In Four Volumes* [ed. Thomas Tickell] (London, 1721), vol. 3, p. 492.
7. Mark Akenside, *The Pleasure of Imagination. A Poem. In Three Books* (London, 1744), Book I, lines 447–9.
8. Dugald Stewart, *Philosophical Essays*, 3rd edn (London, 1818), pp. 274, 279.
9. George Turnbull, *A Treatise on Ancient Painting, containing Observations on the Rise, Progress, and Decline of that Art amongst the Greeks and the Romans* (London, 1740), p. 146.
10. Editorial 'Introduction' to *The Optical Papers of Isaac Newton: Volume I: The Optical Lectures 1670–1672*, ed. Alan E. Shapiro (Cambridge, 1984), pp. 2–4, quoting Robert Boyle, *Experiments and Considerations Touching Colours* (London, 1664), pp. 11, 76.
11. Alan E. Shapiro, 'Artists' colours and Newton's colours', *Isis*, 85 (1994): 600–30; Kemp, *The Science of Art*, pp. 264–84.
12. J.E. McGuire and Martin Tamny, *Certain Philosophical Questions: Newton's Trinity Notebook* (Cambridge, 1983), pp. 432–5.
13. *Correspondence of Isaac Newton*, vol. 1, p. 92.
14. Alan E. Shapiro, 'The spectre of Newton's "spectrum"', in *From Ancient Omens to Statistical Mechanics: Essays on the Exact Sciences Presented to Asger Aaboe*, ed. J.L. Berggren and B.R. Goldstein (Copenhagen, 1987), pp. 183–92.
15. *Correspondence of Isaac Newton*, vol. 1, pp. 95–7; Alan E. Shapiro, 'The evolving structure of Newton's theory of white light and colour', *Isis*, 71 (1980): 211–35.
16. *Correspondence of Isaac Newton*, vol. 1, p. 98.
17. *The Optical Papers of Isaac Newton: Volume I*, ed. Shapiro, p. 543.
18. *Correspondence of Isaac Newton*, vol. 1, pp. 97–8.
19. *Correspondence of Isaac Newton*, vol. 1, pp. 96–7, 173.
20. Isaac Newton, *Opticks: Or a Treatise of the Reflections, Refractions, Inflections & Colours of Light* [Dover reprint based on the 4th edn, 1730] (New York, 1952), pp. 26, 45–6; Shapiro, 'The evolving structure of Newton's theory of white light and colour', pp. 213–14, 233–4.
21. *Correspondence of Isaac Newton*, vol. 1, p. 98.
22. *Correspondence of Isaac Newton*, vol. 1, p. 256; see Shapiro, 'The evolving structure of Newton's theory of white light and colour', p. 223.
23. Hermann Helmholtz, 'On the theory of compound colours', *Philosophical Magazine*, ser. 4, 4 (1852): 519–34, on pp. 526, 528.
24. *Correspondence of Isaac Newton*, vol. 1, p. 100.
25. McGuire and Tamny, *Certain Philosophical Questions*, p. 476; see Alan E. Shapiro, *Fits, Passions and Paroxysms: Physics, Method and Chemistry and Newton's Theories of Coloured Bodies and Fits of Easy Reflection* (Cambridge, 1993), pp. 50–72.
26. Newton, *Opticks*, pp. 198–9, 206, 209.
27. Newton, *Opticks*, pp. 225–35; see Shapiro, *Fits, Passions and Paroxysms*, pp. 89–97.
28. Newton, *Opticks*, pp. 225, 255–6; see Shapiro, *Fits, Passions and Paroxysms*, pp. 111–29.
29. See Shapiro, *Fits, Passions and Paroxysms*, pp. 230–4, 242–67.
30. Edward Hussey Delaval, 'An experimental inquiry into the cause of the permanent colours of opake bodies', *Memoirs of the Literary and Philosophical Society of Manchester*, 2 (1785): 131–256, on pp. 142–4, 146, 155, 171, 208, 250; Shapiro, *Fits, Passions and Paroxysms*, pp. 269–72.

31. Delaval, 'An experimental inquiry into the cause of the permanent colours of opake bodies', pp. 208, 255–6n.

32. John Gage, *Colour and Culture: Practice and Meaning from Antiquity to Abstraction* (London, 1993), pp. 213, 221.

33. John Herschel, 'On the absorption of light by coloured media, and on the colours of the prismatic spectrum exhibited by certain flames', *Transactions of the Royal Society of Edinburgh*, 9 (1823), 445–60, on p. 446; Herschel, 'On the absorption of light by coloured media, viewed in connexion with the undulatory theory', *Philosophical Magazine*, ser. 3, 3 (1833): 401–12, on p. 401; see Shapiro, *Fits, Passions and Paroxysms*, pp. 331–56.

34. *Correspondence of Isaac Newton*, vol. 1, pp. 256, 291; *Isaac Newton's Papers and Letters on Natural Philosophy*, ed. I. Bernard Cohen (Cambridge, 1958), p. 136; see Shapiro, 'The evolving structure of Newton's theory of white light and colour', pp. 224–5.

35. *The Scientific Papers of James Clerk Maxwell*, ed. W.D. Niven, 2 vols (Cambridge, 1890), vol. 1, pp. 411–12.

36. *The Optical Papers of Isaac Newton: Volume I*, ed. Shapiro, pp. 543–7.

37. Gage, *Colour and Culture*, pp. 231–2; Penelope Gouk, *Music, Science and Natural Magic in Seventeenth-Century England* (New Haven, CT/London, 1999), pp. 224–57.

38. Newton, *Opticks*, pp. 126–7.

39. Newton, *Opticks*, pp. 154–7.

40. Isaac Newton, *Opticks*, pp. 122, 133, 151, 157–8; Brook Taylor, *New Principles of Linear Perspective* (London, 1719), Appendix 2, pp. 67–70; Shapiro, 'Artists' colours and Newton's colours', pp. 620–6; Kemp, *The Science of Art*, p. 287.

41. Gage, *Colour and Culture*, pp. 227–32.

42. 'Chromatic', in *Encyclopaedia Britannica*, 3rd edn , vol. 4 (Edinburgh, 1797), p. 721.

43. [Charles Hutton,] 'Chromatics', *Encyclopaedia Britannica*, 3rd edn , vol. 4, pp. 721–41, esp. p. 741; on Hutton's authorship of the article see Shapiro, *Fits, Passions and Paroxysms*, p. 279n.

44. Thomas L. Hankins and Robert J. Silverman, *Instruments and the Imagination* (Princeton, NJ, 1995), pp. 72–85; Kemp, *The Science of Art*, pp. 287–8; Gage, *Colour and Culture*, pp. 234–5; Martin Franssen, 'The ocular harpsichord of Louis-Bertrand Castel', *Tractrix*, 3 (1991): 15–77.

45. Quoted in Franssen, 'The ocular harpsichord of Louis-Bertrand Castel', p. 69.

46. Edmund Burke, *A Philosophical Enquiry into the Origin of Our Ideas of the Sublime and Beautiful* (2nd edn 1759), ed. J.T. Boulton (London, 1958), p. 117.

47. Quoted in Mark Laird, *The Flowering of the Landscape Garden: English Pleasure Grounds 1720–1800* (Philadelphia, PA, 1999), pp. 258, 339–40.

48. It is likely that Robert Waring Darwin 'was largely aided in writing' the paper on ocular spectra 'by his father' Erasmus who 'preserved the polite fiction that Robert wrote the paper on Ocular Spectra'; see *The Collected Letters of Erasmus Darwin*, ed. Desmond King-Hele (Cambridge, 2007), pp. 282, 433.

49. Robert Waring Darwin, 'New experiments on the ocular spectra of light and colours', *Philosophical Transactions of the Royal Society*, 76 (1786): 313–48, esp. pp. 313, 328.

50. Erasmus Darwin, *The Temple of Nature; or, The Origin of Society: A Poem, with Philosophical Notes* (London, 1803), pp. 87–90.

51. [Erasmus Darwin,] *The Botanic Garden, Part II. Containing The Loves of the Plants, A Poem: With Philosophical Notes* (Lichfield, 1789), pp. 127–30.

52. Benjamin Thompson, 'An account of some experiments upon coloured shadows', *Philosophical Transactions of the Royal Society*, 84 (1794): 107–18.

53. Isaac Milner, 'Theory of colours and shadows', in Humphry Repton, *Observations on the Theory and Practice of Landscape Gardening* (London, 1803), pp. 214–19.

54. David Brewster, *Treatise on the Kaleidoscope* (Edinburgh, 1819), pp. 69–70, 134–5.

55. Milner, 'Theory of colours and shadows', in Repton, *Theory and Practice of Landscape Gardening*, pp. 218–19.

56. Kemp, *The Science of Art*, pp. 290–1; Paul D. Sherman, *Colour Vision in the Nineteenth Century: The Young-Helmholtz-Maxwell Theory* (Bristol, 1981), pp. 64–7.

57. J.D. Forbes, 'Hints towards a classification of colours', *Philosophical Magazine*, ser. 3, 34 (1849): 161–78, esp. pp. 162, 165, 168–9.

58. Forbes, 'Hints towards a classification of colours', p. 162; *Letters and Papers of Maxwell*, ed. Harman, vol. 1, pp. 300 note 2 and 301 note 5.

59. Maxwell, *Scientific Papers*, vol. 1, pp. 128, 144, 244; *Letters and Papers of Maxwell*, ed. Harman, vol. 1, pp. 284–5.

60. David Brewster, *A Treatise on Optics* (London, 1831), p. 73.

61. David Brewster, 'On a new analysis of solar light', *Transactions of the Royal Society of Edinburgh*, 12 (1834): 123–36; Hermann Helmholtz, 'On Sir David Brewster's new analysis of solar light', *Philosophical Magazine*, ser. 4, 4 (1852): 401–16.

62. Maxwell, *Scientific Papers*, vol. 1, p. 136.

63. Thomas Young, *A Course of Lectures on Natural Philosophy and the Mechanical Arts*, 2 vols (London, 1807), vol. 1, pp. 440, 786.

64. Forbes, 'Hints towards a classification of colours', p. 172; *Letters and Papers of Maxwell*, ed. Harman, vol. 1, p. 269.

65. Hermann Grassmann, 'On the theory of compound colours', *Philosophical Magazine*, ser. 4, 7 (1854): 254–64, esp. p. 255.

66. *Letters and Papers of Maxwell*, ed. Harman, vol. 1, pp. 268–70; Maxwell, *Scientific Papers*, vol. 1, pp. 131–2, 135.

67. P.M. Harman, *The Natural Philosophy of James Clerk Maxwell* (Cambridge, 1998), pp. 37–48.

68. Maxwell, *Scientific Papers*, vol. 1, pp. 136, 449.

69. *Letters and Papers of Maxwell*, ed. Harman, vol. 1, pp. 326 note 7, 568 note 2.

70. Quoted in Gage, *Colour and Culture*, p. 107.

71. *The Prelude* (1805), Book III, lines 45–60, in *William Wordsworth: Selected Poems*, ed. Nicholas Roe, Folio Society (London, 2002), p. 242; 'Lamia' (1820), Part II, lines 229–37, in *The Poetical Works of John Keats*, ed. H.W. Garrod (Oxford, 1956), pp. 176–7; Percy Bysshe Shelley, 'Adonais' (1821), lines 370, 462–4, in *The New Oxford Book of Romantic Period Verse*, ed. Jerome J. McGann (Oxford, 1993), pp. 626, 629.

72. 'Epitaph. Intended for Sir Isaac Newton, In Westminster-Abbey' (1730), in *The Poems of Alexander Pope*, ed. John Butt (London, 1963), p. 808; Newton, *Opticks*, pp. 168–78.

73. James Thomson, 'Spring', lines 203–12, in *The Seasons* (Oxford, 1981), p. 12; Akenside, *The Pleasures of Imagination*, Part II, lines 103–14; Marjorie Hope Nicolson, *Newton Demands the Muse: Newton's 'Opticks' and the Eighteenth-Century Poets* (Princeton, NJ, 1946), pp. 30–36.

74. Ovid, *Metamorphoses*, Book VI, lines 65–7; Virgil, *Aeneid*, Book IV, line 701; Book V, line 89.

75. *John Constable's Discourses*, comp. and annot. R.B. Beckett (Ipswich, 1970), p. 61.

76. C.R. Leslie, *Memoirs of the Life of John Constable. Composed Chiefly of His Letters* (2nd edn, 1845), ed. Jonathan Mayne (Oxford, 1951), p. 218.

77. *John Constable's Correspondence*, ed. R.B. Beckett, 6 vols (Ipswich, 1962–8), vol. 6, p. 77.

78. *Constable's Correspondence*, vol. 4, p. 433; vol. 6, p. 251; Paul D. Schweitzer, 'John Constable, rainbow science, and English colour theory', *Art Bulletin*, 64 (1982): 424–45; catalogue entry by Timothy Wilcox in *Constable's Clouds: Paintings and Cloud Studies by John Constable*, ed. Edward Morris, exh. cat., National Galleries of Scotland and National Museums and Galleries on Merseyside 2000 (Edinburgh/Liverpool, 2000), pp. 112–15; Gage, *Colour and Culture*, pp. 112–14; John Thornes, *John Constable's Skies: A Fusion of Art and Science* (Birmingham, 1999), pp. 81–8.

79. Quoted in Gage, *Colour and Culture*, pp. 95–6, and in *The Oxford Companion to J.M.W. Turner*, ed. Evelyn Joll, Martin Butlin and Luke Herrmann (Oxford, 2001), p. 273.

80. *The Works of John Ruskin*, vol. 22, p. 212n.

81. *The Works of John Ruskin*, vol. 5, p. 333.

82. Gage, *Colour and Culture*, pp. 114–15; George Landow, 'The rainbow: a problematic image', in *Nature and the Victorian Imagination*, ed. U.C. Knoepflmacher and G.B. Tennyson (Berkeley and Los Angeles, CA/London, 1977), pp. 341–69, esp. p. 369.

83. Carl Boyer, *The Rainbow: From Myth to Mathematics*, new edn (Princeton, NJ, 1987), pp. 294–307.

84. *The Works of John Ruskin*, vol. 5, p. 387.

85. Landow, 'The rainbow: a problematic image', in *Nature and the Victorian Imagination*, ed. Knoepflmacher and Tennyson, pp. 364–5; Allen Staley, catalogue entry in *Pre-Raphaelite Vision: Truth to Nature*, ed. Staley and Newall, exh. cat., Tate Britain 2004, p. 184.

86. George Field, *Chromatics; or, the Analogy, Harmony, and Philosophy of Colours*, new edn, augmented (London, 1845), pp. 4–19, 76.

87. George Field, *Chromatography; or, a Treatise on Colours and Pigments, and of their Powers in Painting, &c* (London, 1835), pp. 35, 39, 42.

88. Field, *Chromatics*, pp. 4, 184.

89. Gage, *Colour and Culture*, pp. 215–21.

90. D.R. Hay, *The Principles of Beauty in Colouring Systematized* (Edinburgh/London, 1845), pp. 25–6.

91. D.R. Hay, *A Nomenclature of Colours, Hues, Tints and Shades, Applicable to the Arts and Natural Sciences; to Manufactures, and other Purposes of General Utility* (Edinburgh/London, 1845), pp. 6–7, 28, 31, 71.

92. *Letters and Papers of Maxwell*, ed. Harman, vol. 1, p. 269 esp. note 6.

93. John Sweetlove, 'The natural philosophy of art', *Art Journal*, new ser., 4 (1852): 6–7.

94. *The Works of John Ruskin*, vol. 33, p. 273.

95. *The Works of John Ruskin*, vol. 3, pp. 279–80, 381.

96. Quoted in *The Oxford Companion to Turner*, ed. Joll, Butlin and Herrmann, p. 106.

97. *The Works of John Ruskin*, vol. 3, pp. 285–8.

98. Newton, *Opticks*, p. 281; Shapiro, *Fits, Passions, and Paroxysms*, pp. 136, 180–1.

99. Lindsay Smith, *Victorian Photography, Painting and Poetry: The Enigma of Visibility in Ruskin, Morris and the Pre-Raphaelites* (Cambridge, 1995), pp. 1–4.

100. *The Works of John Ruskin*, vol. 6, pp. 68–72.

101. *The Works of John Ruskin*, vol. 10, p. 175; Herodotus, *Histories*, Book I, 98.

102. *The Works of John Ruskin*, vol. 7, pp. 415, 418–19; Michael Wheeler, *Ruskin's God* (Cambridge, 1999), pp. 47–9.

103. Quoted in Gage, *Colour and Culture*, pp. 203–4, and Kemp, *The Science of Art*, p. 301.

104. Dennis L. Sepper, *Goethe contra Newton: Polemics and the Project for a New Science of Colour* (Cambridge, 1988).

105. Quoted in Nicholas Boyle, *Goethe: The Poet and the Age. Volume II: Revolution and Renunciation (1790–1803)* (Oxford, 2000), p. 102.

106. Gage, *Colour and Culture*, pp. 201–4; Kemp, *The Science of Art*, pp. 297–304.

107. *The Works of John Ruskin*, vol. 6, pp. 68–9.

Chapter 8   Vital Forces

1. Richard Jenkyns, *Virgil's Experience. Nature and History: Times, Names and Places* (Oxford, 1998), p. 215.

2. Erasmus Darwin, *The Temple of Nature; or, The Origin of Society: A Poem, with Philosophical Notes* (London, 1803), Canto I, lines 129–32.

3. Isaac Newton, *Opticks: Or, a Treatise of the Reflections, Refractions, Inflections & Colours of Light* [Dover reprint based on the 4th edn 1730] (New York, 1952), p. 369.

4. Isaac Newton, *The 'Principia': Mathematical Principles of Natural Philosophy*, trans. I. Bernard Cohen and Anne Whitman (Berkeley and Los Angeles, CA/London, 1999), p. 408.

5. Alan Gabbey, 'Newton, active powers and the mechanical philosophy', in *The Cambridge Companion to Newton*, ed. I. Bernard Cohen and George E. Smith (Cambridge, 2002), pp. 329–57; Gabbey, 'Newton's *Mathematical Principles of Natural Philosophy*: a treatise on "mechanics"?', in *The Investigation of Difficult Things: Essays on Newton and the History of the Exact Sciences in Honour of D.T. Whiteside*, ed. P.M. Harman and Alan E. Shapiro (Cambridge, 1992), pp. 305–22.

6. Newton, *The 'Principia'*, pp. 404–5.

7. Newton, *The 'Principia'*, pp. 794–6.

8. J.E. McGuire, 'Atoms and the "analogy of nature": Newton's third rule of philosophizing', *Studies in History and Philosophy of Science*, 1 (1970): 3–57.

9. Newton, *Opticks*, pp. 245, 255, 260–2, 267, 269; Alan E. Shapiro, *Fits, Passions and Paroxysms: Physics, Method and Chemistry and Newton's Theories of Coloured Bodies and Fits of Easy Reflection* (Cambridge, 1993), pp. 40–48, 125–9; Shapiro, 'Newton's optics and atomism', in *The Cambridge Companion to Newton*, ed. Cohen and Smith, pp. 227–55.

10. *The Correspondence of Isaac Newton*, ed. H.W. Turnbull *et al.*, 7 vols (Cambridge, 1959–77), vol. 3, p. 258.

11. Newton, *The 'Principia'*, p. 943.

12. *Four Letters from Sir Isaac Newton to Doctor Bentley. Containing Some Arguments in Proof of a* DEITY (London, 1756), pp. 25–6, in *Isaac Newton's Papers & Letters on Natural Philosophy*, ed. I. Bernard Cohen (Cambridge, 1958), pp. 302–3.

13. Newton, *Opticks*, pp. 397, 399, 401.

14. J.E. McGuire, 'Force, active principles and Newton's invisible realm', *Ambix*, 15 (1968): 154–208, esp. p. 196.

15. Newton, *Opticks*, pp. 379–80, 399.

16. William R. Newman, 'The background to Newton's chymistry', in *The Cambridge Companion to Newton*, ed. Cohen and Smith, pp. 358–69.

17. *Correspondence of Isaac Newton*, vol. 1, pp. 364–6, 414; the (modified) texts as published in 1744 and 1757 are reprinted in *Newton's Papers & Letters on Natural Philosophy*, ed. Cohen, pp. 180–1, 254.

18. B.J.T. Dobbs, *The Foundations of Newton's Alchemy or 'The Hunting of the Greene Lyon'* (Cambridge, 1975), pp. 204–6.

19. *Correspondence of Isaac Newton*, vol. 5, pp. 298–300.

20. Newton, *Opticks*, pp. 351–2.

21. P.M. Harman, *Metaphysics and Natural Philosophy: The Problem of Substance in Classical Physics* (Brighton, 1982), pp. 8–31.

22. See my articles '"Nature is a perpetual worker": Newton's aether and eighteenth-century natural philosophy', *Ambix*, 20 (1973): 1–25, and 'Ether and imponderables', in *Conceptions of Ether: Studies in the History of Ether Theories, 1740–1900*, ed. G.N. Cantor and M.J.S. Hodge (Cambridge, 1981), pp. 61–83; both reprinted in P.M. Harman, *After Newton: Essays on Natural Philosophy*, Variorum Collected Studies (Aldershot, 1993).

23. Quoted in Robert Kargon, *Atomism in England from Hariot to Newton* (Oxford, 1966), p. 138.

24. Arnold Thackray, *Atoms and Powers: An Essay on Newtonian Matter-theory and the Development of Chemistry* (Cambridge, MA/London, 1970), pp. 8–82.

25. Quoted in Thackray, *Atoms and Powers*, p. 135.

26. Stephen Hales, *Vegetable Staticks; Or, An account of Some Statical Experiments on the Sap in Vegetables* (London, 1727), p. 178.

27. [Herman Boerhaave,] *A New Method of Chemistry: Including the History, theory and Practice of the Art*, trans. Peter Shaw, 2 vols (London, 1741), vol. 1, pp. 173, 208, 223, 359, 362.

28. John Rowning, *A Compendious System of Natural Philosophy* (London, 1744), preface, p. iii.

29. I. Bernard Cohen, ed., *Benjamin Franklin's Experiments* (Cambridge, MA, 1941), pp. 210, 213–14, 233.

30. Gowin Knight, *An Attempt to Demonstrate, That all the Phaenomena in Nature, May be Explained by Two Simple Active Principles, Attraction and Repulsion* (London, 1754), pp. 1–2, 4–5, 56, 66–7.

31. Cadwallader Colden, *The Principles of Action in Matter* (London, 1751), pp. 27–8, 73; R. Lovett, *The Subtil Medium Prov'd* (London, 1756), preface.

32. Quoted in A.L. Donovan, *Philosophical Chemistry in the Scottish Enlightenment: The Doctrines of William Cullen and Joseph Black* (Edinburgh, 1975), pp. 141–51.

33. Quoted in my article 'Ether and imponderables', in *Conceptions of Ether*, ed. Cantor and Hodge, p. 75.

34. P.D. Leslie, *A Philosophical Inquiry into the Causes of Animal Heat* (London, 1778), pp. 119, 124.

35. Adam Walker, *A System of Familiar Philosophy*, rev. edn, 2 vols (London, 1802), vol. 1, pp. 6, 14, 18; vol. 2, pp. 1, 74; Charles Hutton, *A Mathematical and Philosophical Dictionary*, 2 vols (London, 1795–6), vol. 1, p. 473.

36. *The Collected Works of Humphry Davy*, ed. J. Davy, 9 vols (London, 1839–40), vol. 2, pp. 28, 35, 86.

37. *Gentleman's Magazine*, 15 (1745): 193–7; J.L. Heilbron, 'Franklin, Haller, and Franklinist history', *Isis*, 68 (1977): 539–49.

38. Simon Schaffer, 'Natural philosophy and public spectacle in the eighteenth century', *History of Science*, 21 (1983): 1–43.

39. William Watson, 'A letter . . . [on] beatification . . . causing a glory to appear round a man's head', *Philosophical Transactions of the Royal Society*, 46 (1749–50): 348–56; J.L. Heilbron, *Electricity in the 17th and 18th Centuries: A Study of Early Modern Physics* (Berkeley and Los Angeles, CA/London, 1979), pp. 267–9.

40. Benjamin Rackstrow, *Miscellaneous Observations: Together with a Collection of Experiments on Electricity* (London, 1748), pp. 25–6, 56, 58.

41. Edmund Burke, *A Philosophical Enquiry into the Origin of Our Ideas of the Sublime and Beautiful* (2nd edn 1759), ed. J.T. Boulton (London, 1958), p. 39.

42. *Gentleman's Magazine*, 25 (1755): 312, quoted in Schaffer, 'Natural philosophy and public spectacle', p. 9.

43. William Watson, 'Account of . . . Franklin's Treatise . . . *Experiments and Observations on Electricity*', *Philosophical Transactions of the Royal Society*, 47 (1751–2): 202–11; 'A letter of Benjamin Franklin . . . concerning an electrical kite', *ibid.* 565–7; letters by Mazeas, Nollet and Watson, *ibid*: 534–52, 553–8, 567–70; Heilbron, *Electricity in the 17th and 18th Centuries*, pp. 339–46.

44. Joseph Priestley, *The History and Present State of Electricity, with Original Experiments*, 3rd edn, corrected and enlarged, 2 vols (London, 1775), vol. 1, pp. 204, 215; vol. 2, pp. 134–7.

45. *The Yale Edition of Horace Walpole's Correspondence*, ed. W.S. Lewis *et al.*, 48 vols (New Haven, CT/London, 1937–83), vol. 20, pp. 130, 133–4, 140, 154–5.

46. Rev. William Stukeley, 'Concerning the causes of earthquakes', *Philosophical Transactions of the Royal Society*, 46 (1750): 657–69; Rev. Stephen Hales, 'Some considerations on the causes of earthquakes', *ibid*.: 669–81; Stukeley, 'The philosophy of earthquakes', *ibid*.: 731–50; Schaffer, 'Natural philosophy and public spectacle', p. 19.

47. Priestley, *The History and Present State of Electricity*, vol. 1, pp. 401–2, 404–5, 427–38, 447, 454–8; vol. 2, p. 75.

48. Sir William Hamilton, *Campi Phlegraei. Observations on the Volcanos of the Two Sicilies, As they have been Communicated to the Royal Society of London, with 54 Plates*, 2 vols (Naples, 1776), pp. 30–31, 87; Hamilton, *Supplement to the Campi Phlegraei being an Account of the Great Eruption of Mount Vesuvius in the month of August 1779, Communicated to the Royal Society* (Naples, 1779), p. 10.

49. Priestley, *The History and Present State of Electricity*, vol. 1, pp. xiv–xv.

50. Andrew Baxter, *An Enquiry into the Nature of the Human Soul* (London, 1733), pp. 15, 79; John W. Yolton, *Thinking Matter: Materialism in Eighteenth-Century Britain* (Oxford, 1983), pp. 94–6.

51. John Hedley Brooke, *Science and Religion: Some Historical Perspectives* (Cambridge, 1991), pp. 172–3.

52. Joseph Priestley, *The History and Present State of Discoveries Relating to Vision, Light, and Colours* (London, 1772), pp. 390–3.

53. Rowning, *Compendious System of Natural Philosophy* (1744), Part II, p. 6n, Part III, p. 157; William Shakespeare, *Hamlet*, Act II, scene ii, lines 261–2. See Shapiro, *Fits, Passions and Paroxysms*, pp. 226–7; Arnold Thackray, ' "Matter in a nut-shell": Newton's *Opticks* and eighteenth-century chemistry', *Ambix*, 15 (1968): 29–53; and Thackray, *Atoms and Powers*, pp. 53–67.

54. Walker, *System of Familiar Philosophy*, vol. 1, p. 371.

55. Joseph Priestley, *Disquisitions Relating to Matter and Spirit* (2nd edn 1782), in *The Theological and Miscellaneous Works of Joseph Priestley*, 25 vols, ed. J.T. Rutt (London, 1817–32), vol. 3, pp. 218–25, 230, 238, 241. See my article (with J.E. McGuire), 'Newtonian forces and Lockean powers: concepts of matter in eighteenth-century thought', *Historical Studies in the Physical Sciences*, 3 (1971): 233–306, esp. pp. 268–81; reprinted in Harman, *After Newton: Essays on Natural Philosophy*; and J.G. McEvoy and J.E. McGuire, 'God and nature: Priestley's way of rational dissent', *Historical Studies in the Physical Sciences*, 6 (1975): 325–404.

56. John Playfair, 'Biographical account of the late James Hutton', *Transactions of the Royal Society of Edinburgh*, 5 (1805): 39–99, in *The Works of John Playfair*, 4 vols (Edinburgh, 1822), vol. 4, p. 83.

57. James Hutton, *Dissertations on Different Subjects in Natural Philosophy* (Edinburgh, 1792), pp. 175, 218, 221, 233, 245–7, 262–4, 290, 501, 505, 517–19.

58. *Works of John Playfair*, vol. 4, pp. 85–6.

59. Hutton, *Dissertations on Natural Philosophy*, p. 214.

60. James Hutton, 'Theory of the earth; or an investigation of the laws observable in the composition, dissolution and restoration of the land upon the globe', *Transactions of the Royal Society of Edinburgh*, 1 (1788): 209–304, on p. 304; Martin J.S. Rudwick, *Bursting the Limits of Time: The Reconstruction of Geohistory in the Age of Revolution* (Chicago, IL/London, 2005), pp. 169–72.

61. See my article 'Voluntarism and immanence: conceptions of nature in eighteenth-century thought', *Journal of the History of Ideas*, 39 (1978): 271–83, reprinted in Harman, *After Newton: Essays on Natural Philosophy*.

62. [Erasmus Darwin,] *The Botanic Garden; A Poem in Two Parts. Part I. Containing The Economy of Vegetation* (London, 1791), Canto I, lines 363–6, 383–90, Canto II, lines 355–60; and Additional Note V, pp. 10–11.

63. [Darwin,] *The Economy of Vegetation*, Canto II, lines 362–8; Tim Fulford, Debbie Lee and Peter J. Kitson, *Literature, Science and Exploration in the Romantic Era: Bodies of Knowledge* (Cambridge, 2004), pp. 182–3.

64. Frank E. Manuel, *The Eighteenth Century Confronts the Gods* (Cambridge, MA, 1959), pp. 245–70.

65. [Darwin,] *The Economy of Vegetation*, Canto II, lines 327–32, Canto IV, lines 377–80, and pp. 107–8n, 191n; and Additional Note XXII, pp. 53–9; Martin Priestman, *Romantic Atheism: Poetry and Free Thought, 1780–1830* (Cambridge, 1999), pp. 71–3.

66. Darwin, *The Temple of Nature*, Canto I, lines 1–2; and Additional Note I, p. 1.

67. Quoted in Norton Garfinkle, 'Science and religion in England, 1790–1800: the critical response to the work of Erasmus Darwin', *Journal of the History of Ideas*, 16 (1955): 376–88, on p. 386.

68. Darwin, *The Temple of Nature*, Canto I, lines 15–18; Priestman, *Romantic Atheism*, pp. 66–7.

69. Darwin, *The Temple of Nature*, Canto III, lines 207, 230, 257–8; and pp. 100–3n.

70. Darwin, *The Temple of Nature*, Canto IV, lines 384–8, 397–402, Canto II, lines 41–4.
71. Darwin, *The Temple of Nature*, Canto I, lines 235–50.
72. Darwin, *The Temple of Nature*, Additional Note I, pp. 1–3; Canto I, pp. 37–8n.
73. *The Correspondence of Charles Darwin*, ed. Frederick Burckhardt, Sydney Smith *et al.* (Cambridge, 1985–), vol. 11, p. 278.
74. Darwin, *The Temple of Nature*, Canto III, lines 31–4; Additional Note I, p. 2.
75. Darwin, *The Temple of Nature*, Canto II, p. 54n; see Cambridge University Library, CCA.24.64.
76. Darwin, *The Temple of Nature*, Canto I, lines 3–8; Maureen McNeil, *Under the Banner of Science: Erasmus Darwin and His Age* (Manchester, 1987), pp. 43–56.
77. [Thomas Thomson,] 'The Temple of Nature', *Edinburgh Review*, 2 (July 1803): 491–506, esp. 499, 500, 502.
78. *Coleridge's Notebooks: A Selection*, ed. Seamus Perry (Oxford, 2002), p. 3.
79. *The Collected Letters of Samuel Taylor Coleridge*, ed. Earl Leslie Griggs, 6 vols (Oxford, 1956–71), vol. 2, p. 1,034.
80. Garfinkle, 'Science and religion in England, 1790–1800'.
81. Quoted in Trevor H. Levere, *Poetry Realized in Nature: Samuel Taylor Coleridge and Early Nineteenth-Century Science* (Cambridge, 1981), p. 2.
82. *Coleridge's Notebooks*, p. 19.
83. *Coleridge's Notebooks*, pp. 44–5.
84. Robert J. Richards, *The Romantic Conception of Life: Science and Philosophy in the Age of Goethe* (Chicago, IL/London, 2002), pp. 128–51.
85. *Coleridge's Notebooks*, p. 131.
86. Ian Wylie, *Young Coleridge and the Philosophers of Nature* (Oxford, 1989), pp. 25–44.
87. *Coleridge's Notebooks*, p. 149.
88. Priestley, *Works*, vol. 3, pp. 220, 256, 453.
89. *Collected Letters of Coleridge*, ed. Griggs, vol. 1, p. 137.
90. *Coleridge's Notebooks*, p. 5; Thomas McFarland, *Coleridge and the Pantheist Tradition* (Oxford, 1969), pp. 169–77.
91. *The New Oxford Book of Romantic Period Verse*, ed. Jerome J. McGann (Oxford, 1993), p. 120.
92. *Collected Letters of Coleridge*, ed. Griggs, vol. 1, pp. 177, 222.
93. *Collected Letters of Coleridge*, ed. Griggs, vol. 2, p. 706.
94. *Coleridge's Notebooks*, pp. 81, 89.
95. *Collected Letters of Coleridge*, ed. Griggs, vol. 2, p. 709.
96. Quoted in Levere, *Poetry Realized in Nature*, p. 25.
97. *Collected Letters of Coleridge*, ed. Griggs, vol. 3, p. 38.
98. Quoted in Levere, *Poetry Realized in Nature*, p. 35.
99. *The Notebooks of Samuel Taylor Coleridge: Volume 4, 1819–1826*, ed. Kathleen Coburn and Merton Christensen (London, 1990), nos 4,656, 5,464.
100. *The Notebooks of Samuel Taylor Coleridge: Volume 4*, nos 4,516, 4,518.
101. Levere, *Poetry Realized in Nature*, pp. 82–122; Raimonda Modiano, *Coleridge and the Concept of Nature* (Tallahassee, FL, 1985), pp. 138–86.
102. Quoted in Richards, *The Romantic Conception of Life*, p. 144.
103. Quoted in Barry Gower, 'Speculation in physics: the history and practice of *Naturphilosophie*', *Studies in History and Philosophy of Science*, 3 (1973): 301–56, on pp. 311–12, 324–5.
104. *Collected Letters of Coleridge*, ed. Griggs, vol. 4, pp. 767, 883; Samuel Taylor Coleridge, *Biographia Literaria, or Biographical Sketches of my Literary Life and Opinions*, ed. James Engell and W. Jackson Bate, 2 vols (London, 1983), vol. 1, p. 160.
105. 'The Eolian Harp' (1817), lines 26–30, in *Samuel Taylor Coleridge: Selected Poems*, ed. Richard Holmes, The Folio Society (London, 2003), p. 30; M.H. Abrams, 'Coleridge's "A light in sound": science, metascience and poetic imagination', *Proceedings of the American Philosophical Society*, 116 (1972): 458–76.

106. *Collected Letters of Coleridge*, ed. Griggs, vol. 4, pp. 771, 773; Thomas L. Hankins and Robert J. Silverman, *Instruments and the Imagination* (Princeton, NJ, 1995), pp. 102–8.

107. Quoted in Levere, *Poetry Realized in Nature*, pp. 176–7.

108. *The Notebooks of Samuel Taylor Coleridge: Volume 4*, no. 4,648.

109. Levere, *Poetry Realized in Nature*, pp. 103–8.

110. Thackray, *Atoms and Powers*, pp. 218–21; Robert Fox, 'The rise and fall of Laplacian physics', *Historical Studies in the Physical Sciences*, 4 (1974): 89–136, esp. pp. 95–8.

111. Quoted in Jeremy Adler, 'Goethe's use of chemical theory in his *Elective Affinities*', in *Romanticism and the Sciences*, ed. Andrew Cunningham and Nicholas Jardine (Cambridge, 1990), pp. 263–79, on p. 277.

112. J.W. von Goethe, *Elective Affinities: A Novel*, trans. with introduction by David Constantine (Oxford, 1994), pp. 78, 241n.

113. 'Elective Affinities' (1924–5), in Walter Benjamin, *Selected Writings. Volume 1: 1913–1926*, ed. Marcus Bullock and Michael W. Jennings (Cambridge, MA/London, 1996), p. 330.

114. Quoted in Thackray, *Atoms and Powers*, p. 232.

115. *Elective Affinities*, trans. with introduction by David Constantine, pp. xvii, 33–4.

116. 'Preface' to *Frankenstein* and [Walter Scott,] 'Remarks on Frankenstein ...', *Blackwood's Edinburgh Magazine*, 2 (1818): 613–20, in Mary Wollstonecraft Shelley, *Frankenstein; or, The Modern Prometheus*, ed. D.L. Macdonald and Kathleen Scherf (Peterborough, Ontario, 1994), pp. 47, 303–9, esp. p. 306.

117. Shelley, *Frankenstein*, ed. Macdonald and Scherf, p. 364.

118. Darwin, *The Temple of Nature*, Additional Note XII, p. 64.

119. *The Electrical Researches of the Honourable Henry Cavendish, F.R.S.*, ed. J. Clerk Maxwell (Cambridge, 1879), p. 213; Heilbron, *Electricity in the 17th and 18th Centuries*, pp. 487–94; Christa Jungnickel and Russell McCormmach, *Cavendish: The Experimental Life* (Lewisburgh, PA, 1999), pp. 245–8.

120. Iwan Rhys Morus, *Frankenstein's Children: Electricity, Exhibition and Experiment in Early Nineteenth-Century London* (Princeton, NJ, 1998), pp. 126–8.

121. [Erasmus Darwin,] *The Economy of Vegetation*, Canto I, lines 383–8; Shelley, *Frankenstein*, ed. Macdonald and Scherf, pp. 70, 328.

122. Richards, *The Romantic Conception of Life*, pp. 216–61.

123. Levere, *Poetry Realized in Nature*, pp. 46–9; Sharon Ruston, *Shelley and Vitality* (Basingstoke, 2005), pp. 24–73.

124. Shelley, *Frankenstein*, ed. Macdonald and Scherf, pp. 79, 81; Marilyn Butler, 'Introduction' to Mary Wollstonecraft Shelley, *Frankenstein; or, The Modern Prometheus* (London, 1993); L.S. Jacyna, 'Immanence or transcendence: theories of life and organization in Britain, 1790–1835', *Isis*, 74 (1983): 311–29, esp. pp. 312–16.

125. Shelley, *Frankenstein*, ed. Macdonald and Scherf, p. 45; John Milton, *Paradise Lost*, Book X, lines 743–5, in *The Poems of John Milton*, ed. Helen Darbishire (Oxford, 1958), p. 232.

126. Shelley, *Frankenstein*, ed. Macdonald and Scherf, pp. 126, 128.

127. William Godwin, *Enquiry Concerning Political Justice*, in Shelley, *Frankenstein*, ed. Macdonald and Scherf, p. 254.

128. Shelley, *Frankenstein*, ed. Macdonald and Scherf, p. 128.

129. Shelley, *Frankenstein*, ed. Macdonald and Scherf, p. 83.

130. Shelley, *Frankenstein*, ed. Macdonald and Scherf, pp. 75–7.

131. *The Journals of Mary Shelley, 1814–1844*, ed. Paula R. Feldman and Diana Scott-Kilvert, 2 vols (Oxford, 1987), vol. 1, pp. 142–4.

132. Sir Humphry Davy, *Elements of Chemical Philosophy: Part I, Vol. I* (London, 1812), pp. 159, 165, 175.

133. Laura E. Crouch, 'Davy's *A Discourse Introductory to a Course of Lectures on Chemistry*: a possible scientific source of *Frankenstein*', *Keats–Shelley Journal*, 27 (1978): 35–44.

134. Jan Golinski, *Science as Public Culture: Chemistry and Enlightenment in Britain, 1760–1820* (Cambridge, 1992), pp. 194–8.

135. *The Prose Works of William Wordsworth*, ed. W.J.B. Owen and Jane Worthington Smyser, 3 vols (Oxford, 1974), vol. 3, pp. 140–1; Roger Sharrock, 'The chemist and the poet: Sir Humphry Davy and the preface to Lyrical Ballads', *Notes and Records of the Royal Society of London*, 17 (1962): 57–76; Catherine E. Ross, ' "Twin labourers and heirs of the same hopes": the professional rivalry of Humphry Davy and William Wordsworth', in *Romantic Science: The Literary Forms of Natural History*, ed. Noah Heringman (Albany, NY, 2003), pp. 23–52.

136. Humphry Davy, *A Discourse Introductory to A Course of Lectures on Chemistry, Delivered in the Theatre of the Royal Institution on the 21st of January, 1802* (London, 1802), pp. 5, 8, 10–11, 15–19, 22.

137. Shelley, *Frankenstein*, ed. Macdonald and Scherf, pp. 83, 103–4; Davy, *Discourse Introductory*, p. 24.

Chapter 9   Nature and Culture

1. John Locke, *An Essay Concerning Human Understanding*, ed. A.S. Pringle-Pattison (Oxford, 1924), pp. 6–7.

2. *The Yale Edition of Horace Walpole's Correspondence*, ed. W.S. Lewis *et al.*, 48 vols (New Haven, CT/London, 1937–83), vol. 13, p. 181.

3. Cited by Malcolm Andrews, *Landscape and Western Art* (Oxford, 1999), p. 130.

4. Adam Smith, 'The Principles which lead and direct Philosophical Enquiries; illustrated by the History of Astronomy', in *Essays on Philosophical Subjects* (1795), ed. W.P.D. Wightman and J.G. Bryce (Oxford, 1980), pp. 45–6.

5. Cicero, *The Nature of the Gods*, Book II, 152, trans. P.G. Walsh (Oxford, 1997), pp. 102–3.

6. John Dixon Hunt, 'Evelyn's idea of the garden: a theory for all seasons', in *John Evelyn's "Elysium Britannicum" and European Gardening*, ed. Therese O'Malley and Joachim Wolschke-Bulmahn (Washington, DC, 1998), p. 280.

7. Wordsworth, *A Guide through the District of the Lakes in the North of England* (1835), in *The Prose Works of William Wordsworth*, ed. W.J.B. Owen and Jane Worthington Smyser, 3 vols (Oxford, 1974), vol. 2, p. 188; W.H. Pearsall and Winifred Pennington, *The Lake District: A Landscape History* (London, 1973), p. 135; Simon Schama, *Landscape and Memory* (London, 1995), p. 9; Oliver Rackham, *The History of the Countryside* (London, 1986), p. 307; Stephen J. Pyne, *The Ice*, new edn (London, 2003), pp. 67–8.

8. William Cronon, 'The trouble with wilderness; or getting back to the wrong nature', in *Uncommon Ground: Toward Reinvesting Nature*, ed. William Cronon (New York, 1995), pp. 69–90.

9. James G. McKusick, *Green Writing: Romanticism and Ecology* (Basingstoke, 2000), pp. 6–11.

10. Schama, *Landscape and Memory*, pp. 6–7.

11. William Gilpin, *Remarks on Forest Scenery, and the Woodland Views*, 2 vols (London, 1791), vol. 2, p. 166; Francis Jeffrey in *Edinburgh Review*, 18 (May 1811): 1–46, on p. 15.

12. *The Works of John Ruskin*, Library Edition, ed. E.T. Cook and Alexander Wedderburn, 39 vols (London, 1903–12), vol. 3, p. 627n.

13. *The Works of John Ruskin*, vol. 5, p. 234; *The Odyssey of Homer*, translated by Alexander Pope, 5 vols (London, 1725–6), vol. 2, pp. 9–12 (Book V, lines 75–94).

14. *The Works of John Ruskin*, vol. 5, p. 235.

15. *The Odyssey of Homer*, trans. Alexander Pope, vol. 2, pp. 105–8 (Book VII, lines 142–77).

16. *The Odyssey of Homer*, vol. 1, p. 4n.

17. Horace Walpole, *The History of the Modern Taste in Gardening* (2nd edn 1782), in *Horace Walpole, Gardenist*, ed. I.W.U. Chase (Princeton, NJ, 1943), p. 4.
18. *Edinburgh Review*, 18 (May 1811): 15.
19. Edmund Burke, *A Philosophical Enquiry into the Origin of Our Ideas of the Sublime and Beautiful* (2nd edn 1759), ed. J.T. Boulton (London, 1958), p. 58.
20. *Horace Walpole, Gardenist*, p. 27.
21. Archibald Alison, *Essays on the Nature and Principles of Taste* (Edinburgh, 1790), pp. 85–7.
22. *John Constable's Discourses*, compiled and annotated by R.B. Beckett (Ipswich, 1970), p. 68.
23. Francis Hutcheson, *An Inquiry into the Original of our Ideas of Beauty and Virtue*, 2nd edn (London, 1726), pp. 45, 105, 69.
24. Mark Akenside, *The Pleasures of Imagination. A Poem. In Three Books* (London, 1744), pp. v, 37–9n.
25. Adam Smith, *Essays on Philosophical Subjects* (1795), ed. Wightman and Bryce, pp. 45–6.
26. James Hutton, *Dissertations on Different Subjects in Natural Philosophy* (Edinburgh, 1792), pp. 214, 218, 246, 263, 685, 666; and Hutton, *An Investigation of the Principles of Knowledge, and of the Progress of Reason, from Sense to Science and Philosophy*, 3 vols (Edinburgh, 1794), vol. 1, pp. 521–2, 529.
27. *Georgics*, Book II, line 149; Richard Jenkyns, *Virgil's Experience. Nature and History: Times, Names and Places* (Oxford, 1998), pp. 341–86 (on p. 359).
28. *Georgics*, Book II, lines 490, 493; Jenkyns, *Virgil's Experience*, p. 374.
29. *Georgics*, Book II, lines 490–4 in *The Works of John Dryden*, vol. 5, ed. W. Frost and V.A. Dearing (Berkeley and Los Angeles, CA/London, 1987), p. 203, and see also p. 137.
30. Joseph Addison, 'An Essay on the *Georgics*', in *The Works of John Dryden*, vol. 5, p. 146.
31. [Erasmus Darwin,] *The Botanic Garden; A Poem, in Two Parts. Part I. Containing The Economy of Vegetation. Part II. The Loves of the Plants. With Philosophical Notes* (London, 1791), Part I, Canto IV, p. 191 footnote; Erasmus Darwin, *The Temple of Nature; or, The Origins of Society: A Poem, with Philosophical Notes* (London, 1803), Canto IV, lines 7–10, p. 129, where he footnotes Virgil's *Georgics*, Book II, lines 490–2.
32. Perez Zagorin, *Francis Bacon* (Princeton, NJ, 1998), pp. 68–73; Paolo Rossi, *Francis Bacon: From Magic to Science*, trans. Sacha Rabinovich (London, 1968), pp. 73–134.
33. John Brewer, *The Pleasures of the Imagination: English Culture in the Eighteenth Century* (London, 1997), pp. 615–61.
34. Hutton, *Dissertations*, pp. 684–5.
35. Seamus Perry, ed., *Coleridge's Notebooks: A Selection* (Oxford, 2002), p. 43
36. 'Science', *Encyclopaedia Britannica* (Edinburgh, 1797), vol. 16, p. 705; quoted in Russell McCormmach, *Speculative Truth: Henry Cavendish, Natural Philosophy and the Rise of Modern Theoretical Science* (New York, 2004), pp. 3, 18.
37. See my essay 'The scientific revolutions', in *The New Cambridge Modern History. XIII: Companion Volume*, ed. Peter Burke (Cambridge, 1979), pp. 248–70.
38. *The Correspondence of Charles Darwin*, ed. Frederick Burckhardt and Sydney Smith *et al.* (Cambridge, 1985–), vol. 11, p. 403.

Index